D1274040

BOCCACCIO

Genealogie veorum gentuliu av ugonē
melutum veuisalem ¬ capu regē seairbu
Jopem luranum ve certalvo liber prim⁹
macipit feliciter. Prolemium

Isaus ex velatoe vomini parmenstoe e
gregg Ansino tui viera percep. Rex scli
re sumope cupis gyenealogia veorum
gentuliū vkzonum ex eis uñ ficuoes
veteris vescenventau atqz cū pac quid
sub fabulaū tegmine illustres quon
vam se sunnit aut veane a cessi avoine
tua qual expetistau atqz ciubiesli
mū homines in talibs seletii tanto opi
autoie. Sane incomterum vesiveau tui
avouuraoon e poz enī qui vi homines
veer quiv rege moncar putuntani 7 vo
uersus electoones mei quis senta vice
puucta neoū insustinenau mea mon
straueto psubrezstigia arbitreno ipsin
labeni boz os audent. Ad qz av sentena
mei artea impitii op is vetuemū libet
serenssime regū. aq pone z suo omnia
queva salres que inter vomi. tū sisigme
mibel tuū vū nssa tue vlistunvis expli
caret. em 7 isiuenē uerba ut eis plemo
satis trementibus tui uuias 7 temeni
nate meā vum inobeviēta tui maiestati
veuenio. Cuar igz ille sucanus ex sacra
ne solūmtatis studia z opū regu 9 off
aq avuunanva vec nō z insignes atqz
glouosos quosvam tui neis titulos lon
ga vicanate explausis coueuent in
conatui plunmo me iuua sentē avez
cere conaretur. nec unica tui voe similez

ex quibs saom naluc uivebā tū queva ver
postquā tacent tū ruvenvi copia sia est.
sie uter. Arbitrat soasam saute mule⁹ seu
rex tuuo expio nir futuma p stitte veo hāc
isiamā ueteru scilicet aupienvis se hū vini
no z veatos sangume augulū sue mo
au comcasse teā z invicuili quovva ut e
par pauo seuasse teas tractu uieluit z
receiissimū opis sacile colligi posse. Atta
mē bona semp tua pice vicm longe alt
ē. Nam ut omta cicelavos et reliqua eggi
maris insulas achauam zyllmcam atqz
tracias quas penes somēta huu skultue
emicie plunmu z potissime vū grecorū
veo.p. flozuit. Eleuuni maris hellespon
naci z iconu veatei, pamphili. ciliai. pix
miae. z syra atqz egaptau litoza sua ota
egioe insent. Nec expens nir rego z isigne
venis. abixat labe siue limmuo. Sic comes
libie atqz seatii trumuhie oza labesacta
mit z tablanuacos arvui maris siuio.
et remotissimos kespeviii ootvo. Nec me
viteuanei tū maris sue otēn tirouls qui
umo z av icognuto maris nanos eaā pe
nesuir. venvere z sommes hac cū litoralub
accole omis uuli fonte omētis z arene li
bice una cū suo gestibs z antiquissimaz
trkuuzū solituvuoes. nec nō z tupivōs egi
poz atqz garamātos semvus z caleuties
numū usinuqi ethropes. zotoru arabel.p
seq viteo atqz gangnuves ipsi z ingre
vine isignes unvi. babulones z celsa em
casi canmima emioq ni steuubs solem
qz i geluvos artē⁹ sabzosa veriua. caspiui
mare hycamei z cruces zois tmnauo ac
niuosos sep zhelexes z sierbaii z saulta
bubanos. Et eui oueētalis occeam suneth
z niboz maris skeauisu sul ue postremo
.... copua.... z veclmauit. aveo ut vo
.... iomi.... enus offiscata mu
.... gioni.... vio i qui
....vaut
....schut
....reta
....nqua
....stro

BOCCACCIO

A Critical Guide to the Complete Works

Edited by

Victoria Kirkham,

Michael Sherberg, and

Janet Levarie Smarr

THE UNIVERSITY OF CHICAGO PRESS
Chicago and London

VICTORIA KIRKHAM is professor emerita of Romance languages at the University of Pennsylvania. MICHAEL SHERBERG is associate professor of Italian at Washington University in St. Louis. JANET LEVARIE SMARR is professor of theater history and Italian studies at the University of California, San Diego.

The University of Chicago Press, Chicago 60637
The University of Chicago Press, Ltd., London
© 2013 by The University of Chicago
All rights reserved. Published 2013.
Printed in the United States of America

22 21 20 19 18 17 16 15 14 13   1 2 3 4 5

The University of Chicago Press gratefully acknowledges the generous support of the Graduate School of Arts and Sciences and the Department of Romance Languages and Literatures at Washington University in St. Louis, and the Division of Arts and Humanities at the University of California, San Diego, toward the publication of this book.

Frontispiece: Giovanni Boccaccio, *Genealogia deorum gentilium*, MS 100, fol. 11r (late fourteenth to early fifteenth century). Special Collections Research Center, University of Chicago Library.

ISBN-13: 978-0-226-07918-9 (cloth)
ISBN-13: 978-0-226-07921-9 (e-book)
DOI: 10.7208/chicago/9780226079219.001.0001

Library of Congress Cataloging-in-Publication Data

Boccaccio : a critical guide to the complete works / edited by Victoria Kirkham, Michael Sherberg, and Janet Levarie Smarr.
    pages ; cm
  Includes bibliographical references and index.
  ISBN 978-0-226-07918-9 (cloth : alk. paper) — ISBN 978-0-226-07921-9 (e-book)   1. Boccaccio, Giovanni, 1313–1375—Criticism and interpretation.   2. Italian poetry—To 1400—History and criticism.   I. Kirkham, Victoria, editor.   II. Sherberg, Michael, editor.   III. Smarr, Janet Levarie, 1949– editor.
  PQ4294.B63 2014
  853'.1—dc23

                                                                    2013025539

♾ This paper meets the requirements of ANSI/NISO Z39.48–1992 (Permanence of Paper).

CONTENTS

ILLUSTRATIONS

ACKNOWLEDGMENTS

Each of the coeditors of this volume has debts of gratitude to those whose support has helped us bring our project to a successful conclusion. Generous financial subventions were received from Seth Lerer, Dean of Arts and Humanities at the University of California, San Diego; and at Washington University in St. Louis from Gary Wihl, Dean of the Faculty of Arts and Sciences, and Harriet Stone, chair of the Department of Romance Languages and Literatures. Grants from the Rockefeller Foundation Bellagio Center and the Liguria Study Center at Bogliasco gave Victoria Kirkham sabbatical time during the crucial formative period of this project. As it advanced, we had the opportunity, thanks to the Renaissance Society of America, to organize panels in sessions to preview chapters of the book by volume contributors. Comments by the two anonymous readers for the University of Chicago Press, including one of the most remarkably thorough and generous reports we have ever seen, were of essential assistance in the revision phase. The three of us extend special appreciation to our editor at the press, Randy Petilos, for his enthusiastic support of the idea for this book from the beginning and for practical guidance through the calendar of production phases, and our thanks for the patient and thorough copyediting of Marian Rogers. Finally, we thank our contributors, friends, and colleagues in the community of scholars who, knowingly or not, have been part of the five-year dialogue that has seen this collaboration grow from an idea to a reality, an American monument to honor the 700th anniversary of the birth of Giovanni Boccaccio.

CHRONOLOGY OF BOCCACCIO'S LIFE AND WORKS

Victoria Kirkham

1313 Born in Certaldo (*Filocolo* 3.1; *De montibus* 5.368) or Florence (*De montibus* 5.3), the illegitimate son of Boccaccino da Certaldo and an unknown mother; Robert of Anjou is given nominal titular rule of Florence in an alliance between Naples and Florence

Ca. 1320–27 After learning the basics of reading and writing by age six, Boccaccio is enrolled in the school of Giovanni di Domenico Mazzuoli da Strada, father of Zanobi, where he learns elementary rules of Latin grammar and arithmetic

1327 summer–fall Boccaccio and his father, an agent of the Bardi bank, move to Naples

1330–35 Canon law student at University of Naples

1330–36 and later *Zibaldone Laurenziano* (e.g., *Allegorical Epistles*, 1339; letter to Zanobi, 1348; Greek additions, 1360–67)

Ca. 1332–34 Earliest Latin compositions: *Elegia di Costanza* (*Carmina* 1)

Ca. 1333–34 *Caccia di Diana*

1334 Andalò del Negro dies

Ca. 1335 or just after *Filostrato*

Ca. 1336 Expedition led by Lanzarotto Malocello of Genoa reaches Canary Islands

Ca. 1336–38 *Filocolo*

1338–39 Factional wars in Barletta, in Kingdom of Naples

1339 Letter to Francesco de' Bardi in Neapolitan dialect (*Lettere* 1)

Ca. 1339 Four allegorical epistles: "Crepor celsitudinis," "Mavortis milex," "Nereus amphytritibus," "Sacre famis"; *Allegoria mitologica*

Ca. 1339–41 *Teseida delle nozze d'Emilia*

1340s Period of *Miscellanea Laurenziana*, except for *Priapei* and verses by Lovato Lovati, added either after 1346 or after 1351

Late 1340s Autograph manuscript of *Teseida*

1341 Begins *De vita moribus Francisci Petracchi de Florentia*

Early 1341 Moves back to Florence from Naples in wake of European financial crisis

1341 Aug. 28 Letter to Niccola Acciaiuoli from Florence (Epistle 5)

1341 Nov. 15 Letter by Florentine merchants in Seville describing expedition to Canary Islands, partially financed by Alfonso IV of Portugal and led by the Genoese captain Niccoloso da Recco and the Florentine Angelino del Tegghia dei Corbizzi

1341–42 *Comedia delle ninfe fiorentine*

Ca. 1342 (no later than 1345) *De Canaria*, inspired by merchants' letter of Nov. 15, 1341

1342–early 1343 *Amorosa visione*

1342–43 For ten months Walter of Brienne, Duke of Athens (and nephew of Robert of Anjou), rules Florence as tyrant

1343 King Robert of Anjou dies

1343–44 *Elegia di madonna Fiammetta*

1345 Economic crisis in Florence; Boccaccio holds office in Florence as a treasury official

1344–46 (or 1346–47) *Ninfale fiesolano*

Before 1346 Translation of Livy's Fourth Decade, dedicated to Ostagio da Polenta (Boccaccio's authorship is uncertain)

1346 In Ravenna at court of Ostagio da Polenta; may have copied *Eclogues* and Latin poetry of Giovanni Del Virgilio; Boccaccio's patron Ostagio da Polenta dies

1346–47 Famine in Florence; first two eclogues

1346–67 Composes *Buccolicum carmen*

1347–48 Moves to court of Francesco Ordelaffi at Forlì

1348 Poetic correspondence with Checco di Meletto Rossi, Ordelaffi's chancellor; death of Duke of Durazzo at hands of Louis of Hungary

1348 Jan. Writes Zanobi da Strada in Forlì (Epistle 6)

1348 spring–1349 spring Black Death in Florence

1348, after July 8 Death of Ciampi della Tosa, honored in Boccaccio's epitaph for Pino and Ciampi della Tosa (*Carmina* 4)

Ca. 1348–50 Writes *De vita et moribus domini Francisci Petracchi de Florentia*

1349–50 Birth of his third illegitimate child, Violante

1349–51 *Decameron*; under revision until at least 1372

Ca. 1350 First conception of the *Genealogia*, not executed until 1360; (self ?-)portrait, *Boccaccio Lecturing to the Monks*, pasted into a later copy of his *Buccolicum carmen* (MS 34.49, Biblioteca Laurenziana, Florence)

1350 summer Lost Latin poem to Petrarch

1350 Aug.–Sept. Ambassadorial mission to the Romagna and Ravenna; delivers ten gold florins from Florence to Dante's cloistered daughter, Sister Beatrice

1350 early Oct. In Florence, a first brief encounter with Petrarch, who is on his way to the Jubilee at Rome

1350s? Verses on the Arno in *De fluminibus* (*Carmina* "11")

1350–55 (or 1355–57?) Boccaccio's first Dante autograph (MS 104.6, Biblioteca Capitolare, Toledo)

1350 to mid-1360s Compiles *De montibus*

1351 Receives Cicero's *Pro Archia* from Petrarch

1351 Jan. Chosen by lot to serve as chamberlain of Chamber of the Commune of Florence

1351 late Mar. First of four visits with Petrarch, in Padua; perhaps gets verses by Lovato Lovati

1351 Apr. 19 Letter on behalf of Florentine authorities to Petrarch inviting him to teach at new university (Epistle 7)

1351 Dec. 12 Receives letter of credit from Signoria to carry as ambassador to Prince Ludwig of Brandenburg

1351–52 winter Mission to Ludwig in the Tyrol

1351–53 Compiles manuscript (not an autograph) that contains the *Commedia* and a dedicatory poem, "Ytalie iam certus honos," to send to Petrarch

1351 after Mar.–1355 First redaction of *Trattatello in laude di Dante*

Ca. 1351–56 *Zibaldone Magliabechiano* (but *De Canaria* is older, no later than 1345)

1352? Letter to Zanobi da Strada (?) (Epistle 8)

1352 Jan. Chamberlain and delegate of Florence in the ceding of Prato to Florence by the Crown of Naples

1352 Letter to Zanobi da Strada (Epistle 9)

1353 Petrarch moves to Visconti court in Milan

1353 July 18 Angry letter to Petrarch at Milan from Ravenna (Epistle 10)

1354 Giovanni Visconti, Duke of Milan, dies

1354 Apr. 28 Letter from Signoria of Florence recommending Boccaccio as ambassador to Pope Innocent VI

1354 May–June Ambassadorial mission to Innocent VI in Avignon

1354 July Mission to Certaldo to organize citizen resistance against the captain of a mercenary company

1355 Eclogues 7–9

1355 Apr. 10 Petrarch in Milan receives "immense" work of Augustine's *Commentary on the Psalms* in Boccaccio's hand

1355 May 5 Boccaccio's name is drawn to serve from the Santo Spirito neighborhood in the *Ufficio della Condotta* (officials charged with supervising equipment of mercenaries)

1355 May 15 Zanobi da Strada receives laurel crown from Emperor Charles V

1355 November? Boccaccio writes a metrical epistle to Zanobi da Strada, "Si bene conspexi" (*Carmina 7*)

Late 1355, probably after writing to Zanobi Second visit to Naples; at nearby Montecassino Boccaccio discovers Varro's *De lingua latina*; Cicero's *Pro Cluentio*; the Ciceronian *Rhetorica ad Herennium*; Tacitus's *Annales* and *Historiae*

Ca. 1355 *Corbaccio*

Ca. 1355–57 Conception and first draft of *De montibus*; corrections continue to 1374

1355–60 Capponi *Decameron* (MS Ital. 482, Bibliothèque Nationale, Paris), early authorial redaction of the text and first fully illustrated copy

Ca. 1355–60 Redaction A, *De casibus*

1356 Sept. Battle of Poitiers; death of Walter of Brienne

1357 summer Boccaccio back in Ravenna

1359 second half of Mar. Second of four visits with Petrarch (their third meeting, counting Petrarch's passage through Florence in 1350), this one in Milan; plant laurel trees together in Petrarch's garden; *De casibus* perhaps completed by this time up through book 7; small Vaucluse landscape perhaps drawn by Boccaccio in Petrarch's Pliny

1359 June 22 Boccaccio and his brother Iacopo elected ambassadors to Lombardy

1360 First draft of *Genealogia*; first version of *Genealogia* probably finished, dedicated to Hugh IV, king of Cyprus; political turbulence in Florence; friends of Boccaccio plan a coup d'état against the city's reactionary Guelph government

1360 summer Leonzio Pilato arrives in Florence

1360 Nov. Pope Innocent VI legitimizes Boccaccio, who can afterward receive holy orders as cleric

1360 Dec. 30 Boccaccio's friends Domenico Bandini and Nicolò di Bartolo del Buono (dedicatee of the *Comedia delle ninfe fiorentine*) hanged; others take flight and are banished

Ca. 1360 Latin tetrastych marking completed transcription of Dante's *Commedia* (*Carmina 8*)

After 1360 Boccaccio adds Greek alphabet to his *Zibaldone Laurenziano*

1360–62 Studies Greek and Homer with Leontius Pilatus

1360–63 Second autograph transcription of Dante's *Commedia* (MS 1035,

Biblioteca Riccardiana, Florence) with seven illustrations in *Inferno* sometimes attributed to Boccaccio

1360–70 Third autograph transcription of Dante's *Commedia* (MS Chigiano 50.6.213, Biblioteca Vaticana)

July 13, 1360 First documented evidence of *Decameron*'s transmission

Early 1360s Second redaction of *Trattatello* (the "*Compendio*")

1361 Drafts *De mulieribus* in Certaldo, continued in nine successive redactional phases up to 1375, dedicated to Andrea Acciaiuoli; Zanobi da Strada dies

1361 July 2 Boccaccio gives his brother Iacopo his house in the Santa Felicita neighborhood and transfers to Certaldo

1361–62 Winter trip to Ravenna

1361 late–early months of 1362 *Consolatory Epistle to Pino de' Rossi*

1362 Monk brings prophecy from Pietro Petroni in Siena predicting that Boccaccio will die soon unless he renounces poetry

1362 Jan. 2 Boccaccio sends Petrarch his *Vita sanctissimi patris Petri Damiani*, based on the life of Saint Peter Damian by Giovanni da Lodi (*Epistle* 11)

1362 May 15 Letter to his old friend Barbato da Sulmona (Epistle 12)

1362 June Invited by Queen Giovanna's seneschal, Niccola Acciaiuoli, to visit Naples; dedicates *De mulieribus* to Andrea Acciaiuoli, Niccola's sister

1362 Oct.–Mar. 1363 Disastrous trip to Naples at invitation of Niccola Acciaiuoli; discovery at Montecassino of Martial's *Liber de spectaculis*

1363 Guest of Mainardo Cavalcanti for several days in Regno di Napoli; on return from Naples stops in Venice to visit Petrarch at his home on the Riva degli Schiavoni; death of Boccaccio's daughter Violante

1363 June 28 or 30 Letter to Francesco Nelli (Epistle 13)

1363–66 Autograph transcription of *Genealogia* (MS 52.9, Biblioteca Laurenziana, Florence); autograph transcription of Dante's lyric poetry (MS Chigiano 50.5.176, Biblioteca Vaticana)

1365 Serves another term on payroll of Comune of Florence as officer of the Condotta (to review conduct of soldiers)

1365 August 18 (or 19?) Letter from Signoria of Florence recommending Boccaccio as ambassador to Pope Urban V

1365 Aug. 21 Prepares his will (lost)

1365 Aug.–Nov. Ambassadorial mission to the Grimaldi Doge in Genoa and to Pope Urban V in Avignon

1366? Letter to Pietro da Moglio (Epistle 14)

1366 Commissions two altarpieces for his church in Certaldo

1366 May 20 Letter to Leonardo del Chiaro

1367 Eclogues 10–16

1367 spring Third of four visits to Petrarch, in Venice; in Petrarch's absence Boccaccio is welcomed by his daughter Francesca ("Tullia") and son-in-law Francescuolo da Brossano

1367 July 1 Letter to Petrarch recounting spring visit to Venice (Epistle 15)

1367 Oct. 30 Boccaccio's name drawn to serve among officials of the Condotta, responsible for recruiting *condottieri*

1367 Nov.? Second diplomatic mission to Pope Urban V, now back in Rome

1368 Fourth of four visits to Petrarch, in Padua; death of Donato degli Albenzani's son (still living in last of *Eclogues*, which must have been written no later than 1367)

1368 Dec. 1 Pope Urban V writes priors that he has received Boccaccio as an ambassador

1369–70 Publishes his *Buccolicum carmen*

1370 Return to Naples, where he is well received by Queen Joan

Early 1370s Third redaction of *Trattatello*

1370–72 Transcription of Berlin *Decameron*, MS Hamilton 90 (B)

1370–73 Autograph manuscript of *De mulieribus*

1371 Letter to Iacopo Pizzinga (Epistle 19)

1371 Jan. 20 Letter to Niccolò da Montefalcone (Epistle 16)

1371 May 12 Letter to Matteo d'Ambrasio (Epistle 17)

1371 June 26 Letter to Niccolò Orsini (Epistle 18)

1372 April 5 Letter to the jurist and poet Pietro Piccolo da Monteforte (Epistle 20)

1372–74 Letter to Fra Martino da Signa with key to meanings of his pastoral poems (Epistle 23)

1372–75 Revisions of *Genealogia*, books 14 and 15

1373 Redaction B of *De casibus*

Early 1373 Boccaccio stands as godfather to Mainardo Cavalcanti's child

1373 Aug. 12 Petition from citizenry of Florence approved for appointing a "worthy and wise man" to read Dante publicly

1373 Aug. 28 Letter to Mainardo Cavalcanti describing poor health and medical crisis (Epistle 21)

1373 Sept. 13 Boccaccio receives a cup of golden coins from Mainardo

1373 Boccaccio thanks Mainardo for the gift, and a second one of equal value received several days later (Epistle 22)

1373 Sunday, Oct. 23 Begins public readings of his *Esposizioni sopra la "Comedia" di Dante* in the Florentine church of Santo Stefano di Badia, salaried by the city

1373 Dec. 31 Receives from Signoria fifty florins as pay for first six months as reader of Dante

1373–74 Completion of *De casibus*, dedicated to Mainardo Cavalcanti

1374 late Jan. Forced by ill health to stop public readings of *Esposizioni*

1374 July 18–19 Petrarch dies

1374 August 28 Last will and testament

1374 Sept. 4 Receives 178 lire and 15 soldi owed him for public commentary on Dante

1374 Oct. 19–20 Receives notice of Petrarch's death from Petrarch's son-in-law Francescuolo da Brossano

1374 first days of Nov. Reply to Francescuolo da Brossano (Epistle 24)

1374 after Nov. 3 Verses to the *Africa* (*Carmina* 9)

Ca. 1374 Autoepitaph (*Carmina* 10)

1375 Dec. 21 Dies in Certaldo

Fig. 1. Unknown artist, *Giovanni Boccaccio*. Detail from *Portraits of Dante, Petrarch, Zanobi da Strada, Boccaccio*. Fragmentary lunette frescoed between 1375 and 1406 for the Guild-hall of the Judges and Notaries, Palazzo del Proconsolo, Florence (today Umberto Montano's restaurant Alle Murate).

INTRODUCTION · A Man of Many Turns

Janet Levarie Smarr

G iovanni Boccaccio (1313–75) has long reigned as one of the "three crowns" of Italian letters. His admiration for both Dante and Petrarch made him consider himself third among the three.[1] Yet, the enormous variety and wide popularity of his writings among diverse audiences — humanists, merchants, and women — gave him an influence at least as great and enduring as that of the other two "crowns."

Just as Petrarch and Boccaccio were friends in life, so this volume on Boccaccio forms a pair with the centenary volume on Petrarch, published in 2009, also by University of Chicago Press.[2] The mission and format of this volume follow the guidelines of the Petrarch volume, in the way that Boccaccio in his fifteenth eclogue followed Petrarch as a guide up the mountain of the Muses. Thus we have assembled essays on each of Boccaccio's works, grouped in sections, and have given the contributors the same charge as in the Petrarch volume — to discuss "Quid est?" What is this particular work? What did Boccaccio contribute in each case to the traditions he inherited? How did he reenvision genres or topics? How did he redirect the course of literature? His influence on later writers springs from these innovations but is mentioned only briefly. The focus is on Boccaccio as a writer in his own time, seeking to rework inherited models and articulate his own new vision.

Throughout his life Boccaccio experimented continually in all directions. He wrote letters, from serious to burlesque, in Latin, Italian, and even the Neapolitan dialect. He wrote lives of kings and of poets, of men and of women, of ancients and of contemporaries. He wrote fiction in verse and in prose, set far away in the ancient past or in the local present, narrated by male or female figures, by single or multiple narrators. Sometimes the characters are clearly allegorical, and sometimes they are just as clearly historical. He revived classical genres such as the pastoral eclogue, writing it in both Latin and Italian, and then refashioned the mode into a more ex-

1

tended narrative linked to the mythicization of local geographical features.[3] At other moments he turned to more popular genres, such as the anecdote, the short tale, and the longer romance, and rewrote these in a higher style and more self-conscious form. Thus he made the popular literary and the literary popular. He turned his hand to scholarship, writing dictionaries and commentaries on both classical myth and recent Italian poetry, even—like Dante—on his own poetry.

Unlike Petrarch, Boccaccio recognized the importance of the vernacular as the new mode of expression even for classical forms. Where Petrarch attempted an epic in Latin, Boccaccio proudly presented his *Teseida* as the first martial epic in the vernacular. Both Petrarch and Boccaccio wrote Latin eclogues, but it was the innovation of Boccaccio's vernacular pastoral writing that most creatively fired the imagination of subsequent writers and artists. When Boccaccio produced his hundred tales in the vernacular, Petrarch typically translated one into Latin. However, the use of the vernacular opened Boccaccio's works to less educated readers, whether merchants, literate but without Latin, or women. Already in his lifetime Boccaccio in his letter to Mainardo de' Cavalcanti mentions women reading his stories,[4] and he repeatedly uses the figure of the female recipient of his work. In the next few centuries, Boccaccio's writings—because of their use of the vernacular and because of their inclusion of female narrators and readers and of female biographies—would become an important model for women's new experiments in writing. Both in Italy and in France, women would turn to a number of his works as models for their own.[5]

Boccaccio's interest in the development of a vernacular literature and a vernacular literary language sprang from a lifelong devotion to Dante, from the early *Caccia di Diana* (*Diana's Hunt*) with its *terza rima* form to the *Esposizioni sopra la "Comedia" di Dante* (*Commentary on Dante's "Comedia"*) at the end of Boccaccio's life. Petrarch's *Letters on Familiar Matters* 21.15 quotes Boccaccio's claim that Dante was "your first guide and the light of your youthful studies";[6] and Boccaccio's narrator in the *Amorosa visione* (*Amorous Vision*), 6.2–3, calls Dante "il maestro dal qual io / tengo ogni ben" (the teacher from whom I have all that is good). Boccaccio's transcriptions of Dante's lyric poetry and *Comedia* helped to promote not only those works but also the idea of a great and serious literature in the Italian language.[7] Boccaccio added to these transcriptions rubrics ("Argomenti") both in *terza rima* (for the three *cantiche*) and in prose (for each canto) regarding the narrative contents of the poem.[8] The *terza rima* summaries, which sum up the narrative without interpretive commentary, each begin and end with the verses that begin and end Dante's *cantiche*. Boccaccio first wrote them into his transcription of Dante's poem circa 1355 (MS Toledano 104.6) and recopied them in his later transcriptions (MS Riccardiano 1035 and MS Chigiano 50.6.2013) during the 1360s. This last transcription added the prose rubrics for each canto.[9] Giorgio Padoan compares the verse summaries to those Boccaccio had written into his *Teseida*, and the prose rubrics to those of the *Decameron*. Despite his admiring friendship with Petrarch, Boccaccio's love for Dante created this divergent direction of interest and influence and made Boccaccio's own writing the foundational model for prose in the Italian vernacular. Several of this volume's essays—those by Elsa Filosa, Robert Hollander, and Roberto Fedi—attest to the tension for Boccaccio between the pull of Dante and that of Petrarch.

Petrarch's later return to work on and organize his vernacular lyrics, the *Rerum vulgarium fragmenta*, may have been a response to Boccaccio's insistence on the value of the vernacular. In the codex Vat. Chigiano, 50.5.176 (1363–66), Boccaccio transcribed Dante's lyric poetry together with Cavalcanti's famous *canzone* and a version of Petrarch's lyric collection (labeled *Fragmentum liber*), contributing to the creation of a vernacular canon. Petrarch could not have surmised, however, that these vernacular lyrics would become in time the principal foundation of his fame.

At the same time as Boccaccio was developing the Italian literary language, he was also looking back beyond Latin to Greek. Significantly, he would send to Petrarch both a copy of Dante's *Commedia* and a Latin translation of the *Iliad*. Boccaccio had developed an interest in Greek during his youth in Naples, thanks to his acquaintance with the royal librarian Paolo da Perugia and Paolo's friend the monk Barlaam. Already in his early texts Boccaccio played with Greek roots to create significant names for his characters. Despite his recurrent modesty about the value of his writings, he boasts proudly in his *Genealogia* 15.7 about having launched the long-abandoned study of Greek by hiring and prodding the Calabrian monk Leonzio Pilato to produce the first Latin translation of Homer, and by establishing him as Europe's first professor of Greek at the University of Florence. The impact of Boccaccio's interest was precisely in turning the use of Greek from purely religious reading to a rediscovery of classical Greek literature and philosophy. While in Florence during the early 1360s, Leonzio translated and lectured on Euripides and Aristotle as well as Homer. Although Boccaccio argues in the *Genealogia* that "we might profit greatly" from acquaintance with Greek writings,[10] he could not have fully realized how tremendously important this new opening would be for European culture over the next many centuries.

Perhaps it was this very experimentalism that made Boccaccio constantly

doubtful of the value of his own contributions. Petrarch with his Latin epic
and bucolics was following an established model for great, serious poetry
and publicly received a laurel crown. While granting Dante preeminence
in vernacular poetry, Petrarch scorned this path—or at least claimed to.[11]
Seeking Petrarch's approval but unconvinced by his example, Boccaccio
wrote in endlessly new ways, none of which was the obviously right way
to be a great poet and none of which won him a laurel. In *Epistole* (*Letters*)
15.17–21, hearing that Petrarch had finished a collection of letters (*Rerum
familiarum*) including several to Boccaccio, Boccaccio responded that he,
too, had been collecting Petrarch's letters—he never collected his own—
and he hoped that at least Petrarch's volume would preserve Boccaccio's
name. It is impossible to imagine Petrarch making such a comment to Boccaccio. Moreover, although Boccaccio criticized his friend sharply for accepting the patronage of a Milanese tyrant and old enemy of Florence, he
himself for many years longed in vain for the patronage that might free him
from ongoing financial cares to attend completely to his beloved studies.
Thus the recurrent expressions of humility in his writings are not merely a
topos. They express the uncertainty that was both produced by and productive of the writer's multidirectional experimentation.

Given the astonishing variety of Boccaccio's prolific work, our groupings of texts aim to suggest some of their many possible fruitful intercon-
nections. Where the Petrarch volume had six major sections, a sign of the
more centrally focused efforts of Petrarch, this volume has eleven, and
many of the works here arranged under one rubric could have appeared
just as well under another. For example, the *Buccolicum carmen* (*Bucolic Song*)
and the *Comedia delle ninfe fiorentine* (*Comedy of the Florentine Nymphs*) might
be grouped under either allegory or pastoral. The *De mulieribus claris* (*On
Famous Women*) might appear in either the section on women or that on
humanism. Because Boccaccio often came back to earlier works to revise
them (the biography of Dante and the *Decameron*) or developed a project
over many years (the *Buccolicum carmen* and *Genealogia*), it was impossible to
arrange the sections of this volume in a neat chronological order. We have
rejected the old critical divisions of Boccaccio's works into "major" and "minor," or into Italian fictions and Latin humanism. Rather, our groupings
call attention to Boccaccio's many directions of experimentation and to his
frequent reworking—sometimes many years later—of certain projects or
genres, often trying them out in *both* languages. Biography, pastoral, lyric,
letters, commentary, classical mythology, even writings about women, all
appear in both Latin and Italian; and scholars have pointed out how Boccaccio's vernacular narratives are closely connected with narratives in his

Latin texts.[12] The frequency of both Italian and Latin versions of projects is also what makes him so different from Petrarch. Boccaccio was a humanist who tried to recreate classical culture, archaeology, and genres in the vernacular while writing about women in Latin. This introduction will present the essays on Boccaccio's writings within the categories we have created for them while at the same time linking them to an account of Boccaccio's life.

As the Petrarch volume began with the *Canzoniere*, the work for which the poet became most famous, so this volume starts, in part 1, "The Vernacular Master," with the *Decameron* (1349–51), the only text that is the subject of two essays: one presenting a critical reading, and the other a textual history. In "Also Known as 'Prencipe Galeotto,'" Ronald Martinez comments on the rich, complex interplay of sources, styles, and structures, drawn from classical, vernacular, and Boccaccio's own previous writings, that converge in the *Decameron*. He pays attention especially to the various overlapping structures that organize the book. Brian Richardson, in "The Textual History of the *Decameron*," lays out the complexities of the textual traditions in manuscript and print, as well as of the scholarly efforts to reconstruct a correct complete edition and to determine whether Boccaccio himself produced more than one version.

Depending on one's focus of interest, the *Decameron* can be linked with almost anything else Boccaccio wrote. The gathering of a *brigata* in a garden appeared first in his early *Filocolo*, with the garden set in the environs of Naples rather than of Florence. Two of the tales told in that Neapolitan garden reappear in the *Decameron*'s Tenth Day. The *Comedia delle ninfe fiorentine* offers a precursor to the framed set of narratives told by seven women associated with the virtues. The address to women runs throughout the vernacular romances and into the Latin *De mulieribus claris*, dedicated, despite its Latin, to a woman and eagerly picked up by subsequent female readers. The explicit topics of fortune and love and the implicit topic of the pursuit of wealth are displayed pictorially in the *Amorosa visione*, while the power of fortune returns later, this time in Latin, in the *De casibus virorum illustrium* (*On the Downfall of Illustrious Men*). The psychological realism for which the tales have been praised has precursors in the *Filostrato*'s and *Elegia di madonna Fiammetta*'s analyses of long internal reactions to small external events; both of these works deal admirably, for example, with the experience of waiting for someone to arrive. Boccaccio's lifelong devotion to and disagreement with Dante appear in the very opening pages of the *Decameron*, with its subtitle "Prencipe Galeotto" ("Prince Galahalt") and its ascent from a plague-stricken city to a garden on a hill. While the plague links Florence to images near the bottom of Dante's hell, the ascent takes us only to his earthly paradise and not beyond, and the very first tale criticizes the assurance with which Dante assigns souls to heaven or hell.[13] Petrarch's influence, too, can be glimpsed in the desire for fame expressed by Panfilo in his selection of the final day's topic; the *Buccolicum carmen*'s eclogue about the ascent of a mountain, this time following in Petrarch's footsteps, can be seen as one more variation, in Latin, on the *Decameron*'s Dantean opening theme. Although the *Decameron* set a model for vernacular prose, that prose has a syntactical complexity and clausal rhythms based on Latinity, which connects this vernacular masterpiece to Boccaccio's Latin writings. In another stylistic experiment, both the tirade of the wife in *Decameron* 7.8 and the bitter vengeance of the scholar in 8.7 prepare for the *Corbaccio*'s invective, while the *Decameron*'s claim to offer a remedy for those suffering from love has its complement in the *Corbaccio*'s harsher medicine. In a sweeter vein, the songs that end each day contribute to Boccaccio's lifelong production of lyric poetry. The geographical range of the *Decameron* links it to Boccaccio's geographical interests, apparent in his essay on the Canaries as well as in the geographical dictionary *De montibus, silvis, fontibus, . . . (On Mountains, Forests, Fonts, . . .)*. In sum, readers who start with the *Decameron* can readily follow their interests into Boccaccio's other works.

Lucia Battaglia Ricci has noted the richly mixed education that produced the complexity of styles and genres within the *Decameron*: the study of commerce and canon law, of university texts, merchant manuals, and vernacular poetry, and an acquaintance through the Angevin library with the astronomical studies of Andalò del Negro as well as with French romances and Latin classics gave Boccaccio widely diverse models of writing and of inquiry.[14] Written in Florence and with its narrative frame set in and near there, the *Decameron* still owes a great deal to Boccaccio's adolescent years in Naples.

Taken by his father, Boccaccino, to Naples at the age of fourteen,[15] Boccaccio first worked for his father's business with the Bardi bank, and then studied law. As he laments in *Genealogia* 15.10,

> I well remember how my father even in my boyhood directed all my endeavors towards business. . . . For six years I did nothing in his office but waste irrevocable time. Then, as there seemed to be some indication that I was more disposed to literary pursuits, this same father decided that I should study for holy orders, as a good way to get rich. My teacher was famous, but I wasted under him almost as much time as before. . . . But while he tried to bend

my mind first into business and next into a lucrative profession, it came to pass that I turned out neither a business man, nor a canon-lawyer, and missed being a good poet besides.[16]

However, these were not wasted studies. They introduced Boccaccio not only to the world of Italian and international commerce, which would come to life in his *Decameron*, but also to teachers of law such as Cino da Pistoia, who, with personal links to both Dante and Petrarch, connected his student to the latest exciting developments in contemporary literature. Boccaccio's renditions in the *Filostrato* of poetry by Cino da Pistoia (5.62–65) and by Petrarch (5.54–55) are only one indication of Boccaccio's eager if informal apprenticeship in Tuscan literature. Barbato da Sulmona and Giovanni Barrili, Neapolitan friends who had visited Florence while Boccaccio still lived there, would have spoken similarly of Petrarch with enthusiasm. Canon law studies included the writings of Aquinas, who inspired in Boccaccio enough admiration that he gave the saint's name and family to the figure of his beloved lady, "Maria d'Aquino," in the *Amorosa visione* (43.46–59), referring to the saint there as one "che d'ampio fiume di scienza degno / si fece" (who made himself worthy of an ample stream of wisdom). Such studies surely contributed to his reading and explication of Dante. Ideas from Aquinas appear as well in Boccaccio's own writings, as Steven Grossvogel and Victoria Kirkham have pointed out.[17] Even the scholastic training in debating both sides of an issue was turned to literary use in the *Filocolo*'s famous debates about love.

Besides teachers such as Cino who encouraged Boccaccio's interest in vernacular poetry, other learned men were appreciatively remembered by Boccaccio for their formative influence: the teacher of rhetoric Dionigi di Borgo San Sepolcro, the science-minded Andalò del Negro and Paolo dell'Abbaco, and the historian Paolino Minorita.[18] Paolo da Perugia, the court librarian, and his friend Barlaam introduced the young student to the rudiments of Greek; decades later, Boccaccio would inherit and complete Paolo's project of an encyclopedia of classical mythology.[19] For the rest of his life Boccaccio retained friends from his Neapolitan years, visiting and corresponding with them. His experience of the court-centered Naples as well as the merchant-run Florence gave him an awareness of social class issues that has contributed to readers' sense that the *Decameron* offers a new kind of realism. He dreamed for much of his life of returning as an admired writer to bring luster to Naples and its court, until the invitations from Niccola Acciaiuoli decades later turned into bitter and disillusioning experiences, confirming Boccaccio in his life of impoverished independence.[20] When more trustworthy invitations came near the end of his life, he felt too set in his habits by then to move.

Part 2 of this volume, "The Autodidact," covers these early years in Naples with a focus on Boccaccio's youthful Latin writings in verse and prose: the classically inspired *Elegia di Costanza* and verse epistles, the *Allegoria mitologica (Mythological Allegory)* with its use of classical myth to represent biblical narratives, and four allegorical epistles. Boccaccio chose to write Latin verse occasionally throughout his life, either in imitation of classical forms (funereal, pastoral) or when the subject seemed appropriate (poems to and about Petrarch, and a prayer). Giuseppe Velli's essay, "Moments of Latin Poetry," examines an array of Latin verse from early efforts in the resurrection of classical forms to much later expressions of anxiety about the future preservation of Petrarch's manuscripts. In "A Fable of the World's Creation and Phaeton's Fall," Steven Grossvogel discusses the lengthy presentation in the *Allegoria mitologica* of the tale of Phaeton, which seems to allude (fearfully?) to Boccaccio's own literary ambitions. As Jason Houston demonstrates in "A Portrait of a Young Humanist," his analysis of the four unsent letters, we can see already in these early exercises how, by trying out various styles, Boccaccio was beginning to find his own voice.

The years in Naples were crucial to Boccaccio's cultural formation in the vernacular as well as in Latin. It was here that he wrote or at least began a series of what in part 3 we are calling "classical romances." From the *Filostrato* (1335?), his influential stanzaic tragedy set in Troy, to the *Filocolo* (1336–38), his epic-scale prose narrative elaborating a medieval romance and following explicitly in the footsteps of Virgil, Lucan, Statius, Ovid, and Dante,[21] and on to the *Teseida* (1339–41), proudly announced as the first martial epic in Italian (12.84–85) but interested as much in love as in battle, we see the convergence of Boccaccio's enthusiastic discovery of classical learning and his attraction to French romances. David Wallace, in "Love-Struck in Naples," sets forth the *Filostrato*'s combination of classical and romance, literary and popular, features, and the relevance of its classical setting to contemporary interests of the Angevin court. Furthermore, as he notes, Boccaccio's development of the octave as a stanza for narrative verse created a model for Ariosto and Tasso. Elissa Weaver's "A Lovers' Tale and Auspicious Beginning" comments on the novelty of Boccaccio's combination of divergent models in the *Filocolo*, including his importation of Byzantine romance into Italian prose literature. The *Teseida*, a work begun in Naples but finished in Florence, aimed to fill the niche indicated by Dante's suggestion in *De vulgari eloquentia* 2.2.8–10 that of the three main literary themes—love, valor, and salvation—only valor had not yet been treated in the vernacular. In producing the *Teseida* as a twelve-book romance-epic in Italian, Boccaccio, on the one hand, developed the stanzaic narrative verse of the popular *cantari*;[22] on the other hand, he annotated his tale, set in Greek antiquity, with footnotes that attempt to recreate in a scholarly way what could be known about ancient culture, its architecture, and its practices.[23] Boccaccio's glossing of his own poetry in the *Teseida* is perhaps an imitation of Dante, inspired by the *Vita nuova*, although carried out in a quite different manner.[24] Michael Sherberg, in "The Girl outside the Window," discusses the fruitful convergence of classical and romance models in the *Teseida*, with Dante as a linchpin connecting the two.

Part 4, "Allegorical *Terza Rima*," displays the admiration for Dante already evident in Naples and developed further after Boccaccio's return to Florence. Boccaccio tried his hand at Dante's verse form and use of allegory together with other Dantean techniques, such as number symbolism and the use of acrostic. Arielle Saiber's "The Game of Love" shows how the young Boccaccio, in writing the *Caccia di Diana* (1333–34), a Neapolitan work of courtly compliment and moral allegory, was trying to establish himself through its "tour de force combining number games, lore from medieval bestiaries and hunting manuals, troubadoric, stilnovistic, courtly, and classical traditions, . . . [and] textual references and poetic forms." The *Amorosa visione* (1342–43), an obvious imitation of the *Commedia*, features a narrator who follows his guide through a series of scenes teeming with individual examples, and openly celebrates Dante among philosophers and poets famous for their wisdom (cantos 5–6). At this time, too, Boccaccio was copying into his *Zibaldone Laurenziano* (*Laurentian Notebook*) a collection of Dante's writings. Vittore Branca suggests that being in Florence inspired Boccaccio's renewed Dantean efforts as he tried now to insert himself into the Tuscan literary tradition.[25] Jonathan Usher, in "Mural Morality in Tableaux Vivants," emphasizes this new weight of attention to Dante as a model for many aspects of the *Amorosa visione*, along with repeated motifs from Boccaccio's own previous works. He sees the *Visione* as an experiment in which encyclopedic categorizing and static iconography replace dramatic narrative, and which, although not entirely successful, tried out features that would be reemployed in greater works.

The return to Florence, sometime during the winter of 1340–41 but before Petrarch's coronation in Naples,[26] was difficult at first; Boccaccio gives a grim description of the change, near the end of the *Comedia delle ninfe fiorentine* (49.64–84).[27] His father's financial difficulties added depressingly to the loss of friends, royal library, and court culture. While the *Comedia delle ninfe* ambivalently advocates rising above a material focus to more spiritual pursuits, the *Amorosa visione*, which displays the triumph of Fortune over worldly goods and glory, shows Boccaccio's own father among the figures who foolishly waste their energies in seeking to amass wealth (14.34–45). Although Boccaccio's father had wanted his son to pursue a career that would give him an income, either in business or in the church, the experience of his father's financial troubles must have encouraged Boccaccio to pursue his true passions of study and writing in the hope that they would provide more lasting value. That attitude would have been reinforced by the Neapolitan confirmation and Roman coronation of Petrarch as a poet laureate in 1341, which Boccaccio noted with admiration. Nonetheless, Boccaccio remained involved in business matters, collecting rents and purchasing new property, signing contracts, and for the first time holding public office as a treasury official (1345).[28]

Boccaccio's first two works written entirely in Florence are closely inspired by Dante in their use of both allegory and *terza rima*; but in one of them Boccaccio connects this line of endeavor with another project: the revival of pastoral poetry. The *Comedia delle ninfe fiorentine* (1341–42) contained the first pair of eclogues, or shepherd's songs,[29] in Italian, opening up a very fruitful line for later vernacular poets. Borrowing its title from Dante, Boccaccio's *Comedia* elaborates on the seven nymph-virtues of Dante's earthly paradise. The series of narrations by these seven women looks back to the "love questions" of the *Filocolo* (4.16–72) and forward to the storytelling *brigata* of the *Decameron*. In part 5, "New Pastorals," Jane Tylus argues in "On the Threshold of Paradise" that the nymphs' tales with their double audience and double meanings suspend the text between the recreational and transformative (Dantean) possibilities of literature. At the same time, writing or storytelling is defended as pastoral work rather than pastoral leisure or idleness, pastoral work in which even the divine Venus, through a striking allusion, seems to participate.

While Boccaccio was writing pastorals, Florence was experiencing one of its more tumultuous periods politically. Its alliance with King Robert, dating from 1313, was wavering; the brief reign (1342–43) of Robert's nephew, Walter of Brienne, the Duke of Athens, had provoked a popular rebellion. Uncertain about the political leanings of Florence, wealthy Neapolitans sought to withdraw their investments from the Florentine banks; this action, combined with the failure of the French and English kings to repay loans from the Hundred Years' War, precipitated an economic crisis (1345), to which angry mobs responded by burning and looting bankers' mansions. Boccaccio spent 1346–47 not in Florence but in Ravenna, and the following year in Forlì. Meanwhile the death of King Robert provoked a violent power struggle in Naples into which Boccaccio was drawn through his service to Francesco Ordelaffi, ruler of Forlì. Although Boccaccio seems not to have accompanied Ordelaffi's brief military expedition to Naples in support of King Louis of Hungary,[30] his political eclogues comment on these events. The ultimate chaos came in 1348 with the Black Death. Boccaccio was back in Florence for this terrible event, which killed his father, his stepmother, and many of his friends, and left him, at thirty-five, in charge of his remaining family.

During these years of upheaval Boccaccio wrote pastoral verses in both Italian and Latin: the vernacular *Ninfale fiesolano* (*Tale of the Nymph of Fiesole*) (1346–47?) and early portions of the Latin *Buccolicum carmen*, begun during his years in Ravenna and Forlì and added to over the next twenty years. While these projects continued both the use of allegory and the revival of classical genres, they also began to lead the pastoral genre in two divergent directions: on the one hand, toward the use of eclogues for contemporary political and literary commentary; and, on the other, toward the creation of an unallegorized pastoral world of sentiments. The *Ninfale fiesolano* was a truly innovative and remarkable composition. Eschewing the allegorizations of the *Buccolicum carmen* and the *Comedia delle ninfe fiorentine*, it presented its rustic narrative in a newly simple and direct manner, depicting domestic relationships tied to the local geography. Yet it, too, connected to serious concerns of the normal world: as Susanna Barsella argues in "Myth and History: Toward a New Order," "The *Ninfale* transposes into collective terms the evolution from natural to civilized" man displayed in Boccaccio's *Comedia delle ninfe* with specific reference to the origin of Florentine political civilization.

Meanwhile, although under Petrarch's influence Boccaccio was turning away from the light grace of his two Virgilian Latin eclogues to a more ponderous allegorical use of the genre, nonetheless he retained those first two as eclogues 1 and 2 in his *Buccolicum carmen*. In "The Changing Landscape of the Self," David Lummus points out the importance of Ovid along with Virgil as a model and suggests that Boccaccio's series of eclogues is similarly a work of metamorphoses, in which the landscape continually changes meaning. Yet it remains always a place of cares, whether personal, political, or spiritual, while the true *locus amoenus* remains "on its edges," out of reach but beckoning. The place of poetry in a world of political crises and mercantile values is one recurring theme of these poems.

Boccaccio's new responsibilities were not only domestic ones; he started to be employed as well by the Florentine commune for missions of diplomacy. One of the first (1350) was to Romagna, where his personal acquaintance with both Ravenna and Forlì was no doubt useful. He was chosen also to present a gift from Florence to the daughter of Dante in Ravenna, in belated reconciliation with the poet honored after his death by the city that had exiled him. Other political missions followed during the 1350s, some dealing with threats from the aggressive Visconti, others with Florence's own territorial annexations. These missions took Boccaccio not only to other parts of Italy but also beyond to the Tyrol and Avignon; they included negotiations not only with local rulers but with the pope and the emperor. Boccaccio was becoming a respected leader in his community.

When Petrarch passed through Florence on his way to Rome in 1350 for the Jubilee year, Boccaccio invited him to stay and organized a local group of Petrarch admirers to participate in the occasion. It was the beginning of a long friendship between Boccaccio and Petrarch, and also of the social circle of Florentine humanists. Soon after, Boccaccio arranged to have Florence offer to restore Petrarch's patrimony, confiscated upon his father's exile, and to invite Petrarch to assume a professorship at the brand-new University of Florence. He presented these offers to Petrarch in Padua in 1351. Although disappointed that Petrarch turned them down, he was pleased to spend time with this friend, whom Boccaccio's letters repeatedly refer to as "my teacher." During this visit, as during several subsequent meetings, they became further acquainted with each other's writings and ideas, to their mutual benefit. Even Boccaccio's outrage in 1353 (Epis. 9) at Petrarch's decision to accept the patronage of Florence's enemy, the Visconti, could not break this deep friendship, which lasted until the end of their lives.

Part 6, "Woman and Women," highlights another feature of Boccaccio's writing, besides the use of Italian for classical genres, that set him apart from Petrarch: an interest in women's lives and in the use of female narrators. Developing Ovid's *Heroides* into an expanded vernacular prose narrative, Boccaccio created the *Elegia di madonna Fiammetta* (1343–44), which Branca has called "the first modern psychological and realistic novel peopled wholly by middle-class characters,"[31] innovatively set in the voice — and putatively the pen — of its female protagonist. This book, which became an important model for Helisenne de Crenne two centuries later, was also a useful source for *commedia dell'arte* actresses because of its range of emotional expression.[32] In her essay, "An Experiment in the Healing Power of Literature," Annelise Brody notes the confluence of vernacular (especially Dante) and classical sources typical of Boccaccio's writing in the *Elegia*'s exploration of the devastating power of love. She connects the *Elegia di madonna Fiammetta* to the *Decameron*, written soon after, as literature intended to help the reader deal with this destructive passion. Fiammetta fails to find help in the texts she reads, perhaps because of the way she uses them. Despite Fiammetta's appeal for our sympathy, she presents a cautionary example. So, too, does the lusty widow of the *Corbaccio* (c. 1355), seen in this instance from the perspective of a thwarted and humiliated male. Letizia Panizza, in "Rhetoric and Invective in Love's Labyrinth," discusses the *Corbaccio* as an invective therapy for immoderate sexual passion, aimed this time at men. She suggests that the title refers to the invective itself, with its harsh-sounding message. We can see that the *Elegia di madonna Fiammetta, Decameron*, and *Corbaccio*, composed in fairly close succession, all treat the same problem through widely varied genres and tones, another sign of Boccaccio's endless experimentation.

Criticizing his humanist friend, and other previous historians, for writing biographies only of famous men while ignoring the contributions of famous women, Boccaccio launched a model of female biography with his *De mulieribus claris* (1361–) that would have an enormous impact not only on future writings by both men and women but also on women's lives. Over the next few centuries, women received and read copies of this work and its later imitations, finding in them examples of women celebrated for their cultural contributions and even for their governmental and military leadership. When we add the preponderant use of female narrators in the *Decameron* and their equal turns as ruler of the day, we can see why Boccaccio's writings continued to be a model and inspiration for women writers, French as well as Italian, throughout the centuries that followed. However, as the inclusion of infamous women among the biographies, the ironies of Fiammetta's *Elegia*, and the vituperations of the *Corbaccio* (1355) demonstrate, Boccaccio cannot be neatly proclaimed a feminist. In "Doing and Undoing: Boccaccio's Feminism," Deanna Shemek clearly demonstrates the contradictions within the *De mulieribus claris*: "Even Boccaccio's praise in the *De mulieribus* often delivers backhanded swipes at womankind." Drawing heavily on classical examples, and employing the same euhemerist interpretations of myth as in the *Genealogia*, Boccaccio combines moral commentary with humanist scholarship. Shemek suggests that Boccaccio evinces "uneasiness in the multiple agendas of this text."

Boccaccio's biographies deal not with saints or kings but with women and poets. His life of Dante (1351–) can be compared to his biography of Petrarch (1348–50), two men both so important to his ideas about the functions of poetry and scholarship. Appropriately enough, the biography of Dante was written in Italian, and that of Petrarch in Latin. Both lives are treated in part 7, "Devotion to Dante and Petrarch." In the essay "A Life in Progress," Giuseppe Mazzotta indicates the ambivalences in Boccaccio's portrait of Petrarch, whom he seeks both to exalt and to accompany. Seeking to convey the significance of a life that is still ongoing, Boccaccio praises Petrarch for both poetic and moral qualities yet remains puzzled by the nature of his political involvements. In "To Praise Dante, to Please Petrarch," Elsa Filosa discusses how Boccaccio's *Trattatello in laude di Dante* (*Little Treatise in Praise of Dante*) was motivated by the need Boccaccio felt to respond to Petrarch's attitudes about Dante and about the vernacular in general. She notes also that it launched Boccaccio's development of the biography genre, applying the features of hagiography to praise of a poet.

The *Esposizioni* (1373–74), a commentary on Dante's *Commedia*, derived from a commission by the commune of Florence to lecture publicly on Dante's poem, a poem Boccaccio had copied both for himself and as a gift for Petrarch, and which had been formative to Boccaccio's entire career. The lectures and writing were interrupted at *Inferno* 17 by Boccaccio's final illness. Just as Filosa observes the lurking presence of Petrarch in the Dante biography, Robert Hollander, in "Boccaccio's Divided Allegiance," indicates the tension evident in this commentary between Boccaccio's allegiances to Dante and to Petrarch. Furthermore, noting several divergences of Boccaccio's approach to the *Commedia* from Dante's own, Hollander asks: "Did he know that he was disagreeing with Dante himself?"

Part 8, "Historian and Humanist," takes on works in which scholarship predominates. Although Boccaccio's career once used to be thought of as split between youthful fictions and the scholarship of older age, we have come to realize that both interests persisted and merged throughout his life. The enormous project of the *Genealogia* (ca. 1350–), with its combination of historical and philosophical interpretations of mythology, picked up and fulfilled the project begun by Paolo da Perugia, King Robert's court librarian, who had befriended the young Boccaccio in Naples. In his essay, "Gods, Greeks, and Poetry," Jon Solomon examines just how mammoth and unwieldy this project was, which occupied Boccaccio for four decades. Boccaccio made use of sources rarely known to medieval scholars, struggling to fit everything into a genealogical framework, and "the *Genealogy* became the first influential scholarly work in modern Europe to incorporate quotations, translations, and analyses of passages from Greek literature." For centuries it was the handbook of writers and artists seeking information on how to represent and interpret the classical gods. In its last books, Boccaccio also set forth a theory of literature that defends it against the ancient charges of lying and frivolity; he defends as well the study of pagan poets against Christian objections.

The *De casibus virorum illustrium* (1355–) expanded Boccaccio's biographical interest into a series of lives stretching from Adam and Eve to the contemporary Filippa of Catania, involved along with her son and granddaughter in intrigues at the Neapolitan court. As we can see from these framing examples, this book, too, despite its title, includes the occasional woman along with illustrious men. The lives are moralized under the rubric of Fortune, a concept crucial also to the *Decameron* and frequently recurring in Boccaccio's letters; they remind the reader that no height of power or wealth is exempt from the turning of Fortune's wheel. Simone Marchesi, in "Boccaccio on Fortune," points out how Boccaccio's sense of Fortune is quite different from Machiavelli's. Yet he notes also that the surprising "absence of any otherworldly perspective subsuming the history of mankind may be found in Boccaccio's dialogic situating of his work as continuation of and in contrast to Dante's." Boccaccio views history from an earthly perspective, where lives appear caught in recurring cycles.

The *Genealogia* and *De casibus* treat especially the classical past, although the *De casibus* mixes Greeks and Romans with figures from the Hebrew Bible and more recent histories. These works seek above all to make the ancient past relevant to the modern world yet without unduly diverging from a historical understanding—hence the *Genealogia*'s significant rejection of Christian readings of pagan mythology, of the sort promulgated by Bersuire and tried out by Boccaccio himself in earlier years. Taking a euhemeristic approach, Boccaccio often assumes that the gods were historical human beings deified for their contributions to civilization. He also wants to know what these myths might have meant to the ancients themselves, what meanings could have been consciously intended by their poets. Remarkably, given his claim that literature teaches via meanings intentionally hidden beneath a fictional surface, his theory includes even the fables of old women by the fireside as having something to convey: "and not only this, but there was never a maundering old woman, sitting with others late of a winter's night at the home fireside, making up tales of Hell, the fates, ghosts, and the like—much of it pure invention—that she did not feel beneath the surface of her tale, as far as her limited mind allowed, at least some meaning."[33] Thus even in a work that especially required scholarly erudition, Boccaccio did not entirely separate himself from the humble vernacular spinner of tales, but rather recognized a basic affinity and shared function in the human impulse to tell stories.

The lifelong convergence of Boccaccio's interests in the classical or learned and the vernacular or popular may have involved him early in his career in the vernacularization of ancient texts. He has been suggested as one of the translators of Livy, Valerius Maximus, and Ovid. In "Vernacularization in Context," Alison Cornish shows how problematic such attributions are, given the intertwined and multihanded processes of translation, glossing, and transcription. However, as she points out, whether or not Boccaccio produced any of these vernaculatizations, he used them even for texts that he knew in Latin, and evinced repeatedly a general concern for helping readers via one or another form of mediation.

In 1361, while working on several very long projects, Boccaccio moved from Florence and took up residence at a family property in Certaldo. The political situation in Florence at the beginning of the decade had become fraught with violent tension. A planned uprising against the powerful self-aggrandizement of certain families was betrayed, and some of the conspirators—including friends of Boccaccio's—were executed or exiled. This was the occasion of Boccaccio's long *Epistola consolatoria* (*Letter of Consolation*) to the exiled Pino de' Rossi. Regarded with suspicion by those in power, Boccaccio left Florence in disgust at its politics. Freed from civic duties, he found in tiny Certaldo the freedom and peace and quiet necessary for his intellectual labors.

It was in the interests of that freedom that he rejected Petrarch's invitation to come share his home. Later, for the same reason, he would reject other invitations, from the powerful Neapolitans Hugo of San Severino and Niccolò Orsini, and from the king of Maiorca.[34] The only invitation that succeeded in tempting him away came from Acciaiuoli via Francesco Nelli, an admirer of both Petrarch and Boccaccio. Lured by the idea of an honored position at the Neapolitan court, Boccaccio made the journey there late in 1362 only to spend six months in increasing anger and disillusionment. Abandoning the court, where—as he describes in a lengthy and irate letter to Nelli—instead of being treated as a valuable guest he found himself shamefully lodged and fed and generally ignored, he comforted himself with visits to some of his old friends, Mainardo Cavalcanti and Barbato da Sulmona, before returning home.[35] This unhappy experience reinforced his determination to remain independent despite financial constraints.

A combination of journeys and readings led Boccaccio to compose his two geographical works: the *De Canaria* (*On the Canary Islands*) (ca. 1341–42) and the later reference tome *De montibus, silvis, fontibus, lacubus, fluminibus, stagnis seu paludibus, et de diversis nominibus maris* (*On Mountains, Forests, Fonts, Lakes, Rivers, Marshes or Ponds, and on Different Names of the Seas*); these works are discussed in part 9, "Geographical Explorations." The *De montibus*, begun around 1355 and worked on for two decades until the year of Boccaccio's death, was explicitly intended as an aid to reading, especially classical literature and also scripture. In "Between Text and Territory," however, Theodore Cachey notes its double aims: "to elucidate textual references" and "to describe real territories" in "a distinctively Italocentric world." In the *De montibus* Boccaccio recorded his own impressions of areas near Naples and of crossing the Alps as a Florentine envoy; he also showed his appreciation for the tales of other travelers, ancient and recent. Similarly, the *De Canaria*, written shortly after his return from Naples to Florence, was based on the accounts of seafarers who had come upon those previously unknown islands, but also, as James Coleman shows in "Boccaccio's Humanistic Ethnography," on classical notions of the Golden Age. We cannot be surprised that the author of the *Decameron* combined these interests in the classics and in the contemporary, real world.

Part 10, "Miscellanies," gathers together writings never authorially collected into a larger whole: scattered lyric poetry, letters, and the notebooks into which Boccaccio copied texts that interested him. Unlike Petrarch, Boccaccio did not shape a collection of letters or poems. Perhaps he recognized that his forte lay in narrative rather than short verse. His perennial modesty also played a part here, for he collected the poems and letters of Dante and of Petrarch rather than his own. His unorganized writings in verse and prose nonetheless offer us rich insight into his thoughts at different periods of his life. In "Pathways through the Lyric Forest," Roberto Fedi presents the textual history of this poetry in its generic and thematic range, from light and playful, even burlesque, to more elegant and stilnovistic to serious and personally reflective. He argues that through eclectic experiments with various traditional themes and forms, "Boccaccio is seeking an original, or at least autonomous, path within the forest of amorous lyric." In the essay "Personality and Conflict," Todd Boli focuses on the stylistic and topical variety of Boccaccio's letters and shows how the more personal glimpses they offer make clear how different Boccaccio was from Petrarch. The letters also grant insights into Boccaccio's material life, as he struggled with problems of money and of health. Boccaccio lived his late years on a very modest income; although his letters often mention his restricted financial situation, he turned down several offers of support late in life in order to maintain his by-now long habit of solitary independence.[36]

While Boccaccio was visiting Ravenna, Petrarch sent him a request for information on a Saint Peter of Ravenna. Boccaccio's Epistle 11 corrects Petrarch's confusion of two distinct Peters of Ravenna and promises that he is about to send Petrarch his rewriting of a biography of Peter Damian composed by Giovanni da Lodi. Besides improving the style of his source text, Boccaccio added two new chapters: chapter 4 on the mutability of worldly

goods ("the ruin of proud kingdoms, the destruction of cities and large populations, and the vain and futile labors of individuals") and chapter 6 on the
pleasures of a solitary rural life removed from the cares of town and "lived
in full liberty."[37] Although Boccaccio was writing specifically for Petrarch,
he was no doubt thinking also of his own experiences: the plague, and his
escape from the political turmoil of Florence to the freedom and independence of a solitary life: "Nor is what some people often say an objection,
that is, that a holy life in the countryside serves only one's own good. Who
is so mad as not to prefer to benefit himself alone in the woods than to harm
himself while pursuing the good of others in the courts?" (6.3). Boccaccio's
own refuge, however, was intermittent at best. During his last decade, he
traveled both on personal visits, to Venice and to Naples, and on renewed
missions for Florence, such as those to the pope, first in Avignon and then in
Rome. Further civic duties for the Florentines, including his series of public
lectures on Dante's *Inferno*, required periods of residence in the city.

It is unusual good fortune that we possess the notebooks in which Boccaccio copied texts and facts that interested him, from his young school days
until the 1350s. In the essay "Boccaccio's Working Notebooks," Claude
Cazalé Bérard presents these manuscript *Zibaldoni* or notebooks as the heterogeneous "library and literary laboratory" revealing the wide-ranging interests that would fuel a long life of literary experimentation. Besides copies of historical, moral, scientific, and literary materials both classical and
medieval, they preserve the sole surviving copies of three letters by Dante,
Dante's exchange of eclogues with Giovanni del Virgilio, and several of
Boccaccio's early works: his first Latin poem (*Elegia di Costanza*), *De Canaria*, the four allegorical epistles, and the *Allegoria mitologica*. Cazalé Bérard
traces the findings and shifting methodologies of recent research on these
important manuscripts.

One aspect of Boccaccio's prolific creativity has been less recognized
than his writings: the designs and drawings that he penned onto manuscripts. In "A Visual Legacy," Victoria Kirkham gathers all that have been
definitively or controversially attributed to him, from marginal curls and
pointing hands through small portraits of some *Decameron* characters to
larger and more complex illustrations of the *Decameron* and, possibly, of Petrarch's Vaucluse.

It was at his home in Certaldo that Boccaccio ended his days on December 21, 1375. He survived his friend Petrarch by only a year, and the
quick succession of their deaths led Franco Sacchetti to lament that an era
of cultural renovation had now passed.[38] Our volume ends with Boccaccio's
last will. Michael Papio, "An Intimate Self-Portrait," offers the first English

translation and an analysis of the will, which give us a glimpse of the writer's material circumstances and circle of associates at the end of his life.

Although it has surprised readers of the *Decameron*'s anticlerical tales to think of Boccaccio as a member of the clergy, by 1360 he had obtained the status of *clericus*. He was greeted as such in a letter by Pope Innocent VI absolving him of his illegitimate birth so that he could care for souls and receive a benefice from the church.[39] As Boccaccio's will mentions a breviary and the garments of a priest, the poet apparently exercised this papally granted right and probably obtained some modest income from it. His youthful study of canon law had become useful after all.

Despite his Christian faith, Boccaccio believed in the desire for fame as a spur to a virtuous and productive life. This idea recurs in a number of his writings. Panfilo, suggesting his topic for the final day of the *Decameron*, argues that examples of magnanimity will inspire similar behavior in the hearers of these tales, so that

> la vita nostra, che altro che brieve esser non può nel mortal corpo, si perpetuerà nella laudevole fama; il che ciascuno che al ventre solamente, a guisa che le bestie fanno, non serve, dee non solamente desiderare ma con ogni studio cercare e operare. (9, Concl., 5)

> our life, which in the mortal body cannot be other than brief, will perpetuate itself in praiseworthy fame, which every person who does not merely serve his belly, in the manner of beasts, ought not only to desire but also with all zeal to seek and effect. (my trans.)

The *Genealogia* claims in 14.7 and 11 that poets are properly inspired by the pursuit of fame, and in 15.13 cites Cicero on the desire for praise and glory as an incentive for all men. In *De casibus* 8.1, as Boccaccio, weary of writing, wonders whether fame is not an empty reward, Petrarch's spirit appears to him and launches into a speech on the importance of the human impulse to achieve a virtuous fame, which, he claims, even holy men such as Jerome and Augustine desired. This speech rouses Boccaccio to cast off his excuses for laziness and to resume his work.

However, if Petrarch, as Kirkham has suggested, was obsessed with the evaluation of men's worth, especially his own,[40] Boccaccio's self-assessment remained always humble and unsure. Indeed, Petrarch marveled: "Almost all men are deluded by love for themselves and for what is theirs; you alone among so many thousands are deceived in your estimation of your own things by hatred and contempt."[41] In *De casibus* 3.14.10–11, following his

praises of Homer, Virgil, and Petrarch, Boccaccio writes of himself: "I con-
fess that I am not a poet; far be it that I should be so mad as to dare to claim
to be or want to be held to be what I am not; but it is what I wish to be and
what I pursue with effort; whether, however, I shall reach the goal, God
knows. Indeed I judge that my strength will not to be up to such a long
course, since many abrupt ravines and nearly inaccessible peaks intervene."
In his letter to Iacopo Pizzinga (1361), after praising Dante for opening a
brand new pathway to the Muses via the vernacular, and Petrarch for re-
opening the ancient (Latin) pathway and encouraging others to ascend it,
Boccaccio reflects:

> Perhaps, famous man, after all this you expect me to say something
> about myself, since I, too, have long followed poetry. By heaven! I
> come to it not without blushing in mind and in face as I lay open to
> you briefly my weak-mindedness. With great intention, I confess,
> I entered the already beaten path, drawn by the desire of perpetu-
> ating my name and by my faith in the lead of my famous teacher,
> and I took to the road with those same men on whom you, too,
> had relied. But while I allow myself to be drawn hither and thither
> now by domestic and now by public cares, and I look up at those
> peaks almost grazing the sky, I have begun to flag and gradually
> to lose courage and fail in strength, and setting aside the hope of
> arrival, having become lowly and despondent, seeing those whom
> I had taken as guides moving farther and farther ahead of me, now
> white-haired I have come to a standstill, and—what is to me a lam-
> entable evil—I neither dare turn back nor seek to ascend higher;
> and thus, unless some new grace from above be poured into me, I
> will entomb an inglorious name along with my corpse.[42]

Posterity has been kinder to Boccaccio than he dared hope. He was
greatly esteemed already by his contemporaries and has remained admired
and famous ever since. If he never wrote a Latin epic, that was not what
made even Petrarch famous in the long run. Boccaccio became the model
for Italian prose, for fiction, for pastoral narrative, for biographical writing,
for the re-creation (not just revival) of classical genres in the vernacular,
and for the rediscovery of Greek. With attention both to popular culture
and to learning, he combined the prolific efforts of a creative writer and a
scholar. His work has stood the test of centuries, inspiring countless other
writers in many languages. Despite his own doubts, it has well earned him
his place among Italy's "three crowns."

PART I

THE VERNACULAR MASTER

CHAPTER ONE

ALSO KNOWN AS "PRENCIPE GALEOTTO" • (Decameron)

Ronald L. Martinez

Boccaccio's *Decameron cognominato Prencipe Galeotto* (*Decameron surnamed Prince Galahalt*), one of the most influential and accomplished collections of short tales in European and world literature, contains "a hundred stories, told in ten days by seven ladies and three young men" while they are away from Florence during the great plague of 1348.[1] It transmits, in a new Italian vernacular literary form called the *novella*, a rich selection of short narrative that crowns a thousand years of medieval writing. In addition to stories probably of his own devising, Boccaccio exploits many sources: the Latin classics, especially Ovid's *Metamorphoses* and *Heroides* and Apuleius's *Metamorphoses of Lucius*; the lives of the Christian fathers and the popular *Legenda aurea* (*Golden Legend*); didactic medieval compilations like the *Disciplina clericalis* (*Scholar's Guide*) of Petrus Alfonsi; bawdy French *fabliaux*, courtly romances like *Tristan*, and the *lais* of Marie de France; and an Italian collection of short tales, the *Novellino*—all adapted, collected, and placed in a frame story by a single authorial consciousness.[2] In his Proem Boccaccio gives to his *novelle* the alternate names of *favole* ("fables," or fictional tales), *parabole* ("parables," or stories with detectable didactic meaning), and *istorie* ("histories," implying a basis in historical fact). Further complexity comes at each Day's close in a *ballata*, a strophic poem with refrain suitable for dancing, sung by one of the ten narrators, so that the work mixes prose and verse.

Although strikingly original, the *Decameron* benefits from Boccaccio's previous work in manifold ways. The fifteen *quistioni d'amore* in his early prose *Filocolo* (4.16–72) are a germ for the collection, which incorporates two of them.[3] The *Comedia delle ninfe fiorentine* features a protagonist, Ameto, whose adolescent eros is transformed into virtuous love when he hears a set of narratives related by seven beautiful nymphs representing the virtues, and whose allegorical names conceal those of women in existing Florentine families. The prose *Elegia di madonna Fiammetta*, written in the voice of a married woman abandoned by her lover, anticipates the dedication of the *Decameron* to women suffering from love-melancholy (Proem, 9–12). In several early works Boccaccio experimented with ways to fashion a single book out of various parts and paratexts (e.g., titles, rubrics, proems, and arguments). From a thematic perspective, most reflect an attempt to mediate conflicts of love and duty, sexual energy and official morality ingrained in late medieval Christian culture, a tension also discernible in the *Decameron*.[4]

Boccaccio's work on the *Decameron* probably began in 1349 and was substantially complete by 1351; however, it underwent revisions until at least 1372, when he wrote out the whole text in fair copy. Consciously designed to appear as a masterpiece, the 1372 version was set out in double columns in a semigothic book hand, a format reserved for major works of learning like the compilation of pagan mythology he began after completing the *Decameron*.[5] Its inclusion as characters of Tuscan masters like the painter Giotto (6.5) and the poet Guido Cavalcanti (6.9) reflects the Certaldan's awareness of being an artistic innovator.[6] Despite his friend Petrarch's discouragement of vernacular work, Boccaccio's continuing labor on the *Decameron*—even as his humanist vocation led him to write mainly in Latin—makes it clear that his *Centonovelle* (as the work was popularly known) was a bid to emulate the hundred cantos of Dante's *Commedia* and perhaps to rival Petrarch's collection of 366 vernacular lyrics.[7] But where Dante's *Commedia*, despite fielding many characters, has a single protagonist and narrative voice, and Petrarch's is a wholly monological collection, Boccaccio's includes multiple voices, male and female, making his work represent a social community of thought and speech.

While affiliated with Boccaccio's earlier works, the *Decameron* is utterly unlike them in the vivid realism and historical specificity of its characters and situations, and in the bawdy humor of many tales, which mine what Bahktin defined as the carnivalesque "lower bodily stratum." The *Decameron* treats the most urgent topics of the late Middle Ages (love, sexuality, mortality, virtue, fortune, courtliness), as they are lived by a broad range of social groups, from sultans and kings to merchants to cooks, bandits, and pirates. How this leap in range and quality was achieved remains somewhat mysterious, but part of the answer lies in Boccaccio's return to Florence from Naples in 1341, after the failure of the Bardi banking house with which his father was associated. This meant his exposure to the urban, pragmatic, guild-based republicanism of the Guelph regime, so different from the aristocratic leisure of the Angevin court of Naples, and it required his reassessment of Florentine vernacular literature, chiefly Dante's *Commedia*, a work distinguished by a "creatural realism" representing an epochal advance in narrative technique.[8] In Florence, moreover, Boccaccio could size up the future aristocratic, mercantile, and learned audiences of the *Decameron*, as well as the "idle ladies" (*oziose donne*) to whom he dedicates the work in its Proem.[9]

For his large collection, Boccaccio deployed a highly ornate but sinewy artistic prose, far more effective than the often oversweet texture of the *Comedia delle ninfe*, for example. Not only in the Introduction and other authorial passages but throughout the tales there are rhetorical periods of syntactical complexity equal to the Latin prose of Cicero.[10] Flexible enough to accommodate various levels of decorum and a wide spectrum of diction, the style is also multilingual for the sake of parody, as in Madonna Lisetta's Venetian dialect (4.2) and Rinaldo d'Asti's liturgical Latin (2.2.12). In the authorial defense before the Fourth Day, Boccaccio claims the stories are written "in the humblest and most unassuming style that they can be," echoing the language defining the level of the *Commedia* in Dante's *Letter to Can Grande* (*remissus et humilis*), thus a "comic" or middle register.[11] Boccaccio also thought his work to be of mixed genre, at once comic, tragic, and satirical, again after the model of Dante (*Trattatello in laude di Dante* 176), thus requiring the middle style. But Boccaccio's style and diction are more uniform than Dante's,[12] and certainly more restrained, despite the sexual or scatological content of many stories: the use of puns and euphemisms to avoid explicit obscenity is virtually a structural principle of the work.[13] Boccaccio never uses "shit" (*merda*), for example, as Dante does (*Inferno* 18.116), preferring instead the more decorous "dung" (*letame*) (*Decameron* 6.10.21).

Thirty stories set in Florence, twelve more in Tuscany, and six more in which Florentines appear as characters account for nearly half the total, but the book embraces all of Italy. Not surprisingly, given Boccaccio's long residence in Naples, ten stories represent southern Italy, including Salerno, Sicily, and nearby islands. Northern Italy from Milan, Asti, and Treviso to Friuli and the Marche is represented, as are the Atlantic and the Mediterranean from Britain (2.3, 2.8), Portugal (Algarve, 2.7), and Paris (1.2, 3.9, 7.7) to Alexandria (2.6, 2.7, 2.9, 10.9) and Acre in the Holy Land (10.9), including islands from the Balearics and Rhodes to Crete and Cyprus;[14] one story is set in Cathay (10.3). More briefly, we have Italy, the Mediterranean, and the world. In terms of temporal scope, four stories are set in ancient times (5.1, 7.9, 9.9), including one among the Romans of Octavian's day (10.8); one is set in the early seventh century, when the Langobards ruled Italy (3.2). But most tales are set in the period between the First Crusade and Boccaccio's own day (1100–1350), especially between about 1260 and

1330, that is, the period of the Guelph-Ghibelline conflicts that make up the active "memory" of Dante's *Commedia*, and of Boccaccio's recent past.[15]

The geographical limits of the book implicitly frame its material, as when on the first Day Boccaccio sets stories in Genoa (8), in Liguria, Monferrat, and Verona (4, 5, 6), and in Paris and Bologna (2, 10). Genoa was the hub of Italy's seafaring mercantilism; the next three places were known for the cultivation of troubadour lyric; the last pair of cities housed the principal European universities for studies in theology, the liberal arts, medicine, and law. Taken together, they are localities that suggest Boccaccio's appeal to readers from mercantile, aristocratic, and scholarly milieus, respectively.[16] But the *Decameron* also deploys an unprecedentedly elaborate set of explicit frames. The book is like a series of concentric boxes. Circumscribing the whole is the voice of the Author-Narrator in the Proem and Introduction, in the Author's defense before Day 4, and the Conclusion. Individual storytellers in turn, conditioned by the topics imposed by the ruler of eight of the ten Days, narrate stories that can themselves contain tales (e.g., 1.3, 1.6, 5.8, 10.4). The numerous paratexts also serve a framing function. In addition to the work's highly significant titles, the authorial summaries for each Day and for each tale (rubricated in the Hamilton 90 autograph) condition how readers approach the narratives. In the case of 10.10.1, for example, the authorial emphasis in the rubric on Griselda's oppressive husband, the Marquis of Saluzzo, may qualify the usual intense focus by readers on the wife.[17] By inserting the rubricated headings directly into the 1372 version (i.e., not setting them off with full paragraphing, though leaving a space before the beginning of the *novella*) Boccaccio minimizes their disruption of continuous reading but conserves their use as indexing devices for selective perusal.[18]

In the Proem, the Author-Narrator, introducing himself as having survived a love affair thanks in part to the ministrations of others, offers up the book as a remedy for women in love who lack the distractions (hunting, gambling, business) available to men.[19] Displays of compassion, as if following the Narrator's exordial *sententia*, "To have pity for those in distress is human,"[20] recur especially in Day 4, when tragic love stories excite the pity of the seven storytelling ladies. These displays of kindness within the fictional world of the tales contrast with the absence of human compassion (the word is not even used) in the account of Florence devastated by the plague with which the first Day of the work properly begins.[21]

The Introduction relates that the plague reached Florence about March 25, 1348—the feast of the Annunciation—and raged until July. A group of seven ladies assemble in the Church of Santa Maria Novella on a

Tuesday, and the eldest of them, Pampinea, proposes to leave the city for the sake of self-preservation. The detailed account of the rapid progress of the disease, the fraying of social compacts, the wholesale decay of laws, morals, and husbandry, and especially the neglect of decent burial, follows a medieval Latin account of a much earlier plague and is possibly also influenced by Petrarch, whose Latin poem *Epystole* 1.14 on the plague of 1340 was copied by Boccaccio into one of his miscellanies.[22] The title *Decameron* is based on the term *Hexaemeron*, which in patristic works refers to the six days of Creation, and in Boccaccio's case implies that the ten Days of storytelling serve not only for recreation, but for the re-creation, through narrative, of the Florentine polity. Plagues do in fact traditionally give occasion to new institutions.[23] The idea of the plague remains a presence in the collection. The forthright Nonna de' Pulci of Prato is recalled as having died in the current epidemic (6.3.8), and the narrator Dioneo, despite his wish to avoid memories of the afflicted city (1, Intro., 93), recalls the decay of morals during the plague (6, Concl., 8–9); references near the end of the work to the mortality of the narrators (10, Intro. 4; 9, Concl., 5) are in the same spirit. Related to the plague context is the fact that *novella* characters sicken and die, beginning with the first one, Cepparello or Ciappelletto (1.1.20);[24] on Day 4 only the second and the last tale end without at least one dead body.[25]

According to the Author-Narrator (1, Intro., 51) the ten storytellers, hereafter the *brigata*, do not bear their real names, supposedly those of real people, but have sobriquets assigned "not without reason." One reason is their affiliation with other works of Boccaccio: an Emilia is the heroine of the epic *Teseida delle nozze d'Emilia*, a Pampinea is found in the pastoral *Eclogues*, a Panfilo in that precursor of the novel that is *Elegia di madonna Fiammetta*. Other names point to other authors: Elissa is the original name of Virgil's Dido; Lauretta was Boccaccio's name for Petrarch's Laura, Neifile (new love) evokes the *stilnovo* (new style) of poets Guido Cavalcanti, Cino da Pistoia, and Dante. Another reason is allegorical significance: on the model of the seven nymphs of *Comedia delle ninfe fiorentine*, who personify cardinal and theological virtues, Pampinea, who may stand for Wisdom or Prudence, originates the sensible idea of fleeing the plague-ridden city (1, Intro. 92) and dictates the terms under which the *brigata* functions, "never exceeding the limit of reason" (1, Intro. 65), a crucial interpretive parameter for the book.[26]

The exact fit between the seven ladies and their allegorical roles is often subtle. The characters and allegorical roles of the three males who chance upon the ladies in Santa Maria Novella and furnish them their "head" is more transparent, as is their relation to the subjects they choose for the

Days over which they rule. Panfilo, whose name means "all-loving" in approximate Greek, speaks for the rational, Boethian idea of love governing
the universe (*Consolatio philosophiae* 2, m. 8). As the very first narrator, he
makes the gesture of invoking God's name,[27] and he is king of the final Day,
when he calls for tales of magnificent gestures, including those demonstra-
tive of a higher love, charity; he also speaks of the fame that transcends death
(9, Concl., 5). The melancholic Filostrato, whose name means "downed by
love," is dominated by the irascible part of his soul, and so imposes for the
Fourth Day unhappy love stories that suit his dark mood (3, Concl., 5–6).
Dioneo, finally, associated onomastically with Dione, the mother of Venus,
stands for the concupiscent soul, and speaks on behalf of bodily appetites
and social misrule; he commands the Seventh Day, in which women trick
their husbands for the sake of love or self-preservation (6, Concl., 6). The
three male narrators, whose Days of rule frame the work in three parts (1–4,
5–7, 8–10) echo the several guises of the Author-Narrator. As the writer of
the Proem, survivor of an "immoderate love," he is an ex-Filostrato who has
acquired the perspective and compassion of Panfilo, but in his facetious, defensive irony on behalf of his bawdy tales and his "sweet tongue" (4, Intro.,
32–39; Concl., 27), he resembles Dioneo.

Pampinea decrees (with Dioneo's urging) dedication to a festive life,
but—invoking again the topic of self-preservation—notes that a rule must
govern the storytellers if their society is long to endure. Elected the first
ruler by acclaim, Pampinea proposes to avoid envy by instituting a rotat-
ing sovereignty, which in its provision of leadership to all members may
be an idealized reflection of the Florentine republic.[28] Indeed, Filomena
refers to Neifile, the rising queen, as "governing our small polity,"[29] adopting the term historically used for the guild-based Florentine government.[30]
The parallels with secular governance are significant, yet the careful daily
routine established by Pampinea, by which the sovereign apportions according to the canonical hours of tierce, nones, and vespers the times for
eating, sleeping, and recreation—including singing, dancing, chess, reading
and reciting romances, and of course telling stories—is more like a secular
form of monastic life, a life of pleasure so temperate and so well regulated
as to be sacred in its rituality, that "order" (*modo*) that Pampinea claims is
necessary for any entity to survive (1, Intro., 95). Nor is the frame complete
at the outset; it undergoes changes and refinements: at the end of the first
Day (1, Concl., 12) Dioneo requests the privilege of always speaking last,
permitting him to exercise his subversive wit, a departure from rule that
becomes a rule, though one that Dioneo himself does not hesitate to break
at the end of Day 7, the Day of his own regency. Emilia on her Day 9 sets

no prescribed topic. Neifile institutes the custom of abstaining from story-telling on Fridays in honor of the day of Christ's death and on Saturdays to permit personal ablutions, a custom reaffirmed by Lauretta after Day 7 but with greater emphasis on devotions. Only on Day 8, a Sunday, is it reported that the *brigata* attends Mass.

Changes of venue furnish equally consequential innovation. Having left Florence, the *brigata* heads first to a well-appointed villa in the hills a few miles from the city and narrates the tales of Days 1–2 in a meadow bordered by a stream. Before Day 3 Neifile leads them to a walled garden familiar from courtly romance tradition, complete with fountain and reflecting pool. Elissa, before Day 7, shows her fellow narrators a more secluded garden, the Valley of Ladies, a fecund, perfectly circular (though natural) terraced nursery where trees grow that represent all four seasons and where the women and the men serially bathe in the transparent pond at its center. The gardens variously allude to Eden and to the valleys and gardens where Dante's pilgrim pauses in the *Purgatorio*. The walled garden frames the most erotic tales in the collection (but also the storytelling on Days 4 and 5), while the Valley is the exclusive stage for the tales in which women achieve their desires in spite of their husbands. The very subject of Day 7 is decided by means of an innovation, indeed almost a revolution: at the end of Day 5 a dispute breaks out between the servants Licisca and Tindaro on whether the wife of a certain Sicofante was a virgin on her wedding night; Dioneo subsequently borrows his subject for Day 7 from the dispute, so that a narrative topic may be said to enter the collection from both the "lower bodily stratum" and the lower class. Respecting a principle of dialectical balance, Boccaccio frames the generically "comic" squabble of Licisca and Tindaro with allusions to his own "tragic" *Filostrato* and "epic" *Teseida*, as pairs of *brigata* members sing about Troilo and Criseide (6, Intro., 3) and Arcita and Palemone (7, Concl., 6). High tragedy frames, and contains, low comedy.

Despite so many licentious stories told, both the cynical Dioneo (6, Concl.,11–12) and the high-minded Panfilo (10, Concl., 4) acquit the *brigata* of any dishonesty, and Panfilo praises their harmonious consensus as he proposes the return to Florence (10, Concl., 4–5); we recall that Pampinea, to minimize discord, had deliberately chosen storytelling rather than games with winners and losers (1, Intro., 111). One of the last views of the story-tellers has them wearing oaken crowns, the ancient Roman prize for saving the life of a citizen, and the Narrator remarks that anyone who saw them would esteem them immortal, or likely to die happily (9, Intro., 4). By the end of the ten Days Pampinea's principle of self-preservation has acquired the implication of having preserved a civic culture. The contrast between a plague symptom as "certain indication of future death" (*futura morte*, 1, Intro., 12) and the *brigata* "speaking about their future life" (*futura vita*, 10, Intro., 3) is surely thematic.

Although the frame story evolves, Boccaccio has not failed to arrange an articulated spatial form for the *Decameron*. It is best summarized with a diagram:[31]

	1	2	3	4	5	6	7	8	9	10	11	12	13	14	15	16
Total Days	*Tue*	*Wed*	Thu	Fri	Sat	Sun	Mon	*Tue*	*Wed*	Thu	Fri	Sat	Sun	Mon	*Tue*	*Wed*
Story Days, Ruler	I	II				III	IV	V	VI	VII			VIII	IX	X	
	Pamp	Filom				Neif	*Filos*	**Fiam**	Elis	*Dion*			Laur	Emil	*Panf*	
Place	city	meadow				garden				Valley			garden			city
Singer *ballata*							**Filos**		**Elis**							
		Emil	Pamp			Laur		Dion		Filom			Panf	Neif	Fiam	

Although there are ten Days of storytelling, sixteen days pass in all, including the day the *brigata* assembles (Day 1) and the day of departure (Day 16). Because they are Fridays and Saturdays, Days 4–5 and 11–12 are excluded from storytelling. Story Days fall into three sections: 1–2, 3–7, and 8–10, which puts into relief the five consecutive Days in the middle, with Day 5 as the center, and the two Sundays when storytelling recommences (3, 8). The five-Day central series is further articulated by the garden locations, entered beginning Days 3 and 7, that frame Days 4–6 and still further by Filostrato and Elissa, who are the only narrators asked to sing a *ballata* at the end of the same Day over which they rule (Days 4–6), again framing Day 5, which is also "centered" by Day 1, on which Pampinea assigns no topic, and Day 9, on which Emilia prescribes none. Within the five-Day central series, the pair of Days 4 and 5, including tragic loves on Day 4, then stories that skirt disaster but end happily with marriage on Day 5, are a microcosm that reproduces Boccaccio's account of the movement of the *Decameron* as a whole (1, Intro., 2–5), and his characterization of the tales as "pleasant and bitter stories of love" (Proem, 14). In other words, they are a microcosm of the book's comic structure.

In contrast to the emphases on Day 5 as a center, a bipartite structure is suggested by Days 1 and 6, both of which feature tales of swift responses that reverse difficult situations, suggesting that the ten-Day structure may also be viewed as two five-Day halves. There is thus a distinct emphasis on Days 5–6, with the "center" of the whole book, according to this reckoning, falling exactly between the two. The pairing is an understandable one, since these two Days are a Tuesday (*martedì*) and a Wednesday (*mercoledì*), named after the planets Mars and Mercury, traditionally held responsible for the mixture of knightly valor and mercantile ingenuity in the Florentine character: one more way of identifying the *Decameron* with the fortunes of Florence.[32]

Among the consequences of this double articulation is that Day 5, although the chief formal center of the work, must also share this distinction with Day 6. Stories like 5.9 and 6.1 (as well as Dioneo's subversive 5.10) are thus "central," an honored placement borne out by their content. Fiammetta's 5.9, on how Federigo degli Alberighi conquers his lady's heart by nobly sacrificing his falcon, is attributed to the Florentine gentleman Coppo di Borghesi Domenichi, a representative of the *buon tempo antico* (good old days) of chivalrous civic responsibility that Boccaccio, as Dante had done, hopes to rekindle imaginatively with his narrative. Fiammetta's story heralds the all-Tuscan Sixth Day and a rich vein of Tuscan tales in Days 7–9 (twenty-one out of thirty, while Days 4–5 have only three). One of them, Filomena's 6.1, is the most conspicuous metanovella in the collection: a knight offers to bear Lady Oretta on her way on the "horse" of a tale, but he tells it so poorly that she suffers palpitations and, complaining wittily of the story's rough gait, begs to be set down. Furnishing a thumbnail canon of the well-told story, the tale of Madonna Oretta exemplifies the topos of storytelling as conveyance, familiar to Boccaccio from other framed collections, including Apuleius's Latin novel.[33] Fiammetta's first story, on how the Marquise of Monferrat dissuades the king of France from invading her bed by hosting him to a dinner of nothing but chicken, resembles a tale from a version of the *Book of the Seven Sages*, a collection in which storytelling extends the life of a king's son when impeached by his wicked stepmother. Thus storytelling as self-preservation, which lies behind Pampinea's rationale for leaving the plague-ridden city in the first place, is reflected in Fiammetta's first story; in Oretta's case the consequences of unartful narrative for bodily health are obvious.

Story collections are typically didactic, a function recognized in the other chief metanovella of the *Decameron*, the Author-Narrator's own, which he inserts before the Fourth Day in order to defend both his dedication of the

Decameron to women in love, and his cultivation of the Muses, also women.[34] In the Author's tale, the widower Filippo Balducci, having raised his son from infancy in an austere mountain cave, finally takes the boy to Florence, where after accurately identifying most of the sights he swerves from correct denotation and describes women as goslings (*papere*) and "evil things" in an attempt to thwart his son's interest. But the son's natural instinct recognizes the goslings as desirable, indeed more beautiful than painted angels, and he begs his father for one he can take home and feed. The tale is richly symptomatic of the *Decameron*. It is about Florence as a prosperous metropolis, a showcase for early capitalist ostentation, and it exemplifies Boccaccio's unflinchingly parodic use of hagiographic sources.[35] Though verging on obscenity when the father scornfully alludes to the beaks where the "goslings" are fed (*ove s'imbeccano*), the Author's tale remains, thanks to metonymy and metaphor, linguistically chaste, illustrating the Author's view in the Conclusion that nomenclature alters neither things in themselves nor the intentions of speakers or readers (Concl., 7–15).[36] Most suggestively for the tale as a metanovella for the *Decameron*, the boy's preference of the lovely goslings to painted angels recalls the conclusion to Guido Guinizzelli's famous *canzone*, "Al cor gentil rempaira sempre amore" ("Love repairs always to the gentle heart"), one of the founding texts of the poetic movement known as the *dolce stil novo*, in which the speaker imagines himself reproved by God himself for preferring his lady to the Virgin Mary, but responds with metaphysical boldness that he could do no other, given that God had made women as beautiful as angels, thus blurring the distinction between sacred and profane loves. Boccaccio thus enrolls himself—if in his own facetious way—among the poets of preceding generations who enhanced the prestige of love poetry and broadened the scope of the licitly erotic.[37]

Boccaccio's narrators are bound to choose tales that suit the subject of the Day, with the exception of the privileged Dioneo. But Dioneo often conforms (e.g., Rustico and Alibech, 3.10; Frate Cipolla, 6.10; Salabaetto, 8.10) or merely parodies the stories of his fellow narrators, as in 5.10, when he replaces the nuptial conclusions of that Day with a ménage à trois. When Dioneo's tales depart from the subject, they anticipate the Day that follows: in 2.10, Riccardo Chinzica's wife, rather than enduring the sexual fasting her husband demands, enjoys the vigorous attentions of the pirate Paganino, thus anticipating the lovemaking of Day 3; and the cheerful news imparted to Tingoccio by the ghost of his dead friend Meuccio, that no notice is taken in the afterlife of sex with *comari* (godmothers, 7.10.28), jocosely introduces the topic of judgment explored in Day 8. Thus Dioneo's license de jure works de facto to unify the collection.[38]

Not only are the stories over eight Days unified by prescribed themes, each Day's theme follows the astrological suggestion of the weekday. For example, both Wednesdays, 1 and 6, feature tales in which brief, witty remarks serve to avoid harm or to reproach an antagonist. Wednesday is *mercoledì*, the day of Mercury, the messenger-god of eloquence and ingenuity. Boccaccio writes in his *Genealogia* 14.18 that Mercury, who persuaded Aeneas to leave Dido, signifies the stimulus to return to the way of fame. Thus in Elissa's brief ninth story, the shortest in the whole book, the first Latin king of Cyprus is galvanized by a humble lady of Gascony who asks him how he endures his dishonorable sloth. Indeed, because the vices of rulers and of the rich are also civic and social ills that bespeak a failure of leadership, Day 1 shows the just reproof of the powerful in Christendom and the world. The corruption of the pope and his curia (2), an abbot's hypocrisy (4), an inquisitor's avarice (6), the lechery of a French king (5), and the atypical tightfistedness of Can Grande della Scala, the ruler of Verona (7), are all subject to satirical correction.[39]

If Day 6 contains stories on the arts of narrative and oratory (Madonna Oretta in 1, Giotto and Messer Forese in 5, Frate Cipolla in 10) as well as painting (6.5), the mercurial inspiration of the Day means that not only verbal dexterity but the whole range of arts requiring skill (*ingenium*) at which Florentines excelled are on display, from the reply of Cisti, a baker (6.2), to the dialectic mastered by Guido Cavalcanti (6.9). Prominent is the law, represented by Forese, a lawyer (6.5), and by Madonna Filippa's reform of the bad laws of Prato (6.7): laws were among the institutions devastated by the plague (1, Intro., 23, 62; 6, Concl., 9).[40] The archetype of all arts, divine creation, is humorously implicit when Fiammetta explains the ugliness of the Florentine Baronci as resulting from God's first, halting attempts to shape human beings (6.6). Since travel, too, is mercurial, the Day's stories refer to movement in space, from Oretta's "horseback" ride to Frate Cipolla's account of a journey around Florence, dressed up in words to sound like a pilgrimage to the Holy Land; the Day culminates in his tale with a mercurial feat of both travel and impudent folderol.[41]

The second Day is rigorously programmed to display the workings of Fortuna, a topic central to Boccaccio's later work.[42] Four tales have preambles in which Fortuna's "variable movements" (2.6.3) are described by the tale-teller (2.3, 2.6, 2.7, 2.8): in the third tale Pampinea uses words from Dante's set piece (*Inferno* 7.73–96), spoken by Virgil, where Fortuna is portrayed distributing the fate of nations and peoples.

On the third Day, ruled by Neifile, the narrators' presence in a pleasure garden is reflected in four stories (3.1, 3.3, 3.5, 3.8) where a lover reaches his illicit embrace by penetrating an enclosed garden, like the tempter invading Eden. The industry suggested by the two mills in the *brigata*'s garden (3, Intro., 10) is continuous with the "tilling" metaphors of 3.1.18 ("work the plot") and 3.6.36 ("you tilled your own land"), which also parody God's exhortation to Adam "that he care for Eden," *ut custodiret illum* (Genesis 2:15). The symbolism of the workers' "tools" also abounds: Masetto's axe (3.1.13), and the torch and baton carried by King Agilulf when he visits his wife, usurped by the groom who supplants him (3.2.12–13), testify to the male's nether equipment. Boldest to a modern reader is the parody of religious language that describes Masetto's service of the nuns as "putting (t)horns on Christ's crown" (3.1.43) and the description in Dioneo's tale of the hermit Rustico's erection, when he sees Alibech's naked beauty, as the "resurrection of the flesh" (3.10.13):[43] an event that reflects the telling of the tale on a Sunday, the day of resurrection.[44]

With such richly parodic notes the third Day inaugurates five continuous Days of storytelling (Sunday–Thursday), and for the first three of those and the last, love stories predominate. Some seventy stories in the collection touch on love in some form. With Filostrato's imposition in Day 4 of tales where lovers end up unhappy, dismemberment of the body is a persistent signifier. Decapitations hold the center of the Day (4.4, 4.5), while the stories at the extremes (4.1, 4.9) include murders that tear the heart from the body: in the ninth tale, the lover's heart is fed by the husband to the unfaithful wife, who, when informed of the fact, throws herself from a tower and is smashed to pieces ["tutta si disfece"]. The Day centers on Filomena's tale of Elisabetta (4.5), who finds her lover murdered by her brothers, removes the head, and places it in a pot of basil. Isabella's wasting away when deprived of her love is an extreme form of the predicament of the women to whom Boccaccio directs his collection.[45] The Day re-evokes from the plague account the ills to which the flesh is subject, in this case when seized by the amorous or irascible passions, which are Filostrato's psychological province: thus Lauretta's tale warns against a woman's furious anger (4.3.4–7), and the king's story depicts the wrath of Rossiglione against Guardstagno, formerly his best friend (4.9.11).[46]

The Fifth Day corrects the violence and fragmentation of the fourth, as Filostrato himself crowns Fiammetta so that the *brigata* may be "consoled" (4, Concl., 3). Filostrato's own story (5.4) tells how in exchange for a promise of marriage, Lizio da Valbona graces his daughter and her lover after catching them in flagrante (a perilous situation repeated in 5.6 and 5.7), thus fulfilling the Day's theme of tragedy averted and followed by nuptials. With the tale, Filostrato also makes amends for his tyranny of the Day before (5.4.3), as Queen Fiammetta kindly recognizes (5.5.2). A Tuesday (*martedì*), this central Day reflects the influence of Mars, the planet that fosters a tempered fortitude as well as wrath and is thus linked to the first Tuesday, when Pampinea boldly proposed leaving the plague-stricken city, and to the third, the final Day of storytelling, when Panfilo's rule brings out, among other stories, examples of victories over the passions (tales 3–6).

Prestigious source material, classical and vernacular, adorns this central, fifth day: Gianni of Procida's night swims to Ischia to see his beloved Restituta (5.6.5) recall Ovid's Leander crossing the Hellespont for Hero (*Heroides* 19), while Teodoro's refuge with his master's daughter in a ruined church (5.7.12–13) imitates Aeneas and Dido's embrace in a cave in a rainstorm (*Aeneid* 4.165–168). Vernacular antecedents include the capture of the lovers Florio and Biancifiore from Boccaccio's own *Filocolo* (source of 5.6.21–22), and Cimone's enchantment by Ifigenia (5.1.6–10) after the prescriptions of the Tuscan lyric *stilnovo*.[47] Neifile's 5.5, the middle story on the middle Day, is a linchpin: rivals who have come to violence over nubile Agnesa are reconciled when she is recognized as one's lost sibling; this pure distillate of Roman comedy anchors the comic structure of the Day, and of the whole collection.[48]

The Seventh Day, inspired by Licisca's cynicism about wifely chastity (6, Intro., 8–10), offers transgressive stories told within the *Valle delle donne*. Boccaccio includes as apparent instances of female resourcefulness tales that in their original settings are stridently misogynistic — Peronella in 7.2 from Apuleius's *Metamorphoses* 9.4; Tofano's wife in 7.4 from the *Disciplina clericalis* of Petrus Alfonsi. Panfilo's ninth tale, from the medieval Latin *Comoedia Lydiae*, is remarkable for the dizzying ironies that arise from Queen Lidia's ability, in order to allay her servant-lover Pirro's doubts about her love for him, to induce her husband, Nicostrato, to disbelieve the plain evidence of his own eyes. When Dioneo persuades the reluctant ladies to tell stories about tricks played on husbands (6, Concl., 8–15), it raises the question of whether the strategy for ordaining that theme is in fact elaborately misogynistic — a question that for a growing number of readers and critics permeates the entire collection.[49]

The Eighth Day balances the Seventh, allowing tales of tricks played by *both* sexes, and on the Ninth Day, in the absence of a subject imposed by Emilia, the narrators drift along in the same vein. By multiplying the tally of tricks and referring to sexual relations in economic terms (8.1, 8.2, 8.8, 8.10), the narrators sketch a society dominated by avarice, a target of Boccaccio's satire. In the medieval imaginary the account book is also an image of the final judgment, a concept that comes to dominate the second Sunday of tale-telling, Day 8, which thus alludes to the eschatological eighth day, the day of judgment. The theme of judgment, human or divine, is prominent not only in Pampinea's key seventh tale, but in Calandrino's subjection by his pals Bruno and Buffalmacco to the bitter aloes ordeal to determine if he has stolen a pig from himself (8.6), and also in the central tale (8.5), where Florentine cutups humiliate a rustic judge from the Marche in his courtroom.[50] Panfilo's turn to the topics of liberality and magnificence in the Tenth Day is thus a timely corrective for the avarice, mockery, and fractiousness that emerge in Days 8 and 9.

The Eighth and Ninth Days also register a change in how the tales are connected. Elissa's story (8.3) begins a suite that includes the same cast of Florentine characters (the painters Calandrino, Bruno, and Buffalmacco; a ridiculous Bolognese doctor, Maestro Simone, occasionally joins in). The two Days also include nine occasions on which the narrator's tale is cued by that of another (8.5, 8.6, 8.8, 9.3, 9.4, 9.5, 9.6, 9.7, 9.8). These stories thus hint at how a different collection might arise from the storehouse of purely Florentine tales, and in so doing herald the return to Florence of the *brigata*.

Because the *Decameron* generates much of its meaning through its contrasts with Dante's *Commedia*, focus on how that work enters the collection is profitable by way of conclusion. Although Boccaccio names Dante in the *Decameron* only once (4, Intro., 33),[51] virtually no page of the book lacks some trace of Dante's influence.[52] The debts begin with the collection's second title, or *cognomen*, *Prencipe Galeotto* (*Prince Galahalt*), which derives from the description by Dante's Francesca (*Inferno* 5.127–38) of the French romance *Lancelot*, to which she ascribes her perdition, and implies that the *Decameron*, too, is a go-between. Boccaccio's language in the Introduction, referring to the "ponderous and noisome beginning" of the plague description and the "lovely and delightful plain" of its tales, recalls how the title *Commedia* is justified in Dante's *Letter to Can Grande* (*Epistola* 13.10): the poem has a "fetid" origin in hell and a happy conclusion in heaven. The framing of the whole *Decameron* with allusions to Dante is reaffirmed when we find Dante's infernal incontinence, violence, and fraud organizing Boccaccio's description of the scoundrel Ciappelletto in the first tale,[53] and Dante's phrase "mad bestiality" (matta / bestialitade, *Inferno* 11.82–83), adapted to describe Gualtieri's cruelty in the final tale (10.10.3). Boccaccio's choice of three male narrators representing the three faculties of the human soul (rational, irascible, concupiscent) takes a cue from Dante's account of how the three spirits of his soul respond to the sight of Beatrice (*Vita nuova* 2.4–6).[54] But where in the *Vita nuova* the voice of the lowest stratum can only anticipate being scanted of food and drink (as lovers traditionally are), in the *Decameron* the "voice" of concupiscence, Dioneo, is not only given scope and license but remains perhaps the most snugly fitting alter ego of the Author-Narrator.

Dante's presence is also indirect, and sometimes ghostly. The first tale is set in 1301, the year that Charles of Valois invaded Florence and sent Dante into exile. Bologna and Paris (1.2 and 1.10), were for Boccaccio places Dante had studied (*Trattatello* 25). The story of Bergamino and Can Grande (1.7) recalls Dante's *Letter to Can Grande* in that Bergamino is attracted by Can Grande's fame, just as Dante is in the exordium to the letter (*Epistola* 13.1). Maestro Alberto, the wise old man in love of *Decameron* 1.10, recalls the old Dante in love in having a white head and green tail (1.10.17–18; cf. 4, Intro., 33).[55]

At the other extreme, the Tenth Day is virtually woven with Dantean thread: its ascensional order, in which each teller attempts to outdo the previous one in relating acts of magnificence, recalls the ever-higher and more capacious spheres of Dante's Paradise. The Day's competition of virtues, as Francesco Bausi has shown, explores the system of the virtues of Aristotle and Aquinas that Dante also adopted for exploring the virtues in the *Purgatorio*.[56] The presence in the Day's stories of families found in Dante's Hell, such as the Carisendi and Caccianemici (10.4; cf. *Inferno* 31.136, 18.50), and especially Boccaccio's reconciliation (10.2) of Dante's Boniface VIII (*Inferno* 19.53) and Ghino di Tacco (*Purgatorio* 6.13–15), figures who in Dante threaten the peace of Italy, suggest that Boccaccio amends Dante's judgments against them. Dante's incorporation in the *Decameron* does not mean acquiescence in his judgments. Several tales sharply problematize Alighieri's bold claim of representing divine retaliation for human sin, and thus mark Boccaccio's doubts regarding his predecessor's confidence as self-proclaimed prophet. Panfilo, the most rational narrator, suggests Boccaccio's agnosticism in the matter of final judgment when he concludes the first story acknowledging that no one but God can know if the blackguard Ciappelletto is finally a saint or a damned soul, despite the likelihood of the latter (1, Intro., 5–6, 89–90).

Boccaccio raises urgent questions regarding retaliation in both human and divine terms in two stories unmistakably Dantesque: the story of Nastagio degli Onesti of Ravenna (5.8; cf. *Purgatorio* 14.107), and the tale of the scholar and the widow (8.7), the latter using a plotline revisited in the openly misogynistic *Corbaccio*, the Certaldan's last vernacular work.[57] In 8.7, Pampinea narrates how the scholar Rinieri, besotted with a merry but unscrupulous widow, Elena, is inveigled into waiting for her in a courtyard under her window during the night of January 2 and nearly freezes to death; once recovered, he crafts a trap for Elena in early July that results in her being charred by the sun. Rinieri's vengeance is Dantean in the calculated "justice" that opposes summer heat to winter cold, and in the implication that Elena's exposure to the sun anticipates the final judgment, in regard to which the scholar claims to offer her a salutary warning. This longest story in the collection is also resonant for the *Decameron* in that Rinieri's revenge occurs during a storytelling Sunday that is, we saw, a typological day of judgment. Perhaps most significant, in depicting a man cured of love, it recalls, while markedly differing from, the gentler cure undergone by the Author-Narrator. Indeed the *brigata*, Boccaccio's human jury, renders its most complex response to any tale in the collection in both conceding Elena's guilt and judging Rinieri to be cruel (8.8.2).[58] Asking whether the scholar may appropriate the apparatus of divine retaliation for personal ends, the tale calls into question Dante's personal investment in the vengeance meted out in the *Commedia*.[59]

Boccaccio's sense of the limits of human judgments is thus closely associated with his ambivalent reception of Dante. In large measure, this reception was channeled through an instinctive resistance to the older poet's damnation of Francesca. Boccaccio writes his own account of Francesca, sharply different from Dante's, in his commentary on the *Commedia* (1373–74).[60] For Boccaccio, Francesca is deceived as to the identity of her promised spouse, and thus gives her heart, innocently and irreversibly, to her brother-in-law Paolo, rather than to his brother Gianciotto. Boccaccio's mitigation of Francesca's guilt inevitably challenges the justice of Dante's damnation of her.[61] Since Boccaccio's name *Galeotto* for the *Decameron* comes directly from Dante's Francesca, the placement of this title on the book's forehead—to adapt Boccaccio's phrasing (1, Intro., 2)—begins the challenge to Dante's authority on the very first page.[62]

Scholars vigorously debate interpretations of meaning in the *Decameron*. Is the work a revised and expanded (if more earthy) *Comedia delle ninfe*, in which the *brigata*'s virtuous ladies preside over an ascensional pattern from, at the outset, Ciappelletto, "perhaps the worst man ever born" (1.1.15), to the saintly Griselda, in the last tale?[63] Or does Boccaccio's *brigata* in their several gardens affirm a view of existence that allows scope to the natural needs of the body and evades religious prohibitions—as in, for example, Dioneo's first story, showing how a monk outwits his abbot in the pursuit of sexual pleasure—thus advocating a kind of Epicureanism?[64] An influential scholar has explicated the book as a "repertory of the rhetorical forms and traditions of play," privileging the imaginative and the aesthetic over the moralistic.[65] Supporters of the first thesis can point to the magnificent gestures of the Tenth Day in defense of their views, those advancing the second can cite the tale of Filippo Balducci and his son, with its neat inversion of a saint's life, while defenders of the last can point to the Author-Narrator's facetious and ironic Conclusion—in effect the book's last word. Yet, as we saw a few pages back, all three male Decameronian narrators have a share in the complex persona of the Author-Narrator of the collection. The strong voice given Dioneo may seem to correct Dante's sublimated love of Beatrice, but even Dioneo bows to "the limit of reason" Pampinea establishes at the outset, and acknowledges the unimpeachable conduct of the *brigata*. Given the powerful cultural forces the book sets in play, it should not surprise us if Boccaccio's collection is both richly complex and discernibly high in tension—and because of precisely those qualities a satisfying work of the literary imagination.

CHAPTER TWO

THE TEXTUAL HISTORY OF THE
DECAMERON

Brian Richardson

The tale of the text of the *Decameron*, from its elaboration by Boccaccio to its presentation by others across the centuries, is as rich in twists and turns as the collection of *novelle* that it contains. The beginning of the story is shrouded in some uncertainty. The composition of the *Decameron* cannot be dated exactly, and we do not know whether the architecture of the work we now read corresponds with Boccaccio's original conception. The Introduction to Day 1 must have been written after the Black Death, which ended in Florence in spring 1349, and the narrator refers to an extended process of composition (*Decameron* 10, Concl., 20, 27, 29). In the Introduction to Day 4, he mentions the critical reactions of some readers, and it has been suggested that parts of the work, perhaps groups of three Days, circulated independently; but there is no secure evidence for this.[1] The first evidence of the work's transmission dates only from the 1360s. In a letter written in Ancona in 1360, Francesco Buondelmonti, the Florentine nephew of the grand seneschal of Naples, Niccola Acciaiuoli, asked that a copy be sent to him in L'Aquila or Sulmona. The oldest manuscript, datable to the early 1360s, is the *frammento magliabechiano* (Florence, Biblioteca Nazionale Centrale, MS 2.2.8, fols. 20–37), which contains the conclusions of Days 1–9 with a single story, 9.10, concerning Donno Gianni and compar Pietro. A lengthy preface refers to Boccaccio as still alive. The person who transcribed this anthology also wrote a commercial document for Lapa Acciaiuoli, sister of Niccola and mother of Francesco Buondelmonti. The selection could therefore have circulated among rich Florentines linked with the Angevin court, and its connection with the Acciaiuoli circle may explain the choice of the only tale set in Puglia. Also probably from the 1360s are two other manuscripts: Paris, Bibliothèque Nationale, MS It. 482 (P), transcribed by a member of a family prominent in Florentine politics and trade, Giovanni di Agnolo Capponi, in a mercantile script on vellum, with sixteen pen-and-ink illustrations attributed by some to Boccaccio;[2] and the partial text found in MS Vitali 26 of the Biblioteca Passerini Landi, Piacenza, perhaps commissioned by the author.

Boccaccio's own copying of his masterpiece is witnessed by MS Hamilton 90 of the Staatsbibliothek Preussischer Kulturbesitz, Berlin (B), written around 1370–72. Three fascicles are now missing. This is a large-format vellum copy, but the support is of mediocre quality, Boccaccio's semigothic hand is somewhat irregular, transcription progressed in a gradual fashion, and correction was sporadic and incomplete. Even if Boccaccio originally intended to use this as a presentation copy, he seems to have decided to keep it for his own use. The redaction contained in B is now recognized as distinct from that represented by P. Boccaccio replaced some rarer, more antiquated, or popular linguistic forms with more usual ones and made the word order less Latinizing. However, the text was also enriched with non-Florentine or otherwise uncommon or more expressive forms, as when Venetian *marido* replaces *marito* in the story of Frate Alberto (4.2.43). Some alterations improved the logic of the narration. This later version of the *Decameron* was read less widely: about thirty of the extant manuscripts are related to P, about twenty to B.[3] This suggests that the work was diffused quite rapidly after its composition. However, as Marco Cursi points out, the evidence from Boccaccio's lifetime is linked to scribes or owner-readers close to the author, and this may mean that he was keen to supervise publication and also to encourage reading of his stories among those of high social status.[4]

After Boccaccio's death, the *Decameron* was copied both by those who wished to own a copy for themselves and their friends and by professional scribes, and both within and beyond Tuscany. One amateur scribe, Francesco d'Amaretto Mannelli, was to have a major influence on the text's history through his copy, Florence, Biblioteca Medicea Laurenziana, MS 42.1 (Mn), written in a mercantile hand and dated 1384. His exemplar was not B but perhaps a working copy from Boccaccio's desk. Mannelli marked some readings as uncertain or missing, but he aimed to transcribe faithfully and signaled any emendations. He also engaged with the work in a cultured, lively way, noting in the margins parallel passages in other works and his personal reactions. The first identifiable scribe from outside Tuscany was Domenego Caronelli of Conegliano, a notary's son, who transcribed the *Decameron* for his own use in 1395 as well as copying an anthology of extracts perhaps intended as a gift. In the fifteenth century, Tuscans continued to be the main producers of manuscripts. One amateur scribe was Lodovico di Salvestro Ceffini, a well-to-do wool merchant, whose copy, dated 1427 and written "for myself," has ink and watercolor illustrations of each story, in several hands.[5] Another Florentine, Filippo d'Andrea da Bibbiena, transcribed the *Decameron* in the second half of the century "for himself, his relatives, and friends."

The *Decameron* was also copied by professional scribes, working for individuals who required a copy or for stationer-booksellers confident of finding customers for the work. Two copies made by Ghinozzo di Tommaso Allegretti of Siena, one dated 1409, belong to a group of manuscripts that he produced, most probably for financial motives, while exiled in Bologna. The notary Taiuto di Balduccio copied the work in 1438, no doubt at the behest of Lodovico di Cece da Verrazzano, *podestà* of Pisa. Most of the professionals' manuscripts were of medium or low quality. A uniquely prestigious copy, however, is MS Holkham misc. 49 in the Bodleian Library, Oxford, illuminated in about 1467 by Taddeo Crivelli for Teofilo Calcagnini, a favored young courtier, as a gift from Duke Borso d'Este.

This Bodleian copy, produced with exceptional care, demonstrates that the *Decameron* could be prized by readers of high social class. We know that the dukes of Milan had a copy in their library in Pavia and that a cultured Marquis of Mantua, Ludovico III Gonzaga, owned a copy in 1472.[6] However, evidence for the century after Boccaccio's death suggests that most copies were made for nonaristocratic readers. About eighteen of the sixty extant fourteenth- or fifteenth-century manuscripts can be firmly linked to merchant owners, whose role in the reception of the *Decameron* was thus significant but far from dominant. Copying was shared fairly equally between professional copyists and those writing for themselves: of these sixty surviving copies, seventeen appear to have been written on commission and fifteen by amateurs.

In view of the length of the *Decameron*, it is not surprising that its reproduction was taken over almost entirely by printing when this was introduced into Italy. Of the thirteen editions dating from the period up to 1510 of which copies survive, the first, known as the *Deo gratias* from its concluding words, appeared in Naples around 1470; its text is related indirectly to that of B, but its language is influenced by its southern provenance. The text of the earliest Venetian edition, 1471, is generally close to that of the *Deo gratias* but makes occasional use of one or more manuscripts. For the Mantuan edition of 1472, the printer probably used the Gonzaga manuscript mentioned above, and his dedicatory letter shows that he was counting on commercial success. This *Decameron* was, directly or indirectly, the main source for the other editions that appeared in northern Italy at fairly regular intervals over the next four decades: Bologna, 1476; Milan, 1476 (which also made some use of the 1471 edition); Vicenza, 1478; Venice, 1481, 1484, 1492, 1498, 1504, and 1510. The only early Florentine *Decameron* was derived from the edition of 1476 and was produced in 1482–83 at the press of the female convent of San Iacopo di Ripoli; curiously, Boccaccio mentions "le donne di Ripole" in 8.9.97. All these editions were printed in folio format, and all used roman type, with the exception of Milan 1476, set in semigothic type. The 1492 *Decameron* was distinguished by woodcut illustrations imitated in some later editions, and it included the life of Boccaccio by Gerolamo Squarzafico that had first appeared with the Venetian *Filocolo* of 1472.[7] However, no edition shows evidence of any concern to present an accurate text.[8]

A fresh approach to the preparation and presentation of the *Decameron* is marked by two editions that appeared in 1516. Both showed a concern with textual correctness resulting from the rise in status of Boccaccio's prose as the principal model of vernacular usage. The production of these two editions within two months of each other also reflects the intense rivalry developing between Venice and Florence in editing Trecento literature. The first of the pair was brought out in Venice and edited by the patrician Nicolò Delfino (Dolfin), who claimed to have restored the work "to its whole and clear reading," selecting readings from "many very ancient texts"; in practice this meant following the 1472 edition with some recourse to manuscripts. Florence responded with a *Decameron* based on the previous Florentine edition (1483) but making some use of the Florentine manuscript Mn. The anonymous editor or editors declared that the original text had been restored by using copies "transcribed from the original." The cultural context of these two books is also signaled by their use of italic type and quarto format, a combination first used by Aldo Manuzio for Pietro Bembo's *Asolani* of 1505. Delfino's edition proved the more influential. Its text was the main source for the Venetian *Decameron* of 1522, which was then adopted for two further Venetian editions of 1525 and 1526, although both editions gave readers to understand that the text had been improved by collating authoritative copies. A copy of Delfino's *Decameron* was used as the basis for a Florentine edition of 1527, prepared by a group of men who corrected Delfino's text with readings derived from manuscripts including Mn. This assiduously prepared *Decameron* was regarded as authoritative for over two centuries.

Readers now wanted to use the *Decameron* as a prose model as well as for enjoyment. The following three decades thus saw both a marked acceleration in the printing of Boccaccio's work—between 1526 and 1557 an edition appeared about annually on average, against seven between 1501 and 1525—and a shift of emphasis in its editing. The main innovations concerned the provision of paratextual aids to comprehension and imitation, including glossaries, annotations, and other explanations, often intended for non-Tuscan readers. For the text itself, the 1527 edition was the main source used. The Venetian Lodovico Dolce patriotically but perversely based his 1541 text on Delfino's edition of 1516, before modifying his isolated stance in 1552.

The Catholic Reformation brought an entirely new challenge for editors. The Index of Prohibited Books issued in 1559 included the *Decameron* on the grounds of its "intolerable errors"—especially its often unflattering portrayals of the clergy and their practices. The Tridentine Index of 1564 and its successors offered a partial solution: the stories could be printed if they were "purged" with the approval of the Holy Office.[9] The first editors to take on the additional role of censor were Vincenzio Borghini and other Florentines appointed by Grand Duke Cosimo de' Medici to prepare an edition printed in Florence in 1573. These "Deputati" strived at the same time, however, to recover the original form of the text, restoring archaic or unfamiliar forms removed by earlier scribes and editors. Their *Annotationi et discorsi* (Annotations and Discussions), also published in 1573, explain that they used the 1527 edition as their base text but introduced readings from other sources, in particular from Mn, dubbed the *Ottimo* ("best"). One variant set the Deputati wondering perceptively whether Boccaccio might have published two differing texts in succession.[10] As for their expurgation, the Deputati preserved as much of the text as possible by turning members of the clergy into laymen and laywomen. A different typeface was used to indicate words substituted for those of Boccaccio, and asterisks indicated omissions.

The church authorities in Rome soon decided that this censorship had not been strict enough. In 1580, Lionardo Salviati was appointed by Grand Duke Francesco de' Medici to prepare a freshly expurgated text, published twice in 1582.[11] Salviati placed even greater faith in the authority of Mn than the Deputati had done, but brought its spelling more closely into line with contemporary Florentine usage. He went further than the Deputati in indicating disapproval of immoral behavior, for instance by removing stories from the Christian world to a pagan context, making some "wicked" characters meet an unhappy fate, and adding marginal notes to draw attention to actions judged worthy or unworthy. A third expurgated *Decameron*, prepared by Luigi Groto, was published in Venice in 1588. Groto, too, changed clerical characters into secular ones and punished the morally transgressive. He was not interested in establishing a philologically improved text, preferring to adapt Girolamo Ruscelli's Venetian edition of 1552. Groto's *Decameron* appeared again only in 1590 and 1612. Salviati's version enjoyed more enduring success, being printed eight times in Venice between 1585 and 1638.[12]

The nature of the censorships of the Deputati, Salviati, and Groto can be illustrated by their bowdlerizations of the stories of Masetto da Lamporecchio, who pretends to be deaf and dumb while working as a gardener in a Tuscan convent and satisfying the nuns' carnal desires (3.1), and of Nastagio degli Onesti, the young gentleman of Ravenna who, after misspending his wealth in vain efforts to win the love of a lady, turns to his advantage an infernal spectacle of a woman being hunted by the hounds of the man she rejected (5.8). The Deputati simply change the opening of the Masetto story so that it is set in a sort of finishing school run by a widowed countess. They do not intervene in the story of Nastagio. Salviati distances 3.1 further from Christianity: the convent in Tuscany becomes a tower in Alexandria where girls are kept before being sent off to the sultan of Babylon, and Masetto is a Jew whose real name is Massèt. To prevent any reader getting mistaken ideas about the afterlife, the infernal vision witnessed by Nastagio becomes a ruse of the devil; and Boccaccio's concluding tongue-in-cheek remark that the incident made all the women of Ravenna more submissive to men is rendered hypothetical: this *would* have happened if wise men had not (fortunately) revealed the devil's work. Groto turns the story of Masetto into a folktale, albeit a risqué one. After an astrologer tells the king of Sicily and his eight barons that their young daughters will become pregnant before marriage, the girls are enclosed in a remote palace in the middle of a forest; however, a Tuscan lord disguised as the humble Masetto manages to get into the place and ensure that the prediction is fulfilled. He marries the princess and finds noble husbands for the other girls. Groto leaves the tale of Nastagio unaltered but repeats a marginal note from Ruscelli's edition warning that this is a *cantafavola* (fanciful story) and sets out an orthodox position on the spirits of the dead: they have no bodily form and are never allowed out of the place to which they are allocated.

Of the earlier unexpurgated *Decameron*s, that of 1527 retained the highest prestige and was the main source of the Elzevier edition (Amsterdam, 1665). Amsterdam was claimed falsely to be the place of publication of an edition of 1679 probably printed in Geneva or Germany. In the seventeenth century, Italians responded to growing demand for the full text, a demand arising partly from the veneration of Boccaccio by linguistic purists. Amsterdam, again, was used as a false imprint for two editions printed in 1703 and 1718; they actually originated in Naples, and the latter, at least, was produced by Lorenzo Ciccarelli, who was responsible for several editions of works that would appeal to purists but in some cases would also have met with ecclesiastical disapproval. A near-facsimile edition of the 1527 *Decameron* was produced in 1729 anonymously, but in fact in Venice. The London edition of 1725, edited by the poet Paolo Rolli, marked a tentative step forward in the editing of the text, since Rolli altered details of the 1527 text with variants from four other Cinquecento editions and the Holkham manuscript. He dealt with possible objections to the unexpurgated text by citing Boccaccio's dictum beginning "No word, however pure, was ever wholesomely construed by a mind that was corrupt" (*Decameron* 10, Concl., 11). However, adolescents of both sexes had to be protected from details that might provoke what one editor termed "carnal concupiscence" while being helped to study Boccaccio's Tuscan. For such readers, selections of stories judged appropriate appeared in Italy between 1739 and 1754. Surveys of the text's history were offered by Rolli, in his preface, and by the Florentine scholar Domenico Maria Manni in his *Istoria del "Decamerone"* (1742). Manni shared the Deputati's veneration for Mannelli's manuscript, believing the scribe was Boccaccio's godson.

Although the unexpurgated *Decameron* was included in the Index until as late as 1891, it was printed and studied openly in Italy from the papacy of Benedict XIV in the mid-eighteenth century. In 1761, a new edition printed in Lucca and promoted by Pier Antonio Guadagni and Angelo Maria Bandini took Mn as its sole foundation, following the lead of the Deputati in 1573; however, recognizing the prestige that the 1527 text still had, the editors provided its variants and those of its Venetian imitation of 1729. Mannelli's spelling was followed meticulously. This proved too pedantic for Vincenzio Martinelli, who introduced what he considered "true spelling" in his London edition of 1766. Some readings from the 1527 edition were adopted in the "London" (actually Livorno) *Decameron* of 1789–90, yet its principal basis was again Mn. The "London" edition then provided the basis for the Milanese edition of 1803, used by Michele Colombo for his Parma edition of 1812–14, which in turn was the main source for Ignazio Moutier's Florentine edition of 1827–28. More original than this sequence of editions was the Venetian *Decameron* of 1813: it, too, followed Mannelli's manuscript except where the latter was judged evidently incorrect, but based its spelling on the contemporary "living voice" of the people of Tuscany (anticipating the spirit of Manzoni's revision of *I promessi sposi*). This policy was criticized as incongruous by Ugo Foscolo in the *Discorso* that preceded his London edition of 1825, which sought to improve on that of 1813. Pietro Fanfani offered in 1857 a *Decameron* "compared with the best texts," but in practice he, too, remained primarily faithful to Mn.

In the late nineteenth century, attention moved to the manuscript B. After being owned by Apostolo Zeno in the eighteenth century and then passing into the collection of the tenth Duke of Hamilton, it was acquired by the Prussian government in 1882. Studies by Adolf Tobler (1887) and Oskar Hecker (1892 and 1895) concluded that B was the source of Mn and also, Hecker added, the (perhaps indirect) source of the *Deo gratias* edition. Aldo Francesco Massèra followed B in his edition of 1927, modernizing its spelling and using Mn and the *Deo gratias* where B is incomplete or where he believed its readings to be in error. Massèra described his text as a "starting point" for the restoration of the *Decameron* that left Boccaccio's hands, and indeed it proved to be no more than this.[13] In the same year Michele Barbi published a landmark article "Sul testo del 'Decameron,'" in which he argued that a correct text could not be derived from B and Mn alone, that the whole manuscript tradition should therefore be taken into consideration, and that this tradition also revealed evidence of authorial revisions. He doubted whether Mn had been copied directly from B.[14] In 1933, Barbi saw B at first hand with his assistant Alberto Chiari and judged it autograph. However, this crucial discovery was publicized only in the postwar period in short articles by Chiari that lacked supporting evidence and thus failed to convince.[15]

Vittore Branca followed Barbi's lead in his edition of 1951–52 (Florence: Le Monnier), identifying eighty-five manuscripts and selecting eleven for collation together with the *Deo gratias* and 1527 editions. Branca considered the theory of a double redaction of the *Decameron* insufficient to explain the extent of variance among manuscripts. Just as he saw the work as a "merchant epic," so he drew a picture of an unsupervised, "adventurous and irregular" tradition, in which the text was transcribed mainly by amateur and merchant scribes who were liable to tailor copies to their own tastes. Branca believed that some variants did derive from genuine earlier redactions, but he did not yet seek to single these out. At this stage he considered P to be at the same level as B in the genealogy of manuscripts, and sometimes preferred readings of P to those of B. Charles Singleton had been working on a new edition for Laterza since 1936, and it eventually appeared in 1955. He described fifty-one manuscripts and divided them into three groups on the basis of a small number of variants that, he believed, were probably derived at different moments from a single, evolving original copy. His critical text was derived chiefly from B and another manuscript. The full importance of the Berlin manuscript was revealed at last in 1962, when Pier Giorgio Ricci and Branca examined it directly and demonstrated that it had been transcribed by Boccaccio toward the end of his life.[16] After Singleton had edited a diplomatic transcription in 1974, Branca produced in 1976 both a new critical edition and a fully annotated edition in which the text was based on B and, for the sections missing in this manuscript, on Mn, but with modernized punctuation and spelling.[17]

Some important questions remained to be resolved. One was that of Boccaccio's supposed revisions of his masterpiece. In an edition of 1977, Aldo Rossi suggested speculatively that there were two redactions of the *Decameron*, represented by P and B among other manuscripts, and that from the first redaction and an intermediate phase an abridged *"Decameron* of the poor and merchants"* had been derived in the late Trecento.[18] From the early 1990s, Branca, first on his own and then with Vitale (see note 3), established the status of P as an earlier redaction and analyzed the rationale for the revisions that Boccaccio had introduced by the 1370s. Another major question concerned the work's scribal circulation from Trecento to the early Cinquecento; by using the evidence of paleography and codicology, the study by Marco Cursi mentioned in note 1 has (as outlined above) further advanced our understanding of the earlier stages of the story of Boccaccio's text.

We have seen that, from its outset to modern times, this story is unusually complex and in some ways still problematic. At least two versions of the *Decameron* were published by the author, but it has not proved straightforward to recover even one of these entirely. After the work had left Boccaccio's desk, its material presentation and its text could take considerably different forms. Some of this variety can be linked to that of the *Decameron* itself and its ability to attract readers with diverse tastes. The work has been adopted as a model of linguistic usage and moral behavior, yet it has also provoked or offended readers and has even been regarded as dangerous: thus at some moments its text has been altered in line with changing needs, beliefs, and anxieties. Studies of the text failed for a long time to take account of the whole of its tradition and to use sound philological and bibliographical approaches to its editing. However, Branca's editions of 1976 now provide an authoritative text of the final version of Boccaccio's work, and research has gradually enhanced, and is still enhancing, understanding of its evolution and reception.

PART II

THE AUTODIDACT

CHAPTER THREE

MOMENTS OF LATIN POETRY • (*Carmina*)

Giuseppe Velli

As is true of his vernacular *Rime*, Boccaccio never collected the Latin poems he composed from youth to old age. The most recent edition of the *Carmina* gathers ten that remain, chronologically ordered according to their certain or probable date of composition.[1] Six of them, the longer compositions, are central to this essay, but first, in a corpus so scant, even those that are very brief deserve mention.[2] These four occasional poems, too, range over many years and represent the thematic diversity typical of Boccaccio's oeuvre as a whole.

The earliest of the shorter *Carmina* is a twin epitaph for an able Guelph diplomat, Ciampi della Tosa (d. 1337), and his military son, Pino. Only recently noticed in a notebook of the poet's intellectual heir, the chancellor of Florence Coluccio Salutati, this tribute to a pair of Florentine patricians may have been carved on the men's tombstone in Santa Maria Novella. Since Ciampi della Tosa died July 8, 1348, most likely of the Black Death, these four Latin hexameters resonate with the grief that afflicted so many — including Boccaccio, who lost members of his own family in the epidemic — and the historical catastrophe with which the *Decameron* opens, in the very same church that is Ciampi and Pino's burial place (*Carmina* 4).[3]

Another piece has its historical context in the enmity between Florence and Milan, ruled in the Trecento by an aggressively expansionist Visconti dynasty. Against the Viscontis' drive to establish an empire in northern Italy, Boccaccio's monostich puts roaring words into the Florentine lion's mouth. Known as the Marzocco, that kingly beast was a symbol of the republic and its determination to fend off Milanese tyranny:

Nescis posse meum, que sit mea gloria nescis. (*Carmina* 6)

You do not know my power; my glory you do not know.

The poet displays his rhetorical skill, deploying *epanalepsis*, a line with identical beginning and ending. The lion's menace, according to a note in the one manuscript that preserves this single verse, targets specifically Archbishop Giovanni Visconti, ruler of Milan (d. 1354). To forge an alliance against that despot, Boccaccio had traveled to the Tyrol in late 1351, representing Florence as "solemn ambassador" before Ludwig of Bavaria. When Petrarch accepted Giovanni's patronage, beginning an eight-year stay at the Visconti court in 1353, Boccaccio famously wrote him a letter expressing outrage at his friend's decision and deeply compromised position.[4]

Around 1360, Boccaccio composed a tetrastich to mark his completion of a copy of Dante's *Commedia*, one decorated with beautiful drawings that some have attributed to the Certaldan:[5]

> Finis adest longi Dantis cum laude laboris:
> gloria sit summo Regi matrique, precamur,
> quos oro celsas prestent conscendere sedes
> dum supprema dies veniet morientibus egris. (*Carmina* 8)

> Here ends Dante's long, praiseworthy labor; / may it glorify, we
> beseech, the supreme King and Mother, / whose high seats I pray
> they may deign to grant me / when the last day comes to trembling
> mortals.

The admiring Dantista looks to heaven and hopes for salvation. The indefatigable amanuensis who transcribed the entire *Commedia* in three surviving manuscripts nods as well to Boethius, one of his favorite authors, adapting in his third hexameter a verse from the *Consolation of Philosophy*. Traces of Boethian influence run throughout Boccaccio's oeuvre, prominently in the consolatory motif of the proem to his *Decameron*.[6]

Most famous of Boccaccio's short Latin poems is his autoepitaph, preserved in manuscripts dating back to the Trecento:

> Hac sub mole iacent cineres ac ossa Iohannis,
> mens sedet ante Deum meritis ornata laborum
> mortalis vite; genitor Boccaccius illi,
> patria Certaldum, studium fuit alma poesis. (*Carmina* 10)

> Under this stone lie the bones and ashes of John; his spirit / stands
> in the presence of God, adorned with the merits his mortal / labors
> on earth have earned him. Boccaccio sired him; his native / Fatherland was Certaldo; he cherished the nourishing Muses.[7]

He composed these verses for his grave, set into the ground at the center of the nave in the Certaldo church of Saints Iacopo and Filippo, next door to his house. Within just a few years, it was desecrated by partisan conflict that destroyed the marker and scattered his ashes. A small, wall-mounted stone incised with the epitaph, still in situ, dates from before the end of the Trecento. Perhaps inspired by models such as Virgil's epitaph transmitted in medieval versions of the *Vita* by Suetonius, it succinctly frames his life as a Christian poet. He envisions his spirit in the presence of God, his eternal life earned through his hard work as a writer. As for his life on earth, three facts define him—his paternity (son of Boccaccio), his *patria* (Certaldo), and his greatest love (*studium*), the pursuit of literature. In the debate over the place of his birth (Florence or Certaldo), it is significant that all his authorial signatures, from the earliest allegorical epistles, identify him with that ancestral Tuscan hilltop town. Manuscripts he transcribed, such as his *Zibaldoni*, Terence, and Aquinas's *Commentary on the "Nichomachean Ethics,"* consistently present the same toponymic, "Iohannes de Certaldo."[8]

"Elegia di Costanza" (Costanza's Elegy, *Carmina* 1)

The "Elegia di Costanza" is certainly the first poetic composition in Latin of the young Boccaccio, still a student in Naples (ca. 1332–34).[9] Costanza, a Neapolitan maiden not even fifteen, has been struck down by death and addresses her bereaved fiancé, who passes her tomb and bitterly laments her loss. Their brief dialogue, 135 verses, contains the first indubitable signs of the artist's tendency to rely on the already-existing word—that is, an inherited tradition. Boccaccio's elegy owes much to the great Latin poetry of the twelfth and thirteenth centuries: the meter (rhythmic dactylic verses), the mechanisms of construction and assemblage, the very evident *amplificatio* as well as the rhetorical ornaments used to achieve that (*descriptio, interpretatio, expolitio*), and a conspicuous taste for stylistic sound effects. Finally, it reveals in its phrases the massive presence of the models on which he drew for his pastiche (Alain de Lille, Joseph of Exeter, Arrigo da Settimello). The importance to Boccaccio of twelfth- and thirteenth-century Latin poetry remains a less explored aspect of his work.

The elegy takes as its starting point and primary source the epitaph of Homonoea (first century A.D.), which was destined to have great success in the humanistic age. Boccaccio is the first modern author to know and use this brief text, in which the deceased lady addresses from the grave her widowed spouse, Atimetus. How and when the artist saw the ancient epitaph or whether he had access to an early manuscript tradition is unknown.[10] His version retains the tone and level of Homonoea's message as she asks the man who walks by to pause and read the "few words" of her epitaph:

> Tu qui secura procedis mente
> Siste gradum quaeso verbaque pauca lege.

> You who so confidently walk along, / stop a moment, I ask, and read these few words.[11]

In Boccaccio's revisitation the unhappy passerby, Costanza's betrothed, is likewise a reader (*lector*, 45). Her wish that he not suffer because of her death triggers his dramatic response:

> Hic ego sum miser primus qui verba notavi
>   et legi versiculos qui mea danna ferunt.
> Sed male, quod optas, possum, spetiosa puella:
> ponere ploratus, te sine vita iacente. (49–52)

> I am the one, the wretched one, who first saw the words / and read the verses that carry my misfortune, / but I cannot do what you wish, lovely girl: / I cannot abandon tears while you lie without life.

Here the young artist is indeed a prevaricator in the sense that he is inventing, but in this deviation we discover the most hidden textures of authorship. Boccaccio's interpolated creation begins with the bereaved lover's expanded lamentation; here his fantasy enjoys full play, in the central verses of the poem (49–126), where the artist is far from his starting point and on his own ground. The bereaved "reader" thus becomes the speaking protagonist of an author who already is imagining fiction rooted in pathos, long before he would transform this snatch of Latin dialogue into the first-person, fully developed narrative fiction of the *Elegia di madonna Fiammetta*.[12]

Letter to Checco di Meletto and the Eclogue "Tempus erat placidum" ("The weather was calm," *Carmina* 2–3)

Between 1347 and 1348 Boccaccio was in Forlì at the court of Francesco Ordelaffi. Here he engages in a four-part Latin poetic correspondence with the lord's chancellor, Checco di Meletto Rossi, a sequence suggested by the eclogue exchange between Dante and Giovanni del Virgilio. It begins with Boccaccio's "Postquam fata sinunt" ("Since the fates permit [war]"), a metrical epistle in pastoral key, to which Checco replies in kind. There follows Boccaccio's eclogue "Tempus erat placidum," and an answer by Checco completes the sequence.[13] In the bucolic code of this correspondence, the writer Boccaccio becomes "Menalca," Checco is "Meri," and the admired "Mopso" to whom they refer is Petrarch, cast as already famous. The correspondence turns on two issues, which really come down to one, namely, Petrarch's coronation and the meaning that event has for Boccaccio. Emulative tension vibrates from the beginning.

"Mars" ravages Italy, war caused by the arrival in Italy of Ludwig of Hungary, who has come to avenge the death of his brother Andrew, husband of Queen Joan of Naples, the granddaughter and successor to King Robert of Anjou. Although such conditions little suit it, Menalca aspires "to bind our brows with myrtle" (talia cum minime deceant nos timpora mirto / cingere temptantes, 2.4–5) —that is, to converse in a poetic register on the lowest plane of pastoral or amorous poetry. The letter's expressive system runs a gamut characteristic of that genre: from the plant of love poetry, myrtle,[14] to the conversational limits of pastoral and Venus:

> curaque pastorum vel magna Dyonidis arma
> sint calami limen nostri. (2.19–20)

> Let the cares of shepherds or the great arms of Venus / be the limit of our reeds.

It rejects epic, "the labors of men and of gods" (hominumque deûmque labores, 2.26), a form considered the exclusive prerogative of the *Africa*'s author, Mopso-Petrarch, "whose brow we saw crowned with laurel" (cui frontem nectere lauro / vidimus, 2.27–28). Nonetheless, the writer's own ambitions for a laurel crown are at this point clear, for in spite of the disclaimer, his enunciation is clothed at the outset with an epic signifier, "Let . . . the limit of our reeds" (Sint calami limen . . .), a quotation from Statius's *Thebaid*.[15]

Checco's answer meets his interlocutor only halfway. He accepts the proposed literary role assigned to him, but instead of entering the Arcadian world, he insists on the negative aspects of reality (disorder, privations, war), to which he adds his own lament on the death of poetry, borrowed from Petrarch's *Collatio laureationis* (Coronation Oration): "Nothing is less valued than the composition of alluring verse" (nil minus in pretio quam blandus condere versus, 24). Aganippe, the fountain of the Muses, is abandoned (26), and patronage has declined:

Et quondam virides squalent in polvere frondes,
mirtus cum lauris edera ac, que nexibus ambit
arboreum corpus, solitum posuere decorem. (35–37)[16]

And the leaves once green lie dirtied in the dust, / myrtle with laurel
and ivy, which used to be / gracefully set in embraces around the
body of trees.

Ignoring Meri's belief that poetry is no longer possible, Boccaccio continues the dialogue with its third, most robust component, an eclogue. Testili
(the city of Ravenna) breaks the calm of an idyllic setting with her shrieks,
terrified that Faunus (Ordelaffi) is abandoning her for a bear hunt (to enter
the war). Menalca encounters Meri, who explains the reason for Testili's
distress and recites a mournful elegy for the great Argus (King Robert of
Naples). Its source is Petrarch's homonymous eclogue for Robert's death,
sent in a letter of January 17, 1347, to Barbato da Sulmona. Meri then
chronicles under "pastoral veil" Neapolitan events following Andrew's
death. At the end, Menalca suddenly announces a bewildering decision to
abandon the crown of flowers he was weaving and follow Faunus in his
expedition: "But until I return, you, dear, milk the goats" (sed dum venio
mulge tu, care, capellas).[17]

Boccaccio's eclogue obeys a twofold impulse. On one hand, there is the
structuring dimension of the dialogue, through which the poet, with Checco
as his foil, touches on the ethical-social plane of reality (even within the
pastoral life), hints at his own desire for coronation (2.43–46), and provides
a precise justification for poetry in general—not just bucolics, but a more
nuanced impulse to "humanistic" literature. On the other hand, a new fact
suddenly appears: Petrarch's *Argus*, which endorses a formal solution for
the eclogue absent from Boccaccio's initial proposal. The master shows that
pastoral poetry is more than evasion; it can take in the social, political, ethical, and emotional demands of reality through the instrument of allegory.

Boccaccio must not yet have been acquainted with *Argus* when he wrote
the metrical letter to Checco,[18] not only because Petrarch appears there
exclusively as an epic poet, the composer of *Africa* (3.26–27), but also because Boccaccio had suggested restricting the pastoral theme to love, as in
his first two Latin eclogues. The new fact of Petrarch's eclogue does not
oblige Boccaccio to modify his previous compositions. Something similar
occurs in *De vita et moribus domini Francisci Petracchi de Florentia*, which had
been written a few years earlier: here, too, the event represented by the Petrarchan eclogue (partially transcribed, together with the covering epistle

to Barbato, in the *Zibaldone Laurenziano*) occurred when the panegyric had already been written; what Boccaccio records in his notebook does not become a sufficient reason for him to make radical, organic alterations in his *De vita*. The signs of insertion of new material indicate significantly that his intellectual and formal adventure is on the whole open, and not constricted by subsequent revisions.

To Francesco Petrarca, "Ytalie iam certus honos" ("Sure honor now of Italy," *Carmina* 5)

Composed as a dedication for a gift copy of the *Divina commedia* sent to Petrarch,[19] Boccaccio's *carmen* opens with the words "honor of Italy," which refer not to Alighieri but to the laureated addressee, begging him to accept a masterpiece without equal, even though in the vernacular:

> Ytalie iam certus honos, cui tempora lauro
> romulei cinsere duces, hoc suscipe gratum
> Dantis opus doctis, vulgo mirabile, nullis
> ante, reor, simili compactum carmine seclis. (5.1–4)

> Sure honor now of Italy, you whose temples / the Roman senators circled with laurel, receive this work by / Dante, welcome to the learned, marvelous to the common folk; / never before, I opine, in any century was a similar poem composed.

Dante, situated in a line ideally descended from Claudian (ca. A.D. 400), glorifies Florence, mother of the Muses.[20] Were it not for his exile and premature death, Boccaccio asserts, he, too, would have received the laurel. Reaching his peroration, the sender urges Petrarch: "Take up [this learned compatriot], read closely, add to your favorites, cultivate, approve" (suscipe, perlege, iunge tuis, cole, comproba, 5.36). The final verses return full circle to the first, as he bids farewell to the laureate who adorns Rome and the world ("decus Urbis et orbis," 5.40).

The absolute primacy Boccaccio grants Dante as poet, philosopher, and theologian makes "Ytalie iam certus honos" one of the most difficult and complex of his minor pieces, not for a prima facie understanding of its content — obvious except for the usual convolutions of our author in composing Latin verses — but for its ambiguous underlying cultural "knots," or intersections of intellectual preferences and taste. It can perhaps be said that nowhere else in Boccaccio do the differences that irremediably separate him from

Petrarch, against his own will and in spite of often-affirmed loyalty to the latter's humanistic program, emerge with such impetus from their deep existential roots to the light of the word. Boccaccio's defense of Dante's decision to write in Italian, which is also a spirited self-defense, is a polemical stance vis-à-vis Petrarch. In sending the copy of the *Commedia* to his preceptor, he attempts an impossible reconciliation, but his effort may have had a respectable effect on Petrarch's admiration for Dante's poetry, both Latin and vernacular. Boccaccio's *carmen* to Petrarch is crystal clear in its ambiguity.

To Zanobi da Strada, "Si bene conspexi" ("If I have well understood," *Carmina* 7)

Soon after receiving the laurel crown from Emperor Charles IV in Pisa on May 15, 1355, Zanobi, now living near Montecassino, writes Boccaccio a metrical epistle in Latin asking for suggestions of themes on which he could write.[21] Boccaccio, hoping he has "rightly understood" the request, replies somewhat mockingly with ideas for an epic set in the middle period between antiquity and modernity on the Vandals, the Langobards, or the Goths — topics of interest to him in the mid-1350s. Abruptly, however, he changes tack to describe a serious illness in which he struggled with a stubborn fever like Hercules against Antaeus.[22] Having recovered, he closes the letter by urging Zanobi quickly to "pluck his lyre" (Fac, age, tange chelim, 59).

Boccaccio, who had written a somewhat ambivalent letter on friendship to Zanobi in early 1348, came to envy the Stradino for his laurels, but his personal jealousy must not and cannot overshadow the reciprocal esteem of the two intellectuals.[23] This is the only way that we can explain the exchange of the two poems, as well as Boccaccio's interest in copying Zanobi's work — for example, the *sermo* "Audite me" ("Listen to me") in the *Miscellanea Magliabechiana* (fols. 100–103), and the resounding praise for this *sermo* in Epistle 6.[24]

"Versus domini Iohannis Boccaccii ad Affricam domini Francisci Petrarce" ("Verses by *dominus* Giovanni Boccaccio to the *Africa* by *dominus* Francesco Petrarca," *Carmina* 9)

"Verses . . . to the *Africa*" was composed in the last year of the writer's life, probably after the letter of November 3, 1374, in which Boccaccio replied to news of Petrarch's death from the latter's son-in-law, Francescuolo da Brossano.[25] There, after a panegyric to the poet who had been his *preceptor* (teacher), Boccaccio expressed serious preoccupation concerning the fate of his master's library — his unfinished writings and most of all, the *Africa*:

"But what most anguishes me is what has happened to the books he has written and especially that *Africa* of his, which I consider a heavenly work, whether it is still there and will endure or whether it has been burned as he—too harsh toward his own things—often threatened to do while he was alive."[26] Belonging fundamentally to the trite line of direct *ad locutio* to the work (apostrophe), "Versus" reflects fears among Petrarch's admirers that he would never publish the *Africa* and the work would be lost.[27]

Finally, on the initiative of Francescuolo and Petrarch's Paduan circle, Pier Paolo Vergerio made the *Africa* public in 1396 with meticulous respect for the incomplete condition of the work. This event did not justify doubts concerning the Paduans' good judgment that Boccaccio had rather rudely expressed first in his letter to Francescuolo and then in "Versus" 103–6, where the poem is actually invited to flee "the untrustworthy Euganean hills" (dubios . . . euganeos montes) and to seek refuge in Florence. There, at least partially for tactical reasons, the most illustrious exponent of the Florentine side, Coluccio Salutati, himself very close to Boccaccio, awaited the opportunity to release them.[28]

This monument to Petrarch, the longest of the *Carmina* (182 verses), retains importance for several reasons. It is a living expression of the poetic and humanistic ideal that Boccaccio lived in his last years with an almost religious fervor for poetry and letters, represented here as the central force of a civilization that establishes itself by returning to its ancient origins. Petrarch's epic has accomplished just this: "You wish to restore to their natural home the Italic Muses of yore" (in sedesque velis tecum revocare priores Ausonias musas, 9.67–68). It is a question about which the writer has strong, serious feelings and that he treats elsewhere with more straightforward lucidity (*Genealogia deorum gentilium*, books 14 and 15, and the letter to Iacopo Pizzinga). Here it is barely visible, under the uncontrolled flood of words that pour forth in a predictable, monotonous rhetorical scheme (the *descriptio* of Florence in mourning is but one example), rendering the composition heavily inert, almost intolerable. This formal failure, however, finds twofold compensation. On the one hand, it allows a more precise recognition of what the late Boccaccio was reading, including Petrarch's Latin poetry;[29] on the other, it opens a more accurate understanding of his compositional method. Here it should be noticed, as a last point, that the stiffened repetitiveness—or, as I am tempted to call it, a senile anchylosis of style—emphasizes dramatically the poem's component parts, down to expressive formulas from the very young Boccaccio (*Elegia di Costanza*),[30] and especially his lifelong tendency to recycle previous literary material—that is, the Certaldan's vocation to rewrite.

CHAPTER FOUR

A FABLE OF THE WORLD'S CREATION AND PHAETON'S FALL • *(Allegoria mitologica)*

Steven M. Grossvogel

On folios 61r-62r of the *Zibaldone Laurenziano*, MS Plut. 29.8, Boccaccio wrote a historical fable in Latin, which a later hand entitled *De mundi creatione* (*On the Creation of the World*) and Aldo Francesco Massèra would rename the *Allegoria mitologica* (*Mythological Allegory*), the title it has retained.[1] This fable starts with a brief history of the world, beginning with the creation of the pagan universe, followed by a description of the successive periods of the world, from the Golden Age to the Silver, Bronze, and Iron Ages. Most of the material for this part of the narrative (about one-third of the *Allegoria*) is taken from the first book of Ovid's *Metamorphoses*. What Boccaccio chose to borrow from Ovid, however, also echoes the book of Genesis. The unnamed demiurge that creates the universe is a pagan type for the God of Genesis, and the actual creation of the universe is very similar to the Creation in Genesis. So, too, the Arcadian world of Saturn's Golden Age evokes the garden of Eden, and the wrath of Jove at the wickedness of humankind followed by the flood that destroyed everyone except Deucalion and Pyrrha (pagan types for Noah and his wife) clearly recalls events leading up to the Great Flood in Genesis. Again, the Titans' assault of Mount Olympus recalls Nimrod and the Tower of Babel. At the same period of time humankind received its first set of laws from the pagan Phoroneus, an allusion to God giving Moses the Ten Commandments, as Manlio Pastore Stocchi has shown: "Olympus opened itself and from the divine hand laws were given, with which are held in check the people who recognize the kingdom of the gods."[2]

Clearly Boccaccio is creating a typology of pagan figures and events that are meant to evoke similar biblical accounts, much the same way that medieval exegetes saw the Old Testament as prefiguring the New.[3] Boccaccio's reasons for doing so, however, are not self-evident. Is he simply imitating a medieval literary genre—the moralized commentaries on Ovid's

Metamorphoses? If he is rehabilitating pagan myths for use within a Christian context, as we find in the *Ovide moralisé* (probably written between 1316 and 1328) and Pierre Bersuire's popular *Ovidius moralizatus* (dating from the second quarter of the fourteenth century),[4] what was his purpose for doing so? Is his typology meant to carry the same theological subtext that we find in medieval biblical typology?

His narrative of the decline from the Bronze Age to the Iron Age is an example of how Boccaccio apparently wanted to use the pagan texts to conceal a Christian message in a manner similar to that of the medieval my-thographers and commentators.[5] To explain how the noble souls who were descended from Deucalion (pre-Christians) "might renounce the kingdom of Dis and be able to fly on high as a reward for their merits," there ensues a pagan allegory of the advent of Christ and redemption, culminating in a brief history of the church, allegorized as a garden, as Pastore Stocchi has shown.[6] Although this symbolic imagery is common in medieval allegorizations of classical myths, the poet's syncretism of pagan mythology and biblical history is elsewhere cryptic and difficult to decipher.

For example, as time passes, who is the "new pharaoh" with a hardened heart who tries with his cohorts to defeat the "militia of peace" (the Christians now inhabiting the earth)? Could he be, as the *Allegoria's* most recent commentator, Pastore Stocchi, speculates, the Holy Roman Emperor and his antipapal Ghibelline forces? Who is the "Moses" that "Tritonia Pallas" (the Holy Spirit) gives to Gideon (Florence?), the power that rises to oppose "Pharao novus" so that the flowers in the garden (the clergy?) may learn to exercise their virtues and resist their adversaries? Might he be King Robert of Anjou, the Guelph ruler of Naples who was given nominal titular rule of Florence in 1313? And who is "he who does good" (*bona faciens*)? Given the punning name, he seems to be Pope Boniface VIII. When Boccaccio says that this individual "plants new vine shoots and uproots the old ones," does he allude to the pope's attempts to renovate the church, to make it more worldly and increase its temporal power? What about the one "who came by water?" "Qui fuit de aqua latus," Pastore Stocchi points out, is the biblical interpretation of Moses' name. Is he then the same "Moses" alluded to earlier? Why is the "water-borne" man only interested in teaching the virtues and properties of the old flowers in the garden? Do those "old flowers" stand for church doctrine resisting changes proposed by newer, reform-oriented theology? Is the *almus pater* one of Pope Boniface's successors, responsible for moving the papacy from Rome to Avignon and distancing it from Italian affairs? If so, why has he recused himself from cultivating the new flowers? And most importantly, who is the Phaeton who is asked by the inhabitants of Parthenopea (Naples) to reveal the virtues of the new flowers? Still today among scholars, the answers to all these questions remain elusive or speculative.[7]

After the Creation and ages of the world, almost two-thirds of the *Allegoria* is devoted to Boccaccio's recounting of Ovid's myth of Phaeton. Unlike what precedes, the tale of Phaeton does not have the awkward allusions to historical figures disguised in pagan mythology and sounds more like an actual fable, or even a proto-*novella*. Although not as developed as the characters in Boccaccio's subsequent works, the figure of Phaeton is more than a mere exemplum used to illustrate the moral at the end of the *Allegoria*: "Therefore, may everyone remain in his vocation, like Aaron; nor should anyone assume the semblance of a teacher who does not know how to be a disciple if he wishes to avoid the miserable ruin of Phaeton."[8] As Tobias Foster Gittes has pointed out, unlike the Ovidian Phaeton whose divine birth is put in doubt by Epaphus, thereby inducing him to seek his father's acknowledgment of paternity, Boccaccio's young charioteer is motivated by a noble cause.[9] He is moved by the pleas of the Parthenopeans who acknowledge his divine birth and noble upbringing: "You, indeed, the son of the Prince of Stars and the Giver of Joyful Light, raised among the Muses of Mount Helicon, fortified in deeds of valor, true to your father, deign to show us the powers of the new kind of flowers, which bring anguish to our hearts." Later, when Phaeton visits his father, the reason he gives Apollo for wanting to drive the chariot of the Sun—"to remove the fog of their error with your light"—suggests that he is indeed "magnanimus Pheton," unlike his Ovidian counterpart, who is motivated by pride and peer pressure.[10]

Looking at the intricate intertextuality between the Phaeton fable in the *Allegoria* and Boccaccio's later works, as well as Ovid's *Metamorphoses* and *Tristia* and Dante's *Divina commedia*, Jonathan Usher makes a detailed case for interpreting the Phaeton tale in autobiographical terms. He sees the historical summary at the beginning of the *Allegoria* as a standard exordial feature in Boccaccio's works. The Phaeton story itself, he argues, is an extended metaphor of "poetic ambition and cultural discipline" and a "figure of youthful over-estimation of powers, particularly in the intellectual sphere."[11] In this context, the *bona faciens* is probably a major political figure with cultural pretensions (Acciaiuoli? King Robert?). Like Boccaccio, the new Phaeton comes from the north (as Boccaccio had moved from Florence to Naples). The "new flowers," which Usher takes as a symbol of writing, require "association with Pallas" (a symbol for learning in general, and for the study of philosophy in particular). Like both Phaeton and Dante, Boccaccio is also a poet-philosopher who is "nourished amongst the muses of

Mount Helicon."[12] The Boccaccio of the *Allegoria* could have seen in Dante's concluding remarks at the end of the *Vita nuova* his own need for professional development, or as the moral of the *Allegoria* has it, to be an apprentice before he can be a master. Dante had written: "And to come to that I strive as much as I can, as she [Beatrice] truly knows." Just as Dante's vision of the *Commedia*, which appears at the end of the *Vita nuova*, will require greater study on his part ("so that I may more worthily write of her"), so, too, must Boccaccio undertake similar studies in order to write about topics that are currently beyond his faculties.[13]

Victoria Kirkham has suggested that a path to better understanding may come from closer study of the *Allegoria*'s connections with Boccaccio's other writings. As she points out, Usher's reading of the *Allegoria* as poetic autobiography represents a radical departure from the scholarly tradition, which up through Pastore Stocchi has seen the work as a Christian history of the world charged with implications of political power struggles involving pope, emperor, and the house of Anjou—plausible concerns for the new writer, who was a student of canon law. In the contemporary *Filocolo*, for example, his protagonist Florio (traveling as Filocolo) encounters a character named Idalogo, a Boccaccian double who recounts in allegorical disguise the author's idealized poetic autobiography (5.8); soon after in his travels, at Rome Filocolo hears a long lecture on Christian history and the catechism from the priest Ilario (5.53–54). Boccaccio thus mixes history with autobiography, pagan with Christian allegory.[14] Furthermore, as Janet Smarr has pointed out, the opening of the *Filocolo* combines religious history and Neapolitan history in mythological terms. This work seems to be part of Boccaccio's experiments with mythology that he was learning from Paolo da Perugia while in Naples.[15] As Smarr has indicated, it was an experiment to which he returned later with the *Buccolicum carmen*, combining historical, autobiographical, and religious referents by way of mythological allegory.[16] In it Boccaccio retells the Bible via classical vehicles, and some of the same characters and situations in the *Allegoria mitologica* reappear in *Eclogue* 11 (for example, "Deucaliona pium," "Jovis turbatum," and "Foroneum").

Boccaccio's historical fable anticipates by several decades his *Genealogia deorum gentilium* (*Genealogy of the Pagan Gods*), which not only makes extensive use of mythology to narrate history but also discusses the relationship between *istoria* (history) and *fabula* (fiction). According to Boccaccio, history is associated with the literal truth and is often sacrificed in invention by poets. Whereas historians "begin their account at some convenient beginning and describe events in the unbroken order of their occurrence to the end," poets are not constrained by chronology and "begin their proposed narrative in the midst of events, or sometimes even near the end; and thus they find excuse for telling preceding events which seem to have been omitted."[17] Furthermore, poets do not have to portray historical figures the way history has: Boccaccio notes that there are discrepancies between Virgil's Dido and the way history depicted her, and he gives several reasons for them. First, Virgil "desired to bring his hero to somebody worthy of regard who might receive him and urge him to tell of his own fate and that of the Trojans. Such a one above all he found in Dido, who, to be sure, is supposed to have dwelt there not then, but many generations later." Second, Virgil wished "to show with what passions human frailty is infested, and the strength with which a steady man subdues them. . . . So he represents in Dido the attracting power of the passion of love, prepared for every opportunity, and in Aeneas one who is readily disposed in that way and at length readily overcome." The other two reasons Boccaccio gives are that Virgil wished "to extol, through his praise of Aeneas, the *gens Julia* in honor of Octavius," and "to exalt the glory of the name of Rome. This he accomplishes through Dido's execrations at her death; they imply the wars between Carthage and Rome, and *prefigure* the triumphs which the Romans gained thereby."[18]

I believe that, as early as the *Allegoria mitologica*, the young Boccaccio is exercising prerogatives of both historian and poet. Like a *fabula*, the *Allegoria* portrays historical figures not the way history portrays them, but as mythological figures meant to have a symbolic significance. Like Aeneas, Phaeton, too, "is readily disposed . . . and at length readily overcome"; and like Dido, the Parthenopeans are "worthy of regard" and "an attracting power" who "receive him and urge him." As for the cryptic allusions to the *bona faciens* and to *Mose*, these may have been intended as allusive encomia to extol and exalt the court of King Robert of Anjou and "prefigure" the events that would happen at his court.

Yet the young Boccaccio has several of the same attributes as the mature author describing himself in an autobiographical passage in the *Genealogia*, 15.10.[19] Furthermore, like a history (*istoria*), the *Allegoria* begins not in medias res but with the creation of the universe and concludes with Boccaccio's present time. The events that take place between those two moments are similar to history as Boccaccio saw it, according to Vittore Branca: as a series of Viconian *corsi e ricorsi* whereby characters rise and fall on the wheel of Fortuna, the Boethian goddess who so dominates Boccaccio's other works.[20] Phaeton typologically prefigures what happens to young people who are not adequately prepared to undertake lofty endeavors, a theme we find in many of Boccaccio's later works (from Filocolo's nearly disastrous adventure in Alexandria to similar misadventures in several *novelle* in the *Decameron*).

Boccaccio, like many medieval writers, viewed history as having a subjective and moral dimension. Both the character of Phaeton and the events surrounding him are portrayed as exempla.[21] Boccaccio's *Allegoria mitologica* seems to bring together sources at once personal, literary, and historical in creating exempla that serve, among other things, as models of appropriate or inappropriate behavior. The nature of Boccaccio's Latin prose fable not only anticipates the exemplary quality of his vernacular *novelle* but further illustrates how *fabula* and *istoria* are closely intertwined.

For all its shortcomings, the *Allegoria* contains *in nuce* narrative elements that will be developed in Boccaccio's later works. Even though much of what he writes in the *Allegoria* is taken from Ovid and, to a lesser extent, from Dante, Boccaccio was not afraid to sacrifice his two beloved sources to invention. Like the author of the *Ovide moralisé*, Boccaccio reveals the allegorical message at the end of his fable but deliberately leaves unanswered many of the cryptic allusions to historical figures, as if inviting his readers to delve further into his text, something he would insist that they do with all his works.

CHAPTER FIVE

A PORTRAIT OF A YOUNG HUMANIST • (Epistolae 1–4)

Jason Houston

The four epistles collectively called the "allegorical" epistles owe their survival exclusively to the fact that their author, Boccaccio, copied them out in his notebook, the *Zibaldone Laurenziano* (Biblioteca Lauren-ziano, MS Pluteo 29.8). They were written in 1339, as indicated by the dates Boccaccio himself provides in the conclusions of three of the four let-ters, and he copied them into the *Laurenziano* at the time of composition or shortly thereafter, but in any case before his return to Florence from Naples in 1341.[1] While modern editors have organized them chronologically, Boc-caccio grouped three letters (1, 3, 2) together with a later one to his friend Zanobi da Strada (Epistle 6). Boccaccio placed the fourth allegorical epistle later, immediately after three of Dante's letters and the letter of Frate Ilaro to Uguccione della Faggiuola. The presence of these four letters in the *Lau-renziano* attests to Boccaccio's interest in preserving them, at least for his own reference. For the reader of Boccaccio, they offer a hazy portrait of the author *in cursu discendi* (in the course of learning); they record his earliest, and often clumsy, attempts at finding his way among classical and contem-porary authorities.

Scholars who have commented on these letters stand in nearly universal agreement that Boccaccio never intended to send them to their purported addressees.[2] Instead, he composed them as exercises in the literary genre of letter writing. The first letter names Charles, Duke of Durazzo, as the recipient, while the other three do not carry the name of an addressee. As exercises, the letters follow the medieval formulae of the *ars dictaminis* (art of letter writing), which prescribe a five-part division: *salutatio, exordium, narratio, petitio*, and *conclusio* (greeting, opening, narrative, request, and con-clusion). The third letter is an exception; written in an antagonistic spirit to an unfaithful friend, it omits the *salutatio* and abbreviates the *conclusio*. Boccaccio also executes the highly rhetorical metrical structure of the *cursus*, a rhythmical flourish that emphatically terminates select clauses.[3] Finally, each of the first two letters concludes with a vernacular incipit to a poem that supposedly would have accompanied the letter. As Boccaccio never intended to send the missives, there is no evidence that he ever composed these poems.

These four compositions find Boccaccio trying his hand at the various voices of epistolary writing current in the Trecento. He composes three of them in the *stilus rhetoricus* (rhetorical style); that is to say, he writes the letters as if they were formal orations, including emotive flourishes to simulate a passionate delivery. In the remaining letter Boccaccio writes in the *stilus obscurus* (obscure style), employing arcane vocabulary and difficult periodic structure to show off his Latin competency, eclectic vocabulary, and familiarity (however tenuous) with Greek. In all, Boccaccio frequently cites, both directly and indirectly, classical sources to color his prose.

On the other hand, these four letters offer perhaps the earliest evidence for Boccaccio's ongoing intellectual negotiation with more contemporary authorities. Internal evidence in the second letter indicates that he is writing to Petrarch, his lifelong literary model and, eventually, personal friend. On the other hand, as Giuseppe Billanovich first pointed out, Boccaccio models his letters specifically on Dante's, which he had copied out in the *Laurenziano*.[4] Already in these earliest fragments from Boccaccio's career, the profiles of his two masters, Dante and Petrarch, make up the background of his own writings. The letters, taken as a whole and seen as exercises in the *ars dictaminis*, document somewhat chaotically the idiosyncratic literary development of a remarkable humanist.

The young writer addresses his first letter to a figure in the Angevin court of Naples during his tenure there. Boccaccio likely met the Duke of Durazzo in that southern city, where the latter was a charismatic young nobleman and figure of political intrigue until his death at the hands of Louis of Hungary in 1348, an event lamented in "Dorus" from the *Buccolicum carmen*. In this letter, however, the character of the duke stands for an important figure for many authors of the day, the patron. Boccaccio assumes the customary humility of a poor author in the presence of a great noble, whom he flatters with a classical, and conspicuously erudite, salutation. "O heavenly fame of the Epirian Prince, and singular brilliance of Italian nobles," he blurts out roughly in his opening salvo.[5] Boccaccio's flattery and humility quickly give way to the central purpose of the letter to a potential patron, the posing of a question whose obvious answer would favor the letter writer and flatter the recipient. The question allows the patron to assume the role of wise mentor while drawing on the classical trope of magnanimity to encourage munificence. In this case Boccaccio asks the duke, through citations from Seneca and the book of Deuteronomy, what virtue is most important in a lord, clemency or justice, implying that the duke possesses both. The question having been posed and a response timidly requested, the letter quickly fizzles and concludes. Certainly the most conventional and dispassionate of the four letters, Boccaccio's letter to the Duke of Durazzo offers an early glimpse of his serial attempts, and perhaps the reason for his chronic failure, to secure powerful patronage.

By contrast, in the second letter Boccaccio finds his voice as a mediator between the poetic visions of his two masters, Dante and Petrarch. This is the first of the five extant letters that Boccaccio composed to Petrarch, and despite the fact that he did not intend it for the recipient's eyes, it shows the careful reverence he has for Petrarch. The letter opens with ebullient praise before a long enumeration of the classical and medieval models for Petrarch, from Socrates to Ockham. Boccaccio then shifts the register of the letter when he describes the apparition of a beautiful lady:

> But as the night turned to day, and as I walked sure and carefree near the tomb of Virgil, suddenly a woman appeared, bright as a flash of lightning from the sky, I know not how, to my good fortune entirely pleasing to me in beauty and in manners. Oh, how amazed I was at her appearance! So much so that I seemed to become a thing different from myself; no indeed, I thought myself a ghostly image. And thus having taken leave of my senses and driven to insanity, I dreamed while awake; with my eyes open wide, I tried to know if I was awake. Finally my stupor ended because of the terror of the sound that followed. For just as thunder follows immediately behind heavenly bolts, so once I had seen the flame of that beauty, terrible and imperious love held me. Fiercely, just as a lord expelled from his native land returns after a long exile, he killed, exiled, or bound in chains whatever in me was contrary to him.[6]

This allegorical scene depicting the astonishment caused by Love closely follows Dante's letter to Moroello Malaspina but also echoes other sources, including Ovid, Apuleius, Boethius, and Andreas Capellanus; it also prefigures many episodes in Boccaccio's early vernacular fiction.[7] The letter continues as a friend appears to the stunned Boccaccio and consoles him with the suggestion that he read Petrarch as a remedy for his stupor. It closes with a long panegyric to Petrarch as a sacred vessel of poetic wisdom and a model of the virtue of poetry to console the amorously preoccupied young Boccaccio.

Although the letter overtly praises Petrarch, the approach that Boccaccio takes reveals how his own vision of poetic excellence takes root in the fertile soil of Dante's poetic legacy.[8] The figure of the beautiful lady in a vision that enthralls the viewer to love recalls Dante's first vision in the *Vita nuova* (chap. 2). Her befuddling presence, the deep depression at her departure, her ability to spur the poet toward consideration of his poetic craft, the invocation of poetic exile—all of these *topoi*, familiar to Boccaccio through Dante, appear, if cursorily, in this letter. Boccaccio's approach to Petrarch as friend and mentor, which he here inaugurates, coordinates Petrarch's identity as a poet in the Tuscan tradition defined by Dante.[9]

The third letter is difficult to read, at times nearly incomprehensible, and thus easy to categorize definitively as an attempt to write in the *stilus obscurus*. Indeed, in conclusion Boccaccio uses the transliterated Greek verb *katagraphein* to describe his rhetorical mode in the letter: "Catagrafavi enim obscure" (I have composed this letter in an obscure style).[10] Boccaccio peppers his formal epistolary Latin style with an idiosyncratic vocabulary of Latinized Greek forms from his recent reading of Apuleius as well as access to Uguccione da Pisa's *Derivationes*, an etymological compendium. The result is both artificially Hellenic and oddly Italianate, showing Boccaccio the autodidact at work. Although it reads as amateurish, as the effort of a young scholar, it demonstrates a dedication to learning Greek and applying those studies to his own literary production, an early habit that will continue through his entire career, as is clear in his choice of names in some vernacular texts (Panfilo, Filocolo, Dioneo, etc.) as well as in his close work with Leontius Pilatus on the *Genealogia*.[11]

Beyond the difficulties that Boccaccio's Latin presents, this letter, more so than any of the other three, foreshadows his literary style. It purports to record the author's displeasure with a person who has betrayed his friendship. Yet the lament's exaggerated nature, cast in an extravagant vocabulary, suggests a rhetoric of hyperbole. It may remind the reader of the spirit-guide's harangue against his wife for the dreamer's benefit in the *Corbaccio*:

> But in effect you were the opposite, like a deaf asp, you blocked up your ears against therapeutic admonitions, unabashed and foolish; despicably pursuing your ignorance and madness just like the Agriophagi, you scorned the fraternal banquet.

A shrewd doctor cannot always heal every illness or every patient with sweet-smelling ointments, since there are many illnesses and many patients who do not respond to these and who require foul-smelling remedies if they wish to be led back to health; and if there is any sickness which one may wish to purge and cure with foul words, arguments, and demonstrations, ill-conceived love in man is one of them, because in a short time a foul word has more effect on the scornful intellect than a thousand decent and pleasant persuasions poured into the deaf heart through the ears over a great length of time.[12]

Not only do these passages share vocabulary (*surdi/sordo*, *farmaciis/medicato*, *aures/orecchie*), but the linguistic expressionism and expansive lexicon that mark his prose fiction in Italian appear here in early bloom. The vehemence of tone in the *Corbaccio* finds its earliest voicing here.

The fourth epistle raises the most doubts about whether Boccaccio meant it to be purely an exercise or had actually intended to send it. Like its companion, the third letter, this missive addresses a man who has let Boccaccio down in some way. Boccaccio filled the previous letter with venom; this time he assumes the plaintive tone of one who has been neglected by a friend recently elevated to a new circle. After Boccaccio opens his letter by apologizing both for his distance and for daring to bother his recipient, he begins a long catalog of the latter's virtues. So far, the letter adheres to convention. Using the most florid and formal language, Boccaccio recounts the education and then the intellectual and moral qualities of the addressee.

Less than halfway into the letter, however, he changes tack, relating how his friend has turned from the liberal arts to the art of war, at which fact Boccaccio can only express nearly silent dismay: "When I heard one day that you had become a warrior, full of wonder, I said, 'Alas,' emitting a mournful sigh."[13] Boccaccio then goes into details of the political and military exploits of his erstwhile friend in the Apulian city of Barletta, both lamenting his change of character and complaining about being excluded from these matters. While the rest of the letter indulges in erudite invocations of classical references as points of comparison for the martial deeds of his friend, there are also many specifics that suggest, at least to this reader, that Boccaccio penned this epistle with an actual friend in mind.[14] Indeed, nearing his conclusion, he wishes that his friend's wife, Lucina, will bear him a child that Boccaccio might welcome as godfather—a human detail that goes beyond the needs of a rhetorical exercise.

The fourth letter's very intimate tone, and its supplicatory language, prefigure much of Boccaccio's later epistolary production. Indeed, in this letter Boccaccio finds a voice that will persist throughout his life. Just a few years later, in 1341, he writes a letter very similar in tone to his fellow Florentine Niccola Acciaiuoli (Epistle 5). Reproof echoes with more force in Boccaccio's fiery response of 1353 to Petrarch for refusing to return to Florence as *magister* of the *studio fiorentino*, a professor at the Florentine university (Epistle 10). Boccaccio's political disappointment, tangible for the first time here, returns with terrible vengeance in his letter to Francesco Nelli of 1363 (Epistle 13), written after Boccaccio's brief and disastrous tenure as Acciaiuoli's courtier in Naples. And finally, the tenderness that Boccaccio shows to his friend's future child will be even more poignantly expressed for Petrarch's granddaughter Eletta in 1367 (Epistle 15). Even if the fourth letter seems to us to be simply an example of Boccaccio's practice of the *ars dictaminis*, it still provides us with a portrait of the young poet and future humanist, as do its three sister pieces in their own way.

PART III

CLASSICAL ROMANCES

CHAPTER SIX

LOVE-STRUCK IN NAPLES • *(Filostrato)*

David Wallace

The *Filostrato*, composed at Naples in 1335 or just after, is an extraordinary accomplishment for an author in his early twenties. It is at once a simple tale of love won and lost and a self-consciously ambitious experiment in synthesizing diverse literary styles, influences, and *modi agendi*. Such ambitions are immediately announced by the rubric, or gloss, that names the book and then explains the novel Greek-Latin calquing of its title: "Filostrato is the title of this book, for this reason: because it best expresses what the book is about. *Filostrato* is as much to say *a man conquered and beaten down by love*; as was Troiolo, so one can see, conquered by love in loving Criseida so fervently, and then again beaten down by her departure."[1] No autograph of the *Filostrato* survives, but it is clear from the *Teseida* autograph manuscript that Boccaccio was his own rubricator and annotator, employing such means to *authorize* his vernacular compositions, to suggest their finished status as *books*.[2] The disquisition above, leading from simple statement of the book's name to etymological unpacking of that fanciful title, represents the first hint of grander ambitions explored in the extensive glosses to the *Teseida*, and later through Latin encyclopedism. Here, however, Boccaccio's rubricating and annotating serve the fiction of his creating a finished physical object, a book that should come into the hands (*alle mani*) of his lady. Or rather, that it should come *first* into her hands. Clearly his hopes for this work, and his investment in fashioning it, are very high—as evidenced by the elaborate prose with which, in his *Proemio*, he sends it on its way: "And so, worthy lady, I gathered (*ridussi*) these present verses into the form of a little book: perpetual testimony to future viewers both of your worthiness, with which these verses are to a certain extent embellished, and of my sadness; and having gathered them (*ridottole*), I thought it not honest that they should first come into any hands but yours, since you have been their sole and true *causa*."[3]

This is a highly complex Italian sentence, or period. Its first main verb, withheld with Cavalcantian tenacity, finally arrives as *ridussi* (a usage reminiscent of Caxton's Latinate determination to *reduce* texts to English); the period is then immediately extended by *ridottole*, a participial phrase spun from the same verb. The concluding characterization of the departed lady as single and true *cagione* (cause) of all this clearly fails to convince; what moves Boccaccio is egregious literary ambition. The lady who screens such aspirations is herself offered a screen role in the fiction to follow. As the young author is to be identified with young Troiolo, so she may see herself as Criseida. Such identification is problematic, of course: Boccaccio goes on gauchely to suggest that the lady need identify with only the positive aspects of his heroine (good looks, good manners), and "whatever else is praiseworthy in woman."[4]

The supposition developed in the *Proemio* is that the lady of the young, love-struck *Filostrato* author has moved to Sannio, a region of the kingdom lying inland from Naples, beyond the mountains (Pr. 8). Critics have long discounted the romantic biographical schemes favored, especially, by nineteenth-century scholars. No evidence suggests that Boccaccio had an early mistress named Giovanna or Filomena, the dedicatee of this romance, or actually had a beloved called Maria d'Aquino or Fiammetta, who enters his corpus with the *Filocolo*, or that he himself was the product of a liaison in Paris between his father, a Florentine merchant, and a French princess; he was a *povero bastardo* who seems never to have known his own mother.[5] But the notion of being separated at Mediterranean Naples from a beloved lying not too far away fits nicely with romantic imaginings of the Trojan War, with the Greeks camped outside the city. Such a Troy, lyrically Ovidian rather than epically Virgilian, owes much to the traditions of French romance that accentuated affairs of the heart while downplaying the fighting. Boccaccio's most obvious debt here is to Benoît de Sainte-Maure's *Roman de Troie* (ca. 1155–60) and its condensed Latin translation, Guido delle Colonne's *Historia destructionis Troiae* (1287).[6] The *Roman de Troie*, which Boccaccio may have known directly or through the Italian translation of Binduccio dello Scelto, is the first text to focus on the amours of Criseida (providing relief from the steady diet of battles and truces). Benoît devotes most space to Criseida's affair with Diomede, leaving Boccaccio to amplify her relationship with Troiolo and the theme of their separation. Boccaccio cleaves closer to Guido's prose than to Benoît's octosyllabics for matters of detail—perhaps not surprisingly, given Guido's status as a distinguished jurist and poet at the imperial court in Sicily, the island lost by the Neapolitan Angevins to Aragon following the Sicilian Vespers revolt of 1282.

The young Robert of Anjou (1277–1343), held hostage by Peter III of Aragon during the Sicilian Vespers, inherited Naples from his father in 1309, along with extensive territories in northern Italy and southern France. With Sicily under Aragon, the Neapolitan Angevins could only look and dream north and east, across the Mediterranean. Robert's father, Charles I, had been overthrown in Sicily while preparing for a military expedition to Greece, and Angevin interests spread into the Levant. Historical narratives of Troy and Thebes, then, were of more than recreational interest to members of the Neapolitan court in the 1330s. It was in this period that King Robert commissioned a revised redaction of the *Histoire ancienne jusqu'à Cesar*, a capacious prose compendium of human history, beginning at Genesis.[7] Robert's revised version cuts Genesis, begins the historical narrative with Thebes, and imports massively from Benoît's *Roman de Troie*. Boccaccio's decision to compose poetic narratives of Thebes and Troy in the 1330s, then, resonates with the tastes and ambitions of the Neapolitan Angevin court in timely fashion.

Boccaccio had been attempting to move closer to court and literary circles ever since arriving at Naples (following his father's appointment as chief representative of the Florentine Bardi company in April 1328); after some four years working as apprentice merchant or *discepolo*, he abandoned Bardi banking for the study of canon law and for the opportunity to frequent the Neapolitan Studio and improve his Latin. King Robert, following six years of residency at Avignon (1318–24), vigorously promoted Latin learning in Naples, drawing in distinguished scholars such as the astronomer and astrologer Andalò del Negro, the Franciscan universal historian Paolo da Perugia, and (late in 1338) the scriptural and classical commentator Dionigi da Borgo San Sepolcro.[8] The *Teseida*, particularly in its longer prose glosses, shows considerable absorption of this learned Latin culture; the earlier *Filostrato*, however, offers (through its autocommentative rubrics) mere shows and trappings of it. Both these early poems, plus the *Ninfale fiesolano*, are written in a verse form that stands at the far end of the cultural spectrum from the Neapolitan Studio and its Latin learning: they are in *ottava rima*, a verse form sung (to borrow Petrarch's dismissive characterization of Dante's audience) "by ignorant oafs in taverns and market places."[9]

The *cantare* corpus of popular narrative compares closely with traditions of Middle English romance, particularly tail-rhyme (as parodied by Chaucer's *Tale of Sir Thopas*). Such performances generally begin with boisterous appeals for attention, or with pious formulae, make spurious appeals to written authority—"in romaunce as we rede"; "per quel che 'l libro mi mostra" (going by what the book shows me)—and grease the wheels of rhyming with formulaic tags (roses and lilies abound). Syntax is simple and lyricism brief; action and adventure are at a premium, and courtly behavior is generally associated with spending large amounts of money. Trojan tales were popular with *canterini* (*cantari* composers and singers); Benoît's *Roman de Troie* provided material for at least one of them.[10] The *Decameron* was to provide material for no fewer than eighteen *cantare* adaptations: there are five distinct versions of the Ghismonda *novella* (4.1), two starring the piratical Paganino da Mare (2.10), plus one each of favorites such as Masetto (3.1), Nastagio degli Onesti (5.8), and Griselda (10.10).[11] Many *canterini* knew Boccaccio's work well; the Florentine town crier Antonio Pucci, actively composing *cantari* along with other work from the 1330s until his death in 1388, was an assiduous copyist of his writings.[12] And perhaps the bond between Boccaccio and the *cantare* was yet stronger: the *Filostrato*'s *ottave* have been acclaimed as *fons et origo* (font and origin) of the entire tradition.

The earliest datable *cantare* is the *Fiorio e Biancifiore* found in Florence, Biblioteca Nazionale, MS Magliabechiano 8.1416, from 1343—that is, from less than a decade after Boccaccio was reworking the same French-derived materials into his *Filocolo*. For Domenico De Robertis, as for many other critics, *ottava rima* is born not with the *cantare*, but with the *Filostrato*, circa 1335. De Robertis is circumspect *not* to suggest that the *Filostrato* invents *cantare*: it offers, rather, new form and scope for genres already well-attested by popular literary traditions.[13] Paola Rada suggests that the Magliabechiano *Fiorio e Biancifiore* shows signs of deriving from an earlier exemplar, and Armando Balduino sees Boccaccio catching the wave of a preexisting *cantare* tradition, and not as sole inventor of *ottava rima*.[14] Much is at stake in this peculiarly Italian critical debate: Benedetto Croce's clean distinction between high and popular art compounds with the age-old habit of dividing the Tre Corone (Three Crowns of Florence) from everyone else writing in Trecento Italy.[15] Young Boccaccio in Naples had not yet fallen under Petrarch's discriminatory tutelage: his early linguistic promiscuity extended into self-parody in Neapolitan dialect.[16] He was, nonetheless, acutely concerned with matters of social distinction at Naples, as the illegitimate son of a Florentine merchant portrayed among the *avari* (avaricious) of the *Amorosa visione*. Such fears, I shall suggest, play powerfully through the *Filostrato*, but they align imperfectly with more recent critical anxieties concerning the social provenance of literary sources.

Boccaccio deploys his *ottave* in the *Filostrato* across a wide range of literary registers. At certain moments he sounds just like a *canterino*; at others he impresses as a budding practitioner of the most complex, aulic prose. The phrase "if the story speaks the truth" (se 'l ver dice la storia, 1.46.6) bespeaks not bookish reflexivity but the need for a third *b* rhyme. When Criseida "risembrava mattutina rosa" (seemed like a morning rose) she resembles any *cantare* heroine; her appearance as *perla orientale* later in book 2 reflects not so much oriental allure as, again, the need for a third *b* rhyme (2.38.3, 108.6). And there is nothing in the following half stanza to distinguish Boccaccio from any half-decent jobbing *canterino*:

> Troiolo canta e fa mirabil festa,
> armeggia e dona e spende lietamente,
> e spesso si rinnuova e cangia vesta,
> ogni ora amando più ferventemente. (2.84.1–4)

> Troilus sings and parties hearty, / jousts and gives gifts and happily spends money, / and often renews and changes his clothes, / every hour loving more fervently.

Just four stanzas earlier in book 2, however, Boccaccio had opened with an ambitious imitation of the flowery simile at *Inferno* 2.127–32 and ended by glancing at *Purgatorio* 11.4. Motifs and phrasings from Dante and the *stilnovisti* recur throughout the poem, and 5.62–65 is more or less turned over to Cino da Pistoia, so close is Boccaccio's imitation of his most celebrated *canzone*, "La dolce vista e 'l bel guardo soave" ("The sweet sight and the fair, gentle glance"). At other moments, particularly when wishing to move the plot briskly along, Boccaccio resembles a prose chronicler (with rhymes no longer aligning with syntax): "E come che' Troian fosser serrati dalli Greci nemici, non avvenne che per ciò fosser mai intralasciati li divin sacrificii, ma si tenne per ciascun sempre in quelli modi usati" (1.17.1–5, with line breaks omitted to make the point; And although the Trojans were locked in by their Greek enemies, it never happened for that reason that sacrifices to the gods were neglected, but everyone stuck to them in the usual way).[17] Conversely, the prose of his *Proemio* sometimes stockpiles subjunctives that, elsewhere, provide easy rhymes for his *ottave*: "acciocché io vivessi e vi potessi ancora vedere e più lungamente vostro dimorassi vivendo" (Pr. 25: so that I might live and might see you again and might, by living, remain yours for a longer time).[18] Shortly after this knotty expression of his will to live, Boccaccio summarizes the aim of his current work with admirable precision: "cantando narrare li miei martiri" (Pr. 26: singing, to narrate my sufferings). He thus finds, amid this complex prose, a perfect hendecasyllabic line to capture *in nuce* his ambitions for the *Filostrato*: to sustain a tension between *singing* and *narrating* that might serve to express intensely personal emotion. His *cantando* here looks to the *cano* that opens Virgil's *Aeneid* rather than to *cantare* tradition, although it foretells a lyricism that is also foreign to the action-oriented *canterini*. Boccaccio's Troiolo seems always eager to exchange public space for the solitariness of his own room (*camera*), where past actions might be recollected, and private emotions expressed: "tutto soletto / in camera n'andò" (1.33.1–2: all alone / he went to his chamber). Troiolo's *camera* functions like a separate *chamber* of the brain, suggesting inner being that must be differentiated — by physical movement through built space — from the persona presented to a greater public.

Troiolo's retreat into *in camera* reflection is determined by his *filostrato* moment, his being struck by love. Boccaccio's handling of this *innamoramento* has proved hugely influential, inspiring one of Chaucer's greatest scenes, which in turn forms the template for the most famous and disastrous literary *innamoramento* of the twentieth century: that of Ted Hughes and Sylvia Plath.[19] Boccaccio's brilliant realization of falling in love, the moment of the fatal look or gesture, proves deeply compelling to moderns following Troiolo's line of sight to Criseida:

> Ella era grande, ed alla sua grandezza
> rispondeano li membri tutti quanti,
> e 'l viso avea adorno di bellezza
> celestiale, e nelli suoi sembianti
> quivi mostrava una donnesca altezza;
> e col braccio il mantel tolto davanti
> s'avea dal viso, largo a sé faccendo,
> ed alquanto la calca rimovendo.
>
> Piacque quell'atto a Troiolo e 'l tornare
> ch'ella fé 'n sé alquanto sdegnosetto,
> quasi dicesse: "E' non ci si può stare."
> E diessi a più mirare il suo aspetto. (1.27–28.4)

She was big, and in accord with her bigness / all her limbs were well proportioned, / and a face she had adorned with beauty / from the heavens, and in her gestures / there showed forth a womanly *hauteur*; / and with her arm she moved her mantle / from before her face, swishing it widely around herself, / and somewhat moving the crowd backwards. // That action pleased Troiolo, and also the returning / to her original position that she made, somewhat disdainfully, / as if she were saying: "Here one may not stand." / And he gave himself to further gazing at her face.

Translating *grande* as "big" and *grandezza* as "bigness," while clumsy, accentuates that what Boccaccio has in mind here amounts to more than physical height: for that, *altezza* would serve (as it serves just four lines later, albeit with the doubled sense of looking down from a certain height). Criseida is *grande* both physically and in the scope of her gestures: for her sweeping mantle suggests that here is a woman who will allow nobody to stand in her self-designated personal space. Or at least, her gestures *seem* to say this. Troiolo, viewing her from across a crowded temple,[20] is deep into hermeneutics, as that subjunctive (quasi dicesse) suggests. But he is already hooked, gazing increasingly at her face (a più mirare) and then, by the end of the stanza, gazing fixedly (di mirar fiso, 1.28.7). Boccaccio knew from Dante and medieval optics that gazing too fixedly endangers the health (*salute*) of the viewer: a beloved's image that has traveled through the eye to the heart might never be removed. And appearances may deceive; Troiolo's particular tragedy is that Criseida's *grandezza* fails to live up to this initial, fulminating impression. She is not *grande* in rank, a member of the magnate class; nor will she measure up to the standard that Troiolo assumes for her.

Criseida is well aware that Troiolo is *grande*, and that any *gran donna* should be happy with him (2.49.1–2); he is of much higher rank, she reminds herself, than she (di troppo più alta condizione / che tu non sei, 2.76.2–3). She defers to Troiolo's royal splendor (splendor reale, 3.28.6), and Troiolo himself concedes that his own father will consider her *not* his equal (diseguale / a me, 4.69.7–8). But even in his last speech to Criseida before her departure for the Greeks, Troiolo remains chained to his first impression, recalling "your lofty and lordly actions" (atti tuoi altieri e signorili) and her "ladylike disdain" (sdegno donnesco) that apparently finds repellent every "vulgar behavior" (oprar popolesco) (4.165.1–6). This impression carries into her moment of leaving Troy: turning *disdegnosamente* to Diomede, she makes clear her disdain (*sdegno*) for the Trojans letting her go (5.8.1, 5.9.4). The first descriptive term used of Diomede, her new suitor, is *grande* (6.33.1): true in every sense, since he is of royal blood. Meanwhile, back in Troy, Troiolo is surrounded by a circle of royal Trojan women, and it is from within this circle that his sister, Cassandra, delivers an excoriating class critique: Criseida, she says, is a priest's daughter, offspring of a man of little importance (di picciolo affare, 7.87.5). Troiolo responds by reading from the *Convivio* 4 playbook, "There is nobility wherever there is virtue" (7.94.1),[21] and the princess Cassandra is silenced. It is worth noting, however, that within this circle of genuine *grandi* Troiolo effectively talks his way back to health: he goes off to fight the Greeks again at 7.104. All too soon, however, proof of Criseida's infidelity is dragging him down, and Diomede, too, rendering their mutual taunts wicked and base (cattivi e villani, 8.26.1); the very last epithet applied to Criseida by Boccaccio in concluding the storytelling proper is as follows: "cotal fine ebbe la speranza vana / di Troiolo in Criseida villana" (8.28.7–8: such an end had the vain hope placed / by Troiolo in base Criseida). The narrative's last bitter realization is that Troiolo was deluded by that initial sighting: she who was *grande* in person should, by all expectations of medieval aesthetics, have proved morally if not socially *grande*, too. Instead she turns out to be *villana*: churlish, a *villein*, possessed of the moral instincts of peasantry. The moral vocabulary of European vernaculars, now as in the Middle Ages, grounds itself on positive valences of *nobility* and negatives associated with those laboring in fields or with animals. The precocious communal government of Trecento Florence, however, had attempted to curb magnates and promote *popolani*. In fact, magnates—aristocrats claiming descent from the Tuscan feudal nobility—had been banned from most areas of communal government since 1293; only by severing family ties and becoming *popolani* could they effectively reenter public life. All this made trade and diplomatic dealings with northern Europeans difficult for Florentines, since the operative lexicon of honor, trust, and prestige rooted itself lexically in class hierarchy: nobles represented noble principles; *villeins* acted villainously.[22] The bottom-line disquiet over class matters rendered by *Filostrato* 8.28.7–8 suggests, then, ambivalence stemming from the author's own déclassé, illegitimate origins, his promiscuous mixing of high and low art sources, and his wavering attachment to Florentine communal values when confronted by the graceful waft of courtly Neapolitan Angevin *otium*. Such ambivalences, stoking the boiler of a brilliant creative mind, were never to be resolved. The *Decameron* carries the *Filostrato*'s cultural hybridizing forward to imagine a most peculiar Florentine-Neapolitan construct: a communal structure, in which governance is shared by all participants, that is also a monarchy.

Much else carries forward from the *Filostrato* to later phases of Boccaccio's career, most notably perhaps exploration of the distinct possibilities of, and permeable boundaries between, verse and prose. As we have seen, Boccaccio's verse occasionally exceeds end-stopping to assume the modality of prose; and his prose rhythms often seem more poetic than prosaic. The *Decameron* features lyric set pieces, but also finds rhythms in prose movement reflecting Boccaccio's immersion in Latinate culture and his study of *artes dictaminis*, especially *cursus*, that began in Naples.[23] The *Filostrato* also features letter exchanges that improve on the one-sided effusions of Ovid's *Heroides* (a lifelong favorite) by making the intensive study of epistles a received part of the poem's fabric. Troiolo and Pandaro, in particular, subject

Criseida's writing to intensive scrutiny; when fidelity wears thin, Pandaro proposes a kind of trial by hermeneutics: "con iscrittura è da tentar costei" (7.49.2: she is to be tested by writing).

The very last act imagined in and for the *Filostrato*, we have noted, is delivery as a finished text-object,[24] freshly copied and rubricated, into the hands of Boccaccio's absent lover. Tellingly, the poem's ninth and final section addresses itself not to this "donna gentil della mia mente" (9.5.2: noble lady of my mind), but rather to the book itself: the author speaks, explains the work's last rubric, to his work (l'autore parla all'opera sua). The actual transmission or sending out of his text proved successful beyond anything that Boccaccio could have imagined: Branca's edition lists eighty-five manuscripts, with thirty-four in Florence, six at the Vatican, three each in Rome, Paris, and Berlin, two each in Madrid, Modena, Milan, Naples, and Oxford, plus single copies in a host of locales including Dublin, Edinburgh, and London. We can place at least one manuscript in fourteenth-century London, knowing that customs officer and royal appointee Geoffrey Chaucer mined it with great diligence for his own *Troilus and Criseyde*. Scottish schoolmaster Robert Henryson (d. ca. 1490) endows the female protagonist of his *Testament of Cresseid* with leprosy. William Shakespeare, following the template of William Thynne's 1532 *Chaucer*,[25] reads Chaucer and Henryson's stanzas as a continuous sequence; his own *Troilus and Cressida* is hence infused with corruption and disease. This brings us very far from our sunny and youthful point of origin but fulfills Boccaccio's penultimate hope for the work beyond the dreams of avarice: "Or va', ch'io priego Apollo che ti presti / tanto di grazia ch'ascoltata sii" (9.8.6–7: Now go, and I pray Apollo that he may give you / grace enough that you might be listened to).

CHAPTER SEVEN

A LOVERS' TALE AND AUSPICIOUS BEGINNING • *(Filocolo)*

Elissa Weaver

Certo grande ingiuria riceve la memoria degli amorosi giovani pensando alla grande costanza de' loro animi, i quali in uno volere per l'amorosa forza sempre furono fermi servandosi debita fede, a non essere con debita ricordanza la loro fama essaltata da' versi d'alcun poeta, ma lasciata solamente ne' fabulosi parlari degli ignoranti.

Boccaccio, *Filocolo* 1.1.25

The *Filocolo*, a long prose romance, which Boccaccio wrote while he was studying canon law at the Studio (university) in Naples, was the author's first important work.[1] It retells the old French tale of Floire and Blancheflor, Florio and Biancifiore in Italian, but it is much more than this story of love and adventure. The *Filocolo* provides a summa of the learning and interests of the young Florentine merchant immersed in the court and university culture of Angevin Naples. In this youthful work Boccaccio demonstrates a vast knowledge of literature, classical and medieval, and a personal engagement with it, giving a strong indication of literary promise and of the masterpieces to come.

The old French story that Boccaccio retells and greatly embellishes is that of the love of Florio, the son of the king and queen of Spain, and Biancifiore, the orphaned daughter of noble Romans, who are raised together and fall in love. His parents object to the match and separate the couple, sending him away and attempting unsuccessfully to get rid of her by false accusations, the promise of another marriage, and finally by selling her to merchants who take her to Alexandria. After peregrinations throughout the Mediterranean, dangers met and overcome, they are reunited and married. Stopping in Rome on their return, they are baptized and eventually convert all of Spain to Catholicism. Boccaccio enlarges and ornaments the story with detailed descriptions of Florio's travels throughout Italy and the Mediterranean, adding digressions, geographical, historical, and mythological, at each stop and each new encounter; he weaves into the story autobiographical allegories, exotic places, and even a lesson in church history and doctrine. Entertaining additions to the tale, they resist the author's attempts to impose a structural unity on the whole.

The *Filocolo* is divided into five books: the first and last provide a historical and religious context for the love story, which is told in books 2, 3, and 4.[2] As book 1 opens, Juno sets the action in motion with an obvious allusion to the opening episode of the *Aeneid*, suggesting that the tale will be epic in nature, but as Juno here represents the church, that it will be a Christian epic in which Roman Catholicism will triumph. The Angevin victory over Manfred and the Hohenstaufen dynasty is shown to be a contemporary manifestation of the earlier victory to be narrated through the story of Florio and Biancifiore, and it sets the scene for the introduction of the Author.

Having established the historical moment and place of writing of the romance, Naples at the time of King Robert of Anjou, Boccaccio introduces a framing device (1.1–2), to which he will return at the end of book 5, in which the Author reveals the occasion for his writing. He has fallen in love with the king's natural daughter, Maria,[3] who charges him with retelling the beautiful story of the love, faith, and perseverance of Florio and Biancifiore, since it is known, unfortunately, only in versions unworthy of belief and recounted by the unlettered ("fabulosi parlari degli ignoranti").[4] She asks him to tell it in an ennobling style ("versi d'alcun poeta").

Before beginning the story, Boccaccio first addresses his readers, young men and women in love, asking them to learn from the tale: men should be consoled knowing that others have suffered as they do; women will learn from Biancifiore that it is important to love and be faithful to only one man. Following this address, which anticipates elements of the *Decameron* Proem,[5] Boccaccio begins his narration in the manner of the chroniclers, with the story of creation, the fallen angels, redemption, and then the saints, in particular San Iacopo (Saint James) of Compostela. A brief account of the shrine and miracles of San Jacopo provides the necessary background for the vow and pilgrimage of Biancifiore's parents, the subject of book 1, while the story of the fallen angels explains the interventions of the devil (Pluto) in these events.

It is clear from this elaborate opening that the Author's love story will be in some ways reflected in the story of Florio and Biancifiore; indeed his beloved appears again at the heart of the tale, where we are told that the king's daughter, named Maria but called Fiammetta by her friends, is the beloved of Caleon, who is said to be a particularly eloquent young man.

The connection is not made explicit, but the similarity to the Author's love story is indisputable, and this episode is an important stop on Florio's journey. Boccaccio also underscores the relationship between the Author's love story and Florio's and strongly suggests its significance by chosing to call his romance, his labor of love, not *Florio and Biancifiore* but *Filocolo*, the name the protagonist takes for himself as he embarks on his quest to find Biancifiore, and which, according to Boccaccio, means "labor of love."[6]

Boccaccio probably knew and used various accounts of the story of Floire and Blancheflor, both written and oral versions. It is a Byzantine tale of romance, and Boccaccio acknowledges its oriental origin by attributing it to Ilario, a writer and priest belonging to a Greek family, whom the young couple meet in Rome.[7] The accounts that circulated in the West belong to three different textual traditions, two characterized by two old French romances of *Floire et Blancheflor*, the so-called aristocratic and popular versions, and a third tradition whose archetype is unknown but of which an early Spanish chronicle survives, the *Crónica de Flores y Blancaflor*.[8] While the *Filocolo* contains elements that appear in all three traditions, it features characteristics of the third tradition that distinguish this strain from the other two—primarily, its emphasis on the religious conversion theme. The anonymous Italian *Cantare di Fiorio e Biancifiore* also belongs to the third tradition; it was long thought to be Boccaccio's source, but it is impossible to date with accuracy and is probably dependent instead on the *Filocolo*.[9]

Classical and medieval sources of the many other subjects treated in the *Filocolo*, especially those used, often in literal translation, in Boccaccio's depiction of events, along with his use of myth, have been studied, especially by Antonio Enzo Quaglio, who cites them prodigiously in the notes to his critical edition of the work.[10] Primary among them is Dante, together with the classical authors Virgil, Ovid, Lucan, and Statius, all acknowledged in the envoy the Author addresses to his "little book" ("O picciolo mio libretto . . .") in a pose of humility that, however, as it echoes Dante's inclusion of himself in the group of ancient poets in Limbo (*Inferno* 4.67–102), serves to show that he too belongs to that august company.[11] Boccaccio also borrows heavily from Valerius Maximus, the Bible, Jacobus de Voragine's *Legenda aurea* (*Golden Legend*) and other hagiographical works, and those of some of the young Florentine's mentors in Naples, for example, Paolino Minorita, Andalò del Negro, and Cino da Pistoia, who taught civil law at the Studio in the years Boccaccio attended.[12]

Boccaccio was also inspired by French and Provençal courtly literature, readily available to him in King Robert's library, and this influence appears clearly in two of the most famous episodes of the *Filocolo*, that of the "vows on the peacock" in book 2, and the "thirteen questions of love" in book 4. The first is a chivalric ritual performed at the king's feast, in which each courtier in attendance offers to make a grand gesture or perform a great feat to honor the beautiful Biancifiore, who serves the peacock to her adoptive father, King Felice of Spain (2.33).[13] Boccaccio could have known of the chivalric ritual from any of several French poems, but its inclusion in this romance seems to have been an innovation, since it does not appear in any of the other known versions of the tale.[14] The thirteen questions of love are also taken from French and Provençal traditions, vernacular and Latin, in which issues regarding love and its proper conduct in society are debated. An interlude in Florio's quest to find Biancifiore (4.17–71), it is one of the best-known episodes of the romance and was published independently in English, French, and Spanish as early as the sixteenth century. Florio (now called Filocolo)[15] is invited to join a group of young Neapolitans, led by the beautiful daughter of the king, Maria, called Fiammetta. They are gathered around a small fountain in a shady garden to escape the heat of the day and engage in a genteel pastime in which each of the thirteen companions poses a question concerning love.[16] Fiammetta, chosen to lead them in this activity, pronounces judgment in each case after debate. The episode is an early idea of what would become the structure of the *Decameron*.[17]

One of the features of the *Filocolo* that has most troubled critics is Boccaccio's use of pagan deities. Gods and goddesses intervene in the action to resolve or sometimes to create difficulties, and classical myths and Christian religious history are intermixed, the two languages often seen as interchangeable. These interventions of the divine, unnecessary for the progress of the plot, are not always incorporated seamlessly into the action. The strange vision in book 4 (74.1–21), which follows the episode of the thirteen questions of love, is a case in point. Its meaning is clear, but it is an odd admixture of medieval imagery of the cardinal and theological virtues, with scenes reminiscent of Dante's *Vita nuova* and terrestrial paradise, and of the Petrarchan ship in dangerous seas, with a frightening figure of Fortune at the helm.[18] The vision, a brief drama in which Florio (Filocolo) must choose the theological over the cardinal virtues in order to save himself and Biancifiore from disaster and fly with her to heaven, works in conjunction with the episode of the thirteen questions of love. It adds detail but otherwise simply reinforces what Florio has learned in Naples from Fiammetta, and that is, that his love for Biancifiore must be "honest," a love that leads to salvation.[19]

Not all the questions debated by the group of young Neapolitans in Fiammetta's circle apply directly to Florio's situation, but some do, and especially the seventh question (4.44), posed by Caleon, who asks whether one should fall in love. Fiammetta, in response, explains that there are three kinds of love: *amore onesto*, honest love, which she likens to the love God has for his creatures; *amore per diletto*, love for pleasure, erotic love; and *amore per utilità*, useful love, love entered into for personal advantage.[20] Useful love is to be abhorred, and erotic love must be overcome, since it deprives one of liberty and leads to vice. Of the three, only honest love is good, and it is this love that leads to heaven. The dream that follows the encounter with Fiammetta confirms this point, teaching Florio that he must embrace not only the cardinal virtues, as he has, but also the theological virtues in order to unite in honest love with Biancifiore.

The love of Florio and Biancifiore as told in the *Filocolo* is a tender, moving story. Boccaccio dwells at great length and with striking psychological realism on the lovers' emotions: their infatuation with one another, their grief at parting and longing to be reunited, recollections of happy moments spent together, and their fear of losing their beloved to another or to death.[21] These feelings are depicted through long laments, often excessive, sometimes repetitious, but always a convincing portrayal of emotion. Boccaccio stresses the importance of the lovers' imagination and dreams, with which they hold their beloved near even in separation. His depiction is also heavily indebted to literary models, especially to Ovid, and his account of the couple's experiences inevitably includes comparisons with other literary and mythical lovers, evidence of the young author's erudition and, in their excess, of his immaturity. Both Florio and Biancifiore have dreams and visions of beasts and heavenly messengers, portents of what is to come, which seem highly contrived alongside the moving portrayal of their emotions.

The romance includes several secondary love stories, which are all examples of unrequited love. They are recounted but not given the psychological analyses that Boccaccio reserves for his protagonists. In book 3, the courtier Fileno falls in love with Biancifiore, and his cause is promoted by the queen, but Biancifiore is steadfast in her love for Florio. Caleon, in book 4, and Idalogo, in book 5, two characters whom Boccaccio invests with autobiographical allegory, are also unhappy lovers. Caleon is rejected by Fiammetta, the beautiful daughter of the king, and leaves Naples; encouraged by Florio, he founds and eventually governs Certaldo, the city of Boccaccio's birth. Idalogo gives up the study of science in Naples to pursue the love of a woman, and the details of his short biography allude to Boccaccio's experiences during his student years in Naples. Theirs is a passionate love; and so it seems is the Author's for his beloved Maria, for whom he writes and from whom he hopes in reward only that she will gladly receive his little book, hold it in her hands, and perhaps kiss it. It seems that he expects to be rejected like Caleon and Idalogo, and it is not clear how we should understand these unhappy loves in the context of the story of Florio and Biancifiore; what is clear is that Boccaccio represents himself, too, in the romance as a passionate but unhappy lover. In the light of Fiammetta's hierarchy of love, these are examples of the kind of passionate love she denounces, a love that deprives the lover of liberty (4.44). It is perhaps in illustration of that notion that Fileno and Idalogo undergo Ovidian metamorphoses: Fileno becomes a fountain, Idalogo a tree.

Fiammetta's teaching on love—if it is, as it seems, a key to the religious message of the tale—asks us to reimagine the love of Florio and Biancifiore, till now depicted as erotic desire, as a love aroused by the virtue of the beloved. We must read the beauty of their bodies, which sparks their love initially and fuels it throughout books 2, 3, and 4, as a reflection of their virtue. Yet the description of Filocolo's yearning for Biancifiore and his lovemaking with her while she is asleep emphasize the erotic. The guards who arrest them and tie them up derive pleasure from touching Biancifiore's body (4.127.1–2), and a crowd comes to see them bound naked and hanging from the tower (4.127.7). Boccaccio insists on the spiritual allegory, but the story he tells resists this reading. In book 5 he is more convincing: there all mention of sensual pleasure disappears, and the now-married couple, traveling with their child, Lelio, are baptized, return to Spain, and convert the king and queen and all their subjects to Christianity, dramatizing the effects of their honest love, as preached by Fiammetta and symbolized in Florio's vision.

The moral and allegorical readings of the text are clear in book 1, which begins with the promise of a pilgrimage to the shrine of San Iacopo of Compostela, and in book 5, in which the pilgrimage is completed, and the pagan land of Spain is converted to Catholicism by the lovers. With this framing of events, the author shows that the two young lovers are agents in a larger story of providential history, their love and adventures a moment in the history of redemption. Boccaccio in the *Filocolo* is still much indebted to Dante and the stilnovists for his notion of a love that leads to salvation. Yet the eroticism of certain episodes and the depiction of the suffering of lovers when separated or unrequited point to the passionate love that will characterize Boccaccio's later works and that seems a truer reflection of his sensibilities, which he cannot or will not entirely suppress. Indeed, when he tells his readers what they are to learn from his book (men, that they are not alone in suffering from love, and women, that they should love and be faithful to one man), the Author seems to forget for a moment the spiritual message of his romance and appears instead more like his counterpart in the *Decameron*.[22] His devotion to Dante and the *stil novo* struggles against his allegiance to Ovid.[23]

There is a school of Boccaccio criticism today that sees, though not everyone in the same way, an overall coherence in the text provided by its moral allegory.[24] Yet for the most part, critics have found fault with the *Filocolo*, calling it a "rambling romance" and a *centone*, a mixture of erudition and fantasy, accusing it of juxtaposing but not fusing elements of very different inspiration.[25] These were the characteristics of Byzantine romances, from which the tale of Florio and Biancifore derives. Boccaccio embraced that variety and infused it with classical and vernacular erudition. He brought to bear his finely honed rhetorical skills, elegant Ciceronian syntax, and a large dose of his own personality. It is to his enormous credit that the young audacious writer, then and always an innovator, introduced the genre in Italy. The *Filocolo* is the first great achievement in prose of the Italian literary tradition, and on this critics seem to be in general accord.

CHAPTER EIGHT

THE GIRL OUTSIDE THE WINDOW • *(Teseida delle nozze d'Emilia)*

Michael Sherberg

An ambitious work that bridges the late Neapolitan and early Florentine phases of his literary career, Boccaccio's *Teseida* reflects its author's immersion in medieval literary traditions as well as his growing interest in classical culture. Inspired in large part by Statius's *Thebaid* but marked as well by the influence of the *Aeneid*,[1] the poem narrates two adventures featuring Theseus—the conquest of the Amazons and the defeat of Creon—while then taking up its most richly developed story, the rivalry between Arcita and Palemone over the Amazon princess Emilia, and the eventual resolution of that conflict in Arcita's death and Emilia's marriage to Palemone. Structurally the poem mimics the Virgilian and Statian epic models, presenting its story in twelve books, here in *ottava rima*, while also borrowing features from medieval narrative. These include the dedicatory letter to Fiammetta; the framing sonnets—one for the whole poem, one for each book, and two at the end in which the author delivers the poem to the Muses, who then report back on Fiammetta's response to it;[2] rubrics that divide the books into chapters; and numerous glosses of varying length.

While Boccaccio worked on the poem over a number of years, the question of the *terminus post quem* remains unanswered. Alberto Limentani dates the poem to around 1339–41, though he adds a question mark, suggesting his own doubts about this estimation.[3] Lucia Battaglia Ricci is equally speculative, limiting herself to saying that the poem was composed *forse* (perhaps) in part in Naples and in part in Florence, though certainly glossed in Florence.[4] William Coleman, in his registry of the three redactions of the poem, assigns the first to the early 1340s, and with standard biographies dating Boccaccio's return north to the winter of 1340–41, its author could very well have written the poem entirely in Florence. Coleman assigns the last redaction (including the autograph manuscript) to the late 1340s–early 1350s, by which time Boccaccio would already have been working on the

Decameron.[5] Wherever and whenever Boccaccio set pen to paper, the testimony of the three redactions assigns the poem a conspicuous place in the years leading up to the *Decameron*, and the poem itself reflects the Neapolitan culture of Bocacccio's early literary preparation.[6]

Conspicuous, too, is the shadow of Dante. In the poem's *explicit* Boccaccio remarks on its unique status: "ma tu, o libro, primo a lor [the Muses] cantare / di Marte fai gli affanni sostenuti, / nel volgar lazio più mai non veduti" (but you, o book, first make them sing / the struggles endured for Mars, / never before seen in the vernacular of Latium; 12.84.6–8).[7] This claim recalls Dante's observation in the *De vulgari eloquentia*: "As for arms, I find that no Italian (*nullum latium*) has yet treated them in poetry."[8] Boccaccio restates Dante's observation, glossing the verses "E perciò che tu primo col tuo legno / seghi queste onde, non solcate mai / davanti a te da nessuno altro ingegno" (And because you first with your boat / slice these waves, never before plied / by any other genius; 12.85.1–3) with "That is, that never before this has any history of wars been put into rhyme."[9] The geographic range that Boccaccio assigns to Lazio ("Latium is understood here broadly as all of Italy")[10] suggests as well the swell of his ambition, a desire not simply to live in Dante's literary universe but to create one of his own. While examples of Latin epic sat on his desk, Boccaccio did not write in Latin, as did Guido delle Colonne for his account of the Trojan War or as Petrarch would his *Africa*. Dante had proven the expressive power and beauty of the vernacular, and Boccaccio, who in the dedicatory letter claimed to write "in vulgar Latin and in rhyme, so that it might please more,"[11] appears determined to extend its reach. By following the vernacular path paved by Dante, Boccaccio sought to guarantee that the Tuscan tradition would endure and that the new linguistic road paved by the *Commedia* would not reach a literary dead end. The new age continued.

The late characterization of the *Teseida* as a poem of war contrasts, however, with another claim, offered in a gloss to 1.6, that "the author's principal intention in this little book is to write of love,"[12] or similarly, in the dedicatory letter to Fiammetta, that it is "so beautiful for the subject it speaks of, which is love."[13] That these two themes should coexist reflects the influence of the two cultural lines, classical and courtly, Latin and vernacular, into which Boccaccio is simultaneously tapping. The vernacular tradition brings with it the extensively developed courtly and amorous line, which exerts pressure on the story of warfare. In like manner, Boccaccio's appreciation of such Latin models as the *Aeneid* and the *Thebaid*, and more generally of classical culture, impinges on his courtly vernacular side.[14] Dante remains the link to both. If the *Teseida* ends with its claim of filling the empty niche of vernacular war poem, in the dedicatory letter to Fiammetta Boccaccio makes clear allusion to Francesca da Rimini's amorous reverie in *Inferno* 5: "Since past happiness, returning to my mind, in the misery in which I see myself now, is a clear reason for grave pain."[15]

Boccaccio's fusion of the themes of love and war sets a model for Italian narrative poetry that will endure for centuries, from Pulci and Boiardo to Ariosto and Tasso. While today we use the shorthand of "epic" to describe this genre, it may be somewhat risky to apply such a label to the *Teseida*.[16] It is not clear that Boccaccio would have defined epic in this way, or even that he had a stable generic understanding of epic. In his introduction to the poem Limentani lists several characteristics that associate it with the Virgilian and Statian models, including the division into twelve books, the obligatory scenes of warfare and individual battle, allegorical figurations of the realms of Mars and Venus and other mythological elements, the parade of heroes, Arcita's funeral games, the use of speeches, similes, and astronomical references. As he himself admits, however, the heavy infusion of medieval accents and of a sort of Ovidian sentimentalism suggests that the poet is less interested in slavishly copying his antique models than he is in harmonizing them with the poetic concerns of his own times.[17] At the same time, as the plot makes clear, the accommodation of vernacular courtly themes does not undermine the poem's engagement with antique models. Rather, the poem stages the conflict between its so-called epic and romance impulses, with the former undertaking to impose its order on the latter.[18]

While the poem begins with a clear nod to Latin epic antecedents in the episodes involving the defeat of the Amazon women and of Thebes, it hastily cedes its epic ground to a romance plot involving Emilia, younger sister of the defeated Amazon queen Ipolita who has become Teseo's wife, and Arcita and Palemone, two Theban prisoners whom the king has brought back with him to Athens. From the beginning Teseo appears to be more a guarantor of justice than an epic hero; his two great undertakings, the conquest of the Amazons and the defeat of Thebes, have their origins in a problem that requires correction.[19] As the love triangle plot unfolds, the narrative focus shifts away from him, and he assumes the role of arbiter. The final, definitive battle between Arcita and Palemone, engineered by Teseo, does not rise to epic modalities; rather, it concludes ironically, with the victor Arcita dying as Venus avenges Palemone's defeat, and Palemone winning the girl after all.[20] In organizing the showdown Teseo had pointedly minimized its import, as if consciously denying it epic purpose:

qui non è tra costor mortale sdegno,
qui non si cerca di commesso oltraggio
vendetta, ma amore è la cagione,
com'ho già detto, di cotal quistione. (7.7.5–8)

Here there is no mortal disdain between them, / here one is not
seeking a vendetta for an outrage committed, / but love is the reason, / as I have said, for such a question.

Nevertheless, the application of an "epic" solution, the public tournament,
to a "romance" problem suggests what the poem is attempting to accomplish: the reconciliation, through the submission of amorous material to epic
pressures, of two disparate and in many ways opposing narrative impulses.
The key element in understanding that process remains the figure of Emilia,
who unwittingly unleashes conflicts beyond her control and must ultimately
submit to the authority, albeit imperfect, of Teseo as guarantor of order.[21]
    The question of genre cannot remain limited in any event to the poem
in octaves, for the *Teseida* is more than that. The autograph manuscript of
the work contains all its many paratexts, including the glosses.[22] Giuseppe
Vandelli first described these glosses in detail, and Limentani included them
in his edition. They may themselves be of Statian inspiration, for as Vandelli
points out, medieval manuscripts of the *Thebaid*, including Boccaccio's own,
regularly contained glosses attributed to Lactantius Placidus.[23] As Vandelli's published plates show, the *Teseida*'s glosses vary between interlinear
and marginal, depending on their length. In general they reflect the author's anticipation of the cultural information contemporary readers would
require for a fuller understanding of the poem. For example, while he does
not gloss the courtly material, he does regularly offer lengthy explanations
of his many mythological references, suggesting that he expected the latter
to be new information for the poem's earliest audiences.[24] If, as some have
argued, Boccaccio borrows the *ottava* form from an already-established
Tuscan tradition of the *cantastorie*, the glosses and the other paratexts suggest that he sought to distinguish himself from popular tradition through his
display of editorial control and scholarly erudition, and to establish himself
as being part of a literary culture that stood apart from oral transmission.[25]
    Boccaccio plays with the dual notion of poem and book in the verse
proem. To the emphasis on the poet as singer that marks both *Aeneid* 1.1,
"Arma virumque cano" (Arms I sing and the man), and *Thebaid* 1.4, "gentisne
canam primordia dirae" (Shall I sing the origins of the dreadful race?),[26] he
responds by positioning himself as reader, writer, and speaker:

E' m'è venuto in voglia con pietosa
rima di scrivere una istoria antica,
tanto negli anni riposta e nascosa
che latino autor non par ne dica,
per quel ch'io senta, in libro alcuna cosa;
dunque sì fate che la mia fatica
sia graziosa a chi ne fia lettore
o in altra maniera ascoltatore. (1.2.1–8)

The desire has come to me in pious / verse to write an ancient history, / put away and hidden for so many years / that it appears that no Latin author, / as far as I know, says anything about it in a book; / therefore make it so that my efforts / are gracious to whoever might be a reader, / or in any other way a listener of it.

Continuing on in the same vein, in the next octave he begs Venus, Mars, and Cupid: "sostenete e la mano e la voce / di me che 'ntendo i vostri effetti dire" (Hold up my hand and voice, / for I intend to tell of your effects; 1.3.6–7). Mixing the singer's pose with that of the author, he anticipates that his poem will be both read and heard. The differences here are a measure, I believe, not simply of the poet's identity at play, but also of a notion of the work as something materially more complex than its story alone.

It is in this spirit perhaps that Boccaccio executes one of his earliest Statian gestures, which in turn opens a window onto his own poetics. Assuming a pose less certain than that of his predecessor Virgil, Statius opens the *Thebaid* by exclaiming that he does not know where to begin:

Fraternas acies alternaque regna profanis
decertata odiis sontesque evolvere Thebas,
Pierius menti calor incidit. unde iubetis
ire, deae? (1.1–4)

Brothers crossing swords; held by turns, their kingdom vied / for in fiendish hatred; the guilt of Thebes—these my mind, struck / by Pierian fire, burns to unfold: / where do You bid me begin, Goddesses?[27]

The problem, he continues, is that the conflicts at Thebes have a long history, too much for a single poem, so he resolves to limit himself to "Oedipodae confusa domus" (the confused house of Oedipus), leaving any prehistory aside. Early in book 2 Boccaccio's own narrator confronts a similar problem, when he pens a section entitled "Transgression of his own material, to show why Theseus went against Creon."[28] The digression itself lasts only eight octaves, but it comes with an extended gloss that begins as follows:

> After the author has shown above, in the first book, whence and how Emilia came to Athens, in this second [book] he intends to show how Arcita and Palemone arrived there. In order to do this, it is necessary for him to touch on the war that took place between Eteocles and Polynices, and what came of that; but because it goes by very quickly in the text, in order that the following eight stanzas and many things that follow are understood more clearly, I will recount it here as briefly as I can, so that the reason also for the war that follows between Theseus and Creon will be more clear.[29]

So the glossator, "I," lends a hand to the "author," represented as a distinctly other person, the former explicating the verse narrative and specifically detailing the story of the conflict between Eteocles and Polynices. The eight octaves constitute a transgression because they do not pertain directly to the story at hand, which involves Emilia and eventually Arcita and Palemone. Statius's problem—just how far back does one go?—returns here, with Boccaccio suggesting a solution that is rather less arbitrary than Statius's own: the use of annotation.

The distribution of the material depends on degrees of separation. Narratives with one degree of separation from the primary narrative—in this case, the prehistory of Thebes—receive summary treatment in the poem only to the extent required for understanding the primary narrative. The accompanying gloss serves to satisfy those readers whose curiosity transcends the narrative borders of the poem itself. This approach appears to assume that a reader, as opposed to a listener, to whom the poem is read aloud, will approach the work with a greater degree of sophistication and intellectual curiosity. It also puts that reader at an advantage, because material contact with the book gives access to the supplementary material, which can easily remain invisible to a listener, whose access the reader controls.

While the glosses often furnish information with a neutral impact on a reading of the poem, this is not always the case, particularly with regard to the two longest glosses, concerning the houses of Mars (7.30) and Venus (7.50). Each constitutes a brief and carefully constructed essay, the former on the irascible appetite, the latter on the concupiscible. While the reader may understand the allegorical import of the narration simply from the text itself, the glosses offer the benefit of transparency to a discourse that is somewhat more opaque in the octaves. As Robert Hollander points out in his reading of the glosses,[30] Boccaccio's explication of the house of Venus as a locus of desire growing from a reasoned judgment or lack thereof lends much to an understanding of Palemone, who offers his prayer to Venus. Indeed, it is Palemone who pushes the amorous rivalry between himself and his cousin to the breaking point, insisting that they do battle despite Arcita's stated reluctance, and it is Palemone who qualifies that duel as one to determine "chi più diletto / avrà d'amare Emilia" (who will have greater delight in loving Emilia; 5.64.6–7). Boccaccio's insistent classicism, in both the poem and the glosses, thus exposes some of the *Teseida*'s darker implications, both for the history of Thebes, which repeats itself here, and more generally for the way in which the concupiscible appetite threatens social structures. In pushing his rivalry with Arcita to the point of battle, Palemone privileges his desire for Emilia over his friendship with his cousin, the latter representing the last best hope for a reversal of the terrible history of Thebes and the foundation of a new order grounded in homosocial amity.

The glosses constitute but one of a number of paratexts to the poem. One of the more significant is the dedicatory letter to Fiammetta, which recounts the poet's history with his beloved and relates the poem to that history.[31] It turns out that the allusion to Francesca's infernal discourse with which Boccaccio opened the letter was anything but casual. Not only does he develop the theme of the contrast between present misery and past happiness, he does so in a way that recalls Francesca as a reader. He tells Fiammetta that he conceived the idea of offering her a book as a means of rekindling her love for him: "remembering that, in past days that were more happy than long, I heard you wanted to hear and sometimes to read one story or another, and most of all the amorous ones, you being a woman who burned in the fire in which I am burning—and you did this perhaps so that the tedious times with their leisure might not be a reason for thought more damaging."[32] Unlike Francesca, Fiammetta had taken to reading as a means of avoiding carnal danger. That activity offered both vicarious pleasure and a diversion from cupidinous thoughts, ironically the opposite of what the "author" seeks. He goes on, alluding to elements of Dante's poem evocative of their own story, but without elaborating. Finally, he distinguishes her from a broader class of female readers who "because they are not very intelligent usually avoid" writing like his, which he names "history, fable, or closed speech" (storia, favola, o chiuso parlare).[33] Fiammetta, on the other hand, is "by intellect and knowledge of the aforementioned things separated from the crowd of other women" (per intelletto e notizia delle cose predette . . . dalla turba dell'altre separate), so he feels free to write at a more sophisticated level. She thus emerges as an exemplary female reader, open to the full range of allegorical possibilities and susceptible to the poem's erotic force. She is also likely the implied reader of the glosses, because she will not just "hear" but "sometimes read," and because she is endowed with the "intelletto" and *sana mente* capable of appreciating them.

The *Teseida* thus emerges as an experiment designed to create an ideal reading experience for the discerning female reader. The letter concludes with a nod in that direction, as the poet offers a plot summary "so that the work, which seems a little long, is not regretted before it is read."[34] The summary makes Emilia the poem's organizing principle. Having already suggested that Fiammetta see herself in Emilia, the author appears to design his plot as a means both to appeal to and to demonstrate the risks inherent in Fiammetta's narcissism. If the poem operates as a paean to her and to the catalytic power of womanhood, it also shows that the erotic power of women must submit to good social purpose.

The notion of a narcissistic Fiammetta finds its textual coefficient in the narcissistic strain the poem assigns to the Amazon women. Emilia is the younger sister of Ipolita, queen of the Amazons, whom Teseo will marry after defeating her and her army in battle. Introduced immediately after the poem's proem, the Amazons are described as

> crude e dispietate,
> alle qua' forse parea cosa fiera
> esser da' maschi lor signoreggiate. (1.6.2–4)
>
> cruel and pitiless, / to whom perhaps it seemed a brutal thing / to be lorded over by their men.

As events unfold, however, one gets the sense that this resistance to male domination grows less from any objection to a history of patriarchal repression than from the women's own self-absorption. This becomes evident in an early exchange of letters between Ipolita and Teseo. Ipolita's letter is heavy with first-person singular pronouns and possessives: *io, mi, le mie mura*, etc. ("I," "me," "my city walls," and so forth); and she sees the war as her own: "ho ragion d'aver guerra con teco" (I am right to make war with you; 1.99.8). Teseo's letter, on the other hand, begins by speaking on behalf of "Teseo, duca d'Attene, e la sua gente" (Teseo, duke of Athens, and his people; 1.109.4), and it contains a significant number of first-person plurals: *noi, nostro, nostri*, etc. ("we," "ours," "our," and so forth). The repair of the disorder created by the Amazons' defeat of their men implies as well a comeuppance for Ipolita, who does not understand the place of women in the natural order.

This pattern continues with Emilia's entry into the poem. It is spring-time—the zodiac is in Taurus, Venus is powerful—and every dawn the young girl leaves her bedroom for an adjacent garden, where she likes to frolic and sing. It just so happens that on the other side of the garden Arcita and Palemone, captured after the defeat of Thebes, languish in prison. Alerted by the sound of Emilia's singing, Arcita goes to investigate:

> sanza niente dire a Palemone,
> e una finestretta disioso
> aprì per meglio udir quella canzone. (3.11.4–6)

> Without saying anything to Palemone, / he opened a little window desiring / better to hear that song.

Espying Emilia in the garden, he summons Palemone, who comes to watch. The natural scene framed by the window becomes an emblem of the work itself: the frame directs our focus to the girl. The two young men quickly declare themselves wounded by Love's arrows, and upon hearing Palemone's cry, "Omè," Emilia turns and realizes that she is being watched. While she hastens from the scene, the narrator notes her pleasure in being an object of desire:

> e parendole ciò saper per vero
> d'esser piaciuta, seco si diletta,
> e più se ne tien bella, e più s'adorna
> qualora poi a quel giardin ritorna. (3.19.5–8)

> And as it seems to her to know in sooth / that she has pleased [them,] she takes delight, / and holds herself more beautiful, and adorns herself the more / whenever later she returns to that garden.

Her adornments are the equivalent of rhetorical devices: both the girl, and by extension the poem, dress up in order to please their audience.

The performer-audience relationship evolves from there, with Emilia calibrating her behavior to entice her audience and performing for them.

> E se ella vedeva riguardarsi,
> quasi di ciò non si fosse avveduta,
> cantando cominciava a dilettarsi

in voce dilettevole e arguta;
e su per l'erbe con li passi scarsi
fra gli albuscelli, d'umiltà vestuta,
donnescamente giva e s'ingegnava
di più piacere a chi la riguardava. (3.29)

And if she saw herself being watched, / almost as if she had not noticed, / she began to take pleasure by singing / in a delightful and witty voice; / and upon the grasses with few steps / among the bushes, dressed in humility, / in a ladylike way she moved and undertook / to please more whoever watched her.

The description of Emilia evokes Dante's Beatrice, who in the *Vita nuova* is famously described as walking "benignamente d'umiltà vestuta" (benignly dressed in humility).[35] While in his sonnet Dante describes men as not daring to look at her: "e li occhi no l'ardiscon di guardare" (and their eyes do not dare to look at her), here the two men do in fact stare, and she walks not *benignamente* but *donnescamente*, fully aware of her carnal femininity and its rising power. The shift from her spontaneous behavior, before she knew she was being watched, to a more studied performance, suggests how the stuff of nature may be manipulated into an art that affirms and may even increase nature's beauty.

Emilia's willful submission to the male gaze, her play with desire, represents a turning point both for her and to some degree for the tradition. That she enjoys being watched, as opposed to a Beatrice whose beauty discourages the gaze and who remains indifferent to it, makes her into a particularly dangerous figure, capable of manipulating men for her own purposes and without any transcendental intent. The narrator insists that she behaves in this way not out of love but because of a vanity, "che innata han le femine nel core, / di fare altrui veder la lor biltate" (which women have innate in their heart, / to make others see their beauty; 3.30.3–4).

The poem elaborates on the dangerous consequences of her behavior when the friendship between Arcita and Palemone ruptures over her. After years of separation they meet again, both now free from the prison that disciplined their urges, and they fight over Emilia in a recriminative scene that repeats generations of Theban internecine conflict. Palemone asks Arcita to renounce his claim on Emilia in the name of their friendship, demanding that as an alternative they duel; Arcita counteroffers that they both court Emilia and accept her choice. The poem here reaches a crossroads, as the two proposals distill into a choice between an "epic" solution that reasserts a distinctly male order and a courtly one that validates female desire. Their first violent duel ends when Emilia chances upon it and summons Teseo, who determines that the matter will be settled in a public *battaglia* one year hence, with each warrior leading an army of a hundred men into the Athenian *teatro* (amphitheater), and the winner marrying Emilia.[36] Within the economy of the narrative, both the lovers' desire and she must be mastered and channeled for a socially productive outcome.

Teseo's judgment elevates the voyeurism of the garden gaze into full spectacle. Parallel to Emilia's own conversion from unself-conscious subject to self-conscious performer, the spontaneous private duel becomes an orchestrated entertainment before an audience.[37] Inasmuch as all three protagonists of the love triangle belong to groups defeated by Teseo and are therefore subject to his rule, the king's command restores an Athenian order to a situation that had been running on its own fuel. While synthesizing and solving the conflict over Emilia, Teseo's rule also resolves the conflict over the "epic" and courtly impulses that inform the poem. The Athenian king regains his status as the poem's ordering principal, if not its ordering principle.

The narrative of events involving the tournament and its aftermath consumes the second half of the poem and includes a number of elements typically associated with epic: the parade of dignitaries, votive offerings to Mars and Venus by Arcita and Palemone, a careful ordering of the tournament by Teseo that Boccaccio counterbalances with the narrative of the chaos of battle itself, and divine interventions at critical moments. Throughout this portion of the poem Boccaccio also regularly takes care to note Emilia's thoughts and feelings, beginning with her prayer to Diana prior to the tournament. Insisting that she is better suited to hunting than love, she asks the goddess to excuse her from marriage, but then attempts to negotiate the outcome of the battle should she be destined for marriage against her will. She inveighs against Amore for putting her in an untenable position that she never wanted, because the souls of the many who will die—wrongly, she insists—in this battle will forever pursue her and delight in her misfortune, as will their loved ones. Her prayers and reflections conclude with this extraordinary octave:

> Così m'hai fatto, Amore, e più non posso,
> e sanza amare inamorata sono:
> tu mi consumi, tu mi priemi adosso
> per colpa degna certo di perdono;
> tu m'hai il cor, dolorosa!, percosso

con disusato e non saputo trono:
e or pur foss'io certa che campasse
l'un d'esti due e sposa men portasse! (8.109)

Thus have you done to me, Love, and I cannot take it anymore, /
and without loving I am in love: / you consume me, you thrust
yourself upon me / for a fault surely worthy of pardon; / you have
my heart, and I am pained!, struck / with an unusual and unfamiliar bolt: / and now if only I could be sure that one of these two / will
survive and take me away as his wife!

The ideological gulf that separates the lyric Petrarch from Boccaccio distills
into this one octave. Boccaccio gives a voice to Emilia, enabling her to lament the paradox of her situation as well as her despair at being the object
of undesired desire. Petrarch never thought to give such a voice to Laura.

The final paratext of the *Teseida* comes as a tailed sonnet (*sonetto caudato*)
written by the Muses themselves to their "caro alunno" (dear student).[38] In
it they announce that they have brought the poem to that "più tua donna"
(lady most yours) and have witnessed her reading of it. They record her response: "fra sé soletta disse sospirando: / 'Ahi, quante d'amor forze in costor
foro!'" (She said to herself sighing, / "Ahi, how great were the forces of love
in them!"). They go on to report that she implored them "d'amor tututta
accensa" (all burning with love) that the poem reach a wider audience, and
that she had named it "Teseida di nozze d'Emilia." They assure the poet that
they have honored Fiammetta's request and put the poem into circulation.
The sonnet is striking for two reasons. First, adumbrating interests that
will mature in the *Decameron*, it identifies the role played by the Muses as
Boccaccio's go-between, with regard both to Fiammetta and to the wider
reading audience who will now receive the poem.[39] Second, it suggests that
Boccaccio had allowed Fiammetta to name the poem, or that he substituted
the name she gave to it for one of his own. Her somewhat awkward solution
accurately reflects the composite nature of the poem itself, its desire to be
an "epic" tale (the song of Theseus) about a courtly event (the wedding of
Emilia). As it records Boccaccio's efforts to accommodate his classicizing
concerns to medieval themes, it foretells the challenge his poetic successors
will face of reconciling disparate cultural impulses.

PART IV

ALLEGORICAL *TERZA RIMA*

CHAPTER NINE

THE GAME OF LOVE • *(Caccia di Diana)*

Arielle Saiber

B occaccio wrote the *Caccia di Diana* (*Diana's Hunt*), dubbed the most minor of his "minor works," in Naples when he was twenty or twenty-one, delighting in the high life of the Angevin court. This slender poem, only definitively attributed to him since 1938, consists of eighteen cantos in *terza rima*, 1,047 lines total.[1] Considered his earliest vernacular composition (1333 or 1334), and called his "first fiction," it is also the first known Italian imitation of the metrical form Dante invented, *terza rima*.[2] A scant family of six manuscripts transmits the poem, bound with two of his other works in *terza rima*, the *Amorosa visione* (*Amorous Vision*) and the *ternario* "Contento quasi ne' pensier d'amor" ("Content—almost—in thoughts of love").[3] He chose an allegorical mode with a theme that marks the beginning of his career-long juggling of "two Venuses" (erotic and virtuous love) and "two Dianas" (virginal and marital chastity).[4] A tour de force combining number games, lore from medieval bestiaries and hunting manuals, troubadoric, stilnovistic, courtly, and classical traditions, the *Caccia* displays a panoply of textual references and poetic forms revealing the author's erudition.[5] It marks Boccaccio's bid to establish himself as a writer and scholar in dialogue with the world around him. In doing so, he shows a desire to reckon with (and to reckon) the multiple pulls represented by both Venus and Diana. In this poem of accounting, he proves that he can "balance his books" with flare.

The poem begins in bucolic style, with an unidentified narrator recounting how he was languishing in a Campanian springtime in search of refuge from love sickness, when suddenly he heard the voice of a gentle spirit rallying a troop of young Neapolitan noblewomen, both married and maidens, to hunt by Diana's side.[6] He notes each woman's name in a tone of awed celebration. They are the real-life noblewomen of Robert the Wise's Neapolitan court. There are fifty-eight of them, plus an "unnamed woman," and

Diana—no doubt homage to Dante's lost *sirventese* in praise of sixty Florentine women.[7]

Diana groups the women into four contingents and indicates the direction in which to hunt, herself joining the eastward troop, while the "unnamed woman," *la bella donna* (1.46)[8]—who turns out to be not only the narrator's beloved (and the thirty-third of the huntresses called), but a pivotal figure for the action of the poem—is assigned to lead the southern charge.[9] The subsequent bulk of the poem (cantos 3–15) graphically depicts the animals the women slaughter. After the hunting games conclude, and the animal carcasses are piled onto a pyre, the *bella donna* surprises us by refusing to perform the ritual incineration of the dead wildlife in the name of Diana; and with but a few words, she convinces her companions to make the sacrifice to Venus instead.

Immediately, Diana flies off in a huff (*turbata*, 16.57). The women silently pray and place laurel crowns on their heads as they light the pyre. Venus descends on a little cloud, promising to give the women what they really wish for: "someone to love" (facci ancora / alcuno amando, gli animi contenti, 17.27). The goddess then whispers inaudibly to the bonfire, and the dead animals leap from the flames as unclothed young men who dash off into a nearby stream, emerge dressed in red robes, and pair off with the women. But the surprises do not end there: our narrator is now one of these men, having been, it turns out, a stag all along (and apparently out of the huntress's sight). Now changed from "brute beast to rational man" (uom ritornai / di brutta belva, 18.23–24), he is given to his *bella donna*.[10]

Two Venuses + Two Dianas

Fourteen of the poem's eighteen cantos focus on the wildly successful hunt organized and led by Diana. In the end, however, the hunt is not hers alone. Diana's ideal hunt would have been one in which the annihilated beasts (that is, the men) were offered to Jove in her name, thereby freeing the Neapolitan maidens from any risk to their virginity or celibacy. And although her weapons temporarily silence the beasts' passions, the fires of desire are not snuffed out; they begin sparking in the hearts of the women: "Our breasts are enkindled with another fire and our souls are aflame" (accese d'altro foco / abbiamo i petti e l'anime infiammate, 16.52–54).

We do not know the original title Boccaccio intended for his poem, but the ambiguity of the word *caccia* is important. It can be "a hunt" in which something is caught (the men), or it can be something that is "chased away" (Diana, or vice?). The huntresses wish both to "chase away" unvirtuous thoughts from their breasts (16.22) so that their hearts can be "generous and noble" (larghi e gentili, 17.24) *and* to "catch" their men.

Many scholars have characterized the Diana-Venus relationship as an antithesis, noting classical and medieval dialogic precedent in such genres as the *contrasto*, *altercatio*, *tenso*, and *certamina*.[11] The Diana-Venus binary, however, is not as black and white as it might initially seem. Diana departs immediately but without ado. Although irritated, she cooperates with Venus, as she will on behalf of Florio and Biancifiore in the *Filocolo* (written only a year or two after the *Caccia*).[12] In the *Caccia*, Diana prepares the huntresses for the virtuous love and marital chastity that civilizes both beauties and beasts.

Like most medieval retellers of classical myths, Boccaccio often depicted Diana as "vengeful," "savage," "cruel," "antisocial," and not necessarily beautiful, preferring the company of animals to that of humans.[13] She also has the power to turn men into beasts, as Ovid's Actaeon regretfully discovered after seeing her bathing.[14] In the *Caccia*, however, Venus turns beasts into men (the narrator-stag included), and women see men bathing. This flip might suggest that the *Caccia* is about Venus vanquishing Diana: love (carnal) trouncing virginity.

And yet, such an "either-or" binary in the *Caccia* and in Boccaccio's other works is not quite that simple. The beasts the Neapolitan women were hunting were men wounded by the maidens' charms and beauty, but they no doubt delighted in being hunted by the enthusiastic huntresses. Venus (or perhaps her son Cupid, who might be the "gentle spirit" calling the women to the hunt, 1.8) was present before the *Caccia*'s sport began. Diana did not turn the men into beasts, as she had done to Actaeon; nor did she turn them into rivers, as she regretfully would do to the nymph Mensola after Africo raped her in the *Ninfale fiesolano*. Lust had already turned them into beasts. These particular beasts are not *figurae Christi* who offer their flesh for redemption, as Boccaccio, following Fulgentius, later allegorized Actaeon; they are slain by the maidens' arrows in an amorous game.[15] Nor do these beast-men neatly parallel Guido degli Anastagi's woman, cruelly devoured by his hunting dogs in a vision that Nastagio degli Onesti uses to frighten his own lady into returning his love.[16]

The similarity between the Latin for "hunt," *venatio*, and the name for Venus, *Venere*, could not have been missed by Boccaccio.[17] Moreover, Venus undoes her previous doing, *re*-turning them into rational men (18.23–24), converting their past carnal, erotic love into the virtuous love of marriage. Diana has not completely lost out to Venus; rather, she abets the process of moving the women and men from erotic love to virtuous love. She will do something similar in the *Filocolo* and in the *Comedia delle ninfe*, when the lusty protagonist Ameto, tutored by nymphs formerly allied with Diana, is transformed by a "Trinitarian" Venus (*trina*, 41.1–2) into a virtuous, Christian man, purified by fire and water. Venus's threeness seems to be mirroring Diana-as-Trivia.[18]

Still, the double nature of each goddess is central here. As there are two Venuses in Boccaccio's writing, there also seem to be two Dianas, the second being the one who helps the lover learn to love chastely. Just as Venus was conceived as a goddess of both erotic and virtuous love, the virginal huntress was also a goddess worshipped by women who sought to become pregnant or wanted protection during pregnancy and childbirth.[19] Boccaccio notes Diana's attributes of fertility and midwifery in the *Geneaologia* and says that they are due to her having been born before her twin brother, Apollo, whom she helped deliver.[20] Diana is also known as Lucina—invoked at the birthing of Mensola's child in the *Ninfale fiesolano* (403)—while the "other Diana," the one that shines in the daytime, is angered by Mensola's loss of virginity. She reminds the huntresses in the *Caccia* that they were able to capture the beasts due to *her* tutelage (16.38). Diana and Venus, in fact, could be seen as team players with interwoven roles in the creation of family. Venus 1 starts the game by prompting erotic desire; Diana 1 enters, teaching the art of self-control and chastity; Venus 2 joins, encouraging virtuous love and marriage; and Diana 2 ends the game by making the family grow through fertility, childbirth, and rearing. The two (or should we say four?) goddesses work together, albeit in strikingly different ways. The *Caccia* is an early example of Boccaccio's attempt to puzzle out the nature of their collaboration. His later works will continue to struggle with the Venus-Diana volley, and show how difficult it is to have truly balanced, virtuous human relationships.

In writing the *Caccia*, Boccaccio certainly had relationships in mind, especially the one he was seeking to cultivate with the *bella donna*. Biographical interpretations of the *Caccia* have attempted to determine the identity of the woman whom the narrator wins in the end. In decades past, many have thought her to be Maria D'Aquino (an illegitimate daughter of King Robert) or associated her with the *bella lombarda* (Monna Vanna) of the *Amorosa visione* (40.64) and the *Rime* (poem 69) or with *la formosa ligura* (the curvaceous Ligurian) Acrimonia in the *Ameto* (29). Current scholarship, however, tends toward seeing her as either the composite of a number of desirable women in the Angevin court or an idealized precursor to Fiammetta who parallels Dante's Beatrice and Petrarch's Laura, even as a *senhal* coded with a number, as Anthony Cassell and Victoria Kirkham have shown.[21]

That Boccaccio did not dedicate the poem to anyone in particular (as far as we know), nor refer to it in his later works, could imply that it was a piece he wrote to delight that particular woman, or all the women (and men) of the Angevin court, leaving them the pleasure of solving the riddle of the *bella donna*, or at least keeping them guessing. Not all the women listed in the *Caccia* were maidens; some were already married. One wonders, in fact, if the animal-men who paired with married women were actually their husbands. And then there is the question of the two women who do not catch anything,[22] as well as the last of the women to join the hunting team, Zizzola d'Anna, who comes alone, after the groups have completed their hunt. Do they receive men? What we know of Zizzola is that she was much younger than the other women of the hunt, which could explain why she arrived later and failed to slay an animal. It is more difficult to account for the other two. Perhaps they were unappealing, or renowned for being vehemently chaste. Or are they to remind us of Naples herself, Parthenope, the virgin whose tomb was found on the shores of the city?[23]

Animal Nature

The *Caccia*'s slaughter fest contains a large array of animals, some of which could be found in a forest in the Campanian hills or nearby valleys, but also exotic species such as tigers and elephants, and a number of mythical creatures.[24] As the ways of reading the Venus-Diana relationship and the transformation of the men into beasts and back into men are multiple, so are the possible ways of interpreting the animals. On one level, the animals can be seen as emblems of sins (and sometimes virtues), as they were allegorically depicted in medieval bestiaries and in biblical and patristic writings.[25] On another level, they could be evoking qualities of specific men of the Angevin court known to have been "caught" by the very women who slay them in the poem. One could imagine the great delight Boccaccio's cohorts would have taken in seeing how he depicted each young man (a timid hedgehog, a powerful bear) and how each was slaughtered (easily by an arrow to the heart, with great difficulty and persistence). Boccaccio's discussion of Circe in *De mulieribus* 38 is illuminating: "We would thus be right in believing that the men [that Circe enchanted] changed into the kinds of wild beasts appropriate to their misdeeds. . . . If we consider human behavior, we see plainly enough from this instance that there are many Circes everywhere, and many more men whose lust and vice change them into beasts." But would Boccaccio, a Florentine merchant recently admitted into confidence with the Neapolitan nobility, really want to critique his friends so explicitly?

Being compared to a bear (evil connotations aside) would certainly have been flattering, but comparison to a hedgehog might not have felt quite as good. And being depicted as a good huntress or a weak one could likewise have felt exhilarating or depressing. Take, for example, Caterina Brancazza and her sister's pride after catching two tigers (6.1–11) or Beritola Carafa and Sobilia Capece's frustration in their repeated efforts to catch two bears (5.1–33) or the embarrassment of Covella d'Anna at having to receive help to capture an ostrich (15.37–52). The personalities of the Neapolitan court, and how each woman conquered her man, were likely common knowledge. Perhaps Boccaccio wrote this to amuse all, even at the risk of upsetting some. How widely the *Caccia* circulated in the court, however, is not known, and given the lack of discussion of the piece by Boccaccio or his contemporaries, perhaps it was written to delight only a few pairs of eyes. Whose eyes they were, we can only speculate.

The violence of love is a well-worn trope, and although medieval literature is filled with graphic depictions of love pains (not to mention battles, divine retribution, and martyrdoms), many of the kills in the *Caccia* are exceedingly vicious. An example is Caterina Caradente's tussle with a boar:

> Di squama pien, furioso costui
> venia, de' can d'ogni parte addentato
> ed infiammato di nuocere altrui;
>   e nello spiedo a lui innanzi parato
> ferì con rabbia sì che vi rimase
> da una parte in altra trapassato. (3.40–45)

> Bristle-covered, he came raging, bitten all over by the dogs and hotly bent on doing injury. And he so angrily struck the spear brandished before him that he ran himself through on it, shafted from end to end.

Another example is when the *bella donna* tears out the hot heart (*caldo cuore*) of a leopardess and feeds it to her eagle (4.32–33), a clear evocation of Beatrice's meal of Dante's heart (as offered to her by Love itself), and of the first of the three beasts in *Inferno* 1.[26] In yet another chilling moment, the huntresses encounter a snake in a pit, and a protracted, frenzied mission to destroy it ensues. Terrified, but rallying themselves for the kill, they smoke it out of its lair and lop off its head. Shortly after, six baby snakes emerge. The emboldened women defeat them, too—all seven of the deadly sins, with lust instead of pride, perhaps, as the parent-snake here. Classical and Christian allegory are unquestionably at play in some of these more riveting chase scenes.

The allegory of Christian rebirth, through a catechumen's preparation and then baptism in water (and fire, too), is also central to the poem. It underlies both the men-beasts' and the huntresses' conversion or transformation.[27] In preparation for the hunt, Diana has the women dip into a fountain and don olive leaves, flowers, and purple robes. During the hunt, they burn with desire to capture these beasts (conquer sins); after the hunt, they burn, virtuously (16.53–54), with hope for "someone to love" (17.27). The dead men-beasts figure as the inverse of the women. As beasts, they epitomize lust and recall the penitents on the seventh terrace of Dante's Purgatory, made to purify their passion through fire. They complete their transformation in water, emerging with red robes (symbolic of love/charity), but fresh as "lilies" (17.46), thus evoking the symbolic pure white of the newly baptized. The purple robes the huntresses wear at the beginning, linked to the "tepid fire in chaste breasts" ('l tiepido foco / ne' casti petti, 2.22–23), could indicate their connection to the four cardinal virtues (see *Purgatorio* 29), but also that they were not yet ready for the "laurel crowns" the *bella donna* will have them put on before calling on Venus (17.9). Both the beast-men *and* huntress-women need purification — they must love nobly to merit victory (*vittoria*, 17.18) and mercy (*pietate*, 17.51). Such is the hunt of Diana *and* of Venus.

Accountability

When Boccaccio wrote the *Caccia*, he had just left his banking job — the profession his banker father hoped his son would pursue — which he had held since arriving in the Angevin city in 1327. Boccaccio's training in the mathematics needed for commerce was in abacus logistics (basic arithmetical computations);[28] some Pythagorean, Euclidean, and Nicomachean *arithmetica* (number theory, via Boethius);[29] geometry, and perhaps a small amount of algebra.[30] Such study was something he neither chose nor liked very much.[31] He even claimed that his time as banker had been a waste of six years.[32] Yet his mathematical training appears to have contributed noteworthy elements to much of his literary production, as can be seen in his use of number play and symbolism, the combinatorics of his acrostics, and the inclination toward particular geometric patterns in his organization of settings, scenes, and themes. The computational and spatial devices that he employs throughout the *Caccia* reveal a young, mathematically savvy mind wanting to show that "he counts," that he is "accountable" as a poet and person of court, and that he knows how to make things "add up," literally and metaphorically, in this poem.

Kirkham has written extensively on the complex array of numerological devices throughout the *Caccia* and elsewhere in Boccaccio's works; it is to her studies that readers should turn for in-depth discussions of Boccaccio's numerological mechanics.[33] The most prominent number associations in the *Caccia* are those built around the number three (and its multiples), with the Trinity, Dante's *terza rima*, the *bella donna* as the thirty-third woman called to hunt, and the triune associates of Venus and Diana already noted. There is also the peculiarity of Canto 3, which is the only canto in the poem with sixty verses (again recalling Dante's *sirventese*) instead of fifty-eight;[34] and the halfway mark of Canto 9 (three squared, and a Dantean number par excellence), with the arrival of the second troupe of women, who, the narrator realizes after some observation from afar, were not "evil-minded" (*malvagia*, 18). "Diana's number," seven—linked to virginity, the moon, virtues, vices, and the liberal arts—not surprisingly, also receives a great deal of play in this poem.[35]

The *Caccia*'s final canto moves to the present tense and a stilnovistic celebration of the *bella donna*. The narrator even indirectly admits that he has more work to do in his purification and "salvation" (*salute*, the poem's final word, 18.58), as "pride, sloth, greed, and wrath" (18.34) flee from his mind when he looks at her; but not, it would seem, lust or gluttony. He prays to continue to merit honoring her. Then, in a retrospective paralipsis, he says he will not speak of her any longer here, but rather in "a place more praiseworthy" (in parte più di lode degna, 18.50), as Dante had done with Beatrice at the end of the *Vita nuova*. The *Caccia* could be read, in fact, as neither celebrating carnal love (as some see the final cantos doing, since the couples run off to enjoy each other's company) nor parodying its cult (as others have imagined it), but rather as acknowledging passions in both lovers and beloveds and the mutual will to transform and be transformed.

Furthermore, if we see the *Caccia* as homage to Dante's works, or as a "Comedia delle ninfe napoletane"[36] and hoped-for *vita nuova*, we have much to support such a claim. Boccaccio nods to Dante in his metrics, numerology, and theme, and in other ways, too: the poem begins with the narrator who finds himself in a wood; he observes a sort of hell of sins; the huntresses' dogs have Dantesque devil names (such as Graffiacani, 14.5–6); the beasts, and narrator himself (although merely gazing at his beloved from a privileged vantage point, in stilnovistic fashion), are purified by fire and then by water; and the narrator ends his day by refinding himself (mi ri-trovai, 18.8) with the other beasts as a rational man, given to his beloved *bella donna*, and allowed to enjoy virtuous joys in an Edenic field.

The *Caccia* is the first bloom in Boccaccio's intricate garland of musings on the nature of love, both erotic and virtuous. It showcases a young author with an affinity for tying classical learning and elements from the great authors of his time together with number devices, both religiously reverent and delightfully playful. It is, in a way, a word problem that shows the world who he is and what he hopes for: conversion, love, and, ultimately, the laurels with which he has crowned his huntresses.

CHAPTER TEN

MURAL MORALITY IN TABLEAUX
VIVANTS • *(Amorosa visione)*

Jonathan Usher

Written shortly after the *Comedia delle ninfe fiorentine*, the *Amorosa visione* was perhaps a corrective reaction to what Boccaccio, ever restlessly critical of his own output, must have realized was a lack of cohesion between doctrinal intent and narrative energy in his early writings. Now living in Florence, he found himself, not for the first time, at a writerly impasse. As always, the solution attempted was not perseverance with a problematic model but a wholesale change of genre, with a consequent veering toward a different "master" for inspiration. If the earlier works had been written under the classicizing signs of Ovid, Virgil, and even Apuleius, now it was the turn of a modern, vernacular *auctor*, Dante, to guide his pen. Though the choice seems obvious to us now, it was a bold move for somebody of Boccaccio's generation, as the cult of Dante had not yet begun in earnest, and Dante's quirky contrarian political stance still made for uncomfortable reading in Florence. Internal evidence (who among contemporary figures was still alive or dead) dates the *Amorosa visione* to the year 1342 or early 1343.[1]

Instead of attempting once again an arduous synthesis of the competing claims of story line and homily within a cohesive vehicle, Boccaccio would now attempt a work where the narrative element was minimal, the allegorical device as far as possible externalized, and the parade of symbolic values and exemplary elencation paramount. The narrator's job would be merely to transport the reader from instructive tableau to instructive tableau with a minimum of interpretative assistance. Once the reader was transported into the work, what would be on offer would be a serial ekphrasis, a kind of verbalized pictorial dictionary. The *Amorosa visione* has, therefore, in its attempt at sequenced information, a lot in common with the later Latin works, *De casibus virorum illustrium*, *De mulieribus claris*, and even the *Genealogia deorum gentilium*, in that the underlying driver is encyclopedic and categorizing, while any framing narration merely provides the barest presentational excuse for taxonomic organization. Taken alongside the very early *Caccia di Diana*, it suggests that Boccaccio's penchant for catalog and classification was a lifetime constant, rather than some late conversion, post-*Decameron*. Perhaps in compensation for this loss of narrative energy, the strictly formal elements of the *Amorosa visione*, metrical and acrostic structures, are heavily reinforced as a unifying device, for the work marks a return to continuous verse after the mixed *prosimetrum* form of the *Comedia delle ninfe*.

The poem consists of fifty cantos (a consciously humble demi-*Divine Comedy*) in Dantean *terza rima*, which narrate a vision in which a young man is encouraged to reform, morally and spiritually, after being shown, by a guide, a thematically organized exhibition of portraits of personages representing virtues and vices.[2] Beneath the imagery, the formula of the narrator's conversion by exemplum is exactly the same as in the *Comedia delle ninfe*, but with grandiose, static visual iconography replacing the lascivious and lively narrations of voluble nymphs. The new poem is an engine for producing nonstop listings and may well have been inspired by the sculpted terrace of the proud in Dante's *Purgatorio*.[3]

Apart from the Dante-inspired verse form and canto structure, the chief organizational feature of the *Amorosa visione* is a grotesquely ambitious, self-imposed *contrainte* (literary constraint), worthy of some of the more eccentric achievements of the twentieth-century French Oulipians such as Georges Perec. The obstacle-device, a massive preprogramming of the initials of all the tercets of the poem, is a kind of desperate bet that Boccaccio will be able to stick to his aim and subordinate all his various talents (and even more varied subject matter and value systems) to some overarching architecture.

The constraint is purely formal—so formal, indeed, that to satisfy it, Boccaccio will have to make enormous textual accommodations and paradoxically compromise the very unity that he thought the device might ensure. The device itself consists of three introductory *sonetti caudati* ("tailed" sonnets with an added final tercet) that provide an acrostic key to the whole poem and also provide a *sphragis*, or incorporation of the author's signature.[4] Each successive letter in the sonnet sequence provides the opening letter to the next tercet in the main text.[5] Needless to say, such artifice is not always conducive to lyrical inspiration, and frequently there are signs of opportunistic lexical manipulation and mechanical padding in the verse, but Boccaccio must have envisaged it as a healthy challenge.

The narrative outline, such as it is, goes something like this: the narrator is visited in his sleep by a lady sent by Cupid (the Love of the title) to convert him from vain delights to the highest form of happiness. The pair proceed to a noble castle where there is a choice of two gates, a narrow one leading directly to the good life, and a broad one leading to life's pitfalls. It is the classic Pythagorean life-choice topos of the two paths, traditionally known as Hercules at the crossroads, often represented by the letter *Y*.[6] The narrator picks the broad gate. Narratively, if not ethically, this is a wise choice. The narrow gate of virtue has nothing to offer, artistically, for the *Amorosa visione* would tamely and quickly grind to a halt in uninteresting beatitude. What is needed is a kind of *descensus ad inferos*, or exploration of the far more instructive lower reaches of humanity. Perversely drawing his guide with him through the portal of deviance, the narrator wanders through the halls of the castle, which are decorated with edifying frescoes worthy of Giotto.[7]

    In the world of Boccaccio's fiction, at least, such elaborate murals will resist time, for when in the *Decameron* the members of the *brigata* reach their first villa, they will find its interior still "di liete *dipinture* raguardevole e ornata" (elegant and decorated with merry *paintings*, 1, Intro., 90; italics mine). Some of the most amusing characters of the *Decameron*, Bruno, Ca-landrino, and Buffalmacco, are part of a team of painters engaged in such frescoes (8.3, 8.6, and 8.9; 9.3 and 9.5). Another story of the *Decameron*, that of Guiglielmo Borsiere's put-down of Ermino de' Grimaldi's meanness (1.8), actually relates how to choose a symbolic subject for a mural (in this case an atypical "generosity").[8] Boccaccio may have gotten the idea for murals depicting exemplary figures from Alain de Lille's portrayal of the palace in *Anticlaudianus* 1.119–52, where the list of frescoes, arranged in categories, includes philosophers and intellectuals (Aristotle, Plato, Seneca, Ptolemy, Cicero, Virgil, etc.) and then offers examples of straying humanity (Nero, Midas, Ajax, Paris, etc.).[9] Petrarch, too, will imagine a similarly *visually driven* catalogue (in this case statues not murals) when describing the hall of Syphax in the third book of the *Africa*.[10]

    The frescoes in the *Amorosa visione* are much more elaborately conceived than those in the *Anticlaudianus*, and they depict a series of triumphs: of Wisdom, Fame, Worldly Riches, Love, and Fortuna, or Fate. There is evidence, if we look at the space devoted to these themes, that an initial ambition for architectural and thematic symmetry quickly ran into difficulties (whether of inspiration or of suitable biographical material it is unclear), for the space allotted to the subjects is very unevenly distributed.[11] Wisdom is illustrated by 62 examples in two *canti*; Fame, on the other hand, boasts 152 figures spread over twelve *canti*; Worldly Riches offers a mere 18 portraits in two *canti*; Love counts 53 representative passions in fifteen *canti*. Fortuna is a kind of corrective postface, placing, in its eight *canti*, the previous exemplars in a context of redistributive justice. Out of the 50 sets of examples of Fortuna, many are repetitions from earlier tableaux, with a clear majority coming, unsurprisingly, from the triumph of Fame. The rest of the poem, before the complex process of withdrawal from the vision, offers a catalog of contemporaries, particularly women, which reminds one of the *Caccia di Diana*.

Though untidy and ultimately incoherent, Boccaccio's organization here offers an important clue to the genesis of other works. It is clear, for instance, that the ordering of "stories" by motivational categories driving them is a foreshadowing of the patterning of the days of the *Decameron*, as is the oppositional matrix, where a particular force is then countermanded in a reversal. The other work that is clearly heralded is the *De casibus*, as can be seen in Boccaccio's exceptional concentration, in the *Amorosa visione*, on Fame, brought to nought by Fortuna. What will make these later works successful, in contrast to the earlier poem, is the passage from mere catalog to full-scale narrative, whether presented as fiction or as historical biography.

The tableaux of the *Amorosa visione* are crowded with mythological and historical examples. In effect, the poem is a kind of pseudo-illustrated biographical dictionary arranged according to ethical categories. The price for including so many figures is brevity, with only perfunctory detail supplied. In that sense, the poem is a rehearsal or reorganization of knowledge held elsewhere, and which the reader is expected to supply. The sources to enable one to do this do not have to be searched for afar: the triumph of Love is peopled overwhelmingly with characters from Ovid's *Metamorphoses*. Fame, on the other hand, derives its examples from texts with an epic or historical dimension: the Old Testament, Virgil, Lucan, Statius, Livy, the Arthurian romances, and, of course, Dante. Among the catalog of contemporary beauties, Boccaccio will playfully insert Lia and Fiammetta, two of his own creations from earlier work, while the "new Dido" of canto 42.41 may be an anticipation of the Elissa of the Decameron *brigata*.

After viewing the frescoes, Boccaccio's narrator still obstinately goes his own way and heads for the garden, where he meets a group of other ladies, including a drowsy Fiammetta, with whom he is just about to make unconsensual love when he awakens from what has turned out to be a vision within a vision. Empty-handed, he promises he will sing of what he has seen, and then, sheepishly and belatedly, he agrees to follow his guide through the other, narrow gate in search of a life of virtue, fortunately for us omitted from the narration.

The narrator's refusal to follow the guide's advice, and the evident eagerness to experience the pleasures of wayward humanity, initially make one think of a subverted *Divine Comedy* in which the pilgrim turns out not to be Dante but Ulysses. "Ogni cosa del mondo a sapere / non è peccato" (to know everything of the world is no sin) proclaims the young narrator, in an obvious echo of *Inferno* 26.98 and 116, while hurrying through the broad gate of sinful experience. This aspect of unconsidered haste is a constant in Boccaccio's parables of learning: from his very earliest work, the so-called *Allegoria mitologica*, he was dramatizing the risks of premature ambition.[12] Here in the *Amorosa visione*, the guide warns the eager narrator:

Ir si conviene qui di soglia in soglia
con voler temperato, ché chi corre
talor tornando convien che si doglia. (1.82–84)

Here one must proceed from threshold to threshold / with tempered will, for whosoever rushes, / turning back, comes to grief.[13]

This warning is reminiscent of the rules of Dante's ascent of the mountain of *Purgatorio*, but with an important difference. Allegorically, of course, by entering by the broad gate, Boccaccio is adopting a conventional sapiential model where the philosopher has to *descend* into the depths to understand the sinful soul before he can rise to knowledge of the good. It is a program he sketches out on numerous occasions, from the *Elegia di Costanza* and the epistle "Mavortis milex" ("Soldier of Mars") to the *Genealogia deorum gentilium*. In the *Divine Comedy*, the crucial difference between Dante and Ulysses had been the divine dispensation for Dante's journey contrasted with the merely human presumption of the Greek's. Boccaccio does not seem in the *Amorosa visione* to be aware of this distinction: the moral message suffers in clarity as a result.

Boccaccio is still insisting on an overplayed Guinizzellian *stilnovismo* as a literary vehicle for his allegory, with unashamedly terrestrial love as a facile metaphor for spiritual advancement. In essence, the whole elaborate iconographic experience is merely an occasion for stating the somewhat banal tenet that virtue (the guide) is of little worth unless accompanied by passion, the soul's experience of love (Fiammetta). In other words, an initially intellectual perception of virtue has to be followed by an uncompromising, dedicated change of heart. It is a psychological definition of conversion.[14] This is why, ultimately, the prim guide shows herself to be unperturbed at the narrator's errancy, or errant entrance through the wrong gate, and eventual embrace with an apparently more complaisant female figure. As with Boccaccio's previous allegorical program, there is, however, a mismatch between the ethical purpose and the narrative result, with the latter tending to dominate. Indeed, here Boccaccio's representation of love is predictably closer to physical *eros* than charitable *agape*. Even within the newfound discipline of an overtly doctrinal poem, virtuously fettered with acrostic constraints, some of the love scenes get out of hand and become indulgent narrative in their own right: Dido's amorous lament hogs the limelight in cantos 28–29, pushing other equally deserving exemplary figures into the shade.

The influence of Dante is everywhere: in the meter, where Boccaccio, adept at the narrative *ottava*, is determined to prove he can finally master *terza rima*; in the situation of the narrator, who achieves a knowledge of virtue only after an educative journey through vice; in the opening situation of sleep and solitude, where Boccaccio's *liti salati* (salty shores) remind one of the shipwreck image in *Inferno* 1; in the advent of a guide sent by a divine agency — but Boccaccio's sensuality demands a *donna piacente* (pleasing lady) and not Dante's dour Virgil;[15] in the final promise of narrating what he has seen;[16] in the imagery taken from various points in Dante's poem, the "noble castle," the gates, even the frescoes, which present their ethical exempla "as if on film," in much the same way that the sculpted terrace of the proud does in *Purgatorio* 10; even in the lists of exemplary figures, which frequently appear in the same relative order as they do in the *Commedia* (though Boccaccio is not averse to throwing in extras when he feels like it).

Boccaccio's overwhelming debt to Dante is acknowledged in a moving scene in the first hall of the noble castle, where the narrator contemplates a portrait of the great poet himself, surrounded by the figures of the wise. In an effusion of heartfelt admiration reminiscent of Dante-character's hero worship of Virgil in the *Commedia*, Boccaccio's narrator refuses to move along to view the next tableau:

> I' 'l riguardava, e mai non mi sarei
> saziato di mirarlo, se non fosse
> che quella donna, che i passi miei
>   là entro con que' due insieme mosse,
> mi disse: — Che pur miri? forse credi
> renderli col mirar le morte posse?
>   E' c'è altro a veder che tu non vedi!
> Tu hai costui veduto, volgi omai
> gli occhi a que' del mondan romore eredi. (6.19–27)

I gazed at him, and never would I / have tired of contemplating him, were it not / that that lady [the guide], who moved my steps / therein along with those two [fellow pleasure-seekers], / said to me: — "What are you wondering at? Do you perhaps think / to bring back his dead powers by your gazing? / There is yet more to see that you haven't seen! / Now that you have seen him over here, turn / your eyes to those heirs of earthly notoriety."

The reverie is modeled consciously on the wonderment felt by the Croatian pilgrim whom Dante describes as gazing at the Veronica in Rome, finally satisfying himself about the appearance of the Savior (*Par.* 31.103–11). Even the guide's subsequent prompting for the narrator to move on is a reference to Dante-character's idling on the terrace of the proud, where Virgil is obliged to tell him: "Non tener pure ad un loco la mente" (Don't rest your mind on just one spot, *Purg.* 10.46).

Alongside this massive Dantesque presence, it is also easy to identify much material that Boccaccio has reworked from his own previous writing. Visions and dreams have been a constant dramatic and allegorical device in his works, and revelatory visitations on the orders of divine agencies were especially frequent in the *Filocolo.* The element of conversion is another constant: the *Caccia,* the *Filocolo,* and the *Comedia delle ninfe* all make use of improbable last-minute spiritual illuminations, almost as if Boccaccio were always belatedly trying to redeem his books' moral purpose after a bout of lively mimesis, or perhaps, if indeed the ethical intention had remained constant, as though he had suffered last-minute worries about his readers' ability to grasp the interpretative code.

Lists of names are another recurrent feature. Constituting one of the main metrical challenges of the *Caccia,* they had reached a paroxysm of erudite display in the tournament scene of the *Teseida* (there is more than a hint that the knights taking sides there, for Mars or for Venus, are a crude classification of ancient heroes into irascibles and concupiscibles), and here in the *Amorosa visione* the lists acquire that moral distribution pattern that was to inform much of Boccaccio's biographical and mythographic scholarship in the years that followed the *Decameron.* Likewise, the garden scene at the end of the *Amorosa visione* takes up the recurrent *locus amoenus* motif in the *Filocolo, Teseida,* and *Comedia delle ninfe.* It will, of course, become a major constituent of the framing narrative of the *Decameron.* The moment in the garden scene of the *Amorosa visione* when poor Fiammetta wakes up to find herself already in an ardent embrace is a repetition of Florio's meeting with

Biancifiore in Sadoc's tower in the *Filocolo* (4.118). The same fantasy device of aroused male libido contemplating dormant female beauty will recur memorably in the tale of Cimone in the *Decameron* (5.1). A more sinister, ostensibly necrophiliac version had occurred in the thirteenth *quistione d'amore* (question concerning love) in *Filocolo* 4.67, a tale that would be reworked in the story of Gentile de Carisendi (*Decameron* 10.4).

Occasionally in the *Amorosa visione* the back-references to previous works are explicit, as when Boccaccio refers to Lia "che trasse Ameto / dal volgar uso dell'umana gente" (who drew Ameto away from the common habits of mankind, 41.35–36). The inclusion of Lia, the favored nymph of the *Comedia delle ninfe*, is playful because the mythical Lia now figures among a list of *real* ladies, some of them contemporaries of Boccaccio (Lia's immediate neighbor is Margherita, wife of the notorious dictator of Florence, Walter of Brienne). Among Boccaccio's male contemporaries mentioned in the poem, the figure of Robert of Anjou stands out. While in Naples, the young Boccaccio had enjoyed the kid-glove treatment that the Angevins had reserved for the Florentine financiers, their source of ready cash. Robert is consequently portrayed in Boccaccio's earlier works as a model sovereign, virtuously combining statecraft with intellectual patronage. The financial crises that toppled the Florentines from their position of influence and privilege in the kingdom were also probably responsible for Boccaccio's own reluctant departure from Naples. Still freshly smarting from his "exile" to a seemingly uncouth Florence, the poet here punishes Robert with a positively Dantesque *contrappasso*, the punishment being cruelly financial. The king is observed in the midst of an undignified mob scratching at a mountain of precious metals and gems:

> ornato di be' drappi e rilucenti
> il nipote vid'io di quel Nasuto,
> che gloriar si va co' precedenti,
>   recarsi in mano un forte biccicuto,
> dando ta' colpi sopra 'l monte d'oro,
> che di ciascun saria un mur caduto;
>   e d'esso assai levava, e quel tesoro
> in parte oscura tutto il serbava,
> e quasi più n'avea ch'altro di loro. (14.25–33)

Elegant in fine and glittering robes, / I saw the grandson of Him of the mighty snout, / who goes proudly with the ones before, / pick up a great pickax, / attacking the mountain of gold with such blows

/ that each one would have demolished a wall; / and he bore away great chunks, and that treasure / he kept all for himself in a dark place / and had more of it than almost anyone else.

The precisely personal context of Boccaccio's animosity becomes evident when royal ignominy is further compounded by juxtaposing the spectacular money-grabbing and miserliness of Robert with the shabby, small-time avarice of Boccaccio's own father, who never makes it into the big league of money-grubbing, but not for dint of trying. Robert and Boccaccino had been intimately associated in the financial arrangements of the Angevin regime.[17] Now they were forever linked, grubbily, in this symbolic tableau.

Though these cameos, whether of Virgil, Dido, Dante, or Robert of Anjou, momentarily enliven the arid enumeration of categories and characters, the general impression the poem gives is of an ambitious, exciting project weakened by mediocre execution. Doctrinally, its message on love and fate, secular and spiritual goods, is anything but original, being the stuff of conventional sermons. The poem suffers furthermore from an ideological fuzziness that Boccaccio was never entirely able to dispel from this work. Dramatically and narratively, the self-imposed disciplines of the organizational format mean that the poem is rarely able to rise above the artificiality of its conception.

In this sense, the conscious emulation of Dante at all levels serves only to illustrate the wide gap in achievement between the two poets. Not only is Dante able to conceive a theologically profound project; he is also able to bring it artistically to life, giving a real sense of direct experience and curiosity to the narrator-protagonist, while using dynamic, interactive encounters with his characters, not static ekphrases. Boccaccio, however, despite his use of first-person narration, only rarely seems to inhabit, in an imaginative sense, the world of his vision. The text is studded with telltale concessionary formulae like *parevami, così pareva* (it seemed to me, thus it seemed) from the visionary tradition, which reinforce the impression that the narrator is at least partially standing outside his narration, and at best unsure of how to look in.

This exteriority leads to extraordinarily complex presentational problems. At stake is the definition of levels of reality. The narrator expressly states that the whole experience is a vision or dream. Within that dream, the tableaux he sees in the noble castle are but representations (he does not meet the characters in the flesh): in Platonic terms, they are illusions of illusions. In the model Boccaccio was trying to emulate, Dante's sculpted terraces in *Purgatorio*, the pilgrim is so overawed by the supernatural realism of the representations (which are *directly* crafted by God) that he can even synesthetically add the nonsculptural sensations such as smell and hearing to his interpretation. The ploy works in Dante because amazement, almost disbelief at belief, is elevated to being one of the main dramatic ingredients, and it only needs to be maintained for a relatively short part of the poem. It is a brief parenthesis of reality at two removes (or arguably, given the divine artifex, of hyperdirect reality) within a larger work based on only one remove from "reality." Boccaccio, despite all his efforts, does not manage to maintain his levels with any consistency. The juggling the poet is required to perform makes no sense and clarifies only one point, and that is that Boccaccio had not really found a way of dealing with multiple layers of perception.

Reversing Dante's pattern, which moved from single to double illusion, the garden to which the narrator proceeds after the two frescoed rooms is now meant to be a "real" garden (only in the sense that it is real within the dream). During this garden scene, the narrator makes free with the somnolent Fiammetta and is about to reach a selfish climax when he "wakes up" (elsewhere in Boccaccio's fictions, it is the woman who sleeps and wakes up at the crucial moment). Clearly, therefore, the narrator has been having a dream within a dream, but it is unclear at what point he might have "fallen asleep." A generous interpretation might be that Boccaccio's clumsy insistence on the reality of the garden is a device to save him from falling into the even-greater difficulty of creating, or rather admitting openly, a triple illusion, a dream about a dream within a dream.

Despite the allegorical and organizational weaknesses of the work, one element stands out as a very real achievement. Boccaccio's thematic grouping of images and characters into triumphs is iconographically quite alluring. The very stasis and artifice that make the poem unsatisfactory from a dramatic point of view make it exceptionally rich in terms of symbolic possibilities, creating almost a sequence of secular *sacre conversazioni*. What Boccaccio achieves is an expansion of the mystical procession in the Earthly Paradise of Dante's *Purgatorio*. Dante's procession was a disciplined, ritual representation of mankind's divinely ordered, developing relationship with a spiritual truth. Its success lay in the harmony and providential symmetry of the procession as a whole. In the *Amorosa visione*, however, Boccaccio wants to include all kinds of disorderly, heterogeneous experience in his pageant, just as his narrator obstinately refuses to follow any of the direct paths to virtue. The result is a kind of allegorical circus parade rather than a semiliturgical procession, with individual performers often more interesting than Dante's faceless symbolic participants, but where the overall show itself lacks direction. Nevertheless, the *Amorosa visione*, for all its incoherence, or maybe because of it, was to prove irresistible to writers and artists in search of a new combinatory iconography, and the first imitator was to be none other than Petrarch in his *Trionfi*.[18]

Had Boccaccio been known only for the *Amorosa visione*, it would be doubtful if he were to be much read nowadays, or even cited in more than a footnote in literary histories. It might stand alongside the *Fiore*, if the *Fiore* had not somehow been associated with Dante.[19] Within the sequence of Boccaccio's other works, however, it stands as a work of considerable importance, illustrating the way in which crucial questions of genre, of influence, of moral and aesthetic organization, were being worked out, systematically, "in the laboratory." The masterpiece of the *Decameron* or the massive monument of the Latin erudite works could not have been achieved without this very aware process of experimentation. The *Amorosa visione*, completed despite the acrostics, also shows, in contrast to Petrarch's penchant for abandoning works that were not going well, a very serious and unsung side to Boccaccio, one that demonstrates staying power, discipline, and sheer grit.

PART V

NEW PASTORALS

CHAPTER ELEVEN

ON THE THRESHOLD OF PARADISE •
(Comedia delle ninfe fiorentine, or *Ameto)*

Jane Tylus

As the first work Boccaccio wrote on returning to Florence after a delightful decade in Naples, the *Comedia delle ninfe fiorentine* betrays mixed feelings about the author's new home. Such feelings are perhaps nowhere more evident than in the reaction of the young hunter Ameto to a story about the Neapolitan city he has never visited, although he has heard that the land around it is prized for hunting, "abundant with young and lustful does, agile young deer fleet of foot, and mature hinds wary of nets, or dogs, or arrows."[1] Nostalgia aside, this is clearly a reference to Boccaccio's *Caccia di Diana*, to which over a decade later the author now gives the status of an urtext. We have again a woodland setting, lovely ladies, and a cameo appearance by Venus—albeit set in the Florentine countryside rather than outside Naples.[2] And although Ameto seems to be the principal male protagonist, it turns out that, like the *Caccia*, the entire *Comedia* is narrated by a figure who watches from afar. This time, however, the narrator is not a stag who will be changed into a man at tale's end, but an unnamed, unsatisfied lover who laments the nymphs' departure after he has eavesdropped on them all day as they told tales to the delighted listener Ameto: "I returned, grieving over my troubles, to my usual spot."[3] Ameto, on the other hand, *has* been changed, and in a manner that symbolically repeats the metamorphosis at the end of the *Caccia*: "It seems to him that from a brute animal, he had become a man."[4]

Written in 1342, first published in 1478, enormously popular during the Renaissance, earning the status of a *piccolo Decameron* in the eyes of its influential editor, Francesco Sansovino,[5] the *Ameto* stands out as a work "in between," reminding many a recent reader of that other well-known halfway space, Dante's *Purgatorio*, particularly its Edenic garden at the top.[6] At the same time, Boccaccio introduces tensions unknown to Dante's serene terrain that ultimately releases its sojourner from the complexities of terrestrial existence. The *Comedia* remains earthbound, prompting us to question whether a work of literature can transport us beyond itself, and to ask whether this world is, indeed, enough. This would at least seem to be the meaning of Boccaccio's invitation in the first chapter to all who love: "In order to follow Cupid with the consideration owed him, I have gathered together my scattered labors, and whoever reads them with a discerning mind will find nothing to blame in what I have praised."[7]

Far more ambitious than the *Caccia*, the *Comedia* reveals an increasingly sophisticated Boccaccio questioning the role and efficacy of literature in human lives. Does it provide mere recreation, a brief and lovely escape from the depressing monotony of everyday life, particularly a life now spent in Florence? Or can it be transformative, moving its readers and perhaps its author toward intellectual and spiritual revelation? Is it, in short, like that other Florentine *Commedia*, Dante's? The work's very structure points to the difficulties of answering such questions. Roughly two-thirds of Boccaccio's *Comedia* is prose, much of it dedicated to the nymphs' lives and amours. The other third consists of poems that provide in Dantesque *terza rima* moralizing interpretations of the stories that preceded them, shepherds' eclogues, and Ameto's and the narrator's own interior monologues — as well as Ameto's appeals to the nymphs early on in the text and his prayer to Venus toward the end. The work is stuffed full of mythological lore, much of it arcane, as well as fanciful stories, some reminiscent of the later *Decameron*. What exactly are we to make of this work that Boccaccio called the *Comedia delle ninfe fiorentine*, and readers and editors since him the *Ameto*, in honor of the rustic protagonist introduced early on as the *vagabundo giovane* — the wandering young man (3.4)?

"How efficacious beauty is"

The story of the *Comedia* is deceptively simple.[8] Hearing one day a beautiful song after a phenomenally successful hunt, a young Tuscan lad wanders into a grove to discover there women who appear to be goddesses. He comes dangerously close to reliving the venture of another hunter, Actaeon, who had by chance espied Diana bathing in the woods. But the young Ameto's fate will not be that of Actaeon, even as dogs pursue him, and he searches anxiously for a stag's horns on his forehead.[9] Rather, the women, amused, admit him to their place of repose. After a long winter, he returns on a feast day to the site, where eventually seven maidens gather in the heat of the day to exchange tales about the powerful role of Venus in their lives. They move this young man to longing, admiration, and finally understanding, which culminates with his immersion in the nymphs' fountain and a radiant vision of Venus herself. This understanding, it would seem, has to do not simply with his grasp of true love in a Christian world whose nymphs are revealed to be the cardinal and theological virtues,[10] but with Ameto's own identity. Spared Actaeon's fate, Ameto has been preserved for something greater. The question that he asks throughout the text becomes our own: Who am I to see so much beauty, and having seen it, what am I to do with it?[11]

Metamorphosis is thus redemptive rather than tragic. Thanks to the merciful power of Venus, Ameto is saved through the act of storytelling itself.[12] All begins and ends with one nymph in particular, the beautiful Lia whom Ameto first encounters after his hunt and who will ask him to preside over a day of tales. Boccaccio had told stories before, in the fourth book of the *Filocolo*, where he plays Caleone, in love with Fiammetta. There the tales are *quistioni d'amore*, or positions taken in the debate over which she rules. The *Ameto* does not pose sides in scholastic fashion but offers autobiographies and songs of women whose beauty Ameto ponders as they reflect on their own amours in a variety of genres. The story of Emilia, who sees a pale young man on a chariot beside Venus, recalls the medieval vision; that of Agapes, married to a garrulous and impotent old man and who is awakened to true love only with a passionate kiss from Venus herself, is like a raucous *fabliau*. Mopsa's tale, the first, is almost equally graphic. Desire overcomes her for a hapless youth, whom she sees sailing on a boat one day. Alternately pleading and threatening him from afar, she eventually dismisses all shame and undresses to bring him to shore. In this she is not altogether different from the forward women of the *Decameron*, except they are not reciting autobiographies.

These are tales to which admittedly sometimes Ameto does not even listen, being absorbed by "the delicate arms and white bosoms of the women" (28.8) as well as by those physical attributes he cannot see, described in extended blazons that anticipate Ariosto's descriptions of Olimpia and Angelica. Boccaccio accentuates Ameto's reactions with an eye to showing us the *wrong* way to respond to women and to react to *novelle*. And yet these salacious details are also what propel Ameto into the stories, prompting him to identify with the male lover or beloved, wishing that he, too, might find himself in the arms of Acrimonia or Fiammetta or Mopsa. Arguably, he learns how to become such a lover. At the end of the story about the desperate Caleone — the "double" for Boccaccio who returns from the *Filocolo* and who as a last resort sneaks into Fiammetta's bed to surprise her with a confession of love — Ameto expresses admiration for Caleone's audacity, "judging that the bold are helped by Fortune."[13] Even the narrator himself

is not immune from this competitive cycle of identification and envy. Boccaccio probes the links that bind readers to stories, as the eavesdropping
author admits to both self-recognition ("thus in my desires and thoughts I
recognized those of Ameto") and an envy so intense that for one moment he
confesses having considered disrupting the charmed circle by revealing his
presence ("and envious of him, I was sometimes on the point of revealing
myself").[14]

The desire for beauty thus affords Ameto a way into the world of the
tales and the beauty they evoke, nowhere more brazenly than when Mopsa
undresses, or when Caleone likewise disrobes and slips into the same bed
with Fiammetta. And while beauty is increasingly associated with moral
and spiritual qualities, the Venus who triumphs at story's end, "marveled"
over by Ameto and the nymphs as Jason was marveled over by the Argives,
remains visually overpowering.[15] Beauty, of course, had also been central
to the *stil novo*, but the Beatrice of the *Vita nuova* never speaks, and Dante's
project in any case depends on her death. How to make the woman who
is very much alive the impetus to one's spiritual education?[16] Boccaccio's
Venus does not represent "disorderly lust, to whom fools give the name of
goddess," as she herself says when she reveals herself to Ameto. But neither
is she simply the "Angelic Mind" of later Ficinian thought.[17] Movement to
the other life can begin only with responsiveness to *this* life, and it is beauty
that generates such responsiveness, as when Mopsa finally wins over the
resistant Affren.

Unlike Affren, however, Ameto is not fated to possess Mopsa, or for that
matter, Lia. What he *can* possess is language—words if not bodies, while
the bodies themselves are never taken from his gaze. Chapter 31 represents
an important transition. Ameto has just heard the tale of Acrimonia, who
describes in detail the annoying attentions she received from Apaten, a rustic youth much like Ameto himself, who responds to the story with what he
describes as "a more temperate desire." He is, he reflects, no Paris, who saw
the goddesses themselves nude, and he reasons that he must learn to accept
his lot and know what belongs to the realm of "impossible things."[18] By
chapter 46, after he is cleansed in the fountain, he opines that earlier during a more "primitive life," "the nymphs may have appealed to his eye more
than his mind; now they pleased his intellect more than his eye."[19] But even
as lust gives way to intellectual hunger, Ameto becomes subject to another
kind of transition. It is also in chapter 31 that Ameto declares that his truest
blessing would be not to enjoy the nymphs but to be remembered by them
in their stories of love, and thus to become a subject of their future narratives. Coming as this declaration does after the rustic Apaten's successful

wooing of Acrimonia, whom she has turned from a "rough satyr" into an "educated youth" (29.61), the insight is not insignificant. As he sees in Apaten a potential double for himself, Ameto desires to be the figure in a story Acrimonia might tell to other young men. And in fact, Ameto *is* included in a story: the last one and the longest, told by Lia, about the founding of Florence. In her final lines, Lia acknowledges that like Acrimonia, she has drawn her rustic lover out of "mental blindness" toward "the knowledge of priceless lore" (della mentale cechità con la mia luce a conoscere le care cose, 38.117). No longer boorish and uncouth, Ameto is now "competent, civilized, and ready for greater things" (abile, mansueto e disposto ad alte cose). The young men of the tales make a journey that matches his own, from the "wildness and disdain" of Mopsa's young man on the waters,[20] to the sophistication of Lia's beloved.

And yet is this indeed Ameto's highest wish? Desire for integration within others' narratives leads to his wish to *write* a narrative himself, contained in the verses of his last song, for "all who will come after me so that they might fall in love with these ladies—as have I."[21] When Venus descends, she asks the nymphs to unveil Ameto's "clouded and darkened eyes," not only to gaze on her beauty, but "to tell his companions the extent to which she allows humankind to see her, ablaze in love."[22] Her wish for him becomes his own. He ends his hymn to Venus, his last spoken words in the text, consigning to her his pages so they may be preserved from the envious and circulate safe from barbaric hands.[23] Several times Ameto suggests that Actaeon suffered most because he could not narrate what he saw: "Oh, how much luckier am I than poor Actaeon, to whom it was forbidden to tell of that vindictive Diana's beauty; and may my powers to narrate such good as I have known to my dear companions not be taken from me."[24] Only when Venus, "beginning and end of all things" (41.2), chases away Diana, as she did at the end of the *Caccia di Diana*—hence its double-edged title—can the stag be transformed to a man and regain his powers of narration.

"Deus nobis haec otia fecit"

Ameto thus experiences an education into literacy.[25] To put it another way, his coming to terms with his own sexuality through the project of writing is a story of civilization, mirrored in the nymphs' tales, which are not simply autobiographies but at times fanciful mythic accounts of the origins of the cities where they spent their youths: Paris, Athens, Naples, Rome, Florence. The last, subject of Lia's story, finds Boccaccio at his most inventive. He imagines Florence founded by the Greek Achemenides, the companion of Ulysses left to die in the Cyclops's cave, then saved by Aeneas, as told by Virgil in *Aeneid* 3. Achemenides himself is from Thebes, founded by Cadmus—the inventor, among other things, of writing—and it is thanks to his rescue from savagery and arrival in Etruria that this rustic spot will become the sophisticated city of Boccaccio's day.[26] At the same time, the nymphs chart their familial histories from violence—notably, almost all are born of rape—to entrapment in mostly loveless marriages, to active acceptance of genuine love, demonstrating their emergence into more civilized social relations. The *Comedia* thus also traces for us a history of sexuality, from its origins in brute male lust to its control and sublimation for purposes of civilization.

As a civilizing text, the *Ameto* presents a challenge with respect to genre. Numerous allusions to the *Aeneid* suggest its epic aspirations, recapturing a moment when men, women, and gods freely interacted. Yet it has also been called the first pastoral novel. The *tenzone* of Alcesto and Acaten early in the work is certainly the first *egloga* in the vernacular, reminiscent of Boccaccio's later Latin eclogues and those of Petrarch. Giuseppe Velli and Janet Smarr have given convincing readings of the *Comedia* and its influence as pastoral. Lorenzo de' Medici drew inspiration for his youthful "Corinto" from Ameto's appeal to Lia to love him,[27] and Sannazaro was indebted to the Boccaccian text for everything from the alternating prose and verse chapters to the embedded tale of Naples, the city where *Arcadia* is set.[28] Yet while there is no question that Boccaccio has recourse to moments in Virgil's bucolics, the competitive eclogue between Alcesto and Acaten suggests that the pastoral atmosphere of song alone is not enough to sustain serious writing. We witness a debate not between the ascetic, contemplative life of the "good" shepherd and the active life of the 'bad," as some have argued, but precisely the opposite: the watchful labors of the Arcadian Alcesto on the mountain where he is visited by the Muses contrast with the wasteful leisure and apparent negligence of the Sicilian Acaten, who boasts of his "fields bursting with infinite grass," which save him from doing any work at all (14.14–15). The *otium* Virgil's Tityrus enjoys arouses fear in another Boccaccian shepherd, Teogapen, whose song suggests that "should the good [of Venus] cease to be felt in our works, we would become lazy (*oziosi*) and do things in vain" (11.5–6). Lia sings that "to flee idleness (*ozio*), I visit the sylvan gods" (4.40–41), and Pomena chastizes the shepherd Palemone from Virgil's third eclogue for his "strange and abominable ways" (27.23)—presumably for his own inactivity in a poem where he serves simply as an audience and abdicates his role as judge. Agape speaks of the necessity of shunning sloth, while the fire of love makes one work to attain happiness (chapter 33). And so on.

Otium, that is, is ever a threat, with Boccaccio's nymphs defending themselves against activities that would appear to be otiose. Tale-telling (*ragionare*) might logically count as one. But as Lia gathers the nymphs around her on Venus's feast day, she defines tale-telling as a form of *negotium*, or work: "Then let's tell each other our stories, and in so doing we will not pass the day in idleness as wretched women do."[29] Storytelling protects from sleep and laziness, both of which lead to vice. To be sure, in chapter 26—almost the longest of the book and virtually at its middle—Pomena elaborates on the distressing fall from grace that accompanied the age of Saturn and the rise of Bacchus and Ceres. It became an unfortunate necessity for her to impart skills to man and woman as they learned to produce food that once came spontaneously, burrow into the earth for metal and ore, and imitate the art of Ariadne. Yet the chapter as a whole belies Pomena's complaint and paean to a properly "golden age": she initiates the wondering *ninfa* Adiona and her beloved, the formerly degenerate Dioneo, into the marvels of horticulture, and Adiona herself takes pride in learning secrets of the trade so that she can pass them on to others. Ameto, too, seems naturally disposed to an ethics of work. When forced to depart from the nymphs after his first glimpse of them, he resourcefully whiles away a long winter by fixing his nets, sharpening his knives, and training his faithful hunting dogs. Labor for riches' sake is to be avoided; Agape condemns her avaricious parents for forcing her to marry for wealth rather than love. The Florentines are jabbed subtly if continuously for falling prey to greed. Venus and tale-telling alike are redeemed if, far from wasting his time in lascivious activities, Ameto can have something to take away from it.

The beloved Lia herself is a key to Boccaccio's georgic vision of pastoral. While "Lia" has been conjectured to be one "Lucia" long ago loved by the young Boccaccio before he first left Florence,[30] she is principally the biblical Leah, who represents the active life in medieval allegory because of her fertility, while the lovely Rachel represents contemplation. Lia in fact sings of herself in her opening song as the sister and opposite of Narcissus, described as a hunter. But he was "wild and unmoving" in the very thing that Lia, and eventually Ameto, embrace: "love, and others' pleasure" (amore e 'l piacere ad altrui). She looks outward rather than obsessively inward, engaging in what she calls "affanni e . . . diletti" (works and delights, 4.58). And in her final song, she suggests that had Aristotle "understood with working faith" the active life that she herself exemplifies, he would have reached the "happy realms" where Moses and his own followers now reside.[31] Narcissus, in contrast, becomes the self-satisfied figure who opposes love, eventually punished for his selfishness, an unsettling association for a text that supposedly moves us toward the Rachel of heavenly contemplation.

And here is where we might finally turn to Dante. On the final plateau of Mt. Purgatory, and hence on the threshold of gaining the earthly paradise, Dante dreams of Lia, who makes herself a garland and says that while her sister Rachel is happy to gaze at herself, so she, Lia, is content to work with her hands: "She satisfies herself with seeing, I with works" (27.108).[32] This beautiful young woman who appears to Dante at the hour of Venus—when "Cytherea, who always seems aflame with fires of love, first shines upon the mountains from the east"[33]—prepares the pilgrim and writer for another woman and another garden: Matelda, who greets him in the earthly paradise and immerses and cleanses him in the clear waters of Lethe. She thus fulfills the moment of which Dante wrote at the beginning of *Purgatorio*: "I will now sing of that second realm, where the human spirit is purged and made ready to ascend to heaven" (Canterò di quel secondo regno / dove l'umano spirito si purga / e di salire al ciel diventa degno, 1.4–6). Immediately thereafter Dante sees the four lovely ladies, who reveal themselves to be the stars that Dante saw in the first canto, and who are quickly followed by the other three of a higher order: the seven virtues, whom he is now worthy to behold. This is the contemplative "finale," the attaining of Rachel and the end, in effect, of Dante's earthly pilgrimage as he prepares to ascend to Paradise alongside Beatrice.[34]

Dante's Lia is thus the first of several women at the end of *Purgatorio* thanks to whom he will begin to attain his celestial vision, and the parallels with Boccaccio's *Ameto*, as readers have commented, are striking. We might see the songs of the shepherds as an antepurgatorial visit with Casella, and the seven virtues/nymphs as the seven plateaus of Purgatorio. And at the end Ameto is both doused with water and "rendered happy within the fire," and the "lovely planet that is patroness of love," as Dante calls her, will literally appear as Venus herself.[35] The moments that seem most akin to that other Florentine *Commedia*, however, display some of the starkest differences between these two Trecento texts. When Ameto is finally able to apprehend Venus herself, his eyes now cleansed of their mist, so struck with wonder is he that he compares himself to the Argives seized with admiration when they saw Jason pick up the plow to harvest warriors ("gli achivi compagni veduto bifolco divenuto Giansone," 44.4). The mention of Jason and his Argonauts transforms Venus into plowman or *bifolco*, with a curious effect. She not only takes on Ameto's rustic status. She becomes identified with the space of georgic labor that makes her, along with Lia, a figure representing not intellectual contemplation but action, the productive work of a laborer, an odd resonance in what is supposedly the climactic moment of the text.

Complicating matters further is the fact that the passage repeats virtually verbatim a passage from *Paradiso* 2, where Dante famously warns his readers that only a few should follow him in his little boat or *piccioletta barca*, and he continues: "Those glorious ones who passed into the Colchis did not marvel as much as you will do now when they saw Jason turn plowman."[36] This boastful dare makes of Dante the *bifolco* who turns plow into pen, as Peter Hawkins suggests, calling attention to the end of his "georgic" apprenticeship and his beginning as a real epic writer as he takes us into the final *cantica*.[37] That Dante's allusion to Jason occurs at the edge of Paradise suggests that for Boccaccio we are also at such a threshold, and in fact Ameto immediately addresses Venus and the nymphs as "Pegasean goddess" and "lofty muses," asking them to "turn his weak mind to such a great task" as to tell of divine beauty, insofar as human tongue is authorized to do so.[38] Yet if Dante goes on to heaven, Ameto goes home, burning with love, still on earth, still bound by a beauty at once otherworldly and terrestrial. Remorseful over the far-too-hasty departure of the nymphs, he nonetheless nourishes the hope of returning there to see them again ("con isperanza di ritornarvi similemente si parte lieto," 48.4).[39] We must thus ponder whether this pastoral sojourn is a transitional moment to higher realms, or ultimately self-sufficient—albeit as a place of labor rather than of Virgilian *otium*, as Boccaccio attempts to save tale-telling from itself. In many ways, Francesco Sansovino's suggestion that the seven nymphs represent the seven *scienze* or the seven liberal arts is an acute one, as it notes the resistance Boccaccio's text offers to a Dantesque ascent to paradise and an exclusive movement toward contemplation and grace.[40] Ameto's education is by and large an earthly one, his own labors coming to fruition with the pages he writes, not because he has found the portal to a golden age or paradise, but because he has learned to read and to speak. His final hymn to the "divine light" of Venus in the presence of the nymphs is very different from his first song, when he had begged Lia to "descend" from the heights of the mountains where she dwells and bring her lovely choir (8.37).

Lia does repair to a beautiful field to meet Ameto on the feast day at winter's end, and there they remain until nightfall. And the narrating author remains there, too. In the work's final chapter, he turns to his dedicatee—not Fiammetta or fifty-nine Neapolitan women (or, as in the case of the *Decameron*, women readers more generally)—but Niccolò di Bartolo del Buono di

Firenze, about whom little is known other than that he seems to have been sufficiently wealthy for Boccaccio to address him as a Maecenas.[41] In a work indebted heavily to Ovid, Claudian, Virgil, and others, the last myth the narrator mentions invokes "the sad misfortunes of Icarus" (d'Icaro li miseri casi, 50.1), which he has sought to avoid by not overreaching. It is tempting to see in this final allusion to the tragic figure who flew too close to the sun a memory of Dante, whose own work was being criticized by the church that Boccaccio invokes in his closing dedication to Niccolò,[42] and hence to envision the Certaldan choosing a safer route as he largely renounces heavenly speculation for terrestrial labors. While Ameto may have glimpsed a Venus who is said to be a "triune god," any wish on the narrator's part to attain the god's-eye view of the heavens has been long abandoned. All he could do was to "listen furtively to those pleasant, lovely accounts of love and of lovers as told by beautiful nymphs."[43] Caught up in the intense experience of listening, the unnamed narrator experiences a mixture of joy and pain: "la novella fiamma . . . raccese / l'antica," as a new love reawakens an old one. As this line reminiscent of the *Aeneid* suggests, the narrator seems to take his place not among the faithful of paradise but in the realm of Dido and other suffering lovers in hell.[44] His last plea in his closing poem is in fact to ask for a quick death, since he sees no other way to escape from the lengthy suffering provoked by the presumed loss of his love.

And yet amid suffering, beauty is born. In the final chapter of the book, and thus immediately after the narrator's despairing poem, Boccaccio himself "appears" in his own text to offer the gift of a flower to Niccolò: a rose, symbolic of "the beauties of Florence" and "born among the thorns of my adversities."[45] Thus does he engage in a gesture reminiscent of that of Mars when he identified the city of Florenzia with the flowers Venus herself was holding.[46] Might one also see in Boccaccio's metaphor an act of naming, as his return to the city of his youth coincides with a new work, perhaps even a new genre, of literature? Like Ameto and the nymphs, Boccaccio, too, has defeated *otium*, inspired by the beauty to which he has been witness, hiding with his narrator in the thicket and watching "the beauty of Florence" unfold. Thus the *Comedia* began with the request to a Venus who inspired Orpheus to travel to the "house of Pluto" in search of his bride, to stimulate his own "weak wit" so that he may fittingly sing her praises and the power of her realm.[47] While Ameto consigns his pages to Venus, the real work of recounting Ameto's experience to worldly readers is Boccaccio's, as he gathers together "his scattered labors" for a new Florentine audience. His productivity has thus led to a fiction that ideally can teach as well as console, providing earthly delights proscribed by life itself, a life that has taken the young Boccaccio away from the Naples he loved, as he—or his narrator, or both—return to a house that is "dark, and silent, and terribly sad" (oscura e muta e molto trista, 49.77). Indeed, the final question the text forces us to ask is whether the writer Boccaccio shares the pessimism of his narrator as to how long storytelling can fill the void left by unrequited love, or whether he, too, like Ameto, hopes to return to find the nymphs on another day.

CHAPTER TWELVE

MYTH AND HISTORY: TOWARD A NEW ORDER • (*Ninfale fiesolano*)

Susanna Barsella

A reconstruction of the origin of Florentine political civilization, the *Ninfale fiesolano* (*Tale of the Nymph of Fiesole*) contains both an etiological myth and an etymological fable. It is the exemplary story of the origin and identity of a nation and of the forces at play in the passage from an old to a new order, from a nature-based world to political civilization. Like the *Comedia delle ninfe fiorentine* (1341–42), the *Ninfale* transposes into collective terms the evolution from natural to civilized world.[1] The selection of the genre—the mythological fable—seems to be the understandable result of Boccaccio's vision of poetry's role in bringing together the truths of myth and history.

In the works produced between his return to Florence and the *Decameron*,[2] mytho-autobiographical themes, although still present, tend to fade and only indirectly resonate in the political motives underlying the *Ninfale*. Although debated, the date of composition of this little narrative poem in *ottava rima* (eight-verse stanzas, or octaves) is generally set between 1344 and 1346.[3] The financial and political crisis of this period generated an intellectual climate that likely influenced Boccaccio's choice of the subject. Edward III of England's unpaid debts to the bankers of Florence had triggered an unprecedented economic emergency, and the political situation was no less problematic.[4] The city was still in turmoil after the failure and consequent exile of Walter VI of Brienne, the Duke of Athens, in 1343, and it was torn apart by political strife between Guelphs and Ghibellines. The climate only worsened with the famine of 1346–47, immediately followed by the Black Death in 1348. Boccaccio's economic situation was precarious, and in search of adequate positions he possibly spent a period in Ravenna during the lordship of Ostasio da Polenta before moving to the court of Francesco Ordelaffi in Forlì between 1347 and 1348.[5] Boccaccio thus conceives the *Ninfale* in a condition of partial estrangement that perhaps echoes in the wanderings of the outsiders from Fiesole before they integrate, at the fable's conclusion, with the Florentine stock. Intertwining with the biographical and historical threads, the tale of genetic and political reconciliation between two cities and two cultures (the Etruscan-autochthon and the Roman-Florentine) also seems to weave in its legendary fiction the contemporary tensions dividing Florence and Rome.

By investigating the historical and geographical identity of his roots, Boccaccio celebrates the contribution of the Fiesolans, and the archaic culture they represent, to the greatness of Florence.[6] Born of a family originally from Certaldo, Boccaccio possibly projects in this celebration his own desire to reconcile and ennoble the *genti nove* Dante had despised (*Inferno* 16.73).[7] This desire perhaps plays a nonsecondary role in the *Ninfale*, where, unlike contemporary historiography, Boccaccio rejected a vision of national identity as coinciding with pure-bred Roman lineage.

Considered Boccaccio's most accomplished work before the *Decameron*, the *Ninfale* takes its pastoral setting and mimetic form from the classical bucolic models perfected in antiquity by Theocritus and Virgil and revived in Boccaccio's time by Dante and Petrarch. Boccaccio, however, further explored and renewed the genre. In the *Ninfale*, as in his first pastoral work, the prosimetrum of the *Comedia delle ninfe*, the bucolic setting maintains and further develops its function of "oblique exploration of the world," as Giuseppe Velli notes, in a poetic interrogation of the origins of civilization.[8] Unlike the *Comedia delle ninfe*, however, the *Ninfale* abandons medieval allegorization. The ostentatious erudition and Alexandrine plot complexity that had marked previous works such as the *Filocolo* also disappear in favor of a new linear syntax and simplified lexicon, contributing to an essential style that announces the prose of the *Decameron*. Furthermore, its linear narrative style where myth, legend, and history fuse in a poetic synthesis offers a model for the mythological fables of the Quattrocento.[9] These elements are perhaps the strongest arguments in favor of dating the *Ninfale* to not long before the *Decameron*, and of valuing it as Boccaccio's most successful literary enterprise before his masterpiece.[10]

Although presenting typical traits of the pastoral, the *Ninfale* resists a precise classification by including and transgressing pastoral, bucolic, etiological, and mythological genres.[11] The text blends them all and reflects in its composite literary language the theme of the origin of populations resulting from different races, perhaps also showing in its aesthetics a distant critical response to Petrarch's cultural purism. The geographical area delimited by the three rivers that flow from the hills of Fiesole to the Arno in Florence (Mugnone, Africo, and Mensola) is the true protagonist of the story. The tragic love of the nymph Mensola and the shepherd Africo serves the etymological and etiological narrative of the origins of the fluvial names and of the two rival cities of Fiesole and Florence. The historic-geographic theme provides continuity to the structure of the *Ninfale*, which emerges as a "political" poem narrating the birth of a civilization that—as in the biblical account of Creation—coincides with the naming of its objects.[12]

The poem unfolds in 473 octaves ideally divided into thirty-four episodes by rubrics.[13] It opens to four proemial stanzas, textured with Sicilian and stilnovistic topoi that reinterpret Dante's theme of Amor who "dictates within" (ditta dentro, *Purgatorio* 24.54). Love compels the author to write "a very ancient tale of love" (un'amorosa storia molto antica) to overcome the resistance of a "proud lady" (donna altera). The following 431 octaves illustrate the vicissitudes of Africo with one of Diana's nymphs, Mensola, centering on the protagonist's violent victory over her resistance.[14] Africo wins Mensola's soul with his words, as the author hopes will happen with his lady, but in a typical Boccaccian narrative reversal, it comes about only after the mythical rustic violates his nymph's body. The last 37 octaves are dedicated to the rise and fall of Fiesole and Florence, linked fictionally to the *gens* descended from Africo and Mensola. Thus the *poemetto*'s love story supports political implications that guarantee a homogeneous conceptual structure to the narrative.

In the woods of Fiesole, Africo falls in love with Mensola. His father, Girafone, warns him against the perils of seducing Diana's nymphs and tells him the tragic story of Mugnone, Africo's grandfather, and Cialla, both killed by the goddess. Untouched by Mugnone's example, Africo invokes Venus's assistance and pursues Mensola without success until, dressed in feminine clothes, he succeeds in deceiving the nymphs and eventually possessing Mensola.[15] Seduced by Africo's rhetoric, the girl returns his love and consents to a second intercourse, from which she conceives a child, Pruneo. Refusing to marry Africo even after voluntarily breaking her vows to Diana, Mensola breaches her promise to see him again and chooses to remain consecrated to the goddess. Desperate, Africo kills himself in a river that will take his name. Diana eventually discovers Mensola's disloyalty and transmutes her into water as she crosses a stream trying to flee from the goddess's vengeance. Africo's parents raise the child, Pruneo, who, after being educated at the court of King Atlas, becomes the first ruler of Fiesole, the city Atlas founded on the hills where the three rivers flow.[16] Centuries later the Romans destroy Fiesole and found Florence. The Fiesolans scatter in the countryside and in time mix with the Florentines until Totila razes the city to the ground and rebuilds Fiesole, binding those willing to return to an oath of unflinching enmity toward the Romans.[17] Refusing to inhabit the new barbarian Fiesole, the "African" people disperse again in the countryside. When Charlemagne eventually rebuilds Florence, Africo's descendants gradually return, intermix, and eventually assimilate with the Florentine people, contributing valuably to its glory and fame.

The mythological tale of Mensola's resistance and defiance is the generative nucleus of the etiological fable and provides the basis for interpreting the story of "African" lineage and its relation to Florence. This narrative revolves around two episodes of rape, the first prefiguring the second: that by Africo's grandfather Mugnone of the nymph Cialla, and Africo's of Mensola. These two episodes are connected through the kinship relation between Mugnone and Africo and the episodes' representation of the symbolic steps in the process that led from natural to political forms of associated life. While Cialla is a victim of violence, Mensola eventually returns Africo's love, though maintaining her radical refusal of marriage, an institution the *Ninfale* places at the root of civil life.[18]

Along the lines of a mythological rendition of historical facts, the poem implicitly affirms the special place literary invention may claim in reconstructing the truth of events whose reality has been transformed in and by collective memory. The mythological fable rooted in historical facts reveals that only the fictional reality of poetry where myth, legend, and history are conflated can reconstruct what is lost to collective memory and yet still live in the present.[19] As later in the *Genealogia deorum gentilium* (and the same pattern can be observed in the *De mulieribus claris* and the *De casibus virorum illustrium*), in the *Ninfale* Boccaccio historicizes myth and mythologizes history to present the origin of civilization as resulting from the admixture of different people — Etruscans, Romans, and "barbarians."[20] In this "myth of miscegenation," as Tobias Foster Gittes suggestively calls it, reconciliation of nations prevails over the stern defense of a Florentine purity of Roman lineage.[21] Yet Boccaccio does not create a purely irenic myth set in an allegorical landscape. The mythologized account of the historical birth of a nation follows the epic pattern of Roman historiography. As Rome was founded on the amalgam of Latins and Trojans, so is Florence mixed. In both cases the mix is the result not of a peaceful and harmonic encounter but rather of violent clashes, for the establishment of a new order always involves crisis, fracture, and disruption. The *Ninfale* thus presents more than a mythological reconstruction of the origins and nature of the Florentine people. Almost with a Lucretian-Epicurean sense of history, it offers a vision of historical progress as a dialectics between new and old forces ever struggling to achieve balance.[22] In this perspective, it illustrates how in any beginning the past opposes the new and lives on as a foreign body that the new tries to expel. This tension between new and old surfaces in the very landscape of the *Ninfale*, where nature is artificially metamorphosed and concretely embodies the signs of punishment of transgression.[23]

Unlike the *Comedia delle ninfe*, the *Ninfale* depicts an archaic society but not an idealized, Edenic, allegorized, atemporal age. Boccaccio describes the community of sparse family units such as that of Africo's parents (Girafone and Alimena) with realistic details of domestic life. Archaic and political worlds are not in opposition; rather, they show a degree of permeability that emphasizes their continuity. The balance of mythological and realistic elements stresses the dynamic interaction between historical truth and imaginative veil. Realism emerges particularly in the descriptions of places and actions, in the subtle psychological analysis of the characters, in Boccaccio's refined narrative use of the octave, and in the adoption of a middle style that creatively blends popular and classical accents while wedding stilnovistic musicality to the beat of the canterine tradition.[24]

Two main themes dominate in the poem: that of the "ubi pacta fides?"[25] related to Mensola's betrayal of Africo and Diana; and the theme of water metamorphoses, representing the dissolution of the "old" in a regenerated "new." The breach of the pacts is a necessary moment in the evolution of the story and symbolically relates to the conflicts that precede the passage to a new social order. Transgression is the force that upsets unstable equilibria and triggers this passage.[26] This force finds expression not just in the violence of rapes, wars, and destruction but also in the disruptive power of love: Africo lies, disobeys, feigns false appearances, and rapes; Mensola breaches all pacts.

Boccaccio adapts various myths of water—Ciane, Arethusa, Egeria, Apollo and Daphne, and Narcissus among the most significant—to the central role that transformation and admixture play in the *Ninfale*'s vision of history. A relevant and attested source is also Ovid's *Metamorphoses*, which underlies the myth of origin as a myth of "miscegenation."[27] The water metamorphoses are connected to the naming of the rivers and to the idea of change that lies at the heart of Boccaccio's vision of history. Girafone narrates the first one when Africo, to account for his lovesickness, claims there is a beautiful doe that eludes him. Girafone, understanding the true meaning behind his son's story, reminds him of Mugnone's tragic rape of Cialla:

> Quivi usò forza e quivi violenza,
> quivi la ninfa fu contaminata,
> quivi ella non potè far resistenza. (90.1–3)

Now he used force and violence. Now she could offer no resistance. Now he defiled the nymph.

Believing the nymph was consentient, Diana shoots a dart, piercing their hearts with a single arrow. The episode insists on the symbolic elements of blood and water, staging at the same time love and death, destruction and regeneration, in a new form. The traditional topos of *ars bellandi* (art of war) as a reflection of *ars amandi* (art of love), typical of medieval romance, is no longer mere aesthetic artifice. Rather, it becomes the central nucleus of the myth of racial assimilation in the poem. Mugnone, as later Africo, does not undergo metamorphosis: he dies spilling his blood into a river that later people will name after him, and his death parallels in a sort of *contrappunto* that of his nymph. Diana takes Cialla's body and carefully collects her blood so that it may not mix with that of Mugnone, and transforms her into a spring that flows parallel to the river.

The event prefigures the fate of Africo and Mensola and delineates a pattern that connects both episodes to the archetypal Apollonian chase and Daphnean escape. In Boccaccio's reinterpretation of the lover's chase (Daphne's metamorphosis saves her while Mensola's is a punishment) two dimensions coexist: the realistic succession of desire, chase, rape, and final death of the masculine protagonist; and the mythological metamorphosis of the female protagonist.

Like Mugnone, Africo sees Mensola sitting with her companions by a spring at the foot of Monte Ceceri. Immediately seduced by her beauty, Africo is torn between the fantasy of a legitimate union and the impulse of violence:

> E fra se stesso dicea: "Qual saria
> di me più grazioso e più felice,
> se tal fanciulla io avessi per mia
> isposa? Ché per certo il cor mi dice
> ch'al mondo sì contento uom non saria;
> e se non che paura mel disdice
> di Diana, i' l'arei per forza presa
> ché l'altre non potrebbon far difesa." (27.1–8)

Then he thought, "Who would ever be more favored or happier, than I had I that maiden for my wife? Truly, my heart tells me, there would be none in all the world. And if fear of Diana did not deter me, I would take her by force, for surely the other nymphs could not protect her."

This tension between the desire to win Mensola either with love or with violence remains a fundamental feature in the binary structure of the story. Prostrated by his failed attempts to approach the nymph, Africo decides to follow the counsel Venus gives him in a dream and disguises himself as a girl (Venus appears to Africo in two dreams), enters the circle of the nymphs, and wins Mensola's affection. The goddess urges him not to fear Mensola's resistance and almost incites Africo to take the nymph by force. Following her advice, Africo waits for the right moment to unveil himself and his love. The climactic scene occurs in the water. When the nymphs bathe naked in a small pond, Africo, forced to reveal himself, runs into the water after Mensola and, as the nymphs flee, violates her. Boccaccio describes the scene of the rape in a series of narrative octaves dense with erotic metaphors. Although the language rendering the sexual act is comic, the scene is realistically violent and intensely dramatic:

> Mensola, le parole non intende
> ch'Africo le dicea, ma quanto puote
> con quella forza ch'ell'ha si difende,
> e fortemente in qua e 'n là si scuote
> dalle braccia di colui che l'offende,
> bagnandosi di lagrime le gote;
> ma nulla le valea forza o difesa,
> ch'Africo la tenea pur forte presa. (243)

> Mensola could not understand the words Africo uttered, but she defended herself with all her strength as long as she was able. As her cheeks streamed with tears, she wrenched violently one way and then another against the arms that clutched her. But neither opposing nor resisting would avail her, for Africo still held her in his power.

Placed at the structural center of the poem (stanza 237 out of 473), the rape in the water is a turning point in the story, marking the limit of the parallelism between Mugnone and Africo. While in the first event the goddess mistakes the rape for a love encounter, here Diana is absent. While before Diana had kept the symbolic liquids of life—water and blood—separated after death, here they mix. Still, this is not yet a new beginning. Immediately afterward, with passionate rhetoric (the words Cupid dictates to him), Africo moves Mensola to return his love (249–77) and seduces her, confused and willing to die, into a second intercourse in a nearby thicket, from which she conceives Pruneo.

The two erotic episodes link in a unitary picture the elements that constitute the central myth of the *Ninfale*, that of the passage from old to new order, in which violence and rupture seem as necessary as union. Central in both is the metamorphosis and dissolution, sign of necessary penetration, of the female protagonist, which ideally prefigures the destiny of Pruneo's descendants before mixing with the Florentine lineage.[28]

It has been noted that the Ovidian myths of Ciane (*Metamorphoses* 5.409–37), Egeria (15.547–51), and Arethusa (5.572–641) might have provided models for Boccaccio, although in all these cases Diana intervenes to protect and not to punish her nymphs.[29] When the river Alpheus chases Arethusa (the name of Alfenide, the older among the nymphs chosen by Diana to rule in her absence, signals a reminiscence of this myth), Diana hides her in a cloud and then melts her into water. Although the context is different, there is an important common trait relevant to Mensola's myth: as Arethusa progressively liquefies, her waters mix with Alpheus's ("et se mihi misceat").[30]

Like Arethusa, Mensola first escapes but then accepts the union with her lover. Boccaccio stresses as "conversion" the moment of her physical solution into the natural element:

> La sventurata era già a mezzo l'acque,
> quand'ella i piè venir men si sentia,
> e quivi, sí come a Diana piacque,
> Mensola in acqua allor si convertia. (413.1–4)

> The wretched girl was already in mid-current when suddenly she felt her legs grow numb; and there, as it pleased Diana, she dissolved into the water.

Like Arethusa, Mensola loses her human form by melting down into the water. Unlike Arethusa's, however, her "spring" does not reemerge in a faraway place but rather assumes the concrete form of a child, who leads his people from mythological woods to political civilization.

The intimate coherence of the *Ninfale* appears evident when Boccaccio's mythography is considered.[31] In the etiological poem, myth does not simply develop from a primordial oral tradition of lost archetypes related to an origin so far away in time as to have become irrelevant to the construction of a new identity, and tragically looking backward. Rather, the narrative concerning gods and heroes is here a bridge from one *logos* to another, from myth to history and to poetry. The vicissitudes of Mugnone, Africo, Mensola, and Pruneo do not represent the aesthetic recovery of a lost golden age but take from the past motifs, themes, and structures that Boccaccio transforms and makes available for the present. If the essence of myth lies in the relation between sacred and origin, and if we follow the convincing idea that myth is a "function," a working of the human mind to deal with limits that every epoch needs to overcome in order to establish new ones, then Boccaccio's use of Ovidian myths in his account of the origin and identity of the Florentine people shows the emerging need to rewrite and create the new with the symbolic function of reconstructing the archetype of the "new": the new society, the new man, the new civilization.[32]

CHAPTER THIRTEEN

THE CHANGING LANDSCAPE
OF THE SELF • *(Buccolicum carmen)*

David Lummus

The *Buccolicum carmen*, the single major poetic work in Latin by Boccaccio, is arguably also the most ambitious poetic work in his corpus.[1]
Boccaccio himself seems to claim as much in the *Genealogia deorum gentilium*
when he defends the opinion that poets often hide meanings beneath the
veil of stories, citing himself along with Virgil, Dante, and Petrarch.[2] Petrarch's pastoral poem, he tells us, gives readers more than enough evidence
in its *gravitas* and exquisite elegance to deduce that the fantastical names of
the characters have allegorical meanings in consonance with the moral philosophy of his *De vita solitaria* and other writings. With typical understatement, Boccaccio mentions that he could also offer as evidence of a philosophical poetry his own *Buccolicum carmen*, but that he is not yet important
enough to be considered among such a distinguished crowd; besides, it is
proper to leave the commentary on one's own works to others. Despite the
apparent modesty of Boccaccio's self-mention, the parallel with Petrarch
places him among the ranks of the modern philosophical poets descended
from Virgil. Perhaps it is even an invitation to his contemporaries to write
a commentary on his poem, such as those Servius and Nicholas of Trevet
had written on Virgil's *Bucolica* and those on Petrarch's *Buccolicum carmen* by
Donato degli Albanzani, Benvenuto da Imola, and Francesco Piendibeni da
Montepulciano.[3]

Such commentaries on Boccaccio's *Buccolicum carmen*, however, were
never written, and in the history of criticism on the pastoral, Boccaccio's
poetry remains a footnote to Petrarch's better-known endeavor to revive
the bucolic genre. Composed between 1346 and 1367,[4] the story recounted
by the *Buccolicum carmen* follows Boccaccio's life from his initial infatuation
with love poetry to the political, ethical, and theological issues of his later
life. It may seem at first glance that Boccaccio restructures the arc of his life
to coincide with the ideal of the Christian conversion story, familiar from

Paul, Augustine, and Dante, among others, since the subject of the poem turns away from love and worldly affairs toward concern for the fate of the soul.[5]

In a letter to the Augustinian friar Martino da Signa, written sometime between 1372 and 1374, Boccaccio explained the work's place in the history of pastoral and addressed the allegorical significance of the titles and character names of most of the sixteen hexameter poems that comprise the work.[6] The letter contains a short definition of the bucolic genre meant to situate Boccaccio's work chronologically and ideologically. He begins with a brief mention of Theocritus, who invented the bucolic style (according to Boccaccio), and who did not write allegorically charged poetry (*nil sensit*); then Virgil used the pastoral mode to communicate *some* hidden meanings but did not always (*non semper*) do so.[7] Although Boccaccio was certainly aware of late antique and medieval examples of the pastoral, he skips over them, saying that between Virgil and Petrarch only unimportant writers tried their hands at the genre.[8] Petrarch followed Virgil by ennobling (*sublimavit*) the humble bucolic style to the status of epic. Unlike Virgil, Petrarch always (*continue*) allegorized the names of the pastoral characters.[9]

In the history of the bucolic genre thus far traced, Boccaccio presents his reader with three adverbial alternatives for understanding the meanings intended by the author: *nil*, *non semper*, and *continue*. Boccaccio's own poetry, he goes on to explain, follows the Virgilian alternative, since some of the names of the interlocutors in his poems have no meaning whatsoever.[10] Thus, Boccaccio aligns himself with Virgil in this history and distances himself from Petrarch.[11] Boccaccio claims to engage directly with the poetics of Virgil's pastoral work, the *Bucolica*, which was thought to be more humble in style and aspiration than his later epic poem, the *Aeneid*. In this he could even be seen as establishing a humanistic poetics in direct competition with that of the Aretine poet, as the modern successor of Virgil. If Petrarch's *Africa* was a modern *Aeneid*, and his twelve-book *Bucolicum carmen* sought to sublimate the bucolic to the heights of epic, then Boccaccio situates his own pastoral work as the modern-day standard-bearer of the ancient *modus humilis*.[12]

After a summary of the sixteen poems that make up this work, an overarching narrative of transformation can be seen to emerge, a narrative that unites the Boccaccian corpus and lays proud claim to the low style of the bucolic genre. With the *Buccolicum carmen* Boccaccio shows himself to be a master of classical poetry, of Latin style, and of heuristic imitation, as he negotiates influences as far afield as Dante, Virgil, Petrarch, Ovid, and others. As an allegorical narrative the work succeeds in reconciling the eclectic diversity of Boccaccio's literary and political career within a landscape of transformation and self-discovery.

The first eclogue, entitled *Galla*, takes up where Virgil's tenth eclogue left off; that consolation for the love pangs of Cornelius Gallus turns into a pseudo-autobiographical consolation of the poet's own love pangs. In an elegiac dialogue between the shepherds Damon (Boccaccio) and Tindarus, the former laments the betrayal of his beloved nymph Galla, whom he compares in beauty to Galatea. As Damon, in despair, invokes death, Tindarus invites him—in Virgilian fashion—into his cave to rest, tell his story, and lighten his mind.[13] Despite Tindarus's efforts to pull Damon back from despair, the latter concludes pessimistically that love is savage and ruins the minds of the young.

The second eclogue, *Pampinea*, is Palemon's soliloquy, as retold by Melampus, of his hopeless love for the nymph Pampinea, who abandoned him for the shepherd Glaucus. Palemon compares his love experience to those of Jupiter, Phoebus, and Argus, but also to that of Corydon for Alexis recounted in Virgil's second eclogue, which Boccaccio's eclogue echoes throughout.[14] Yet instead of Virgil, Palemon (presumably Boccaccio's pastoral double) claims that it was Nasilus (a thinly veiled Ovidius *Naso*) who taught him. By the end he begs for death, imploring the forest oaks to fall down on him.

The next seven eclogues are more or less thinly veiled allegories for key political events between 1347 and 1355 and were presumably influenced by the obscure political allegories of Petrarch's own bucolic poems.[15] The third eclogue, *Faunus*, is a revised version of an autobiographical poem (the third of his *Carmina*) written in 1348 to Boccaccio's friend in Forlì, Checco di Meletto Rossi, and modeled primarily on the second of Petrarch's eclogues, *Argus*.[16] Palemon and Pamphylus listen to Meris sing of recent events in Naples and mourn the death of King Robert of Anjou. The third eclogue concludes with Palemon's negation of the idyllic landscape, which, he says, is better suited to old men, and his decision to follow Faunus, a mask for Francesco Ordelaffi of Forlì, to the aid of Naples during the Hungarian invasion.

The dark fourth eclogue, *Dorus* ("Bitterness"), also refers to events surrounding the Hungarian invasion of Naples. It opens with the hemistich "Quo te, Dorus, rapis?" (Where are you rushing, Dorus?), based on the incipit of Virgil's shadowy ninth eclogue, whose pessimism it captures throughout with its insistence on dispossession and defeat.[17] This invective-style dialogue takes place between Dorus, a mask for King Louis of Sicily; Montanus, later identified as "any inhabitant of Volterra"; and Phytias, the

Grand Seneschal of Naples Niccola Acciaiuoli. Dorus laments to the hospitable Volterran about the terrible chaotic state of the Kingdom of Naples following the death of King Robert (Argus) and of his own forced flight from the kingdom, while Phytias plays the calm adviser.

Vittore Branca has pointed out that the invective of the fourth eclogue turns into the elegy of the fifth, *Silva cadens* ("Falling Forest"), and the paean of the sixth, *Alcestus*.[18] In the fifth, for the most part a monologue on the negative state of Naples after the flight of King Louis, Boccaccio opens with an echo of the *incipit* to Virgil's first eclogue.[19] The sixth, *Alcestus*, is a song of triumph about Alcestus's (i.e., King Louis's) return from Provence to Naples with his court.

The seventh, eighth, and ninth eclogues turn to the subject of Florentine politics and become progressively more negative. The seventh, *Iurgium* ("Quarrel"), is an allegory for the difficult relations between Emperor Charles IV and Florence (Daphnis and Florida). The eighth, *Midas*, should be read as the poem that connects the series on Naples with this series on Florence. It is a political allegory about Niccola Acciaiuoli (who was Phytias in the third eclogue), under the pastoral disguise of Midas, the famously greedy king of Phrygia. The dialogue between the unidentified shepherds, Phytias (presumably Boccaccio) and Damon (perhaps fellow humanist Barbato da Sulmona), recounts Phytias's anger at the greedy man and Damon's efforts to calm his rage.[20] The ninth, *Lipis* ("Anxiety"), in many ways a continuation of the seventh, recounts the dialogue between a wayfarer (Archas) and a personification of the Florentine character (Batracos, from the Greek for "frog"). Like the seventh, it highlights the poet's distrust of emperors and his biting representation of the Florentine demeanor.

Excluding the final eclogue, which is the envoy and dedication of the previous fifteen eclogues to Donato degli Albanzani and appropriately entitled *Aggelos* ("Messenger"), the remaining poems leave aside specific political concerns for simultaneously more personal and more cosmic subjects. The tenth, *Vallis opaca* ("Dark Valley"), recounts the moral and political dissolution of the pastoral universe, while the eleventh, *Pantheon*, follows loosely the matter of Virgil's sixth eclogue, in which the drunken Silenus sings myths about the creation of the universe, by using the pastoral frame for Glaucus's (Saint Peter's) song about biblical history to Mirtilis (the church), a song divided between the Old and the New Testament.[21]

In the twelfth and thirteenth eclogues, poetry is the subject. In the former, entitled *Saphos* for the Lesbian poet, Boccaccio stages himself as Aristeus, caught by the muse Caliopes in the laurel grove before he is ready. The muse sends him to Silvanus (Petrarch) for help in ascending the peak.

In the latter, *Laurea*, Boccaccio stages a singing contest between a merchant (Stilbon) and a poet (Daphnis) over the merits of their respective vocations. The shepherd Critis is asked to judge between them, but they conclude in a draw.[22] The fourteenth eclogue, *Olympia*, recounts a dream-like encounter of Silvius (Boccaccio) with Olympia (his deceased five-year-old daughter, Violante). Olympia sings a song of heavenly revelation that outdoes all the classical poets (Orpheus, Calliope, Virgil, and Homer). Finally in the fifteenth eclogue, *Phylostropos*, Boccaccio figures a conversation between himself (Typhlus, a blind shepherd and everyman figure) and Petrarch (Phylostropos, glossed by the author as "conversion to love"). In it Typhlus is gradually convinced by Phylostropos that he should abandon his current domain of worldly pleasure for a forest ruled over by God.[23]

With these eclogues the focus of the *Buccolicum carmen* turns back toward the self, but this time within a pastoral landscape of much greater depth. Boccaccio's professed engagement with a Virgilian model seems to have been contaminated by Petrarch's more "sublime" allegorical bucolic mode. The caves, woods, fields, and mountains have taken on a cosmic and theological meaning yet are still related to the pastoral landscape of the earlier poems, both amorous and political. It should be clear enough from these quick summaries that the shift in concern in the *Buccolicum carmen* is one of depth of form, not one of substance.

When Boccaccio claimed to have followed Virgil's bucolic model, he meant that he would not transplant into the humble pastoral universe the high allegorical meanings that belong to epic. Petrarch had included twelve eclogues in his own *Bucolicum carmen*, an epic number.[24] From where, then, does Boccaccio's choice of sixteen derive? Perhaps the "fifteen ewes" he dedicates to Donato degli Albanzani recall the fifteen books of Ovid's *Metamorphoses* and that etiological epic's engagement with the pastoral genre.[25] Palemon, masking the young Boccaccio, did say in *Pampinea* that his master was Nasilus (2.86). If the *Metamorphoses* does represent a model for the structure of Boccaccio's bucolic endeavor, then the *Buccolicum carmen* must tell a story of transformation. With this in mind, one might say that the narrative follows the Pythagorean principle that concludes Ovid's epic: "And, as the pliant wax is stamped with new designs, does not remain as it was before nor preserve the same form, but is still the selfsame wax, so do I teach that the soul is ever the same, though it passes into ever-changing bodies."[26] The bodily forms and worldly concerns represented by the pastoral characters and landscape take on different, more profound meanings across the fifteen poems, but the spirit of the author remains the same.

This is to say that Boccaccio's cares remain consistently within the valleys and forests of the material world and are mapped onto the pastoral landscape as if it were an ever-changing yet continuous topological space. The Edenic mountains and green pastures of the highlands remain inaccessible to him, whether they are the fertile fields beneath Vesuvius or the green wood ruled over by God. He never leaves behind the valleys of care completely, even though he eventually separates them from more perfect, unreachable *loca amoena*, and thereby dispossesses them of any illusory salvific power. The ambiguity of the pastoral landscape, with its liminal position between history and imagination, provides the perfect theater for Boccaccio to reflect on his literary, political, and theological selves and to seek out the point where they converge.

That the matter of the *Buccolicum carmen* is narrated by its very landscape is hinted at in the opening lines to the first eclogue, when Damon, the embittered lover, addresses Tindarus with this question:

> Tindare, non satius fuerat nunc arva Vesevi
> et Gauri silvas tenera iam fronde virentes
> incolere ac gratos gregibus deducere rivos
> quam steriles Arni frusta discurrere campos? (1.1–4)

> Tindarus, would it not have been better / to inhabit now the green fields of Vesuvius / and tender leafing woods of Gaurus Mountain / and draw down streams so pleasing to the flocks, / than vainly roam the Arno's sterile plains?

The historical references to the geography of Boccaccio's life are clear,[27] but Tindarus's answer explains to some extent the figurative meaning of the landscape, set in opposition to a more removed, carefree world:

> quantum sibi quisque beavit
> qui potuit mentis rabidos sedare tumores
> et parvas habitare casas, nemora atque remota! (1.8–10)

> Happy is he who has been able / to calm the rabid swellings of the mind / and dwell in humble huts and groves remote!

The traditional *locus amoenus* is beyond the scope of this work's landscape.[28] Instead, Boccaccio's shepherds inhabit an imperfect world in exile from the ideal, as Tindarus laments (1.1): "Quod nequeam, dure de me voluere sorores" (That I cannot be such a man as this / the cruel sisters willed for me).

The pastoral world into which Boccaccio introduces his readers is a world of care and fatigue, a hostile world. Far from the ideal *locus amoenus*, Boccaccio's shepherds offer repose to one another within their dwellings according to the ethics of friendship that rules the Virgilian Arcadia.[29]

On the shady shores of the Arno, Palemon, lamenting the loss of his beloved in the second eclogue, juxtaposes his own state of affairs with that of the surrounding wood:

> Nunc tacet omne nemus, subeunt vineta cicade,
> omne pecus radios cessat, cantare volucres
> desistunt et colla boum disiungit arator
> fessus et umbrosos querit per rura recessus:
> me miserum male sanus Amor per devia solum
> distrahit et longos cogit sine mente labores
> ut subeam victusque sequar vestigia nondum
> cognita Pampinee. (2.5–12)

> Now all the wood is hushed; the crickets hide / among the vines; the herd yields to the rays; / the birds have ceased to sing; the weary plowman / unyokes the oxen's necks and seeks the shade. / Yet I alone am driven by mad love / through wandering ways, insanely to endure / long labors, wretched victim, and to follow / my Pampinea's as yet unfound footprints.

Here as in the previous eclogue, the original *loca amoena* have been changed into landscapes of care (*labor*) by the false promises of earthly desire. The first two eclogues are songs of vituperation and lament, and at the end of the second, Palemon wishes for the collapse of the landscape in pity for his state of anguish:

> O veteres quercus, ylex annosa nemusque
> perpetuum, voces miseri Palemonis amaras
> suscipite et morte hos agile mollite dolores!
> . . . .
> Si qua igitur vobis pietas sub cortice duro est,
> irruite et grandi misero sub pondere mortem
> ferte, precor. (2.123–25, 128–30)

> O ancient oaks, o ilex full of years, / eternal forests, hear the bitter words / of wretched Palemon: soften these pains / with death! /. . . . /

If you, therefore, / have any pity under that hard bark, / fall down
on me and bring death to a wretch / beneath your mighty weight,
I pray.

For the lover in pain, the only comfort that the landscape of the *locus amoenus* can offer is its own collapse and the destruction of the memories that it
holds on its hard bark, on which Palemon and his beloved Pampinea had
once carved signs of love:

> Sed tu que dulcia falce,
> dum tibi solus eram, signabas cortice fagi
> furta. (2.140–42)

> But you who with your blade / cut signs of sweet thefts in the
> beechtree bark / while I alone was yours.[30]

These first two eclogues set the stage for the landscape of the rest of
the work, in which the hills and vales of the pastoral are far from the ideal
locus amoenus and are continually shaded by the cares and concerns of an
engaged poet. Even though unrequited love will no longer be the subject
of that engagement, Boccaccio will superimpose the collapsing forests and
burnt fields of these two poems on the political worlds, the personal anguish, and the theological concerns of an ever more complicated reality,
becoming more and more attracted by the removed, evergreen forests and
paradisiacal mountaintops that reside on its edges.[31]

Nevertheless, he never abandons the earthly concerns—both public and
private—that make the whole forest tremble and shake. The initial verses
of the third eclogue juxtapose the quiet of the shepherds' world and the
forest's eruption with political unrest. The landscape of love becomes the
landscape of politics:

> Tempus erat placidum; pastores ludus habebat
> aut somnus lenis; paste sub quercubus altis
> ac pastulis passim recubabant lacte petulcis
> ubera prebentes natis distenta capelle;
> ast ego serta michi pulchro distinguere acantho
> querebam, servanda tamen dum fistula gratos
> nostra ciet versus Mopso, cui tempora dignis
> nectere concessum, lauro et vincire capillos;
> ocia cum subito rupit vox improba meste
> Testilis. (3.13–21)

The day was clear; the shepherds played or slumbered. / Beneath the tall and spreading oaks, the shegoats / well-fed lay here and there, now offering / milk-swollen udders to their butting young. / But I was picking garlands of acanthus, / to be preserved as long as my reed utters / verses pleasing to Mopsus, who with laurel / has had his temples bound and locks entwined / by worthy men; when suddenly sad Testilis' / persistent voice broke in upon our leisure.

The idle pleasures of the *locus amoenus* in which the poet writes his verses are denied by a political unrest that will eventually threaten the forest with collapse. In *Silva cadens*, the woods and "flowering countryside" of Sicily are juxtaposed to the wood that metaphorically represents the city of Naples and its ruin:

> Iam tacte fulmine pinus,
> et pecudes prostrasse canes noctisque per umbram
> ex septis ululare lupos audisse, nefandum
> prodigium dederant. (5.13–16)

Already have the pines been struck by lightning, / the dogs have killed the sheep, and through night's shadows / I heard wolves howling from the folds; all these / had given horrid omen.

The pastoral landscape's destruction recalls more than just the political exile and dispossession of the king; it evokes a decadent moral state as well. As Caliopus declares at the end of his monologue, "Omne decus periit luctusque laborque supersunt" (All beauty here has perished, / but grief and care remain, 5.115). The aesthetic ideal of the pastoral landscape comports with an ethical ideal as well. As the *locus amoenus* is transformed into a *locus horridus*, the inhabitants of the ancient wood turn their world into a kind of hell.[32]

The ruin turns out here to be only a temporary threat, since the next eclogue, *Alcestus*, begins with the restoration of bucolic idleness in the *locus amoenus*.[33] In the three Florentine eclogues that follow, Boccaccio largely leaves aside the attention to landscape that is so present in the first six eclogues. The shift in structure and the increasingly moralizing tone suggest that he may be taking Petrarch's political eclogues as a model at this point.[34] The landscape returns to prominent titular position, however, in the tenth eclogue, *Vallis opaca*, where the falling forest is transformed into the "dark valley" of hell itself.

This tenth eclogue is one of the most difficult to decipher.[35] It is the conversation between a once-great tyrant (Lycidas) and a shepherd confined to imprisonment in a cave (Dorilus), but Boccaccio gives no hint of its historical referents. Thomas Hubbard has described it as a "macabre takeoff on Virgil's poems of political dispossession," *Eclogues* 1 and 9.[36] Given the Dantean allusion in the title, it is more likely, however, that this eclogue signals a move away from the Virgilian landscape of political disenchantment of *Silva cadens* to a more morally charged landscape of disenchantment with the worldly affairs (love and now politics) that are allegorically bound to the pastoral's *locus amoenus*. In it Dorilus laments:

> Iuppiter a celso prospectans cardine campos
> prostravit feriens ignito fulmine fagum
> his celebrem silvis: sonitu perterrita tellus
> ingemuit, tremuere greges ac arbuta dumis.
> Pastores sese comperta fraude vicissim
> in caveis clausere malis. (10.6–11)

> Great Jupiter from high on heaven's pole / has flattened the fields, with fiery thunderbolt / striking a beech tree famous in these woods. / In terror at the sound, earth groaned, the flocks / and leaves all trembled mid the briars; in turn / the shepherds shut themselves in, with fraud disclosed, / in evil caves.

The ethics of care on which the values of Arcadia are founded has become so debased that the threat of hell is imminent. Lycidas, the soul of a tyrant, visits Dorilus in order to warn him of such an infernal landscape and to console him with a presage of future pastures restored: "teque tuis linquet campis: sic vincula solves" (and he / will leave you in your fields, your chains thus loosed, 10.171). With this eclogue, Boccaccio's political anxieties have turned into deeper ethical preoccupations that are quickly becoming theological. The fallen forests and the valleys of *labor* to which his shepherds were condemned in earlier eclogues risk becoming the dark valleys and forests of the *Inferno*. This infernal eclogue ends with a prayer by Dorilus:

> Numen honoratum silvis, Pan, te precor, assis,
> et veniat lux illa michi: tibi pinguior agnus
> ex grege quippe tuas ultro ferietur ad aras
> quas statuam, ludosque traham tibi carmine sacros. (10.172–75)

> Divinity long honored by the forests, / O Pan, I pray, be present, let that day /

come to me: from the flock a fatter lamb / you may be sure will
gladly be struck down /
upon the altars which I'll raise to you, / and I'll prolong your sacred
games with song.

By now Pan, the god of the wood, clearly refers to the Christian God, and
the landscape across which Palemon swore to seek out Pampinea in the
second eclogue has become an allegory for the created world.[37] Thus in
Pantheon, the eleventh eclogue, when Glaucus recounts the history of creation, the landscape of a restored pastoral order has come to resemble the
order restored to history by revelation. Christ is the ideal shepherd, whose
"labores . . . cunctis voluit prodesse creates" (labors were meant to help all
creatures, 11.36–37).

The scale of the two eclogues that follow is less grandiose, yet the landscape continues to adapt itself to Boccaccio's purposes, especially in *Saphos*,
where the *nemus*, or "wood," is specifically a laurel grove. Aristeus (Boccaccio) sacrilegiously invades the sacred grove in search of Saphos, who
signifies the laurel crown of poetry and whom only the poet Silvanus (Petrarch) has earned the right to see. Aristeus is informed of the mysterious
nymph's remote whereabouts when he is stopped by Caliopes, guardian of
the grove:

Panis nata dei celsum tenet optima Nyse
Saphos, gorgonei residens in margine fontis. (12.100–101)

Pan's dearest daughter, Saphos, stays upon / the heights of Nysa,
dwelling by the brim / of the gorgonean spring.

When he asks the easiest way to reach Saphos, Caliopes informs him that
the landscape prohibits an easy ascent:

Turbavere quidem vestigia longa viarum
et nemorum veteres rami cautesque revulsi,
implicite sentes pulvisque per ethera vectus;
velleris atque fames et grandis cura peculi
neglexit latos montis per secula calles.
Hinc actum ut, scrobibus visis, in terga redirent
iam plures peterentque suos per pascua fines. (12.176–82)

Old branches of the woods and fallen rocks / and tangled briars
and the wind-blown dust / have marred the lengthy traces of the

paths; / and greed for fleeces and the great concern / for wealth have caused the wide paths of the mountain / to be neglected now for centuries. / Hence it has come about that many men, / seeing the gulleys, have turned back already / and sought their object in the pasturelands.

Only the high poetry of Silvanus-Petrarch has granted a modern man access to the inaccessible peak, so the muse advises Aristeus-Boccaccio to approach him in order to find out what friends and what paths he used in order to reach it. In the meantime, however, Boccaccio must be among those who seek out their glory in the pasturelands. Finally, from the valley of hell to the garden of creation, Boccaccio's gaze meets again the mountains that were denied the shepherds at the beginning of the first eclogue, and that have now metamorphosed into Parnassus, the sacred mountain of the Muses.

In the fourteenth and fifteenth eclogues, the inaccessible places of the pastoral landscape mutate once more, this time into the mountains of salvation and terrestrial paradise. In *Olympia* the sylvan landscape is invaded temporarily by the supernatural appearance of the deceased young daughter of Silvius (Boccaccio). Unnatural lights, scents, and sounds fill the forest before her appearance, transforming it into the aromatic forests of Sheba. Upon seeing her, Silvius remembers the circumstances of her death (14.52–53), "calcidicos colles et pascua lata Vesevi / dum petii" (while I sought / Chalcidian hills and the wide pasturelands of Mount Vesuvius), the same fertile landscape denied to the shepherds in the first eclogue.[38] She predicts that Silvius will one day ascend to Elysium, which is situated on a distant mountain that

> Est in secessu pecori mons invius egro
> . . . .
>   cui vertice summo
> silva sedet palmas tollens ad sydera celsas
> et letas pariter lauros cedrosque perennes,
> Palladis. (14.171, 173–76)

is impassable to sickly sheep . . . upon whose peak a forest raises tall palms to the stars / and happy laurels too and longlived cedars / and Pallas' olives.

Here and in the lines that follow, Olympia is describing paradise in pastoral terms as a new forest that will replace that of earthly tribulations. This description of an otherworldly forest does not, however, push Boccaccio's concern away from the world at hand. In fact, Olympia's last words of advice for finding the way and wings to enter the mountain paradise indicate that Silvius should continue to take care of his world and its inhabitants:

Pasce famem fratris, lactis da pocula fessis,
assis detentis et nudos contege, lapsos
erige, dum possis, pateatque forensibus antrum. (14.275–77)

Feed your brother's hunger, to the weary / offer cups of milk, visit the prisoner, / clothe the naked; when you can, raise up / the fallen, let the entrance of your cave / be open to all.

Her words blend the cares of the pastor with the acts of mercy, superimposing Christian ethics on the rules of hospitality from Virgil's Arcadia; they reinforce the poet's dedication to and care for the world of history.[39]

Similarly, in the fifteenth eclogue, Phylostropos (Petrarch) describes another perfect *locus amoenus* beyond the confines of human history:

Surgit silva virens celi sub cardine levo,
aspera dumetis et saxo infixa rubenti. (15.156–57)

A green wood rises under the left pole / of heaven, rough with thickets and infixed / with ruddy stone.

Although Typhlus recognizes his desire to reach this new wood and to leave behind his worldly forest of nymphs and satyrs that is destined to turn cold and hostile, he is frightened, weak, and prone to quit before he even begins. In the end he promises to follow Phylostropos and to leave his earthly, decadent wood where Crisis (Gold) and Dyon (Desire) rule, but the end of the journey is relegated to the future, to the unknown:

Urgeor, insistam; tu primus summito callem
. . . .
imus ut ex syrio carpamus litore palmas. (15.219, 221)

I will press on; I'll enter on the journey; / but you go first; . . . / . . . we go in order / that we may pluck palms from the Syrian shore.

The promise that Typhlus-Boccaccio makes to Phylostropos-Petrarch at the end of the fifteenth eclogue is never completely fulfilled by Boccaccio within the poem.[40] The high places that Petrarch's presence in the *Buccolicum carmen* represents are not the ending place of its journey; they remain always on its edges. In the course of the narrative of Boccaccio's bucolic poem, the erotic is transformed into the political, which is in turn transformed into the moral and spiritual. A closed set in constant reformation, the landscape remains a place of care and sometimes of grief; it never transforms itself into a completely removed place of leisure or salvation. Boccaccio's work is continually in dialogue with the world of care, even up to the final envoy of the poem, *Aggelos* ("Messenger"), which describes him as having nothing else to do but

> patrios ni spectet in agros
> . . . .
> torpendum est igitur seu vomere vertere glebas. (16.72, 74)

> look after his paternal fields / . . . / he must be idle or else plow the soil.

Differently from Petrarch, whose poetic ambitions take him first to the mountain of the Muses and then to the mountain of salvation, Boccaccio's poetry keeps to the world at hand. In poverty, the poet is content with small things and basks in the freedom offered in creation by the generosity of God:

> paucis contentor munere Panis.
> Silvestres corili pascunt, dat pocula rivus,
> dant quercus umbras, dant somnos aggere frondes,
> cetera si desint, lapposaque vellera tegmen
> corporis effeti; quibus insita dulcis et ingens
> libertas, que, sera tamen, respexit inertem. (16.133–38)

> I am content with little. By Pan's gift / the sylvan ivyberries offer food, / the stream gives drinks, the oaks give cooling shade, / a heap of leaves gives rest, if other things / are lacking, and a burr-infested fleece / offers a cover for my weakened body. / To these is added sweet, great liberty, / which, although late, has looked at last upon / an artless man.

When, in his letter to Fra Martino, Boccaccio contrasts his own approach to the bucolic genre with that of Petrarch and simultaneously insinuates that they are equal heirs to antiquity, he is establishing the terms for his own, more modest posterity. The closing words of the final eclogue express the hope that his own version of the humanist enterprise of interpreting, rewriting, and reinventing the themes and language of classical literature, as voiced in the *Buccolicum carmen*, might live on in the future. They even suggest that the fragility of his work might be the sign of its fertility:

> Claudicet esto,
> nam pregnans video, prolem sperasse iuvabit
> et cepisse novam. Surgunt ex montibus altis
> sydera; sis mecum. Nostro hoc tu iungito, Solon. (16.141–44)

Perhaps that ewe is limping now because, / as I perceive, she's pregnant; I'll enjoy / having awaited offspring and then gotten / a newborn. From the high peaks stars are rising; stay with me. Solon, join this flock with ours.

Alluding simultaneously to the appearance of the morning star (*Lucifer*) at the end of book 2 of the *Aeneid*, as Aeneas flees with his father and son from a besieged Troy, and to the rising of the evening star (*Hesperus*) in the final verses of Virgil's *Bucolica*,[41] Boccaccio leaves the *Buccolicum carmen* an open-ended work. The motif of epic rebirth mixes with the bucolic conclusion to the day, granting it the tenuous possibility of a future in the hands of another shepherd. With the prospect of the birth of the new from the old, the final transformation of the poem—the metamorphosis of the self into the work of art—coincides with the ascent of the stars from behind the mountain peaks in the distance. Boccaccio entrusts his work to the world and finally lifts his gaze from the tribulations of the earth.

PART VI

WOMAN AND WOMEN

CHAPTER FOURTEEN

AN EXPERIMENT IN THE HEALING POWER OF LITERATURE • *(Elegia di madonna Fiammetta)*

Annelise M. Brody

Although its exact date is unknown, Boccaccio composed the *Elegia di madonna Fiammetta* (*The Elegy of Lady Fiammetta*) before the *Decameron*, most likely between 1343 and 1344.[1] Thus it is of a piece with other works written in the years leading up to the *Decameron* and developing themes that will find their way into the masterpiece, in the case of the *Elegia* the power of literature to heal the wounds of love and ultimately the inadequacy of certain models — those of classical literature and courtly love — to attain this goal. In addition, as Boccaccio moves away from his early classical settings, he also seems to point out that a possible solution for mitigating the pangs of love might lie in the values of Christianity. These values include compassion and the choice through free will of a more perfect form of love than "amore per diletto" (love for the sake of pleasure).[2]

Fiammetta tells her own story, a simple one. A Neapolitan lady blessed by the good fortune of possessing both wealth and beauty, she falls in love with a handsome young man whom she calls Panfilo. Despite her supposedly happy marriage and against the wise counsel of her nurse, she decides to yield to her ardent passion and become Panfilo's mistress (chap. 1). The pair enjoys some happy time together, but eventually Panfilo grows tired of her and decides to leave Naples with the excuse that his old, sick father has summoned him home to Florence. Panfilo promises the dismayed Fiammetta that he will return in four months (chap. 2). Fiammetta, believing his words, prepares herself for his long absence; when thinking his return near, she readies herself to embrace him again (chap. 3). Predictably, he fails to appear, leaving Fiammetta to conjecture what might have become of him. She finally admits, realistically, that since everything in this world is subject to change, Panfilo has most likely now fallen in love with another lady (chap. 4). In addition to her continuous self-deception, she also receives the dismal news that Panfilo is now married. The tearful reaction of another woman who overhears this announcement indicates that Fiammetta was not the only recipient of Panfilo's love during his stay in Naples. Full of despair, Fiammetta prays in vain to Venus and God to restore her lover to her. Her husband, worried by her unhealthy state, tries all possible remedies; but neither medicine nor a vacation seems to work any effect. Moreover, her lost beauty and very chaste way of dressing indicate to most people (ironically) her new devotion to God (chap. 5). Eventually Fiammetta receives more news of her recalcitrant lover: although he did not marry, he has indeed found a new lover (chap. 6). Erroneous news of Panfilo's return brings Fiammetta new joy, but when she learns it is the wrong Panfilo, she relapses into her previously wretched state (chap. 7). Finally, comparing herself to women of antiquity and stating the superiority of her pain to theirs, Fiammetta sends forth her book, dressed in "vile clothes," among women (chaps. 7, 8, 9).

Because of its modernity, this "novel,"[3] written in the first person with a female narrator, has stirred lively critical debate. The camouflage of the author behind a female narrative voice, although with literary antecedent in Ovid's *Heroides*, motivated some early critics to conjure an autobiographical interpretation.[4] This was challenged and dismissed in later years by Vittore Branca,[5] while more recently critics have pursued the idea of the *Elegia* as a psychological novel, applying a Freudian reading.[6] More radically of late there has been a tendency toward a feminist reading of the *Elegia*,[7] although this has been challenged by the analyses of Victoria Kirkham.[8] As a response to the feminist debate, Michael Calabrese's critique brings into the light the questions of the impossibility of female expression of desire and the unconscious internalization of man-made sexual culture in the medieval woman.[9] From a stylistic perspective, critics have highlighted the *Elegia*'s innovative aspects with respect to both medieval and classical referents, seeing this experiment as the fruit of an ongoing literary engagement with Dante's *Vita nuova*, Ovid's *Heroides*, and Seneca's *Phaedra*.[10]

As the title announces, Boccaccio wrote his *Elegia* in neither the high style of tragedy nor the low style of comedy, but in the median, elegiac style. The narrator-protagonist, a lady fictitiously named Fiammetta in the courtly tradition of the *senhal* (poetic "sign" or code name), calls herself "wretched" (*misera*). This is a key term for linking her account to a famous passage in Dante's *De vulgari eloquentia*, where he distinguishes in a hierarchical way the three genres of the literary tradition: tragedy, comedy, and elegy. Of elegy he states:

Then, when dealing with the various subjects that are suitable for poetry, we must know to choose whether to treat them in tragic, comic, or elegiac style. By "tragic" I mean the higher style, by "comic" the lower and by "elegiac" that of the unhappy. If it seems appropriate to use the tragic style, then the illustrious vernacular must be employed, and so you will need to bind together a *canzone*. If, on the other hand, the comic style is called for, then sometimes the middle level of the vernacular can be used and sometimes the lowly: and I shall explain the distinction in Book Four. If, though, you are writing elegy, you must only use the lowly.[11]

Luigi Surdich writes, "The elegy speaks of a state of the soul and not of human actions,"[12] which is true of Fiammetta as she begins her book of love sorrows: "Unhappy people customarily take greater pleasure in lamenting their lot when they see or hear that someone else feels compassion for them. Therefore, since I am more eager to complain than any other woman, to make certain that the cause of my grief will not grow weaker through habit but stronger, I wish to recount my story to you, noble ladies, and if possible to awaken pity in you, in whose hearts love perhaps dwells more happily than in mine."[13]

The *Elegia* is full of references to the literary tradition, from Ovid and Virgil to Seneca, and, of course, Andreas Capellanus, the author of *De amore* (*The Art of Courtly Love*, ca. 1185), as well as Guido Cavalcanti, Dante, and the poets of the *stilnovo*. These references betray in Boccaccio the anxiety both to confront and to move beyond his models. Certainly none of the literary works to which Fiammetta has recourse in her attempt to identify with the heroines of yore and lessen her love pangs seems to be successful in helping her heal. As Suzanne Hagedorn notes, "Fiammetta's vicarious participation in the lives of these heroines does not free her from her own pain, but rather makes her dwell obsessively in it."[14] This insufficiency or lack of efficacy of the previous literary tradition motivated Boccaccio to experiment with the healing power of words in the *Elegia*. Driven by the *Elegia*'s failure to cure Fiammetta, Boccaccio started to conceive the *Decameron* as a work addressed uniquely to women, with the goal this time of furnishing concrete help to readers struck by lovesickness.

There is little doubt that in the Middle Ages the melancholy of erotic love was treated as a disease. From the eleventh century onward the medical analyses of love came from both Greek and Latin medicine of late antiquity to medieval Islam.[15] This Arabic tradition was inherited through the translation of Avicenna.[16] However, the remedies for lovesickness prescribed at the time, in the form of wine consumption, merry company, music, poetry, and visiting gardens, are those deemed by Fiammetta as ill-suited medicine for curing her pains.[17] Moreover, she indicates that in such therapies lie the origins of her sickness:

> Oh what an ill-suited medicine my husband was using for my pains!. . . . There, for the most part, time is spent in idleness . . . there people consume nothing but delicacies, and the finest old vintage wines strong enough not only to excite the sleeping Venus but also, if she were dead, to bring her back to life inside every man, and those who have tried the powers of the baths know to what extent their beneficial effects also contribute to this. There the beaches, the lovely gardens . . . love songs. . . . Therefore in this place those who can should be on guard against Cupid, who, insofar as I know, in that very place, which seems to be his choice domain, exercises his powers with little effort.[18]

Having thus dismissed the traditional medical cures for lovesickness, Fiammetta turns to other remedies.

As Dante claimed that his words had the power to make people fall in love—"Amor sì dolce mi fa sentire / che s'io allora non perdessi ardire, / farei parlando innamorar la gente"[19]—so Boccaccio explores how the words of a literary work can effectively comfort, heal, and bring some relief from the torments of love. The fact that the *Elegia* does not come to resolution leads to an even deeper suspicion about the experimental nature of the work. The book does indeed end, but the story itself remains open: in the final chapter (chap. 9), Fiammetta is still looking for a solution to her pain, having failed to reunite with her lover, to commit suicide, wholly to embrace the superior form of love in her marriage, or to find further comfort in the literary works of the ancients. Indeed the *Elegia* can be read as a failure of a quest either to cure love sorrows or to attain a higher form of love.

Where the *Elegia* failed, however, the *Decameron* succeeded. Pampinea and her brigade manage, unlike Fiammetta, to experience love and to talk about love without "trespassing the sign of reason."[20] Kirkham indicated in this phrase a fragment of conversation in which Dante talks to Adam in Paradise (26.115–17), obtaining information about the Fall. Adam and Eve "trespassed the sign," that is, they "overstepped a moral limit."[21] In the *Elegia*, however, Fiammetta's understanding of "trespassing the sign"[22] is confined to a concern about displaying an honest decorum to salvage her honor; she thus misses entirely the ethical point of the affirmation. Since the Fall for Fiammetta means nothing more than social disgrace, once she has averted the dangers of having her affair exposed in public, she is troubled no more and happily embraces Panfilo's love.

The gnomic opening of the *Elegia* is itself nothing other than an adaptation of a passage in Dante's *Vita nuova*, in which Dante describes being led astray by the lady of the window: "And because whenever an unhappy person sees someone take pity on him, he is all the more easily moved to tears, as if taking pity on himself."[23] The *Vita nuova* and the *Elegia* share a circular structure. Charles Singleton has emphasized how the reader is aware of Beatrice's death from the beginning of the *Vita nuova*.[24] So, too, in the *Elegia* we anticipate from the first chapter the unhappy ending of Fiammetta's love. The fundamental difference between Dante's work and Boccaccio's is that in the latter there is no inner transformation of the main character. In fact, in the *Vita nuova* love becomes the path to a spiritual elevation; from despair following the lady's death through *caritas* it is a means of reaching God. In the *Elegia*, on the other hand, Fiammetta remains frozen in a state of perpetual pain.[25] She does, however, consider her book as an exemplum for future female readers, whom she admonishes to become more cautious in the matter of love after seeing what happened to her because of her misplaced trust in an unworthy lover.[26] Boccaccio makes clear a similar intent in the Proemio of the *Decameron* when he states that his female readers will find in the book both solace and useful counsel.[27] Fiammetta does not have the guidance of a book like the *Decameron* that claims to teach women what ought to be followed and avoided. On the contrary, Janet Smarr has noticed that the examples available to Fiammetta from classical sources are all negative ones: "Paris, Helen, Clytemnestra, Aegisthus, and Dido follow among others. Treachery, murder, and suicide are the immediate associations with their names."[28]

As with many of the characters of the *Decameron*, Fiammetta's fault is not necessarily in the extramarital quality of her love. In the *De amore* Andreas Capellanus theorized that love can exist only outside of marriage. Instead, Fiammetta's undoing lies in a ruthless extramarital passion that almost drives her insane. Boccaccio utilizes the justification of the *De amore* not only to legitimize Fiammetta's extramarital love,[29] but also to excuse her disregard for her husband, who is young, caring, and handsome, unlike many husbands in the *Decameron* whose old age and impotency often drive the young wife to find a more suitable companion. In fact, in the *De amore* we read that "the easy attainment of love makes it of little value; difficulty of attainment makes it prized."[30] Likewise Fiammetta affirms: "Usually only things which one easily possesses are demeaned, though they may be of great worth, while those hard to obtain are considered very precious, even if they are of very little value."[31] However, even Andreas's advice does not lead to any improvement in the case of Fiammetta. Monica Bardi notes that neither Panfilo's lies nor his infidelity, which Andreas indicates as behaviors apt to sober the lover from the intoxication of love, work to free Fiammetta from her passion. Moreover, Andreas encourages lovers not to flee love because of their sufferings, since after overcoming harsh trials love will bring forth the much-sought prize. There is, however, no such prize for Fiammetta, and her hypothesis that she has endured trials to show her worthiness of Panfilo does not withstand the test of reality.[32]

Fiammetta recognizes the limits of her wit and intelligence. She informs us of the *folle estimazione* of her heart,[33] and then states that she is unable to understand the secrets the gods revealed in her dreams because her mind is too simple: "But I complain no less about those gods who reveal their secrets to obtuse minds in such obscure ways that they can be said to be almost unrevealed until they have come true."[34] As she prepares to participate in the town's festivities, she compares herself to the peacock, a foolish bird, full of vanity, who uses the beauty of his feathers to hide the foul nudity of his rear, as stated by Boccaccio in the *Genealogia deorum gentilium*.[35] Fiammetta presents herself as a creature of stunning beauty, in fact, a victim of her own comeliness (in a precursory depiction of the later character of Alatiel in *Decameron* 2.7), when she says: "I became aware that my beauty in particular, an unwelcome gift to anyone who wishes to live virtuously, set afire young men my own age."[36] Unfortunately, for all her charms, Fiammetta is not equally endowed with intelligence and wit.

More than a comic figure, as Robert Hollander has it,[37] Fiammetta is a pathetic one, and her moral weakness is made worse by the idleness she enjoys. Indeed, her nurse openly accuses Love of dwelling in the wealthy homes of idle minds.[38] Similarly, the *Decameron* recognizes that the loving women who sit in idleness and enjoy little freedom are the ones who need most the diversion that literature can provide.[39] Conversely, the nurse asks: "Now don't we often see the most blessed Venus dwelling in very modest homes, useful for the exclusive fulfillment of our procreation?"[40] Such a love, however, presented in these terms, pales by comparison to the enticements offered by the son of the earthly Venus. One could argue that the nurse, wearing the clothes of reason, is lacking in strength of persuasion. She argues that love will deprive Fiammetta of discernment and freedom. Already lacking in the former, Fiammetta can hardly understand the latter, since as a woman she can already enjoy very little of it.[41] The nurse can show Fiammetta the dangers of submitting to such love, but she is unable to show the rewards of following the right path.[42] Once Fiammetta has secured her reputation with secrecy, she cannot see why she should run away from the pleasures that Venus promises her.[43]

Her Venus, however, represents a dangerous power of erotic love pushed to extreme limits, very different from the goddess of procreation.[44] Walter Pabst highlights a fusion between Fiammetta's Venus and Hell's Fury Tisiphone.[45] The very structure of the *Elegia*, divided into nine chapters, suggests the infernal quality of the matter treated in the book.[46] Fiammetta's disregard for the negative aspects of such a love proves all the more the force of its spell: like a modern Phaedra she is taken by a raging passion, burned by a fire she never felt before.[47] Fiammetta follows too the shameless nature of Dido's love, her vocation to death, and her irrational gestures of a blind love.[48] "Dido is on fire with love and has drawn the madness through her veins."[49] Love as *furor* is unknown in Dante's repertoire but is present in the Provençal tradition of the *folor* and *fole amor* of the Breton romances.[50] Although their magical elements are absent from the classicizing *Elegia*, it shares their perception of love as an inexorable fate that subjugates the mind and spirit. The identity between love and furor comes to Boccaccio above all from Seneca's tragedy *Phaedra* (one of the most prominent sources for the *Elegia*),[51] which provides a precedent for the protagonist's loss of reason.

Because love is portrayed as having such a tremendous power, in the *Elegia* Boccaccio's aim remains neither to condemn nor to consent to the practice of illicit love. Observing that passion as *furor* is an extreme state afflicting many human beings, Boccaccio introduces an innovation, shifting the focus from a moralizing response to a more helpful one. He raises the question of how literature can alleviate such dire consequences and possibly provide remedies through the diversions of storytelling. In so doing, he starts in the *Elegia* along the path of compassion that he will further develop in the *Decameron*. "Sometimes (if I had no other obligations)," Fiammetta writes, "I gathered my maids together in my chamber and recounted, or had them recount, all sorts of stories, and the further from the truth they were — as most of these people's tales are — the greater power they seemed to have in chasing my sorrows away and making me a cheerful listener, and there were many times when I laughed about them with great pleasure in spite of all this melancholy."[52] The element of therapeutic laughter, introduced here as a novelty with respect to both Ovid and Seneca, will be a principal pursuit in the *Decameron*, where the comic element is extended to the characters of the *cornice* as well and provides much needed relief from the horrors of the pestilence. Fiammetta, moreover, does not stop at storytelling to find diversion from her pains: "I looked in various books for other people's miseries, and by comparing them to mine, I felt as if I had company, and so the time passed less tediously."[53]

The *Elegia* marks the author's transition from narratives in classical settings to a contemporary world, allowing the audience to identify more directly with the stories and their characters. The *Decameron* accomplishes this fully in that it starts precisely in 1348, while the *Elegia* presents a strange double time. Although the story takes place in an era of pagan gods, the reader knows that the period is contemporary under a classical disguise and can therefore see Fiammetta as a lady of the fourteenth century. How otherwise could Fiammetta affirm that she was reading the French romances of Tristan and Iseult?[54] As Smarr has rightly observed, Boccaccio uses classical allusion to introduce the distance between the author and the narrator and to work moral warnings into the text, which the narrator disregards but are understood by readers.[55]

In its complexity the *Elegia* not only unfolds in "double" time but constantly offers a double view of love: the Christian and the secular, the lofty and the sinful, the heavenly and the infernal. However, the central conflicts that drive events are nature's force versus civil society's rules, or on an individual level, the struggle between reason and appetite. Smarr writes: "When the nurse of the *Elegia*, seeing that all remonstrances are useless, actively helps Fiammetta arrange her adulterous affair, we are presented allegorically with the subservience of reason to the appetite. Reason may protest but is impotent to redirect the will or to counteract the attractive power of lust."[56] This raises the Christian question of free will in matters of love. Is it possible to resist the overpowering force of love? Can a "mere" (and not particularly intelligent) woman resist by herself what stronger and cleverer men have failed to resist? Again we are presented with two opposite alternatives. For the nurse it is difficult but possible.[57] Fiammetta, by contrast, believes: "Love takes possession of our entire mind, and lords it over us with his divinity, and you know that it is not safe to resist his powers."[58] Like Phaedra and Dido, fateful figures of mad love, she is unable to break free from the spell. All three appear to be exactly alike, except in their final fate—death for the ancient ladies and for Fiammetta a failed suicide. Yet Fiammetta, had she not been so blinded, could have had another option. Hollander's view is that "the difference between Phaedra and Fiammetta is the classical dramatic fatality and the Christian medieval 'drama of choice.' The 'moral drama' of Fiammetta concerns her unwillingness to make the correct choice."[59] Phaedra and Dido—as well as Ovid's letter-writing heroines and Andreas Capellanus—then become literary foils for Boccaccio to suggest obliquely a Christian alternative in matters of love and will. Fiammetta remains trapped in a pagan world and the values of courtly love, which Boccaccio perceives as insufficient. A speech by Venus brings into the text a direct confrontation with the Christian tradition on free will. The goddess forcefully shows Fiammetta the uselessness of her meek attempts to resist the power of Venus's son Love, and she makes no distinction between men and animals when she says: "What are you running away from so madly? If so many gods, so many men, and so many animals have been conquered by him, will you be ashamed to be conquered by him?"[60] Venus here places gods, men, and animals on the same level. This lack of differentiation stands in contrast to the Christian view on free will. In the *De libero arbitrio*, for example, Augustine states that the difference between man and animal is man's rational quality, otherwise defined as mind or spirit. It is the rational quality that allows man to choose well. For Augustine, not only does every man possess it, but it is also the origin of man's freedom of choice.[61] However, Fiammetta (if not Boccaccio) adroitly elides the Christian position on free will with regard to passion by employing the camouflage of the ancient gods and classical literature.

That Fiammetta does so with the intention of exculpating herself or lessening the magnitude of her sin in the eyes of the reader is doubtful, since she later accuses herself of being a contemptible female, fully deserving of her torture.[62] Again the author presents the reader with a double-edged sword: the knowledge of evil and the apparent impossibility for some of avoiding it. Through his ironic perspective, we can distinguish between Fiammetta's purpose in writing the book and Boccaccio's. His ultimate goal lies in the ethical purpose of the book—to serve as a warning to other women. Fiammetta as a female narrator is like the women of Ovid's *Heroides* because her degree of literacy has allowed her to give vent to her depressed state. For her, too, literature is a means of nurturing her sorrow: "And if one song referred to troubles similar to mine, I listened attentively, wishing to learn it so that by repeating it to myself I would and could sometime lament in public in a more orderly and covert language."[63] Petrarch had affirmed that "singing, the pain becomes less bitter."[64] Fiammetta searches for literary relief in the works of others, from the classics to the romances and songs of courtly love.

In the last chapter of the *Elegia*, as she bids her book farewell, the still-disconsolate Fiammetta leaves behind all the literary baggage of the past, addressing her contemporaries. Quite rightly Cesare Segre notes that up to then she "seems to wander in a cold gallery of statues: the characters to whom in the intensity of her drama she had asked for comforting words, gestures, and examples came back to her with the consistency of marble, dusty and silent."[65] Francesco De Sanctis sums it up this way: "When she looks for solace in finding companions for her sorrow, she compiles a treatise of ancient history, narrating thus all the unhappy lovers among both gods and heroes."[66] The lifeless parade exemplifies Boccaccio's own leave-taking in his vernacular fiction from ancient literature with his recognition of its insufficiency to fulfill one of poetry's highest tasks: bringing comfort and relief to modern readers in pain. The theme of compassion in the *Elegia* necessitates incorporating Christian values (to be both parodied and commended) for a literary task achieved more fully in the later *Decameron*. In the *Elegia*, Boccaccio realizes the force of such compassion when it is channeled into the cathartic power of storytelling. For readers who can see beyond Fiammetta's self-centered point of view, opening their eyes to the broader perspective of the author who created her, storytelling can break the cycle of sorrows and ideally heal from lovesickness.

CHAPTER FIFTEEN

RHETORIC AND INVECTIVE IN LOVE'S LABYRINTH • (Il Corbaccio)

Letizia Panizza

On its surface, Boccaccio's *Corbaccio* reads as a misogynistic blast with insults added to injuries, scurrilous terminology, imagery descending to the pornographic, bad puns, and unrelenting lists of female vices far beyond the limits of decency or plausibility. The two main characters in dialogue are sour aging men on whom no modern woman in her right mind would wish to waste a word, let alone seek their company. Set in its literary context, however, *Il Corbaccio* belonged to a particular genre, that of invective, acceptable and practiced from antiquity to the Middle Ages, the Renaissance, and beyond; most important of all, it was governed by rhetorical norms that readers and writers of those ages took for granted. From this perspective, Boccaccio's treatise has its fascination for several reasons: it is a highly wrought example of invective; it engages with contemporary polemics about love poetry; it develops Dante's severe moral attitude to earlier courtly love poetry and romance; and it offers a therapy for dealing with immoderate sexual passion.[1]

A glimpse at the story line gives us a more precise understanding of Boccaccio's aims. The Narrator, hopelessly infatuated with an apparently adorable widow, and then realizing he has been taken in by a two-faced hussy, has to sever his inordinate attachment in order to save his soul. The task of disillusioning him is given to a spirit from purgatory sent by divine authority in a dream, none other than the ex-husband of the widow, and therefore someone supremely qualified to open the eyes of the dazzled Lover-Narrator. The Spirit's discourse is therapeutic, working on the Lover's imagination, emotions, and will. The woman in question is never allowed to argue her side; all accounts of what she looks like, what she says, or what she does come from the mouths of merciless, angry men. In *Il Corbaccio*, bestial imagery defines women's condition, while rational, almost angelic properties define men.

The title itself, *Il Corbaccio*, offers a typical medieval play on Boccaccio's name. It inverts the first part, turning *bocca*, "mouth," into *corba*, "crow" or "raven," and keeps *-accio* as a suffix qualifying the noun, suggesting something huge, ugly, coarse, or unpleasant. Boccaccio playfully inverts his name, transforming a "big, vulgar writer of *novelle*" into a "big, ugly, coarse crow/raven" bearing harsh news. The jury is out on to whom or what else the title refers,[2] though I incline to see it as referring to invective itself, whose subject matter is harsh and sometimes repulsive. (The title *Il Corbaccio*—with the definite article—resembles titles such as *The Iliad* or *The Aeneid*, which refer to all the material about Ilium or Aeneas.) The dating of *Il Corbaccio*—whether it was composed just after the *Decameron* or later in Boccaccio's life, after 1360, when he was admitted to Holy Orders—is a moot point, as he was accustomed to write several drafts of his works, each time adding to or altering the text.[3] What can be said is that it expresses austere moral values befitting one who has taken clerical orders, or at least is making a case for such a decision, which would require the questioning of dominant cultural attitudes with regard to love poetry, women, and sex.

What is invective? What are its features? And what does it purport to do? *Il Corbaccio* finds analogues in a long tradition of Christian writings from Jerome to Petrarch, tinged with Stoic hues. In his autograph *Zibaldone Laurenziano*, Boccaccio himself copied out three examples of invective that found their way into *Il Corbaccio*, two from ascetic sources, Jerome and Valerius (the latter based on Jerome and Juvenal), and one from Cicero.[4] Boccaccio explicitly labels the first two as invectives, not against women as such, but against taking a wife, appropriate for clerics who took vows of celibacy. Called *An uxor ducenda* (Whether to take a wife), this genre of invective had been practiced since Greek and Roman antiquity, when it had as its target philosophers and scholars.[5] It should be pointed out that while classical authors deprecated marriage as a social institution with burdens and distractions inimical to study, they did not condemn sex; ascetic Christian writers in Boccaccio's time denigrated both. Lust or mere physical love leads men and women astray; the straight and narrow path leading to spiritual "perfection" calls for strenuous vigilance of all the senses, and the suppression of *carnale amore*, the phrase used by Boccaccio.

During the time when rhetoric was the instrument of communication governing formal speeches and all written genres, invective was one of a pair of opposites, called in Latin *laus* and *vituperatio*, praise and blame, which could be directed at a person, a group, a particular course of action, a city or state, a religion, or an abstract concept.[6] Invective and its twin went under other names: an attack or a defense; a *persuasio* or a *dissuasio*; a debate *pro* or *contra*; an *apologia*. Invective pushes differences to extremes, using exaggeration and its opposite, understatement (*hyperbole* and *litotes*), for dramatic impact. In a dialogue, different speakers could hold forth on both sides; it was a sign of excellence for the same orator to speak convincingly on both sides of a question, even on a solemn concept like justice, with its contrary, injustice (this was the specialty of Socrates, Plato's master). Teachers of oratory, hoping to avoid the frequent accusation that orators did not care about the truth or morality—they could make black seem white and the reverse—were careful to insist that the orator must be a good man.[7]

Like the orators, Boccaccio could hold forth on either side of a question. If he could compose *Il Corbaccio*, he could also compile *Famous Women*, written in Latin as *De mulieribus claris* (after he became a cleric, between the summer of 1361 and the summer of 1362). The Latin gives these memorable examples of the female sex added dignity and defines the book as serious scholarship. The work has been hailed as "innovative; . . . the first collection of biographies in Western literature devoted exclusively to women."[8] Moreover, even a cursory reading of Boccacccio's *Decameron* and his multitudinous earlier verse and prose encounters a dazzling variety of women: beautiful and ugly, generous and mean, kind and spiteful, lovers of men and haters, bold and timid, impudent and modest, courageous and withdrawn. In both the *De mulieribus* and *Il Corbaccio*, Boccaccio holds up a Stoic-Christian ascetic ideal he had come to admire first in Dante, and then in Petrarch, the grand moral philosopher of the time, his friend and correspondent.[9]

Structurally speaking, *Il Corbaccio*'s speeches resemble loosely arranged concentric rings with a core at the center in which the two male voices dialogue as in a debate: the Lover-Narrator, in need of treatment, and the Spirit, a guide, father figure, spiritual director, confessor, savior, and doctor of the soul. The two to some extent complement each other, the Narrator being the voice of irrational emotion; the Spirit, his alter ego, the voice of reason. To emphasize their roles as types, neither character is given a personal name. The roles have been likened to those of Boethius and Lady Philosophy in the *Consolation of Philosophy*; or, with greater resemblance, to those of poet and saint in Petrarch's *Secretum*, where the troubled poet, in a state of moral crisis, unburdens himself about his not-always chaste adoration of Laura to an imaginary Saint Augustine. Like a stern Christian spiritual director, Augustine puts Petrarch through an examination of conscience to pin down the two "chains" that hold him back from making spiritual progress: Laura is the main one. While Petrarch's dialogue, however, is inconclusive, since he is unable to renounce Laura completely, Boccaccio's is triumphant because the Narrator does renounce his wicked woman, the *malvagia femina*.[10]

The outermost ring, a brief but vital frame holding all the rest in place, is a miracle story of the Blessed Virgin Mary, a *legenda*, in which the Narrator gives thanks to God for his conversion from sin to the state of grace granted by the intercession of the Virgin, who sent the Spirit to warn and rescue him. The Proemium announces that the miracle has already taken place: "I intend to set forth in the following humble treatise, a special grace which was recently granted to me, not because of my own merit, but solely by the beneficence of Her, Who implored it from [Him]."[11] This outer ring closes with an apostrophe to his "little work" or *picciola operetta*, the *congedo* or *envoi* (farewell, dismissal), and a final rhetorical flourish. *Il Corbaccio* is now instructed to spread its message of redemption further afield, to a lower target age: "Strive to be useful to those—and especially the young—who, with eyes closed, set out without a guide through unsafe places, trusting too much to themselves."[12] Just as in a sermon, this invective will enable *young* men to hear an exemplum of the great favors one sinner received from the Mother of God and be forewarned about the wiles lurking in women's company. Note that readers are meant to consider whether the invective has the desired effect on men or not, rather than whether it is objectively true or not. As for female readers, the invective is told: "Above all, see that you do not come into the hands of evil women."[13] A puzzling recommendation: does the Narrator (and the author?) fear that otherwise the invective's offensiveness and mendacity would be clearly seen and damned, while a "good" woman would take it all approvingly?

In the next concentric ring, the Narrator describes his life *before* conversion, bemoaning his failure to become a suitor in the court of Love, not through his own fault, he insists, but because the woman he had so carefully chosen to be his *donna* made a fool of him. Not only did she reject him; she broke another tenet of the courtly love code, secrecy. He found out that she was gossiping about him to other women in the street, and, worse still, to her current lover, with whom she made fun of his gushing love letter. Such grievous loss of face caused his present affliction. Was death not preferable to such humiliation? Our courtly lover manqué sighs, weeps, blurts out the key words *gentile* and *gentilezza* (noble, nobility), characterizing the refined, spiritually ennobling kind of love, which found its most sublimated expression in Dante's poetry of the *dolce stil novo*, codified half a century before and followed with more ambiguity by Petrarch. But the Narrator proves just the opposite of what a courtly lover should be — and so, it turns out, does his *donna*. He is interested in the thrill of conquest and sex, *carnale amore*.

Crazed by wounded *amour propre*, the Narrator lashes out at the widow without mercy: "I concluded that through no fault of mine I had been cruelly ill-treated by her whom I had chosen in my madness as my special lady."[14] Attempting to settle his emotional turmoil, he resorts to giving himself a good talking to by means of a personified Thought (Pensiero), a trope used by Dante and Petrarch in their poetry. The therapy here is to stiffen his jelly-like will and begin the process of detaching himself from his *donna*, now enemy number one: "Oh, poor fool! Where is the meager power of your reason (no, rather, the expulsion of your reason) leading you? . . . If you will only be a man, you can chase [these contrary feelings] away — something which would not happen with eternal woes [in hell]."[15] This has no effect. The malady is too serious, and only the appearance of the Spirit in a heaven-sent dream-vision will accomplish the desired separation.

It has hitherto escaped critics that with the introduction of the words *gentile* and *gentilezza* we are being led to the heart of a decisive reformulation of medieval courtly love ethics based on sexual passion and adulterous relationships. For Dante and his coterie of vernacular love poets, it was codified by the phrase *dolce stil novo* (a revolutionary and inspired way of writing about love) and linked love with virtue, and both to a divine source. In Dante's poems, *gentile* and *gentilezza* now refer not to aristocratic lineage but to nobility of soul: virtue, decency, good sense, kindness, empathy, and refined manners.[16] Why in *Il Corbaccio* should the Narrator's demand of reciprocal love from his *donna* make him deserving of eternal punishment in hell? A glaring response can be found in Dante's *Divine Comedy* (*Inferno* 5) and in Boccaccio's commentary; Boccaccio firmly commends Dante's divine justice for damning Francesca and her lover Paolo even for a single passionate kiss. In support, Boccaccio gravely cites Aristotle, who distinguishes three kinds of love: virtuous, enjoyable, and for a useful purpose (*onesto, dilettevole, utile*). Theirs is the second kind, associated with Cupid, to whom poets attribute extremely strong powers (*grandissime forze*). Since this first kiss came about while Francesca and Paolo were reading the romantic but adulterous tales of those archetypes of courtly love, Lancelot and Arthur's wife, Queen Guinivere, Dante is in effect condemning literature that extols sexual passion as well, especially sexual relations outside marriage. Boccaccio is sure that when Dante faints, emotionally overwhelmed by Francesca's story, he fears for his own salvation.[17] In *Il Corbaccio* the Narrator's admission of *carnale amore* puts him and his *donna* in a parallel and alarming situation; furthermore, he blurts out that he has neither the right lineage nor experience in chivalry, thus revealing that his is no true *gentilezza*, but mere parody. He has failed to grasp that Dante and others in his circle had vigorously denied in their poetry that noble lineage and wealth had anything to do with *gentilezza*. Nevertheless, there is one crucial circumstance in the Narrator's favor: he is still alive and has time to repent and save his soul.

Boccaccio's denunciation of *carnale amore* and false *gentilezza* in *Il Corbaccio* corresponds not only to what he says in his commentary on the *Commedia*, but even more so to his *Trattatello in laude di Dante*. Theology, philosophy, and poetry are fused in the highest degree in Dante, who comes closer than any other human being to a sage, a prophet, a divinely inspired poet (*vate*), and a saint. On only one count did Dante fail: his involvement in public affairs by getting married and taking part in Florentine politics. Boccaccio uses the same invective of Jerome, and Jerome's citation of Theophrastus, to lament his hero Dante's lowering his dignity as a philosopher and hindering his poetic genius by taking a wife. "Let those who would be philosophers leave getting married to foolish rich men, to aristocrats, and to common laborers; let them take delight in philosophy, a much better bride than any other."[18] Dante's family was to blame, for they thought marriage would help Dante overcome his grief at the death of Beatrice; and even more blameworthy were seductive Florentine women in general: "Women! What can't they do in us men?"[19] Further on, Boccaccio enters into praise of poetry as the most sublime gift to mankind, resplendent in Dante.

The central core of *Il Corbaccio* is the lengthy dream-vision sent by divine command. Falling asleep, the Lover-Narrator finds himself in a landscape recalling Dante's own vision of the outskirts of Hell: a desert, fog, mountains, dark woods. His ears are assailed by cries, roars, and yelps from wild animals, all causing fear and loneliness.[20] Just as the Narrator is about to give up all hope, a reassuring Spirit appears. With features of both Virgil and Cato in the *Commedia*, stern but kind and fatherly, he is white-haired, imposing, dark-skinned, clad in an ample crimson robe, and aged about sixty. This venue, he explains, has many names, all denoting abandonment of reason to sexual passion: "Some call it the 'Labyrinth of Love,' and others the 'Enchanted Valley,' and a good number the 'Pigsty of Venus,' and many the 'Valley of Sighs and Woe.'"[21] The resemblance of these names to allegorical topography in courtly romances, referring to the joys and tears of lovers' infatuation, should not blind us to the sinister reality indicated by the Spirit. Our Narrator recognizes his weakness: "Such great contrition and repentance for my evil deeds came upon me . . . that my heart melted into water, just as snow in sunshine."[22] The image of his heart melting fits well the etymological meaning of contrition reiterated in religious tracts: a grinding down, pulverizing, or dissolving of a rock-hard heart.

Governing this central core's rhetorical strategy is an argument by contraries hammered out by the Spirit to overturn false illusions. He trounces what the Narrator clings to about Love and *gentilezza*, shaming him: as a middle-aged scholar who has studied venerable philosophers, what is he doing falling in love like an adolescent? He should have been persuaded of the depravity of *carnale amore*: "Love is a blinding passion of the spirit, a seducer of the intellect which dulls or rather deprives one of memory, a dissipater of earthly wealth, a waster of bodily strength, the enemy of youth, and the death of old age, the parent of vices, and the inhabiter of inane breasts, a thing without reason or order, without the least stability, the vice of unhealthy minds, and the stifler of human liberty."[23] With heavy ammunition from two sources, the written "authorities" of eminent men of letters, ancient and modern, pagan and Christian, and his own irrefutable experience of his ex-wife, the Spirit achieves a metamorphosis in the Narrator, who goes from "bad" to "good" understanding, while his view of the widow goes in the opposite direction, from the subjective opinion of "good" to the "correct" opinion of "bad." And, of course, the heavy style and linguistic register of the invective stands in contrast to those of love poetry and romances. The Spirit justifies his coarse, abusive language, playing on the double meaning of *ɟalute* in Italian — bodily health, and spiritual salvation: "A shrewd doctor cannot always heal every illness and every patient with sweet-smelling ointments; . . . [many patients] require foul-smelling remedies."[24]

As for what a woman is *really* like, the Spirit spews forth an endless list of epithets, associated with derogatory animal imagery, and even viler, lewd descriptions of female genitalia. The reduction of woman to a bundle of well-worn clichés of Aristotelian origin concentrates on her animal irrationality:

A female is an imperfect creature excited by a thousand foul passions, abominable even to remember let alone to speak of. If men considered this as they should, they would go to them in the same way and with the same desire and delight with which they go to any other natural and inevitable necessity. . . . No other animal is less clean than a female; the pig even when he is most wallowed in mud, is not as foul as they. If perhaps someone would deny this, let him . . . search the secret places where they in shame hide the horrible instruments they employ to take away their superfluous humors.[25]

Though her vices are infinite, the Spirit has time for only a few. He alights first on *malizia*, a mixture of malice aforethought dosed with spitefulness and cunning. Specifically, she thinks of nothing else but deceiving her husband. Like a famished wolf, she devours his possessions and thinks nothing of robbing family and friends. Lust she has aplenty, though directed not toward her husband, but to other men. Toward them, she burns with lust, insatiable: "The servant, the miller, the workman, even the black Ethiopian, each is good provided he is up to it."[26] She also frequents brothels in disguise, and her execrable deeds include getting rid of unwanted offspring by abortion and infanticide.

Women's tempers, furthermore, are uncontrollable, sparing no one. "As instinctively as animals, they immediately fly into such a temper that tigers, lions or snakes have more humanity than they do when enraged."[27] The Spirit deems it a great miracle that God himself puts up with them! In addition, he cannot help mentioning fickleness, gluttony, envy, ambition, and an intellectual vanity that leads women to think they know everything after they have heard a sermon or two. Grudgingly, the Spirit admits there have been a few, very few, women who can be counted among the Virgin Mary's companions. In their case, however, Nature has made a mistake: they are *virili*, "manlike," and really men at heart.

The rhetorical purpose of this degradation and strange isolation of Mary from nearly all of womankind becomes apparent when the Spirit turns to the Narrator to present the contrary praise of man. The lower woman has been pushed down, the higher he is raised up. "Your studies should have reminded you . . . that you are a man made in the image and likeness of God, a perfect animal, born to rule and not to be ruled." As for Eve, "her gluttony, disobedience and persuasions were the cause and origin of all our miseries."[28] The Spirit plays fast and loose with Genesis to suit men, whitewashing Adam's part in the Fall and blackening Eve with Satanic attributes. Invective borders on blasphemy with the depiction of a God who hates the female sex that he created.

Worse is to come as the Spirit, turning to experience, describes life with his ex-wife. The beauty that first attracted him and so besotted the Narrator is now revealed in all its falsity. Female flesh is putrid; it stinks like rotting vegetation. Her breasts resemble "two puffed and blighted plums, which were once perhaps two unripe apples," and which are "so beyond measure lengthened and dislocated from their natural position that . . . if she let them droop they would reach her navel, empty and wrinkled like a deflated bladder."[29] The Spirit dwells on those "secret" parts he alone saw, and which are rarely broached in polite love stories, introducing geographical metaphors of a perilous journey from which no man returns alive. If at the center of the Cretan labyrinth there is the Minotaur devouring his victims, here at the center of "the labyrinth of love" there is a hidden female whirlpool sucking and crushing a man's virility: "I do not know where I should begin to speak of the Gulf of Setalia, hidden in the Valley of Acheron beneath dark woods often russet in color and foaming with foul grime and full of creatures of unusual species. . . . The mouth through which the port is entered is of such a size that . . . I might have made room for a companion sailing with a mast no less than mine. . . . A wondrous thing is that never a boat entered it without perishing and without being hurled forth from there without being vanquished and exhausted. . . . That gulf then is certainly an infernal abyss."[30] These ludicrous, grossly exaggerated images may suggest a pathological fear of female sexuality to a modern reader, but in their rhetorical context, they are invective's final dose of nasty medicine for the Narrator's malady, the contrary of his previous ravings about the female body in courtly love poetry that delicately skipped from blond hair, dark flashing eyes, ivory teeth, and rosy cheeks—and barely a hint about luscious, firm apples—to graceful hands and feet, leaving the rest to imagination.

Having driven out false *gentilezza* from the Narrator, the Spirit now jeers sarcastically at *her* misunderstanding, if not travesty, of the term. A dyed-in-the-wool hypocrite, she goes to church to eye the holy friars: "Her prayers and paternosters are French romances and Italian songs in which she reads of Lancelot and Guinivere, Tristram and Isolde, and of their great exploits, their loves, jousts, tournaments and battles; and when she reads that Lancelot, Tristram or someone else meets with his lady secretly, and alone, in her bedchamber, she goes all to pieces because she thinks she can see what they are doing, and would willingly do as she imagines they do. . . . She reads [the song of] *Florio and Blanchefleur* and many other such things."[31] In other words, she is reading just the kind of medieval courtly love stories that Francesca and Paolo were reading when they were all alone, imagining how Lancelot and Guinivere were kissing, and then imitating them. If such amiable young lovers ended up in hell, surely the fate of the *malvagia femina*, presented as the icon of anti-*gentilezza*, will be even lower down. We note that Boccaccio as author is condemning the kind of popular romances and *cantari*, or songs performed in the piazzas, that he sought to ennoble in his own early love literature when he wrote of Florio and Biancifiore in his *Filocolo*.[32] What this is all about becomes clearer when the Spirit, now closing the central core, launches into didactic mode on the true nature of *gentilezza*, echoing the stilnovist mantra: "Nobility first came into the world from virtue."[33] Applied to the social-climbing widow, this judgment is a big nail in her coffin. Applied to the Narrator, it allows him to realize that as a man he has far more claims to nobility than he first thought, and certainly more than she has.

The Narrator's dream concludes with the Spirit reasserting his therapeutic aims, explaining that the very words of his invective will engender emotions of revulsion, disgust, and hatred that will cast out lust, sexual attraction, and sensual pleasure:

> You must act in the opposite way to what you have done; but this must be understood correctly. What you have loved you must hate; and whatever you were ready to do to earn someone's love, you must be ready to do the contrary so that you gain hatred. . . . You loved that woman because you found her beautiful and because you hoped she would grant you carnal pleasure. I wish you to hate her beauty, since it was the cause of your sin, or could be in the future. I wish you to hate everything about her which you judged sensually attractive. I want you to love and desire the salvation of her soul.[34]

The Spirit orders former words of praise for the woman's beauty—a fundamental topos of medieval love poetry—to acidify into hatred: "Prepare yourself to belittle and vilify this deceiving woman, just as you were ready to exalt her. . . . As far as you are able, make her see herself and likewise expose her to others with your words."[35] The Narrator agrees enthusiastically to this new diet of hatred, revenge, and public shaming: "Unless a premature death robs me of the time, in order to show her that not all men are to be mocked in the same way, I shall make her realize her stupidity, . . . so vituperating her baseness that she will wish she had never set eyes on me."[36]

What are we to make nowadays of *Il Corbaccio*? Modern readers will be pleased to know that down through the ages objections to *Il Corbaccio* have focused on its misogyny, although during the Renaissance alone it was clearly labeled an invective and sometimes just "Il laberinto d'amore." It was a popular work, if its relatively numerous editions are anything to go by: from the 1487 *editio princeps* to 1597, I have seen at least sixteen editions in the British Library and the Cambridge University Library alone.[37] While an editor of 1520 found it an excellent defense for young people against Cupid's arrows, he also judged the vituperation excessive.[38] Lodovico Dolce praised the famous publisher Giolito for a new 1545 edition on the grounds that everything by a great writer should be printed. Saints and philosophers, too, have found fault with women, says Dolce, implying that while Boccaccio's misogyny is objectionable, it is not entirely beyond the pale.[39] Not surprisingly, *Il Corbaccio*'s misogyny found favor with a Jesuit censor, Antonio Ciccarelli, who in 1584 purged Castiglione's *Book of the Courtier*, quoting what Boccaccio had written on sexual passion to refute Castiglione's portrait of innocent Platonic love between a courtier and a lady of the court.[40] By contrast, both Castiglione and Ariosto would adapt a story about a Greek heroine from Plutarch, Camma, to counter the accusation found so blatantly in Boccaccio that wives do not love their husbands.[41] And in her pioneering polemic, *The Nobility and Excellence of Women and the Defects and Vices of Men* (1601), Lucrezia Marinella sized up *Il Corbaccio*'s repulsiveness with a meaty chapter titled "Boccaccio's Opinion Adduced Here and Destroyed." She understood the rhetoric of invective perfectly and righted the imbalance by praising women's virtues and condemning men's far more numerous and serious faults.[42]

Hollander's mapping out of the main issues in *Il Corbaccio* in *Boccaccio's Last Fiction* has set the critical agenda. As his title indicates, he has deftly laid to rest an overliteral reading that the use of the first person "I" encouraged in earlier critics. He sees the work as a palinode and a companion piece to the *Decameron*, much as Ovid's *Remedia amoris* is a palinode to his *Ars amoris*, in neither case a serious indictment of women and *carnale amore*. This view is hard to square with a recurrent antifeminist strain in Boccaccio, which surfaces even in some tales of the *Decameron*. For Hollander, the work is "playful," and the two interlocutors "male hysterics."[43] Elaborating this approach, Millicent Marcus has suggested that Boccaccio has written not a straight invective but an ironic spoof of the genre itself, an example of black humor that discredits itself. For the modern reader, there is indeed much in the conversations of the Narrator and the Spirit/Guide that strikes one as grotesquely absurd rather than shocking.[44] Yet this interpretation and Hollander's additional one, that *Il Corbaccio* is un-Christian because of its emphasis on hatred, vilification, and revenge, are difficult to maintain, for they mean ignoring the conversion story, ignoring the distinction between moral and immoral *gentilezza*, and ignoring Christian culture of the time. Two Dominicans, Domenico Cavalca and Iacopo Passavanti, contemporaries of Boccaccio, wrote many treatises and sermons full of invectives, as well as *novelle* railing against the world, the flesh, the devil—and women. *Il Corbaccio* is part of this invective tradition.

CHAPTER SIXTEEN

DOING AND UNDOING: BOCCACCIO'S FEMINISM • *(De mulieribus claris)*

Deanna Shemek

In 1361, at the age of forty-eight and following several years of active public life, Boccaccio withdrew to the Tuscan countryside of Certaldo where, he reports, he took refuge from the *inerti vulgo* (vulgar mob) and welcomed the freedom and mental tranquility to write.[1] The "slim volume in praise of women" that resulted from his efforts in this moment, *De mulieribus claris* (*Famous Women*), was the first collection of female biographies to be produced in the post-classical West. As such it is a landmark of European literature.[2]

The high number of extant manuscripts in Latin (over one hundred, including one bearing Boccaccio's own witness) and the proliferation of early translations (in Italian, French, German, Middle English, Spanish, and English), together with the record of its printed editions, suggest that early modern readers engaged widely with this book.[3] After about 1600, however, the *De mulieribus* shared the fate of most writings from this period by and about women, standing silent and undisturbed on library shelves for centuries. Edited in 1967 for the first time in four hundred years, it came to prominence again in the early 1980s when it emerged as a key document in feminist historiography and cultural criticism.[4] Boccaccio's remark of his own surprise at "how little attention women have attracted from writers of this genre" (Preface, 3), and his decision to remedy this lack by collecting biographies for the *De mulieribus*, are in fact inextricably bound to a striking development in early modern humanism, which Boccaccio helped to found, for that movement would serve as the principal context for an unprecedented number of writings praising, instructing—and condemning—women over the following three centuries.[5] Though this text, like all of Boccaccio's other works, resides in the shadow of the *Decameron*'s fame, the *De mulieribus* stands as one of the most ideologically controversial works in Boccaccio's corpus, precisely for its peculiar relation to Renaissance feminism.

In the late twentieth century, scholars aiming to chart the long history of Western misogyny and to discern a genealogy of women's resistance to patriarchal oppression took their cue from the European writer who first articulated a systematic critique of male-centered history: the Venetian-born French poet and humanist Christine de Pizan. Christine wrote her foundational text, the allegorical *Le livre de la cité des dames* (*Book of the City of Ladies*, 1405), to refute misogynist ideas, especially those appearing in the fourteenth-century *Romance of the Rose*.[6] Like virtually all later writers on this subject, she relied heavily on the *De mulieribus* for her material, following Boccaccio's example of compiling brief biographical profiles of noteworthy women from ancient history and myth. Boccaccio explains from the outset that he aims to take as his model books about noteworthy men and interpret broadly the word *claris* (famous); he thus includes in his volume both good and bad examples of female notoriety, and he condemns many of his subjects' deeds. Christine's book features many of Boccaccio's same women, but, explicitly correcting her predecessor, she replaces negative details and commentary with adamant praise for all of their actions. Her polemical composition of the *Cité des dames* as a counterdiscourse to Boccaccio's marks the commencement of the lengthy Renaissance debate over women's "worth" known as the *querelle des femmes*.[7] Though Boccaccio's book provided material for both the pro- and antiwoman sides in this dialogue, his heavy-handed moralizing and his relentless insistence on women's chastity, silence, and familial devotion have relegated his book to the misogynist list in contemporary feminist historiography.[8] To be sure, the *De mulieribus*, like his earlier *Corbaccio*, complicates considerably our sense of Boccaccio's gender ideology; and from a feminist perspective it is something of a scandal. Yet while the author of the *De mulieribus claris* is difficult to reconcile with that of Boccaccio's earlier works, the path from those writings to the *De mulieribus* traces a discernible intellectual itinerary that is of interest for readers of Boccaccio and students of humanism as well as for scholars of early feminism.

The *De mulieribus* consists of 106 chapters arranged in approximate chronological order, each profiling a woman of renown. All but the first (about Eve) and the final six (which are devoted to medieval women) recount the memorable deeds of women from Greco-Roman antiquity. Ranging in length from less than a page to just under eight pages (chapter 42, on Dido, is the longest), each chapter bears a heading noting the subject's name and usually her title (e.g., "Nicaula, Queen of Ethiopia"), patronymic link

("Portia, Daughter of Cato Uticensis"), marital bond ("Sabina Poppaea, Wife of Nero"), or occupation ("Leaena, a Prostitute"). Several of these rubrics situate the women in multiple ways ("Flora the Prostitute, Goddess of Flowers and Wife of Zephyrus"); a few present women who remain nameless ("A Young Roman Woman"); and two are collective ("Wives of the Minyans"; "Wives of the Cimbrians"). Boccaccio's general procedure is to introduce the women in a sentence or two followed by brief remarks about what made them famous (a virtue, a vice, a bad or good deed). Then follow narratives in which Boccaccio's gifts as a storyteller come to the fore. Also appearing in high relief is Boccaccio the scholar, who in many chapters foregrounds his research by referring to conflicting accounts related by different sources. In some cases he admits being unable to determine which version is correct; in others he chooses among conflicting narratives, sometimes on the basis of circumstantial post-factum evidence. Typical is his handling of Europa's abduction by Jupiter:

> But the ancients do not agree as to the time of this abduction. Those who date it the earliest say that it happened when Danaus was king of Argos. Others say it occurred during the reign of Acrisius. Authorities who place it more recently declare that it transpired during the reign of Pandion. . . . Some sources simply report that. . . . The majority say. . . . Other sources could be cited, but most of them agree that Europa became famous through marriage to a great divinity. . . . I concede that Europa was a woman distinguished for her virtues, not only because of the name she has given to the world, but also because of the remarkable bronze statue dedicated to her in Taranto by the illustrious philosopher Pythagoras. (9.5–7)

Boccaccio the historian consistently euhemerizes the Greek and Roman pantheon by situating figures from classical myth emphatically in the context of political, social, and cultural history, even as he draws moral and historical meaning from their legends.[9] In the passage above, for example, Jupiter is no god; he is a "powerful man" who trapped an unsuspecting maiden while she was tending her father's sheep. Following the book's opening chapter, "Eve, Our First Mother" (in which Boccaccio does not question Eve's status as the first female human or her expulsion from paradise), chapter 2 presents Semiramis, queen of the Assyrians. "Time has obliterated any knowledge of her parents," we read, "except for the legend of the ancients that she was the daughter of Neptune, who, they falsely maintained, was the son of Saturn and god of the sea. We should not believe this story, but it is nonetheless an indication that Semiramis was born of noble parents" (2.1–2). Of Juno, goddess of kingdoms, we learn that "she and that Jupiter of Crete (whom the ancients wrongly imagined to be the god of heaven) were born twins" (4.2). Boccaccio continues: "Later the fictions of poets and the extravagant folly of the ancients made this woman, who had been a mortal queen, into the queen of heaven" (4.5). Minerva, the subject of chapter 6, Boccaccio portrays as a famous inventor who devised weaving, the olive press, the four-horse chariot, iron weapons, armor, battle strategy, the concept and use of numbers, the reed flute, and the bagpipe. He explicates Minerva's iconography (her piercing eyes, helmet, cuirass and lance, and crystal shield) as a set of poetic symbols. "The owl was placed in her keeping to indicate that the man of sagacity sees in the darkness as well as in the light," but Minerva was not a deity, he avers. Rather, "antiquity, that lavish dispenser of divinity, made Minerva the goddess of wisdom on account of these numerous inventions" (6.7).

Presenting Medusa as the daughter of the wealthy king Phorcus, whose realm was located "in the Atlantic Ocean," Boccaccio describes her exquisite beauty as a force that rendered people who gazed on her "almost immobile and forgetful of themselves." Medusa was also a shrewd manager of her father's wealth, "so much so that informed persons believed her to be the richest of all Western rulers" (23.1–5). Medusa's fame inspired young Perseus to kidnap her and escape on a ship whose standard bore an image of the horse Pegasus. All of these events, Boccaccio explains, gave rise to a number of poetic fictions: that Medusa could turn to stone those she gazed upon, that her hair was turned to snakes by an angry Minerva, and that her sexual union with the god Neptune resulted in the birth of a winged horse named Pegasus. Boccaccio ends his Medusa chapter with some moral commentary: "The possession of gold brings unhappiness. If the gold is kept hidden, it is of no use to the owners; if displayed, it gives rise to a thousand plots on the part of those who covet it. . . . If by some chance [the rich man] loses his wealth, the miser, now a pauper, is tormented by anxiety while the gentleman calls him fortunate, the envious man laughs, the poor man offers consolation, and the vulgar all turn the tale of his grief into a song" (23.8).

The addition of moral instruction to be drawn from the biographies is a consistent feature of the *De mulieribus*. Following his gorgeous retelling of the tragic tale of Thisbe, who took her own life in grief upon discovering that her lover Pyramus, thinking her dead, had killed himself, Boccaccio draws some lessons for his readers:

To love while in the flower of youth is a fault, but it is not a frightful crime for unmarried persons since they can proceed to matrimony. The worst sin was Fortune's, and perhaps their wretched parents were guilty as well. Certainly the impulses of the young should be curbed, but this should be done gradually lest we drive them to ruin in their despair by setting up sudden obstacles in their path. Passionate desire is ungovernable; it is the plague and the disgrace of youth, yet we should tolerate it with patience. Nature intends us, while young and fit, to feel spontaneously the procreative urge; the human race would die out if intercourse were delayed until old age. (13.12–14)

The commentary above suggests some continuity with the erotic sympathies evident in Boccaccio's earlier, vernacular works, where lovers abound and are often valorized, but in significant ways the *De mulieribus* marks a turning point in Boccaccio's moral and intellectual orientation. Certain features of the *De mulieribus* signal its emphatic participation in a new humanist culture and chart a clear shift away from the medieval tradition to which Boccaccio's vernacular works belong.[10] Indeed, after drafting the *Decameron*, excepting the misogynist *Corbaccio* (ca. 1355), Boccaccio never wrote another fictional or playful work and, as one biographer notes, "The final third of Boccaccio's life is characterized by its seriousness."[11]

The *De mulieribus* is in Latin, the official language of early humanist learning that not only bound together its adherents and excluded all but the most highly educated from their circles, but also became the medium for thoroughgoing stylistic renovations among humanist writers. Boccaccio opens his preface by signaling his studies of antiquity and invoking the leading intellectual of humanist reform, Petrarch: "Long ago there were a few ancient authors who composed biographies of famous men in the form of compendia, and in our day that renowned man and great poet, my teacher Petrarch, is writing a similar work that will be even fuller and more carefully done" (Preface, 1).[12] He continues, articulating the humanists' recursive agenda for the critical study of history as well as their forward-looking fascination with enduring fame and the possibility that they themselves might achieve such a legacy: "This is fitting. For those who gave all their zeal and their lives in order to surpass other men in illustrious deeds have certainly earned the right to have their names remembered forever by posterity" (Preface, 2). Compatible with the humanists' scholarly agenda is also Boccaccio's choice largely to exclude Hebrew and Christian heroines from his collection. Though his book is in fact saturated with Judeo-Christian morals, he prefers to focus on pagan women, whose merits (unlike those of biblical women and the Christian martyrs) "have not been published" (Preface, 11).

Boccaccio's early writings were poems and prose romances in Italian that drew on popular and courtly traditions, incorporating ancient myths as well as medieval materials. These texts, the *Caccia di Diana, Filocolo, Filostrato,* and *Teseida* of his Neapolitan youth as well as the *Comedia delle ninfe fiorentine (Ameto), Amorosa visione, Elegia di madonna Fiammetta,* and *Ninfale fiesolano* of the Florentine years, valorize Christian virtues to varying degrees, but in their different ways they also all revolve positively around themes of love and sensual pleasure. The culmination of Boccaccio's vernacular career and his greatest contribution to literature is unquestionably the *Decameron,* a book he dedicated to women in love and which he populated with female characters whose unabashed erotic proclivities the *Decameron* celebrates as a vital force—a power that delivers his storytellers from the misery and death inflicted by the plague—even as the text's framing structure underscores the virtues of moderation and restraint. The *Decameron's* one hundred *novelle* feature tonal swerves, from the medieval hazing comedy of the *beffa* tales to the tragic reports of youthful passions thwarted by paternal and fraternal negation, and from fables of divine providence to blasphemous displays of cynical cunning and marvelous wit. Within this variety, a set of consistent values nonetheless pulses through the collection: beauty, intelligence, youth, and humor, passionate love, rhetorical virtuosity, and amorous pleasure— for both men and women—are the *Decameron's* heartbeat. The book's Author figure defends himself explicitly against contemporary critics who deduce from his stories that he likes women too much (*che voi mi piacete troppo*), and offers, in his introduction to the Fourth Day's tales, an additional "part of a *novella*" (the tale of Filippo Balducci), the moral of which is that no amount of social or moral engineering can suppress the natural inclinations of human beings toward erotic pleasure.[13] He goes still further, reflecting ironically on the motives of those who, while attacking his book, profess concern for his well-being or question the veracity of his stories. Finally, he declares that he will persevere in his efforts to please women, for opposing the force of nature can result in "grandissimo danno" (enormous harm), and after all, earthly women—not the Muses of Parnassus—are his greatest inspiration. Women are the ostensible inspiration, as well as the subject, of the *De mulieribus claris,* too, but readers may be forgiven for doubting that the later work's author still likes women too much. The Boccaccio of the *De mulieribus* is a stern advocate of female humility, chastity, and silence who finds women in general to be constitutionally flawed.

His positive exemplars are women who somehow exceed the limitations of femininity. In recounting the mutual suspicions that lead to the accidental killing of Pocris by her husband, King Cephalus, Boccaccio offers a moral to both men and women: "Leaving aside the unbridled love of gold to which we are almost all foolishly attracted, I shall ask those who fall prey to such blind jealousy to tell me what advantage, what praise or what glory they get from it. In my opinion, jealousy is a ridiculous sickness of the mind caused by the pusillanimity of the people who suffer from it; we see it only in those who deem themselves of such little worth that they stand ready to admit that anyone else takes precedence over themselves" (28.9–10). He introduces Pocris's portrait, however, by claiming that "her greed gained her in equal measure the hate of honest women and the approval of men, because through her example the faults of her sex were revealed" (28.1). Semiramis, "like all others of her sex . . . was constantly burning with carnal desire" (2.13). Even Boccaccio's praise in the *De mulieribus* often delivers backhanded swipes at womankind. The hyperbolic legend of Busa, the Apulian woman of Canossa, for example, recounts her astonishing generosity and magnanimity in feeding, sheltering, clothing, and giving money to ten thousand Italian soldiers fleeing their defeat by Hannibal. Comparing Busa favorably with Alexander the Great, whose generosity was legendary, Boccaccio elaborates: "Alexander was a man, Busa a woman, and stinginess is as habitual, or rather innate, to women as is their lack of boldness" (69.6). For this reason, he implies, Busa is to be especially commended.

As many readers have remarked, numerous examples in the *De mulieribus* of women's laudatory achievements set the bar staggeringly high for the women of Boccaccio's day, effectively prohibiting their emulation of his examples unless they resort to prodigious displays of virtue and self-sacrifice. Boccaccio takes the heroism of Argia, wife of Polynices, who braved entry onto a forbidden battlefield in order to retrieve her husband's dead body and perform his burial rites, as a springboard for unfavorable comparison with most women. Other women may commiserate with their husbands' tribulations, but their devotion does not meet Boccaccio's standard: "While hope of a kindlier fortune remains and when fear of a crueler one is removed, many women weep over the illnesses, imprisonment, poverty, and numerous misfortunes of their husbands. This may seem praiseworthy, but one cannot claim that it is overwhelming proof of love, as can be said of Argia's last rites for her husband" (29.6–7).

Boccaccio's inclusion of the Greek prostitute Leaena among his positive models, and his assertion that prostitutes "are not always to be remembered with scorn" (50.3), appear to offer an opening for less-than-perfect examples of female virtue. Indeed, he goes to some length to excuse Leaena's profession: "Who will deny that fortune was to blame for Leaena's life in the brothels?" (50.5). But Leaena also provides an opening for Boccaccio's criticisms of other women, even noble ones: "Virtue found in [prostitutes] shames wanton queens, while queenly vice excuses the debaucheries of whores" (50.3). Leaena in fact supplies Boccaccio's most vivid and brutal image of praiseworthy feminine silence, since her claim to fame is that she bit off her own tongue in order to avoid revealing under torture the names of her male coconspirators against the cruel tyrant, Hipparchus. He ends her story by positing silence as the feminine equivalent of masculine eloquence: "In my view, this woman may have gained no less glory by holding, then biting off her tongue than Demosthenes earned from his compatriots by all the flowers of his eloquence" (50.6).[14]

Chief among the offenses for which Boccaccio condemns women are ambition and the failure to remain chaste. His treatment of Clytemnestra (36) is typical. Though he refers to multiple sources and versions of her story, Boccaccio omits many details from the wretched cycle of revenge killings leading up to the murder of Clytemnestra's husband, Agamemnon; most glaringly Boccaccio says nothing of the king's blood sacrifice of their daughter, Iphigenia, instead portraying the queen of Mycenae as a reckless, power-hungry adulteress who deserved to be murdered at the hands of her son, Orestes.[15] While the theme of women's chastity runs throughout the *De mulieribus*, most striking is Boccaccio's insistence that widows not remarry.[16] Lauded alternatives to second marriages include suicide attempted or achieved (90; 94), self-seclusion in the home (89), or dropping dead from grief (81). Boccaccio also praises the widows Marpesia and Lampedo (11; 12), who responded to their husbands' murders by founding a tribe of Amazons. He reserves particular praise for Dido, queen of Carthage, whose story he selectively narrates as one of wifely devotion, steely cunning, and military strategy. Dido's suicide to avoid a second marriage permits Boccaccio once again to compare her ancient heroism with the pale excuses contemporary women offer for accepting new husbands. He speaks in apostrophe to Dido:

> I wish that women who have lost their husbands would turn their eyes upon you and that Christian women in particular would contemplate your strengths. . . . Our women show great acuity in ex-

cusing themselves, so I believe that someone will reply: "I had to marry again: I had been abandoned; my parents and my brothers were dead; suitors were urgent in their flattery; I couldn't resist; I'm made of flesh, not iron." How ridiculous! . . . Perhaps another woman will rise and say: "My domains stretched far and wide, I had a beautiful house, royal furnishings, and great wealth. I wanted to be a mother so that this great fortune would not end up among strangers." What an insane desire! (42.18)

The journey from the *Decameron*'s worldly playfulness to the harsh rigors of the *De mulieribus claris* is less a sudden leap than a programmatic shift of emphasis resulting from steady changes in Boccaccio's intellectual and moral investments. Following the devastating and quite possibly transforming experience of the 1348 plague, Boccaccio inclined increasingly toward the *gravitas* of what would come to be recognized as early humanism. The dedication to the *De mulieribus* already signals a certain ambivalence, the mark perhaps of self-revision. After noting his flight from the *inerti vulgo*, the author professes to have written this book "more for my friends' pleasure than for the benefit of the broader public," yet his aim in later dedicating the work is to obtain a patron's goodwill so that his text will not "languish idly" (*marceret ocio*) in his possession and might reach a wider audience. Boccaccio opens his dedication in a conventionally complimentary vein, observing that since women are the subject of this book, he thought it ought to have a female dedicatee. He then explains to Andrea Acciaiuoli, Countess of Altavilla, that he chose her for this honor in order not to aim too high, for example at a patron like Joan, queen of Sicily and Jerusalem, whose "royal luster" would have eclipsed the "flickering flame of [his] little book so small and weak" (*opusculi tenuis et fere semisopita favillula*). Still, he resumes, Andrea has her good qualities: her probity, her elegant speech, her generous soul, and her powerful intellect far surpass those of most women. The equivocal flattery continues, unrelentingly tin-eared: come to think of it, God endowed Andrea with so many good qualities, and she rises so far above the natural weaknesses of her sex, that this must explain her name, which recalls the Greek word for "men" (*andres*). Here we have the humanists' supreme compliment to women, the assertion that they embody the superior qualities of men. Far more than a damning exposure of bad faith or of the "real" project behind his book, however, Boccaccio's clumsy dedication, together with the image of the "flickering flame" of his "little book so small and weak" and his choice not to have a powerful woman eclipse it, may point to an uneasiness in the multiple agendas of this text.

Gestures of doing, undoing, and doing incompletely appear throughout the *De mulieribus*, a book that itself participates in a partial "undoing" or "redoing" of Boccaccio's earlier literary career. The author writes a monument to women's achievements, but in many cases he disapproves of their actions. He writes for private circulation but seeks a reading public. He seeks the favor of a remarried queen as his patron but includes in his book a number of attacks on queens and widows who remarry. On the one hand, Boccaccio's project to compose a catalog of heroic women—to inscribe them into history as agents and examples—is inspired by the humanist drive to recover the classical past. On the other hand, he also hopes to publish his research and to reach out—in Latin—to a resolutely male, homosocial intellectual community into which he wants to be accepted. His book as a whole, moreover, anticipates an ambivalence at the heart of the later humanist Renaissance regarding women. It was indeed the humanists who first extolled women in numerous, systematic writings defending their intellectual and moral capacities against the slanders of men. It was also the humanists who later educated a privileged class of women to speak out on their own, in print, effectively affording women discursive tools for their own liberation. Yet the humanist fascination with women also betrayed anxieties about the security of male supremacy, especially as women rose increasingly to positions of real agency and power. Boccaccio's *De mulieribus claris*, remarkably, is both feminist and misogynist. In this sense, it may be considered a quintessentially humanist work.

PART VII

DEVOTION TO DANTE AND PETRARCH

CHAPTER SEVENTEEN

A LIFE IN PROGRESS • *(De vita et moribus Francisci Petracchi de Florentia)*

Giuseppe Mazzotta

It was roughly around 1348, and probably even a couple of years earlier, that Boccaccio wrote what is known as *De vita et moribus Francisci
Petracchi de Florentia* (*On the Life and Mores of Francesco Petrarca of Florence*),
a biography of a contemporary poet, Petrarch, who is presented as if he
were already a classic or an epoch-making figure.[1] Above all, he is a "character" to whom Boccaccio relates as an author does—struggling to grasp
his intellectual and moral mettle—while also viewing him as a projection
of Boccaccio's own self-consciousness. Boccaccio's *Life* of Petrarch tells of
the growth of the poet-humanist as well as the faintly adumbrated perplexi-
ties the poet arouses in the biographer. Because so much is at stake—not
the least Boccaccio's own real and wished-for relationship with the senior,
famous Petrarch—we cannot be surprised to find out that the narrative is
marked by attentiveness to the deepest, most fundamental questions of poetry and poetry's (and the poet's) relationship to life, ethics, and politics. Yet
the biography does not provide an overview of Petrarch's life, accomplishments, and thought as a whole. Nor could it. Petrarch is at this time in his
mid-forties, and Boccaccio cannot but produce a work in progress that by
its very nature gives itself an open-ended process of becoming.

There is no reason, however, to believe that the necessarily inconclusive,
provisional structure of the biographical text lacks the precision that a definitive version would in all likelihood display. Boccaccio, brilliant prose
stylist that he is, makes apparent his complex, coherent assessment of Petrarch's life and works in spite of the open-endedness of his account. The
specific formal structure shaping the narrative emerges in its last paragraphs
(28–30). Boccaccio sets out to recapitulate the poet's production, ranging
from the epic poem *Africa* (which, though left in a fragmentary state, is
mentioned as if it were already completed) to the *Secretum*, to the eclogues,
and to the lost comedy *Filostrato*. The paragraphs conclude with Boccaccio's

admission that he interrupts his telling in the persuasion that future biographers will probe more fully into Petrarch's life and achievements.

For all his authorial modesty and the consciousness of the radically unfinished quality of this biography (like the *Secretum*, which is also viewed as finished), Boccaccio is in fact drawing attention to the relation between fragments and totality and to the peculiarity of the biographical genre. Can one divine the shape of the whole from a fragment? The answer to the question is found in his understanding of biography as an ongoing commentary on a writer's life and works, as an interpretive depiction of the essential traits Petrarch exhibits in his so-far unfinished intellectual project. The reader thus finds himself on the horns of a dilemma: whether to confront the biography as a definitive celebration or to consider it only a contingent, partial view of Petrarch. It logically follows from the ambiguities of the text's structure that we should read Boccaccio's narrative as a paradoxically fragmentary totality, and this paradox demands that we look at *what* he says and *how* he says it.

Boccaccio's understanding of the conceptual implications of the biographical genre reflects his familiarity with the widespread traditions of the Provençal *vidas* of poets, of reverential hagiographies or legends of saints (such as Saint Jerome's *Lives of Illustrious Men*, which is modeled on Plutarch), and of classical portraits of poets, such as Donatus's *Life* of Virgil.[2] As he eventually will find out when writing his *De casibus virorum illustrium*, the narrative of a life is notoriously slippery. Biographies tell the story of an individual life, and in doing so they fuse together fiction and history (literature and facts), and, unavoidably, they raise the question of whether or not the character whose life is narrated is a "world-historical" individual. From this perspective, a number of dramatic difficulties inhere in the structure of the biographical genre: as a study of a personality, a biography aims at representing a private human experience, in itself often unfathomable, within a larger public framework. At the same time, a biography seeks to see through the muddy waters of history via the lenses of private lives (or to nullify the thought of any such relation).

In its general outline, Boccaccio's *Life* of Petrarch faces and brings to a head the contradictory impulses potentially lodged within this rhetorical mode. Its purpose is to shed light on two correlated aspects of Petrarch's life, his poetry and his mores, in the belief that the two dimensions involve and complement each other. The opening lines read: "The poet Francesco Petrarca, a famous man and eminent for both his life's conduct and knowledge, enjoyed a most glorious fame all over the world at the time of the pontificate of Benedict XII."[3] We cannot but be struck by the comprehensiveness and subtlety of the facts put forth with the profuse and yet controlled, trenchant generosity of a writer who stylizes himself as an admiring disciple and friend. Petrarch, so Boccaccio implies, is not one of his contemporaries' number. He is exceptional in that his fame transcends all national boundaries and stretches to the farthest points of the Christian lands. More precisely, the *De vita Petracchi* appears to be both an ethical portrait (*de . . . moribus*) of Petrarch's virtues (and, implicitly, a careful critique of the possible moral and political shortcomings of the story's character) and a biographical sketch of his existential choice to be a poet and heed the irresistible call of the Muse of poetry. Because Petrarch is primarily acknowledged as a *poeta*, the narrative focuses at the start on relating his intellectual history and background and on highlighting his engagement with the classical literary tradition (Virgil, Horace, Ovid, Lucan, Statius, and Juvenal) (par. 8).

Boccaccio stresses Petrarch's poetic apprenticeship in order to account for his public recognition on the world stage as a poet. He can be exemplary in that his education is rooted in and stems from the soil of the ancient classical culture and includes poetry, rhetoric, and the canons of moral philosophy (Seneca), as well as the physical sciences. This traditional curriculum, crystallized in the circle of the liberal arts, is supplemented by the teachings of Neoplatonic theology (Plato and Ambrose are coupled together for their rhetorical mellifluousness) (par. 18). The implication is clear: Petrarch's personal understanding and practice of poetry followed in the path traced by Christian humanism, which originated, as Boccaccio says, with the "apostle" Paul and encompassed the double inheritance of the Latin classical tradition and Christian doctrine. In the life of Petrarch, so Boccaccio implies, these two thematic strains, the poetic and the moral spheres, may often clash and differ profoundly from each other, but at the start the text unfolds on the premise of their possible coexistence.

The intertwining of the two dimensions is not entirely unproblematic. In reality, the point of departure of the biography betrays the presence of an oblique tension in Boccaccio's own narrative posture. The circumstances surrounding the composition of the text help us frame the diffraction in his posture. At this point in his life, Boccaccio had not yet personally met Petrarch, although he had already heard of him from the Augustinian theologian at the University of Paris, Dionigi da Borgo San Sepolcro.[4] Boccaccio also knew that Petrarch had received the crown of poet laureate on the steps of the Capitol in Rome on April 8, 1341. And although Boccaccio had not yet written the *Decameron*, he had by this time completed his *Filocolo* (1336–38), his *Filostrato* (ca. 1335 or after), his *Teseida* (ca. 1339–41), the *Elegia di madonna Fiammetta* (1343–44), and the *Ninfale fiesolano* (1344–46).

These powerful romances of characters misled in the labyrinth of love's paths, and Boccaccio's insight into love as the pivot of the universe, certainly made him feel akin to the poet-humanist Petrarch. Further, the two men shared an abiding interest in classical culture. Nonetheless, the prestigious, international recognition Petrarch had received, indeed the reception of his thought and work, could only be seen as signs of the enormous distance between Boccaccio and his contemporary. The *De vita Petracchi* is consciously shaped as an account of the relation of distance and closeness between the author and his character. And it is possible to suspect that Boccaccio is aware that the biographical project provisionally overturns his genuine sense of subordination to the "character" that he, as the author, is constructing.

The distance between them is dramatized by the reference in the text (pars. 14–20) to the public ceremony of the coveted poetic coronation, which in Boccaccio's consciousness acquires the status of a decisive event. Thanks to this historic occurrence, he says, it seemed that the Golden Age had returned to the land. Nothing like this had happened since the emperor Domitian crowned Statius (par. 16). The elevation of Petrarch to "poet laureate" is evidence that he had deservedly attained the heights of fame and, what is more, won international acclaim while living abroad. In short, Petrarch is a legend, nothing less than the reincarnation of Virgil (par. 8), one to be counted the equal of Cicero and Seneca (par. 9). But this sense of a gulf separating the more provincial author from his cosmopolitan character, Boccaccio from Petrarch, is attenuated as Boccaccio obliquely expresses his intense desire for a possible personal and intellectual closeness between the two of them.

A first sign of this impulse to draw Petrarch within the circle of Boccaccio's own intellectual life appears as he stresses the geographical and historic kinship between them. After the pithy encapsulation of Petrarch's fame, the narrative situates him within the historical context of his family origins. As a native of Certaldo, Boccaccio stresses Petrarch's birth in Arezzo on July 20, 1374, of Florentine parents, Ser Petracco and "Letta" (Eletta Canigiani). And in a move that characterizes Boccaccio's desire to forge what I would like to call the "the myth of Tuscany," he stresses the Florentine origin of his family and the civil war that forced the whole family into exile in Avignon (pars. 1–2).

Boccaccio did hope that a new dawn would finally follow the night of Florence's civil war, and his myth of Tuscany, with its emphasis on the cultural and natural bonds the new generations shared, was a way of transcending the political divisions of the past and holding open the possibility of a general reconciliation. His reference to the political turbulence in Florence, therefore, casts an ambiguous light on the perplexing connection between Petrarch and the noble man-at-arms Azzo of Correggio. Their friendship is recorded in stark language: "Having then obtained his coronation as poet laureate, he went to Parma with Azzo of Correggio, and here, joined to him by a sincere friendship, he lived with him for some time, and lives with him up to the present day."[5] The obscure political link between the poet and the man-at-arms (or generally, the nexus between poetry and power) constitutes a unifying thread of the biography, and the mystery of that connection is never dispelled. Nor is the political theme, which hovers over the representation of Petrarch, and is bracketed when Boccaccio reflects on the fascination Petrarch exerts on himself. The fascination for the master is born of a spirit of nationalist pride in Petrarch's achievement. And Boccaccio focuses on his own competitiveness, which is cast not as rivalry but as desire to emulate Petrarch, as the constructive emulation of a poet by another poet.

The meaning Boccaccio assigns to the notion of *poeta* emerges sharply from the reference to the examination administered to Petrarch by King Robert of Anjou in Naples (pars. 12–14). Poetry rises from within the depths of the tradition of wisdom, and it flourishes on the horizon of moral philosophy, history, theology, and politics. To be a poet means to inaugurate a new style of thinking and feeling. Above all, it means possessing the power to rebel and break away from the mold and expectations of others, such as one's own natural family, and to claim the freedom with which the poetic exercise is identified. Specifically, we are told that Ser Petracco, the poet's father, sent his gifted son to Bologna to study law, but Petrarch—much as Boccaccio himself had done—showed himself indifferent to his father's wishes and, like Boccaccio, disregarded jurisprudence in favor of poetry.

The common turn their vocations have taken becomes the point of departure for Boccaccio's careful expression of his friendly equality with and, implicitly, even ambivalences toward Petrarch's supposedly superior rank. As befits a biography's effort to capture the living reality of its subject, Boccaccio provides a series of objective facts about Petrarch: his looks (tall), his complexion (dark), his mild and affable manners, his austere deportment, his powers of speech and prodigious memory, and his musical taste and knack for singing. And although Petrarch was deeply religious, he wrote most elegant poetry for "Laurettam quamdam" (par. 26), "a certain Lauretta," whom he ardently loved. To be sure, Boccaccio adds, this love for Laura may have to be interpreted *allegorice* (allegorically). The libidinal, sensual drive torturing Petrarch himself (which the author of labyrinthine romances such as the *Elegia di madonna Fiammetta* and the *Filostrato* certainly well understands) abolishes the assumption of any crucial hierarchical difference between the author and his subject.

The critique of Petrarch, however, goes beyond the cautious recognition of his incapacity to live by the standards of the ascetic ideals he pursued and of the allegorical disguises within which he masks his sexual desires. Boccaccio's critique centers not on personal morality but on the political choices Petrarch made, such as befriending Azzo. The fundamental problem for Boccaccio is the disparity between, on the one hand, Petrarch's cultivation of the intellectual and spiritual life and, on the other, the inexplicable, puzzling bond he develops with Azzo and, generally, with princes.[6] If Petrarch's earlier role at the Avignonese court is reconstructed and framed in terms that do not preclude the cultivation of poetry and the freedom it embodies, the role of Azzo in Petrarch's life becomes the inexplicable event in the biography, an incomplete story and an emblem, portrayed in chiaroscuro, of the poet succumbing to the sinister, secret fascination of power.

It turns out that Petrarch, this most meticulous reader of himself and of others' representations of him, must have felt the biting force of Boccaccio's early, stringent account. He responded to it and sought to refute Boccaccio's arguments in his own *Posteritati* and in the epistle to Guido Sette (*Seniles* 10.2). For Boccaccio, however, the biography of Petrarch amounts to the discovery of a stranger whom he wants to befriend. Yet the biographer is caught in a quandary: he is both fascinated and bewildered by the luster and enigmas of the character he draws, and this ambivalence prefigures the trajectory of their relationship, which is marked both by Boccaccio's love for Petrarch and by the misunderstandings to which love is forever vulnerable.

CHAPTER EIGHTEEN

TO PRAISE DANTE, TO PLEASE
PETRARCH • *(Trattatello in laude di Dante)*

Elsa Filosa

The *Trattatello in laude di Dante* (*Little Treatise in Praise of Dante*) is the first extensive biography of a "modern" poet in the vernacular, one that would have a lasting influence in Italy on the genre of the literary *vita*.[1] It is also one of Boccaccio's first efforts in a form that he would come to master, especially through his Latin works *De casibus virorum illustrium* (*The Downfall of Illustrious Men*) and *De mulieribus claris* (*Famous Women*). Boccaccio twice revised the Dante biography, producing three different versions: 1351–55, early 1360s, and probably early 1370s.[2]

The motivation for this innovative work as well as its successive redactions sprang respectively from Boccaccio's admiration for Dante and from his discussions with Petrarch.[3] In late March 1351 Boccaccio visited Petrarch in Padua as an ambassador from Florence to offer him a chair at the University of Florence. At this crucial meeting the two new friends discussed the value of poetry and probably also began a debate, left unresolved, about Dante and his work.[4] Boccaccio could not believe that the library of the "excellent teacher" did not contain the works of Dante.[5] To remedy this absence, as a gift to Petrarch Boccaccio compiled a manuscript between 1351 and 1352 that contained the *Commedia* and a dedicatory poem, *Ytalie iam certus honos* (Sure honor now of Italy),[6] an assertive outburst about the greatness of Dante and his poetry. He wants Petrarch to agree with his judgment: "That Dante—whom you praise and justly worship; whom Florence, mother of great poets, produced and honors with applause—will be the second after the other [Claudian]."[7] He concludes with five hortatory imperatives: "take it up, read through it, join it to your own favorites, worship it, approve it" (*suscipe, perlege, iunge tuis, cole, comprova*). As the poem's editor Giuseppe Velli has written, Boccaccio's "defense of Dante is a self-defense, even in the face of Petrarch's overbearing assertiveness."[8]

It is in this context that we must locate the origin and composition of the *Trattatello in laude di Dante*—as Boccaccio himself informally names it in the *Esposizioni sopra la "Comedia"*[9]—which actually carries, in its first and longest redaction, a Latin title: *De origine, vita, studiis et moribus viri clarissimi Dantis Aligerii florentini, poete illustris, et de operibus compositis ab eodem* ("The origins, life, habits, and studies of the most illustrious poet Dante Alighieri of Florence, and the works he composed"). Boccaccio originally planned Dante's *vita* as an *accessus ad auctorem*[10] of a *liber Dantis* (Dante book) that would include the *Vita nuova*, the *Commedia* (as well as *Argomenti*, or canto summaries, by Boccaccio in tercets), and fifteen *canzoni*.[11]

The *Trattatello*, or *De origine*, reflects Boccaccio's intention to build a verbal monument for Dante, given that Florence—contrary to ancient custom—had never done anything for her extraordinary son, after sending him contemptuously into exile:

> Although I, with my paltry powers, am not fully fitted for the task I am undertaking, I will try to do what the city, with its magnificent resources, has not done. . . . I shall not express his honor with a statue or with splendid rites (a custom that is no longer among us, and for which my strength would not be sufficient), but with words—even though they may not be equal to this enormous task. I do have plenty of these, and I shall use them so that other nations, whether in whole or in part, may not claim that his native land was totally ungrateful to a poet of his great stature.[12]

This monument consisted not only of the *Trattatello*, but also of the whole Dante book that creates a canon in the manuscript tradition and rescues for posterity the fifteen songs.[13]

The work begins in a polemical vein, opening with a maxim from Solon, a recognized font of wisdom, that every republic has to walk on two feet:

> The right foot had to see that no act of wrongdoing would go unpunished, while the left foot had to reward every good deed. He added that, if either of these operations was hindered by vice or negligence or was less than well carried out, a republic that functioned in this manner would go lame; and if, through some catastrophe, it should be deficient in both operations, Solon would have to consider it in all certainty to be unable to stand on its feet.[14]

With this opening Boccaccio begins a vehement attack on Florence not only for having exiled Dante but also for proving to be a culturally insensitive city. As the son of a merchant enlightened and driven to poetry by the *Commedia*, his work on the poet's life is a due tribute to his first inspirational flame.

By rehabilitating Dante, Boccaccio returns the Muses to within the walls of Florence. He defends literary culture itself and, by extolling Dante's vernacular poetry, affirms the status of Italian as a literary language. Indeed, the *Trattatello* includes two great digressions: one is the political invective against Florence, the other his statement on the nature and origins of poetry.[15] These sections may appear at first sight unconnected, but they actually share a single objective: the defense and glorification of vernacular poetry and of the poet's character.

After its polemical opening, the structure of the work largely follows the life of Dante: ancestors and parents (1.11–16); birth (accompanied by a premonitory dream of his mother) and childhood devoted to studies (1.17–27); his love for Beatrice (1.28–38); his grief upon Beatrice's death, and his ensuing marriage—accompanied by an antiuxorial invective (1.39–59);[16] his political career and exile (1.60–85); his last years in Ravenna, his death and funeral, and the epitaph by Giovanni del Virgilio (1.86–91); a second invective against Florence (1.92–110); physical portrait, habits, and character of Dante (1.111–26); digression on poetry (1.127–62); qualities and flaws of Dante (1.163–74); his literary works (1.175–204); interpretation of Dante's mother's premonitory dream, and epilogue (1.205–28).

Today's reader, accustomed to modern biographies, may be disappointed by the sparse personal data in this literary *vita*. Indeed, as Boccaccio confirms in the *Esposizioni sopra la "Comedia,"* this "little treatise" aims to magnify the character of the poet and of poetry, even at the expense of truth. One need only compare this life of Dante with a modern biography of the poet to see that Boccaccio's chronology is dubious.[17] For example, in the *Trattatello* Dante's marriage takes place after Beatrice's death, whereas in fact he married Gemma Donati in 1285, and Beatrice is said to have died in 1290. Some details are difficult to prove and are even unlikely, such as Dante's debated stay in Paris; others are clearly legendary, such as his mother's dream. Nevertheless, whether truthful or fictitious, all reflect a deliberate plan to exalt Dante as a poet.

To understand the structure of the *Trattatello* in greater depth, one must identify its literary subtexts. First, Boccaccio wanted to reconnect Dante's vernacular poetry with the classical tradition—a wish that emerges immediately in the choice of a Latin title—and to tie the life of Dante to that of Virgil, as the author of the *Commedia* had himself done in choosing Virgil to be his guide and in making himself "sesto tra cotanto senno" (sixth among such intellects) in Limbo (*Inferno* 4.102). Already in the *Amorosa visione*, written a decade earlier, between 1342 and 1343, Boccaccio has Dante crowned by the Muses—perhaps influenced by Petrarch's coronation at Rome in the same period—after a list of Greek and Roman writers headed by Virgil.[18] It is unsurprising therefore that the first and most substantial model visible in the *Trattatello* relates the work to the *Lives of Virgil* circulating in the Middle Ages, especially those by Donatus and Servius, in order to create continuity with the classical world and to identify Dante as the new Virgil. Scholars have noticed numerous details that link the two biographies.[19] For example, according to Boccaccio, Dante dedicated the three books of the *Commedia* to three noblemen: the *Inferno* to Uguccione della Faggiuola, the *Purgatorio* to Moroello Malaspina, and the *Paradiso* to Frederick II of Aragon, who became King Frederick III of Sicily (1.193). Similarly, the *Lives of Virgil* report that the *Eclogues* were dedicated to Asinius Pollio, the *Georgics* to Maecenas, and the *Aeneid* to the emperor Augustus.[20] Chronology, too, could have been influenced by the *Lives of Virgil*, according to which the *Eclogues* were composed over three years, the *Georgics* over seven, and the *Aeneid* over eleven, for a total of twenty-one years. Likewise the *Commedia* is given as begun in 1300 and completed in 1321, the year of the author's death.[21] Virgil is said to have studied in many cultural centers, as is Dante, including Paris (probably a fiction suggested by Giovanni Villani's *Chronicle*).[22] Finally, the premonitory dream of Dante's mother recalls Virgil's mother's dream of a laurel bush; the *Trattatello* offers a more complex oneiric account, whose allegorical exegesis comes at the work's conclusion.[23]

This premonitory dream introduces another model underlying Boccaccio's biography: hagiography.[24] His intention is to cloak the "divine" poet, and especially his masterpiece, with a sacred destiny. Thus the composition of the *Commedia*, though repeatedly interrupted, reaches completion. The first seven cantos, left behind in Dante's escape from Florence, would be miraculously returned to him by the grace of God ("We certainly must believe that Fortune can work nothing contrary to what God ordains").[25] Also, after his death Dante appears in a vision to his sleeping son in order to reveal the hiding place where he had stored the last thirteen cantos of the *Paradiso*. This postmortem miracle is typical of hagiography.

His mother's dream is followed by the choice of his name, which foretells his destiny: Dante, "he who gives." The author of the *Trattatello*, in high style, passionately exclaims that Dante is responsible for the rebirth of poetry in Italy:

> This was that Dante who gave purpose to this commentary. This was that Dante who was granted special grace by God in our times. This was that Dante who was the first person to pave the way for the return of the Muses, who had been exiled from Italy. It is his great works that lend nobility to the Florentine language, and it is because of him that the beauty of our vernacular poetry received its proper rhyme and meter. Because of him it can also justly be said that poetry was brought back to life from death. All these things, when duly considered, will show that he could not have carried any other name but that of Dante [The Giver], a most deserved reputation.[26]

With this "high" moment of the *Trattatello* begins the biography proper of Dante, marked by the protagonist's definition as a literary hero. This heroic portrait is something new, that of a man who makes poetry the center of his life and who must constantly struggle against adversity for both poetry and the vernacular tongue to triumph. From his earliest childhood, contemptuous of all other pursuits, Dante abandoned himself to the study of the liberal arts, poetry, and theology, "heedless of heat, of cold, of sleeplessness, of fasts, of any other bodily discomfort."[27] Furthermore, while "academic endeavors . . . usually require solitude, freedom from anxiety, and tranquility of mind . . . almost from the beginning of his life and up to the day of his death . . . he had to endure an uncontrollable passion for love, a wife, a family and civic duties, exile, and poverty."[28] Despite all these adversities, our hero managed to complete his *Commedia*, enabling the victory of vernacular poetry and achieving eternal glory for all posterity.

In his blending of classical, hagiographic, and anecdotal traditions with a heroic narrative of the poet's character in a vernacular work, Boccaccio appears to aim for a diverse audience. The poem to Petrarch, *Ytalie iam certus honos*, defined Dante as both pleasing to the educated (*gratum doctis*) and admirable for the masses (*vulgo mirabile*). Here Boccaccio extols Dante as a holy and heroic poet for an audience of Florentine merchants, but he also writes for the clergy, at least some of whom were unwilling to accept the *Commedia* as "divine." He further targets an audience of intellectuals who in the *Trattatello* could find in Dante a new Virgil, and he undoubtedly addresses a particularly sophisticated reader in Petrarch.

Perhaps this last is the one we should imagine as the *Trattatello*'s ideal reader. It is no coincidence that Boccaccio opens the work with Solon's maxim, which translates almost verbatim *Familiares* 8.10, addressed to the citizens of Florence as unable to safeguard justice.[29] This opening, with Boccaccio's invective against Florence, may be an appeal to the *Magister* for sympathy. As Petrarch attacks Florentines for leaving crimes unpunished, so Boccaccio attacks them for not rewarding those who deserve it. If the *Trattatello*'s first digression finds its source in a letter from Petrarch, similarly the second digression, on the nature and origins of poetry, derives mostly from *Familiares* 10.4, written around 1349, and known to Boccaccio from his Paduan stay of 1351. This second digression makes clear that Boccaccio accepted the theories of the humanistic circle in Padua, which stressed the essential compatibility between poetry and theology. In Boccaccio's eyes Dante was the poet who perfectly personified the theological poet, and he hoped that Petrarch could see him the same way.

In 1359, a few months after his third meeting with Boccaccio, this time in Milan, Petrarch wrote *Familiares* 21.15. It was a response to what he calls his friend's "apologetic epistle," written after the latter's return to Florence.[30] As Carlo Paolazzi writes, "Petrarch's letter refers to a clearly defined 'corpus' of praise, equally available for the two epistolary interlocutors"—very likely the *Trattatello*—"whose author Boccaccio, fearful of having praised Dante at the indirect expense of Petrarch, submits to the latter's judgment, begging him to examine and to evaluate the work, while Petrarch deflects any suspicion of jealousy by approving the praise of Dante, encouraging Boccaccio to polish and to publish it."[31]

Familiares 21.15 is crucial to the history of the *Trattatello* because of its connection with cuts and corrections in the second edition of the work.[32] This time the title is vernacular: *La origine, vita, costumi e studii del chiarissimo poeta Dante Alighieri di Firenze, e dell'opere composte da lui* (On the origin, life, habits, and studies of the most famous poet Dante Alighieri of Florence, and the works composed by him). This second redaction is commonly called the *Compendio*, as it is shorter than the previous version, but it is a definite rewriting, with greater sobriety. Gone is the invective and the tone of resentment toward Florence.[33] Boccaccio also drastically reduces his praise of Dante, and the narrative is tighter, free of digressions. Even the theme of poetry has been retouched. While in the first edition poetry is identified with theology, in the second it is only "similar" (*simigliante di quella*, 2.91).

There is no doubt that many cuts aimed to temper enthusiasm for Dante.[34] Expunged, for example, is the laudatory paragraph 19, cited above, which "had come straight from the heart," as Pier Giorgio Ricci observes.[35] But perhaps Boccaccio sought also to gratify *Magister* Petrarch and to advance the latter's humanistic program. Take, for example, his comparison of Dante, Homer, and Virgil. In the first version of the *Trattatello*, Boccaccio declares that Dante "exalted [the vernacular] to prestigious heights among us Italians, just as Homer had done among the Greeks or Virgil among the Latins."[36] In a passage from *Familiares* 21.15 that Paolazzi defines as "very bold" (*audacissimo*), Petrarch defends himself against accusations of jealousy toward Dante (whom he never cites except indirectly in the entire epistle) by completely overturning Boccaccio's claims: "How can someone who does not envy Virgil envy someone else, unless perhaps I envied him the applause and raucous acclaim of the fullers or tavern keepers or woolworkers who offend the ones whom they wish to praise, whom I, like Virgil and Homer, delight in doing without?"[37] Petrarch polemically establishes a dual relationship between Latin poetry for an intellectual audience, on the one hand, and vernacular poetry for a simple audience, on the other. This places Dante on a level of irreparable inferiority before the triad Homer-Virgil-Petrarch. In the Chigi second redaction, the Homer-Virgil-Dante comparison disappears.

Undeniably influenced by Petrarch's letter of 1359, the shortened Chigi version nevertheless amplifies the narrative considerably on at least one point, when Boccaccio, after recounting obstacles overcome by Dante in his dedication to study, considers that his hero is the exact opposite of those who allow themselves to be disturbed by a "slight murmur" (*leve murmur*) (*Familiares* 21.15.8).[38] Here Boccaccio adds the following gloss:

> What will those say now whose houses are not sufficient for their studies and who thus seek solitude in the forests? Or those who have complete repose, and whose ample faculties without any anxiety are supported by every opportunity? Or those who, free from wife and children, have as much leisure as they desire? Many of those are such that, if they were not sitting in comfort, or if they were to hear a murmur, they would not be able to read or write, let alone reflect, if their elbow were not at rest.[39]

The diametrical opposition between the unfortunate Dante and the "blessed" ones is cloaked in an "ironic gibe against excessively delicate minds,"[40] transforming Petrarch's reference to a "slight murmur" into the disturbances of everyday life. As Giuseppe Velli notes, "Even apart from the 'solitude of the forest,' and from 'the continuous repose,' was it not Petrarch who had 'ample faculties,' and who was 'free from wife and children'? This is not a malicious question on our part: the ambiguity is in the text itself. The least that can be said is that it escapes the absolute control of its author."[41] It is in this irony, whether deliberate or unintentional (and in any case instinctual), that we can see Boccaccio's autonomy as a writer and thinker, an intellectual who largely stands up to Petrarch's authority.

From Petrarch's humanistic perspective, aimed at establishing standards of evaluation based on the philological recovery of classical Latin literature, Dante had no role and no place. It is a role and place, though, that Boccaccio, in a literary vision that is inclusive, not exclusive, cannot bring himself to withhold from Dante and the vernacular, however faithful he remains to Petrarch's program. It is in accordance with this inclusive vision that Boccaccio composes the Chigiano manuscript, bringing together Dante's *Commedia* and Petrarch's *Rime sparse*, in an important early anthology of vernacular Italian literature, whether the *Magister* wishes it or not.[42] Therefore, "Boccaccio's responses are not simply reactive, and it is essential to note that he constantly attempts to juxtapose Dante and Petrarch and to make them complement one another, as he does earlier in the *Life of Petrarch* and later on the pages of his Chigi manuscript."[43]

These editorial activities demonstrate that Boccaccio possessed a sharp philological awareness, which he was able to apply to Dante's works: "It was an approach that applied an incipient humanist textual sensibility to the vernacular sphere, one that represented the beginning of a response to Petrarch's worries about the uncontrolled nature of the transmission of vernacular texts."[44] As a result, whereas Boccaccio after his encounter with Petrarch would turn to Latin, Petrarch after his encounter with Boccaccio would pay more attention to his vernacular *nugellae*.[45]

It is by virtue of this defense of Dante's poetry that Boccaccio has been defined by Giorgio Padoan as "Dante's loyal follower,"[46] after Giuseppe Billanovich had called him "Petrarch's greatest disciple."[47] This "resistance" in the name of Dante is also a defense "of his own role up till now (late 1350's) as an almost exclusively vernacular writer/poet."[48] In the 1370s Boccaccio would compose a third redaction of the *Trattatello*, an amplified version of the second (his *Compendio*), probably just before beginning his lectures on the *Commedia* for the people of Florence, yet one more sign of his undimmed devotion to Dante and his works.[49] After all, in *De casibus virorum illustrium* (8.1.6) Boccaccio may call Petrarch "my excellent and reverend teacher" (*optimum venerandumque preceptorem meum*), but Dante is addressed as "excellent father" (*pater optime*) in *De casibus* 9.23.7, whereas Dante calls him "my son" (*fili mi*). At least until Petrarch's death, Boccaccio establishes an exclusive line of descent, as if it were literally a blood relationship, with Dante as his "first guide and light" for his love of poetry.

CHAPTER NINETEEN

BOCCACCIO'S DIVIDED ALLEGIANCE
• *(Esposizioni sopra la "Comedia")*

Robert Hollander

Giovanni Boccaccio is perhaps the only author, great in his own right, to spend considerable effort working to augment the glory of not just one but two of his contemporary or near-contemporary fellow poets, Dante and Petrarch. As is frequently noted, his public attention to Dante is overwhelming. From the first pages of the *Caccia di Diana* (1334?) the presence of Dante in and behind Boccaccio's poems has been perceptible to almost all readers. The same may be said of all his later poetic production. However, it was only in 1982 that two scholars, Attilio Bettinzoli and I, in the same volume of *Studi sul Boccaccio*, would independently make concerted cases for the large presence of Dante's poetry in the *Decameron*'s prose, a position now shared by many and most recently supported by Kristina Marie Olson.[1] There is virtually no practicing *boccaccista* who will deny that Giovanni wrote anything without Dante very much present in his active memory. Eventually, he turned from one kind of service (imitating the words and concepts of his predecessor in his own poems and stories) to another, that of biographer and commentator. The *Esposizioni*, his readings of the *Divina Commedia* divided canto by canto into "literal" and "allegorical" expositions, are the final manifestation of this second vocation, which has an earlier expression in the *Trattatello*, a combination of literary biography and praise for the poet (1351–55).[2] The writer's public work on Dante seems to have been stimulated by the beginning of his relationship with Petrarch (1350), with whom he enjoyed a series of discussions (at times, debates) about Dante's worth and importance.[3] The *Trattatello* was twice revised, thus indicating its importance to its author. This first public expression of a critical interest in Dante's work occurred in the wake of his finishing the *Decameron* — if the dates we have happen to be accurate. While, apart from Michael Papio's translation, there has been relatively little recent work on the *Esposizioni*, there has been quite a lot of important work done, from varying perspectives, on the *Trattatello*, the concerns of which a reader of the *Esposizioni* will probably also share. It is for this reason that this corpus is briefly represented here: Carlo Paolazzi is convinced that the *Trattatello* was written in answer to Petrarch's negative evaluation of Dante in *Familiares* 21.15; Giuseppe Velli offers the reminder that, as early as 1341, Boccaccio may have been composing his first "life of a poet" (in that case, of Petrarch); Todd Boli discusses the way in which Boccaccio, in fact, represented Dante as resembling Petrarch; Victoria Kirkham notices how often Boccaccio's Dante is presented as resembling Virgil; Karen Elizabeth Gross offers perhaps surprising evidence that Boccaccio made use of details from the life of Saint Thomas in his portrait of Dante.[4]

The dates traditionally assigned to the composition and delivery of the *Esposizioni* are a mixture of guesswork and fact. The first lecture was presented on Sunday, October 23, 1373, in the church of Santo Stefano in Badia. There are numerous testimonies to this *datum*, including notice from Benvenuto da Imola of the location, if not of the date, and of the fact that the edifice was in derelict condition, "as I saw while listening to my venerable instructor Boccaccio of Certaldo interpreting this noble poem in that church."[5] If that was the date that Boccaccio actually began lecturing, when did he begin *preparing* the lectures? That is somewhat more difficult to establish. And since the manuscripts themselves are not autographs, questions about the dates of their production and about their exact form are unlikely to be resolved. However, if he had waited for consummation of his contract with the *Comune* (for the princely sum of one hundred gold florins), he would not have begun to compose his commentary before October 18. What was included in Boccaccio's first *lectura* in Santo Stefano that day and in his next *lezione*? Did they contain, as does the preface to the printed version, the *Accessus*, or introduction to the author (eighteen pages in Giorgio Padoan's edition)[6] and/or a portion of the *esposizione litterale* of *Inferno* 1 (thirty-five pages)? *Lezione* 3 begins with an explanation of Virgil's words "poeta fui" (*Inf.* 1.73, *esp. litt.*), thus allowing for the possibility that Sunday was devoted to the *Accessus* and Monday to *Inferno* 1.1–72. We may choose to theorize about such things (perhaps surprisingly no one seems to have done so), but we shall probably never resolve the issue. Thus for the *terminus a quo* of the writing, as distinguished from the lecturing, we have a fairly open earliest date but a firm latest: October 22, 1373—at least if we believe that Boccaccio wrote before he spoke, which is probably a reasonable view. When did Boccaccio finish or, at least, terminate the lectures? Here there is a generally shared understanding. The lecture to Canto 17 is broken off abruptly, after moving through vv. 1–17 in less than the space provided by two fairly short pages. This would clearly imply that, in his public *lezioni*, Boccaccio did not get past Canto 16, if indeed he got that far.

A question that few have entertained concerns the length (an hour? two or three times that?) and the number of his presentations in the church. If the *terminus a quo* for these is October 23, 1373, the *terminus ad quem* is, by nearly common consent, the first few days of January 1374, when Boccaccio became a shut-in in the house in Certaldo that now serves as his memorial, both library and museum. He would never leave it until he was carried just up the street to the Church of Ss. Iacopo e Filippo to be buried in its pavement, where his tomb may still be found.[7] Guyda Armstrong and Vika Zafrin are of the opinion that "although records are scarce, it seems from the manuscript evidence that Boccaccio gave about fifty-five lectures in total before he fell ill."[8] In fact, his contract with the *Comune* called for him to lecture every day except holidays. This schedule almost certainly required residence in Florence, since spreading as many as fifty-nine lectures over seventy-five days (eight in October, thirty in November, thirty-one in December, possibly as many as a half dozen in January) would have been an arduous enough undertaking without "commuting" by carriage from Certaldo. When we realize how long the entire project was as planned, we also understand that Florentine residence was a necessity. Padoan's edition includes references to numbered *lectiones* throughout the text. Do these replicate marks that Boccaccio himself made in the original manuscript either before or, as seems more likely, after he had given the lectures? Let us see where these indications lead us.

Padoan's edition averages some 375 words per page. The *siglum* "L" (*lectio*, or "lecture, lesson, reading") followed by a Roman numeral runs through the entire text. The first of these indications is "L. III" on page 33. Seven of the sixty are missing (in addition to I and II, also not present are the markers for VII, XII, XVIII, XXIII, XLV).[9] Several interesting facts emerge from a consideration of these materials. First, fewer than one-third of the breaks occur where we would expect them, that is, at the points of clear and important formal divisions: only seventeen of the fifty-three passages marked "L" coincide with the beginnings of the twenty-nine *esposizioni*, whether literal or allegorical. Such an arrangement probably points to the likelihood that writing preceded presentation rather than the reverse. Second, there is a certain consistency in the lengths of the *lectiones*. Twenty-eight are between eight and twelve pages; nine are longer than that, and five are shorter (the reader is reminded that the absence of seven of the sixty *sigla* makes these calculations less exact than one would like). Third, it thus seems likely that Boccaccio had written the *esposizioni* as consecutive prose and indicated the contents of the individual *lectiones* only once he had delivered them. If one assumes that these are annotations indicating what in fact the commentator had "covered" in each *lectio* (and that seems a reasonable assumption), the enormous size of the original project begins to be apparent: more than three hundred *lectiones* to be delivered in a calendar year![10] One may then tentatively conclude that Boccaccio had given his roughly sixty lectures in not many more days than that (no more than seventy-five, as we calculated above). It is probably fair to say that few students of the question seem to realize that the lectures were presented over so short a period, that they poured forth in such a rush. Most studies devoted to the details of Boccaccio's *vita* allow a reader to understand that the lectures were given in 1373 and 1374, with no sense that only less than the last quarter of 1373 and a tiny sliver of the beginning of 1374 were involved.

Such details have considerable effect on our sense of the project that Boccaccio was undertaking. He was, as he knew very well, only another in an already long line of Dantean exegetes; he was probably aware of at least a dozen commentators who had preceded him in the barely more than fifty years since Dante's death. His project was undertaken as a series of lectures in the form of a commentary. As opposed to the *Trattatello*, which may very well be the first modern renewal (at least in prose) of an ancient form, the "life of the poet" (in Virgil's case, Suetonius and Aelius Donatus were the model authors), Boccaccio's *Esposizioni* had no such humanistic originality: the *Commedia* itself had already summoned into existence its own postclassical commentary tradition.

It is instructive that the first literary reference made by Boccaccio at the opening of his *Accessus* is to Plato's *Timaeus*. This is in keeping with his aim to "detheologize" Dante, while presenting him as a worthy Christian philosopher.[11] Several have noted the indubitably clear references in Boccaccio's *Accessus* to the *Epistle to Cangrande*, Dante's thirteenth epistle. (In the dispute over its authenticity, it little matters that Boccaccio either did not realize that Dante was its author or, for whatever reason, wanted to deny his paternity.)[12] He treats the material as a necessary appurtenance to his discussion, which may indicate that he found it in whatever ancillary material was contained in one of the manuscripts of the poem he consulted. To boil this important distinction down to a few words, Boccaccio treats Dante not as *theologus-poeta* (as the epistle insists) but as *poeta-theologus*.[13] This distinction reflects a decision, either conscious or instinctive, to insist on the "traditional humanist" defense of poetry as literally untrue but, through allegory, capable of being understood as consistent with the highest truths. Such an approach to the defense of poetry is a notable feature of Italian fourteenth-century discussions of poetic truth. Dante, whose *Convivio* embraced this "humanistic" approach, had gone his own (and very different) way in the *Commedia*; both Petrarch and Boccaccio, the latter most notably in his *Genealogia deorum gentilium*, aligned themselves with the traditional defense of poetry as literal untruth that yields a higher meaning, one reconcilable with the teachings of theology.

In most cases, the text of each examination of a canto is divided into two parts, or *esposizioni*, the first *litterale*, the second *allegorica* (exceptions are *Inf.* 10–11, 15–16, none of which contains an "allegorical exposition"). Each "literal exposition" begins formulaically, as the first of these reveals a pattern to which the author will return at the beginning of each new canto. Boccaccio begins the *Esposizioni* with the major *divisioni* of the entire poem (the three *cantiche* of *Inferno*, *Purgatorio*, and *Paradiso*), to which he need not return subsequently. He proceeds to divide *Inferno* into two parts, *proemio e trattato* (proem and treatise): that is, Canto 1 and the rest of the canticle. He then divides the first canto itself into two large blocks, vv. 1–60 (the *ruina*, or fall, of the protagonist) and vv. 61–136 (his *soccorso*, or succour, Virgil), both of which are in turn broken into six parts. Boccaccio commits himself to analyses of the literal meanings of words and phrases as he proceeds from "Nel mezzo del cammin" (1.1.3–5), vv. 1–6 (1.1.6–8), vv. 7–9 (1.1.9), and so forth, until he reaches canto 1, verse 73 and the magic word "poeta," which causes by far the longest "pause" in the consecutive treatment of the literal sense we have yet experienced, running ten pages in Padoan's edition (1.1.69–112) and apparently containing the only material presented in the third *lectio*. *Lectio* IV (1.1.113) returns to line-by-line analysis, which continues to the end of the canto. There is perhaps a single gloss that stands out for its idiosyncrasy: at 1.1.154 Boccaccio glosses the pronoun *lei* in v. 123, "con lei ti lascerò nel mio partire" (with her [or him, apparently] I shall leave you when I depart), not, as everyone else in the history of Dante studies has done, as Beatrice, but as Statius, a fascinating but demonstrable error.

Boccaccio's initial practice, strict attention to all of the literal sense of the text, is rigidly adhered to throughout. There is also a certain digressiveness at individual "hot spots." For example, at v. 40, *le cose belle*, the "beautiful things" that form the fixed stars in the eighth heaven, are sufficient cause for a discourse on the ancient astronomers (1.1.25–31); at v. 68, the word *lombardi*, designating Virgil's parentage, gives Boccaccio leave to indulge his recognized and familiar proclivity for geography (1.1.53–58); at v. 71, Virgil's autobiographical remark *vissi a Roma* (I lived in Rome) allows Boccaccio his chance to counter history with the myth of Virgil's life and activities in Naples, which he learned during his own lengthy stay in that city in the 1330s (1.1.61–65). From the preceding paragraph the reader has observed the lengths to which Boccaccio will take divagation once he reaches a triggering word in Dante's text (in that case *poeta*). Continuing his line-by-line analysis with the adjoining phrase *e cantai* (and I sang of), the commentator immediately digresses again, on a related theme, that of Virgil as "singer" (1.1.113–18). His last digression of any length is devoted to Camilla (v. 107).

When we turn to the *esposizione allegorica* of the first canto, we find Boccaccio aligning himself, not with the theological spirit that Dante claimed for himself in so many ways, both large and small, but with that of Macrobius in *De somnio Scipionis* (1.2.8–9). It is not surprising to find him, in the first *esposizione allegorica*, aligning himself (and Dante!) not with the poet's own position, represented by oblique and teasing claims of direct divine inspiration,[14] but with the less disturbing "traditional" defenses of poetry, portrayed as fiction that could be interpreted in philosophical, even "theological," ways. The passage (1.2.18–21) is nothing other than a fairly faithful translation (with the key passages of *Ps.* 113 left in Latin) of the *Epistle to Cangrande* 20–22.[15] The most pertinent observations concerning Boccaccio's direct knowledge of the epistle remain those of Luis Jennaro-MacLennan.[16] It is amusing and instructive to watch Boccaccio come upon the document that we (at least some of us) recognize as Dante's epistle and convert it to material for building a case for the less-than-theological nature of Dante's poem. Against Padoan's notion that Boccaccio did not recognize Dante as the author of the epistle, Jennaro-MacLennan argues that he did realize that Dante was its author but disagreed with him about crucial things, including that the poem is to be considered a comedy, which Boccaccio disputes (*Accessus* 24).[17] Immediately before this citation of the epistle Boccaccio had encapsulated his (mis)interpretation of what that document calls for by turning (1.2.22) to Gregory's *Moralia on Job* to present the idea that the truths found in the *Commedia* are *artificiosamente nascose* (artfully hidden). Padoan's note offers an interpretive paraphrase of this phrase: "mediante le belle finzioni poetiche" (by means of beautiful poetic inventions). Where Dante insists that his poem is literally "true," Boccaccio is pleased to insist that it cannot be. The question remains, Did he know that he was disagreeing with Dante himself?

Having clarified his theoretical bearing by distorting the views put forward in the epistle in order to make them conform to the more usual sort of allegoresis that almost all of Dante's early exegetes embraced, the allegorist sets to work.[18] Perhaps, as Boli has argued from a position that this reader finds intriguing but not convincing, it was the banality of such allegoresis that eventually caused Boccaccio either to reduce the number of allegorical explanations or to abandon the whole project.[19] Having finished the proemial part of the first "official" allegorical explanation of elements encountered in the first canto, he now moves into lengthy explanations of (1) the nature of the protagonist's *sonno*, or "sleep" (1.11; 1.2.29–36); (2) how the world, the flesh, and the devil may lead us into being drawn to that *sonno* (1.2.37–46); (3) the allegorical meaning of the *via* (1.3; 1.2.47–50); (4) the grace that led the author to realize that he had lost that true way (1.3; 1.2.47–63); (5) why it is more likely for a sinner to lose his way *nel mezzo del cammin* than at any other time (1.1–3; 1.2.64–69); the significance (6) of the *selva oscura* (1.2; 1.2.70–77); (7) of the early hour (1.37; 1.2.78–80); (8) of the sun rising over the mountain (1.38; 1.2.81–86); (9) of the diminished fear felt by the protagonist (1.41–43; 1.2.87–89). The tenth and apparently final *esposizione allegorica* is devoted to the three beasts (1.32, 45, 49; 1.2.90–143). It runs away with its author and may have broken his systematic grasp of his material. No longer does he "number" his allegoresis formulaically (each of the previous ten items began with identical phrasing: *La prima cosa, La seconda cosa,* etc.).

This insistent attention to allegory begins to attenuate some three-quarters of the way along in this second part of that treatment of the first canto. The last sections of the *esposizione allegorica* involve a much freer formal arrangement, as Boccaccio moves from considering the evils that Dante had to face, as reported in the first sixty verses, to the "health" sponsored by God, the demarcation marked, according to the glossator, by the verse "Mentre ch'io ruvinava in basso loco" (While I was fleeing to a lower place, 1.61; 1.2.144–45). And now Boccaccio turns his attention to the allegorical significance of Virgil, first seen as *grazia cooperante* and then, as is more usual in the commentary tradition, as *ragione* (1.2.146–58). Virgil, as reason, exhausts for now Boccaccio's allegorical interests. He draws toward his conclusion (1.2.158), presenting Dante as eventually to be instructed by "la guida della teologia, le cui ragioni e dimostrazioni la nostra ragione non può comprendere" (the guidance of theology, whose reasonings and demonstrations our reason [i.e., Virgil] cannot fathom). One senses a provisional ending being written: "Ed in questo mi pare consista la sentenzia dell'allegoria di questo primo canto" (And in this, it seems to me, consists the meaning of the allegory of this first canto). And then (1.2.159–83) Boccaccio finds himself come a cropper where many another has and probably will founder as well: on the meaning of the *veltro* (the hound at 1.101). As he himself admits (1.2.164), he does not understand Dante's riddle. He goes on to assemble a number of other commentators' proposed solutions: (1) he mentions Christ—but he immediately proceeds to distance himself from that hypothesis (1.2.165–68); (2) he recycles the old notion of *feltro* as being some sort of coarse material, and thus humility versus the arrogance of acquisition (1.2.169–71); (3) he then turns to another possible reference—the felt tents of the Tartar kings (1.2.172–77)—which has a certain subsequent history among commentators. It is what comes after these three unlikely (even to Boccaccio) hypotheses that is most compelling. The entirety of the conclusion (1.2.178–83) is a call for restraint in allegorizing, a call eventually placed under the auspices of Saints Jerome and Augustine, with citations of their warnings against unnecessarily fanciful analyses of texts. One is thus aware, at the very outset, of Boccaccio's awareness of the difficulties involved in the avowed second purpose of his exegetical effort.

The rest of the *esposizioni* reveal nothing that is different in method from what we see in the twofold treatment found in the first canto. Perhaps an effective means of demonstrating the balance between Boccaccio's two genres of exposition is found in the following chart:[20]

	Esposizione litterale (Parts)	*Esposizione allegorica* (Sections)
Canto 1	six	twelve
Canto 2	six	three
Canto 3	seven	none
Canto 4	four	none
Canto 5	six	two
Canto 6	five	four
Canto 7	four	none
Canto 8	four	none
Canto 9	five	five
Canto 10	four	none
Canto 11	seven	none
Canto 12	six	two
Canto 13	nine	three
Canto 14	eight	two
Canto 15	two	none
Canto 16	nine	none
Canto 17	three	???

The last glosses to *Inferno* 10 (vv. 133–36) and 11 (v. 115) report, in a matter-of-fact and unsurprised way: "Questo canto non ha allegoria alcuna" (This canto contains no allegories).[21] Again, in responding to Canto 11, Boccaccio insists that "in questo canto non è cosa alcuna che nasconda allegoria" (there is nothing in this canto that might conceal an allegorical meaning). At the conclusion of the last gloss to *Inferno* 15 (vv. 121–24) he promises that there will be allegorical glosses regarding the sinners punished here in the comments to Canto 17, thus making the absence of any excuse in the equally allegory-less Canto 16 more excusable: "L'allegoria del presente canto . . . si dimostrerà nel XVII canto, dove si dirà di tutta questa spezie de' violenti" (where all this sort of violent sinners will be discussed). A similar statement confronts us at the end of the commentary to 16.136, explaining at greater length that since the sins treated in these neighboring *canti* (14–17; sins of violence, we reflect, against God in three forms: blasphemy, homosexuality, usury) are related, they will be treated together in the next *esposizione*. There is no reason to believe Boccaccio did not intend to furnish these glosses. However, as we know, he stopped glossing altogether with Canto 17, which was barely begun before it was abandoned. His behavior as glossator *litteralis* in what we have of his notes to that canto shows no change in his comportment. In other words, in the text itself there is no sign that Boccaccio did not plan to finish all one hundred cantos. This is important to know, since it has become fashionable to speak of a "crisis" of nerve on Boccaccio's part to account for the sudden cessation of the work. While it is true that, from his *esposizione allegorica* of the first canto onward, there is a marked sense of frustration with the need for "allegorical" explanations of what he might have considered the most important metaphors in Dante's text, his method of studying the literal sense of the poem is confidently untroubled from the outset and continues into that final broken-off annotation to 17.16–17, talking about who the Tartars are, "Sono i Tartari . . ."

If Boccaccio's performance as allegorist is curious, defective, and spotty, the reader should be aware of this extraordinary fact: in all his *esposizioni litterali* that have come down to us, there is not a single line or a single word of Dante's text that the glossator omits; every word that appears in the poem also appears in the commentary.

Petrarch is mentioned by name only five times in the *Esposizioni* but still manages to loom over Boccaccio's enterprise on behalf of Dante, especially near its outset. Discussing the origin of the word *poeta* (1.1.73), he turns to "il mio padre e maestro" (my father and teacher) Petrarch, who, in his letter to his brother Gherardo, explained that the ancient Greek poets devised hidden ways of speaking of the divine mysteries. Among these *illuminati* were Musaeus, Linus, and Orpheus. Boccaccio continues: "E, perchè ne' lor versi parlavano delle cose divine, furono appellati non solamente 'poeti', ma 'teologi'" (And, because in their verse they spoke of things divine, they were referred to not only as "poets" but as "theologians"). Then, at *Inferno* 2.7, the first invocation, Boccaccio mentions Dante's precursors in invocation, Virgil (*Aeneid* 1.8), Ovid (*Metamorphoses* 1.2–3), Homer (*Iliad* 1.1 —as translated by Horace), and then, putting Petrarch in a class with Virgil, Ovid, Homer, and Dante, Boccaccio says: "Così similemente il venerabile mio precettore messer Francesco Petrarca fece nel principio della sua *Africa*" (And in just this same way my venerable teacher messire Francis Petrarch wrote at the beginning of his *Africa*). Then Boccaccio cites the first verse and three words of the second of Petrarch's Latin epic. Boccaccio's way of handling this moment may represent an intentional effort to "promote" Petrarch over Dante, making him part of a five-person *bella scola* (*Inf.* 4.94), where Dante's own list included six illustrious poets, himself last among them (after Homer, Virgil, Horace, Ovid, and Lucan). Horace and Lucan are sacrificed (perhaps without grief) to make room for Petrarch.

These first two references to Petrarch are quite enough to have captured his imagined goodwill, particularly since Boccaccio has ventured from his naturally more narrowly defined service to Dante. Had the *Esposizioni* been finished, we can imagine it containing many other references to Petrarch's excellence. As things are, we still hear his name resound three more times in two later passages. At *Inferno* 4.130–32, glossing "'l maestro di color che sanno" (the master of those who know), Boccaccio identifies Aristotle, goes on to refer to Plato, and continues by saying that "appresso il mio venerabile maestro messer Francesco Petrarca" (in the house of my venerable teacher Francis Petrarch), he had seen Plato's writings, "o tutti o la maggior parte o almeno i più notabili, scritti in lettera e gramatica greca in un grandissimo volume" (either all of them or the greater part or at least the most notable, written in Greek characters and grammar in a very large volume) — one wonders what Petrarch, Greekless, had told his admirer that that codex contained. And at *Inferno* 15.120, "nel qual io vivo ancora" (in which I yet do live), Boccaccio's response to Brunetto's claim that he has made himself immortal in his *Tresor* (or, as seems more likely to some of us, *Tesoretto*) is to think that "il nostro carissimo cittadino e venerabile uomo e mio maestro e padre, messer Francesco" (our most dear fellow citizen and that venerable being, my teacher and father, messire Francis) will, along with Dante, enjoy such immortality. Then, slamming those who oppose poetry because of its failures to deal with "practical" things (a familiar Boccaccian hobbyhorse), he goes on to praise again the work of "nostro venerabil messir Francesco Petrarca."

While one can easily imagine the nervousness Boccaccio felt in assembling this book, the stuff of his public lectures, under the very watchful eye of Petrarch, one also imagines his sense of how greatly offended Dante himself would have been to find his disciple's praiseful attention shared by this newcomer who disparaged writing in the vernacular (despite his own ample adhesion to it) and who claimed that Dante was really not all that original or impressive a writer.[22] Surely Boccaccio had some sense that in the view of his hero Dante, Petrarch would never have passed muster. And yet his own urgent allegiances to both his dead master and his living one made the effort necessary. As a result, this commentary, intended to cover the entire *Commedia*, is inscribed in loyal adherence to Petrarch's membership in the very small pantheon of great classical writers and now two—and only two—contemporary ones. Of the three crowns of Florence, only Boccaccio may be considered to have attained at least a modicum of modesty.

Probably the last compositions that Boccaccio was to write (sonnets 122–26 of his *Rime*), as he lay bedridden in his dropsical condition (alluded to in 122.9–13), are directed to Dante (122–25) and to the recently deceased Petrarch (126): "Or sei salito, caro signor mio" (Now you have gone above, dear my lord). The four sonnets addressed to the spirit of Dante all express shame for the prostitution of Dante's poetry, of which Boccaccio now admits himself guilty, confessing to having strewn Dantean "pearls" before the Florentine "swine," as the beginnings of the four sonnets make plain: "S'io ho le Muse vilmente prostrate / nella fornice del vulgo dolente" (If I have vilely cast down the Muses among the goings and comings of the miserable commonfolk, 122.1–2); "Se Dante piange, dove ch'el si sia / che li concetti del suo alto ingegno / aperti sieno stati al vulgo indegno, / come tu di', della lettura mia" (Should Dante be weeping, wherever he may find himself, because the conceptions of his lofty genius have been opened to the unworthy commonfolk, as you say, by my interpretations, 123.1–4); "Già stanco m'hanno et quasi rintuzzato / le rime tua accese in mia vergogna" (In an already exhausted and almost defeated me your verse has kindled shame, 124.1–4); "Io ho messo in galea senza biscotto / l'ingrato vulgo, e senza alcun piloto / lasciato l'ho in mar a lui non noto / ben che sen creda esser maestro et dotto" (I have put onto a galley, without hope of even a biscuit, the ungrateful commonfolk; without a pilot, incapable of crossing this unknown sea, even if they think themselves masterful and learned, 125.1–2). These little poems are a disturbing conclusion to the final stage (1350–74) of Boccaccio's life as a writer, which was marked at either end by a devotional gesture toward Dante, the first great modern poet, accompanied by another necessary salute to that other prince of modern letters, Petrarch.

PART VIII

HISTORIAN AND HUMANIST

CHAPTER TWENTY

GODS, GREEKS, AND POETRY • *(Genealogia deorum gentilium)*

Jon Solomon

Boccaccio's *Genealogy of the Pagan Gods* (*Genealogia deorum gentilium*) offers a comprehensive study of pagan mythology (books 1–13) justified by an impassioned but reasoned defense of the study of ancient poetry (books 14–15). The mythological genealogy includes 723 entries, most of which Boccaccio supplements with detailed allegorical, historical, and scientific analyses. The work is so comprehensive and entices its studious reader in so many different directions that this essay will necessarily be limited to brief evaluations of Boccaccio's scholarly achievement, his use of sources, and how the two medieval methodologies—genealogical organization and euhemeristic analysis—helped shape his understanding of ancient divinities and mythical heroes.[1]

The *Genealogy* was in many ways Boccaccio's most challenging scholarly project. In the initial *Prohemium* he specifies that its size and scope made him reluctant to accept the commission from Hugo IV, king of Cyprus and Jerusalem. He laments that the "foolishness" (*insania*) of the ancients—that is, in tracing their ancestry back to divinity—spread geographically across the Mediterranean basin from the Black Sea to Numidia and chronologically from the time of Abraham to the Trojan War, was recorded in numerous lengthy books difficult to access and required a degree of reading comprehension, memory, and organization beyond his ability: "And upon my shoulders you want to add, not the heavens they bore, but both the earth and the seas, and even the heavenly dwellers themselves along with their distinguished companions. This is to wish nothing upon me other than that I be crushed by their weight and perish."[2] Despite Boccaccio's use of this literary conceit to flatter his royal patron, the result is impressive. He researched, organized, and created a single, immense genealogy consisting of not just the 723 entries but scores of additional mythological personages, creatures, and fables.[3] Even more significant in Boccaccio's own opinion were his detailed allegorical, historical, and scientific analyses, which often dwarf the mythological data.

The effort he poured into this tremendous undertaking spanned most of his adult life. During the 1330s Boccaccio was already studying pagan mythology and collecting information and learned opinions in Naples, while studying with Paolo da Perugia. As the Angevin court's head librarian, Paolo was in a position to provide Boccaccio with access to a number of Latin sources, and as an associate of the Calabrian Greek Barlaam, Paolo also introduced the young Boccaccio to a variety of ancient Greek sources, including such obscure Greek authors as Pronapides, the archaic Athenian who was alleged to have been Homer's tutor, and Chrysippus, the important Stoic logician whose body of work has been reduced to fragmentary status. Paolo seems also to have introduced Boccaccio to Theodontius's extensive and often atypical variants and interpretations of pagan myths.[4] Of the approximately 200 passages in which Boccaccio relies on Theodontius, the most fundamental to the *Genealogy* is that in which Demogorgon, the divine mind dwelling deep within Mother Earth, whose name was too sublime for ancient Arcadian peasants to utter, is cited as the progenitor of the entire genealogy (1, Preface 2.14–3.4). Also identifying Eternity and Chaos as Demogorgon's companions, and Strife, the three Parcae, and Pan as his direct progeny, these unparalleled teachings of Theodontius enabled Boccaccio to complete the earliest links in his genealogical chain before reaching Erebus (1.14) and genealogical territory more familiar from classical Latin literature.[5]

Of course, Boccaccio's most important Greek source was Homer, whom he cites in 217 passages and quotes directly in 45.[6] To gain access to Homer in the early 1360s Boccaccio undertook the study of the ancient Greek language in his own house with Leontius Pilatus. As a result of this laborious process the *Genealogy* became the first influential scholarly work in modern Europe to incorporate quotations, translations, and analyses of passages from Greek literature.[7] Leontius also offered Boccaccio an assortment of eccentric etymological analyses of Greek names and mythological interpretations. He derived "Demogorgon," for instance, not from Plato's *demiourgos* (worker [*ergos*] of the people [*demos*]) but from *daimongorgon* (god [*daimon*] of the earth [*georgos*]). In a characteristic euhemeristic analysis (2.2.1), Leontius is the source of the elsewhere unattested fable—certainly not Athenian in origin—that an Arcadian named Lysanias introduced legal and public institutions to the primitive Athenians who in gratitude made him king and worshipped him as (one of the several gods named) Jupiter.

After decades of preparation Boccaccio finally produced a handsome autograph (Laurenziana Plut. 52.9).[8] He carefully differentiated its hundreds of entry titles with red ink and highlighted the names of his sources by listing them again in the margins. He punctuated its 161 folios with thirteen individually designed, half- or full-page genealogical trees painted with variously shaped and angled leaves in a variety of colors.[9] Before rubricating his autograph's initial capital letters, however, Boccaccio presented his "unfinished" (non perfectum) Genealogy to a group of Neapolitan humanists, including the distinguished jurist Pietro Piccolo da Monteforte, who wrote a number of corrections in the margins.[10] Careful manuscript analysis by Vittorio Zaccaria in the 1980s and 1990s revealed that Boccaccio incorporated these and additional material into at least one subsequent redaction that circulated in the early to mid-1370s.[11] By the time of his death in 1375 he had been developing the project for four decades.

Giuseppe Billanovich discovered a number of verbal parallels between Pietro's suggestions and the final two books of the Genealogy,[12] and Zaccaria, who published his exemplary edition in 1998, hypothesized that those two books circulated separately in the 1370s.[13] This suggests that after decades spent developing his sources, compiling the mythological genealogy, editing hundreds of poetic quotations, and composing variegated analyses, Boccaccio's focus had now shifted to a challenge of equal magnitude, the defense of the value of poetry in general and of his extensive use of pagan poetry in particular. Against the "enemies of the name of poetry" (poetici nominis hostes) Boccaccio argues that poetry provides an allegorical accounting of divine truths, whether these truths are theological, physical, or historical.[14] Boccaccio's defense of poetry, particularly in book 14, would become a landmark in the history of literary criticism, but, as Giovanni Gullace observes, he "never departs from orthodox Christian principles in the evaluation of works. For him poetry is of divine origins; it never occurs to him that poetry may be simply and entirely a human product. He does not introduce a humanistic concept of poetry, but tries instead to re-interpret the medieval concept. Therefore, in his 'defense of poetry,' he does not go beyond medieval tenets."[15] Zaccaria and Billanovich have pinpointed the revision of books 14–15 to the period between the return of the autograph from Naples in 1372 and Boccaccio's death near the end of 1375. This marks the chronological period during which Boccaccio finalized his embrace of such a (late) medieval conception of poetry. During that same period his methodological approach to the genealogical material was subject to an equally contemporary conception. That is, although Boccaccio's Genealogy qualifies as the first work of modern European scholarship to make significant use of Homer, it also represents a culmination of the medieval study of ancient mythology.

His arguments in book 15 would seem to provide an early template for humanist scholarly methodology. At 15.7.3, for example, Boccaccio justifies his use of ancient Greek poetry by pointing out that he is imitating the practice of such esteemed Latin authors as Cicero, Apuleius, and Macrobius, insisting that he and his contemporaries have much to learn from the ancient Greeks. But in the fourteenth century he actually had very little extant Greek literature at his disposal. Without direct access to Hesiod or the epic fragments, the archaic lyric poets (especially Stesichorus, Pindar, and Bacchylides), and the Attic tragedians, let alone pseudo-Apollodorus's comprehensive collection (*Bibliotheca*) of Greek myths, Boccaccio had to rely for specifically Greek information on Leontius, the reports of ancient and medieval Latin authors and commentators, Theodontius, and the teachings of Paolo da Perugia.[16]

As a result, the landscape of Boccaccio's Greco-Roman mythological world looked very different from the one developed by subsequent scholarship. He could relate myths familiar to us directly from the ancient Roman and medieval Latin traditions, but then he had to combine them with the more obscure or unparalleled tales derived from his eclectic Greek sources. While collecting and assembling this disparate material, he encountered still another medieval limitation — the genealogical methodology. If his sources assigned no lineage to a mythological character, then he had to exclude that character from the genealogical format, which, at the behest of Hugo, he traced back to a single progenitor, the infamous Demogorgon. Thus, the fatherless Pandora in the *Genealogy* is a man and has no "jar," and the parentless Babylonian Pyramus and Thisbe are nowhere to be found, even though Boccaccio tells their story in detail in *De mulieribus claris* (chap. 13). In some instances he has to dig deeply for a genealogical connection, often citing one of his Greek sources. At 3.10–12 he cites Paolo as the source that says the personified Victory was the daughter of the river Styx, Theodontius and Paolo as the sources that say that Victory was the mother of Honor, and Ovid as the source that identifies Honor as the mother of Majesty. His research uncovered other rarities: the autograph (fol. 31r) contains a marginal addition, obviously a late insertion (which also has a differently painted leaf on fol. 22r) from Pliny's *Natural History* (7.56.201), that says that the otherwise unknown Scythes was a child of Jupiter (2.76).

Boccaccio employs the unique combination of Homeric, arcane Greek, and traditional Latin sourcing in the complex of mythological characters and tales involving Agamemnon. For the Cassandra episodes (6.16.2–3), he relies on the Homeric *Odyssey* and Seneca's *Agamemnon*, not Stesichorus or Aeschylus, but he also writes an entry on the otherwise-unknown Antiphus and Isus, the two sons of Priam whom Agamemnon slays in the *Iliad* (11.101–21).[17] Unaware of or rejecting the tradition in which Aërope is the mother of Agamemnon and Menelaus, he cites Agamemnon, along with Priam and Aeneas, as examples of famous men whose (mortal) mothers' names are obscure (6.53.23). He cites Leontius's assumption that it was Palamedes who perpetrated the intrigue between Clytemnestra and Aegisthus (12.10.2), which leads to a citation of Dares Phrygius, who represents the anti-Homeric medieval Trojan tradition and says that Palamedes inherited Agamemnon's position as commander in chief of the Greek forces at Troy (10.59–60). In the entry on Helen (11.8.5–6), Boccaccio discusses a chronological discrepancy between Eusebius and Homer: in Eusebius's *Chronicle* Paris abducts Helen in the first year of the reign of Agamemnon, and Troy was destroyed fifteen years later, while in the last few lines of the *Iliad* (24.765–66) Helen says she has been at Troy for twenty years. Although to moderns it might seem an absurd exercise to discuss a chronological discrepancy between an archaic mythological poem and a late ancient/early medieval compilation of dubious historical accuracy, Boccaccio demonstrates the greatest respect for both authors throughout the *Genealogy*. One was the revered ancient Greek poet to whom Boccaccio had new and almost exclusive access; the other he regarded as the medieval standard for chronological precision.[18]

For modern readers, artists, and scholars, Agamemnon's genealogy is a simple matter sourced primarily from Homer and the three Attic tragedians: Pelops fathers Thyestes and Atreus; Thyestes fathers Aegisthus; Atreus fathers Agamemnon and Menelaus; and Agamemnon fathers Orestes and Electra.[19] In contrast, Boccaccio offers a much more complex genealogy of the Tantalids (12.1–23). Citing primarily Seneca, Lactantius Placidus, Theodontius, and Eusebius, but also Homer, Varro, Lucretius, Cicero, Virgil, Ovid, Dares, Dictys, Solinus, "Anselm" (Honorius of Autun), Paolo, and Barlaam (and Thucydides via Barlaam), he incorporates additional siblings and progeny, most notably Phistenes (Plisthenes). The mythological tradition has passed down at least four different Tantalids named Plisthenes—a son of Pelops, a son of Atreus, a son of Thyestes, and a son of Menelaus. Multiple applications of names are not an uncommon result of the fluid mythological tradition of Greece. Playwrights, local historians, and mythographers assigned such names as Merope and Lycus to multiple personages, in some instances belonging even to different families, but in attempting to include most of the names mentioned by his sources—he does not cite Hyginus's account—Boccaccio attributed four children to Pelops (Lysidice, Atreus, Thyestes, and Plisthenes),[20] two to Plisthenes (Agamem-

non, Menelaus), three to Atreus (Alceon, Melampus, and Eviolus), and five
to Thyestes (Tantalus, Plisthenes, Harpagiges, Pelopea, and Egisthus).
Theodontius had access to a larger cache of source material. At least,
in citing the variant that Atreus was not the natural father of Agamemnon
and Menelaus but a guardian who served in a parental capacity after the
death of his natural father Plisthenes (son of Pelops) (12.11.1), Theodontius demonstrates his knowledge of the Greek tradition that circulated in
seventh-century epic, sixth-century lyric, and fifth-century dramatic poetry, through the Hellenistic and subsequent scholarly tradition to pseudo-
Apollodorus (3.2.2).[21] Similarly, where Boccaccio (12.8.1–2) cites Seneca's
Thyestes (717–27) for the names Tantalus and Plisthenes, two of the three
sons slain in the play, Theodontius provided the name of the remaining
brother, Harpagiges, who is otherwise unattested but almost certainly
derived from the name of the Median Harpagus discussed by Herodotus
(1.108–19) and Justin (1.5). The obvious link here is the story Herodotus
tells about Harpagus's son, who, like the three sons of Thyestes, is murdered, boiled in a stew, and fed to his father.[22]

Theodontius clearly had access to fairly exotic sources that gave accounts
of the earliest strata of divine and human existence as well as the farthest
regions of the eastern Mediterranean basin and its Eastern neighbors, recalling Boccaccio's initial description of the scope of the proposed project.
We have already seen that in the earliest entries in book 1 Boccaccio cited
Theodontius for information about Demogorgon, his companions Eternity
and Chaos, and Demogorgon's immediate offspring. Following primarily
Theodontius, Boccaccio also describes as inventions and discoveries of the
"most ancient Arcadians" (*vetustissimorum Arcadum*) the discovery of natural philosophy (1, Preface 2.10) and animistic religion and divine worship
(1, Preface 3.3–5), and the invention of musical pipes (1.4.7). In book 2
where Boccaccio discusses the considerable progeny of the first Jupiter
(the Jupiter whom Leontius associated with the Arcadian Lysanias), he
frequently cites Theodontius as he works through the lineage of Epaphus,
his son Belus, and the offspring of the latter's sons Danaus, Aegyptus, and
Agenor (2.19–33). This is the predominantly Eastern branch of the Greek
mythological tradition. It begins in Egypt with Io (a veritable Greek hypostasis of Isis) and her son Epaphus (i.e., Apis), and then extends eastward
with the latter's son Belus, the Greco-Latin human reduction of the god
Bel Marduk whom Boccaccio correctly associates with Babylonia of the
Chaldeans (2.21.2–3).

The latter passage gives us an appreciation for Boccaccio's attempt to
record, distinguish, and report on such otherwise inaccessible sources. Be-

cause many of the accounts of Theodontius, Leontius, Paolo, and Barlaam cannot be verified, it is natural to suspect that they may have misremembered, misinterpreted, misrepresented, or even fabricated mythological and quasi-historical material. This does not necessarily mean, however, that their value must be discounted or that Boccaccio should be criticized for employing them or not being able to sort them out definitively. Quite the opposite is true, for Paolo echoes a euhemerized account that assigns to Belus Priscus the discovery of astronomy in Egypt, a discovery so valuable that he was honored with a temple in Egyptian Babylonia. Theodontius explains that the third ("Cretan") Jupiter then expanded his pool of worshippers by having temples built in his name in numerous allied kingdoms. Boccaccio concludes by citing "others"—whether Paolo or Theodontius cited these other sources cannot be determined—who say that the temple was not built in Egyptian Babylonia but in Babylonia of the Chaldeans, and not by Belus Priscus but by Ninus, king of the Assyrians.

Boccaccio here is dovetailing sources and information rarely found or accessed in medieval Europe. While it may read like a confused mythological hodgepodge of gods (Jupiter), kings (Belus Priscus, Ninus), places (two Babylonias, Assyria), and cultures (Egyptian, Babylonian, Assyrian), the cults of the celestial male divinity known variously as Bel or Ba'al spread widely in the second and first millennia B.C. along extensive Babylonian, Phoenician, and Assyrian trade and diplomatic networks. As polytheists, neither the Greeks nor the Romans concerned themselves with distinguishing between these cults or tracing them to a common ancestry. They were content to syncretize them with the names of their celestial male divinities Zeus and Jupiter. It was perhaps Euhemerus himself (ca. 300 B.C.) who proposed that Jupiter/Zeus traveled throughout the earth establishing cults to himself, albeit with different names.[23] For monotheist Christians it had been a long-standing tradition to euhemerize pagan divinities, strip them of any semblance of their cultic essence, and render them as humans. This meant that the myths, rituals, and epithets associated with a divinity who was worshipped for several thousand years over the vast territories stretching from Mesopotamia to the Levantine coast and whose impact was felt in Egypt, Cyprus, Crete, and Greece had to be distributed among a number of human fabrications. At the end of the entry on Agenor, Boccaccio reveals his own sense of the problems inherent here: "From this we can understand that because of the similarity of names there may also be a mistake in the time period, so that he who was the son of the Syrian Belus was believed to be the son of the Egyptian Belus. But whichever Belus was his father, I have a mind here to follow the opinion of Theodontius and Paolo, since no author is sufficiently clear about the former. And so they say that he left Egypt for the Syrian shores, ruled the Phoenicians, and was famous for his numerous and noble offspring."[24]

I would argue that sorting through these names, especially since they were for the most part passed on to Boccaccio via Paolo and Theodontius, demonstrates Boccaccio's scholarly maturity. He was caught in a convergence of euhemerized divinities and genealogical homonyms from the eastern Mediterranean. It is evident here that Boccaccio was confronted with the chronological, historical precision of Eusebius's *Chronicle*, which seemed to confirm the historicity of the most important of these names, and Cicero's division of the Greco-Roman divinities into multiple euhemerized individuals, hence the insertion of "Cretan" Jupiter into the mix. Because Boccaccio's mythological methodology here is, like his approach to poetic theory, medieval and not yet humanistic, for an author who needs to silence critics who find the study of the pagan gods reprehensible and to reconfirm his Christian faith throughout the work it would be almost impossible to abandon the euhemeristic and genealogical methodologies of medieval mythological studies. And so we cannot expect him to approach the pagan divinities as genuine but now neglected objects of historical cults.

The rest of book 2 provides three exemplary segments as it shifts among the divine, historical, and mythological human strata sourced originally from the eastern Mediterranean, while maintaining its driving genealogical logic. Agenor fathers seven predominantly Levantine children, including Cilix, the eponym of Cilicia, who fathers Pygmalion, king of the Cypriots, and the rest of the Cypriot tradition through Adonis (2.44–53). Once again Boccaccio depends exclusively on Theodontius and Paolo to make a critical connection, here filling the gap from Cilix and Pygmalion to the eponym Paphos, which enables him to incorporate the well-known but genealogically isolated Ovidian tales of Pygmalion, Myrrha and Cinyras, and Venus and Adonis (2.49–53).[25] The progression leads from the aforementioned euhemerized versions of Ba'al to the Ovidian humans. For Adonis, however, the last in the series, Boccaccio cannot ignore the wealth of material from Cicero, Macrobius, Lactantius, Augustine, and Justin's *Epitome* of Pompeius Trogus that correctly identifies Adonis as the object of a historical Eastern cult. Similarly, Eusebius treats Phoenix, another eponym, as a historical king; Theodontius identifies him as the father of Philistine, who as a priest of Hercules, that is, Tyrian Melqart, founded the western Phoenician colony of Cadiz and became the grandfather of Sychaeus, husband of Dido, another Phoenician colonizer of the western Mediterranean (2.61). Lastly, from Cadmus, another son of Agenor, Boccaccio follows the branch of the genealogy that transports the strain to Thebes on the Greek mainland (2.63–75).[26] Following Palaephatus and Eusebius, Boccaccio discusses the historical aspects of Cadmus as well as the Ovidian story of Europa, and then proceeds to the Labdacids. Again he relies on Theodontius and Paolo to connect Agenor to Laius via Labdacus, but in contrast his discussions of Oedipus, Antigone, Ismene, Eteocles, and Polynices, despite a cursory citation of Statius's *Thebaid*, are noticeably lacking in literary support.[27] He introduces Polynices (2.74), for instance, by saying simply: "It is well known (*notissimum est*) that Polynices was the son of Oedipus and Jocasta."

We can see in these examples that in general the genealogy tends to proceed from divine to human, the very process Boccaccio described as "foolishness" at the outset of his *Prohemium*. Book 8 proceeds in a similar fashion as it follows the lineage from Saturn through his daughter Ceres to the progeny of Picus, whose lineage through his son Faunus elicits a discussion about the Arcadian fauns, satyrs, and *silvani*, leading ultimately to such mortals as King Latinus and Lavinia. Book 9 accounts for the lineage descended from Saturnian Juno, including a juxtaposition of Mars and Cupid leading ultimately to the most famous and chronologically most human of the Roman offspring of Mars, the quasi-historical Romulus and Remus. Books 11–13 progress from the third Jupiter to such mortals as Ulysses' son Auxonius (11.53), sourced from the two historians Paul the Deacon and Livy, and the quasi-historical Tullius Servilius (Servius Tullius; 12.70–79) and his two daughters described by Livy. The final entry in the final book of genealogy offers Boccaccio's explanation for why he does not include either Alexander the Great or Scipio Africanus as a son of Jupiter (13.71), ultimately determining that Alexander would have been a more admirable human if he had not claimed that his mother, Olympias, had intercourse with Jupiter in the guise of a serpent.

A larger fractal proceeds from Theodontius's Demogorgon in the *Prohemium* of book 1 to the labors of Hercules in book 13.[28] Associated with the Platonic demiurge (*Timaeus* 40c) that was developed into a spiritual force in later Platonic and Gnostic thought, Demogorgon also represents the earlier type of ineffable, invisible god that proliferated in the ancient Near East but lacked the usual mythological elements and votive epithets associated with anthropomorphic Greco-Roman gods.[29] In contrast, Hercules, the Hellenic Heracles, was a widely worshipped, opposite-gendered hypostasis of the earth goddess (Hera), a male antagonist who battled the beasts she nurtured, and suffered her punishments but ultimately underwent apotheosis and married her virgin aspect (Hebe). Of course Boccaccio, still caught in the euhemeristic mind-set, could not have even begun to apply any of these modern, analytical mythological or theological categories, which have taken centuries of philological, historical, and archaeological investigation to develop. The genealogical method, however, had a lengthy pedigree of its own dating back to antiquity and proliferating in the thirteenth century, and, as we have seen, Boccaccio produced a well-researched, cleverly developed, and elaborately detailed product dependent on this method.[30] Because euhemerized gods by definition cannot be categorized into the divine hierarchy of supreme and lesser gods, demigods, heroes, and mortals, Boccaccio busied himself with collecting sources rather than distinguishing them.

In his defense of poetry (14.9.5–8), Boccaccio discusses fiction and distinguishes four categories dependent on the amount of truth the fiction obscures or reveals: (1) fables involving nonhuman speakers, (2) those that infuse some human history into what we might call myth, (3) those that convey more human history than myth, and (4) those that have no bearing on the truth whatsoever. He argues that those who dismiss fiction as superficial do not understand the truths it contains, and, after simply eliminating the fourth category, he cites as examples of the first three categories tales in Aristotle, Homer, Virgil, and, more importantly, the Old and New Testaments. If we apply these categories to genealogical fiction and eliminate the first as irrelevant to euhemerized divinities, they proceed throughout the Genealogy from beginning to end, ranging from an aniconic supreme divinity like Demogorgon to quasi-historical, anthropomorphic divinities like Jupiter and Hercules to mortal fabrications like the fables that claimed that Alexander and Scipio were gods.[31]

CHAPTER TWENTY-ONE

BOCCACCIO ON FORTUNE • *(De casibus virorum illustrium)*

Simone Marchesi

Hic Pirrus 'Heram' vocabat fortunam, quam causam
melius et rectius nos 'divinam providentiam' appellamus

Dante, *Monarchia* 2.9.8

Boccaccio's *De casibus virorum illustrium* (*The Downfall of Illustrious Men*)
is a nine-book encyclopedic history devoted to a review in a moralizing vein of Fortune's impact on both individual and collective destinies.
The scope of the Latin work is totalizing, stretching from the inception of
mankind, with Adam and Eve's fall, to the author's present, the most recent
event mentioned in the work being the defeat of John II the Good (and
Walter of Brienne's death) at the battle of Poitiers in 1356. In the Proem
to the first book, Boccaccio synthesizes both the ethical-political task and
the boundaries of his work. His survey of history, he states, will bring out
"what almighty God, or—to use their language—Fortune could and did do
to those set on high . . . from the origin of the world to our own day."[1]

The history of the work is marked by two different redactions and perhaps two distinct phases of elaboration of the text. Regarding the shape of
the text as it is printed, Pier Giorgio Ricci and Vittorio Zaccaria provide a
thorough review of the evidence, leading us to conclude that two versions
of the work were circulated: the A redaction, composed between the mid-
1350s and 1360, and the B redaction, dating to 1373 and containing the
dedicatory epistle to Mainardo Cavalcanti.[2] Furthermore, if one were to
interpret in a biographical vein the narrative excursus with which Boccaccio opens book 8, in which he "relates" a conversation between the figure
of the depressed author (a deadly form of *ignavia*, or idleness, being what
he laments in 8.1.1) and an enthusiastic Petrarch on the as-yet-unfinished
and "back-burnered" work, the incitements of Boccaccio's avowed *magister*

to continue working on the project may actually reflect the situation of the text. It was left unfinished until 1359 (when, in March, Boccaccio was to meet Petrarch in Milan), and then was taken up again and brought to fruition with the last two postclassical books.[3]

In narrative terms the *De casibus* is loosely organized as a series of "visions" depicting in a triumph-like scenario a vast array of historical figures who march before the meditating author and lament their sufferings at the hands of Fortune.[4] Among each group of querulous characters the author decides to tell the story of one, deemed the most "exemplary" figure, in greater detail. The treatise thus reads as a series of short catalogs of unfortunate characters, reviewed in brief summary style, followed by longer narrative analyses of individual stories.[5] A third constant element in what tends to become a series of compositional triptychs is a usually highly rhetorical and stylized section reserved for the author's invective against a specific vice or class of people in some way connected to the preceding narrative. The declared task assigned to these sections is to introduce variety, "lest an uninterrupted series of histories cause the reader discomfort."[6] In the earlier books (1–3), this element is more developed and more consistently marked off from the narrative sections that precede it. In the later books, it becomes a less standard feature of the work's compositional rhythm; the most explicitly and tangentially moralizing tirades tend to be summarized and embedded in the final paragraphs of the second section. In this case, they usually take the form of a highly elaborated period, organized as a series of parallel anaphoric pronominal clauses, each marking off by contrastive language and syntax the moment of "fair" from that of "foul" fortune in a given individual's life. One example, from book 5, chosen quite randomly among the many possible ones, may suffice to convey the rhetorical quality of Boccaccio's technique of point-by-point comparison and contrast:

> Thus, he [King Jugurtha of the Numidians] who had killed his brothers by fraud, and by fraud prolonged war, and by fraud deceived the Romans, was trapped in his own fraudulence. He who had put all his trust and pleasure in his wealth and in the magnificence of his kingdom — and in power rather than in virtue — was rendered by someone else's power poor, obscure, powerless, and, what is worse, a prisoner. He who had climbed to the summit of kingship by shedding his brothers' blood, descended to the bottom of the river, by being cast off a cliff. And thus he who had burned with too much desire was made more temperate by the coldness of the river.[7]

Acting in a retributive mode, Fortune responds to moral shortcomings by curbing each individual's ethical disequilibrium, and Boccaccio's syntax takes upon itself to do precisely the same thing. In the central clauses just cited, wealth is syntactically matched by poverty, magnificence by obscurity, power by impotence, self-reliance by someone else's power; similarly, the climb to the top is matched by a descent to the bottom, bloodshed by "being shed" off the Tarpeian Rock.[8] The paragraph concludes, triumphantly, on a peculiar QED: Those who trust more in themselves than in virtue are bound to suffer harsher blows from Fortune (15). If, however, the moral of the work is that all who have been exalted will be humbled, what role is left for "virtue" to play?

Fortuna and *Virtus*: A (Still) Unlikely Polarity

Book 5 had opened with a similar, though positive, statement involving *virtus*. Here is what Boccaccio has to say about the historical predominance of the Roman people, which he sees in relation to the heroism of some of their early citizens (the latest of whom is Regulus, whose story has just been reviewed): "Why should I wonder that the Romans had an empire bound only by the Ocean, when I see that their state had such great citizens? Certainly Fortune was powerless against them; and this should count as a proof, for those who want to see it, that where there is virtue, Fortune has no share."[9] The issue is of no small moment, since understanding the nature of Fortune is the work's main purpose. Taking our cue from Zaccaria's introduction and dealing for a moment in generalities, we may realize that Boccaccio's humanism is more "medieval" than his innovative juxtaposition of *fortuna* and *virtù* in this passage might suggest.

Zaccaria's comment points out that, notwithstanding the "Machiavellian flavor" of Boccaccio's sententious statement (and Zaccaria is most likely thinking of formulations in chapters 24 and 25 of *The Prince*), "we are not in a humanistic realm, since the notion of what is Good rather than what is Expedient dominates Boccaccio's reasoning," and because the historical framework in which the relation of Fortune and Virtue is made to play out is one "of providential order and universal harmony."[10] Zaccaria's point is well taken, but it may be further refined. Indeed, two essential elements in Boccaccio's treatment of Fortune work against any humanist understanding of his juxtaposition. First, both in this passage and throughout the work, for Boccaccio Fortune is *not* the cipher of unpredictability that it would be in Machiavelli. Quite the contrary, her ways are the most predictable, almost mathematically certain, element in human life. Fortune's work ethic, as it were, has one single rule: whatever she elevates, she eventually brings down. The iconographic subconscious of Boccaccio's treatise (which comes closest to the surface in 5.13.1) associates Fortune with the predictable motion of her wheel rather than with the much more erratic river or wind imagery that will dominate later understandings of the same concept. The medieval "wheel of Fortune," inspired by Boethius (*Consolation of Philosophy* 2.1.10), is not a figure for blind mechanical randomness, but a philosophical embodiment or a rhetorical personification of the providentially ordained, constant change affecting all sublunary destinies. If anything, medieval Fortune is something—actually, one may even argue, the *only* thing—on which one can count in this world.

Second, when Boccaccio contrasts Fortune and virtue in the case of the irresistible ascent to world domination of the Roman Empire, he does not seem to be hinting at the possibility that human beings have to shape their destiny by seizing the few favorable occasions that Fortune affords them while preparing to withstand her backlash by making proper defensive arrangements in advance, as Machiavelli would have taught his Prince.[11] The point made in the *De casibus* is much more "medieval" in quality, as well as in cultural points of reference. In the case of the Roman people, Boccaccio is moving on recognizably Dantean ground. When he muses on the lofty destiny of Rome, he adopts the same elective principle that Dante had a few years earlier, arguing in his *Monarchia* 2 (and before that in *Convivio* 4, and then again in *Paradiso* 6, always in the same terms) that *virtù* was the Roman quality that made Providence choose that particular nation to bring peace and unity to the world, a necessary step for Christ's incarnation to take place and for Christ's passion to work as a universally cleansing sacrifice. Polemically engaging the theocratic party of his day, Dante had been adamant on this point. It was neither sheer force nor *fortuna*—"a cause which we better and more correctly call divine providence" (as he writes in *Monarchia* 2.9.8)—that had propelled the Roman people to world dominance, but their exceptional *virtus*. This is, in essence, what Boccaccio is asserting in the passage quoted above. His point is intended much more as a backward glance at his compatriot's argument regarding the synonymy of Fortune and Providence than it is a premonition of the oppositional relation the humanists will see in the *fortuna-virtù* dyad.

To clarify the "ethical" dimension that Zaccaria sees at work in Boccaccio's conception of Fortune, it might be useful to consider the role that the classical tradition assigns to the four cardinal virtues (Prudence, Fortitude, Temperance, Justice), as potentially forming a system to be carefully kept in balance. Cicero presents them in this light in *De officiis* (1.5.15–1.6.19), a text Boccaccio makes use of in his *De casibus*.[12] For Cicero Fortitude and Wisdom, the two individualizing virtues emerging from his dissection of the rules for appropriate action, could come into play as partial antidotes to the work of Fortune. Fortitude *in rebus secundis* (when fortune is propitious, as opposed to *in rebus adversis*, in adversity) teaches that a healthy measure of self-control should accompany one's good fortune, just as Prudence, the foresight-related aspect of wisdom, should help the ethical subject be aware of the momentary quality of any earthly success. Whether potentially curbing pride or instilling reasonable and healthy doubts about the transient quality of any worldly accomplishment, these attitudes are certainly not alien to Boccaccio's own repeatedly stated didactic goal and oft-sounded warning that only humility, as a moral as well as topographical stance, is a real guarantee against the *casus* (downfall) that Fortune has in store for each one of her subjects. Similarly, in the parabolic graphs of the many individual life-stories Boccaccio traces, Justice and Temperance are the community-oriented virtues whose systematic abuse marks the beginning of the end for each personality who has benefited from Fortune's benign face. The paradigmatic life-cycle is so often repeated in the *De casibus* as to become an ethical-historical standard. Boccaccio quite regularly insists either on the excessive desires of the individuals who have risen to the top of the social ladder (usually in the form of a "desire to increase the size of their kingdoms") or on their falling into a sloth-induced excess of carnal satisfaction.

In literary and iconographical terms, in sum, Boccaccio makes each character's Fortune-propelled and irresistible ascent to power culminate with the highest earthly success. This is the *regnabo-regno* quadrant-section, familiar to us from wheel of Fortune depictions. The vertex of the parabola acts, however, also as the tipping point, with a moral flaw (in the form of a habit or a morally questionable action) that brings about the individual's downfall along the quadrant *regno-regnavi*. The final resting place of each character's story is the condition of *sine regno sum*, in Boccaccio's account, leading to or often simply consisting in a miserable death. The four stations in the turning of the wheel of Fortune are labeled here according to the value system encapsulated in the mnemonic Leonine hexameter from *Carmina Burana* 19, "Regnabo, regno, regnavi, sum sine regno" (I will have a kingdom, I have a kingdom, I used to have a kingdom, I am without kingdom), but they appear to match well Boccaccio's standard *modus narrandi*.[13]

History and the Individual Stories

The overall effect of the *De casibus* is that of reading a vast examination of human history, marked by epicyclical individual destinies that are studied in various degrees of detail, each life story consisting of a minimal historical revolution around and along the larger trajectory of history as a whole. As far as this larger trajectory is concerned, it is perhaps striking that readers are left without any eschatological recapitulation of human history as a whole. Focused as it is on individual happenings, and clear-mindedly framed as a systematic debunking of any illusory trust in earthly success, Boccaccio's treatment of history in the *De casibus* does not seem to need any theological underpinning. If history already proves *ad abundantiam* (if not *ad nauseam*) a moral point, there seems to be no need to go beyond it to find its meaning. History has become a much more complex affair than any consolatory *translatio*-theory may encompass, and there seems to be no room for any transfiguration of human struggles on the metaphysical plane. Thus, the work affords its readers no end-of-days perspective, either in the form of a reconciliation of individual destinies within the larger providential progress of time or in that of a potentially eschatological final resolution. Both moves were perhaps to be expected by a passionate reader and advocate of Dante, whose *Commedia* relies exactly on that foundational double shift in focus.

A possible reason, tentatively advanced here, for the absence of any otherworldly perspective subsuming the history of mankind may be found in Boccaccio's dialogic situating of his work as continuation of and in contrast to Dante's. Firmly rooted in the realm of ethical and political action rather than that of speculation, Boccaccio's treatise is apparently interested in investing its subjects (both the characters and the readers reading about them) with full responsibility for the choices they make in their earthly destiny. This ethical parameter is certainly not alien to Dante's own understanding of the task of his work, since the *Commedia*, according to the *Epistle to Cangrande* 13.40.16, clearly articulates its goal as "not speculation, but action" (non ad speculandum, sed ad opus). Boccaccio's way to go about achieving that same ethical thrust, however, differs from Dante's. What in Dante's *Commedia* was a "view from the ending" becomes for Boccaccio a "view from the present"—which is a provisional and tactical, not a metaphysical and absolute, vantage point.

A spiritual dimension is, of course, present in Boccaccio's treatment of Fortune as a worldly affair. Incidentally, it is the same spiritual dimension that may be detected in his literal gloss of Dante's handling of *Fortuna* in the *Esposizioni* (Canto 7 (i).74–76). There too, Boccaccio's moralizing insistence on human free will is paramount, since our free will is precisely the spiritual agent capable of undoing Fortune's permutations of material goods. In both the Latin treatise and the vernacular commentary, however, the ethical dimension that Boccaccio achieves is based on the strategic bracketing of any metaphysical temptation. Fortune, being inessential to the destiny of human souls, which are created "above" the realm of material objects (the only domain in which Fortune has jurisdiction), is a matter of this world, or, as the *Decameron* puts it, an utterly *umana cosa* (human thing). While she is conceived as one among the angelic intelligences or as a misnomer for divine Providence, in other words, Fortune is also strategically confined to the realm in which ethical action is possible and called for. In this sense, human free will rather than any pre-Machiavellian *virtù* is her antagonist and antidote.

When we look at Boccaccio's generally pessimistic understanding of human history within this framework, the title of the work may acquire additional resonance. If the word *casus* refers primarily to the topographical dimension of the individual downfall from high to low station in society, both a juridical and a rhetorical valence of the term may be detected in the title. The *casus* in point are not only the archetypal "fall" and its iterations throughout history, but also the sum of the "cases," the incidents and happenings in personal and collective history. These "facts" have a value that should be determined by a judgment, and in this sense the *casus* are also the "cases" that are made, in the juridical domain and with the tools of rhetoric, in order to adjudicate their value.[14] History from the point of view and for the use of human beings is the ultimate object of meditation for this work, which had opened by striking a strong political note in its dedicatory incipit and was eventually to inspire a blossoming of unmetaphysical ethical manuals.[15]

Further (Re-)readings

What follows should be taken as an invitation to read this challenging text again, along two promising lines. In addition to affording an inquiry into Boccaccio's craft as a Latin narrator, in stylistic appeal and rhetorical brilliance rivaling his vernacular counterpart,[16] certain sections of the *De casibus* could respond both to a metaliterary reading and to a closer canvassing in a Dantean vein.

Let us begin with the latter. When reading the *De casibus*, one runs across a few instances in which Boccaccio's Latin seems to translate memorable passages from Dante's *Commedia*. There are a few predictable cases. In 2.12,

"Nondum Sardanapalus . . . venerat" echoes "non v'era giunto ancor Sardanapalo" (Sardanapalus had not yet come) in *Paradiso* 15.107; in 1.12.26, "Hecuba . . . latrantemque canum more" is a strong rendering of Dante's "latrò sì come cane" (she barked like a dog) in *Inferno* 30.20; in 7.3.51 (a quarrel among Tiberius, Caligula, and Messalina), "criminum cognitor Minos" is based on the tag "conoscitor de le peccata" (knower of sin) in *Inferno* 5.9; and finally, in 9.14.3 (on William III), "Ioachinus quidam, calaber, prophetico dotatus spiritu," translates Dante's "Il calavrese abate Gioacchino / di spirito profetico dotato" (Joachim from Calabria, endowed with prophetic powers) in *Paradiso* 12.140–41.[17] In some other cases, as in this last example, Dante's phrases are intriguingly reassigned. In 2.11 ("In Praise of Dido"), "Paucos quippe qui future vite superesse poterant annos" (the few years of future life, which may be left to us) could well be considered an audible echo of Ulysses' "questa tanto piccola vigilia . . . ch'è del rimanente" (whatever little is left of this life of ours) in *Inferno* 26.24–25; similarly, in 4.15.18 ("On Arsinoe"), "et cum festum omne versum esset in luctum" appears to redeploy the Dantean tag "che i lieti onor tornaro in tristi lutti" (so that happiness and honor turned into sadness and mourning) in *Inferno* 13.69, or perhaps two, since "noi ci allegrammo, e tosto tornò in pianto" in *Inferno* 26.136 is a plausible candidate as well; finally, in 8.6.16 ("On Zenobia"), "Ite igitur humane conditionis immemores et scandite celsa" (Go now, forgetful of the human condition, and climb on high) might be read as a corrective reprisal of *Purgatorio* 12.70–72: "Or superbite, e via col viso altero, / figliuoli d'Eva, e non chinate il volto / sì che veggiate il vostro mal sentero" (Go now proudly, children of Eve, with your brow raised; keep your gaze high, so as not to see your evil path). Other intersections, finally, appear to be the product of a thematic reconsideration. In 2.18 ("A Few Words on Dreams"), "maximum quoddam divinitatis occultum infixum mortalium animis est, eoque agente curis soluti seu minus corporea depressi mole, plura . . . audimus videmusque futuri" (Something of the divine is hidden in, and bound to the human soul, and thanks to it, when we are free from cares and least weighed down by the burden of the body, . . . we see and hear many things of the future) seems to be a meditated reworking, in a Macrobian vein, of "la mente nostra, peregrina / più da la carne e men da' pensier presa, / a le sue visïon quasi è divina" (Our mind, farthest away from the flesh and least occupied by thoughts, is in its vision almost divine) in *Purgatorio* 9.16–18. With significant variation and an epic effect, in 7.8.1 ("On the Destruction of Jerusalem"), "tot viros quot fere naturam rerum produxisse vix extimasse potuissem" revisits Dante's *Inferno* 3.55–57: "sì lunga tratta / di gente, ch'i' non averei creduto / che morte tanta n'avesse disfatta" (in T. S. Eliot's rendering, "a crowd of people; so many, I had not thought death had undone so many"). One of the Italian editors of the work might have already picked up on this feature of Boccaccio's humanistic Latinizing style, when he invitingly rendered the clause "summa reverentia dignum" (said of Petrarch appearing to the author in 8.1.5) with the Italian "degno di somma reverenza in vista" (incidentally a hendecasyllable), which diverges, but not very much, from Dante's own line "degno di tanta reverenza in vista" (appearing worthy of so much reverence), said of Cato in *Purgatorio* 1.32. In this particular case, of course, the implicit gloss Zaccaria entrusts to his rendering is not fully binding (the added tag "in vista," which would really clinch the allusion is of the Italian editor's devising). Zaccaria's translation, however, should be credited with having brought out the latent or occasional Dante-ism of Boccaccio's diction.[18]

Of a more complex nature is the call to readers perhaps contained in at least one of the moralizing digressions in the treatise, the *Adversum nimiam credulitatem* (Against any excess of credulity) (1.10). Inserted as a commentary on Theseus's credulity in the matter of Phaedra versus Hippolytus, the excursus contains a series of caveats for powerful political figures, those who can easily put their will into action. Organized on a grid of indirect interrogative clauses, the examining technique Boccaccio recommends is patently rhetorical-juridical in quality. Before adjudicating a question, he writes, the judicious man should ask himself: "Who is speaking, why, who has acted against whom, where, when, in a fit of rage or cold-bloodedly, and whether he is an enemy or a friend, whether of good or bad reputation."[19]

This passage has one element that provides it with potential metaliterary significance. After having discussed the pernicious effects of Theseus's royal credulity, the chapter appears to trail off and moves to introducing one of the misogynistic tirades for which the later Boccaccio has become famous.[20] To be sure, the chapter stays on target, since the antiuxorial commonplaces come into play specifically as a character argument against Phaedra's certainly objectionable profile. Yet, the way in which general advice against believing denigrating arguments is paired with a wide assortment of them may cast some reasonable doubt on their ultimate cogency.

It might be interesting to try following Boccaccio's advice and apply the grid he proposes to one of his characters, the narrator of the misogynistic *Corbaccio*. The experiment would be, of course, for purely rhetorical and juridical purposes. Rather than unveiling the "psychology" of that character, what would be interesting to see emerge from this kind of reading are the conditions that make some of us readers all too ready to be convinced. By keeping in mind what in the context of the *De casibus* appears basic to hermeneutics, we might be in a better position to examine our own judgments while we formulate them. The questions that should have led Theseus *not* to trust his wife against his son were most likely not intended as a "decoder," a sort of Enigma machine designed to unriddle the misogynist stance of the narrator in the *Corbaccio*.[21] They were more probably offered as a modest reminder that narrators should be scrutinized before we accept their claims. The message is not new. Articulated from a different but no less incisive viewpoint than, say, the one found in the *Decameron*, it is the same Ovidian lesson to which Boccaccio tirelessly, if subtly, draws our readerly attention. Every speaker has an agenda, and so does every reader, this one included.

CHAPTER TWENTY-TWO

VERNACULARIZATION IN CONTEXT
• *(Volgarizzamenti* of Livy, Valerius Maximus, and Ovid*)*

Alison Cornish

To Boccaccio have been attributed vernacular translations (*volgarizza-menti*) of parts of Titus Livy's *Ab urbe condita* (*History of Rome*), several translations of Valerius Maximus's *Factorum et dictorum libri* (*Memorable Deeds and Sayings*) with glosses also in multiple versions, and one of the three Tuscan versions of Ovid's *Ars amandi* (*Art of Love*) with glosses. While the Certaldan has been mentioned as translator of Livy at least since the fifteenth century, his role in versions of Valerius Maximus and of Ovid's amorous books is a twentieth-century supposition. Currently only one part of Livy (the fourth decade) is still thought to be possibly by Boccaccio; the translation of Valerius Maximus has been dated to before 1326, making Boccaccio's authorship highly unlikely; and the identification of Boccaccio with the self-described "rough scholar" who glossed and updated a version of Ovid's *Ars* remains tentative. Boccaccio's authorship cannot be proven in part because it has become clear that no one person could be responsible for all the different versions of these texts and their glosses. Yet it cannot be excluded that he might have played some role in some stage of their production and circulation because of their proximity, even quite close verbal proximity, with his other works.

In his fifteenth-century history of Latin literature, Sicco Polenton claimed that Boccaccio put three decades of Livy into the speech of his homeland. About a hundred years later Pietro Bembo referred in two letters to "a decade of Livy translated into the vernacular by Boccaccio."[1] The text of Titus Livy's *Ab urbe condita* survives in units of ten books referred to as "decades" since late antiquity. Only three (books 1, 3, and 4) of the original fourteen were known in Boccaccio's day. Though the Italian versions of the three surviving decades, all produced during the Trecento, eventually circulated together, even Bembo could tell right away that the first could not be by Boccaccio.[2] It is full of borrowings from French and even untranslated

255

French words, indicating its derivation from a prior French translation that does not survive.[3] The translators of the other two decades not only worked directly from the Latin; they are generally also more Latinate in their lexicon and syntax. In the nineteenth century Attilio Hortis traced stylistic similarities between the proem to the translated fourth decade and Boccaccio's other works, noting the proem's dedication to the lord of Ravenna, Ostagio da Polenta (d. 1346), under whose patronage Boccaccio had lived.

The translation of Livy is very much at the nexus of a cultural shift between the vernacularization movement and Latin humanism, which followed upon it. Livy's work was revered but not well read in the Middle Ages, because of both its imposing size and its preimperial ideology. Giuseppe Billanovich saw in the revival of Livy starting in the thirteenth century with Lovato Lovati, Albertino Mussato, and Riccobaldo of Ferrara the "origins of humanism." Moreover, he identified Petrarch's own copy of Livy in the British Library, which showed how as a young man Petrarch undertook to collect, collate, and correct all the surviving books. In addition, Billanovich made the fundamental discovery that this very exemplar, or a copy of it, was used for the Tuscan translations of the third and the fourth decades.[4] Billanovich's student Maria Teresa Casella made a comprehensive study of the manuscripts of the vernacular Livy and their verbal correspondences with Boccaccio's other works and concluded that he himself was the translator.[5]

The first suspicion that Boccaccio might have had something to do with a vernacular version of Valerius Maximus came from passages in the *Filocolo* deriving from it. Salvatore Battaglia noticed that in the *Filocolo* Boccaccio used the contemporary *volgarizzamento* of Valerius Maximus rather than the original.[6] Vittore Branca concluded that in his youth Boccaccio read Valerius mostly in translation, which Antonio Enzo Quaglio confirmed with a series of textual comparisons.[7] Casella argued that the resemblances arose because, here too, Boccaccio himself was the author of the translation, as well as of several redactions of accompanying glosses.[8] Giorgio Padoan went on to find verbal resemblances between the second redaction of the vernacular Valerius and the tale of Tito and Gisippo (*Decameron* 10.8), which he attributes to the memory of the translator rather than a dependence on other people's translations.[9]

Casella's theory encountered a major difficulty when a manuscript of the vernacular Valerius Maximus was recovered with a gloss describing events of 1326 as "today"—when Boccaccio was just thirteen years old.[10] Yet already in 1986 Giuliano Tanturli mounted a critique of these attributions, starting with Billanovich's assumption that similarities, a shared original, and even dependence between the translations of the third and fourth decades of Livy necessarily meant they were authored by the same person. The proem to the fourth decade announces its intent to translate those ten books without referring to a prior undertaking. In fact, Tanturli demonstrates by means of misreadings in the fourth decade that its translator could not have, or at least not yet, translated the third, since he seems not to know events and personages recounted in the earlier books.[11]

The very anonymity of these translations suggests a certain self-disdain, or at least indifference to fame, on the part of those responsible, whoever they were. Thinking about Boccaccio's possible engagement with vernacular translation of classical texts also entails thinking about the characteristics of *volgarizzamento* in this place and time.[12] In essence, *volgarizzamento* is a space of anonymous and multiple rewriting. While it may be a difficult thing to establish authorship in such a space, it is nevertheless one in which Boccaccio operated.

The translator's proem to the fourth decade of Livy bears particular comparison with Boccaccio's other works, expressing an intent to make available to those ignorant of Latin ancient stories useful to civic life.[13] Typical of early Italian translators, the author of this proem explains that the limitations of his audience and their idiom are what necessitate his departure from the text he is trying to translate:

> Nor is it my intention (*intendimento*) in the exposition of the aforesaid decade always to adhere closely to the letter of the author because, doing that, I do not see how I could properly arrive at the intended purpose (*fine intento*), which is wanting to make clear the meaning (*intenzione*) of Tito Livio to those who do not understand (*a' non intendenti*). Because not just in one place but in many he writes so precisely that if only his words, with nothing added, were put down, the vernacular version (*il volgare*) would remain cut short to those, I mean, who are of not too subtle perception, so that they would understand as little from the translated text (*volgarizzato*) as from the original (*per lettera*). Thus in order that all of his meaning can be fully understood even by the roughest people, without departing from his own meaning, I think that it is useful in some places to fill out his words with more.[14]

Simone Marchesi regards the attitude toward antiquity in the proem as intermediate to Dante's optimistic Limbo, where the modern poet can walk and talk with five ancient ones, and Petrarch's "diachronic despair," symbolized by his literal sewing back together of Livy's dismembered decades.[15]

Scholars have observed that, despite the proem's preemptive apology for departing from the original in the translation in order to make it more comprehensible to the *non intendenti*, this vernacular fourth decade is not very accommodating to vulgar readership. Assuming the translation we have is the one referred to by the author of the proem, this inconsistency suggests some ambivalence about the project. Carlo Dionisotti supposed that such ambivalence might be the cause of the persistent anonymity in the manuscripts of this and other translations that in more recent times have been ascribed to Boccaccio.[16] If his contemporaries knew Boccaccio was the author, it is hard to imagine how the manuscripts could "forget" it, or why his known works of translation would circulate less as their author became more famous. Dionisotti concludes that the translator deliberately hid his identity and distanced himself from his early vernacularization work, just as he distanced himself from vernacular composition in general as he came under the spell of Petrarch.

The philological rigor brought to bear on recovering the text of Livy is antithetical to and "intolerant"—as Dionisotti put it—of the impulse of *volgarizzamento*. That Boccaccio would put Petrarch's labors to such a use demonstrates a resistant discipleship: one that uses such a philological advance (a painstakingly emended text) to revert to the old approximative practice of vulgarization, demanded by the avid but semiliterate readership of the urban mercantile class. The ready availability of this vernacular version is thematized in the *Trecentonovelle*, where Franco Sacchetti depicts a prominent Florentine citizen and respected contemporary of Boccaccio's reading his *Titolivio* on a Saturday afternoon.[17] The humor in the tale, where the amateur reader of Livy rants incomprehensibly at workmen in his house about an episode in Roman history, derives presumably from the fact that by Sacchetti's time (d. 1400), such vulgar readers of classical texts looked faintly ridiculous.

Yet there is already, within the vernacular translation of Livy itself, a perceptible movement away from domestications more fully familiar to the reader unschooled in Latin, and toward foreignizations that in a sense refuse to be translated. By focusing on the translation of the word *miles* (soldier), Tanturli observed that the third decade regularly uses the Latinism *milite*, and only rarely the circumlocution *uom d'arme* (man of arms). The fourth decade instead falls back on the more traditional and anachronistic term, *cavaliere* (knight). The author of the third decade is aware, that is, of the historical difference between a Roman foot soldier and a medieval knight, which the author of the fourth decade elides—an equivocation that Leonardo Bruni would take pains to dissect in his *De militia (Civic Knight-*

hood). Similarly, the third decade uses the vernacular *segno* to translate *signum* (military ensign or standard) in order to avoid equating it with *bandiera* (flag), as the translator of the fourth decade regularly does. Lorenzo Valla seized upon the dyad *signa atque banna* in the Donation of Constantine, which ignorantly equated the Roman *signum* with the medieval *bandiera*, as proof of its non-Roman origins.[18] As we saw, the translator's proem to the fourth decade apologizes in advance for having to depart from the text and add explanatory material. The third decade, in contrast, does not explain and at times does not even translate what it does not find as equivalent between the two cultures, thus refusing the domesticating practice of the older *volgarizzamenti*. The refusal to translate is symptomatic of a kind of "diachronic despair," a kind of pathos of distance between the ancient and modern worlds of which humanism becomes aware.

A similar trend is apparent also in the various vernacular versions of Valerius Maximus. A translator explains in the proem, present in two manuscripts, that he was obliged to retranslate the text when he went to gloss it, because of just such a new awareness:

> Valerius Maximus . . . which another time I brought over from Latin into this vulgar tongue, but certain wise religious men, considering the affection laypeople bear toward this book because of narrations of the deeds and sayings worthy of memory that are in it, and considering the brevity of these stories that the author touches on, which instills thirst in listeners for a more expanded style, made on this book certain writings, like glosses. So, because when I was asked to put those glosses onto this text and especially because in many places I did not understand the same thing the glossators do because of the poverty of my ability, I had better bring it over again into said language together with the necessary and useful glosses. Therefore no one should be surprised to see this second *volgare* different from the first.[19]

This translator's earlier attempt has usually been identified with the most widely circulating redaction (surviving in twenty-nine manuscripts and four sixteenth-century editions), and hence called the "vulgate," which is full of errors of translation as well as awkward and sometimes impenetrable phrases.[20] In addition to the revision preceded by the proem quoted above, preserved complete only in a single Florentine manuscript, there is a third version preserved in two witnesses, which Concetto Marchesi had first attributed to a later, "unknown and incompetent redactor," but which Adriana Zampieri has demonstrated to be the oldest of all three, blaming its abundance of errors in large part on a poor Latin exemplar. For Zampieri as for Casella, similarities between the earliest and latest versions are explained by a persistence in the memory of a single translator, who recalled some of his earliest attempts to translate the text even as he was working on his second revision.[21] This busy translator and retranslator would be Boccaccio himself.

Yet the manuscripts of the translation of Valerius Maximus and its vernacular glosses also tell another story. Some manuscripts of the vulgate are accompanied by glosses transcribed in the same hand as the text, indicating that they were linked already from an early date. The witnesses we have of the revised translation, apparently motivated, as we are told in the proem, by the encounter with the commentary of learned clerics, contain a different set of glosses. Their content makes evident their derivation from the Latin commentary on Valerius Maximus that the Augustinian friar Dionigi da Borgo San Sepolcro, friend of both Boccaccio and Petrarch, dedicated to Cardinal Giovanni Colonna sometime after 1327. These new vernacular glosses are found most fully in two witnesses of the revised version of the text, both containing the proem announcing a retranslation inspired by the encounter with learned commentators.[22] However, contrary to expectation, the vernacular text of Valerius Maximus cited in the marginal glosses is not the same as the vernacular text they are set around. These new glosses were working with yet another version that has not come down to us. As the revised glosses do not go with the revised text, they were not likely authored by the same person.[23] Rather, the complex manuscript tradition of translation and glosses suggests the work of quite a number of independent agents, building on the work of their predecessors and near contemporaries.

The third vernacularization of a classical author associated with Boccaccio is the Tuscan translation of Ovid's *Ars amandi*, which also survives in multiple redactions. Vanna Lippi Bigazzi has proposed that Boccaccio be identified as the self-described "rough scholar" (*scolaio rozzo*) who added a second prologue to the most widely circulating one. Lippi Bigazzi has brought into relief the crowded layers of retranslation, revision, and reglossing in the tradition of the Tuscan versions of both the *Ars amandi* (*Art of Love*) and the *Remedia amoris* (*Remedies of Love*), so that even if Boccaccio is involved, he would again be only one of many agents. The *volgarizzatore* himself (whom Lippi Bigazzi thinks is Andrea Lancia) says in his own prologue to the *Arte d'amare* that he "retranslated" (*rivolgarizzato*); and in the prologue to the same redaction of the *Rimedi d'amore* he says he glossed the text as well as translated it more than once. Even after the modifications and stylistic adjustments of the self-described "rough scholar," the text of the translation received further emendations on the basis of a Latin text different from the one used by the original translator. Lippi Bigazzi is content to leave the attribution to Boccaccio a mere possibility, encouraged by similarities between some glosses on the *Arte d'amare* and those of Boccaccio on his *Teseida*, as well as by the importance of Ovid's amorous books to Boccaccio's canonical works.

Whether or not we want to confirm or deflate Boccaccio's authorship of any particular translation or all of them, Boccaccio's engagement with vernacular translation remains certain. In addition to the vernacular Valerius Maximus, the *Filocolo* also makes use of Andrea Lancia's vernacular compendium of the *Aeneid*.[24] Resemblances have been identified between several of Boccaccio's works (*Filostrato, Filocolo, Teseida*, and *Rime*) and the *volgarizzamento* of Ovid's *Heroides* together with the Italian version of Benoît de Sainte-Maure's *Roman de Troie* (*Romance of Troy*), *Istorietta troiana* (*Little History of Troy*), both of which are preserved in a fourteenth-century manuscript also containing a partial copy of Andrea Lancia's *Eneide*. These similarities suggest that Boccaccio was working, if not with this particular codex, then with one very much like it.[25] Use of a vernacularization, even by as accomplished a Latinist as Boccaccio, does not signify authorship. What it does signify is a readiness to use, or even a preference for, vernacularizations.

The anonymity of the vernacularizations that have been ascribed to Boccaccio may suggest his ambivalence about a project that went against Petrarch's new cult of a return to Latin originals, but it may also simply be symptomatic of the enterprise of vernacularization. If neither Boccaccio nor any other single individual can be the author of these vernacularizations in all their different versions, then the project of vernacularization has to be seen as the product of many agents and authors, or readers and scribes who become coauthors. Anonymity is not the sign of no authorship, but of multiple authorship. Vernacular translation does not attempt to replicate, only to explicate. Whether translating or not, this is what Boccaccio was most often up to.

PART IX

GEOGRAPHICAL EXPLORATIONS

CHAPTER TWENTY-THREE

BOCCACCIO'S HUMANISTIC ETHNOGRAPHY • *(De Canaria)*

James K. Coleman

The Canary Islands represented, for the ancients, the westernmost limit of the known world. Pliny and other classical geographers identified them with the Fortunate Isles (or Islands of the Blessed), where, according to Greek and Roman myth, the departed heroes enjoy an eternal, blissful existence.[1] For most of the Middle Ages there were no recorded successful attempts by Europeans to reach the Canaries, and all knowledge of these islands was based entirely on the authority of ancient authors. The Canaries were, effectively, brought back within the known world of the Europeans around the year 1336, when an expedition led by Lanzarotto Malocello of Genoa succeeded in reaching the islands, inaugurating a new phase of European exploration. Malocello's voyage was followed in 1341 by a larger expedition, financed in part by King Alfonso IV of Portugal and led by Niccoloso da Recco (a Genoese captain) and Angelino del Tegghia dei Corbizzi (a Florentine).[2] This 1341 voyage gave rise to the first surviving description of the islands since antiquity—Giovanni Boccaccio's *De Canaria et insulis reliquis ultra Ispaniam in Occeano noviter repertis (On Canaria and the Other Islands Newly Discovered in the Ocean beyond Spain)*.[3]

Boccaccio declares that his source for the account of the voyage is a letter that certain Florentine merchants living in Seville had sent to Florence on November 15, 1341. It would appear that Boccaccio managed to gain early access to information about the expedition through his connections at the bank of the Bardi, who had probably received this letter from Florentines working at the bank's large branch in Seville. Since no trace of the letter mentioned by Boccaccio has survived, it is impossible to determine precisely how Boccaccio reworked his immediate source—consisting, most likely, of vernacular anecdotes relayed by sailors and bankers—into the Latin prose of the *De Canaria*. The resulting literary text contains elements that reflect mercantile interests as well as humanistic values. To the former category we may assign, for example, the list of commodities that the sailors brought back to Europe from the Canaries. The humanistic character of the text (reflecting, undoubtedly, the values of Boccaccio, perhaps shared to some degree by his sources) is evident above all in two areas, as the remainder of this essay will show: on the one hand, the text's open and sympathetic presentation of the human qualities and society of the native islanders; on the other, the recourse to classical literary precedents—particularly the topoi of the Golden Age and of the noble savage—to shape this ethnographic presentation.

The same voyage described in Boccaccio's *De Canaria* also captured the interest of Petrarch, whose *De vita solitaria* expresses his reactions to the rediscovery of the islands. Theodore Cachey, in his excellent comparative study of these two texts, has cautioned that the discussions of the Canaries by Petrarch and Boccaccio represent fundamentally different viewpoints and cannot be characterized as a unified "humanist" response to the discovery.[4] Petrarch enters into a brief discussion of the Fortunatae Insulae in order to clarify that the inhabitants of this newly discovered land, while living in isolation, cannot be considered to enjoy the benefits of true solitude, which requires a certain capacity for contemplation. The lonely existence of these people is due, in Petrarch's view, to the absence of the customs and culture that would allow for the development of social structures. Guided only by their natural instincts, they lead aimless, atomized lives comparable to the wanderings of beasts. Although he uses the name Fortunatae Insulae to designate the Canaries, Petrarch (in contrast with Boccaccio, as we shall see) makes no real attempt to connect newly reported facts about the islands with the Golden Age myths that had traditionally been associated with them. Petrarch summarily concludes that the islands' paradisiacal reputation and name are bitterly ironic in light of the poor natural and human conditions that he says prevail there.

Boccaccio's deep knowledge of classical myths plays an important, if tacit, role in the composition of the *De Canaria*. Manlio Pastore Stocchi, in what he regards as a sign of the Certaldan's increasingly erudite interests, observes that Boccaccio's *De Canaria* "sembra influenzato da miti esclusivamente colti, come quello del buon selvaggio."[5] The observation merits more detailed study and calls for an assessment of the specific sources Boccaccio was able to draw on for versions of the major primitivist myths of the Golden Age and the noble savage.

The Golden Age myth that recurs throughout classical literature derives ultimately from Hesiod's *Works and Days*.[6] Hesiod recounts that during the time when heaven was ruled by Cronos (identified by the Romans with

Saturn), the earth was inhabited by a race of men who knew nothing of toil, evil, or sorrow, living on the fruits of an abundantly fertile land. Four successive ages produced increasingly degenerate races of men, except for the penultimate age, that of the heroes, who were granted by Zeus an eternal home in the Islands of the Blessed, where Cronos still rules. While Boccaccio did not have access to Hesiod's *Works and Days*, he was deeply influenced by versions of the Golden Age myth composed by numerous Roman authors: especially Ovid and Virgil, but also Horace, Seneca, Juvenal, and Boethius.[7]

Early medieval Christian authors appropriated this classical mythology but understandably looked askance at the notion that the bountiful islands celebrated by these pagan authors could be identified with any earthly paradise. Isidore of Seville's discussion of the *fortunatarum insulae* was particularly influential in the Middle Ages; he situates the islands "in the Ocean, against the left side of Mauretania, closest to where the sun sets," and describes a typically paradisiacal setting of fertile fruit trees, grapevines, and spontaneously growing crops. However, he objects to the "mistake of pagans and the poems by worldly poets, who believed that these isles were Paradise because of the fertility of their soil."[8]

Connected to the classical topos of the persistence of Golden Age conditions in distant lands like the Fortunate Islands is the tendency of classical authors to idealize the lifestyle of specific remote or "primitive" peoples. The myth of the noble savage, which would achieve marked prominence in European discourse from the sixteenth century on, has its roots in antiquity, when Greek and Roman authors criticized the ills of their own societies by reporting on the moral rectitude and other admirable qualities of tribal "primitives" such as the Scythians, Germans, and Hebrideans.[9] Boccaccio would have known versions of this topos by Cicero, Horace, Virgil, Seneca, and Solinus, among others.[10] Classical authors often employ motifs of the Golden Age myth in descriptions of the simple but happy existence of tribes presented as noble savages; for example, Pliny claims that the Hyperboreans, whom he regards as a real people, are not only without discord but also completely free from disease.[11]

In *De Canaria* Boccaccio does not assert that the newly discovered islands are identical to the paradisiacal Fortunate Isles referred to in ancient texts. Rather, his account aims to establish the specific ways in which the society of the island's natives does or does not correspond to the Golden Age societies described in classical literature. Boccaccio's particular interest in ethnographic details that resonate with traditional facets of the Golden Age and noble savage myths is especially evident in the detailed discussion of the four native men who were taken back to Lisbon as captives. Although these men could not understand any European languages and were therefore able to communicate with their captors only through gestures, the *De Canaria* states that they are "very intelligent, as can be determined" (magni intellectus ut comprehendi potest), and observes with clear admiration: "They seem to be extremely trustworthy and just. For whenever any food was given to one of them, he would divide it into equal parts and give these portions to the others before tasting the food himself."[12] The text also observes that this noteworthy degree of mutual concern and respect occurs within the context of what appears as a harmonious social structure: "They honored one another reciprocally, although they honored one more than the rest; this man had a loincloth made of palm leaves, painted yellow and red, whereas the rest had loincloths made of rushes."[13] From the classical origins of the topos on, praise for the noble savage has always functioned, implicitly or explicitly, as a critique of contemporary "civilized" peoples. The praise for the natives in Boccaccio's text clearly serves this function at points: "They sing sweetly, and dance almost in the French manner. They are cheerful and lively and quite sociable—more so than many Spaniards are."[14] His barb against the Spanish is a particularly clear example of this critical function in Boccaccio's text, though in this instance the target is not civilized man generally but one particular European people.

Echoing another feature consistently ascribed to Golden Age societies in classical literature, the *De Canaria* reports that the natives have no knowledge of gold, silver, or edged weapons: "Gold and silver coins were shown to them, and these items were totally unfamiliar to them. . . . Gold jewelry, decorated vases, swords and sabers were shown to them, but it does not appear that they have ever seen such items, nor that they themselves possess any."[15] The presence of this detail reflects, on the one hand, the mercantile interests that play a role in the text's contents—from this point of view the natives' lack of familiarity with such items would be a disappointing indicator for the possibility of profitable trade with the islands. On the other hand, the absence of gold and of weapons is a conventional element of literary accounts of the Golden Age, to be taken in most cases as a concrete demonstration of the nonexistence of greed and warfare in such societies. According to Ovid's *Metamorphoses* (1.150–57), for instance, in the Golden Age men possessed (somewhat paradoxically, it might be said) no knowledge of precious metals; "destructive iron and harmful gold" were unearthed together in the Iron Age, corresponding to historical time.

While the *De Canaria* describes the garments worn by some of the island natives, the text also contains numerous references to their nudity.

The first island that the sailors visit is described as "filled . . . with naked men and women" (habundantem . . . nudis hominibus et mulieribus). Of the same four prisoners whose garments are described, Boccaccio also writes that "they go about naked" (nudi incedunt). Freedom from feeling shame at one's own nudity is, clearly, a quality that Boccaccio would have associated with paradisiacal environments, being one of the salient characteristics of the prelapsarian state of Adam and Eve in the garden of Eden. That the islanders' lack of self-consciousness about their own nakedness is to be taken as a sign of innocence and purity is demonstrated by the fact that, in Boccaccio's account, this quality is displayed especially by virgins: "Among this people the women enter into marriage, and those women who have had relations with men wear loincloths, as the men do; the virgins, however, go about completely naked, and experience no sense of shame going around like this."[16]

Classical descriptions of the Golden Age generally feature a superabundance of food; in many versions of the myth, humans in the Golden Age subsist on foods that are nourishing and very easy to procure, though decidedly simple or even austere, such as acorns.[17] The food of the Canary natives is described in similar terms: the sailors find "dried figs in palm baskets—very good, as we judge those to be that are grown in Cesena—and grain that was much more beautiful than our own, since it had longer and thicker kernels than our grain has, and was very white. . . . The grain and cereals they either eat in the manner of the birds or they make flour which they eat without making it into bread at all, just drinking some water with it."[18] On another island the sailors find a great abundance of doves, which are presented as an ideal food source: not only are they larger and perhaps tastier than the doves familiar to European hunters; they are also such easy prey that the sailors can hunt them using stones and sticks.

The *De Canaria* reports that the islanders possessed no boats of any kind, so that each island populace was isolated not only from European civilization, but even from neighboring islands. In many classical literary texts, blissful ignorance of navigational technology is presented as a positive feature of Golden Age society.[19] The chorus of Seneca's *Medea* evokes that lost age, laments its passing with the advent of navigation, and prophesies a future in which the ocean "shall uncover new worlds": "Unsullied the ages our fathers saw, with crime banished afar. Then every man inactive kept to his own shores and lived to old age on ancestral fields, rich with but little. . . . Now, in our time . . . any little craft now wanders at will upon the deep. All bounds have been removed . . . : the Indian drinks of the cold Araxes, the Persians quaff the Elbe and the Rhine. There will come an age in the far-off years when Ocean shall unloose the bonds of things, when the whole broad earth shall be revealed, when Tethys shall disclose new worlds."[20] Boccaccio, in the proem to the tenth book of the *Genealogia*, seems to allude to and subvert this Senecan passage, which some came to view after Columbus's voyages as a sort of prophecy of the discovery of the New World:

> What indeed is one to make of ships, with the help of divine illumination, designed by human ingenuity and built by artifice. . . . By means of this active voyaging on this sea it has come about (and this is no small benefit for the whole of the human race) that the Cimberi and the Celts in another corner of the world sometimes hear about who the Arabs are . . . and in this way too the Spaniard and the Moor, having been visited, may visit the Persians and the Indians and the Caucasus; and the most distant Thule may tread the shores of Sri Lanka. And while they exchange their goods reciprocally, it not only comes about that they marvel at one another's customs and laws and habits, but it even can happen that one who, while he looks at the other and considers how he comes from another world, and how he is not encircled by the same ocean with him, mixes rites, gives credit for merchandise, forms friendships.[21]

The expedition to the Canaries provided Boccaccio with the means to observe the customs and lifestyle of a previously unknown human society. His humanist perspective, and his deep familiarity with the Golden Age myth in classical literature, made him receptive to the possible existence of a remote society worthy of admiration, with which Europeans might, as he puts it, "mix rites." His perspective is not, however, that of an integral primitivist. The practice of navigation itself is an example of an advanced human technology that Boccaccio praises unequivocally, in the name of these same humanistic values.

The encounter between the Canary Islanders and the Europeans is often cited as an anticipation or prototype of the pattern of exploration, conquest, and colonization that would be repeatedly inflicted on New World peoples following Columbus's voyage. It is rarely recognized, though, that Boccaccio's account of the initial phase of this encounter likewise anticipates a major strand of the European literary response to the exploration of the New World. Montaigne's "Des cannibales," for instance, shares with the *De Canaria* a reliance on the classical myths of the Golden Age and the noble savage to interpret and give literary form to ethnographic reports about the inhabitants of new worlds.[22] While the *De Canaria* was not a direct source for Montaigne, this connection is not merely coincidental. The values of the humanist movement that Boccaccio helped to establish, and that Montaigne inherited, account for the analogous approaches taken by the two authors. After Montaigne, as is well known, the noble savage topos would become a central element of European discourse about "primitive" peoples, especially among eighteenth- and nineteenth-century romantic writers. Thus the *De Canaria*, beyond its value as a historical document, reveals Boccaccio's place as precursor of a major intellectual current often traced only from the sixteenth century forward.

CHAPTER TWENTY-FOUR

BETWEEN TEXT AND TERRITORY
- *(De montibus, silvis, fontibus, lacubus, fluminibus, stagnis seu paludibus et de diversis nominibus maris)*

Theodore J. Cachey Jr.

M odern scholarship has repeatedly highlighted Boccaccio's profoundly original and pioneering literary contributions across an impressively broad spectrum of genres and literary forms. Nevertheless, the innovative character of the geographical dictionary or gazetteer containing nearly two thousand alphabetically ordered entries that Boccaccio compiled between 1350 and the middle of the 1360s, the *De montibus, silvis, fontibus, lacubus, fluminibus, stagnis seu paludibus et de diversis nominibus maris* (*On Mountains, Forests, Fonts, Lakes, Rivers, Marshes or Ponds and on the Different Names of the Seas*), has yet to receive adequate critical assessment.[1] This is due to a general tendency among readers primarily to consider the *De montibus* as the expression of an early humanist philological preoccupation with toponyms found in classical *auctores*. Manlio Pastore Stocchi, in the introduction to his edition of the text, characterizes the emphasis of the work as falling not on geography but on history and poetry, asserting that "Boccaccio did not intend to traverse material places but rather places of memory by rendering affectionate homage to a strictly literary universe of springs, forests, mountains. . . ."[2] A recent review of the specifically geographical contribution of the *De montibus*, however, has called into question this generally accepted view by illustrating the work's preoccupation with geographical knowledge in its own right and with the geographical description of the contemporary world. In fact, Claudio Greppi has argued that a geographical mode of analysis proves to be much richer than an antiquarian approach to the text and merits further development.[3] For example, the geomorphological criteria that govern the sequence of the sections, so that the section on fonts precedes that on lakes and rivers, since the latter derive from the former,[4] represents an innovation with respect to Boccaccio's classical sources, and in particular the arbitrarily ordered sections of Vibius Sequester's modest geographical dictionary.[5] Moreover, the brief introductions to the respective parts are distinguished by their discussion of specifically geophysical matters, such as the difference between a marsh and a pond,[6] to say nothing of the evidently map-aided geographical analysis that informs the highly original presentation of the earth's seas in the work's final section, "De diversis nominibus maris."[7]

While the perspective of the geographer has provided a welcome and perhaps overdue corrective to the critical *vulgata* on the *De montibus*, the question of whether Boccaccio primarily intended to elucidate textual references or to describe real territories should not be too rigidly drawn. In fact, an unstable equilibrium or tension between the interrelated realms of literary text and geographical territory is intrinsic to both Boccaccio's intention and his achievement in the *De montibus*. A critical reevaluation of the work might therefore usefully focus on the tension between text and territory at the heart of the work's original conception, as a means of resituating it within the context of the transition from the medieval to the modern history of literature and of geographical knowledge that it epitomizes.

Boccaccio's disingenuous claim in the introduction that he compiled the *De montibus* as a relaxing pastime, "desiring to restore myself with leisure,"[8] was probably intended, as Pastore Stocchi first noted, to excuse or to distract attention from a characteristic of the work that renders it uniquely modern among Boccaccio's other Latin works of erudition, namely, the lack of any moralistic or allegorical dimension such as characterized the more or less contemporary *De mulieribus claris*, the *De casibus virorum illustrium*, and the *Genealogia deorum gentilium*.[9] Boccaccio manages to foreshadow a modern philological attitude in the *De montibus* by focusing solely on the historical or literal sense of texts; Pastore Stocchi notes that in this respect the *De montibus* can be considered a precursor of Ermolao Barbaro's *Castigationes Plinianae* (*Plinian Emendations*, 1492) and *Castigationes in Pomponium Melam* (*Pomponius Mela Emended*, 1493).[10] But the extent to which Boccaccio's "literal" approach in the *De montibus* expresses a modern geographical curiosity that transcends the literary antiquarianism of the author's original intention should not be underestimated. Indeed, a tension or underlying aporia between the work's explicitly philological and literary aim and a concern with geographical knowledge is implicit in Boccaccio's statement of purpose in the introduction. He announces that he intends to provide an aid to humanist readers of the *auctores*, particularly of the best "gentile," or pagan, authors,[11] so that the error of mistaking the name of a mountain for that of a river, or of locating that mountain or river in the west when it is actually located in the east, can be avoided.[12] In other words, the text is concerned with both names and places, with both philology and geography. And one could plausibly argue that the tension between the ostensibly philological and antiquarian remit of the work and its no less compelling and underlying concern with geographical knowledge is ultimately resolved in favor of the latter.

As Pastore Stocchi was the first to note, rather than mine the poets directly as sources, Boccaccio utilizes primarily encyclopedic and geographical works such as Pliny, Pomponius Mela, and Vibius Sequester as his sources for the entries. This procedure suggests a scope or range of geographical reconnaissance that went beyond the simple aim of providing an aid to the interpretation of toponyms found in the texts of the gentile poets and historians. A substantially lower proportion of entries derives directly from the poets, and many of these provide no more information than what was already available in the original text, and thus appear to serve no other purpose than to contribute to the impression of a complete geographical coverage of classical sites.[13] Equally, the alphabetical ordering of the geographical entries itself tends to have the effect of suggesting implicitly a comprehensive or encyclopedic range of territorial coverage from *A* to *Z*. By blending information from Pliny, Livy, Vibius Sequester, and other sources in a single entry, as Boccaccio typically does, he produces the inevitable result of privileging place itself, above and beyond any particular textual reference or source concerning it. An overwhelming sense of the "placedness" of the literary tradition in its geographical rather than its textual dimensions forcefully emerges from Boccaccio's encyclopedic procedure and characteristic handling of his sources. Having set out to provide a philological support for readers of Roman and Greek literature, Boccaccio ultimately exceeds the original purpose of the work and produces something more akin to a geographical index for a map of the world, a written supplement or gazetteer to accompany the coeval *mappaemundi* of a Paolo Veneto or a Pietro Vesconte.[14]

In fact, despite Boccaccio's claim in the introduction to be primarily concerned with gentile poets and historians, the effective canon of authors from which the entries derive includes not only Horace, Livy, Ovid, Virgil, Statius, and the newly available Homer,[15] but also the scriptures, whose Holy Land loci such as Mt. Sinai are culled from Jerome's Latin translation of Eusebius's *Onomasticon*, with additional information provided by Flavius Josephus as well as modern pilgrims.[16] There are also entries that attest to Boccaccio's knowledge and consultation of modern travelers to the East such as John of Plano Carpine and William of Rubruk.[17] Dante represents an especially significant addition to the canon of *auctores*, particularly regarding the representation of the Italian Peninsula (but not only of Italy). The "places" of the other two great moderns, Petrarch and Boccaccio himself, are also prominently featured in the *De montibus*, including lengthy entries on the Sorgue and various Neapolitan sites, including Baia, which was celebrated also by Petrarch.[18]

While the entries directly linked to the "Three Crowns" are relatively few, they nonetheless serve to orient the overall ideological thrust of the work. Rather than carrying out a purely antiquarian exercise in textual philology, Boccaccio performs through the *De montibus* an act of contemporary cultural territorialization, particularly as regards the Italian Peninsula. The explicit and implicit presence of the moderns and of contemporary Italy in key entries scattered throughout the *De montibus* cumulatively demonstrates that Boccaccio was not so much engaged in recovering the lost geographical world of the ancients as he was in establishing a modern literary territorial identity that still had a connection to that world. The disproportionate number of entries and the special care dedicated to Italian mountains, forests, fonts, lakes, rivers, marshes, swamps, and seas reinforce a distinctively Italocentric world. Boccaccio represents the Tuscan-centric embodiment and modern continuation of this Roman legacy.[19]

Boccaccio's access to the Italian geography covered by the dictionary, in fact, is in many cases firsthand, as he states explicitly in his introduction to the lengthiest section of the *De montibus* (over nine hundred entries, nearly half of the entire work), dedicated to rivers: "I will especially speak about those [rivers] that by the diligence of the ancients are known to us, and about those that we, traveling in various regions, have seen with our own eyes."[20] In fact, among the most remarkable entries are those dedicated to the Po, where Boccaccio largely sets aside the ancients and a concern for classical poetry and history in favor of geographical description. The entry on the Po delta is a tour de force, with its focus on the diverse characteristics of each of the seven mouths of the river. It is based on an original collection of information that, while bearing in mind the classical sources, reflects nonetheless the contemporary situation where Boccaccio "bases himself on what appears to be extensive personal knowledge of the places."[21]

In order to situate the *De montibus* more precisely within the context of the transitional moment in literary and geographical history from which it emerged, it is necessary to revise somewhat the traditional view that has deemed the work to be perfectly parallel or even subsidiary to Petrarch's humanist geographical interests. In fact, it should be recognized that the cofounders of humanism assume somewhat different attitudes toward geographical knowledge. For example, confronted with the rediscovery of the

Canaries during the first half of the fourteenth century, in a passage of the *Vita solitaria* Petrarch identified them as the same as Horace's Fortunate Islands and invested them with an antiprimitivist allegory. Boccaccio, on the other hand, ignored the putative identification of the "newly discovered islands" with the Fortunates and inaugurated a new Atlantic genre of discovery literature by writing in his *Zibaldone Magliabechiano* the Latin translation of a vernacular letter reporting on an early expedition there, the *De Canaria*.[22] Petrarch's engagements with geography are unfailingly related to consolidating his own literary identity and subject position, most famously in the letter describing the ascent of Mt. Ventoux (*Familiares* 4.1). But there is also the letter on Thule (*Familiares* 3.1), among many other texts, that could be cited to illustrate the distinctiveness of Petrarch's characteristic approach, one that rigorously subordinated geographical knowledge of the outside world to interior self-exploration and the interpretation of the poets.[23] Boccaccio's geographical explorations in the *De montibus*, on the other hand, are unhindered by preoccupations with interior space or moral allegories. He was thus freer to express a genuine curiosity about the geography of the world that pushed beyond the relatively narrow confines of the Petrarchan humanist subject.[24]

Indeed, there is some evidence that Boccaccio was aware of and somewhat anxious about exceeding the limits of an appropriately Petrarchan approach to his geographical subject. The work ends with a passage in which Boccaccio expresses in an exaggerated form his fear that Petrarch may have undertaken a work of geographical erudition that will put his own modest contribution to shame, and concludes by deferring to the greater authority of his master.[25] Just as the modesty topos at the beginning of the work provided rhetorical cover for Boccaccio's discomfort at presenting a geographical dictionary that had no moralizing or allegorical gloss, so the vignette at the end of the work represents a no less excessive expression of modesty designed to excuse Boccaccio for having entered into territory where his master had not trodden and was unlikely ever to tread.

While the original inspiration and format of the *De montibus* lie in Petrarchan humanism, the work is also indebted to Dante's *mappamundi* and the cartographic mode of writing that Dante pioneered, not only for the location of the island of Crete at the intersection of the three continents, as Ambrogio Camozzi has recently noted,[26] but especially for Dante's mappings of the Italian Peninsula in the *De vulgari eloquentia* and in the *Inferno*. The entry for the Apennines, for example, as Greppi notes, is perhaps the most noteworthy (and lengthiest entry by far) among the 568 mountains. Pastore Stocchi notes that while Boccaccio was perhaps inspired by classical sources (Pliny 3.5.48), his description of the track of the Apennines is "substantially original" and is based in large part on a direct knowledge of the places. However, in the entry for the Apennines Boccaccio is also indebted to Dante, who among the moderns first divided the right and left side of the peninsula (after Lucan) between "upper" (Adriatic) and "lower" (Tyrrhenian) seas as separated by the mountain chain in the *De vulgari elo-quentia*. He follows Dante also in the cartographic style of the entry, written from the same "bird's-eye" perspective that the geographer Farinelli has characterized as foreshadowing a modern conception of the peninsula as a territorial unity.[27]

Similarly, in the entry on the Arno, Boccaccio describes a major feature of Italian geography not so much through the lens of classical as modern sources, by associating Dante, Petrarch, and himself with the river. Since it lacked fish, depth, and good water, as Benvenuto da Imola would later observe, it had little to recommend it besides its association with Dante, Petrarch, and Boccaccio. Only in the case of the Arno, in fact, does Boccaccio provide the adornment of a Latin poem (thirteen verses by him at the entry's conclusion) and depart from alphabetical ordering by featuring the river first of the more than nine hundred treated. It enjoys priority because it is the river of the author's homeland, "and it was the first I knew before all others from infancy."[28] The expression has a distinctly Dantean flavor. It recalls Dante's most emphatic assertion of his own Florentine origins in the *bolgia* of the hypocrites:

E io a loro: "I' fui nato e cresciuto
sovra 'l bel fiume d'Arno a la gran villa,
e son col corpo ch'i' ho sempre avuto." (*Inferno* 23.94–96)

"In the great city, by the fair river Arno,"
I said to them, "I was born and raised,
and I am here in the body that was always mine."[29]

In what might be termed the signature entry of the work, Boccaccio describes the Arno in a substantially original manner, "as is demonstrated by the partially modern toponyms and the apologetic references."[30] In fact, while Boccaccio's description of the course of the river can be said to be in the tradition of Dante (see especially *Purgatorio* 14.16–21), he adds an element of Petrarchan literary geography in recalling that the river passes by "Incisa, a town of the Florentines, ancient home of the ancestors of the excellent star Francesco Petrarca, a noteworthy poet."[31] At the same time that he associates himself with the Tuscan river that was so central to Dante's life and poetry,[32] Boccaccio graciously includes Petrarch in a revised itinerary of the river. By inscribing himself (via Dante) alongside Petrarch within a characteristic landscape, Boccaccio illustrates the complex and profoundly interrelated nature of the interactions of the textual and the territorial as orders of space—namely, the ways in which literature becomes associated with geographical place, on the one hand, and how geography itself is made visible by means of literary acts of inscription, on the other. Boccaccio effectively canonizes the "Three Crowns" of Tuscan literature through an act of literary geographical territorialization.

In the final analysis, the *De montibus* offers insight into the processes by which a humanist culture that was initially primarily concerned with literary and historical texts progressively developed a more direct concern with geography as an object of study in its own right. Just as the *De montibus* foreshadows the philological advances of later humanists such as Ermolao Barbaro and Agnolo Poliziano in terms of the study of geographical places in classical literature, so too does the work anticipate the later achievements of humanists in the study of geography, when, for example, in the early Quattrocento, the fascination with Ptolemy's rediscovered *Geographia* stopped being primarily literary and started to inspire and inform the planning for and mapping of the new geographical discoveries of the Renaissance.[33] At the intersection between text and territory, Boccaccio's *De montibus* is worth further investigation and discussion aimed at fully appreciating its innovative character both within the context of Boccaccio's oeuvre and within the larger context of the history of geographical literature and the cultural production of space.

PART X

MISCELLANIES: LYRICS, LETTERS, NOTEBOOKS

CHAPTER TWENTY-FIVE

PATHWAYS THROUGH THE LYRIC
FOREST • *(Rime)*

Roberto Fedi

Unlike his friend and close contemporary Petrarch (1304–74), Giovanni Boccaccio never decided to organize his numerous lyrics into
a genuine *canzoniere*, that is, a collection conceived, chosen, and ordered
by its author. Yet, as bears noting here, in his fundamental prose work, the
Decameron, Boccaccio had taken minute care to organize the one hundred
tales as a series. He even went so far as to enclose them in a frame story, or
cornice — not his invention, but a form descended from, to cite one example,
the *Thousand and One Nights*. The *Decameron* begins with the grievous event
of the European plague that struck Florence in 1348 (the same one in which
Laura died, as Petrarch painfully noted), and it holds all the tales together
in an organization that is nothing short of miraculous.

This fact is not without importance. For Boccaccio, by all evidence, the
composition of lyrics did not fall into a diary-like or roughly biographical
"series." It appears rather, over the arc of about forty years (from the early
1330s until his old age),[1] as a normal concession to contemporary practice,
one with its own internal evolution, too, although largely cleansed or at
least freed of philosophical or doctrinal considerations. In this Boccaccio
appears to stand in the middle, not only historically but truly conceptu-
ally, between Dante and Petrarch. Removed by now from considering poetry, and above all lyric poetry, as a medium for philosophical reflections or
statements of poetics, he remains at the same time distant from the great,
wholly Petrarchan invention of the personal "diary," framed in a life story
and continuously searching for its own internal equilibrium. All of this, for
Boccaccio, is the unique privilege of prose; poetry can still be a place, spa-
cious but not defined, for private meditation in ways that, if not random, are
at least sporadic. One should in any event revisit the old notion that Boccaccio's is an eclectic anthology of occasional lyrics, brought together as a

mere stylistic exercise and therefore substantially minor. Likewise, another entirely misleading notion, attributable not only to Boccaccio alone but by now almost a commonplace, is that the author had such scarce consideration for his lyrics that he destined them for the fire, a claim that Vittore Branca took care to belie.[2]

The principal reason for such critical, not to mention editorial, misfortune (only three important editions in the twentieth century—very few, considering that the author is one of the absolute classics of Italian literature) is likely to be found in the vexed philological situation of the texts themselves. The manuscripts that transmit them mix them more or less randomly, since as we said at the outset, the author never imposed an order on them. Even the principal source of transmission, the so-called Raccolta Bartoliniana, compiled in the sixteenth century by Lorenzo Bartolini, is structured in this way. He derived it in part (101 sonnets) from the collection made by Ludovico Beccadelli, and for a very small section from another anthology by Giovanni Brevio.[3] The Massèra edition (1914), the first to confront the problem in modern times, tried to order the lyrics according to a highly questionable chronological-biographical pattern. Branca's 1992 edition, which in large part replicated Massèra's organization, appears to the most recent editor, Antonio Lanza, to be valuable, but questionable precisely because of this somewhat arbitrary order, which suggests an eclecticism that after due consideration seems quite gratuitous. Moreover, this latest edition undertakes finally to exclude from the lyric corpus those poems that were attributed to Bocccaccio surely by error, and it reintegrates into the author's corpus some texts that Massèra had relegated to dubious status. According to the Lanza edition, at present the following texts are of certain attribution: 1–127 (*Rime di sicura paternità boccacciana*, "Poems surely authored by Boccaccio"); to these are added other texts considered dubious (19 compositions), and still others surely not by Boccaccio (in all 28 texts). The first section, that of securely authorial texts, today consists of seven groups, organized (for lack of an alternative) along thematic-stylistic lines: stilnovistic poems (1–20); comic-realistic poems inspired by Cecco Angiolieri (21–27); late Gothic lyrics (28–77); lyrics in a gnomic-realistic style (78–79); epistolary lyrics, both true (80–82, 125, 126, 127) and fictitious (83); Petrarchist lyrics (84–106); and moral and religious lyrics (107–24).[4]

Even in this order, not pseudobiographical but stylistic and thematic, it appears that Boccaccio, who presumably (at least according to a long critical tradition) began to pen lyrics around 1334–35, therefore around the time of the *Caccia di Diana* and more than a decade before beginning the *Decameron*, initially cultivates a type of poetry that was inevitably of one school or another: there appears in it a generic base of stilnovistic stamp, showing the influence of Dante (including his *Rime petrose* [*Stony Rhymes*]), Cavalcanti, Cino da Pistoia, and Petrarch.[5] The motifs and genres are fairly traditional: typologies like those of the *plazer* or its opposite, the *enueg*,[6] are frequent, as are the celebration of the lady and the account of the "steps" involved in falling in love, and obviously, by way of contrast, the tears shed for her obstinacy and cruelty. Some motifs, however, are less traditional, or at least more personal: the marine landscape—in some ways an echo of Dante's sonnet "Guido, i' vorrei," ("Guido I should like")[7]—some less predictable Neapolitan landscapes (the place of the young Boccaccio's first poetic formation), and a few small portraits of courtly sentimental life, which have given rise to the definition of these poems as "late Gothic," reflecting a practice not inconsistent with the "major" Boccaccio. In this sonnet, for example, the young women busy talking in a garden can call to mind similar *ragionamenti*, or conversations, in the frame story of the *Decameron*:

> Intorn'ad una fonte, in un pratello
> di verdi erbette pieno e di bei fiori,
> sedean tre angiolette, i loro amori
> forse narrando, ed a ciascuna 'l bello
>   viso adombrava un verde ramicello
> ch'i capei d'òr cingea, al qual di fuori
> e d'entro insieme i dua vaghi colori
> avolgeva un suave venticello.
>   E dopo alquanto l'una alle due disse
> (com'io udi'): "Deh, se, per avventura,
> di ciascuna l'amante or qui venisse,
>   fuggiremo noi quindi per paura?"
> A cui le due risposer: "Chi fuggisse
> poco savia saria, co'tal ventura!"[8]

Around a fountain, on a little meadow / full of green tuftlets of grass and fair flowers, / sat three little angels, perhaps telling of their loves, / and a green branchlet / that encircled her golden hair / shaded each one's fair face, around which a soft little breeze / wove together from without and within / the two lovely colors. // And after a while one said to the two / (as I heard): "Ah, if by chance / each of our lovers should now come here, / would we flee hence out of fear?" / To which the two replied: "She who flees / would hardly be wise, with such good luck!"

This is a typical sonnet of late Gothic coloration, sketched in a solar landscape of intense and brilliant chromatic quality, into which are set three young and very blond women (a topos of the lyric tradition)[9] as a sort of resplendent flash, exemplifying the lady-of-light (*donna-luce*) typical of late Gothic taste. The insistent presence of diminutives and endearments (*pratello, angiolette, ramicello, venticello*, all in rhyme, as if to increase the symbolic value of a representation that is unusually gentle and lighthearted) must not obscure, though, cleverness of style and the technique of *enjambement* between vv. 4 and 5, sign of an already advanced and mature mastery, even though this was probably written in Boccaccio's youth.[10]

In the course of his experimentation (and this seems to be the nature of many of his lyrics), Boccaccio does not overlook the playful and burlesque register either, even though in the absence of reliable information it is not possible to attribute those texts to a particular phase in the author's life — say, the youthful Neapolitan period. Indeed, avoiding the suggestion that this production be relegated to a still ingenuous or immature moment in Boccaccio's poetic experience, one could in my opinion more reasonably think that it is intertwined with the "major" work.[11] Moreover, historically we are at a moment in which the lyrical-courtly and burlesque could still coexist (only Petrarch is immune to this sort of generic mixing):

> Cader postù in que' legami, Amore,
> ne' quai tu n'hai già molti aviluppati;
> rotte ti sien le braccia, ed ispuntati
> gli artigli, e l'ali spennate, e 'l vigore
>   tolto, e la deità tua sia 'n orrore
> a quei che nasceran e che son nati,
> e sianti l'arco e gli strali spezzati,
> ed il tuo nome sia sempre Dolore!
>   Bugiardo, traditore e disleale,
> frodolente, assassin, ladro, scherano,
> crudel tiranno, spergiuro, omicida!
>   ché, dopo il mio lungo servir invano,
> mi proponesti tal ch'assai men vale:
> caggia dal ciel saetta che t'occida![12]

May you fall victim to those ties, Love, / in which you have already bound many of us; / may your arms be broken, and your claws / unsharpened, your wings unfeathered, and your vigor / taken, and may your godliness strike horror / in those who will be born and have been born, / and may your bow and arrows be broken, / and may your name always be Pain! / Liar, traitor, and untrue, / fraud, assassin, thief, troublemaker, / cruel tyrant, false witness, murderer! / for after my long useless service, / you put ahead of me one who is worth far less: / may a thunderbolt fall from the sky and kill you!

This is an obvious, almost stock case of *vituperium* of Cupid, a genre that Boccaccio, moreover, will confront again in other lyrics (for example, in the sonnet "S'io veggio il giorno, Amor, che mi scapestri," derived from Petrarch).[13] The image of Love with his plucked wings and broken arrows, also present in Petrarch's *Triumphus Pudicitie* (*Triumph of Chastity*),[14] turns here in a burlesque, not lyrical, direction, following a model of the type found in Cecco Angiolieri. This vituperative style will return powerfully at times in the mature Boccaccio as well (one need think only of the *Corbaccio*, which is certainly not a youthful work), and it clarifies for us the broad crop of stimuli, not merely lyrical, that are at work in Boccaccio as poet and experimenter. In this sense, his poetic production, not coincidentally largely composed of sonnets, is of singular importance for filling some lacunae in the fourteenth-century panorama, occupied almost overwhelmingly by the powerful figure of Petrarch, a "leveler" of lyric history before and during his time.

It is not easy, as we have said, to reconstruct a possible timeline for the poetic compositions. While a good number of them with a moralizing or religious tone probably belong to Boccaccio's older age, even if we can hypothesize that this type of poetry is "spreadable" over his entire life as a writer, it is fairly certain that the little group of rhymes of stilnovistic intonation, listed by numbers above, belongs to a chronologically "remote" phase, probably back to back with the poetic experience of Dante for one. In a sonnet like the one now numbered 19,[15] the stilnovistic heritage leaps into view:

O miseri occhi miei più ch'altra cosa,
piangete omai, piangete, e non restate!
Voi di colei le luci dispietate
menasti pria nell'anima angosciosa,
    ch'ora disprezza; voi nell'amorosa
prigion legaste la mia libertate;
voi con mirarla più raccendevate
il cor dolente, ch'or non truova posa.

Dunque piangete, e la nemica vista
di voi spingete col pianger più forte,
sì ch'altro amor non possa più tradirvi.
Questo desia e vuol l'anima trista,
perciò che cose grave più che morte
l'ordisti già incontro nel seguirvi.

O eyes of mine, wretched beyond all else, / cry henceforth, cry, and do not stop! / You first led the pitiless eyes of her / into my anguished soul, / which she now disdains; you in the amorous / prison bound my freedom; / you by looking at her kindled more / the sorrowing heart, which now finds no rest. // Therefore cry, and reject the inimical sight / with even more crying, / so that another love can never betray you. / This the sad soul desires and wants, / because things worse than death / you were already plotting against her[16] when she was your follower.

As one can see, it is a sonnet with dramatic movement that develops in emotional tones a theme recurrent in stilnovistic lyric, above all, Cavalcanti's and Cino's.[17] The poet accuses his own eyes, which are guilty of having made him fall in love with a pitiless woman whose eyes are cruel (the *luci dispietate* of v. 3). One finds the theme authoritatively in Dante as well, in the double *sestina* "Amor tu vedi ben" (Love, you see perfectly well) from the *Rime petrose* (*Stony Rhymes*), where the phrase appears at v. 36 in all its clarity:

così dinanzi dal sembiante freddo
mi ghiaccia sopra il sangue d'ogne tempo,
e quel pensiero che m'accorcia il tempo
mi si converte tutto in corpo freddo,
  che m'esce poi per mezzo della luce
là onde entrò la dispietata luce. (31–36)[18]

Just so, before her expression that is all cold, / my blood freezes over always, in all weather, / and the care that so shortens my time for me / turns everything into fluid cold / that issues from me through the lights / where her pitiless light came in.

This is a reference of great importance. The presence of the "stony" (*petroso*) Dante, and also naturally that of Cavalcanti, indicates the search for a lyric possibility that, if not an alternative, is certainly less predictable, often painful, certainly anguished, and by now fairly distant from the more normal stilnovistic sequences (not even Petrarch will remain immune from this: the adjective *dispietata* appears five times in the *Rerum vulgarium fragmenta*,[19] and once in the *Triumphi*, but never together with *luce*; the phrase is therefore exclusively Dantesque, a "trademark" easily identifiable by contemporary poets as well). What is more, Boccaccio's sonnet, even with the learned references it presents, also has its own noteworthy originality, especially in the invitation to reject the lady's *nemica vista* (v. 9) through increased tears and harshened weeping. In other words, in his hypothetical eclecticism, even in the *Rime* Boccaccio is seeking an original, or at least autonomous, path within the forest of amorous lyric that is contemporary or immediately prior to him. It is a path, later abandoned for other and more important efforts no longer lyric, on which his friend Petrarch will set out walking or was already walking during these same years, while a resident in Provence or in his first Italian years.

Clearly, poems like the one just cited belong to a lyric order that may be experimental but is surely not biographical. They signal instead his searching and selecting from the vast amount of material that was coming to him from a recent but foundational tradition, one he came to know during his Neapolitan sojourn and then, more strongly and firsthand, in Florence after his return home. In this way, and with an ear well attuned to contemporary tendencies, the author of the *Decameron* was traveling—completely independently—a road that was not all that different from Petrarch's, uninterrupted or at least unneglected except for the time of composing his major work.

In this broadly experimental poetry (in the sense of an obvious approach to the most disparate genres, without any constructive intention of the type that we could *a posteriori* call Petrarchan), those compositions of a moral type or that meditate on life already lived, seen always as irremediably lost, assume a certain importance. One example is sonnet 116 (Branca, no. 56), likewise not datable, and only because of an inevitable suggestion, attributable to the final moment of his life:

> Quante fiate indrieto mi rimiro,
> m'accorgo e veggio ch'io ho trapassato,
> forse perduto e male adoperato,
> seguendo in compiacermi alcun desiro,
>   tante con meco dolente m'adiro
> sentendo quel ch'a tutti sol n'è dato
> esser così fuggito, anzi cacciato

da me, che ora indarno ne sospiro.
    Né so s'è conceduto che 'mia danni
ristorar possa ancor di bel soggiorno
in questa vita labile e meschina,
    perché passato è l'arco de' mia anni,
e ritornar non posso al primo giorno:
e l'ultimo già veggio s'avicina.[20]

As many times as I look back, / I realize and see what I have passed
over, / perhaps lost and poorly used, / following some desire to
please myself, / so many do I in pain grow angry with myself /
feeling that what alone is given to all / has thus fled, indeed been
chased / from me, who now sigh for it in vain. / Nor do I know if
it shall be granted that I make up for my losses / by a more worthy
residence / in this fleeting and paltry life, / because the arc of my
years has passed, / and return I cannot to the first day: / and the last
I see already approaching.

The impulse, from the very first verse, is absolutely Petrarchan. Compare *Canzoniere* 281, which begins:

Quante fiate al mio dolce ricetto
fuggendo altrui et, s'esser po, me stesso,
vo con gli occhi bagnando l'erba e 'l petto.[21]

How many times, fleeing others and, if it is possible, myself, do I
seek my sweet hiding place, bathing with my eyes the grass and my
breast.

Petrarch's sonnet is almost certainly datable to the period following his return to Vaucluse in 1351–52, and the *dolce ricetto* is surely the solitary little
town in Provence where Petrarch had established his household. In the
Canzoniere, this sonnet numbers among those of regret and of the search
for solitude after Laura's death. In Boccaccio, the memorializing impulse
is directed at the past, and with a certain originality the text rejects the
theme of return to search for a lady now lost. In Petrarch that theme was
very strong: "cercando col penser l'alto diletto / che Morte à tolto, ond' io la
chiamo spesso!" (seeking with my thought the high delight / that Death has
taken, so that I often call for Death! vv. 7–8). Boccaccio's poem morphs into
a text of existential reflection.
    Therefore, Boccaccio's intervention is not purely following a "school"

text. Rather, it derives from an intelligent intersection of Petrarchan elements, as the author "contaminates" the memory of *Rerum vulgarium fragmenta* 281 with that of 298:

> Quand'io mi volgo indietro a mirar gli anni
> ch' ànno fuggendo i miei pensieri sparsi,
> et spento 'l foco ove agghiacciando io arsi,
> et finito il riposo pien d'affanni,
>   rotta la fe' degli amorosi inganni,
> et sol due parti d'ogni mio ben farsi,
> l'una nel ciel et l'altra in terra starsi
> et perduto il guadagno de' miei damni,
>   i' mi riscuoto, et trovomi sì nudo.
>   (298.1–9)

When I turn back to gaze at the years that fleeing have scattered all my thoughts, and put out the fire where I freezing burned, and ended my laboring repose, / broken the faith of amorous deceptions, and turned all of my wealth into two parts only (one is in heaven, the other in the ground), and destroyed the profit of my losses, / I shake myself and find myself so naked.

Boccaccio makes from these two sonnets a new text, one in which what is remembered is no longer—nor could it be for him—a lost lady, but more generically and morally the time that has been lost or wasted.

Let us again consider the insistent recourse in Boccaccio's texts to strophic *enjambement* between the first and the second quatrains, as this too is a technical "sign" that should not be overlooked in an itinerary under construction toward not only a poetics, but also his own stylistic monogram. Probably, indeed almost certainly, dating to after he began writing the *Decameron* (given the dates of the Petrarchan sonnets to which it refers), sonnet 116 is relevant because of its "hinge" function, if not biographical then surely intellectual, between the more stilnovistic or playful texts and those of more insistent moral reflection. And so, even if, as we have noted repeatedly, it is very difficult if not impossible to trace a biographical arc in the sequence of the *Rime*, a sonnet like 112 (Branca, no.107), in which the poet traces a clear distinction between his "jocund" rhymes and the more dignified ones, is certainly not entirely scholastic. As a text it is provocative, not to mention important, and represents a sort of rethinking that recalls Epistle 20 of 1372 (to Pietro da Montefiore):

Mentre sperai e l'uno e l'altro collo
trascender di Parnaso e ber dell'onde
del castalïo fonte e delle fronde
che già più ch'altre piacquero ad Apollo,
    adornarmi le tempie, umìl rampollo
de' dicitori antichi, alle gioconde
rime mi diedi; e benché men profonde
fosser, cantâne in stil leggero e sollo.
    Ma poscia che 'l cammino aspro e selvaggio
e gli anni miei già faticati e bianchi
tolser la speme del sù pervenire,
    vinto, lasciai la speme del viaggio,
le rime e i versi e i miei pensieri stanchi:
ond'or non so, com'io solea già, dire.[22]

While I hoped to ascend both one peak and the other / of Parnassus and drink from the waters / of the Castalian font and with the
branches / that Apollo liked more than any other, / to adorn my
temples, humble offspring / of the ancient poets, to jocund rhymes /
I gave myself; and although they were / less profound, I sang them
in a light and easy style. // But after the harsh and savage road / and
my years already worn out and white / took away the hope of arriving up there, / defeated, I left my hope of the voyage, / my rhymes
and verses and tired thoughts: / so that now I know not, as I once
did, how to make poetry.

Almost certainly a late lyric, one in which the Dantesque and Petrarchan
language and a symbolically traced itinerary of salvation already outlined
in the *Commedia* condition the poetry, it is a text of passage, as it were, a
"closing of accounts" with the past. It derives, of course, from illustrious
examples, but with a personal pursuit of intimate reflection all its own in
the admission of the inability to make poetry, which is much more than a
generic *apologia*.

It seems thus appropriate to conclude with one of the securely datable
sonnets of the collection, sonnet 127 (Branca, no. 126), dedicated to the
death of his friend Petrarch, which occurred during the night between
July 18 and 19, 1374. This text is certainly influenced by Petrarch's sonnet
on the death of Sennuccio del Bene,[23] who is cited here, and what is more
cited along with Cino and Dante, who are united as two indivisible crowns.
The poem points to a serious, experimental lyric journey, tied to masters of

past and present, which lacks only—but here Petrarch would be an absolute innovator—the obstinate search for unity that Boccaccio had in any event reserved, innovating in his own way, for the geometric, absolutely solid construction of the *Decameron*:

> Or sei salito, caro signor mio,
> nel regno al qual salire ancor aspetta
> ogn'anima da Dio a quell'eletta
> nel suo partir di questo mondo rio.
> Or sè colà dove spesso il desio
> ti tirò già per veder Lauretta;
> or sei dove la mia bella Fiammetta
> siede con lei nel cospetto di Dio.
> Or con Sennuccio e con Cino e con Dante
> vivi, sicuro d'eterno riposo,
> mirando cose da noi non intese.
> Deh, s'a grado ti fui nel mondo errante,
> tirami drieto a te, dove gioioso
> veggia colei che pria d'amor m'accese![24]

Now you have risen, dear my lord, / into the realm where every soul expects / to rise who has been chosen for it by God / in its departure from this wicked world. / Now you are there where often desire / drew you to see Lauretta; / now you are where my fair Fiammetta / sits with her in the presence of God. // Now with Sennuccio and with Cino and with Dante / you live, certain of eternal rest, / gazing upon things not understood by us. / Ah, if I pleased you in the errant world, / pull me up behind you, where joyous / I might see her who first inflamed me with love!

CHAPTER TWENTY-SIX

PERSONALITY AND CONFLICT • *(Epistole, Lettere)*

Todd Boli

Boccaccio's twenty-four surviving prose epistles represent but a small share of a lifetime of letter writing.[1] They are a heterogeneous group spanning a number of decades and marking the most diverse moments of his biography. Some are communications about practical matters, some are angry letters, and some come to us only as fragments or as vernacular translations of their Latin originals. Most reflect Boccaccio's use of the late medieval *ars dictaminis*, the stylistic and organizational procedures conventionally prescribed for the Latin prose epistle. The letters Boccaccio wrote in his maturity more often depart from medieval formulas and exhibit a less structured approach that reflects the influence of Petrarch. Unlike Petrarch, however, Boccaccio never collected his epistles, and thus his letters are remarkable for their many gaps, in particular their paucity of references to individual literary projects. Yet for all that Boccaccio's epistles may lack in cohesion and continuity, they more than make up with their variety and range. They give expression to his ideas, fears, aspirations, and desires, an expression all the more vivid because it comes from the pen of as emotional, determined, indignant, and enthusiastic an author as Boccaccio. The following touches on fourteen of these letters, a sampling which focuses on Boccaccio's unremitting search for financial security, and the ups and downs of his friendship with Petrarch.

The earliest letter is really two, one written in the Tuscan vernacular introducing the second written — strikingly — in the Neapolitan vernacular. Both are addressed to Boccaccio's fellow Florentine Francesco de' Bardi, and both are written as coming from Boccaccio and from his and Francesco's friends in Naples, the second letter having purportedly been prepared with those friends' assistance. The letter was written in 1339, when Boccaccio's fortunes were at a turning point. Boccaccio's father, who had brought his son to Naples thirteen years earlier as he pursued work with the Bardi bank, had by then separated from that firm and returned to Florence, leaving Boccaccio behind to attend to family business. Nevertheless, the bond between Francesco de' Bardi and Boccaccio evidently remained strong. The Tuscan part of the letter is ennobled with the same stately rhythms prescribed for Latin, and it was soon found circulating, without the more colloquial letter that it covered, in sample books offering models of vernacular prose. The Neapolitan part drolly recounts the baptism of a boy recently born to a young lady whom Francesco de' Bardi apparently admired. While joking good-naturedly at Francesco's expense, the letter also targets Boccaccio, who appears in the third person as "Abbot Giovanni Boccaccio,"[2] a studious loner who "neither by day nor even at night does anything but write."[3] This mock-serious self-representation as scholar is counterbalanced by his comical self-portrait as the fun-loving narrator who whimsically signs the letter "Jannetta di Parisse" (Neapolitan for "Giovanni of Paris").[4] The persona of Boccaccio immured in his study, however facetious, is one Boccaccio would don throughout his life. Even in the much later *Genealogia deorum gentilium* (*Genealogy of the Pagan Gods*), Boccaccio defends himself against the same charge of aloofness that his merry double, Jannetta di Parisse, lodges against him in this early letter. Slight but cleverly crafted, the letter exemplifies the "bifrontality" (to use Vittore Branca's term)[5] of the celebration of popular culture and erudite learning that characterizes Boccaccio's art throughout his life, and the letter is indeed, as Francesco Sabatini calls it, a "little, precocious masterpiece."[6]

Epistle 6, addressed to Zanobi da Strada, is Boccaccio's earliest extant Latin letter, and it exhibits the conventional rhythmic prose cadences prescribed in the late Middle Ages for epistolary compositions, namely, the *cursus* in its various forms.[7] Written in January 1348, the epistle gratefully acknowledges some unspecified favor that Zanobi has done for Boccaccio, perhaps procuring the unnamed book mentioned therein. Zanobi was already competing with Boccaccio for the favors of Niccola Acciaiuoli, with whom Boccaccio would come to have a prickly relationship, and a certain boastful element can be read between the lines of this ostensibly friendly missive. The exaggerated assertions of friendship seem only to sharpen the almost spiteful note of pride that creeps into Boccaccio's letter, especially where he goes out of his way to inform Zanobi that not only does he enjoy Francesco Ordelaffi's literary patronage but that "at my aforesaid lord's command, I myself will be accompanying him, not as a common soldier, but as his arbitrator, as I may say, of needful matters."[8]

Epistle 7, written to Petrarch in 1351 on behalf of the city of Florence, advises that Florence will restore to Petrarch the real estate confiscated

from his exiled father, Ser Petracco, and invites him to come teach in the
city's new university. Although the letter refers to Boccaccio in the third
person, he is clearly its author. The letter says that Florence has decided to
found a school of higher learning, "since of late we perceived that without
liberal studies our city limped along as though lame on its right foot."[9] The
figure of the lame city is evidently drawn from Boccaccio's personal copy of
a letter from Petrarch to the city of Florence and is one he will use again in
the *Trattatello in laude di Dante* (*Little Treatise in Praise of Dante*). What betrays
Boccaccio's authorship most tellingly is the letter's assertion that Florence's
offer to Petrarch is an exception to "the laws and customs of our city," an
offer such as "we scarcely recall having ever been extended to another."[10]
However much these words may stress the generosity of Florence's offer,
they also give voice to Boccaccio's abiding indictment of Florence's cruelty
in refusing to extend any similar offer to the heirs of Ser Petracco's companion in exile, Dante. Boccaccio traveled to Padua to deliver the letter to
Petrarch in person, but Petrarch had already decided to accept an invitation
to join the papal court in Avignon. When Florence learned that Petrarch
would decline its offer, it promptly reconfiscated Ser Petracco's property.[11]

In 1353, Petrarch, no longer finding suitable patronage from a new pope,
left Avignon and went to Milan, where he shocked his friends by accepting
the protection of Italy's most powerful and aggressive despot, Archbishop
Giovanni Visconti. Among the letters of protest directed to Petrarch by his
friends is Boccaccio's Epistle 10. It recalls that on the occasion of Boccaccio's visit to Petrarch in Padua in 1351, Petrarch had deplored how Milan's
tyrant was allowed to ravage northern Italy and threaten the liberty of Florence and had called for his overthrow. Now Petrarch's sudden readiness to
don the tyrant's yoke brings disrepute not only to himself but to Boccaccio
and his other friends and supporters. Boccaccio speculates that Petrarch
may have repudiated his ancestral city because of Florence's withdrawal of
its pardon of his father, and says he shares Petrarch's indignation. Nevertheless, he cannot excuse a man who embraces his country's enemies simply
because he claims to be "moved by righteous indignation."[12] That in less
than three years Petrarch had twice embarrassed Boccaccio with the city of
Florence doubtless made Boccaccio's displeasure all the keener. At bottom,
though, Boccaccio's acrimony springs mainly from his and Petrarch's contrasting situations: Boccaccio proudly enjoys his Florentine freedom but is
meagerly compensated as the employee of a democratic republic; Petrarch
is generously compensated and is free to pursue his studies but is shamefully compromised by his subservience to autocratic patrons.

In Epistle 11, written in Ravenna in 1362, Boccaccio answers Petrarch's request for an account of the life and works of Saint Peter Damian by announcing that he has penned his own version of the saint's life, and this biography, now partially lost, presumably accompanied the letter. Boccaccio's eagerness to collaborate with Petrarch pays homage to his mentor, and the biography's treatment of a Christian subject in a learned style reflects Boccaccio's humanism in its flower. In 1361, it had been discovered that friends of Boccaccio's were planning a coup d'état against Florence's reactionary government. After some were beheaded and others exiled, Boccaccio left his house in Florence to his half brother and with evident circumspection retreated to the relative safety of Ravenna and then to his hereditary Certaldo. When Epistle 11 cryptically closes by calling Ravenna "the sewer" of northern Italy, it may well be referring to the psychological morass to which Boccaccio feels his personal danger has consigned him.

In early 1362, the *Epistola consolatoria a Pino de' Rossi* (*Consolatory Epistle to Pino de' Rossi*) addresses the recent conspiracy directly as Boccaccio seeks to comfort a friend who has been exiled for alleged involvement in the failed coup. Although Pino de' Rossi's social rank is superior to Boccaccio's, and Rossi's exile is compulsory while Boccaccio's is voluntary, their situations are comparable enough, the letter explains, to prompt Boccaccio to try to console his fellow exile with reasoned advice and examples of others who have similarly suffered. Written in the vernacular, the *Consolatory* nevertheless borrows its argument and most of its examples from two of Boccaccio's recently drafted Latin works, the *De casibus virorum illustrium* (*The Downfall of Illustrious Men*) and the *De mulieribus claris* (*Famous Women*). The choice of the vernacular may be found in two great works of exile to which the *Consolatory* is greatly indebted: Dante's *Convivio* and *Commedia*. Like both these works and, for that matter, the *Trattatello*, the *Consolatory* employs the Florentine idiom to address a Florentine audience on a Florentine issue. That audience is not limited to Rossi, for Boccaccio asks him to share with his fellow exiles "the consolations that I give to you,"[13] thus authorizing the epistle's circulation. Before closing the epistle, Boccaccio gives a brief account of his own voluntary exile in Certaldo, shrewdly turning the epistle into a public platform for his own self-defense. When the *Consolatory* describes the bucolic poverty of Boccaccio's life in Certaldo, it may superficially echo Petrarch's *De vita solitaria*, but it resonates more deeply with the self-justifying Dante of the *Paradiso*. When the *Consolatory* calls "leaving the country you loved" the "first arrow that exile shoots,"[14] it quotes *Paradiso* 17.55–57 almost verbatim: "Tu lascerai ogne cosa diletta / più caramente; e questo è quello strale / che l'arco de lo essilio pria saetta" (You shall leave everything beloved most dearly; and this is the arrow which the bow of exile shoots first).[15]

In 1362, Boccaccio writes Epistle 12 to his old friend Barbato da Sulmona in answer to a letter from Barbato, which enclosed a letter written by Boccaccio's problematic patron, Niccola Acciaiuoli, and two Orsini noblemen, Napoleone and Niccolò, to urge Petrarch to publish his *Africa*. Barbato's letter expresses the belief that if Boccaccio forwards the enclosed letter with his recommendation, it will be more persuasive. In his epistle, Boccaccio says he will reply only to Barbato, because while Barbato is sincere and genuinely learned, Acciaiuoli and his friends are shallow and self-serving. Boccaccio will not, he says, forward their request, because he himself has already tried to convince Petrarch to publish the *Africa* and failed. Boccaccio, who has recently abandoned Ravenna in financial straits and been looking to Petrarch for help in securing a position, now says with self-pity that he is ready to renounce his whole career. He had wanted to go to Padua to receive Petrarch's "final instructions"[16] and then head for Naples to meet with their friend Francesco Nelli and stop along the way to see Barbato, but now the uncertainty of finding Petrarch in Padua and news that Nelli is in Sicily with Acciaiuoli oblige him to defer the trip.

Concluding, Boccaccio says that he has written more than he meant to, "so greatly have my feelings driven me."[17] It is precisely here that Boccaccio draws back the curtain on how stubbornly material necessity threatened the achievement of his literary and artistic ideals. For Boccaccio, the vexing paradox was that Petrarch often could not or would not offer him practical assistance in any way adequate to the poetic goals that Petrarch inspired him to strive for. Petrarch had reasons for disappointing Boccaccio, and not least among them was the intransigent and capricious Niccola Acciaiuoli. Petrarch was clever enough to stay beyond Acciaiuoli's reach, but he was not strong enough to replace Acciaiuoli as a source of support and preferment for Boccaccio. When Petrarch resisted Nelli and Acciaiuoli's pressure to add his luster to the Neapolitan court, Nelli prevailed on Acciaiuoli to invite Boccaccio to Naples instead. After stipulating his conditions and receiving "broad promises" in Acciaiuoli's own hand,[18] Boccaccio warily accepted the invitation and set out for Naples.

Epistle 13, written in 1363 to Francesco Nelli, is by far Boccaccio's longest. Except for the last four sentences of the Latin original, Boccaccio's epistle survives only in a vernacular translation. It is apparent, though, that the original was some five times as long as Boccaccio's next longest Latin epistle. The letter complains of Boccaccio's treatment at Acciaiuoli's hands, and it turns Nelli into a kind of surrogate for Boccaccio's bête noire. It thus shares with the *Consolatory Epistle to Pino de' Rossi* the topos of a *historia cala-mitatum* to which late Trecento and early Quattrocento middle-class read-ers liked to turn for moral edification (compare the "Lament of Jeremiah, the Passion of Our Savior, and the Plaint of the Magdalen" wryly recom-mended in the "Author's Conclusion" of the *Decameron*[19]). Epistle 13 was probably translated into the vernacular precisely to make it more accessible to those middle-class readers, and its very length promises that its readers' appetite for examples of misfortune will be amply indulged.

The epistle recounts how Nelli's preparations for welcoming Boccaccio to Naples miscarried and how Boccaccio ended up being alternately abused and ignored by Acciaiuoli. After receiving an unpromisingly cool greeting from Acciaiuoli, Boccaccio found the quarters Nelli had arranged for him so squalid that he compares them to the bilge of a ship.[20] Moreover, he was left to eat with Acciaiuoli's household staff, while Nelli dined at Acciaiuoli's table. When an influential Florentine friend in Naples rescued Boccaccio by taking him to his own home, Acciaiuoli pretended not to notice. When Boccaccio followed Acciaiuoli's household out of the city for the Christmas holidays, he was again consigned to "a stinking little chamber."[21] Finally, when the household returned to Naples, Boccaccio was left behind with all his belongings. When Boccaccio complained of being treated "like a miser-able slave,"[22] Nelli accused him, the letter famously relates, of being made "of glass."[23] Boccaccio says he refused to return to "the bilge" and stayed instead with his friend until, after fifty more days of being ignored by Ac-ciaiuoli, he abandoned Naples altogether. The epistle exhibits the ruthless invective whose analogue is encountered throughout Boccaccio's oeuvre, from the *Decameron*'s story of the scorned scholar to the *Corbaccio* and the sonnets written against the detractors of Boccaccio's lectures on Dante. What sets the epistle apart, however, is how it places the supreme value of Boccaccio's poetic calling above his sense of personal injury. The epistle makes clear that the quarrel of Boccaccio's critics is with his art: "And you call me, a child of the Muses, a person made 'of glass?'"[24] Acciaiuoli is not Boccaccio's enemy, but the enemy of the Muses: "And the enemy of the Muses, shall I call him my friend?"[25]

Epistle 15 was written to Petrarch after Boccaccio's journey to Venice in the spring of 1367. He had hoped to find Petrarch there, and although Pe-trarch had left for Pavia, Boccaccio stayed to visit Petrarch's daughter and become acquainted with her husband, Francescuolo da Brossano, whom he had never met. The letter describes how Petrarch's daughter greeted him as though he were Petrarch himself, and "welcomed me with a certain modest and filial affection."²⁶ As Francesca was inviting Boccaccio to make full use of her father's house and library, Boccaccio was greeted by Petrarch's little granddaughter, who touchingly reminded him of his own much mourned daughter. Boccaccio is full of praise for Petrarch's son-in-law and relates how on Boccaccio's departure from Venice, Francescuolo tactfully took him aside and, "grasping my spindly arm with those gigantic hands of his,"²⁷ obliged Boccaccio to accept a generous gift, presumably to help him pay for his journey home. Boccaccio concludes by saying that he is assembling a collection of the letters that Petrarch has sent to him and, indicating that there are several "which I never received,"²⁸ asks Petrarch to send him copies. That Boccaccio collected Petrarch's letters without ever collecting his own is a reminder of how steadfastly Boccaccio doubted that his abilities could ever compare with those of his serenely self-confident mentor. The irony is all the keener for Epistle 15's exceptional expressiveness, which breaks free from the old medieval format and, in keeping with its addressee, employs a manner of argument much like Petrarch's own, with an organization that is more spontaneous, discursive, and direct and a style that is at once more reserved and more intimate. When Petrarch copied it for his own library, he headed it with the annotation "one of a thousand."²⁹

In Certaldo in 1371, Boccaccio received an invitation from Niccolò Orsini to live as his guest on the Argentario promontory near Tuscany's border with Latium. In Epistle 18, Boccaccio explains why he must decline. He relates how he has been obliged to turn down similar offers, since in every case "my liberty, which I wish to enjoy completely unconditioned, seemed to be bound by some hidden restraint."³⁰ Boccaccio writes that he must offer Orsini the same reply he has made to the others, and adds that "my advanced age, accustomed to liberty, will no longer suffer me to bend my neck to a yoke."³¹ Throughout most of Boccaccio's life the aristocratic values of princes and courts contended with the democratic values of merchants and towns, but in Epistle 18 the contest now seems to be decided, at least in practical terms, in favor of the values summed up by Florence's one-word motto, *Libertas*. Boccaccio will serve the prince, but only from the liberty of his Certaldo hilltop: "If in any case I can offer service fitting to your splendor from the place where I am, command and your servant is ready."³²

Epistle 20 was written in 1372 in answer to the jurist and poet Pietro Piccolo da Monteforte, whose recent letter praised Boccaccio's defense of poetry in the *Genealogia deorum gentilium* and his generosity in letting his books circulate, especially while Petrarch refused to do the same. Like Boccaccio's earlier Epistle 12 to Barbato da Sulmona, this one defends Petrarch's refusal to publish his works before they are ready. Boccaccio commends

Monteforte for deflating "with true and sacred arguments" the presumption that leads certain self-appointed judges to condemn poetry without having read it,[33] and thanks him for his helpful suggestions for improving the *Genealogia*. He regrets, however, that the book was still unfinished when he was persuaded to leave it in Naples and that it "has circulated so as to deny me all hope of editing and improving the imperfect work."[34] Boccaccio's understanding of Petrarch's motives is thus clear when he responds that in holding back his compositions until they are perfect, Petrarch is doing no more than what the great poets of antiquity did. In the "insults" that the one published passage of the *Africa* has already received,[35] Petrarch foresees the viciousness with which the entire poem will be attacked. Boccaccio reminds Monteforte of how Petrarch, with his *Invective contra medicum* (*Invectives against a Physician*), had to answer a physician who carped about his other works, and asks him to contemplate with what zeal the same critic would attack Petrarch's masterpiece. Finally, with a self-deprecation as touching as it is extreme, Boccaccio insists that he must not be blamed for so "profusely and carelessly" doing what Petrarch refuses to do, because "the faintness of my fame eclipses and covers my many faults, where his resplendent glory would call even the slightest flaw to account."[36] In conclusion, Boccaccio assures Monteforte that not only will he urge Petrarch to publish his *Africa*, but he will do so in person and is planning, "unless prohibited by unforeseen circumstances, to visit him in Padua around the end of this month or the beginning of the next."[37] However, as Epistle 21, written four months later, makes clear, a serious illness would oblige Boccaccio to forgo the trip.

Epistle 21, written in 1372 to an earnest admirer of Boccaccio's, Mainardo Cavalcanti,[38] in fact reveals the infirmities of Boccaccio's advancing age. It describes how a long list of ailments "and a gloomy outlook on everything" have denied Boccaccio the company of the Muses.[39] "In brief," he adds, "everything that is mine turns toward unhappiness."[40] If Cavalcanti could see him, he writes, he would find Boccaccio's "skin so pressed onto my bones, that I resemble more Erysichthon than Giovanni."[41] Cavalcanti now knows why Boccaccio has not written sooner, what Boccaccio is feeling, and what he desires—presumably his death, which will bring "the end of all my ills before I become an even greater burden to my friends."[42] The letter continues after a two-week interval during which Boccaccio says he suffered a fever so extreme that "I believed I was altogether headed toward my end."[43] Yielding to his neighbors' urgings, Boccaccio set aside his disdain for physicians and called for a country doctor whose aggressive ministrations quickly brought the patient around.

Boccaccio sent his letter on August 28, 1372, and in a mere matter of days, on September 13, he received from Cavalcanti a reassuring response accompanying a gold cup full of gold florins; a few days later, as Boccaccio says in his letter of reply, Epistle 22, he received "a second token of your generous spirit, a gift, if you please, that was equal to the first."[44] The older, more scholarly Boccaccio seems embarrassed to accept the young noble-man's charity, and so when Cavalcanti ingenuously confesses that he him-self "has not yet read my stories"[45] but hastens to reassure Boccaccio that the women in his house have been enjoying them, Boccaccio dissembles his position as supplicant by assuming the role of mentor. Perhaps Boccaccio had recommended the *Decameron* to Cavalcanti because he understood that the gentleman's pretensions were far from erudite. "You write," Boccaccio replies, "that you will nevertheless get to it this winter, which I approve, if you have nothing better to do."[46] However, Boccaccio continues, "I cer-tainly do not approve that you permit the worthy women of your household to read my trifles, wherefore by your faith I must sincerely implore you not to do it."[47] In citing how much in the *Decameron* is contrary to decency and how likely it is to lead women to think indecent thoughts, Boccaccio bor-rows ideas and language from the "Author's Conclusion" of the *Decameron*, while turning the argument there on its head. The difference between how lovingly Boccaccio edited and recopied the *Decameron* as recently as 1371 and the nearly contemporaneous reservations expressed in Epistle 22 may find its explanation in the circumstances of the epistle. Boccaccio has ad-vised Cavalcanti on a religious matter concerning his upcoming marriage — his future bride was a distant relative — and for this he has just received double compensation, although not without the embarrassment of having to ask for it, and Epistle 22's equivocal position on the *Decameron* allows Boccaccio to rescue his dignity by asserting opinions that affirm his status as a clergyman and scholar.[48] In late December, as Boccaccio had deemed likely, Cavalcanti received the papal dispensation sanctioning his marriage. Boccaccio then stood as godfather at the baptism of Cavalcanti's child in early 1373, and not long thereafter, he inscribed to Cavalcanti the *De casibus virorum illustrium*, which he had once thought of dedicating to the now de-ceased Niccola Acciaiuoli.

Boccaccio wrote Epistle 24 on the three first days of November 1374, in response to Francescuolo da Brossano's letter, received on October 20, announcing the death of Francescuolo's father-in-law and Boccaccio's clos-est friend, Petrarch. Petrarch died on July 18, and Boccaccio had already learned of his death, in all likelihood from Coluccio Salutati.[49] In the letter Boccaccio says he would like to have come to Arquà (where Petrarch had been living since 1369) to pay his respects and offer his condolences. However, the illness that he has been suffering for the ten months "since I was publicly reading Dante's *Comedia* in Florence" has made it impossible for him to travel.[50] "Woe is me," he exclaims, "for I would seem to you far other than the person you saw in Venice!"[51] On reading Francescuolo's letter, Boccaccio says that he wept for a whole night, not for Petrarch, whose salvation is certain, "but for myself and his friends forsaken on this seething earth."[52] To Francescuolo, who is going to bury Petrarch in Arquà, Boccaccio replies that Florence is to blame for not being chosen as the final resting place of its great son: "Alas, shameful city, to whom it has not been given to watch over the remains of so illustrious a son! . . . Truly, of such a splendor you are unworthy, for when he lived, you neglected to draw and clasp him to your bosom as he deserved!"[53] If there is friendship in heaven, Boccaccio believes Petrarch will love him there, "not, I swear, because I deserve it, but because it was his wont, once he had made a friend his own, always diligently to keep him so, and I was his for forty years or more."[54] Then Boccaccio thanks Francescuolo for sending him the legacy Petrarch has left him, which according to the delicately worded item in Petrarch's will was the significant sum of "fifty gold florins, for a winter cloak against his nightly studies and contemplations."[55]

In the three months that passed after Petrarch's death without word from Francescuolo, Boccaccio doubtless grew anxious over the fate of his mentor's papers and books, and it is to this concern that the rest of Epistle 24 turns. Boccaccio tells Francescuolo that he especially wants to know whether the *Africa* still exists or whether Petrarch has consigned it to the flames, which as "an excessively severe judge of his own things, he very often threatened to do when he was alive."[56] Boccaccio implores Francescuolo to inform him regarding the fate of the rest of Petrarch's works, especially the vernacular *Trionfi*. Boccaccio also asks for a copy of the letter Petrarch wrote him in reply to his own letter urging Petrarch to retire from his studies, "and also a copy of the last of my stories [i.e., *Decameron* 10.10], which he has embellished with his eloquence."[57] Both, he reports, were lost by their couriers. Then in closing, Boccaccio declares that because of his illness "I have spent nearly three full days writing this brief epistle" and signs himself, "Your Giovanni Boccaccio, if that is anything."[58]

In scarcely more than a year after Epistle 24 was written, Petrarch's death was followed by Boccaccio's own, and the concern that the epistle expresses for Petrarch's library and papers marks the twilight of Boccaccio's lifelong campaign of championing Petrarch's works. That Boccaccio pleads on behalf of not only Petrarch's Latin *Africa* but also his vernacular *Trionfi* is emblematic of how his embrace of Petrarch's accomplishments took no account of Petrarch's own ambivalence regarding vernacular literature. Boccaccio's insistence on the compatibility between the *Africa*, written in Virgil's hexameters, and the *Trionfi*, written in Dante's *terza rima*, parallels Boccaccio's unrelenting insistence on the parity between Petrarch, who wrote chiefly in Latin, and Dante, who wrote chiefly in Italian. The assertion of the two poets' parity is discernible even in Epistle 24's condemnation of Florence for having refused to embrace Petrarch, which echoes Boccaccio's *Trattatello* and its equivalent condemnation of Florence's neglect of Dante. That Boccaccio censures equally the relentless persecution inflicted on Dante and the far less harsh treatment received by Petrarch betrays a fundamental tenet of Boccaccio's thinking, namely, that popular and learned poetry are identical insofar as they are both poetry, and its corollary, that Petrarch and Dante are poets of equal merit.

Boccaccio's judgment of his own contribution, alas, is less bold. The parity he asserted for Dante and Petrarch he could never extend to himself. Although throughout his life Boccaccio had always called Petrarch his "preceptor," only now that his illustrious mentor was gone could he tentatively add the more intimate appellation of "father." "I received your sorrowful letter, most loving brother," he says in his letter to Petrarch's son-in-law, "and as I read your name I immediately sensed what I was going to read of in it: the blessed passing of our illustrious father and preceptor."[59] However, the parity Boccaccio points to by calling Petrarch his father is once again between Petrarch and Dante, for Boccaccio similarly calls Dante his "excellent father" (and has Dante call him "my son") at the end of the *De casibus virorum illustrium*.[60] As Petrarch's son, Boccaccio is at once his heir and his subordinate. It was left to Barbato da Sulmona, Niccola Acciaiuoli, Napoleone Orsini, and Niccolò Orsini to recognize Boccaccio's parity with his mentor when, as related in Epistle 12, they turned to Boccaccio for assistance in urging Petrarch to publish the *Africa*. The equivalence they recognized would not be established as a commonplace of Italian literary thinking until 1525 in Pietro Bembo's *Prose della volgar lingua*.[61]

Boccaccio's epistles attest amply to the great debt that posterity owes him, for having (among other things) safeguarded Petrarch's legacy, secured the establishment of Dante's reputation, and nourished Italian literature with the rich genius of his own many masterpieces. However, Boccaccio's epistles also attest to a modesty that at times bordered on terrifying doubt. Petrarch, in signing his very last dated letter, which was addressed to Boccaccio, wrote with decisive finality: "Farewell, friends! Farewell, epistles!"[62] Boccaccio, in signing his last surviving letter, which was addressed to Petrarch's son-in-law, looked at his name—the name his own gifts and exertions had made immortal—and wondered if it was anything at all.[63]

CHAPTER TWENTY-SEVEN

BOCCACCIO'S WORKING NOTEBOOKS
* *(Zibaldone Laurenziano, Miscellanea Laurenziana, Zibaldone Magliabechiano)*

Claude Cazalé Bérard

The *Zibaldone Laurenziano*, the *Miscellanea Laurenziana*, and the *Zibaldone Magliabechiano* are three autograph manuscripts studded with notes, compendia, original and others' texts, from Boccaccio's philological and literary apprenticeship, both in Naples and in Florence. These *Zibaldoni* (Notebooks) represent the library and literary laboratory of the author in his first years. In addition to preserving in their sole surviving copies three letters by Dante, Dante's exchange of eclogues with Giovanni del Virgilio, Boccaccio's own *Elegia di Costanza* (*Elegy for Costanza*, his first Latin poem), his *De Canaria* (*On the Canary Islands*), his four *Epistole allegoriche* (*Allegorical Epistles*), and his *Allegoria mitologica* (*Mythological Allegory*, on the creation of the world), they contain a cross section of texts copied from other manuscripts that reflect his wide-reaching curiosity as autodidact: moralizing maxims, epigraphs, chronicles, the Hebrew and Greek alphabets, patristic excerpts, a record of Petrarch's coronation as poet laureate, letters by Petrarch, and various other correspondence. As an object of research they allow us to follow the methods of medieval paleography and codicology, of philology and textual criticism, up to the use of electronic technology for the conservation, editing, and transmission of texts.[1]

Methodological Questions

Initially the critics' attention, bestowed first on the *Zibaldone Laurenziano*, was oriented toward two types of investigation: one codicological, regarding the questions of attribution and authorship; the other philological, dedicated to identifying authors and texts considered of primary importance for literary history, including Dante, Giovanni del Virgilio, Petrarch, and Boccaccio himself, and unique witnesses of the classical and medieval tradition, in such entries as *Ibiʃ, Lamentatio Bertolði* (*Bertolð'ʃ Lamentation*), *Verʃuʃ beati Thome ðe Aquino* (*Verʃeʃ by the Bleʃʃeð Thomaʃ Aquinaʃ*). Recently, research has focused on the recognition and mapping of graphic typologies and textual content in the codices in order to uncover Boccaccio's methodology and systems of knowledge and writing.

Because the *Zibalðoni* constitute the author's memory archive as well as an exercise manual and a provisional encyclopedia, it was necessary to turn to scholars from different disciplines in order to offer a pertinent and exhaustive description of the materials and genres (*auctoritateʃ*, treatises, historical and ecclesiastical reports, repertoires of names, facts and sentences, proverbs, etc.), writing praxis (signature, marginalia, alphabets, etc.), discursive techniques and rhetorical procedures (*abbreviatio, amplificatio*, etc.), methods of rewriting (citations, excerpts, interpolation, etc.), stylistic choices (comedic, elegiac, satirical, etc.), and narrative models and schema.

Credit for the first systematic study goes to Henri Hauvette, in 1894, followed by Oscar Hecker in 1902 and Antonio Traversari in 1905; Guido Biagi and Enrico Rostagno for the *Zibalðone Laurenziano* facsimile of 1913; and Giuseppe Vandelli, who definitively attributed the *Zibalðone Magliabechiano* to Boccaccio's hand in 1926.[2] Within sight of the 1975 sixth centennial of Boccaccio's death, new studies were undertaken by Filippo Di Benedetto, Bianca Maria Da Rif, and Aldo Maria Costantini,[3] and that same period saw publication of the manuscript catalog preserved in the *parva libraria* (Santo Spirito, Florence).[4] More recently, the International Seminar entitled "The *Zibalðoni* of Boccaccio: Memory, Writing, Rewriting," organized in Florence under Vittore Branca, confirmed the importance of the corpus as an irreplaceable testimony to Boccaccio's precocious, eclectically erudite, literary, historiographic, and critical activity.[5] The seminar's new, rigorously scientific approach sought to base itself on the dual principles of structure and system. Every single text would be studied as a structure (or microstructure) produced by the combination of factors that belong to multiple systems (graphic, linguistic, stylistic, thematic, symbolic, and ideological), and as a constitutive element of the author's system.

The Three *Zibalðoni*: Handwriting, Dating, Composition

The three codices appear to conserve the characteristics that Armando Petrucci attributes to *libri ða banco*, the scholarly university book, large in size, containing a collection of many texts copied in one or two columns, with large margins, in library script (*littera textualiʃ*) but with wide variation of graphic execution (the *Magliabechiano* is in cursive).[6] Actually, they carry the genre well past the limits of its model in terms of content and organization of the material, enough to justify the definition of "author's book/archive."[7] Nevertheless opinions have been divided on the *Zibaldone Magliabechiano* (for which Hauvette denied the paternity of the cursive) and the two "twin" Laurentian codices, considered for the most part synchronous and attributed either partially or entirely to Boccaccio's hand. The autography of the *Miscellanea* (*Miscellany*) was rapidly ascertained, but that conclusion was long in doubt for the *Zibaldone Laurenziano* because of its heterogeneity, both in handwriting and content.

While the two Laurentians used to be considered separately according to a traditional historical-philological viewpoint, Stefano Zamponi, along with Martina Pantarotto and Antonella Tomiello, undertook — starting from the pioneering work of Virginia Brown on the Beneventan palimpsests — to review the *Zibaldone* and the *Miscellanea* on the basis of paleography and codicology, in order to reconstruct the composition of the whole and retrace the genesis of the corpus, later separated into two codices.[8] Even if both manuscripts contain palimpsest pages from the same parchment volume of origin, the investigation confirms the diversity of composition of the two codices. "At first glance the *Miscellanea Laurenziana* appears to be above all a meaningful documentation of Boccaccio's interest in classical Latin authors and an important witness to the tradition of certain classical masters, while the nature of the *Zibaldone Laurenziano* immediately reveals its greater complexity."[9] The very multiplicity of the texts long prevented a complete reconstruction of the writing activity of those years: the *Zibaldone Laurenziano*, containing letters from Dante (of which it was the only exemplar), Petrarchan texts, original compositions by Boccaccio, and texts by minor fourteenth-century authors, was considered a composite, in part because of the variation in handwriting. Not until 1971 was it entirely attributed to Boccaccio. Furthermore, analyses of and attempts to date single texts or sections, according to the specializations of the scholars involved, developed but were always based on a traditional approach. From the period of Boccaccio's first scholarly training in Florence (before 1327) to the end of the 1340s, the only certain transcription date in the *Zibaldone Laurenziano* is that of the letter from Boccaccio to Zanobi da Strada (fol. 50v), written in Forlì in 1348. For the *Miscellanea*, more homogeneous and less problematic, everyone agrees on a dating around the 1340s, with the exception of the *Priapei* and the verses by Lovato Lovati, added either after 1346 or after 1351.[10]

Virginia Brown recognized the profound links between the *Zibaldone Laurenziano* and the *Miscellanea Laurenziana* and demonstrated that both come from a unique Beneventan liturgical codex, a gradual from the end of the thirteenth century. This permitted dating that pertained to certain sections of both manuscripts.[11] Nevertheless, the task remained of evaluating the overall stratification of the materials collected in the *Zibaldone Laurenziano* and the *Miscellanea Laurenziana*; the different writings had to be situated and collated at various diachronic intervals.[12]

This approach does not limit itself to comparing the shapes of the letters in Boccaccio's hand but rather examines his writing as a system and a structure. Boccaccio's writing, in those codices, can be brought back to the *littera textualis*—common to scholars, schoolteachers, and legal practitioners in the fourteenth century—but it shows a notable degree of autonomy and individuality. Even the systematic codicological examination of the principal aspects of the construction of the two codices allows us to recognize quite precisely a dense series of relationships. The result is a detailed stratification that helps us to reconstruct with precision the genesis of the manuscripts: "At the beginning of the 1350s Boccaccio possessed a series of homogeneous parchment gatherings, 18 quartos and 1 terno, in which were written, without discernible order, texts written over a twenty-year period, containing in addition to classical and medieval authors a collection of scholars from the fourteenth century, among them Dante, Petrarch, and Boccaccio himself. . . . Probably this series of gatherings was not definitively bound while in Boccaccio's keeping; certainly its primitive organization was subsequently altered, in order to conform to choices dictated by cultural and practical norms."[13] The current ordering of the gatherings is the result of a radical reorganization by its last owner, Antonio Petrei, the sixteenth-century canon of San Lorenzo who created two volumes by moving blocks of the text. When it passed into the Medici library, in 1568, the single volume was divided into two codices: *Zibaldone Laurenziano*, an anthology of fourteenth-century texts; and *Miscellanea Laurenziana*, an anthology of classical texts.

The paleographic and codicological analysis has in large part confirmed the presence of three groups of gatherings in the *Zibaldone Laurenziano*, as suggested by Di Benedetto:[14]

1. fols. 2r-25r: Andalò del Negro, *Tractatus sphaerae* (*Treatise on the Sphere*, fol. 2r) and *Tractatus teorice planetarum* (*Treatise on the Theory of the Planets*, fols. 14r-25v), datable to circa 1330–1336, which will donate content to the *Filocolo*;[15]

2. fols. 26r-45r: Medieval texts on morality or history, collected during the years of Boccaccio's tenure at grammar school in Florence;

3. fols. 45v-77r: Moral and literary texts copied between 1339 and 1348:

1. St. Jerome's *Contra Jovinianum* (*Against Jovinianus*, fol. 52v) and Walter Map's *Dissuasiones Valerii ad Rufinum* (*Valerius to Rufinus That He Not Take a Wife*, fols. 53r-54r), the little "antimatrimonial dossier" that fed two opposing lines: the misogyny of the *Corbaccio*, and the exaltation of virtuous, wise women in the *De mulieribus claris* (*Famous Women*). The fragment by Jerome is represented in the vernacular in the *Esposizioni sopra la "Comedia"* (*Expositions on Dante's "Comedy"*), where Boccaccio discusses Dante's episode of Iacopo Rusticucci (*Inferno* 16).

2. Literary texts organized into two types of repertoires: prose and verse epistles by Dante, Petrarch, and Boccaccio (fictional and composed around 1339);[16] poems, with the eclogue-like correspondence between Dante and Giovanni del Virgilio, the *Argus* by Petrarch (with the letter to Barbato), and the first draft of Boccaccio's eclogue *Faunus*.

Dennis Dutschke, comparing the Petrarchan model of the "author's book," observed in reference to the third part: "I believe that one can pick out a composition of the book that distances itself from the scholastic tradition and moves toward that Boccaccian mosaic of erudition and literature that, as a whole, determines a change in the development of the new form of the book, called the humanist book by Petrucci and, let us go ahead and say it, the *Libro d'autore*, or author's notebook. This is an entirely Boccaccian literary form, ignored by Petrarch, but which had an illustrious follower in Poliziano."[17] The *Zibaldone Laurenziano* is not a disorganized or casual compilation of literary notes, but rather a pointed selection of materials attentively evaluated and chosen for their arguments, and destined for a vast program of reuse, rewriting, and creative production according to the complex dynamic of *imitatio/emulatio* that carries Boccaccio from Dante to the "master" Petrarch. Petrarch himself, instead of using the form of the miscellany, proceeded differently, even in his harvesting of examples, as Dutschke points out.[18] Boccaccio, when long past his youth, will still recognize in the *Genealogia* his inability to organize his compiled materials according to the standards of the master; as Dutschke notes, "If Petrarch's progress is concentrated, centripetal, Boccaccio's is expansive, centrifugal. Those *fragmenta* that Petrarch makes an effort to unite in a single volume and in a single voice, Boccaccio tends rather to collect in their singularity, or—to stand with Dante—in their multiplicity that spreads out through the universe."[19]

The *Miscellanea Laurenziana*, studied by Da Rif, contains primarily texts of classical origin: six satires by Persius annotated by Boccaccio and three compositions in Latin verse (*Appendix Virgiliana: Culex, Dirae, Lydia*).[20] The citations from Livy, Ovid, Valerius Maximus, Horace, and Juvenal demonstrate Boccaccio's mastery of the classical tradition, even if the manuscript reveals some errors. Robert Black observes, in his study on Boccaccio's marginal annotation of the three pseudo-Virgilian components of the *Appendix Virgiliana*, that Boccaccio's annotations recall medieval classroom practice:[21] even if a literal explanation was most often preferred, some texts allowed room for allegorical interpretations (Virgil, Ovid's *Metamorphoses*). As Black notes, "Boccaccio's *Virgiliana* can be described as transitional texts, looking back to his school studies as well as anticipating his mature endeavors as a humanist."[22]

The *Zibaldone Magliabechiano* is a paper codex written in cursive and, according to the majority of critics, dating to 1351–56.[23] The history of its attribution to Boccaccio and of its authentication was complex, until Vandelli's examination settled the question.[24] The more recent descriptions by Costantini, Di Benedetto, Giancarlo Savino, and Gabriella Pomaro have exhaustively completed the codicological information.[25] Pomaro's contribution provides further indications about the page order, handwriting, and ornamentation, indispensable for establishing a more precise chronology of the various sections that are clearly related to Boccaccio's mature interests. By the redaction of the *De casibus virorum illustrium* (*The Downfall of Illustrious Men*) that closely resembles it, the final part of the notebook can be ascribed to 1356.

Costantini immediately recognized "a composite and substantially bipartite nature" in this *zibaldone*. While in some ways "it is the result of a collection—systematic in the intention of the scholar—of historical sources that cover a space of several centuries (from ancient Rome to Angevin Naples), branching off into religious and genealogical asides," in others it is "a rather disorganized series of literary texts that revolve more or less strictly around the author's centers of interest, around his cultural biography."[26] We can even hypothesize with Pier Giorgio Ricci that the collection was gathered for use in the *De casibus*.[27]

Two sections are particularly interesting: the anthology from Seneca's *Ad Lucilium* (fourteen fols., 147r-160v) and the interrupted transcription of the Sallustian monograph on the Catiline conspiracy. The Seneca anthology "benefits from a diligent, punctilious, ordered organization; every statement is corroborated by precise bibliographical indications."[28] The transcription of the Sallustian *De coniuratione Catilinae* (*On the Conspiracy of Catiline*) "extends for only four pages (107r-108v) and the following folio (109), which remained blank." The copy breaks off at the twenty-seventh chapter. For

Costantini that text did not represent part of the general historical design of the *Zibaldone Magliabechiano* but would be collocated "in that *pars minor* (smaller part) that offers literary and ethical material. The 'little hand' with the pointing finger (*manicula*) indicates passages of ethical interest, memorable and memorizable judgments for future use."[29] A note on Sempronia (*Nota hic de Sempronia muliere*) seems to anticipate the comment on that figure in *De casibus* 1.17, "In mulieres" (On women). Vittorio Zaccaria's critical edition had in fact underscored the dependence of that treatise on the *Zibaldone Magliabechiano* in other references (Orosius, Martinus Polonus, Paolino Veneto). The loss of several pages prevents us from identifying with certainty the origin of the texts used by Boccaccio: the first nineteen pages are missing for the compendium of imperial history that occupies the first third of the manuscript; another loss of twelve pages (fols. 277–88) interrupts Hayton's *Flos historiarum terre Orientis* (*Flower of Histories of the Orient*), transcribed with notable diligence and precision.

The most lively section is that in which Boccaccio transcribes ample extracts of the *Compendium* or *Chronologia magna* (*Great Chronology*) of Paolino Veneto (fols. 164r-263v), accompanying it with marginalia that expose the copyist's critical spirit. His most vehement attacks and asides decry the Venetian's contradictions, confusion in the collection of data, his incapacity for historical analysis, and his despicable linguistic habits ("imbractator": dauber, splatterer; "venetus bergolus": blabbermouth Venetian). The thematic organization of the transcription (no longer exclusively chronological like its source) proves Boccaccio's intention to create for himself a repertory organized according to plans for later works, possibly correcting and completing the collected information. Isabelle Heullant-Donat, basing her work on the *Compendium*, suggests that Boccaccio compared and completed his text with other sources (the description of Jerusalem could not be drawn only from Paolino's little map). Furthermore, Boccaccio adds to the list of *Doctores* figures not cited by this source, but worthy of memorializing—Dante, Petrarch, Zanobi da Strada, Giotto, and others. According to Heullant-Donat, the editing would have been done in two stages: the first in Naples (1335–40) for the collection of data; the second probably in Florence (1351–56) for the reordering of material and the joking comments and negative judgments, attributable to his critical distance and greater maturity.[30]

The *Genealogia deorum* of Paolo da Perugia transcribed in the *Zibaldone Magliabechiano* and studied by A. Teresa Hankey both confirms Boccaccio's affinity for mythological material and demonstrates the diversity of his approach with respect to the learned librarian of Angevin Naples.[31] Paolo's work, organized as a genealogical repertory in order to facilitate the reading of the classics, could not satisfy a Boccaccio who sought commentary and allegorical interpretation like that in Paolo's lost *Liber collectionum* (*Book of Collections*), closer to the Vatican mythologists, which is the most likely reason for his interrupted transcription of it.

Boccaccio's Laboratory: Handwriting, Writing System, Designs, Drawings

Much of the *Zibaldoni's* fascination resides in the numerous graphic images in Boccaccio's own hand, part of the complex system of writing, punctuation, notes, and drawings (marginalia, *manicule*, etc.). Giovanni Morello retraces the chronological stages of Boccaccio's marginal drawings up to the definitive confirmation, by Vittore Branca, that both text and catchword images in the Berlin manuscript Hamilton 90 of the *Decameron* are autograph. Di Benedetto (1971) and the centenary catalog of the exhibition in Florence (1976) dedicated considerable space to Boccaccio's variegated activity ornamenting his manuscripts, in which it is possible to distinguish thematic developments: from the watercolor designs in the Berlin manuscript to the freaks of nature that he drew in the *Zibaldone Magliabechiano*; from the little pointing hands to the crowns or tiny busts of historical characters, all either decorative elements or intended to facilitate the reading of the text, such as colored and decorated initial letters or binding references (catchwords) for the gatherings.[32]

We pass "from the geometric simplicity of a rectangle enhanced by little red globes" in the Vatican codex of the *De consolatione philosophiae* (*The Consolation of Philosophy*) by Boethius, attributed to Boccaccio's youth, to a more elegant elaboration in the *Zibaldone Laurenziano*, where the astronomical treatises by Andalò del Negro are accompanied by numerous drawings and illustrations (including little humanized suns). Likewise attributed to Boccaccio, because of their unity of placement and realization, are the *ductus* (formation of the letter stems) made by the quill pen as well as the writings inserted into or encircling the geometric and astronomical drawings.[33] These interventions are striking to scholars for their surprising modernity and uncommon artistic sensitivity. In the case of the pointing hands, Morello observes that those attributed to Boccaccio are particularly refined, with the addition of decorative details.[34]

Signatures and erasures, too, can be significant. For the 1996 seminar, Victoria Kirkham confronted the question of the author's signature as a fleeting and mutable face behind friendly and misleading masks.[35] In Boccaccio's first epistolary experiments (transcribed in the *Zibaldone Lauren-ziano*), the name "Johannes de Certaldo" seems to have been erased from the letters' closings. By whom, if not himself? And if this is the case, for what reason? According to Di Benedetto, it was the author as a strict censor of his own youthful works.[36] In Kirkham's view what he did can rather be compared to his putting himself (or Certaldo), during the same period, at the center of his own novel, clothed as the protagonist (Florio-Filocolo), but leaving to the reader the work of decoding. Thus the situation is rather a knowing and refined artistic strategy—even, paradoxically, the first step toward an authorial awareness.

The study of the handwriting and writing system in the *Zibaldoni* should represent part of a more global study applied to all autograph manuscripts, as Giovanni Morello hoped, including the problems of transcription errors both ancient and modern.[37] Yet Giancarlo Savino insists on how much the prejudicial view of a distracted or sloppy Boccaccio-copyist—and the comparison with Petrarch's library style and stable, unchanging handwriting—impeded the recognition of autograph manuscripts or books annotated by Boccaccio, involved rather in continuous experimentation. The "concordant and severe evaluation of bad transcriptions that Boccaccio made of his own writings," as expressed so categorically by Giuseppe Billanovich, had lasting consequences, and for a long time Boccaccio's hand remained "hidden."[38] The chronology of the casual discovery and identification of the *Zibaldone Magliabechiano* by Sebastiano Ciampi, in 1827, is a sign of the resistance of traditional methods. The scholar's first reaction, in the case of a work by a conspicuous author, was to attribute the codex to Petrarch. The same scholar refused to recognize Boccaccio's library handwriting in the Laurentian *Zibaldone*.[39]

Patrizia Rafti, studying Boccaccio's *usus distinguendi* (editorial articulation of a text), demonstrates the utility of an overall approach that underlines "the multiform, polyvalent, and multicolored reality of Boccaccio-the-author's distinctive formal writing system, above all as a copyist of his own *Zibaldoni*."[40] This Boccaccio is an "aesthetically sensitive copyist" who characterizes his text with an unmistakable taste, which he expresses through marginal designs or ornamental friezes in his manuscripts.

Boccaccio's Library: Intertextual System and Strategies of Rewriting

Michelangelo Picone, co-organizer of the seminar on the *Zibaldoni*, beginning with the theory of *auctoritas* forged in the thirteenth century, described the parabola traced by a young Boccaccio who wished to become a full-fledged author, and for whom the *Zibaldoni* play an inaugural and foundational role.[41] The *Zibaldoni*, as "author's archive-notebooks," act as a net of links that unite threads from various materials, styles, and genres in order to be reactivated gradually according to multiple modalities and literary keys. From this there descends a system, simultaneously paradigmatic and syntagmatic, of the most erudite works: the *Genealogia deorum gentilium* (*Genealogy of the Pagan Gods*); the repertoire of the lives of illustrious men and women, the *De casibus* and the *De mulieribus*; the unfinished *Esposizioni*. Furthermore, the *Genealogia* and the *Esposizioni* offer an original poetics and also a historiographic and critical approach to literature.

Boccaccio reuses his collected materials while demonstrating a continuity of intent and absolutely exceptional interests, but also a capacity and adaptability that allow him to use these materials on different levels and for different purposes. Whether we speak of erudite or explanatory works, such as *De montibus, silvis, fontibus, lacubus, fluminibus, stagnis seu paludibus et de diversis nominibus maris* (*On Mountains, Forests, Fonts, Lakes, Marshes or Ponds and on the Different Names of the Seas*) and *De Canaria*, or poetic or narrative fiction, in vernacular or in Latin, for the purpose of edification or amusement, the reference covers various functions: from the guarantee of *auctoritas*, to clever and refined *imitatio*, to parody, joke, and even polemic in regard to the canonical tradition.

Di Benedetto undertook a systematic census of the minor texts in order to point out their variety. His study is supported by an updated table of contents for the *Zibaldone Laurenziano*.[42] The census reveals—other than the strictly literary, historical, or geographical interests of its composer and the necessary proofs of his authorship (*Elegia di Costanza*)—an antique collector's curiosity that embraces epitaphs, epigraphs, and oracular texts. While the *Comedia Lidie*, included in the *Miscellanea Laurenziana* and studied by Picone, foretells the *vis comica* (comic power) of the *Decameron* and one of its most famous tales (7.9); the *Lamentatio Bertoldi*—a scholastic patchwork of classical and medieval Latin quotations from Ovid to the *Pamphilus* to Hugo Primat of Orléans—anticipates the tale of Primasso (1.7), in which the character represents "the image of the author projected into the text, and thus reflecting the new *auctor* within the old."[43] The most important and interesting works for the formation of the short-story teller are the three elegiac comedies—the *Geta et Birria* by Vital de Blois (67v-69r), the *Alda* by William of Blois (69r-71v), and the *Comedia Lidie* by Matthew of Vendôme (71v-73v). These are adapted not in their theatrical dimension, but as repertoires of rhetorical effects distributed throughout the *Decameron*, from the microtexts to the macrotext of the frame narrative, and as sources of fantastical narrative plots.

In terms of authorial apprenticeship, among the most seductive discoveries is that Boccaccio's transcription of Ovid's *Ibis* (independent of the fact that this copy of an extremely difficult text contains a noteworthy number of errors), as studied by Robert Hollander, confirms the Certaldan's taste for satire, which will erupt in the *Corbaccio*. Ovid's text also informs Fiammetta's outbursts in the *Elegia di madonna Fiammetta*, as Carlo Delcorno has noticed, which means that editing of the *Zibaldone* could date back to 1340 or to as late as the period of the *Decameron*.[44]

In his examination of the *Elegia di Costanza*, Pier Massimo Forni demonstrated the "relevance of this complex and fascinating shelter for the fantastic archeology of Boccaccio," whose imaginative phenomenology and technical procedures are recognizable in his rewriting of classical material from the *Filocolo* to the *Decameron*. The two first narrative exercises of the *Zibaldone Laurenziano* (the *Elegia di Costanza* and the *Allegoria mitologica*),[45] which already knowingly put into practice the Aristotelian functions of *memoria, inventio, dispositio*, and *elocutio*, are no longer geared principally toward persuasion and moral edification, but composed according to an erudite interest and aesthetic pleasure in source recognition, an appreciation of the process of re-elaboration and virtuosity in quotation, and an enjoyment of combinatory and syncretistic unpredictability.[46]

The EDIC Project: Diplomatic Interpretative Encoded Edition

Partial critical editions and the selective study of a few texts excerpted from the *Zibaldoni* (epistles, Latin poetry, *Allegoria mitologica*) have been undertaken,[47] with the inevitable loss of supporting information about the writing technique and compositional system. It therefore seems auspicious to suggest an integral publication of the textual corpus that both respects and bears witness to the complex structure that can be considered "prehypertextual," in that it is constructed on the basis of a net of intertextual, intratextual, and extratextual relationships. Only an electronic edition (encoded and not just reproductive) can describe and represent dynamically the multidimensional and multisignificant structure of a manuscript, with its stratifications and levels of codification (graphemes, graphic organization of the page, textual typologies). At the 1996 seminar Tito Orlandi presented principles of electronic codification and procedures for working with digitized manuscripts, stressing the necessity of capturing both the implicit and the explicit aspects of the text, and subjecting them in advance to a critical interpretation of the observed phenomena, all with reference to the virtual text "that is obtained by examining the material text in light of the competence of its producer."[48]

Thus, beginning with the criteria of textual philology and in light of the principles elaborated by Orlandi and his school, Raul Mordenti has conceived the project of a digital edition of the *Zibaldone Laurenziano*,[49] whose complexity respects that of the codex itself—an "author's book," a "progressive text," "a repertoire text of writing and culture," a "book-archive of the author"—that is, the features of the codex that have made a paper edition impossible. As he writes, "the *Zibaldone* (like any other manuscript, for that matter, but on a larger scale) is movement, whereas the printing press aspires to install in the text a definitive fixity (*ne varietur*)."[50] The stratified construction of the text, the uncertainty of the limits and disposition of the fragments, the mix of genres, styles, and editing phases, the superimposition of glosses and erasures, require in reality an editorial treatment that does not erase but rather underscores the various functions of writing and rewriting.

There are four objectives of an electronic edition scientifically conceived: to preserve the text; to restore and retrieve the integrated text in its original structure; to make the text accessible and readable; and to facilitate further research. We can thus explain (with scientific rigor) the phases of copying the material, organizing the page, and distributing the compositional elements of the entire corpus, traced in its development according to the intentions of the author, while, at the same time, putting programs in place to record, collate, classify, and compare the author's letters, variants, notes, and corrections, and the illustrations in his hand, thus offering the instruments necessary to those who study variants in texts transmitted from the past.

As a first step toward the goal of creating a digital *Zibaldone Laurenziano*, there is now an online edition provided by the Edizione Diplomatica Interpretativa Codificata (or EDIC) that includes the texts of Saint Jerome's *De non ducenda uxore* (*On Not Taking a Wife*, fol. 2v) and the *Elegia di Costanza* (fols. 60r-60v).[51] As the project grows, it will open to a wide public this fascinating manuscript that has survived in Florence for more than 650 years. Its contents, a library and laboratory of Boccaccio in his early years as a reader, note taker, and writer, will become for scholars a site for continuing research on the methods of medieval writers and the fruits of their cultural mnemonics.

PART XI

EPILOGUE

CHAPTER TWENTY-EIGHT

A VISUAL LEGACY • (Boccaccio as Artist)

Victoria Kirkham

Boccaccio, founding master of Italian fiction and Petrarch's eager companion in early humanism, left another legacy, neither vernacular nor classical, but in the language of images. This "third language" appears in manuscripts that he transcribed, owned, borrowed, or studied. Largely unsuspected until the second half of the twentieth century, it "speaks" along a conceptual continuum from dots or marks of a single stroke to small marginal portraits, amusingly decorated catchwords, and complex family trees of the pagan gods, bursting with color across whole folios. Critical tradition—overreaching, as some have begun to say—has further credited him with a half-folio self-portrait, as well as sophisticated multiepisodic narrative scenes in manuscripts of the *Decameron* and *Divine Comedy*.[1] While art historians continue to argue attributions with tools of stylistic analysis, literary scholarship can review the visual evidence as it connects with a manuscript's verbal contents. In a capital initial elegantly pen-flourished or in incipit letters with "scratched out" internal decoration (*sgraffito*), text and image merge.[2] The text *is* the image. And what about the countless but puzzling pen strokes hovering near the written words, neither text nor decipherable figure but nonetheless deliberate, that may be reminders for the author or aids to the reader?[3] Or marginal cues that are perfectly understandable, like the pointing index finger (the "manicule," *manicula*),[4] or coronets beside royal names in a genealogical list?[5] When does such conventional signage end and personal expression begin? Fascinated by the notion that Boccaccio was not only a poet but an artist, scholars have pored over the spectrum of graphic enhancements in more than a dozen of his autographs and nearly as many older manuscripts, attempting to date and indentify the hand. Initial enthusiasm stretched his corpus to 150 drawings, but the most recent scholarship is inclined dramatically to reduce that total. Doubts and outright denials have surfaced, especially surrounding attributions of programmatic image cycles that seem to be the work of profession-als, not the product of a talented amateur.[6]

The poet's drawings in his *Zibaldone Laurenziano* accompany treatises he transcribed by Andalò del Negro (d. 1334), astronomer to the Angevin court, whose science finds poetic reflections in Boccaccio's Neapolitan writings. Astrology is powerful in his *Filocolo*, where the autobiographical Idalogos speaks in a pastoral mode of his learning under "Calmeta, shep-herd of great solemnity" (Andalò). The *Teseida*, in twelve books as befits a new classic, follows a medieval astrological program tied to the twelve signs of the zodiac.[7] In the *Zibaldone*, neatly charted grids with small flo-ral embellishments and marginal diagrams of the planets that humorously personify the sun (he makes faces from cocky to curmudgeonly) denote an aesthetic eye. A tiny drawing *bas-de-page* profiles a well-sexed bull in full stride to illustrate the definition of *colure*, or celestial meridian, as defined in Andalò's *Treatise on the Spheren* (fol. 5r; fig. 2): "Colure takes its name from *colon* [clause of a sentence, member of a strophe], which is a 'member,' and *uros*, which is a wild ox, because it appears to us in the manner of an erect ox tail, which is its member. It makes in its erection a semicircle."[8] Boccaccio writes behind the ox-bull's horns "example of a semicircle" (*exemplum semi-circuli*), extending to the tassel-like tip of its semicircular tail. Its placement is a visual pun, since the Latin *cauda* means both "the tail of an animal" and "the last letter of a word."[9] This bull's long, raised tail carries another play on words as an "erect member" that almost appears to be ejaculating. The animal's true male member protrudes conspicuously from his underside in a sort of vertical symmetry with his sturdy, pointed horns.

Although the artist knew bulls from agricultural life and the zodiacal Taurus, his bovine speaks a visual language distinctly Boccaccesque. Its simple outline, a pictograph, communicates the etymology of *colure* and a meridian's "erect" appearance. Perhaps the poet liked to amuse himself dur-ing the tedious task of transcription by pausing now and then for a little artistic tangent.[10] Here, to the technical text of another author, he brings his own creative cast of mind with its inclinations toward erotic voyeurism and the salacious anecdote: Florio hides in Biancifiore's bedroom and slips into her sleeping arms (*Filocolo* 4.110–21); Caleone manages to steal the same pleasure from Fiammetta, when the sight of him standing in her chamber *nudo, bellissimo* undoes the last shreds of her resistance (*Comedia delle ninfe fio-rentine* 35.62 and 35.113); eighty obscene Latin poems in the *Zibaldone Lau-renziano* honoring male deities of fertility, the *Priapeia*; and a stunning recent

Fig. 2. Boccaccio, *Zibaldone Laurenziano*. Quasi catchword with bull illustrating Andalò del Negro, *Tractatus spere materialis*. Florence, Biblioteca Medicea Laurenziana, MS. Plut. 29.8, fol. 5r. By permission of the Ministero per i Beni e le Attività Culturali. È vietata ogni ulteriore riproduzione con qualsiasi mezzo.

discovery at the Ambrosian Library that brings to light another autograph rife with obscenity, the *Epigrams* by Martial, which Boccaccio transcribed with relish.[11] Finally, in its small way, the Laurentian bull anticipates those well-known punning euphemisms that dot the *Decameron* — Alatiel's visit in the nunnery dedicated to St. Stiffen-in-the-Hand (2.7.109), Bartolomea's "mortar sin" with her buff kidnapper Paganino da Monaco (2.10.37), and Alibech's desert lessons on putting the devil in hell (3.10).[12]

Boccaccio habitually framed his catchwords, even if only with dots, but sometimes he pauses, as he did on the bull, to answer an artistic impulse.[13] Giuseppe Vandelli, in a still-valuable description of the *Teseida* autograph (1340s), notes in a lower margin its curious little shield with crown, flowers, and *F*—for the Angevin princess Fiammetta? Boccaccio planned for it an extensive visual apparatus, leaving spaces for many illustrations.[14] Only the first was painted, an abraded watercolor with the author kneeling, who presents his book to Fiammetta (fol. 1r). This and full-color initials with stylized acanthus leaves in tempera at the incipit of the prologue and book 1 (fols. 1r, 3r) reveal the hand of an unknown professional artist, perhaps commissioned by Boccaccio.[15]

Whimsical catchword decorations—leaves, fruits, a crown, grotesque faces—recur in the autograph of *Famous Women* (1370–73). One of the grotesques encloses the catchword "he had painted" (*pinxerat*), referring to the failed efforts of Zeuxis fittingly to portray Helen of Troy, legendary for her beauty: "What he 'had painted' was but a simulacrum of her celestial grace." In ironic contrast to context, behind wide-open eyes and a thick, flat nose, pointed doglike ears flap on either side of the ugly catchword face. The topmost lines (sparse hair?) suggest spindly horns or antennae. Below the cavity inside its flaring cheeks, sprouting with scraggly strands of a beard, in place of a chin (Lat. *mentum*) a tongue hangs down like a pendulous male member (*mentula*). The word *pinxerat* is inside the creature's gaping mouth, as if it were being spoken, perhaps to carry another pun: Zeuxis "had painted," but Boccaccio draws.[16]

Boccaccio's catchword art culminates with half-figure drawings of characters in the *Decameron* for his painstakingly transcribed late autograph (1370–72), MS Hamilton 90 in Berlin.[17] Drawn and color-washed with the same inks that served for text and rubrication, dominantly brown, these comic sketches conjoin copyist and illuminator.[18] Far from the courtly International Style seen in Simone Martini's frontispiece for Petrarch's Virgil and luxury copies of the *Divine Comedy*,[19] this *Decameron* asserts the popular register of caricature, playing on such earthy forms as breasts, beards, horns, and tongues.[20] Princess Alatiel's low-cut bodice emphasizes her ample bosom, across which parade the letters of the word *vivere*.[21] What better than "to live" for the sultan's daughter, who coupled with "eight men perhaps 10,000 times" during her four-year Mediterranean odyssey as Fortune's toy? On the Fourth Day a night guard in Brescia, who arrests Andreuola with the dead body of her secret husband Gabriotto, bears a shield that reads: "be bold" (*sia ardito*) (fig. 3). A formidable metal helmet, prominent nose, and jutting beard complete his aggressive stance, apt for a tool of the town's evil judge (*podestà*). Like *pinxerat*, these catchwords belong to a narrative context with meaning quite contrary to their pictorial implications. Alatiel, in fact, suffers through multiple kidnappings in foreign countries where, not knowing the languages, she is forced "to live" like a deaf mute (2.7.80); Andreuola courageously retorts to the patrol: "Let none of you 'be bold' enough to lay a hand on me" (4.6.32).

Verbal and visual codes interact, turning catchwords into commentary. In *Decameron* 1.4 the monks' escapades take place at a monastery "in

Fig. 3. Boccaccio, *Decameron*. MS Hamilton 90, fol. 55v: Catchword "sia ardito" depicting a soldier of the Signoria (*Decameron* 4.6). Staatsbibliothek der Stiftung Preussischer Kulturbesitz, Berlin.

Lunigiana"—where, specifically, the catchword of their abbot tells (fig. 4). With a face suggesting both lechery and the life of a bon vivant, his robe identifies the Pulsanese Benedictines, who had only one house in that region, at Santa Croce del Corvo, above Lerici. A cloudlike white patch on his brown robe reads "mind" (*mente*), which in the *novella* is part of an Italian adverb describing how he "quietly" (*piana*mente) enjoyed women in the night, but as a label for the image, it declares how astute he was, using his "mind" to solve a need for country wenches in the cells.[22] The privateer Landolfo Rufolo (2.2) wears a hat pointing down on one side and up on the other, allusive to Fortune's vagaries, theme for Day 2. A portrait of

Fig. 4. Boccaccio, *Decameron*. MS Hamilton 90, fol. 8v: Catchword "mente" depicting the abbot (*Decameron* 1.4). Staatsbibliothek der Stiftung Preussischer Kulturbesitz, Berlin.

the arch-hypocrite "Tedaldo" degli Elisei (3.7) insinuates his duplicity. Costumed in the "hood and cloak" of a pilgrim from the Holy Sepulcher (which he is not), he reconquers his married lady with deceitful sophistry. Boccaccio first painted his beard as a long, narrow triangle, but in what appears as a *pentimento* he added a second point that flows starkly beyond the figure's outline, symbolic of a "forked tongue."[23] Gianni Lotteringhi (*Decameron* 7.1; fig. 5), convinced that his wife's lover is a ghost, has a slack mouth with red tongue sticking out and a huge pair of curving horns, simpleton and *cornuto* that he is.

Finally, there is the image of a lady that scholars have always identified as "Neifile," but who might better be renamed Bartolomea. Her story concludes on the verso of the page facing the folio whose recto contains the catchword *licentia* (fig. 6). It comes when Neifile takes the crown and announces less "license" in storytelling for Day 3, that is, a narrower theme than before (2, Concl., 8). Nevertheless, the dejected appearance of the lady depicted hardly fits Neifile, a young woman who sings gladly of love in her ballad (9, Concl., 8). None of the other surviving catchwords portrays a frame narrator. A better candidate is on the folio just opposite, Bartolomea, mismatched wife to a doddering Pisan judge, whose calendar of abstinence reduces her to "grave melancholy" (2.10.10). Drawn with downcast face and an oddly dangling sleeve, she becomes a rebus for her husband's impotence and the "license" of her sexual liberation with the lusty pirate Paganino. These visual double entendres, descendants of the distant little bull in the *Zibaldone*, are in the same comic spirit as the obscene euphemisms that lace Boccaccio's *novelle*.

Humor can be broad or high, and it rises to a serious register with a full cycle of illustrations for the Capponi *Decameron*, so named after the family friend who copied its pages in twin columns of mercantile script.[24] The oldest illustrated *Decameron* (ca. 1355–60), it preserves sixteen ink drawings lightly shaded in a wash of the same brown color. They open on a single grand panel, deftly executed in an imaginative tripartite spatial conception (fol. 4v; fig. 7). Dominating the foreground, set on two steps, is a hexagonal fountain reminiscent of a more complex predecessor in the delightful garden of Boccaccio's *Amorosa visione* (cantos 38–39). From lively waters a slim column rises, spouting from delicate animal mouths and topped by a nude statuette of Venus, chastely posed in a Gothic sway. A serving woman of a certain age leans over the rim to draw water with her jug. At left rear stands a country house with crenellated roof, its tall door open to a shady interior. Midground the *brigata* sits in a circle ruled by Pampinea, facing out with scepter and laurel crown. Going by the text, at her right sits Panfilo

Fig. 5. Boccaccio, *Decameron*. MS Hamilton 90, fol. 79v: Catchword "pare" depicting Gianni Lotteringhi (*Decameron* 7.1). Staatsbibliothek der Stiftung Preussischer Kulturbesitz, Berlin.

frontal (1, Intro., 115), but he must also remind us of Dioneo's wit because the artist, perhaps supervised by Boccaccio, has costumed him with a suggestively placed *scarsella*. Darkly colored, this purse hung on a belt stands out against his tunic and tights, caught over his crotch in a visual pun. An idyllic landscape with thickly tufted grass, framed front and rear by small

Fig. 6. Boccaccio, *Decameron*. MS Hamilton 90, fol. 31v: Catchword "licentia" depicting Bartolomea (or Neifile?) (*Decameron* 2.10 or 3, Intro.). Staatsbibliothek der Stiftung Preussischer Kulturbesitz, Berlin.

trees with balloon-shaped branches, completes this visual gateway to the *Decameron*.

As in the words on the pages of the book, realistic detail opens to possibilities of symbolism. Taken alone, the woman at the well could belong to a genre scene, but in the context of a hexagonal basin surmounted by the

Venus *pudica*, she and the fountain—front and center—announce the frame narrators' decorum and anticipate the Valley of the Ladies, first visited late on Day 6 and encircled by six "little mountains."[25] Chastity controls sensuality, at which the artist winks when positioning one male narrator's purse. The domicile manifests an urban world of civilization that reaches the country, where the *brigata* imposes a rationally ordered, new society triumphant over plague and death.[26] The image does not merely decorate or illustrate. It captures the spirit of the book and interprets its meanings.

The page facing opens with a boxed rectangular drawing of two couples confronted on horseback (fol. 5r). Just above the rubric, "Here begins the book called *Decameron*, surnamed Prencipe Galeotto," Lancelot and Queen Guinevere lock in the embrace pandered by Sir Galeotto. Filtered through Dante's Paolo and Francesca, whose own go-between ("Galeotto") had been that same Arthurian romance, the image announces tales from a chivalric

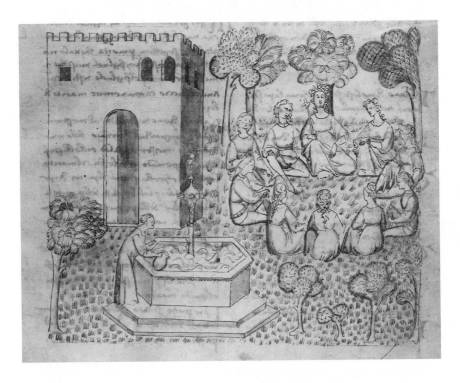

Fig. 7. Boccaccio, *Decameron*. MS ital. 482, fol. 4v: the *brigata*. Bibliothèque Nationale de France, Paris.

world.[27] Below the rubric, a large historiated *H* ("Humana cosa è . . .") holds the scene canonical for a manuscript incipit, an author portrait. A cleric ensconced in a carved stall chair, beneath Cupid fluttering with cocked bow, reads to expectant young women. It sums up the promise of the Proem, stories for love-struck ladies. *Mutatis mutandis* the format is identical to the Boccaccio portrait pasted into a copy of his *Buccolicum carmen* (ca. 1379?), where a plump author *in cathedra*, robed as a cleric, reads to a circle of Augustinian Eremite monks. This time the presence hovering overhead is his Muse, with whom he exchanges dialogue in Latin verses that stream diagonally between them and forecast his good prospects for fame (fig. 8).[28]

In the Capponi images, as in Boccaccio's prose, pattern with variation is the rule. Always at the top of the page, almost all run across the double columns of text. Typically they visualize the Day's first novella.[29] The last, the narrators' return to Florence, is a visual epilogue, symmetrical counterpart to the Proem illustration. Some picture strips form a diptych or an evenly partitioned triptych, while others are more complex in their narrative flow, with diegetic "props" functioning simultaneously as dividers and transitions between scenes. No less than five episodes crowd into the space allotted for the tragic tale of Ghismonda. A central rocky mass opens vertically to Guiscardo's secret passageway, one side of which serves partly to hide the lovers in bed, as if stones had morphed into a blanket to imply the secrecy of their tryst. Their embrace is the scene's focal point, highest on the picture plane and perfectly centered, with two episodes on either side — at left, Guiscardo receives Ghismonda's message in a hollow cane, then clambers up the cleft on a rope; at right, Ghismonda receives his heart, then tips to her mouth the poisoned chalice. The image reveals an artist on intimate terms with the text, unlike one Flemish-speaking illuminator, who could imagine only the palace chimney as a clandestine means of arrival.[30]

Symmetries, internal centers, and frames in these drawings replicate visually structures that articulate the Gothic plan of the *novelle*. So trees of an Arthurian forest cluster at the center and lean in from either side of the Proem's "mounted" lovers; for the Author's conclusion, the *brigata* grouped midscene trots along against a backdrop picturesque with hilltop tower and trees exploding in little bursts of branches. Behind at far left stand the same palace and fountain that had appeared large in the gateway image; ahead awaits Florence, tightly walled around its proud landmarks — the Baptistry, Palazzo Vecchio, Giotto's campanile. Depicted as only a Florentine could do, this is the city already seen from the inside, as the setting to Filippo Balducci's return with his grown son, excited by the wonderful "goslings"

Fig. 8. Boccaccio, *Buccolicum carmen*. Boccaccio author portrait, his Muse, and Augustinian monks. Florence, Biblioteca Medicea Laurenziana, MS. Plut. 34.49, fol. 1v. By
permission of the Ministero per i Beni e le Attività Culturali. È vietata ogni ulteriore
riproduzione con qualsiasi mezzo.

(*papere*), and beside them, a long-eared pack ass bearing supplies for their
retreat on Mt. "Asinaio."

Discussions of Boccaccio's visual corpus have paired the Capponi *Decameron* with a second major narrative cycle, seven drawings in one of his
three autograph manuscripts of Dante's *Commedia* (ca. 1360–63).[31] Incom-

plete, they reach only as far as *Inferno* 17.[32] Here in a prevailing Tuscan style of Giottesque naturalism, the images are all *bas-de-page* with figures classical in their sculpturesque lines and three-dimensionality. Eerie background emptiness contrasts sharply with the Capponi *Decameron*, where realistic details fill the picture reels, both in depth and in breadth. A minimal prologue scene depicts Virgil, marked as an ancient sage by his toga, baldness, and white beard, who speaks inside a shadowy V-shaped valley dense with trees (fig. 9). Beside him a youthful Dante gestures surprise, confronted by three beasts on a faintly indicated desert slope: a spotted leopard, the kingly lion, and the she-wolf blocking his progress, her underbelly heavy with swollen teats. They remind us of Boccaccio's fascination with animal lore from the time of his first fiction, *Diana's Hunt*, which he stocked with a menagerie from the bestiaries.[33]

The images that follow fall at random intervals, as if the artist had decided to draw what he liked best. Paolo and Francesca hover midair (*Inferno* 5). Phlegyas (canto 8), hairy-chested and horned, poles his ferry.[34] Three Furies, horrifyingly snake-infested, crest the gate of Dis (*Inferno* 9), a wild trio not unlike the women wailing ritualistically over Filippo Balducci's dead wife in the Capponi *Decameron*. The club-wielding Centaur Nexus

Fig. 9. Dante, *Inferno*. MS 1035, fol. 4v: Dante, Virgil, the three beasts (*Inferno*, canto 1). Biblioteca Riccardiana, Florence.

(canto 12) rears up hirsute and horned, his equine half recalling the *Zibaldone* bull (fig. 2) and the she-wolf (fig. 9). Finally, a reptilian Geryon waits at the brink of the abyss while the pilgrim turns to the three usurers, their money bags huge with a heraldic zoo: a great white goose, a clawing lion rampant, and a fat sow (*Inferno* 17.54–65).[35] Horned Phlegyas and Nexus have a bicornal feature in common with the Laurentian bull, the cuckolded Gianni Lotteringhi (fig. 5), and a miniature horned Moses sketched in a history book Boccaccio consulted, the *Jewish Antiquities* by Josephus.[36]

Fascinated by the poets, history, myth, and *mirabilia*—from the marvels of Rome to mores on the Canary Islands, from Dripetrua born "with a double row of teeth" to the nesting habits of vultures—Boccaccio scattered tiny pictures in manuscripts he both owned and did not (such as the Josephus).[37] Ovid looks out wide-eyed with anxiety from the margin of his *Tristia*.[38] "Seneca" is among the small figures that decorate Boccaccio's Martial.[39] Freaks of nature accompany historical notice of their birth in his *Zibaldone Magliabechiano*: two sets of conjoined twins, one male and one female; an armless, sightless creature with a lower body like a fish tail.[40]

Small but telling "signatures" from Boccaccio appear as well in manuscripts that belonged to Petrarch: a collection of Claudian's poetry,[41] and a much discussed late thirteenth-century copy of Pliny's *Natural History*. In the latter, interpolated remarks on the magical powers (*virtutes*) of the vulture drew both men's attention. Properly used, the dead bird's parts drive out devils, make thieves friendly, assist in childbirth, cure foot ache (both right and left), and make all wishes come true—only, however, if one speaks the formula "Angelus Adone Habraham" before chopping off the bird's head. Beside the passage, Petrarch wrote *vultur*, and above he drew a manicule. Directly level with the word "Abraham" is a small portrait of him by Boccaccio, who must have been captivated by this amazing conjunction of bestiary lore with a venerated biblical patriarch.[42] Their clustered marginalia "speak" of the two early humanists absorbed in conversation over Pliny.[43]

Their companionable reading accounts for the most celebrated drawing in the manuscript, a picture of Vaucluse (fig. 10). Once assumed to be Petrarch's, it has found advocates for a Boccaccian paternity. Where Pliny speaks of the source of the Sorgue, an ascending rocky height surmounted by a sanctuary has been drawn. At its base from a dark cavern flows the river, down to marshland, where cattails grow, and a heron holds in its beak a fish. Beneath it Petrarch has written: "My most delightful Transalpine solitude." Boccaccio could have sketched this small vignette on a visit in 1359 to his friend, by then at Milan, who nostalgically described it from memory.[44]

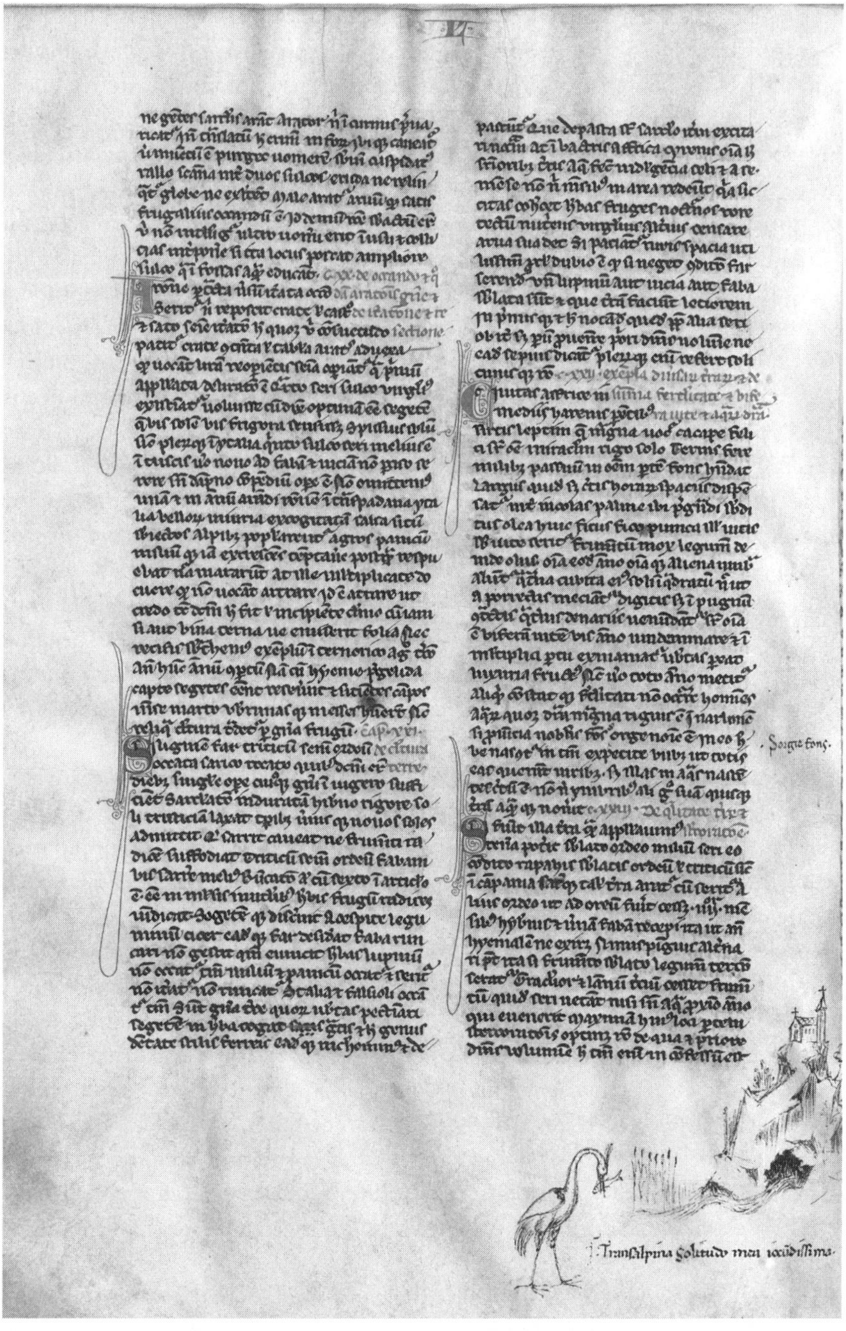

ꝟ

Transalpina solitudo mea iucundissima·

Sorgue fons·

Fig. 10. Pliny, *Natural History*. MS lat. 6802, fol. 143v: Petrarch's Vaucluse, source of the Sorgue. Bibliothèque Nationale de France, Paris.

Boccaccio's most minuscule drawings dwell among the folios of his autograph *Genealogy of the Pagan Gods* (1363–66), a treasure that more importantly displays his most expansive art, family trees exploding into full-page,
brightly colored, curvilinear designs to document "Demogorgon" and all
his posterity (fig. 11). As "richiami," or *signes-de-renvoi*, tiny images (and
other markings—e.g., a Greek theta) connect passages in the main text to
marginal notes: a bee, a lily, a flower, a fly, a lion head, a butterfly, a hare, an
ant, a bird with rabbit ears. Some are fanciful hybrids; some are amazingly
naturalistic, idly observed by the scribe sitting at his desk. Like footnotes
or hyperlinks, his figural code connects information of at least three kinds:
Greek passages to a Latin translation, text to gloss, text to a marginal insertion. Moving from marginalia to page center, we meet the magnificent
trees that open the first thirteen books of this great mythological encyclopedia. Each one's branches curl differently with medallions and morphologi-
cally distinct leaves, outlined in ink and colored around spaces left open for
names in a palette typical of the amanuensis—brown, red, purple, green,
yellow, dragon's blood.[45] Influenced by such related paradigms as consan-
guinity trees (Boccaccio would have seen them as a student of canon law)
and the Tree of Jesse with Christ's ancestry, his arboreal families became
archetypes for later copies, among them the University of Chicago manuscript 100, which provides the images for the cover and frontispiece of this
volume.[46]

An indefatigable copyist, Boccaccio imprints himself in manuscript *mise-
en-page*, the layout of information—text, glosses, and miniatures—that makes
every folio a singular object and turns the book's faces double-spread into
wondrously varied viewscapes.[47] In his *Miscellanea Laurenziana* marginal
glosses actually become "concrete" words: circles, a rectangle, diamond,
triangle, phytomorphic forms, and even a pitcher (fig. 12). Whoever leafs
through his *Teseida* autograph can see how he planned it, contrary to most
scribes with their *horror vacui*, so that each of the epic's twelve books heads
a page. Against the dark ink of text and glosses, multiple features collaborate to make a surface at once highly encoded and pleasing to behold. Each
double-faced view of the open codex is unique, with variables of rubrication, a Gothic hierarchy of initials alternating in red and blue, other letters
splashed with yellow, and distinctive offset paraphs (paragraph signs).[48]
His artistic talents supplement the text, guide the reader, and aesthetically
enliven the folio.

Dante, Petrarch, and Boccaccio all clearly appreciated art, but only the
Certaldan was himself an artist.[49] Of Dante, no autograph or art survives.
Petrarch, wealthy enough to purchase fine books, hire illuminators, and

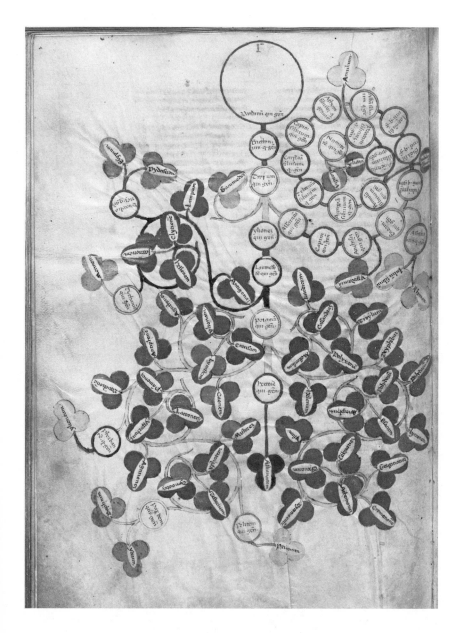

Fig. 11. Boccaccio, *Genealogia deorum gentilium*. Family tree of Dardanus. Florence, Biblioteca Medicea Laurenziana, MS Plut. 52.9, fol 65v. By permission of the Ministero per i Beni e le Attività Culturali. È vietata ogni ulteriore riproduzione con qualsiasi mezzo.

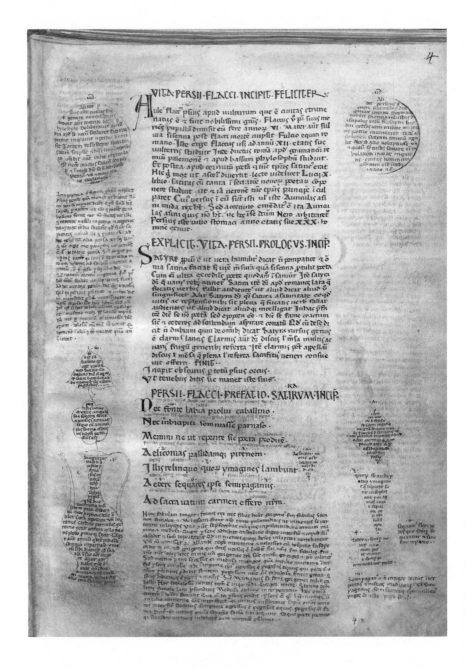

Fig. 12. Boccaccio, *Miscellanea laurenziana*. "Concrete" glosses. Florence, Biblioteca Medicea Laurenziana, MS Plut. 33.31, fol. 4r. By permission of the Ministero per i Beni e le Attività Culturali. È vietata ogni ulteriore riproduzione con qualsiasi mezzo.

own a *Madonna* by Giotto,[50] left copious annotations in his manuscripts as
well as occasional drawings, but their quality is far inferior to the finesse
of Boccaccio's figurative marginalia. Petrarch's manicules, for example,
sometimes displayed six or even seven fingers. Boccaccio's, emerging from
elegant buttoned cuffs, are so distinctive that they are like fingerprints telling us that he, too, seven hundred years ago, put his eyes and his hands on
a precious book. Not until the artist-poets of the Renaissance—men like
Michelangelo, Bronzino, and Cellini—can anyone in the Italian tradition
compare to Boccaccio, a poet-artist whose double talent created the patrimony that enshrines his cultural identity.

Appendix of Manuscripts: With Boccaccio's Drawings and Decorations*

1. Autographs
   Berlin, Staatsbibliothek der Stiftung Preussischer Kulturbesitz, MS
   Hamilton 90 (*Decameron*)
   Florence, Biblioteca Laurenziana, MS Plut. 29.8 (*Zibaldone Laurenziano*)
   Florence, Biblioteca Laurenziana, MS Plut. 33.31 (*Miscellanea
   Laurenziana*)
   Florence, Biblioteca Laurenziana, MS Plut. 38.17 (Terence)
   Florence, Biblioteca Laurenziana, MS Plut. 52.9 (*Genealogia deorum
   gentilium*)
   Florence, Biblioteca Laurenziana, MS Plut. 54.32 (Apuleius)
   Florence, Biblioteca Laurenziana, MS 90, sup. 98[1] (*De mulieribus claris*)
   Florence, Biblioteca Laurenziana, MS Acquisti e Doni 325 (*Teseida*)
   Florence, Biblioteca Laurenziana, MS Ashburnham App. 1856 (Trojan
   history)
   Florence, Biblioteca Nazionale, MS Banco Rari 50 (*Zibaldone Magliabe-
   chiano*)
   Florence, Biblioteca Riccardiana, MS 1035 (*Divina commedia* with seven
   images once attributed to Boccaccio, but perhaps by a fifteenth-
   century Venetian artist)
   Florence, Biblioteca Riccardiana, MS 1232 (*Buccolicum carmen*)
   Milan, Biblioteca Ambrosiana, MS 204 part. inf. (Aristotle's *Ethics* with
   commentary by Aquinas, the latter Boccaccio's autograph)
   Milan, Biblioteca Ambrosiana, MS C 67 sup. (Martial)
   Toledo, Archivo y Biblioteca Capitulares, MS Zelada 104.6 (*Trattatello*

in laude di Dante, Vita nuova, Commedia, Argomenti in terza rima, Quindici canzoni dantesche)
Vatican City, Biblioteca Apostolica Vaticana, MS Chig. 50.5.176 (*Vita di Dante, Vita nuova, canzoni*; Cavalcanti's "Donna me prega," Boccaccio's Latin poem "Ytalie iam certus honos," Petrarch's *Rerum vulgarium fragmenta*, Chigi form)

2. Manuscripts Not Autograph but with Traces of Boccaccio's Figural Intervention

Florence, Biblioteca Laurenziana, MS Plut. 29.2 (Apuleius)
Florence, Biblioteca Laurenziana, MS Plut. 34.39 (Juvenal)
Florence, Biblioteca Laurenziana, MS Plut. 34.49 (Boccaccio's *Buccolicum carmen* and *Epistle to Fra Martino* with suppositious self-portrait of Boccaccio reading his work to monks)
Florence, Biblioteca Laurenziana, MS Plut. 35.23 (Lucan)
Florence, Biblioteca Laurenziana, MS Plut. 38.6 (Statius)
Florence, Biblioteca Laurenziana, MS Plut. 66.1 (Josephus)
Florence, Biblioteca Riccardiana, MS 489 (Ovid)
Paris, Bibliothèque Nationale, MS ital. 482 (*Decameron* with complete cycle of illustrations whose attribution to Boccaccio is now questioned)
Paris, Bibliothèque Nationale, MS lat. 5150 (Historical miscellany)
Paris, Bibliothèque Nationale, MS lat. 6802 (Petrarch's Pliny)
Paris, Bibliothèque Nationale, MS lat. 8082 (Claudian)

*The most up-to-date and authoritative information on Boccaccio's autographs, which arrived as this volume was going to press, is the entry by Marco Cursi and Maurizio Fiorilla, "Giovanni Boccaccio," in *Autografi dei letterati italiani: Le origini e il Trecento*, ed. Giuseppina Brunetti, Maurizio Fiorilla, and Marco Petoletti (Rome: Salerno Editrice, 2013), 43–103.

CHAPTER TWENTY-NINE

AN INTIMATE SELF-PORTRAIT • *(Testamentum)*

Michael Papio

Although we know that Boccaccio prepared a will in 1365, that document is lost.[1] What does survive is his final will and testament, dated August 28, 1374. An Italian version of the latter appeared in a volume of commentary, *Annotazioni e discorsi sopra il "Decameron"* (*Annotations and Discourses on the "Decameron"*), prepared by the Deputati (Deputies), a committee of churchmen headed by Cardinal Vincenzo Borghini, who had been charged with expurgating the *Decameron* after the Council of Trent.[2] Borghini himself had conducted a lengthy search for the document, and the idea to print it was probably his. The book's editors, Filippo and Iacopo Giunti, whose colleague Giuliano Lapi had discovered it, claimed it as the original autograph. We do not know where it was when Lapi found it, but Giovambattista Ubaldini claimed to have read it in the Santo Spirito library, where it was shown to him by Giovanni Battista Deti (also known as *il Sollo*), one of the founding members of the Accademia della Crusca.[3] If this is true, we cannot discount the possibility that the Italian version was not an initial draft, but the transcription (albeit rather slapdash) that Boccaccio himself had ordered, together with the inventory of his books, for the benefit of the convent's friars.[4]

Similarly mysterious are the first two centuries or so of the official Latin version translated here.[5] By the sixteenth century, however, it was in the possession of Giovan Battista Muzzi (or Muti) of Poggibonsi, professor of theoretical medicine and philosophy at the University of Pisa from 1557 to 1581.[6] Muzzi, wishing to do Ippolito Agostini Balì of Caldana a favor, sent it to him in 1591 together with a dedicatory letter. According to Milanesi, the will and the letter remained among Agostini's possessions until his death, at which time they went to Agostini's daughter and sole heir, Anna Eleonora, who married Annibale di Rutilio Bichi. The will remained in the Bichi family's archive whence it was edited by Milanesi and published in

1853 with the patronage of Senator Scipione Borghesi Bichi.[7] Upon his death, it passed with the rest of the Bichi-Borghesi collection into Siena's Archivio di Stato, where it remains today.

Unlike that of his revered friend and teacher, Petrarch, Boccaccio's will offers relatively little insight into the personality of its author. Petrarch had used his last legal document as yet another opportunity to address subsequent generations and as a "final and truly unforgettable self-portrait according to the medieval model of *imitatio Christi*."[8] Boccaccio, however, clearly conceived of his last testament chiefly as a sober list of final instructions regarding the distribution of his belongings. If this list sheds less light than we would like on the literary personality of its author, it nonetheless does give important clues to our understanding of his final years and his Florentine circle. Its simplicity and the scarcity of possessions mentioned have long encouraged scholars to consider it evidence of Boccaccio's religious piety, a perspective advanced in order to combat the widely held opinion formed by readers of the *Decameron* that he was more ribald than reverent in his personal life. In fact, the *Deputati*'s *Annotationi* present the Italian version of the will to their readers so as to "wash away the stain [of being placed on the Index of Prohibited Books] from the memory of him" (purgare da questa macchia la memoria sua) and to demonstrate that he was "not only a faithful Catholic, but also very pious and religious" (non solo fedele & Cattolico: ma molto anchora pio & Religioso). Similarly, Aldus Manutius the Younger included it in its entirety in his 1583 commentary on Cicero's *De officiis* 3.10,[9] a chapter that contains reflections on one's obligations to friends.

Over four centuries removed from the initial printing of the Index and several generations from the last serious considerations of the will, we can now reflect in a presumably more objective manner on the limited data the will contains. In the course of the following translation, Manni's findings are supplemented with information that a modern reader of Boccaccio may wish to know in order to understand somewhat better the cultural climate in which his last will and testament took shape.[10]

In God's name, amen. During the twelfth indiction, according to the Florentine calendar and custom, and the time of Gregory XI, pope by divine providence, on the twenty-eighth day of the month of August, A.D. 1374. Completed in the church and parish of Santa Felicita in Florence, in the presence of Pazzino di Alessandro de' Bardi of the parish of Santa Maria Sopr'Arno in Florence, Angelo di Niccolò of the said parish of Santa Felicita, Andrea di Biancardo, Orlandino d'Iacopo, Burando di Ugolino, Francesco di

Tommaso, all of the said parish of Santa Felicita, and Brunellaccio Bianchini of the Florentine county of Certaldo, witnesses to the following who were each verbally called and requested by the undersigned testator to be present and to serve together with the others mentioned above.

The list of witnesses, perhaps not surprisingly, contains names of several people who have long since vanished into oblivion. Pazzino di Alessandro de' Bardi seems to have been a son of Alessandro, the famous banker, who was one of the Otto della Guerra (Commissioners of War), appointed in 1376, during the so-called Guerra degli Otto Santi (War of Eight Saints), and the father of Lorenzo de' Medici's paternal grandmother, Contessina de' Bardi. We do not know, though, if this Pazzino was the son of the same Alessandro who was likely the father of Franceschino de' Bardi to whom Boccaccio wrote the famous 1339 letter containing a page of Neapolitan. There is a letter from Guidetti Orlandino di Iacopo in the Datini archives in Prato dated 1392, but no demonstrable connection between him and this Orlandino d'Iacopo. Francesco di Tommaso has not been definitively identified, in part because there were very many men with this name, even one among the Bardi family.

Whereas nothing is more certain than death and more uncertain than the hour of that death, and whereas, as attested to by truth, it is necessary to remain vigilant, insofar as we know neither the day nor the hour at which a man shall die, the venerable and distinguished gentleman Giovanni son of the late Boccaccio of Certaldo in the Val d'Elsa, being of sound mind, body, and intellect, therefore arranged through the present nuncupative testament, and not otherwise in writing, for the distribution of his belongings in the following manner.

To wit, first commending his soul to God Almighty and to Holy Mary ever the Glorious Virgin, the testator has chosen for the burial place of his body, should he die in the city of Florence, the Church of Santo Spirito of the Order of Eremite Friars of St. Augustine in such a place as seems fitting to the venerable master Martino, Master in Sacred Theology, who is a member of the said Order. Should it happen that he die in the castle of Certaldo, he has requested that his body be buried in the Church of San Iacopo in Certaldo in such a place as seems fitting to his townsmen and neighbors.

The first paragraph here contains standard testamentary language. The second, however, includes a reference of particular importance. Friar Martino da Signa (d. 1387) was best known as the addressee of Boccaccio's

Epistle 23, which contains a series of self-glosses on the pastoral poems, and as the recipient of Boccaccio's library, discussed below. Though much work remains to be done on the relationship between the two men, it is generally recognized that Martino was a significant link between Boccaccio and the Augustinian order, an affinity shared by Petrarch as well. Some scholars underscore Martino's role in establishing at Santo Spirito the group of Plato students that, under the direction of Luigi Marsili, would become a jewel in Florence's Quattrocento crown.[11]

> *To wit, he bequeaths to the Church of Santa Maria Reparata of Florence ten soldi in small florins.*
>
> *To wit, he bequeaths to the construction of the city walls of Florence ten soldi in small florins.*
>
> *To wit, he bequeaths to the Compagnia di Santa Maria of Certaldo five lire in small florins.*
>
> *To wit, he bequeaths to the construction of the church, or Opera di San Iacopo, of Certaldo ten lire in small florins for the relief of his soul and that of his relatives.*

This section deals quickly and efficiently with Boccaccio's civic obligations. Indeed, the bequeathal to Santa Maria Reparata, required of all Florentines, may have been viewed as a sort of tax.[12] At any rate, these bequests demonstrate Boccaccio's shared allegiance to Florence and Certaldo, inasmuch as donations of this type were very much expected from someone of Boccaccio's status. That said, we should not disregard the sincerity of Boccaccio's pious commitment to his parish, in which he was buried.[13]

> *To wit, he bequeaths to Bruna, daughter of Cianco da Montemagno, who has long dwelled with him, the bed in which she normally slept while at the Castle of Certaldo, with bedding, blanket, down bolster, a small white blanket to be used with the said bed, a set of sheets, and the bench that normally stood alongside the said bed.*
>
> *Also, a small walnut table for eating on and two ordinary shelves three braccia in length for general use.[14]*
>
> *Also, two small tablecloths.*
>
> *Also, a flask that holds three draughts of wine.*
>
> *Also, a dress of reddish brown cloth with purple sendal lining, a matching tunic and robe, and a hood, and to the same Bruna the remainder of what is owed of her salary by the testator.*

We know very little about this Bruna, and even less about her father. She is apparently the servant girl (*ancillula*) mentioned in Boccaccio's 1372 letter to Mainardo Cavalcanti (Epis. 21.19).[15] Pier Giorgio Ricci notes that the Latin name Fusca (of *Buccolicum carmen* 14.51) translates the Italian Bruna, and both could be one and the same, but there is no proof.[16] She was not his "wife," as claimed recently by David Slavitt.[17] In fact, both the Giunti Italian version and the Latin version specifically note that, in the event of Boccaccio's death, Bruna's salary is to be paid off.

To wit, he commits, disposes, transmits, and bequeaths to all and each man and person listed in a certain register of his labeled "A" who are due to receive or possess anything of the said testator and to all others who legitimately demonstrate that they are due something despite not being listed in said register whatever is required to satisfy their claims, by way of his executors herein undersigned, to be taken from the property, belongings, and goods of the said testator, with the exception of the said testator's books, and especially from the house located in Certaldo, which is bounded on the first side by the street called Borgo, on the second by the property of Fornaino di Andrea di ser Bengo de' Rossi, on the third by Via Nuova, and on the fourth by another property owned by the said testator that is to be sold by his executors, or the majority of them, and, if that is not sufficient, they may also sell other belongings of his.

To wit, he bequeaths to the venerable Friar Martino da Signa, Master in Sacred Theology, of the Convent of Santo Spirito of the Order of Eremites of St. Augustine, all his books, with the exception of the testator's breviary, on the condition that the said Master Martino may, for as long as he shall live, use the said books and provide a copy of them to whoever desires one. In exchange for this, he shall be required to pray to God for the soul of the said testator and, upon his death, he shall be required to bequeath to the Convent of the Friars of Santo Spirito the said books, which must, without reduction in their number, be placed within a cabinet in the said place and remain there in perpetuity so that anyone of the said convent may read and study the said books. There in that place, they shall have the style and form of the present testament transcribed and an inventory made of the said books.

The short paragraph related to the bequeathal of Boccaccio's books is without doubt the single most important section of his will. One of the first bits we have regarding it comes from Niccolò Niccoli (1363–1437), humanist book hunter and friend of Poggio Bracciolini, who paid for bookshelves to be set up in Santo Spirito so that these volumes could be removed from the cabinet (*armarium*) mentioned here.[18] It was believed for some time that the fire that engulfed a large portion of the convent in 1470 or 1471 (depending on who tells the story) had destroyed what remained of the library, a notion corrected by Adolfo Gaspary and others.[19] Because of the inherent importance of knowing which texts Boccaccio possessed, there have been several attempts to reconstruct this library. The most authoritative is that of Antonia Mazza, whose conclusions have clarified several uncertainties in previous studies.[20] Shortly after Boccaccio's passing, it became clear that the *Esposizioni*, being contained not in a single volume but in twenty-four notebooks and fourteen notepads, was not easily identifiable by the phrase "all his books" (*omnes suos libros*). There then arose a legal dispute between Fra Martino and Boccaccio's half brother Iacopo, inasmuch as each claimed a right to this unfinished work. The text remained in the possession of one of the other executors, Francesco di Lapo Bonamichi, until the final judgment was passed in court. The man who handed down the verdict, Parente di Corrado da Prato, decided in favor of Iacopo, who was supported in the suit by both Barduccio di Cherichino and Agnolo di Torino Bencivenni.[21]

> To wit, he bequeaths and orders that his undersigned executors, or the majority of those who are surviving, donate and deliver to the Monastery of the Friars of Santa Maria del Santo Sepolcro del Poggetto or della Campora outside Florence's city walls each and every one of the holy relics that said Giovanni managed to obtain, over a long period of time and with great effort, from different parts of the world.
>
> To wit, he bequeaths to the members of the Opera of the Church of San Iacopo of Certaldo, who shall receive them on behalf of the church, one alabaster tablet of the Virgin Mary, one chasuble with a stole and maniple of red sendal, one small altar cloth of red fabric together with an altar cushion and three corporal burses.
>
> Also, a tin container for holding holy water.
>
> Also, a small cloth made of fabric lined with yellow sendal lining.[22]
>
> To wit, he bequeaths to Sandra, wife of Francesco di Lapo Bonamichi, a small panel on which is painted the image of the Virgin Mary with her Son in her arms and, on the other side, the skull of a dead man.

After the brief lines regarding Boccaccio's library, this next series of bequeathals has drawn the most attention on account of its undeniably religious content. Any serious consideration of this passage must inevitably take into account Giuseppe Billanovich's study entitled "Il Chierico Giovanni Boccaccio,"[23] in which he suggests that these objects were not simply "pious possessions" but had served him frequently in his capacity as cleric. Though too much has perhaps been made of Boccaccio's religious inquietude addressed in Petrarch's uplifting humanistic epistle to his friend (*Seniles* 1.5), it is certain that our modern lay attitudes do us a disservice in assessing the precise importance of these articles. The Church of Santa Maria del Santo Sepolcro (deconsecrated in 1434 and now known as the Villa del Corona) was constructed on the Colombaia ridge just south of Florence in 1348, and its adjacent monastery was finished two years later. The church's origins are tied to a Pistoian hermit named Bartolommeo di Bonone who, having formed a small group of like-minded followers, obtained permission in 1334 from Cardinal Giovanni di Gaetano Orsini, Apostolic Legate to Tuscany, to form there an Augustinian order. In November 1372, less than two years before Boccaccio wrote his testament, a certain Alfonso Fernández, once bishop of Jaén, successfully appealed to Pope Gregory XI to be allowed to form within that tiny community an order dedicated to Saint Jerome. In November 1373, the order of Hieronymite friars was born.[24] Since the relatively new Augustinian church benefited between 1372 and 1375 from a remarkable outpouring of support from several Florentines, including numerous gifts and bequeathals, it should not surprise us that Boccaccio chose the order as an appropriate destination for his relics.[25] We know very little about this Sandra, however.[26]

Additionally, with regard to all his other assets present and future, movable and immovable, the testator establishes as his sole heirs in equal measure his nephews Boccaccio and Antonio, sons of Iacopo of the aforementioned Boccaccio of Certaldo, and all other children, male and female, now alive or yet to be born, of said Iacopo by the legitimate wife of said Iacopo, who shall share his inheritance equally, on the condition that the profits and the revenues from the belongings of the said testator be brought into the house of said Iacopo, in the quantity that said Iacopo desires, so that he may be able to support himself and his wife and the children whom he has at that time and, furthermore, on the condition that his above-mentioned heirs are not able, do not attempt, and do not presume, directly or indirectly, tacitly or expressly, to sell or alienate the said testator's belongings until they have reached thirty years of age, and then only with the consent of said Iacopo, their father, if he is living, except in those cases in which they wish to provide a dowry for one or more of their sisters and wherein they shall first receive permission from their undersigned guardians.

Similarly, he has stipulated that his heirs designated below shall not at any time, for as long as there are found to be existing descendants of Boc-

caccio di Chelino, the father of the said testator and of said Iacopo in the male line, even should such descendants be illegitimate, be able, attempt, or presume to sell or alienate the house of the said testator, which is located in the parish of San Iacopo in Certaldo and is bounded on the first side by the public street called Borgo, on the second by the property of the said testator, on the third by Via Nuova, and on the fourth by the property of Guido di Giovanni Machiavelli.

Also, a piece of arable land partially planted with vines, situated in the commune of Certaldo in the said parish of San Iacopo in a place called the Valle Lizia, bounded first by il Fossato, second by the property of the said testator and that of Niccolò Rustichelli, third by that of the said testator, and fourth by that of Andrea, also known as Migliotto.

A reasonably good amount of information has been discovered regarding Boccaccio and his relationship with his half brother Iacopo, Boccaccio di Chelino's only legitimate child.[27] Iacopo's first wife, Diana, died before having any children. Iacopo's second wife, Piera, had come to the marriage with a significant dowry, but we do not know from which family. Bice, the couple's first child, was initially named after Boccaccio's stepmother, Bice di Ubaldino di Nepo dei Bosticchi, but she came to be known as Piera after her mother's death. She was certainly the niece Boccaccio had in mind when he makes reference here to a dowry, but she died in 1383, apparently before marrying. Iacopo's third wife, Bianca (daughter of Geri di Simone Donati),[28] gave Iacopo three children: Boccaccio and Antonio, who were both young children at the time of Boccaccio's death, and Giovanni, born only months after the completion of this will, who was named after our author.[29] Sometime shortly after 1384, Bianca and her three children all died. Iacopo then married Taddea (daughter of Giovanni di Arrigo Sassolini), who gave him two children, Taddea and Giovanni (nicknamed Vanni),[30] before her own early death. With his fifth and final wife, Filippa, Iacopo had no children before his death in 1391. These two remaining children are listed as his sole heirs by Iacopo in his testament of 1384.

We know that Boccaccio's father possessed several properties in and around Certaldo.[31] The property mentioned here, which is now the location of the Ente Nazionale Giovanni Boccaccio, is the more important of two adjacent houses belonging to Boccaccio in the center of Certaldo and was closer to the church in which he was buried. The second, which stood alongside that of the de' Rossi family, is listed above. These two neighboring lots were still listed in the 1384 last will and testament of Iacopo Boccaccio.[32] In the Olivetan documents published by Domenico Tordi, however, we discover that Iacopo had, contrary to his brother's wishes, already sold both houses by 1391.[33] There is ample evidence to suggest that Iacopo was a poor money manager throughout his life. Indeed, it may well be on account of this that Boccaccio left his properties directly to his nephews and not to his brother, a strategy that was not ultimately successful. It seems that the agricultural property listed here did in fact remain in the family until Iacopo's death.[34]

Though not required to do so by law, the testator appoints, assigns, and commits to have as the tutors or guardians of the said heirs Boccaccio and Antonio: Iacopo di Lapo Gavacciani, Piero di Dato de' Canigiani, Barduccio di Cherichino, Francesco di Lapo Bonamichi, Lionardo di Chiaro di Messer dalle Botte, Iacopo di Boccaccio, and Agnolo di Torino Bencivenni, Florentine citizens, and [should some of them die] the majority among them who shall still be living.

Additionally, he appoints, assigns, and commits to have as executors of the said last will and testament: the aforementioned Friar Martino da Signa, Barduccio di Cherichino, Francesco di Lapo Bonamichi, Agnolo di Torino Bencivenni, and Iacopo di Boccaccio, Florentine citizens, and [should some of them die] the majority among them who shall still be living. The said testator hereby gives and concedes to his said executors and the majority among them, above-mentioned items notwithstanding, full authority and unrestricted power over the belongings of the said testator to carry out the realization and fulfillment of his bequeathals through the sale and alienation of the belongings of the said testator and to receive payment for them, to enter into agreements in their regard, to issue quitclaims for them and assure through the eviction thereof the deed and the physical possession of the property to be sold, to surrender the rights of sale and alienation pursuant thereto, to request and accept any sum of money in exchange for its sale and quittance and, if necessary, to testify in its regard as plaintiff or defendant in the presence of any witness whatsoever, and to engage in or initiate all other legal actions in his name, and, should it be ordered by the court, to do everything that is appropriate with regard to the foregoing.

The testator has affirmed that this is his last will and has stipulated that it serve legally as his testament, which, if it otherwise did not, or will not, serve as his testament, indeed would or will henceforth serve as such. Additionally, he has commanded that the foregoing so serve as his official testament and has stipulated that this testament substitute by codicillary right any and all other last wills whatsoever and be held to prevail over them, annulling, overturning, and rescinding all other last wills and testaments hitherto prepared by the testator, regardless of any other contrary statement or statements contained therein, which the same testator hereby declares withdrawn. Additionally, he has ordered that the present last will and testament prevail over any other testaments hitherto prepared by him, and that this testament may now and in the future be held to serve better and more greatly in that function.

I, Tinello son of the late messer Bonasera of Passignano, Florentine citizen, ordinary judge by imperial authority and notary public, was present during the elaboration of all the foregoing statements and was engaged in that capacity to record and register them, in faith of which I hereby sign.

The assignment of guardians for his nephews is perhaps most interesting because it gives us an idea not only of Boccaccio's sense of familial responsibility but also of the social status of his immediate circle in Florence.[35] Iacopo di Lapo Gavacciani was the son of Lapo di Giovanni Gavacciani, one of the priors of Florence in 1327–28 and 1333–34.[36] In 1335 Lapo founded the Spedale e Oratorio di Santa Maria a Malavolta and, after his death in 1338, was buried in Santo Spirito.[37] Because Iacopo died without children, his property was added to the rest of his belongings, which were split upon his death in 1376 between the Compagnia di Santa Maria del Bigallo and the Oratorio di Orsanmichele. Iacopo was the Florentine vicar in Pescia in 1369 when Charles IV entered Italy and *podestà* of Pistoia in 1375. He was again Florentine vicar in Pescia when he died in 1376.[38] Piero di Dato de' Canigiani, onetime friend and ally of Niccola Acciaiuoli, was Florentine ambassador to Faenza and was the man charged with delivering a message of congratulations to Bernabò Visconti in 1365, when the latter's son Ambrogio was elected "capitano generale del banco [mercenary army] di San Giorgio di Genova" (an event he had foreseen months earlier when the idea of not rehiring the English mercenaries had first been debated in Florence).[39] Piero was *podestà* of San Gimignano in 1366 and again, with Giovanni di Lerisio de' Mozzi, in 1377, in addition to being a prior in Florence at least twice, in 1356 and 1363.[40] During the winter of 1377–78, Piero was one of the most encouraging supporters of Catherine of Siena's visit to Florence. He even contributed materials to the construction of her house in Florence. His house and that of his son Ristoro (who fled Florence during the plague of 1363, bound for Bologna, where he wrote *Il ristorato*) were burned during the Ciompi revolt in the summer of 1378, after which he was stripped of privileges and fined 2,000 florins.[41] He appears in *Decameron* 8.10 and as "Pietro da Lucanajano" in Boccaccio's Neapolitan dialect letter to Franceschino de' Bardi. Barduccio di Cherichino, a banker and statesman from the Santo Spirito parish, was *gonfaloniere della giustizia* in

1410 and 1413. He died in 1416 and was buried in the Church of Santa Felicita, where Boccaccio's testament was signed. Lionardo di Chiaro was the same hometown friend to whom Boccaccio wrote while the former was working as a banker in Avignon.[42] Agnolo di Torino Bencivenni was a poet, a compiler, and the author of religious texts.[43] Among his works are a 1342 poem intended to instruct Walter of Brienne, the Duke of Athens, on the proper modes of government (and another shortly thereafter expressing disappointment), the *Brieve meditazione sui beneficii di Dio*, and the *Trattato della miseria dell'umana condizione*. Described by one of his editors as a man of "exemplary life and the severest of habits,"[44] he has long enjoyed the reputation of being an austere character who was rather more talented as a moralist than as a writer. He enjoyed the company of such men as Luigi Marsili, Giovanni dalle Celle, Carlo di Battifolle, and, of course, Giovanni Boccaccio.[45] In short, Boccaccio, despite his poverty, seems to have had among his close friends several who were wealthy and influential.

What emerges, then, from this brief legal document is a snapshot of Giovanni Boccaccio's life sixteen months before his death on December 21, 1375. Having left behind the experiment of the *Esposizioni* approximately seven months earlier and having already suffered through two serious periods of ill health, he may have been moved to write his last testament by the news of Petrarch's death in August 1374.[46] In Boccaccio's subsequent letter of November 3 to Francescuolo da Brossano, he describes his deteriorating physical condition with forlorn hopelessness. By then he had already traveled back to Certaldo with the help of friends and knew, no doubt, that the end was near. We can imagine him during his last days in his sparsely furnished home on Via Borgo (now Via Boccaccio), attended by Bruna, his servant girl, and perhaps also by his brother, absorbed in thought and prayer when not distracted by his maladies. Though such a conclusion may seem quite sad, we can console ourselves with some of the same words Boccaccio himself wrote to Francescuolo da Brossano in the wake of Petrarch's passing: "He did what all of us, who are born to die, shall do. He did not simply die, but preceded us" on our final journey.[47]

NOTES

Introduction

1. Petrarch in *Seniles* 5.2.32 chides Boccaccio for his discontent with being third but also reinforces the idea: "I hear that that old man of Ravenna, who is not a bad judge of such matters, whenever he speaks of these always assigns you third place." *Res Seniles, Libri V-VIII*, ed. Silvia Rizzo (Florence: Casa Editrice Le Lettere, 2009), my trans. Giorgio Vasari's "Portrait of Six Tuscan Poets" similarly places Boccaccio behind Dante and Petrarch, though more central than the remaining three poets. See also Boccaccio, *Buccolicum carmen*, XII "Saphos"; and the end of this introduction. See also Jonathan Usher, "'Sesto tra cotanto senno' and *appetentia primi loci*: Boccaccio, Petrarch, and Dante's Poetic Hierarchy," *Studi sul Boccaccio* 35 (2007): 157–98. Victoria Kirkham, in "Le tre corone e l'iconografia del Boccaccio," forthcoming in proceedings of the international conference sponsored by the Ente Nazionale Giovanni Boccaccio, *Boccaccio letterato (Firenze-Certaldo 10–12 ottobre 2013)*, demonstrates Boccaccio's presence in verbal and visual canons from the fourteenth century through the Renaissance.

2. *Petrarch: A Critical Guide to the Complete Works*, ed. Victoria Kirkham and Armando Maggi (Chicago: University of Chicago Press, 2009).

3. See esp. Giorgio Padoan, "Giovanni Boccaccio e la rinascita dello stile bucolico," in *Il Boccaccio, le Muse, il Parnaso e l'Arno* (Florence: Olschki, 1978), 151–98.

4. Epis. 22.19–24.

5. Christine de Pizan drew from both the *De mulieribus claris* and the *Decameron* for her *Book of the City of Ladies*; the *Decameron* also inspired both Moderata Fonte and Marguerite de Navarre to gather a group of or including women for discussions; Helisenne de Crenne looked to the *Elegia di madonna Fiammetta* for her first-person narrative of illicit love. See Janet Smarr, "Boccaccio and Renaissance Women Writers," *Studi sul Boccaccio* 20 (1991–92): 279–97.

6. The translation is from Francesco Petrarca, *Letters on Familiar Matters: Rerum familiarium libri XVII-XXIV*, trans. Aldo S. Bernardo (Baltimore: Johns Hopkins University Press, 1985), 202.

7. See Jason M. Houston, *Building a Monument to Dante: Boccaccio as Dantista* (Toronto: University of Toronto Press, 2010).

8. The "Argomenti e rubriche dantesche" are edited with an introduction by

Giorgio Padoan, in *Tutte le opere di Giovanni Boccaccio*, ed. Vittore Branca, vol. 5, pt. 1 (Milan: Mondadori, 1992), 145–92.

9. Padoan, in Branca, *Tutte le opere*, vol. 5, pt. 1, pp. 147–48, 152, 153.

10. *Genealogia* 15.7; cited from the translation of Charles Osgood, in *Boccaccio on Poetry* (Indianapolis: Bobbs-Merrill, 1956), 119.

11. *Rerum familiarum libri* 21.15. The classic essay on Petrarch's views on Dante is Aldo Bernardo, "Petrarch's Attitude toward Dante," *PMLA* 70 (1955): 488–517. The issue has since been much enriched and complicated: see Zygmunt G. Barański and Theodore J. Cachey Jr., eds., *Petrarch & Dante: Anti-Dantism, Metaphysics, Tradition* (Notre Dame, IN: University of Notre Dame Press, 2009), esp. the long bibliography at 93–94 n. 1.

12. See, for example, Vittorio Zaccaria, *Boccaccio narratore, storico, moralista e mitografo* (Florence: Olschki, 2001); Elsa Filosa, "Intertestualità tra *Decameron* e *De mulieribus claris*: La tragica storia di Tisbe e Piramo," *Heliotropia* 3.1–2 (2005–6); and Filosa, *Tre studi sul "De mulieribus claris"* (Milan: Edizioni Universitarie di Lettere Economia Diritto, 2012), "I rapporti con il *Decameron*," 89–140.

13. Millicent Marcus, "Pseudo-Saints and Storytellers," in *An Allegory of Form: Literary Self Consciousness in the "Decameron,"* Stanford French and Italian Studies 18 (Saratoga, CA: Anma Libri, 1979), 11–26.

14. Lucia Battaglia Ricci, "*Decameron*: Interferenze di modelli," in *Autori e lettori di Boccaccio: Atti del Convegno internazionale di Certaldo (20–22 settembre 2001)*, ed. Michelangelo Picone (Florence: Franco Cesati Editore, 2002), esp. 180.

15. For a discussion of the dating, see Vittore Branca, *Boccaccio: The Man and His Works*, trans. Richard Monges (New York: New York University Press, 1976), 10–12.

16. Trans. Osgood, in *Boccaccio on Poetry*, 131–32.

17. See, for example, Steven Grossvogel, *Ambiguity and Allusion in Boccaccio's "Filocolo"* (Florence: Olschki, 1992), 31, 132–39; Victoria Kirkham, *The Sign of Reason in Boccaccio's Fiction* (Florence: Olschki, 1993), esp. 11–12. Ambrosiana codex A 204 is a Latin text of Aristotle's *Ethics* with Boccaccio's transcription of Aquinas's gloss. See also Francesco Bausi, "Gli spiriti magni: Filigrane aristoteliche e tomistiche nella decima giornata del *Decameron*," *Studi sul Boccaccio* 27 (1999): 205–53.

18. For tributes to these men, see *Genealogia* 14.8 and 15.6; for Dionigi, Epis. 5.

19. Boccaccio cites and praises him repeatedly in the *Genealogia*, from its preface to its last books.

20. See also note 35.

21. *Filocolo* 5.97.4–6.

22. For a review of the debate concerning Boccaccio's relation to the origins of

the *ottava*, a form he had used already in the *Filostrato*, see Armando Balduino, *Boccaccio, Petrarca e altri poeti del Trecento* (Florence: Olschki, 1984), 88–92 and 93–140; and David Wallace's comments in this volume.

23. On Boccaccio's classical studies and attempts to recreate classical culture, see James McGregor, "Boccaccio's Athenian Theater: Form and Function of an Ancient Monument in *Teseida*," *MLN* 99 (1984): 1–42; and McGregor, *The Image of Antiquity in Boccaccio's "Filocolo," "Filostrato," and "Teseida,"* Studies in Italian Culture 1 (New York: Peter Lang, 1991).

24. Robert Hollander, "The Validity of Boccaccio's Self-Exegesis in His *Teseida*," *Medievalia et Humanistica* n.s. 8 (1977): 164 and 168, suggests that Boccaccio produced the text with a gloss to make it look like an "instant classic."

25. Vittore Branca, introduction to the *Amorosa Visione*, in Branca, ed., *Tutte le opere*, vol. 3 (Milan: Mondadori, 1974), 4; Branca, *Boccaccio*, 59.

26. Branca, *Boccaccio*, 50–52, 54.

27. See also the *Elegia di madonna Fiammetta*, 2.6.20–21, where she cites Panfilo's criticisms of the Florence to which he must return, in contrast to the positive qualities of Naples.

28. Branca, *Boccaccio*, 71.

29. In imitation of Virgil's alternating eclogue forms, one is a dialogue and one a monologue.

30. King Louis of Hungary sought justice for the suspicious death of his brother Andrew, the husband of King Robert's granddaughter and heir, Queen Joan.

31. Branca, *Boccaccio*, 68.

32. In a prologue by Domenico Bruni, cited in Robert Henke, *Performance and Literature in the Commedia dell'Arte* (Cambridge: Cambridge University Press, 2002), 46–47, the prima donna of a *commedia* company calls for a copy of "Boccaccio's *Fiammetta*" to study.

33. *Genealogia* 14.10, trans. Osgood, in *Boccaccio on Poetry*, 54.

34. Boccaccio lists these invitations, including Petrarch's, in his response to Orsini's offer, Epis. 18.

35. His long letter to Francesco Nelli, Epis. 13, bitterly describes this sojourn in Naples during the fall and winter of 1362–63, which ended after six months with Boccaccio's irate departure. It was, he laments, the second time he had believed the false promises of Niccola Acciaiuoli, having been previously disappointed by an invitation to Naples in 1355. At last, in 1363, Boccaccio renounced this dream for good.

36. Epis. 18 and 19.

37. *Vita sanctissimi patris Petri Damiani heremite* 4.1 and 6.2; edited, annotated, and translated into Italian by Renata Fabbri, in Boccaccio, *Tutte le opere*, vol. 5, pt. 1, pp. 889–93 and 912–37. The only surviving manuscript, which is not an

autograph and breaks off after the incipit of chapter 14, is in Modena, Biblioteca Estense, α R 6.7 (lat. 630, formerly IV D 26). And see Susanna Barsella,
"Boccaccio, Petrarch, and Peter Damian: Two Models of the Humanist Intellectual," *MLN* 121 (2006): 16–48.

38. Franco Sacchetti, *Rime*, sonnet 181: "Or è mancata ogni poesia / e vòte son le
case di Parnaso," in *Il libro delle Rime*, ed. Franca Brambilla Ageno (Florence:
Olschki, 1990), 255–60.

39. Branca, *Boccaccio*, 111, 119, and 125; Giuseppe Billanovich, "Il chierico Giovanni Boccaccio," in *Restauri boccacceschi* (Rome: Edizioni di Storia e Letteratura, 1947), 167–80.

40. Kirkham and Maggi, *Petrarch*, 1–2, 8.

41. *Seniles* 5.2.5.

42. Epis. 19.38–39, my trans.

Chapter One

1. Boccaccio, *Decameron*, ed. Vittore Branca, in *Tutte le opere*, vol. 4 (Milan:
Mondadori, 1976), Proem, 1: "cento novelle in diece dì dette da sette donne e
da tre giovani uomini." Although a half century later, Franco Sacchetti could
refer to it as "a coarse thing"—see his *Il trecentonovelle*, ed. Antonio Lanza
(Florence: Sansoni, 1993), 1—the sixteenth century proclaimed it the sole
standard of prose style in Italian, and in spite of bowdlerizations imposed by
the Catholic Reformation, the book inspired a multitude of early modern imi-
tators. For more on the book's fortunes, see the essay in this volume by Brian
Richardson. There are brief accounts of the *Decameron* by Pamela Stewart
in the *Cambridge History of Italian Literature*, ed. Peter Brand and Lino Pertile
(Cambridge: Cambridge University Press, 1999), 76–85; and by Victoria
Kirkham, in the *Encyclopedia of Italian Literary Studies*, ed. Gaetana Marrone
(New York: Routledge, 2007), 1:247–52; see also David Wallace, *Boccac-
cio's "Decameron,"* Landmarks of World Literature (Cambridge: Cambridge
University Press, 1991). Among influential studies of the work in English
are Guido Almansi, *The Writer as Liar: Narrative Technique in the "Decameron"*
(London: Routledge & Kegan Paul, 1975); Millicent Joy Marcus, *An Allegory
of Form: Literary Self-Consciousness in the "Decameron"* (Stanford, CA: ANMA
Libri, 1979); and Giuseppe Mazzotta, *The World at Play in Boccaccio's "Decameron"* (Princeton, NJ: Princeton University Press, 1986); see also the works
mentioned in notes 4, 5, and 18.

2. See, e.g., *Decameron* 5.3 for Ovid's *Metamorphoses*; 5.6 for the *Heroides*; 5.10
and 7.2 for Apuleius; 3.10 and 4, Intro., 13 for hagiographic models; 7.4 for
The Scholar's Guide; 3.8 for the *fabliaux*; 5.1 for the romance; 4.1 and 4.2 for
Marie's *lais*; and 1.3 for the *Novellino*. Branca's edition reports sources for

individual *novelle*; recent work has added and reexamined many attributions: see Michelangelo Picone, *Boccaccio e la codificazione della novella: Letture del "Decameron"* (Ravenna: Longo, 2008); and Michelangelo Picone and Margherita Mesirca, eds., *Introduzione al "Decameron"* (Florence: Franco Cesati, 2004). See also Costanzo Di Girolamo and Charmaine Lee, "Fonti," in *Lessico critico decameroniano*, ed. Renzo Bragantini and Pier Massimo Forni (Milan: Bollati Boringhieri, 1995), 142–62. Simone Marchesi's *Stratigrafie decameroniane* (Florence: Olschki, 2004) explores Boccaccio's use of classical (Livy, Horace) and scriptural sources.

3. *Decameron* 10.4 and 10.5, the tales of Gentil de' Carisendi and Madonna Dianora.

4. For the relation of early works to the *Decameron*, see especially Janet L. Smarr, *Boccaccio and Fiammetta: The Narrator as Lover* (Urbana: University of Illinois Press, 1986); and Victoria Kirkham, *The Sign of Reason in Boccaccio's Fiction* (Florence: Olschki, 1993), esp. 17–116.

5. This is the Hamilton 90 autograph (another authorial redaction is known, MS ital. 482, Bibliothèque Nationale, Paris). For the text, see Richardson in this volume, and for the early copies and copyists, Rhiannon Daniels, *Boccaccio and the Book: Production and Reading in Italy, 1340–1520* (London: Modern Humanities Research Association and Maney Publishing, 2009); also Lucia Battaglia Ricci, *Boccaccio* (Rome: Salerno, 2000), 122–28.

6. Boccaccio also mentions Cavalcanti and Dante in *Decameron* 4, Intro., 33–34; and see the Author's Concl., 6, comparing his own artistic license to that of painters. Dante anticipated these matters by discussing poets, fresco painters, and manuscript illuminators in *Purgatorio* 11.79–108. Cf. Paul F. Watson, "The Cement of Fiction: Giovanni Boccaccio and the Painters of Florence," *MLN* 99 (1984): 43–64.

7. Boccaccio was aware of Petrarch's lyric collection well before 1350, when the two met; Branca notes that the opening lines of the Proem resemble the opening of the first sonnet in the *Rerum vulgarium fragmenta*. Petrarch disparages vernacular writing in *Familiares* 21.15 and *Seniles* 17.3–4, although in *Seniles* 5.2 he grants Boccaccio second place among Italian poets. See Jonathan Usher, "'Sesto tra cotanto senno' and *appetentia primi loci*: Boccaccio, Petrarch, and Dante's Poetic Hierarchy," *Studi sul Boccaccio* 35 (2007): 157–98.

8. The formula "creatural realism" is Erich Auerbach's term for Dante's representational mode in the *Commedia*. See Auerbach's essay "Frate Alberto," in *Mimesis: The Representation of Reality in Western Literature*, trans. Willard Trask (New York: Doubleday, 1957), 177–203. Notoriously, Auerbach's reading of *Decameron* 4.2 denies that Boccaccio adopted this same mode, and underestimates the work's seriousness. For a partial critique, see Albert R. Ascoli,

"Auerbach fra gli epicurei: Dal Canto X dell'*Inferno* alla VI giornata del *Decameron*," *Moderna* 11 (2009): 135–52.

9. Branca's emphasis on amateur copyists from mercantile social groups as the core of Boccaccio's early audience has now been qualified. Early copies of the *Decameron* represent mercantile and professional (or learned) copyists and readers equally. See Daniels, *Boccaccio and the Book*, 172–77.

10. Boccaccio's prose adopts the *cursus*, the system of accentual patterns used in medieval Latin epistolography for concluding phrases in periodic sentences; clauses also often fall into an eleven-syllable rhythmic scheme, after the standard measure of Italian narrative verse—all untranslatable effects.

11. *Decameron* 4, Intro., 3: "umilissimo e rimesso quanto il più si possono." Auerbach's discussion of Boccaccio's style in "Frate Alberto" remains indispensable.

12. See Alberto Asor Rosa, "*Decameron* di Giovanni Boccaccio," in *Letteratura Italiana: Le opere*, vol. 1, *Dalle origini al Cinquecento* (Milan: Einaudi, 1992), 579–83.

13. See Mazzotta, *World at Play*, 105–30.

14. Cyprus, Venus's birthplace figures in five *novelle* and is mentioned twenty-six times in all, as if the island were the erotic axis of the sea (fourteen uses are in the story of Alatiel, 2.7).

15. For the geography and history of the tales, see Asor Rosa, "*Decameron*," 545–48, 551–52. See also Roberta Morosini, ed., *Boccaccio geografo: Un viaggio nel Mediterraneo tra le citta, i giardini e . . . il 'mondo' di Giovanni Boccaccio* (Florence: Mario Paglia, 2010), with contributions by nine scholars.

16. See Michelangelo Picone, "The Tale of Bergamino (I.7)," in *The "Decameron" First Day in Perspective*, ed. Elissa B. Weaver (Toronto: University of Toronto Press, 2004), 165.

17. See Jonathan Usher, "Le rubriche del *Decameron*," *Medioevo Romanzo* 10 (1985): 392–418, esp. 412–17.

18. On the frame narrative, see Joy Potter, *Five Frames for the "Decameron": Communicative and Social Systems in the Cornice* (Princeton, NJ: Princeton University Press, 1982); Kirkham, "An Allegorically Tempered *Decameron*," in *Sign of Reason*, 131–72; Asor Rosa, "*Decameron*," 492–509; Franco Fido, "Architettura," in Bragantini and Forni, *Lessico critico*, 13–33; Battaglia Ricci, *Boccaccio*, 141–61; and Michelangelo Picone, "Il *Decamerone* come macrotesto: Il problema della cornice," in Picone and Mesirca, *Introduzione*, 9–34.

19. Kirkham, *Sign of Reason*, 119, quotes in English Boccaccio's source in Ovid's *Heroides* 19.5–16 (Hero to Leander), for the predicament of women in love deprived of distractions.

20. Proem, 1: "Umana cosa è aver compassione degli afflitti."

21. On the theme of compassion, see Teodolinda Barolini, "The Wheel of the *Decameron*," in *Dante and the Origins of Italian Literary Culture* (New York: Fordham University Press, 2006), 224–44, esp. 225–31.

22. For Paulus Diaconus's *Historia langobardorum* on a sixth-century plague in Liguria, see Vittore Branca, *Boccaccio medievale e nuovi studi sul "Decameron"* (Florence: Sansoni, 1990), 301–8.

23. Gregory the Great developed the great litany to pray for deliverance during the plague of 590, and the Roman historian Livy reports that the plague coincided with the initiation of Roman sports and games, *ludi*. See Mazzotta, *World at Play*, 40.

24. Others are at 2.5.63 (Bishop Filippo Minutolo, died October 24, 1301); 2.8.70; 7.10.15.

25. For the medical-therapeutical aspects of the book, see Massimo Ciavolella, "La tradizione della 'aegritudo amoris' nel *Decameron*," *Giornale Storico della Letteratura Italiana* 147 (1970): 496–517; Glending Olson, *Literature as Recreation in the Later Middle Ages* (Ithaca, NY: Cornell University Press, 1982); Mazzotta, *World at Play*, 13–46; Esther Zago, "Women, Medicine, and the Law in Boccaccio's *Decameron*." In *Women Healers and Physicians: Climbing a Long Hill*, ed. Lilian Furst (Lexington: University Press of Kentucky, 1997): 64–77; and Massimo Riva, "*Hereos/Eleos*: L'ambivalente terapia del male d'amore nel libro *chiamato Decameron cognominato Prencipe Galeotto*," *Italian Quarterly* 38 (2000): 69–106.

26. Kirkham, "Allegorically Tempered *Decameron*," comprehensively explores the allegorical implications of the narrators' names and behavior.

27. This is the topos of *exordium in deo*, also used in the Proem to the *Genealogia*, citing Plato and Boethius.

28. Wallace, *Boccaccio's "Decameron,"* 24–25.

29. *Decameron* 2, Concl., 2: "questo picciol *popolo* governare" (italics mine).

30. Various administrations also "command" (for *comandare* see Elissa, 4, Concl., 1, and Lauretta, 7, Concl., 1), "rule" (Dioneo, 3, Concl., 2, says he will "reggerò il regno"), and exert "lordship" (for *signoria*, see 3, Concl., 4).

31. For other accounts of the book's symmetries, see Janet L. Smarr, "Symmetry and Balance in the *Decameron*," *Medievalia* 2 (1976): 159–87; and Smarr, *Boccaccio and Fiammetta*, 174–91; Barolini, "Wheel of the *Decameron*," esp. 239–41; Kirkham, "Allegorically Tempered *Decameron*," 148–49, 166–71; see also note 18, above.

32. The martian and mercurial influences in Florence's horoscope at its refoundation (A.D. 801) are noted in Giovanni Villani, *Cronica* 4.1; for astrology in Boccaccio's texts, see Janet L. Smarr, "Boccaccio and the Stars: Astrology in the *Teseida*," *Traditio* 35 (1979): 303–32; and Victoria Kirkham, "'Chiuso parlare' in Boccacio's *Teseida*," in *Sign of Reason*, 17–54.

33. For the reliance of Oretta's story on a Latin version (*Compilatio singularis exemplorum*) of material from the "Book of Delights" (Sefer Šaašùìm), a miscellany by the Jewish physician Joseph ben Meir Zabara of Barcelona, see Alan Freedman, "Il cavallo del Boccaccio: Fonte, struttura e funzione della metanovella di Madonna Oretta," *Studi sul Boccaccio* 9 (1975): 225–41. For the *novella*'s centrality see Pamela Stewart, "La novella di madonna Oretta e le due parti del *Decameron*," in *Retorica e mimica nel "Decameron" e nella commedia del Cinquecento* (Florence: Olschki, 1986), 19–38; and for its metaliterary quality in context, see Franco Fido, "*L'ars narrandi* di Boccaccio nella sesta giornata," in *Il regime delle simmetrie imperfette* (Milan: Franco Angeli, 1988), 73–89. Apuleius uses the topos of the story as conveyance (*Metamorphoses* 1.20–21), and his novel furnishes models for *Decameron* 5.10 and 7.2 but has also left traces on 2.5, 4.6, 8.7, and 10.10. See Giovanni Vio, "Chiose e riscritture apuleiane," *Studi sul Boccaccio* 20 (1991–92): 139–65; Jonathan Usher, "Desultorietà nella novella portante di Madonna Oretta (*Decameron* VI.1) e altri citazioni apuleiane nel Boccaccio," *Studi sul Boccaccio* 29 (2001): 67–103; Igor Candido, "Amore e Psiche dalle chiose del Laur. 29.2 alle due redazioni delle *Genealogie* e ancora in *Decameron* X.10," *Studi sul Boccaccio* 38 (2009): 171–96.

34. For Boccaccio's interest in classical and originally oriental frame-story collections, see Picone, *Boccaccio e la codificazione della novella*, esp. 76–80, 89–96, 257–68.

35. The story has a well-known source in the framed tales of Baarlam and Josaphat, a version of the life of Buddha as a Christian saint received into the popular collection of saints' lives *Legenda aurea* (*Golden Legend*, ca. 1270); there is also a version in the vernacular *Novellino*, tale 14, where the father calls women *domoni* ("demons"), as in some earlier versions; see *The "Novellino," or, "One Hundred Ancient Tales": An Edition and Translation Based on the 1525 Gualteruzzi Editio Princeps*, ed. and trans. Joseph P. Consoli (New York: Garland, 1997), 35, 136.

36. For questions of denotation and signification in the *Decameron*, see Giovanni Sinicropi, "Il segno linguistico del *Decameron*," *Studi sul Boccaccio* 9 (1975–76): 169–224.

37. Boccaccio echoes Guinizzelli's poem at Concl., 11 and 7.8.46 (possibly via Dante's *Convivio*). See Asor Rosa, "*Decameron*," 569. On parodic reference to the Tuscan *stilnovo*, esp. in 5.1 and 4.2, see Louise George Clubb, "Boccaccio and the Boundaries of Love," *Italica* 37 (1960): 188–96; and Millicent J. Marcus, "The Sweet New Style Reconsidered: A Gloss on the Tale of Cimone," *Italian Quarterly* 81 (1980): 5–16.

38. See Teodolinda Barolini, "*Le parole sono femmine e i fatti sono maschi*: Toward a

Sexual Poetics of the *Decameron* (*Decameron* 2.9, 2.10, 5.10)," in *Dante and the Origins*, 281–303.

39. Kirkham, "'Chiuso parlare,'" and Smarr, "Boccaccio and the Stars," offer the most suggestive studies of astrology in Boccaccio's works, which for the *Decameron* lacks systematic treatment. A chapter is dedicated to each Day in the omnibus edited by Picone and Mesirca, *Introduzione*; some of these are specified below.

40. In the *Paradiso*, Dante places in the sphere of Mercury Justinian, the sixth-century Roman emperor who promulgated the code of laws bearing his name. Madonna Filippa's case has been compared to legal cases and *consilia*; see Nella Giannetto, "Madonna Filippa tra *casus* e *controversiae*," *Studi sul Boccaccio* 32 (2004): 81–100; and Michael Sherberg, *The Governance of Friendship: Law and Gender in the "Decameron"* (Columbus: Ohio State University Press, 2011), 92–99.

41. See Mazzotta, *World at Play*, 63–67; Marcus, *Allegory of Form*, 64–78.

42. See Simone Marchesi on *De casibus virorum illustrium* and Deanna Shemek on *De mulieribus claris*, in this volume.

43. Ferondo's stay in "Purgatory" in 3.8, while the lecherous priest who put him there entertains Ferondo's wife, also ends with a "resurrection": as if preparing these resurrections, the lay friar Puccio's penitential exercise in 3.4.17 is a "crucifixion."

44. See Mazzotta, "Allegory and the Pornographic Imagination," in *World at Play*, 105–27; Kirkham, "Love's Labors Rewarded and Paradise Lost," in *Sign of Reason*, 99–115; Marilyn Migiel, "Beyond Seduction: A Reading of the Tale of Alibech and Rustico (*Decameron* III.10)," *Italica* 75 (1998): 161–77; Jonathan Usher, "Industria e acquisto erotico: La terza giornata," in Picone and Mesirca, *Introduzione*, 99–113.

45. See Roberto Fedi, "Il regno di Filostrato: Natura e struttura della giornata IV del *Decameron*," *MLN* 102 (1987): 39–54. On Isabella and the pot of basil, see Millicent J. Marcus, "Cross-Fertilizations: Folklore and Literature in *Decameron* 4.5," *Italica* 66 (1985): 383–98; Picone, "La ballata di Lisabetta," in *Boccaccio e la codificazione della novella*, 215–34.

46. Several tales stage violence between couples or kinsmen (4.1, 4.3, 4.4, 4.5, 4.9), and corruption by officials investigating the deaths is rife (4.3, 4.6, 4.7, 4.10). Domestic and public spheres are thus in decline, as in plague-ridden Florence.

47. Marcus, "Sweet New Style," 5–16.

48. The plot of 5.5 resembles that of Plautus's *Epidicus*, in fact. For satirical elements in the work, see note 56.

49. For some the complexities of Dioneo's strategy, see Albert R. Ascoli, "Pyr-
    rhus' Rules: Playing with Power from Boccaccio to Machiavelli," *MLN* 114.1
    (1999): 14–57; and Ronald L. Martinez, "Apuleian Example and Misogynist
    Allegory in the Tale of Peronella (*Decameron* VII.2)," in *Boccaccio and Feminist
    Criticism*, ed. Thomas C. Stillinger and Regina Psaki (Chapel Hill, NC: An-
    nali d'Italianistica, 2006), 201–16. Among contributions focusing on gender in
    the *Decameron* are Claude Cazalé Bérard, "Filoginia/misoginia," in Bragantini
    and Forni, *Lessico critico decameroniano*, 116–41; Marilyn Migiel, *A Rhetoric of
    the "Decameron"* (Toronto: University of Toronto Press, 2003), important for
    its critique of traditional claims for Boccaccio's feminism; Barolini, "*Le parole
    son femmine e i fatti son maschi*," in *Dante and the Origins*, 281–301. See also the
    full collection of essays in Stillinger and Psaki, *Boccaccio and Feminist Criticism*;
    and more recently, Sherberg, *Governance of Friendship*. On Day 7 in general see
    also Cesare Segre, "Funzioni, opposizioni e simmetrie nella giornata VII del
    Decameron," in *Le strutture e il tempo* (Turin: Einaudi, 1974), 117–43.

50. For readings of stories told on Day 8, see Marcus, *Allegory of Form*, 79–92
    (8.3); Mazzotta, *World at Play*, 192–99 (8.3, 8.9); Kirkham, "Painters at Play
    on the Judgment Day," in *Sign of Reason*, 215–36 (8.9).

51. For Boccaccio's activity as copier, expounder, and biographer of Dante, see
    Jason Houston, *Building a Monument to Dante: Boccaccio as Dantista* (Toronto:
    University of Toronto Press, 2010); and in this volume the essays by Robert
    Hollander and Elsa Filosa.

52. See Attilio Bettinzoli, "Per una definizione delle presenze dantesche nel
    Decameron II: Ironizzazione e espressivismo antifrastico-deformatorio," *Studi
    sul Boccaccio* 14 (1983–84): 209–40; Franco Fido, "Dante personaggio man-
    cato nel libro Galeotto," in *Il regime delle simmetrie imperfette*, 111–23; Robert
    Hollander, *Boccaccio's Dante and the Shaping Force of Satire* (Ann Arbor: Uni-
    versity of Michigan Press, 1997), esp. 21–52; Luigi Surdich, "La memoria di
    Dante nel *Decameron*: Qualche riscontro," *Letteratura Italiana Antica* 7 (2006):
    325–40. See also, recently, Kristina Marie Olson, "Resurrecting Dante's Flor-
    ence: Figural Realism in the *Decameron* and the *Esposizioni*," *MLN* 124 (2009):
    45–65; Michael Papio's introduction to his translation of Boccaccio's *Exposi-
    tion on Dante's "Commedia"* (Toronto: Toronto University Press, 2009): 3–39;
    and Houston, *Building a Monument to Dante*.

53. Compare *Inferno* 11.22–90 and *Decameron* 1.1.10–13 for Cepparello's sins of
    counterfeiting, homicide, and gluttony. See also Jonathan Usher, "A 'ser'
    Cepparello, Constructed from Dante Fragments (*Decameron* I.1)," *The Italia-
    nist* 23.2 (2003): 181–93.

54. For Boccaccio's use in the *Teseida* of traditional divisions of the soul into high,

middle, and low functions, variously named, see Kirkham, *Sign of Reason*, 38–39, where Aristotle and Scholastic philosophers are cited.

55. See Picone, "Il *gabbo* di Maestro Alberto," in *Boccaccio e la codificazione della novella*, 25–35.

56. See Francesco Bausi, "Gli spiriti magni: Filigrane aristoteliche e tomistiche nella decima giornata del *Decameron*," *Studi sul Boccaccio* 27 (1999): 205–53. Robert Hollander, with Courtney Cahill, "Day Ten of the Decameron: The Myth of Order," in *Boccaccio's Dante*, 109–63, argue that the eulogistic (or, as the authors say, "eupeptic") character often claimed for the Tenth Day is complicated by ethical inconsistencies in the behavior of the characters; Boccaccio's work, they claim, shows a consistent satirical streak.

57. See Guyda Armstrong, "Boccaccio and the Infernal Body: The Widow as Wilderness," in Stillinger and Psaki, *Boccaccio and Feminist Criticism*, 83–104. Boccaccio may have explored both sides of the question precisely because he was profoundly ambivalent about it, just as he was about Dante's judgments.

58. For the story of Nastagio, see Cesare Segre, "La novella di Nastagio degli Onesti (*Decameron* V.8): I due tempi della visione," in *Semiotica filologica: Testi e modelli culturali* (Turin: Einaudi, 1979); 87–96; and for the story of Rinieri and the widow, Robert M. Durling, "A Long Day in the Sun: *Decameron* 8.7," in *Shakespeare's "Rough Magic": Renaissance Essays in Honor of C. L. Barber*, ed. Peter Erickson and Coppélia Kahn (London: Associated University Presses, 1985), 269–75.

59. The tale of Guido Cavalcanti (6.9) also probes Dante's schemes of judgment. See Robert M. Durling, "Boccaccio on Interpretation: Guido's Escape (*Decameron* VI.9)," in *Dante, Petrarch, Boccaccio: Studies in the Italian Trecento in Honor of C. S. Singleton*, ed. Aldo S. Bernardo and Anthony L. Pellegrini (Binghamton, NY: Medieval & Renaissance Texts & Studies, 1983), 273–304.

60. See Boccaccio *Esposizioni*, Canto 5.1, Esposizione letterale, 146–55. Boccaccio goes so far as to claim that Dante was not well informed when giving his account of Francesca's life. For Boccaccio's ambivalence about unveiling the *Commedia* to a broad audience, see *Boccaccio's Expositions*, ed. Papio, 3–37.

61. In 1373 Boccaccio described his *Decameron* as unfit reading for the wife and daughters of his correspondent Mainardo Cavalcanti (*Epistola* 22, partially translated in Kirkham, "Allegorically Tempered *Decameron*," 118–19); thus it is striking that the contemporary account of Francesca is so strongly anti-Dante.

62. For visual evidence of the reception of the title *Prencipe Galeotto*, see Daniela Delcorno Branca, "Il sottotitolo illustrato nel parigino it. 482," *Studi sul Boccaccio* 23 (1995): 79–88.

63. Germs of the ascensional pattern were proposed by Ferdinando Neri, "Il disegno ideale del *Decameron*," in *Storia e poesia* (Turin: Chiantore, 1944): 73–82; and adapted by Vittore Branca in the preface to his edition (*Decameron*, xvii–xviii), which gave the idea wide currency.

64. For statement of the "Epicurean" argument, see Battaglia Ricci, *Decameron*, and especially her *Ragionare nel giardino: Boccaccio e i cicli pittorici del "Trionfo della morte"* (Rome: Salerno, 2000); a partial forerunner of this approach is Aldo D. Scaglione, *Nature and Love in the Late Middle Ages: An Essay on the Cultural Context of the "Decameron"* (Berkeley: University of California Press, 1963). For a reading of 1.4 in this vein, see Ronald L. Martinez, "The Tale of the Monk and His Abbot (I.4)," in Weaver, *"Decameron" First Day*, 113–34. Thomas M. Greene, "Forms of Accommodation in the *Decameron*," *Italica* 45 (1968): 297–313, balances Scaglione's proposals with emphasis on the work's investment in social order.

65. Mazzotta, *World at Play*, 9. Marcus, in her *Allegory of Form*, in part develops Mazzotta's approach but resolves possible divergences between ethics and aesthetics with her argument that the tales, by virtue of their self-consciously realized artistic form, imply allegorical meanings or "moralities," though oriented not to providing a consistent ideological message (as does, for example, Dante's *Commedia*) but rather to interrogating claims of authority, facile belief, and univocal meaning.

Chapter Two

1. Giorgio Padoan, "Sulla genesi e la pubblicazione del 'Decameròn,'" in *Il Boccaccio le Muse il Parnaso e l'Arno* (Florence: Olschki, 1978), 93–121. Major studies of the manuscripts, used in the following discussion, are Vittore Branca, *Tradizione delle opere di Giovanni Boccaccio*, vol. 1, *Un primo elenco dei codici e tre studi*; vol. 2, *Un secondo elenco di manoscritti e studi sul testo del "Decameron," con due appendici* (Rome: Edizioni di Storia e Letteratura, 1958, 1991); Marco Cursi, *Il "Decameron": Scritture, scriventi, lettori; Storia di un testo* (Rome: Viella, 2007); Rhiannon Daniels, *Boccaccio and the Book: Production and Reading in Italy, 1340–1520* (London: Legenda, 2009), 76–101.

2. Discussions of these illustrations include Maria Grazia Ciardi Dupré Dal Poggetto, "L'iconografia nei codici miniati boccacciani dell'Italia centrale e meridionale," in *Boccaccio visualizzato: Narrare per parole e per immagini fra Medioevo e Rinascimento*, ed. Vittore Branca (Turin: Einaudi, 1999), 2:3–52, 66–72 (11–16); Lucia Battaglia Ricci, "Edizioni d'autore, copie di lavoro, interventi di autoesegesi: Testimonianze trecentesche," in *"Di mano propria": Gli autografi dei letterati italiani*, ed. Guido Baldassarri et al. (Rome: Salerno Editrice, 2010), 123–57 (145–57); Victoria Kirkham, "A Visual Legacy," in this volume.

3.   Armando Petrucci, "Il ms. Berlinese Hamiltoniano 90: Note codicologiche e paleografiche," in Giovanni Boccaccio, *Decameron: Edizione diplomatico-interpretativa dell'autografo Hamilton 90*, ed. Charles S. Singleton (Baltimore: Johns Hopkins University Press, 1974), 647–61; Branca, *Tradizione delle opere*, 2:211–62; Maurizio Vitale and Vittore Branca, *Il capolavoro del Boccaccio e due diverse redazioni*, vol. 1, Vitale, *La riscrittura del "Decameron": i mutamenti linguistici*; vol. 2, Branca, *Variazioni stilistiche e narrative* (Venice: Istituto Veneto di Scienze, Lettere ed Arti, 2002) (reviewed by Victoria Kirkham and Jonathan Usher in *Heliotropia* 2.1 [2004], http://www.heliotropia.org/); Cursi, *Il "Decameron,"* 39–42, 161–64.

4.   Cursi, *"Il Decameron,"* 43–44. It has been traditionally suggested that Boccaccio discouraged women from reading his work; for another view, see Rhiannon Daniels, "Rethinking the Critical History of the *Decameron*: Boccaccio's Epistle XXII to Mainardo Cavalcanti," *Modern Language Review* 106 (2011): 423–47.

5.   Ciardi Dupré Dal Poggetto, "L'iconografia," 24–31, 104–14; Paul F. Watson, "Gatherings of Artists: The Illustrators of a *Decameron* of 1427," *TEXT: Transactions of the Society for Textual Scholarship* 1 (1981): 147–55.

6.   Branca, *Tradizione delle opere*, 2:144–45; M. Faloci Pulignani, "L'arte tipografica in Foligno nel secolo XV," *La Bibliofilia* 2 (1900–1901): 23–35 (34–35).

7.   Joseph Allenspach and Giuseppe Frasso, "Vicende, cultura e scritti di Gerolamo Squarzafico, alessandrino," *Italia Medioevale e Umanistica* 23 (1980): 233–92.

8.   On the early printed editions, see Paolo Trovato, *Con ogni diligenza corretto: La stampa e le revisioni editoriali dei testi letterari italiani (1470–1570)* (Bologna: Il Mulino, 1991); Brian Richardson, *Print Culture in Renaissance Italy: The Editor and the Vernacular Text, 1470–1600* (Cambridge: Cambridge University Press, 1994); Daniels, *Boccaccio and the Book*, 101–25.

9.   J. M. de Bujanda, *Index de Rome, 1557, 1559, 1564: Les premiers index romains et l'index du Concile de Trente* (Sherbrooke, QC: Centre d'études de la Renaissance, 1990), 384, 827.

10. *Le annotazioni e i discorsi sul "Decameron" del 1573 dei Deputati fiorentini*, ed. Giuseppe Chiecchi (Padua: Antenore, 2001), 275.

11. Gustavo Bertoli, "Le prime due edizioni della seconda 'Rassettatura,'" *Studi sul Boccaccio* 23 (1995): 3–17; Marco Bernardi and Carlo Pulsoni, "Primi appunti sulla rassettatura del Salviati," *Filologia Italiana* 8 (2011): 167–200.

12. Giuseppe Chiecchi and Luciano Troisio, *Il "Decameron" sequestrato: Le tre edizioni censurate nel Cinquecento* (Milan: Unicopli, 1984).

13. *Decameron*, ed. Aldo Francesco Massèra (Bari: Laterza, 1927), 350.

14. Reprinted in Michele Barbi, *La nuova filologia e l'edizione dei nostri scrittori da Dante al Manzoni* (Florence: Sansoni, 1973), 35–85.

15. The events are recounted by Singleton in Boccaccio, *Decameron*, ix–x.
16. Vittore Branca and Pier Giorgio Ricci, *Un autografo del "Decameron": Codice hamiltoniano 90* (Florence: Olschki, 1962).
17. Giovanni Boccaccio, *Decameron: Edizione critica secondo l'autografo Hamiltoniano*, ed. Vittore Branca (Florence: Accademia della Crusca, 1976); and Boccaccio, *Decameron*, vol. 4 of *Tutte le opere*, ed. Branca (Milan: Mondadori, 1976). For Singleton's edition of the holograph, see above, note 3. Branca's review of this edition in *Studi sul Boccaccio* 8 (1974): 321–29, judged its methodology outdated and its execution flawed.
18. Giovanni Boccaccio, *Il Decameron*, ed. Aldo Rossi (Bologna: Cappelli, 1977); Aldo Rossi, *Il "Decameron": Pratiche testuali e interpretative* (Bologna: Cappelli, 1982).

Chapter Three
Victoria Kirkham assisted in the adaptation of this essay for an English-language audience. She drafted the prologue on the four shorter Latin compositions, drawing on Velli's introduction and notes for his edition of the Carmina. *Translations are hers unless otherwise indicated.*

1. Boccaccio, *Carmina*, ed. Giuseppe Velli, in Boccaccio, *Tutte le opere*, vol. 5, pt. 1 (Milan: Mondadori, 1992). This edition (to which the *Carmina* numbers refer), accompanied by a facing Italian translation, carries an introduction, textual notes, and commentary that are the basis for this essay. It updates Boccaccio, *Opere latine minori (Buccolicum carmen, Carminum et Epistolarum quae supersunt, Scripta breviora)*, ed. Aldo Francesco Massèra (Bari: Laterza, 1928). Isolating verse from Boccaccio's other Latin works, the Velli edition of the *Carmina* establishes a canon for the first time. The vernacular Boccaccio has attracted far more attention from scholars, who in past have either treated the Latin compositions as a corpus within the corpus, the classic being Attilio Hortis, *Studj sulle opere latine del Boccaccio con particolar riguardo alla storia della erudizione nel medio evo e alle letterature straniere aggiuntavi la bibliografia delle edizioni* (Trieste: Libreria Julius Dase, 1879), or otherwise subdivided it—into "minor works" (the eclogues, the epistles, the *Allegoria mitologica*, the brief biographies of Saint Peter Damian, Livy, and Petrarch), as Massèra did, with an implicit "major" complement (the encyclopedic Latin histories, the *Genealogia*, and the geographical gazetteer).
2. Since 1992, when Velli published his edition, scholars have welcomed an eleventh Latin poem into this small corpus, thirteen verses in the *De montibus* (1350s?) that adorn the entry on "Arno." First of the rivers Boccaccio catalogues (*De fluminibus* 3–4), the Arno has the privilege of breaking alphabetical order. It precedes 121 other postponed rivers—such as "Achelous," "Acher-

ontus," "Alpheus,"—receiving not only priority of placement but an exceptionally long treatment that echoes with literary allusions. (See the essay by
Theodore Cachey in this volume.) This *carme*, "Rupibus ex dextris tenuis pro-
funditur Arnus, / Appennine, tuis . . . ," complements the literary Latin prose
it follows by tracing the Arno's course, from deep in the Apennines through
the rocky Casentino, to Arezzo, Florence, and Pisa, and mingling finally with
the waves of the Tyrrhenian Sea.

3. Major battles were fought in 1325 and 1336 at the Tuscan town of Altopascia,
famous for its pilgrimage hostel on the Francigena (the route from France to
Santiago de Compostela, a destination that figures prominently in Boccaccio's
Filocolo). The Della Tosa burial marker that survives today is a sixteenth-
century replacement without the epitaph. When tensions were high between
Guelphs and Ghibellines, Pino's political activity included efforts to protect
Dante's ashes, buried in Ravenna. That would have pleased Boccaccio, as
would his service to King Robert of Naples, briefly the titular ruler of Florence. For excellent background, see Domenico De Robertis, who rediscovered and researched the epitaph, "Un nuovo carme del Boccaccio: L'epitaffio
per Pino e Ciampi della Tosa," *Studi sul Boccaccio* 9 (1975–76): 43–101. Salutati transcribed on the same folio, reproduced by De Robertis, the Tosinghi
commemorative verses, followed by Boccaccio's autoepitaph and the first
verse of his own epitaph for Boccaccio, the latter two carved complete on an
ancient stone in Boccaccio's Certaldo burial church, SS. Iacopo and Filippo
(originally dedicated to SS. Michele and Iacopo). The autograph Salutati
codex is Florence, Biblioteca Medicea Laurenziana, MS Ashburham 574.

4. Todd Boli's essay in this volume discusses the letter to Petrarch. On Boccaccio's embassy to Ludwig, see Vittore Branca, *Giovanni Boccaccio: Profilo biografico*, 2nd ed. (Florence: Sansoni, 1992), 86. This verse survives in only one
manuscript, transcribed by Boccaccio's friend Agnolo Torini (d. 1398), who
copied it on the same folio as the poet's autoepitaph and Salutati's epitaph for
Boccaccio. See Velli's commentary, pp. 461–62 and 480; and the catalog of
the exhibition for the sixth centenary of Boccaccio's death, *Mostra di manoscritti, documenti e edizioni: Firenze-Biblioteca Medicea Laurenziana, 22 maggio–31
agosto 1975* (Certaldo: Comitato Promotore, 1975), vol. 1, p. 96, no. 77. This
same Agnolo Torini sided with Boccaccio's half brother Iacopo in the dispute
after the poet's death over claims to his unfinished *Esposizioni*. See the essay
by Michael Papio in this volume, notes 21 and 43.

5. Florence, Biblioteca Riccardiana, MS 1035. The manuscript, with seven
illustrations of the *Inferno*, is discussed by Victoria Kirkham in her essay at
the end of this volume, chap. 29. The question of artistic attribution remains
open, but scholars increasingly doubt the drawings are Boccaccio's.

6. Velli, primed in the classical tradition, notes the debt to Boethius in his commentary, pp. 483–84: "Da, pater, *augustam* menti *conscendere sedem*" (*De consolatio Philosophiae* 3, meter 9). *De consolatio* figures among Boccaccio's autograph manuscripts. For this and his three copies of the *Commedia* (at the Vatican, the Riccardiana in Florence, and the Biblioteca Capitular of Toledo), see Ginetta Auzzas, "I codici autografi: Elenco e bibliografia," *Studi sul Boccaccio* 7 (1973): 1–20.

7. The translation is by Thomas G. Bergin, from his study of the poet's life and works: *Boccaccio* (New York: Viking, 1981), 64.

8. See the chapter "Signed Pieces" in Victoria Kirkham, *Fabulous Vernacular: Boccaccio's "Filocolo" and the Art of Medieval Fiction* (Ann Arbor: University of Michigan Press, 2001), 76–134 (133); and Kirkham, "Ioannes de Certaldo: La firma dell'autore," in *Gli zibaldoni di Boccaccio: Memoria, scrittura, riscrittura; Atti del Seminario Internazionale di Firenze-Certaldo (26–28 aprile 1996)*, ed. Michelangelo Picone and Claude Cazalé Bérard (Florence: Franco Cesati, 1988), 455–68. For the tomb, see the entry on Gian Francesco Rustici's high-relief marble bust, *Boccaccio with His Book* (1503): Kirkham, "L'immagine del Boccaccio nella memoria tardo-gotica e rinascimentale," in *Boccaccio visualizzato: Narrare per parole e per immagini fra Medioevo e Rinascimento*, ed. Vittore Branca (Turin: Einaudi, 1999), 1:85–144 (1:119–20).

9. The Italian title is a modern editorial addition to the dialogue, which begins under the rubric "Verba puelle sepulte ad transeuntem" ("Words of the buried girl to the passerby").

10. The funeral stone is now in the Capitoline Museum, C.I.L.VI 12652.

11. *Carmina latina epigrafica*, ed. Franz Buecheler (Leipzig: Teubner, 1897), 2:459, no. 995; reprinted in Velli's notes to the *Carmina*, 467.

12. Vittore Branca first called attention to this early poem and demonstrated compellingly that Boccaccio was its author; see Branca, "Il più antico carme del Boccaccio," in *Tradizione delle opere di Giovanni Boccaccio*, vol. 1, *Un primo elenco dei codici e tre studi* (Rome: Edizioni di Storia e Letteratura, 1958), 201–29. See further Giuseppe Velli, "Sull'"Elegia di Costanza,'" *Studi sul Boccaccio* 4 (1967): 241–54; repr. in Giuseppe Velli, *Petrarca e Boccaccio* (Padua: Antenore, 1995), 118–32; and for analysis and examples of how Boccaccio uses his source material, "L'*Elegia di Costanza* e l'*ars combinatoria* del Boccaccio," in Velli, *Petrarca e Boccaccio*, 133–42.

13. The first, second, and third components exist as autograph by "Johannes de Certaldo" in Boccaccio's *Zibaldone Laurenziano*, as does the four-part eclogue exchange between Dante and Giovanni del Virgilio. See the index of that notebook's contents in Filippo Di Benedetto, "Presenza di testi minori negli Zibaldoni," in Picone and Cazalé Bérard, *Gli zibaldoni di Boccaccio*, 13–28.

Cf. further the essay by Claude Cazalé Bérard in this volume. Boccaccio's sojourn in territory near Ravenna, Dante's last refuge in exile and a city that preserved memories of him, likely inspired his idea for this literary experiment.

14. Krautter appropriately quotes from the exemplary Ovid, *Amores* 1.1.29–30: "cingere litorea flaventia tempora myrto, Musa, per undenos emodulanda pedes" (to bind your golden head with seashore myrtle, Muse, composing an eleven-foot meter); here, too, Ovid explicitly sets aside epic poetry. See Konrad Krautter, *Die Renaissance der Bukolik in der lateinischen Literatur des XIV Jahrhunderts: Von Dante bis Petrarca* (Munich: Fink, 1983), 69–80.

15. *Thebaid* 1.16–17: "Limes mihi carminis esto Oedipodae confusa domus" (Let the limit of my song be the disordered house of Oedipus).

16. For the text of Checco's eclogue, "Iam medium lucis," first published by Hortis, *Studj sulle opere latine*, 353–53, see Massèra, *Opere latine minori*, 290–92.

17. Boccaccio seems not, in fact, to have joined Ordelaffi in a battle campaign. For a clear outline of the complex history following Robert's death, see Boccaccio, *Eclogues*, trans. Janet Levarie Smarr (New York: Garland, 1987), xiv and 201–3.

18. This hypothesis was first proposed by Guido Martellotti, "La riscoperta dello stile bucolico," in *Dante e la cultura veneta*, ed. Vittore Branca and Giorgio Padoan (Florence: Olschki, 1966), 335–46 (344); it was more articulately elaborated by Krautter, *Die Renaissance der Bukolik*.

19. The *carme* appears in final form in Vatican City, Biblioteca Vaticana, MS Chigiano 50.5.176, fol. 34r, Boccaccio's autograph miscellany of Dantean material: *Trattello in laude di Dante*, Dante's *Vita nuova*, Cavalcanti's "Donna me prega" with Dino del Garbo's commentary, and Dante's fifteen *canzoni*. The first draft of "Ytalie iam certus honos" must date from shortly before 1351–53, when Boccaccio introduced some marginal retouchings.

20. Owing to a misreading, the Egyptian Claudian was known in the Middle Ages as "Florentine." See *Carmina*, ed. Velli, commentary on 7.1–2 (pp. 480–81). Boccaccio's praise for Florence here contrasts sharply with his condemnation of the city for sending Dante into exile. See *Trattatello in laude di Dante* 1.92–109.

21. For the text of Zanobi's inquiry, see Boccaccio, *Opere latine minori*, ed. Massèra, 298–99.

22. He says it began before the sun left Leo, that is, before August 17, and lasted for several months, perhaps until November. Those internal details help date this letter.

23. Zanobi, from the village of Strada just south of Florence (hence the reference to Zanobi as "lo Stradino"), enjoyed the patronage of Niccola Acciaiuoli, who

sponsored his coronation. Boccaccio, neglected by Niccola, would sour in his friendship with Zanobi, especially after his journey to Naples in late 1355, a failed courtly venture, but a great scholarly success for his rediscovery at nearby Montecassino of important ancient manuscripts. See the essay by Todd Boli in this volume, especially on letters 6 and 13.

24. On the miscellany, see Bianca Maria Da Rif, "La miscellanea laurenziana XXXIII 31," *Studi sul Boccaccio* 7 (1973): 59–124.

25. Giuseppe Billanovich proposes this dating in *Petrarca letterato* (Rome: Edizioni di storia e letteratura, 1947), 292.

26. Boccaccio, *Epistole*, ed. Ginetta Auzzas, in *Tutte le opere*, vol. 5, pt. 1, 24.32: "sed quod me potissime angit est quod de a se compositis libris et maxime de *Affrica* illa sua, quam ego celeste arbitror opus, consultum sit, an stet adhuc et mansura perduret an igni tradita sit quem illi, innotuit, sepissime severus nimium rerum suarum index minatus est vivens."

27. Among them was the pathetic Domenico Silvestri, who, in a letter of 1359 to the master, expressed his longing to see *Africa* published, even at the cost of its author's death.

28. Vincenzo Fera's works *La revisione petrarchesca dell'"Africa"* and *Antichi editori e lettori dell'"Africa"* (Messina: Centro degli Studi Umanistici, 1984) now give us wide-reaching and intelligent information on the vicissitudes of the publication of the *Africa* and its text.

29. The sources most visibly used in "Versus" are Petrarch's *Africa* and *Epystole* and two pseudo-Virgilian compositions, *Ergone supremis* and *Temporibus laetis*. For texts of the latter two see *Anthologia latina*, ed. Franz Buecheler and Alexander Riese (Leipzig: Teubner, 1894–1926), nos. 672 and 242, in vol. 1, pt. 2, pp. 145–48; and vol. 1, pt. 1, p. 198.

30. See *Carmina* 9.44, referring to the dreadful possibility that the epic's brilliant "father" and global fame, will disappear into nothingness: "heu! flentes ibunt tecum tua fata sub umbras!" (Alas! Weeping for your fate, they will disappear with you into shadows!). The verse recalls "Elegia di Costanza" 118, where the young man wants to join his dead lady in death, "et teco ibo sub umbras" (and I shall go with you into the shadows), borrowed in turn from Joseph of Exeter's *De bello troiano* (On the Trojan War) 6.847, part of Hecuba's lament over the body of Priam. See Velli, *Petrarca e Boccaccio*, 135–36.

Chapter Four

1. Boccaccio, *Opere latine minori (Buccolicum carmen, Carminum et epistolarum quae supersunt, Scripta breviora)*, ed. Aldo Francesco Massèra (Bari: Laterza, 1928), 231–37 and notes, 360–62. Massèra improved the text as editor, working from the foundation laid by Attilio Hortis, who had demonstrated Boccaccio's pa-

ternity and first published it in his monumental classic, *Studij sulle opere latine del Boccaccio* (Trieste: Julius Dase, 1879), 323–27 and 357–61. The most recent editor, here cited throughout, has brought minor retouching to Massèra, a close Italian translation, and a useful commentary: Boccaccio, *Allegoria mitologica*, ed. Manlio Pastore Stocchi, in *Tutte le opere*, vol. 5, pt. 2 (Milan: Mondadori, 1994), 1091–1123. All English translations are my own.

2. Boccaccio, *Allegoria mitologica* 7: "Hinc Olimpus aperitur et sacra manu canones conceduntur, quorum virtute populi deorum regna sequentes artantur." See also pp. 1119–20 nn. 23–24.

3. For the interpretation of Old Testament characters and events as foreshadowing characters and events in the New Testament, see Jean Daniélou, *From Shadows to Reality: Studies in the Biblical Typology of the Fathers*, trans. Wulstan Hibberd (Westminster, MD: Newman Press, 1960); and A. C. Charity, *Events and Their Afterlife: The Dialectics of Christian Typology in the Bible and Dante* (Cambridge: Cambridge University Press, 1966).

4. Robert E. Kaske, *Medieval Christian Literary Imagery: A Guide to Interpretation* (Toronto: University of Toronto Press, 1988) 124–25; Ovid, *Ovide moralisé: Poème du commencement du quatorzième siècle*, ed. Cornelis de Boer (Amsterdam: J. Müller, 1915–38) ; Pierre Bersuire (Petrus Berchorius), *Reductorium morale*, bk. 15, *Ovidius moralizatus*, chap. 1, *De formis figurisque deorum*, ed. Joseph Engels, Werkmateriaal 3 (Utrecht: Instituut voor Laat Latijn der Rijksuniversiteit, 1966); and Bersuire, *Reductorium morale*, bk. 15, *Ovidius moralizatus*, ed. Engels, chaps. 2–15, Werkmateriaal 2 (Utrecht: Instituut voor Laat Latijn der Rijksuniversiteit, 1962). See also Ovid, *Metamorphosis Ovidiana moraliter . . . explanata: Paris, 1509 / Pierre Bersuire, Libellus: Basel, 1543 / Albricus*, ed. Stephen Orgel (New York: Garland, 1979).

5. For an extensive bibliography on medieval mythography, see Kaske, *Medieval Christian Literary Imagery*, 104–29.

6. Boccaccio, *Allegoria mitologica* 8: "Non erant igitur vires Deucalionidum, qui iam de ere ad ferrum pervenerant, tales quibus Ditis regna dimissa possent ad alta suis meritis convolare"; see also Pastore Stocchi's introduction to the text, p. 1094.

7. Boccaccio, *Allegoria mitologica*, annotated by Pastore Stocchi, pp. 1120–21, who reads "Pharao novus" as perhaps the emperor, n. 33, and "bona faciens" undoubtedly as Boniface VIII, n. 36; "Tritonia Pallas" certainly as the Holy Ghost, n. 32; "Gedeon," less certainly, as Florence, n. 34; the new Moses, very tentatively, as Robert of Anjou, n. 35; "qui fuit de aqua latus" as the meaning of Moses, n. 39; the "almus pater" in connection with the Avignon papacy, n. 40. On the old and new flowers in the garden ("sed bona faciens . . . novos palmites plantet veteres elicendo"), he accepts (intro., p. 1095) a proposal

made by Francesco Torraca, *Giovanni Boccaccio a Napoli, 1326–1339* (Naples: L. Pierro e Figlio, 1915), 185–87.

8. Boccaccio, *Allegoria mitologica* 39: "Maneat igitur unusquisque in sua vocatione tanquam Aaron, nec sibi magistri formam assummat qui non novit esse discipulus, si Phetontis ruinam cupit miserabilem evitare." We find a similar moral in Giovanni di Bonsignori da Città di Castello, *Ovidio Metamorphoseos Vulgare*, ed. Erminia Ardissino (Bologna: Commissione per i Testi di Lingua, Casa Carducci, 2001), 153: "La verità della istoria fu che anticamente uno chiamato Fetonte, che in greco viene a dire 'speculativo,' cercò e disse del corso delle pianete e delle stelle, e, non sapendo l'arte deritta, mise molti errori per lu mondo e così lo onnipotente Dio per le sue peccata l'uccise con saetta fulgorea." Although Bonsignori's work was probably written after Boccaccio's *Allegoria*, it seems to follow the same interpretative strategies that one finds in the anonymous *Ovide moralisé* and the *Ovidius moralizatus* of Pierre Bersuire.

9. Tobias Foster Gittes, *Boccaccio's Naked Muse: Eros, Culture, and the Mythopoeic Imagination* (Toronto: University of Toronto Press, 2009), 10.

10. Boccaccio, *Allegoria mitologica* 16: "Tu enim filius stellarum principis porrectorisque lucis amene, nutritus inter montis Elicone Musas, in operationibus validis roboratus, a patre non devians, nobis digneris ostendere florum generis novi virtutes, circa quas noster animus ansiatur"; 21: "ut sibi tua luce sui erroris nebulas declararem."

11. Jonathan Usher, "An Autobiographical Phaethon: Boccaccio's *Allegoria Mitologica*," in *Petrarca e Boccaccio: Modelli letterari fra Medioevo e Umanesimo*, ed. Annalisa Cipollone and Carlo Caruso (Alexandria: Edizioni dell'Orso, 2005), 55 and 81.

12. Usher, "Autobiographical Phaethon," 73–74.

13. Dante Alighieri, *Vita nuova*, ed. Domenico De Robertis, in Dante, *Opere minori*, vol. 1, pt. 1 (Milan: Riccardo Ricciardi, 1995), 30.42.1–2: "a tanto che io potesse piú degnamente trattare di lei . . . E di venire a ciò io studio quanto posso, sì com'ella sae veracemente."

14. I am grateful to Victoria Kirkham for bringing this to my attention.

15. Janet Smarr, *Boccaccio and Fiammetta: The Narrator as Lover* (Urbana: University of Illinois Press, 1986), 34–36.

16. I am grateful to Janet Smarr for bringing this to my attention.

17. Boccaccio, *Boccaccio on Poetry: Being the Preface and Fourteenth and Fifteenth Books of Boccaccio's "Genealogia Deorum Gentilium,"* trans. Charles Osgood (Indianapolis: Bobbs-Merrill, 1956), 14.13.

18. Boccaccio, *Boccaccio on Poetry*, 14.13 (my emphasis).

19. Usher, "Autobiographical Phaethon," 59–62. Throughout his works Boccac-

cio knowingly manipulates his personal experiences, as well as those of others, and does this in accordance with medieval cultural paradigms, as Vittore Branca has demonstrated in *Boccaccio medievale e nuovi studi sul "Decameron,"* 5th ed. (Florence: Sansoni, 1981), 243.

20. Branca, *Boccaccio medievale*, 34.

21. Ernst Robert Curtius, *European Literature and the Latin Middle Ages*, trans. Willard R. Trask (New York: Harper, 1963; Princeton, NJ: Princeton University Press, 1990), 59–60: an exemplum could be both an "'exemplary figure' (*eikon, imago*), that is, 'the incarnation of a quality'" and "an interpolated anecdote serving as an example."

Chapter Five

1. On these letters in the *Zibaldone Laurenziano*, see Stefano Zamponi, Martina Pantarotto, and Antonella Tomiello, "Stratigrafia dello Zibaldone e della Miscellanea Laurenziano," in *Gli zibaldoni di Boccaccio: Memoria, scrittura e riscrittura; Atti del Seminario Internazionale di Firenze-Certaldo*, ed. Michelangelo Picone and Claude Cazalé Bérard (Florence: Franco Cesati, 1998), 181–258.

2. For a discussion of the purpose of these letters as well as a full bibliography on their philological and interpretive history, see the introduction and notes of the following critical edition: Boccaccio, *Epistole e lettere*, ed. Ginetta Auzzas, vol. 5, pt. 1, in *Tutte le opere*, ed. Vittore Branca (Milan: Mondadori, 1992). All translations are my own.

3. For the *ars dictaminis* in the Middle Ages, I have relied on Ronald G. Witt, "The Arts of Letter-Writing," in *The Cambridge History of Literary Criticism: The Middle Ages*, ed. Alastair J. Minnis and Ian Johnson (Cambridge: Cambridge University Press, 2005), 68–83.

4. Giuseppe Billanovich, *Restauri boccacceschi* (Rome: Edizioni di Storia e Letteratura, 1947), 47–78.

5. *Epistole e lettere* 1.1: "Crepor celsitudinis Epyri principatus, ac procerum Ytalie claritas singularis."

6. *Epistole e lettere* 2.3–5: "subito suda mulier, ceu fulgur descendens, apparuit nescio quomodo, meis auspitiis undique moribus et forma conformis. O! quam in eius apparitione obstupui! Certe tantum quod magis aliud videbar esse quam ego, ymmo quod admodo larvale simulacrum me sciebam; et sic exterminatus animi actonitus in amentia vigilans sonniabar, districtis adeo diu pupulis an vigilarem scire querebam. Tandem stupor subsequentis thonitrui terrore cessavit. Nam sicut divinis corruscationibus illico subcedunt tonitrua, sic inspecta flamma pulcritudinis huius, amor terribilis et imperiosus me tenuit atque ferox, tanquam dominus pulsus a patria post longum exilium sola in sua repatrians, quidquid eius contrarium fuerat in me vel occidit vel expulit

vel ligavit." This translation was completed with reference to the translation by Victoria Kirkham in *Fabulous Vernacular: Boccaccio's "Filocolo" and the Art of Medieval Fiction* (Ann Arbor: University of Michigan Press, 2001), 69.

7. Auzzas lists the following similar passages in Boccaccio's other texts: *Filostrato* 1.20–30, *Filocolo* 1.1.17–22, *Comedia delle ninfe fiorentine* 35.105–6, *Amorosa visione* 44.31–51, and *L'Elegia di madonna Fiammetta* 1.6. The *Amorosa visione* and the *Filocolo* offer the closest parallels in Italian to this Latin topos.

8. This same passage has received the only notable commentary in English of any of these four letters. Kirkham comments on the Dantean nature of this passage as well as the letter's relationship to Petrarch (*Fabulous Vernacular*, 56–57, 69).

9. Boccaccio continues this tactic until his death. Consider one of his last poems, Rime 126, "Or sei salito," in which Petrarch meets Dante in heaven, along with other Tuscan poets and "Lauretta."

10. *Epistole e lettere* 3.21.

11. On Boccaccio's work with Leontius to learn Greek, see Agostino Pertusi, *Leonzio Pilato fra Petrarca e Boccaccio: Le sue versioni omeriche negli autografi di Venezia e la cultura greca del primo Umanesimo* (Venice: Istituto per la Collaborazione Culturale, 1964).

12. *Epistole e lettere* 3.8: "Sed in effectu contrarius, ritu aspidis surdi, farmaciis monitis aures obturabas, et sine castimonia babillusque, veluti agriofagite tuam baburram ac baccaniam prosequens cathafronitus, agapem contempsisti"; Boccaccio, *Il Corbaccio*, ed. Giorgio Padoan, in *Tutte le opere*, vol. 5, pt. 2 (Milan: Mondadori, 1994), 276–77: "Dèi dunque sapere né ogni infermità né ogni infermo potere essere sempre dal discreto medico con odoriferi unguenti medicato; per ciò che assai sono e di quelli e di quelle che nol patiscono e che richeggiono cose fetide, se a salute si vorranno conducere. E [se] alcuna n'è che con cotali argomenti e vocaboli e con dimostrazioni puzolenti purgare e guarire si vogliono, il mal concetto amore dell'uomo è una di quelle: per ciò che più una fetida parola nello intelletto sdegnoso adopera in una piccola ora, che mille piacevoli e oneste persuassioni, per l'orecchie versate nel sordo cuore, non faranno in gran tempo." Translation from Boccaccio, *The Corbaccio*, trans. and ed. Anthony K. Cassell (Urbana: University of Illinois Press, 1975), 52.

13. *Epistole e lettere* 4.14–15: "cum te una die subito belligerum audivi, fuit admiratione repletum, et dicens 'heu!' emisi suspiria luctuosa."

14. Auzzas also suggests that the letter was likely written, like the first and second letters, to a specific person. She points to a likely acquaintance of Boccaccio's at the court of the house of Anjou in Naples. See Boccaccio, *Epistole e lettere*, ed. Auzzas, 767 n.1. The most important detail that would link this letter with a specific person is the reference to the factional wars in Barletta (a city in the

Kingdom of Naples) that took place in 1338 and 1339. The addressee of this letter certainly took part in King Robert's attempt to resolve that crisis.

Chapter Six

1. Boccaccio, *Filostrato*, ed. Vittore Branca, in Boccaccio, *Tutte le opere*, ed. Vittore Branca, vol. 2 (Milan: Mondadori, 1964), title rubric: "Filostrato è il titolo di questo libro, e la cagione è questa: per ciò che ottimamente si confà con l'effetto del libro. Filostrato tanto viene a dire quanto uomo vinto e abbattuto d'amore; come veder si può che fu Troiolo dall'amor vinto sì ferventemente amando Criseida e sì ancora nella sua partita." The text cited throughout is *Filostrato*, ed. Vittore Branca, in *Tutte le opere*. All translations are my own.

   Precise dating remains uncertain. See Pier Giorgio Ricci, "Per la dedica e la datazione del *Filostrato*," *Studi sul Boccaccio* 1 (1963): 333–47. In reviewing the question in his *Boccaccio* (New York: Viking, 1974), 105–7, Thomas G. Bergin notes that Muscetta puts it in 1340, even after Boccaccio had begun the *Teseida*. Warren Ginsberg, *Chaucer's Italian Tradition* (Ann Arbor: University of Michigan Press, 2002), 150n, argues that it follows *Filocolo*. Branca, ed., *Filostrato*, intro., 3–4, believes it predates the *Filocolo*, the first work to feature the poet's lady Fiammetta, because there is no trace of her in his tale of Troiolo and Criseida, dedicated to a Filomena. Filomena is a *senhal*, or poetic code name, hiding the lady's real name "full of grace" (il vostro nome di grazia pieno, Pr. 16), which gives in Italian "Giovanna." See Branca's introduction and commentary as editor.

2. The autograph manuscript of the *Teseida delle nozze d'Emilia* survives in Florence, Biblioteca Mediceo-Laurenziana, MS Doni e Acquisti 325. See further Rhiannon Daniels, *Boccaccio and the Book: Production and Reading in Italy, 1340–1520* (London: Legenda, 2009), 41–75.

3. *Filostrato*, Pr. 32: "Adunque, valorosa donna, queste cotali rime in forma d'uno picciolo libro, in testimonianza perpetua a coloro che nel futuro il vedranno, e del vostro valore, del quale in persona altrui esse sono in più parti ornate, e della mia tristizia, ridussi; e ridottole, pensai non essere onesta cosa quelle ad alcun'altra persona prima pervenire alle mani che alle vostre, che d'esse siete stata sola e vera cagione."

4. *Filostrato*, Pr. 34: "qualunque altra cosa laudevole in donna."

5. Vittore Branca, *Giovanni Boccaccio: Profilo biografico* (Florence: Sansoni, 1977), 7–8.

6. See Piero Boitani, ed., *The European Tragedy of Troilus* (Oxford: Clarendon Press, 1989).

7. See Marilynn Desmond, "History and Fiction: The Narrativity and Historiography of the Matter of Troy," in *The Cambridge History of French Literature*,

ed. William Burgwinkle, Nicholas Hammond, and Emma Wilson (Cambridge: Cambridge University Press, 2011), 139–44 (142–43).

8. See Francesco Sabatini, *Napoli angioina: Cultura e società* (Naples: Edizioni Scientifiche Italiani, 1975); *Chaucer's Boccaccio*, ed. and trans. N. R. Havely (Cambridge: D. S. Brewer, 1980), 1–12; David Wallace, *Chaucer and the Early Writings of Boccaccio* (Woodbridge, UK: D. S. Brewer, 1985), 23–35.

9. *Familiares* 21.15, as translated by Kenelm Foster, *Petrarch: Poet and Humanist* (Edinburgh: Edinburgh University Press, 1984), 29.

10. See Pio Rajna, "Il cantare dei cantari e il serventese del maestro di tutti l'arti," *Zeitschrift für Romanische Philologie* 2 (1878): 220–54, 419–37 (esp. 231–45); Wallace, *Early Writings*, 76–90.

11. See Paola Rada, *Cantari tratti dal "Decameron"* (Pisa: Pacini, 2009), 17; *Cantari di Griselda*, ed. Raffaele Morabito (L'Aquila: L. U. Japadre, 1988).

12. Pucci's *Reina d'Oriente*, a *cantare* composed before 1375, tells of epic battles between his eponymous oriental queen and the emperor of Rome, the marriage of their two daughters (featuring a miraculous sex change), and a concluding battle between oriental women and the malign *donna della Spina* (woman of the thorn). His *Cantari di Apollonio di Tiro* elaborates the famous *novella* familiar from, inter alia, the *Gesta Romanorum* (Deeds of the Romans); his *Brito di Bretagna* adapts an episode from the *De amore* (*The Art of Courtly Love*) of Andreas Capellanus. See Antoni Pucci, *Cantari della Reina d'Oriente*, ed. Attilio Motta and William Robins (Bologna: Commissione per i Testi di Lingua, 2007); Pucci, *Cantari di Apollonio di Tiro*, ed. Renzo Rabboni (Bologna: Commissione per i Testi di Lingua, 1996); *Poeti minori del Trecento*, ed. Natalino Sapegno (Milan: Riccardo Ricciardi, 1962).

13. De Robertis, "Nascita, tradizione e venture del cantare in ottava rima," in *I cantari: struttura e tradizione*, ed. Michelangelo Picone and Maria Bendinelli Predelli (Florence: Olschki, 1984), 9–24; "[Il cantare] offriva nuova forma e nuovo spazio a generi ben collocati nella tradizione" (12).

14. See Rada, *Cantari*, 11; Balduino, "Le misteriose origini dell'ottava rima," in Picone and Predelli, *I cantari*, 25–47.

15. See a work as recent as *The Cambridge History of Italian Literature*, ed. Peter Brand and Lino Pertile (Cambridge: Cambridge University Press, 1999), where the Trecento section is divided among "Dante," "Boccaccio," "Petrarch," and "Minor Writers." See further Benedetto Croce, *Poesia popolare and poesia d'arte* (Bari: Laterza, 1930), plus the early review by Domenico Vittorini, commending Croce's distinction between these two kinds of poetry, "quella popolare spontanea ed elementare, quella d'arte complessa e più conscia di sè" (*Italica* 12 [1935]: 139–41 [at 140]).

16. See his letter to Francesco de' Bardi (1339), in *Epistole e lettere*, ed. Ginetta Auzzas, in *Tutte le opere*, vol. 5, pt. 1, 860–65.

17. See further, for example, 4.6; 4.112.

18. For spectacular accumulation of subjunctive verb forms in verse, see 2.31.1–6.

19. See *Troilus and Criseyde* in *The Riverside Chaucer*, ed. Larry D. Benson (Boston: Houghton Mifflin, 1987), 1.155–322; Ted Hughes, "St Botolph's," in *Birthday Letters* (London: Faber, 1998).

20. This moment looks back to the *Vita nuova* and finds equivalents in *Filocolo* and Petrarch, *Rime sparse*, 3: see Victoria Kirkham, *Fabulous Vernacular: Boccaccio's "Filocolo" and the Art of Medieval Fiction* (Ann Arbor: University of Michigan Press, 2001), 54–56.

21. This line, "È gentilezza dovunque è virtute," opens the sixth stanza of the *canzone* introducing Dante's *Convivio*, book 4; the line following adds the crucial caveat "but not virtue wherever there is nobility" (*Il Convivio*, ed. Maria Simonelli [Bologna: Prof. Riccardo Pàtron, 1966], *canzone terza*, lines 101–2). Such sentiments were greatly to the liking of merchant-class readers; Chaucer's Wife of Bath borrows freely from *Convivio* 4 in telling her tale.

22. See David Wallace, *Chaucerian Polity: Absolutist Lineages and Associational Forms in England and Italy* (Stanford, CA: Stanford University Press, 1997), 15–16.

23. See Vittore Branca, *Boccaccio medievale e nuovi studi sul "Decameron,"* 6th ed. (Florence: Sansoni, 1986), 45–85.

24. I adopt this phrase from Daniels, *Boccaccio and the Book*, 14–15.

25. See *The Workes of Geffray Chaucer newly printed*, ed. William Thynne (London: Thomas Godfray, 1532), fol. ccxix (r.), where Chaucer's rhyme royal stanzas end and Henryson's begin (with nothing to indicate a change of author).

Chapter Seven

"Certainly it does great disservice to the memory of the loving couple, given the great constancy of their souls, who because of the strength of love were equally firm in their faith to one another, if the fame they deserve is not recorded and exalted by the verses of a poet but is only known through the fanciful tales of the unlettered."

1. All quotations of the *Filocolo* are from Boccaccio, *Filocolo*, ed. Antonio Enzo Quaglio, in Boccaccio, *Tutte le opere*, ed. Vittore Branca, vol. 1 (Milan: Mondadori, 1967). All English translations are mine. Although outdated in its romanticized introduction and marred by infelicities of translation, there is one complete English version: Boccaccio, *Il Filocolo*, trans. Donald Cheney with the collaboration of Thomas G. Bergin, Garland Library of Medieval Litera-

ture, no. 43, series B (New York: Garland, 1985). The order of Boccaccio's early work, written during his Neapolitan period, is uncertain. For Vittore Branca, *Giovanni Boccaccio: Profilo biografico*, rev. ed. (1967; Florence: Sansoni, 1997), 41, the *Filocolo* was written after the *Caccia di Diana* and the *Filostrato*. Most critics agree that it was completed by 1339 and begun some years earlier. See Luigi Surdich, *La cornice d'amore: Studi sul Boccaccio* (Pisa: ETS, 1987), 77–117; and Francesco Bruni, *Boccaccio: L'invenzione della letteratura mezzana* (Bologna: Il Mulino, 1990), 169–73. See Nicolas J. Perella, "The World of Boccaccio's *Filocolo*," *PMLA* 76 (1961): 330–39, for a sensitive reading of the merits of the *Filocolo* that make it Boccaccio's most significant and interesting work before the *Decameron*.

2.   Bruno Porcelli suggests that Boccaccio may have had in mind the five-book structure of the *Ephesian Tale*, a Greek romance (second century A.D.) by Xenophon of Ephesus that narrates the story of the love and adventures of Anthia and Habrocomes; see Porcelli, "Strutture e forme narrative nel *Filocolo*," *Studi sul Boccaccio* 21 (1993): 207–33, esp. 207 and note. The form of this novel known in the West in five books may be an abridged version of the original. Vittore Branca cites this romance also as a partial source of two *Decameron* stories (10.4 and 10.5). Victoria Kirkham, *Fabulous Vernacular: Boccaccio's "Filocolo" and the Art of Medieval Fiction* (Ann Arbor: University of Michigan Press, 2001), 157–62, connects the five-book structure with the importance of Pentecost in its fictional calendar and the Pythagorean marriage number 5.

3.   No evidence has been found of the existence of Maria. Once believed by Boccaccio's critics, the story of Boccaccio's love for the king's natural daughter and the many other references Boccaccio makes in his works to his life are now generally considered fictional, though they may contain a germ of truth. They are figures in an autobiographical allegory. Janet Levarie Smarr, *Boccaccio and Fiammetta: The Narrator as Lover* (Urbana: University of Illinois Press, 1986) traces this fictional framing throughout Boccaccio's works.

4.   *Filocolo* 1.1.25. By adopting Dante's term *parlare fabuloso*, found in *Vita nuova*, chap. 2, Boccaccio from the outset presents himself as a follower of Dante, suggesting, beyond the linguistic borrowing, that both tell a worthy tale for a lady whose love ennobles the author. See Kirkham, *Fabulous Vernacular*; and Michelangelo Picone, "Tipologie culturali: Da Dante a Boccaccio," *Strumenti Critici* 10 (1976): 263–74, esp. 268–73.

5.   I refer to the reference in the *Decameron* Proem to the importance of comforting those who suffer from love, as the Author says he has, and especially ladies, who suffer more because of having fewer diversions than men available to them.

6.   *Filocolo* (labor of love) is one of Boccaccio's several erroneous etymologies. He knew very little Greek and wrote: "Filocolo è da due greci nomi composto,

da 'philos' e da 'colon': e 'philos' in greco tanto viene a dire in nostra lingua quanto "amore" e "colon" in greco similemente tanto in nostra lingua risulta quanto "fatica": onde congiunti insieme si può dire, trasponendo le parti, fatica d'amore (3.75.5)." ("Filocolo" is a combination of two Greek nouns, "philos" and "colon": and "philos" in Greek is "love" in our language and "colon," likewise in our language, becomes "labor": hence, taken together and transposing their order, one can say "labor of love.")

7. *Filocolo* 5.96.3–97.10. See Porcelli on Boccaccio's acquaintance with Byzantine literature. During his stay in Naples Boccaccio had access to the royal library of King Robert of Anjou, and there he came in contact with a scholar of encyclopedic knowledge, Paolo da Perugia, acquainted with Greek and Byzantine culture (Branca, *Giovanni Boccaccio*, 32–33). The fictitious author, Ilario, is the priest responsible for Florio's conversion, that of his family, and all of Spain (5.52–82). Boccaccio writes that Ilario, because of his intimate knowledge of Florio's story, has written it down in Greek: "il reverendo Ilario. Il quale . . . con ordinato stile, sì come colui che era bene informato, in greca lingua scrisse i casi del giovane re" (5.96.3).

8. Madrid, Biblioteca Nacional, MS 7583, *1400 — 1500: Alfonso X; Estoria de España; Primera crónica general*. The first section is the *Crónica fragmentaria*, Castilian, thirteenth–fourteenth century, cited in Patricia E. Grieve, *Floire and Blancheflor and the European Romance* (Cambridge: Cambridge University Press, 1997), 16 n. 2 and 211.

9. For a recent and thorough study of the sources, see Grieve, *Floire and Blancheflor*, 139–56. She discusses the features shared by the *Crónica de Flores y Blancaflor* and the *Filocolo*. The two early French versions of *Floire et Blancheflor* have appeared in several modern editions, and in modernized editions and translations; see Grieve, 212, 214. For the *cantare*, see Vincezo Crescini, ed., *Il cantare di Fiorio e Biancifiore, edito e illustrato* (Bologna: Romagnoli-Dall'Acqua, 1889–99; reprint, Bologna: Editrice Forni, 1967; and Commissione per i testi di lingua, 1969, Scelta di curiosità letterarie inedite o rare dal secolo XIII al XVII), 233, 249. On the problem of dating the *cantare*, see Domenico De Robertis, "Problemi di metodo nell'edizione dei cantari," in *Studi e problemi di critica testuale* (Bologna: La Commissione per i Testi di Lingua, 1961), 119–38.

10. Boccaccio, *Filocolo*, ed. Quaglio, cited above, note 1. See also Quaglio,"Valerio Massimo e il *Filocolo* di Giovanni Boccaccio," *Cultura Neolatina* 20 (1960): 45–77; Quaglio, "Tra fonti e testo del *Filocolo*," *Giornale Storico della Letteratura Italiana* 139 (1962): 321–69, 513–40; 140 (1963): 321–63, 498–551; and "Boccaccio e Lucano: Una concordanza e una fonte dal *Filocolo* all'*Amorosa visione*," *Cultura Neolatina* 23 (1963): 153–71. For a few incisive pages on Boccaccio's re-elaboration of his sources and his predilection for Ovid, see Bruni,

Boccaccio, 174–78. See also Ernesta Cocco, *Il "Filocolo" del Boccaccio e le sue fonti* (Naples: An. Chiurazzi & Figlio Editori, 1935). Almost everyone who has discussed the *Filocolo* has noted Boccaccio's homage and debt to Dante.

11. *Filocolo* 5.97.1. On Boccaccio's writerly pantheon and his relationship to it, see Jonathan Usher, "'Sesto tra cotanto senno' and *Appetentia primi loci*: Boccaccio, Petrarch and Dante's Poetic Hierarchy," *Studi sul Boccaccio* 35 (2007): 157–98, esp. 158–63.

12. Paolino Minorita, a Venetian, was papal nunzio to the Angevin court in Naples in 1316 and in 1324 was named bishop of Pozzuoli. He is the author of a *Compendium*, or *Cronologia magna*, a chronicle of the world from Adam and Eve to King Robert of Naples, and is remembered by Boccaccio in the *Genealogia* (14.3) as an exceptional historian (historiarum investigator permaximus) and also producer of a lot of hot air (dicacitate prolixa), cited in Vittore Branca, "Giovanni Boccaccio: Profilo biografico," in Boccaccio, *Tutte le opere*, 1:35). On Andalò del Negro (b. Genoa ca. 1260; d. Naples, before June 29, 1334), a Genoese astronomer and astrologer, whom Boccaccio met in Naples and who figures as Calmeta, his teacher of science, in one of the autobiographical allegories found in the *Filocolo* (5.8.16–36), see Antonio Enzo Quaglio, *Scienza e mito nel Boccaccio* (Padua: Liviana, 1967).

13. The vows are eventually fulfilled, some at the wedding feast in Alexandria (4.162) and others upon the couple's return home (5.83).

14. The "vows of the peacock" (*vanti del pavone*) is an ancient chivalric tradition in which knights, on important occasions, compete with one another, promising grand deeds. For Boccaccio's possible literary sources, see *Filocolo*, ed. Quaglio, 2.33, p. 778 n. 7, who cites the *Huon Chapet* and other French poems, such as Jacques de Longuyon's *Les voeux du paon*, *Les voeux de l'épervier*, and *Les voeux du hairon*; there are also Spanish versions, for example, *Los votos del Paon*. The episode, however, does not appear in the other known European versions of the story of Floire and Blancheflor. Kirkham, *Fabulous Vernacular*, treats this episode extensively in chap. 5, "The Poisoned Peacock."

15. See note 6 above.

16. This pastime is based on the French and Provençal *joc partit*, or *jeu parti*, and *partimen*. These were a form of *tenzone*, or literary exchange and debate, generally on erotic subjects. This sort of game appears also in Andreas Capellanus's Latin treatise *De arte honesti amandi*, where the author refers to ladies who give judgment on love questions (2.7). On the thirteen questions, see especially the study by Pio Rajna, "Le questioni d'amore nel *Filocolo*," *Archivum Romanicum* 31 (1902): 28–81. Rajna first discusses briefly the Spanish, French, and English translations of the episode, then the medieval sources of each question, directly and indirectly known by Boccaccio, including, besides

French and Provençal sources, indirect influences of the *Thousand and One Nights*. See also *Filocolo*, ed. Quaglio, who at 4.17, p. 853 n. 8, mentions specifically Andreas Capellanus's *De amore*, Peire Guillem's *La cour d'amour*, and the *fablel* of *Hueline et Aiglantine*. Among those who have commented extensively on the meaning of the episode for the hero's quest, see Paolo Cherchi, "Sulle 'quistioni d'amore' nel *Filocolo*," in his *Andrea Cappellano, i trovatori e altri temi romanzi* (Rome: Bulzoni, 1979), 210–17; Kirkham, *Fabulous Vernacular*, chap. 4, "Reckoning with Boccaccio's *Questioni d'amore*"; and Roberta Morosini, *"Per difetto rintegrare": Una lettura del Filocolo di Giovanni Boccaccio* (Ravenna: Longo Editore, 2004), chap. 2, "Le *quistioni d'amore*."

17. In the *Decameron*, Boccaccio will also reuse expressions and topics found in this episode, e.g., the election of a ruler to take charge of the activity and impose an order on it ("Acciò che i nostri ragionamenti possano con più ordine procedere e infino alle più fresche ore continuarsi . . . ordiniamo uno di noi qui in luogo di nostro re, al quale ciascuno una quistione d'amore proponga" [4.17.8: So that our discussions may proceed in a more orderly way and continue into the cooler hours . . . we will select one of us to serve as our king, and to him each of us shall propose a question about love]); two of the questions, the fourth and the thirteenth, will become *novelle* in the *Decameron*, 10.5 and 10.4, respectively. *Decameron* 5.6, the tale of Gian di Procida and Restituta, is based closely on the story of the *Filocolo* from the beginning of the protagonist's travels to find Biancifiore to their discovery, condemnation, recognition, and freedom (*Filocolo* 4.80–165), with, however, the names, places, and historical setting changed.

18. In *Fabulous Vernacular* Kirkham finds an explanation in Boccaccio's sources for each instance of the intervention of the pagan gods, in the dreams, visions, and in all the seemingly superfluous passages, and she demonstrates that they all contribute to the providential history in which the love story participates. I am convinced by her arguments that she has found the key to their meaning in the text. I remain unconvinced that Boccaccio succeeds in imposing this spiritual reading on the love story.

19. This notion of love, found also in the *Comedia delle ninfe fiorentine*, seems out of keeping with the sentiments expressed in the Author's dedication of his book and, indeed, throughout most of the love story, and it will disappear in Boccaccio's later works. It is a sign of Boccaccio's indebtedness at this point in his career to Dante and to the stilnovist tradition. For a discussion of Boccaccio's contrasting conceptions of love in the *Filocolo* and elsewhere, see Robert Hollander, *Boccaccio's Two Venuses* (New York: Columbia University Press, 1977).

20. The three types of love, a commonplace in medieval thought, derive from Aristotle's discussion of friendship in the *Nicomachean Ethics* 1156.

21. See Perella, "World of Boccaccio's *Filocolo*," for a perceptive close reading of the love story and for an analysis of themes central to it that, he argues, are fundamental for an understanding of the text: love, fortune, beauty, and courtliness.

22. For another view of the unreconciled views of love in the *Filocolo*, see Janet Levarie Smarr's seminal article, "Boccaccio's *Filocolo*: Romance, Epic, Allegory," *Forum Italicum* 12.1 (1978): 26–43.

23. The young couple fall in love reading "Ovid's holy book" (1.45.6; il santo libro d'Ovidio; also 2.4.1), and in the envoy addressed to his "little book" the Author recommends that lovers follow Ovid's lessons, which he says his book promotes: "E chi con molta efficacia ama, il sermontino Ovidio seguiti delle cui opere tu se' confortatore" (5.97.5).

24. Robert Hollander, Victoria Kirkham, James McGregor, Janet L. Smarr, and Steven Grossvogel read the *Filocolo* as a moral and ethical work and see many of what others call digressions as an integral part of the overall plan; not all argue in the same way for its coherence. See especially Hollander, *Boccaccio's Two Venuses*; Smarr, "Boccaccio's *Filocolo*" and *Boccaccio and Fiammetta*; Kirkham's several essays, now collected and augmented in *Fabulous Vernacular*; James McGregor's two studies of the significance of Boccaccio's use of Virgil: *The Image of Antiquity in Boccaccio's "Filocolo," "Filostrato," and "Teseida"* (New York: Peter Lang, 1991) and *Shades of Aeneas: The Imitation of Vergil and the History of Paganism in Boccaccio's "Filostrato," "Filocolo," and "Teseida"* (Athens: University of Georgia Press, 1991); and Steven Grossvogel, *Ambiguity and Allusion in Boccaccio's "Filocolo"* (Florence: Olschki, 1992). Morosini, *"Per difetto integrare,"* takes a different approach, finding unity in the aesthetic attention to modes and motives of telling and retelling.

25. See Branca, *Giovanni Boccaccio*, 40–46; Mario Marti, in Boccaccio, *Giovanni Boccaccio, Opere minori in volgare*, ed. Mario Marti (Milan: Rizzoli, 1958), 1:25. This opinion is widely held. Perella says it best in "World of Boccaccio's *Filocolo*," 330: "Perhaps the clearest indication that the *Filocolo* is an immature work lies in the fact that it tries to be too many things at the same time, and, rather than a fusion too often we find mere juxtaposition or confusion of widely differing traditions and tendencies, an inordinate pouring out of everything the young enthusiastic Boccaccio was imbibing by way of culture and of what was already in him."

Chapter Eight

1. For excellent treatments of Virgilian and Statian influences in the poem, see David Anderson, *Before the "Knight's Tale": Imitation of Classical Epic in Boccaccio's "Teseida"* (Philadelphia: University of Pennsylvania Press, 1988); and

James H. McGregor, *The Shades of Aeneas: The Imitation of Vergil and the History of Paganism in Boccaccio's "Filostrato," "Filocolo," and "Teseida"* (Athens: University of Georgia Press, 1991), 44–110.

2. The sonnets also represent something of a bridge between classical and medieval literary culture. As Giuseppe Vandelli points out in "Un autografo della *Teseide*," *Studi di Filologia Italiana* 2 (1929): 5–76, manuscripts of the *Thebaid*, including one Boccaccio surely used because he restored its missing parts in his own hand, regularly contained thirteen twelve-line hexameter summaries of the material, one for the whole poem and twelve for each of the twelve books, authored by someone other than Statius.

3. Boccaccio, *Teseida delle nozze d'Emilia*, ed. Alberto Limentani, in *Tutte le opere*, vol. 2 (Milan: Mondadori, 1964), editor's intro., 231.

4. Lucia Battaglia Ricci, *Boccaccio* (Rome: Salerno Editrice, 2000), 94–95.

5. William E. Coleman, "Appendix: Three Redactions of the *Teseida*," in *Sources and Analogues of "The Canterbury Tales,"* ed. Robert M. Correale and Mary Hamel (Cambridge: D.S. Brewer, 2005), 2:120. For details on the manuscript tradition, which Coleman summarizes, see Edvige Agostinelli, "A Catalogue of the Manuscripts of *Il Teseida*," *Studi sul Boccaccio* 15 (1985): 1–83. Agostinelli (17–18) dates the autograph, MS Doni e Acquisti 325 of the Biblioteca Medicea Laurenziana in Florence, to 1348–50.

6. On this last point, see Rita Librandi, "Corte e cavalleria della Napoli angioina nel 'Teseida' del Boccaccio," *Medioevo Romanzo* 4 (1977): 53–72. While Librandi's essay needs revision in light of more recent work on the poem, it still makes useful points about the Boccaccio's Angevin experience.

7. All translations are mine. The only complete translation based on Limentani's edition, *The Book of Theseus: Teseida delle Nozze d'Emilia*, trans. Bernadette Marie McCoy (New York: Medieval Text Association, 1974), was unsuitable for the present purposes. Vincenzo Traversa has published a translation of the poem and some of the glosses: Boccaccio, *Theseid of the Nuptials of Emilia (Teseida delle Nozze di Emilia)* (New York: Peter Lang 2002), but it is based on a manuscript of the poem owned by him, which he also published in that volume. It is judged inaccurate and idiosyncratic by Martin Eisner in his review, *Heliotropia* 5.1–2 (2008), http://www.brown.edu/Departments/Italian_Studies/heliotropia/05/eisner.pdf. William Coleman and Edvige Agostinelli edited and translated 173 octaves that Chaucer used in the "Knight's Tale"; see Coleman, "The Knight's Tale," in Correale and Hamel, *Sources and Analogues*, 2:136–214. They are also preparing an edition and translation of the poem for the Chaucer Library (forthcoming from University of Georgia Press), though based on a manuscript that most closely resembles the one Chaucer owned and used, as well as new print and digital editions of the poem based on the Lauren-

tian autograph as well as a manuscript housed at the Biblioteca Oratoriana del Monumento Nazionale dei Girolami in Naples (MS CF.2.6 [Pil. X. 36]). Finally, readers interested in the translation challenges presented by the poem may wish to consult Osamu Fukushima, *An Etymological Dictionary for Reading Boccaccio's "Teseida"* (Florence: Franco Cesati, 2011).

8. "Arma vero nullum latium adhuc invenio poetasse" (*De vulgari eloquentia* 2.2.8). Battaglia Ricci, *Boccaccio*, 96, believes that Boccaccio likely read the *De vulgari* only after returning to Florence in late 1340, in which case Dante's observations about vernacular poetry, rather than inspiring the poem's composition, may become a sort of *ex post facto* rationale for it. The bibliography of the *Teseida* includes a number of studies that plumb its relationship with Dante. See, for example, Ronald L. Martinez, "Before the *Teseida*: Statius and Dante in Boccaccio's Epic," in "Boccaccio 1990: The Poet and His Renaissance Reception," ed. Kevin Brownlee and Victoria Kirkham, special issue, *Studi sul Boccaccio* 20 (1991–92): 205–19; and Susan Noakes, *Timely Reading: Between Exegesis and Interpretation* (Ithaca, NY: Cornell University Press, 1988), 68–97.

9. *Teseida* 12.85.2, gloss: "cioè, che mai in rima non è stata messa, prima che questa, alcuna istoria di guerre."

10. *Teseida* 12.84.8, gloss: "lazio s'intende qui largamente per tutta Italia."

11. *Teseida*, "A Fiammetta," p. 246: "in latino volgare e per rima, acciò che più dilettasse."

12. *Teseida* 1.6.1, gloss: "la principale intenzione dell'autore di questo libretto [è] di trattare dell'amore."

13. *Teseida*, "A Fiammetta," p. 246: "bella sì per la materia della quale parla, che è d'amore."

14. Other readers have made analogous points. Robert R. Edwards, "Medieval Literary Careers: The Theban Track," in *European Literary Careers: The Author from Antiquity to the Renaissance*, ed. Patrick Cheney and Frederick A. de Armas (Toronto: University of Toronto Press, 2002), 104–28, sees the poem as "a transposition of the *Thebaid* into the framework of medieval aristocratic culture, which traced its origins to antiquity" (112). For Winthrop Wetherbee, "History and Romance in Boccaccio's *Teseida*," in Brownlee and Kirkham, eds., "Boccaccio 1990," 173–84, "it is also inescapably a romance grafted to the epic tradition, and its romance qualities continually subvert its pretentions to epic seriousness" (175). In Eren Hostetter Branch's view, "Rhetorical Structures and Strategies in Boccaccio's *Teseida*," in *The Craft of Fiction: Essays in Medieval Poetics*, ed. Leigh A. Arrathoon (Rochester, MI: Solaris Press, 1984), 143–60, the poem "presents itself as a debate on the values of the pagan world. In this debate, or argument *in utramque partem*, Boccaccio does not oppose pre-Christian values to Christian ones; rather he delineates,

within his particular classical framework, a double perspective on the values of that world" (155). Finally, Guido Di Pino, "Lettura del 'Teseida,'" *Italianistica* 8 (1979): 26–37, locates a "bipolarità dell'opera" in the themes of arms and love (31).

15. *Teseida*, "A Fiammetta," p. 245: "Come che a memoria tornandomi le felicità passate, nella miseria vedendomi dov'io sono, mi sieno di grave dolore manifesta cagione."

16. Exemplary of this anachronistic tendency is Boitani's claim that "it was precisely to write an 'heroic poem' in Tasso's sense of the word that [Boccaccio] had set about composing the *Teseida*." Piero Boitani, "Style, Iconography, and Narrative: The Lesson of the *Teseida*," in *Chaucer and the Italian Trecento*, ed. Piero Boitani (Cambridge: Cambridge University Press, 1983), 185. In like manner Maria Luisa Meneghetti writes: "Boccaccio intendeva in verità mettere mano al primo poema epico del Medioevo volgare—poema epico alla maniera classica, si vuol dire, e non tradizionale *chanson de geste*." See her essay "Epico, romanzo, poema cavalleresco," in *Manuale di letteratura italiana: Storia per generi e problemi*, ed. Franco Brioschi and Costanzo Di Girolamo (Turin: Bollati Boringhieri, 1993), 1:729. That Meneghetti then goes on to detail all the ways in which Boccaccio compromises the classical model calls into question, first, his intentions as she describes them, and second, whether he had a stable notion of the epic genre.

17. *Teseida*, Limentani's intro., 232. Boccaccio's concerns significantly include both numerology and astrology. For the former see Victoria Kirkham, "'Chiuso Parlare' in Boccaccio's *Teseida*," in *Dante, Petrarch, Boccaccio: Studies in the Italian Trecento in Honor of Charles S. Singleton*, ed. Aldo S. Bernardo and Anthony L. Pellegrini (Binghamton, NY: Medieval and Renaissance Texts and Studies, 1983), 305–51; reprinted in Kirkham, *The Sign of Reason in Boccaccio's Fiction* (Florence: Olschki, 1993), 17–53; and for the latter, Janet Smarr, "Boccaccio and the Stars: Astrology in the *Teseida*," *Traditio* 35 (1979): 303–32.

18. My reading differs from that of Francesco Bruni, for whom the poem willfully balances its epic and romance impulses rather than resolve them in favor of one or the other. See Bruni, *Boccaccio: L'invenzione della letteratura mezzana* (Bologna: Il Mulino, 1990), 188–201.

19. Janet Smarr, *Boccaccio and Fiammetta: The Narrator as Lover* (Urbana: University of Illinois Press, 1986), 66, identifies Teseo as a Jupiter figure, as he embodies the same virtues of temperance and reason that are associated with the divinity. She cites Bernard Silvester's *Commentum super sex libros Eneidos*, wherein he offers the following etymology for the name Theseus: "*theos* is god, *eu* good. Through this we understand the rational and virtuous man." See *The Commentary on the First Six Books of the "Aeneid" Commonly Attributed to Bernar-*

Dis Silvestris, ed. Julian Ward Jones and Elizabeth Frances Jones (Lincoln: University of Nebraska Press, 1977), 88; the English translation is Smarr's.

20. Giuseppe Velli's essay on the poem, "L'apoteosi di Arcita: Ideologie e coscienza storica nel *Teseida*," in *Petrarca e Boccaccio: Tradizione — memoria — scrittura* (Padua: Editrice Antenore, 1995), 143–77, locates that apotheosis in Arcita's arrival in heaven, not in any earthly glorification of the hero. While the poem does celebrate Arcita's life in book 11, dedicated to his funeral and the attendant games, his untimely death prevents him from attaining the sort of historical importance that Virgil assigns, for example, to Aeneas. Arcita's principal contribution appears to have been that he conveniently got out of the way of Palemone and Emilia, generously insisting on his deathbed that Palemone marry Emilia in his stead. As Bruni, *Boccaccio*, 192, points out, "La vittoria nel torneo risulta inutile al buon esito dell'avventura amorosa, il successo nelle armi non è più condizione necessaria del successo amoroso."

21. McGregor, in *Shades of Aeneas*, 44–76, highlights Teseo's failures, convincingly explaining as proof of Boccaccio's point that pagan *pietas* is insufficient in the absence of Christian providence.

22. Studies of the glosses include Limentani, "Tendenze della prosa del Boccaccio ai margini del 'Teseida,'" *Giornale Storico della Letteratura Italiana* 135 (1958): 524–51; and Robert Hollander, "The Validity of Boccaccio's Self-Exegesis in His *Teseida*," *Medievalia et Humanistica*, n.s., 8 (1977): 163–83.

23. Vandelli, "Un autografo," 75.

24. Hollander, "Boccaccio's Self-Exegesis," 165, points out that the mythographic material is largely Ovidian, though likely mediated by medieval compilers, such as Paolo da Perugia. One noteworthy exception, however, would come in the description of Venus's house, based on Claudian's *Epithalamium de nuptiis Honorii Augusti* (*Epithalamium of Honorius and Maria*). For the latter debt, see Bruni, *Boccaccio*, 195.

25. On the question of the invention of the Italian octave, see Battaglia Ricci, *Boccaccio*, 91–94, who provides a thorough bibliography. For a different theory on the intentions of the glosses, see Hollander, "Boccaccio's Self-Exegesis," 168, who argues that "to herald the rebirth of epic in a modern tongue it was only fitting that the instant classic be born *cum commento*." See also Jeffrey Schnapp, "A Commentary on Commentary in Boccaccio," *South Atlantic Quarterly* 91.4 (Nov. 1992): 813–34, published in an expanded Italian version as "Un commento all'autocommento nel *Teseida*," in Brownlee and Kirkham, "Boccaccio 1990," 185–203.

26. Virgil, *Aeneid*, trans. H. R. Fairclough, 2 vols., rev. ed. (Cambridge, MA: Harvard University Press, 1986); Statius, *Thebaid*, trans. J. H. Mozley, 2 vols. (1928; reprint, Cambridge, MA: Harvard University Press, 1967).

27. I cite from Jane Wilson Joyce's translation: *Statius, Thebaid: A Song of Thebes* (Ithaca, NY: Cornell University Press, 2008).

28. *Teseida* 2.10, rubric: "Transgressione dalla propria materia, per mostrare qual fosse la cagione per la quale Teseo andasse contra Creonte."

29. *Teseida* 2.10, gloss: "Poscia che l'autore ha dimostrato di sopra, nel primo libro, donde e come Emilia venisse ad Attene, in questo secondo intende di dimostrare come Arcita e Palemone vi pervenissero. Alla quale cosa fare, gli conviene toccare la guerra stata tra Etiocle e Pollinice, e quello che di quella adivenne; ma perciò che brevissimamente trapassa nel testo, acciò che le seguenti otto stanzie e assai cose che apresso seguitano s'intendano più chiaramente, quanto più brievemente potrò qui la racconterò, acciò che la cagione, altressì della guerra che segue tra Teseo e Creonte sia più manifesta."

30. Robert Hollander, *Boccaccio's Two Venuses* (New York: Columbia University Press, 1977), 53–65. Victoria Kirkham points out that these two descriptions fall at the central points in the poem—the central chapter and the central rubric; 7.30 is the central stanza, and 7.50 is the central chapter (rubric). See Kirkham, "'Chiuso parlare,'" 37–38.

31. I do not intend to revisit here the question of the historicity of Fiammetta. Within the context of the *Teseida* she remains a construct as fictional as that of the author's voice. Readers interested in the question of Fiammetta's identity should consult Kirkham, "Maria a.k.a. Fiammetta": The Men behind the Woman," in *Boccaccio and Feminist Criticism*, ed. Thomas C. Stillinger and F. Regina Psaki (Chapel Hill, NC: Annali d'Italianistica, 2006), 13–27. Smarr, *Boccaccio and Fiammetta*, 63, makes an important point in this regard: "The narrator's remarks tell the reader nothing about who Fiammetta might be historically. From the manner in which the poet addresses her, we can assume that Fiammetta has a higher social rank than he, as consistent with the situation established in the *Filocolo* and with the lover-poet tradition in general."

32. *Teseida*, "A Fiammetta," p. 246: "ricordandomi che già ne' dì più felici che lunghi io vi sentii vaga d'udire e tal volta di leggere una e altra istoria, e massimamente l'amorose, sì come quella che tutta ardavate nel fuoco nel quale io ardo—e questo forse faciavate acciò che i tediosi tempi con ozio non fossero cagione di pensier più nocevole."

33. *Teseida*, "A Fiammetta," p. 247: "sì come poco intelligenti ne sogliano essere schife." The meanings of the terms *storia*, *favola*, and *chiuso parlare* remain uncertain. For Kirkham they "all imply an allegorical intent" (*Sign of Reason*, 18), while Smarr appears to limit that function to *chiuso parlare*: "The narrator's assertion that his book is written with 'chiuso parlare' [closed (or secret) speech]—although true in a number of ways—seems to refer for the narrator only to his concealment of his own love history in the tale, a ruse neces-

sary to 'coprire ciò che *non è onesto* manifestare' [cover what is not honest to reveal]" (*Boccaccio and Fiammetta*, 62). The listing of three different terms is reminiscent of Boccaccio's later characterization of the *novelle* of the *Decameron* as "cento novelle, o favole o parabole o istorie che dire le vogliamo" (Pr. 13), which scholars have variously endeavored to interpret, generally distinguishing the one from the other. Two of the terms in the *Decameron* appear as well in the *Teseida* letter, and one might apply the definitions developed from the latter work to the former, with *storia* indicating a work grounded in history, and *favola* one with moralistic intent. *Chiuso parlare* is a unique term that clearly indicates something hidden beneath the textual discourse, probably something allegorical in a generic sense.

34. *Teseida*, "A Fiammetta," p. 247: "acciò che l'opera, la quale alquanto par lunga, non sia prima rincresciuta che letta."

35. In the famous sonnet "Tanto gentile e tanto onesta pare."

36. Eren Hostetter Branch makes some excellent observations about the difference between the initial woodland setting for the duel and the later theatrical setting; see Branch, "Rhetorical Structures and Strategies," 143–60. On Boccaccio's notion of the Athenian theater, see James H. McGregor, "Boccaccio's Athenian Theater: Form and Function of an Ancient Monument in *Teseida*," *MLN* 99 (1984): 1–42.

37. Bruni, *Boccaccio*, 191, reaches a similar conclusion: "La ferocia del duello senza testimoni è regolamentata da Teseo in una direzione rituale e spettacolare, nello scontro alla presenza di spettatori e di Teseo stesso, giudice al di sopra delle parti."

38. *Teseida*, "Risposta delle Muse," p. 664.

39. The sonnet brings us full circle to the author's initial invocation to the Castalian Sisters, "O sorelle castalie" (1.1.1), with its gloss, the first in the epic, "Nel principio del suo libro fa l'autore, secondo l'antico costume de' compositori, una sua invocazione, e chiama le Muse." In this regard Bruni, *Boccaccio*, 189, notes that the *Teseida* is the only work by Boccaccio in the "registro mezzano" (middle style) to invoke the Muses.

Chapter Nine

1. For the text see Boccaccio, *Caccia di Diana*, ed. Vittore Branca, in Boccaccio, *Tutte le opere*, ed. Vittore Branca, vol. 1 (Milan: Mondadori, 1967); and Boccaccio, *Diana's Hunt / Caccia di Diana: Boccaccio's First Fiction*, ed. and trans. Anthony K. Cassell and Victoria Kirkham (Philadelphia: University of Pennsylvania Press, 1991). On the attribution, see Vittore Branca, "Per l'attribuzione della *Caccia di Diana* a Giovanni Boccaccio," *Annali della R. Scuola Normale Superiore di Pisa* 2.7 (1938): 287–302; reprinted in Branca, *Tradizione*

delle opere di Giovanni Boccaccio (Rome: Edizioni di Storia e Letteratura, 1958),
1:144–98, together with "Nuove note sulla *Caccia di Diana*," 121–43. We do
not have an autograph copy, nor does Boccaccio refer to this poem by name
in his later works or letters. There are six known manuscripts of the *Caccia*.
Four call it *Caccia di Diana*, one the same, but in Latin, and one titles it simply
Caccia. For information about the manuscripts and an annotated bibliography of studies on the *Caccia* up through the 1960s, see Branca, *Tradizione
delle opere*, 1:18 and 148–49; and his notes in *Caccia di Diana*, 679–81. The first
edition of the poem did not appear until the nineteenth century: "*La caccia di
Diana*," *poemetto di Giovanni Boccaccio, ora per la prima volta pubblicata*, ed. Ignazio
Moutier (Florence: Stamperia Magheri, 1832). On the question of the title,
see also Thomas G. Bergin, *Boccaccio* (New York: Viking Press, 1981), 70.
Branca (*Tradizione*, 1:167) cites the first known reference to the poem: it is
called "venatione dyane metricos" in an early fifteenth-century manuscript on
Boccaccio's life (Milan, Biblioteca Ambrosiana, MS S, 72 sup.).

2. Cassell and Kirkham, *Diana's Hunt*, p. 153.

3. For the text of the *ternario*, see Boccaccio, *Rime*, ed. Vittore Branca, in Boccaccio, *Tutte le opere*, ed. Vittore Branca, vol. 5, pt. 1 (Milan: Mondadori, 1992),
poem 69. Bergin, *Boccaccio*, 208, calls it a "pocket version of *Diana's Hunt*."

4. Boccaccio, *Teseida delle nozze d'Emilia*, ed. Alberto Limentani, in Boccaccio,
Tutte le opere, ed. Vittore Branca, vol. 2 (Milan: Mondadori, 1964), 7.50.1,
gloss: "Venere è doppia" (Venus is double). See Robert Hollander, *Boccaccio's
Two Venuses* (New York: Columbia University Press, 1977).

5. On the multiplicity of its sources, see Cassell and Kirkham, *Diana's Hunt*,
4–21; Anthony K. Cassell, "Boccaccio's *Caccia di Diana*: Horizon of Expectation," *Italian Culture* 9 (1991): 85–102 (86); Antonio Illiano, "Per una rilettura
della *Caccia di Diana*," *Italica* 61 (1984): 312–34; and Branca, *Tradizione delle
opere*, 1:122.

6. Boccaccio calls the women "le donne e le pulcelle" in canto 16.12 and "donne
gentili e donzelle" in 16.35.

7. For the count, see Cassell and Kirkham's "Glossary of the Huntresses," in
Diana's Hunt, 196–218.

8. Also called the *donna gentile*. See 2.32; 4.1, 4.11, 4.31, 4.56; 16.46; and 17 and
18 passim.

9. Hollander, *Boccaccio's Two Venuses*, 133, sees the south being opposed to the
east in terms of a moral compass. See also Cassell and Kirkham, *Diana's Hunt*,
note to verses 2.33 and 4.3.

10. See also Boccaccio, *Comedia delle ninfe fiorentine*, ed. Antonio Enzo Quaglio,
in Boccaccio, *Tutte le opere*, ed. Vittore Branca, vol. 2 (Milan: Mondadori,
1964), 46.5, where the protagonist Ameto undergoes a similar transformation:

"d'animale bruto, uomo divenuto essere egli pare"; Boccaccio, *Filocolo*, ed. Antonio Enzo Quaglio, in Boccaccio, *Tutte le opere*, vol. 1 (Milan: Mondadori, 1967), 3.67.12 (echoing *Inferno* 26): "noi non ci nascemmo per vivere come bruti, ma per seguire virtù"; and *Teseida* 2.44: "non per esser tristi—come bruti animali."

11. The terms all describe medieval literary genres that stage dialogue or a contest between contrasting positions in debate. For the list see Branca, *Caccia di Diana*, intro., 6. On Diana, see Enrica Gambin, *Trivia nelle tre corone: I volti di Diana nelle opere di Dante, Petrarca, Boccaccio* (Padua: Il Poligrafo, 2009). See Illiano, "Per una rilettura," 320, however, for the position that Venus picks up where Diana leaves off; and Bergin, *Boccaccio*, 69. Cassell and Kirkham, *Diana's Hunt*, 59, see the goddesses as "inimical on the surface" but cooperative in terms of allegory ("pagan myth as vehicle for a Christian moral"), preparing the catechumen for baptism.

12. See *Filocolo* 3.53.

13. *Comedia delle ninfe* 31.8: *vendicatrice*; *Amorosa visione* 42.75: *insensata*; *Ninfale fiesolano* 94.7: *crudele*; *Teseida* 7.50.1, gloss: *incivile*; and *Filocolo* 5.21.3, where it is suggested that she was not beautiful. In the *Genealogia deorum gentilium*, ed. Vittorio Zaccaria, in Boccaccio, *Tutte le opere*, vols. 8–9 (Milan: Mondadori, 1998), there are numerous discussions of Diana. See especially 2.6 and 2.31; 4.16 and 4.20; 5.2, 5.3, and 5.49; 9.20 and 9.35; 10.50; 11.17 and 11.19; 12.16. Boccaccio does not include Diana, however, in his *De mulieribus claris*, although he does include Venus.

14. For the Actaeon myth, see Ovid, *Metamorphoses* 3.138ff. The interpretations of the Diana-Actaeon myth are multiple. In one reading, the hunter Actaeon is innocent, and Diana—angry that he saw her bathing—turns him into a stag that is subsequently devoured by his dogs. In another interpretation, Actaeon happens upon Diana but immediately feels lust at seeing her bathing; it is actually he who turns himself into a stag (beast) devoured by his dogs (own thoughts). On Actaeon in Boccaccio's works, see Vittore Branca, "L'Atteone del Boccaccio fra allegoria cristiana, evemerismo trasfigurante, narrativa esemplare, visualizzazione rinascimentale," *Studi sul Boccaccio* 24 (1996): 193–208. See, for example, *Comedia delle ninfe* 2.18; 18.18; 24.5; 31.8–9; *Teseida* 5.57.6; 7.79.5; 9.34.2; and *Filocolo* 5.19.1; 5.21.3.

15. See Branca's discussion of Boccaccio's use of Fulgentius and the Third Vatican Mythographer for his interpretation of the myth of Actaeon in "L'Atteone del Boccaccio"; and Cassell and Kirkham's introduction to *Diana's Hunt*.

16. *Decameron* 5.8.

17. See Isidore of Seville, *The Etymologies*, trans. Stephen A. Barney et al. (Cambridge: Cambridge University Press, 2006), 8.11.76–79 and 10.5.279–83. See

also Ovid, John of Salisbury, Andreas Capellanus, and others, as discussed by Cassell and Kirkham, *Diana's Hunt*, 20.

18. See *Genealogia* 4.16.5 and book 14, and the Boccaccio-Glossator of *Teseida* 7.80; Ovid, *Metamorphoses* 2.401–16, 7.74; Virgil, *Aeneid* 4.511; and Dante, *Paradiso* 23.25–27.

19. *Genealogia* 4.16.16.

20. *Genealogia* 4.20.2, 4.16.15; 5.2.7.

21. Cassell and Kirkham, *Diana's Hunt*, 8.

22. Caterina di Rincione and Lariella Caracciola.

23. See *Comedia delle ninfe* 35.2–18. Other legends hold Parthenope to have been a Siren who washed ashore onto the tiny island of Megaride (where Castel dell'Ovo is today) after despairing over not being able to enchant Ulysses. Still others say she was a Greek maiden who ran away from home with her lover and settled in the environs of what is today Naples. Boccaccio does not include Parthenope in his *De mulieribus claris*, but she does appear in *Genealogia* 7.20.

24. For a discussion of the animal allegories, see Cassell and Kirkham's introduction to *Diana's Hunt* as well as their notes to the poem; and Cassell, "Boccaccio's *Caccia di Diana*." See also Branca, "L'Atteone del Boccaccio."

25. See Cassell's discussion in "Boccaccio's *Caccia di Diana*" of the texts to which the poet would have had access in the royal library in Naples. See also the introduction to Cassell and Kirkham, *Diana's Hunt*, 13–21, 37–68.

26. See Dante, *Vita nuova* 2; and *Inferno* 1.31–43.

27. See Cassell and Kirkham's discussion of the baptism symbolism in *Diana's Hunt*, 51–61, and notes to the poem.

28. He would have been enrolled at one of the many *botteghe d'abbaco* (abacist schools) that dotted commercially active cities, such as Florence, in the early fourteenth century. In his *Genealogia* Boccaccio mentions that he studied arithmetic as a boy because his father wanted him to become a merchant (15.10.7). The kinds of tasks a young banker would have performed were weighing money, changing money, paying credit letters, and keeping balance registers. See Vittore Branca, *Giovanni Boccaccio: Profilo biografico* (Florence: Sansoni, 1977), 13–14, 18.

29. This is not to be confused with "logistics" (basic arithmetic as we know it today) or the third-century *Arithmetica* by Diophantus, which was a collection of algebraic problems. *Arithmetica* had its roots in Pythagorean thought, as expounded on in antiquity by Euclid (books 7, 8, and 9), Nicomachus, and Theon of Smyrna, among others; and in the Middle Ages especially by Boethius in his *De institutione arithmetica* (which is essentially a translation of Nicomachus's *Introduction to Arithmetic*) and later authors such as Isidore of

Seville and Rabanus Maurus. This branch of mathematics considered the properties of numbers, relationships between numbers, and what happens when they are "operated" on by multiplication, division, subtraction, and addition. Numbers were thought to have qualities such as shape (square, triangular, rectangular, etc.), and could be perfect, superfluous, or diminutive. They could be discrete or continuous, composite or incomposite, prime or relatively prime. They could be rational or irrational (like the area of a circle). They could be part of a fascinating series, such as the prime numbers, or that named for the twelfth-century mathematician Fibonacci (Leonardo Pisano). Boccaccio could have learned some number theory in his abacist studies as young boy in Florence but would have encountered more complex topics with Andalò del Negro, one of his teachers in Naples. On Andalò see the *Genealogia*, especially 1.6.4; 4.16.11; 8.2.9; 15.6.4. See also Boccaccio, *Esposizioni sopra la "Comedia" di Dante*, ed. Giorgio Padoan, in Boccaccio, *Tutte le opere*, vol. 6 (Milan: Mondadori, 1965), on *Inferno* 5.62–63.

30. See Warren Van Egmond, *Practical Mathematics in the Italian Renaissance: A Catalog of Italian Abbacus Manuscripts and Printing Books to 1600*, Supplement to Annali dell'Istituto e Museo di Storia della Scienza (1980), fasc. 1, monograph 4 (Florence: Istituto e Museo di Storia della Scienza, 1980), 21–26; and Raffaella Franci, "L'insegnamento dell'aritmetica nel medioevo," *Scienze matematiche e insegnamento in epoca medioevale, Atti del Convegno Internazionale di Studio, Chieti, 2–4 maggio, 1996*, ed. Paolo Freguglia, Luigi Pellegrini, and Roberto Paciocco (Naples: Edizioni Scientifiche Italiane, 2000), 112–51.

31. *Genealogia* 15.6.10.

32. *Genealogia* 15.10.7.

33. See Victoria Kirkham, "Numerology and Allegory in Boccaccio's *Caccia di Diana*," *Traditio* 34 (1978): 303–29; and Kirkham, "'Chiuso parlare' in Boccaccio's *Teseida*" (1983), reprinted in *The Sign of Reason in Boccaccio's Fiction* (Florence: Olschki, 1993), 17–53.

34. For a larger discussion of the number fifty-eight, see Kirkham, "Amorous Vision, Scholastic Vistas," in *Sign of Reason*, 109.

35. See Kirkham's "'Chiuso parlare,'" 26ff., for a discussion of the number seven in the *Teseida* and Boccaccio's other works.

36. See Kirkham, "Numerology and Allegory," 328.

Chapter Ten

1. The poem's modern editor discusses internal evidence for dating it in his introduction: Boccaccio, *Amorosa visione*, ed. Vittore Branca, in Boccaccio, *Tutte le opere*, ed. Branca, vol. 3 (Milan: Mondadori, 1974), 6–8. Eight manuscripts preserve the text in what Branca termed the "A" version. He believed

that Boccaccio had returned to revise the poem some ten years later in a "B" version represented solely in the *editio princeps*, edited by Girolamo Claricio (Milan, 1521). "B" serves as the basis for the bilingual Italian-English *Amorosa visione*, trans. Robert Hollander, Timothy Hampton, and Margherita Frankel (Hanover, NH: University Press of New England, 1986). The Hollander volume includes a useful introduction by Branca, based closely on that in his Mondadori edition, which condenses information from his major essay, *"L'Amorosa Visione* (tradizione, significati, fortuna)," *Annali della Reale Scuola Normale Superiore di Pisa (Lettere, Storia e Filosofia)*, ser. 2, 11 (1942): 263–90. For the date and publisher of the first edition, see Branca's "L'editio princeps dell'*Amorosa visione* del Boccaccio," *Bibliofilia* 40 (1938): 460–68. In the following year, Branca published the first twentieth-century edition of the poem, *Le rime, L'amorosa visione, La caccia di Diana* (Bari: Laterza, 1939). From the beginning, other scholars raised doubts concerning the attribution of "B" to Boccaccio, and the weight of philological evidence by now compellingly explains its textual variants as interventions and updatings made by the Milanese humanist who first published it in 1521. For the critical debate and arguments in favor of Claricio's "authorship," see especially Vincenzo Pernicone, "Girolamo Claricio collaboratore del Boccaccio," *Belfagor* 1 (1946): 474–86; Ezio Raimondi, "Il Claricio: Metodo di un filologo umanista," *Convivium* 17 (1948): 108–34, 258–311, 436–59; Marco Santagata's introduction to Petrarch, *Trionfi, Rime estravaganti, Codice degli abbozzi*, ed. Vinicio Pacca and Laura Paolino (Milan: Mondadori, 1996), xxix-xxx; Giorgio Padoan, *"Habent sua fata libelli* I, Dal Claricio al Manelli al Boccaccio," in Padoan, *Ultimi studi di filologia dantesca e boccacciana*, ed. Aldo Maria Costantini (Ravenna: Longo, 2002), 69–122; Marco Veglia, "La filologia di Zadig," *Ecdotica* 4 (2007): 134–57, revised for the introduction to Ezio Raimondi, *Il Claricio: Metodo di un filologo umanista*, ed. Marco Veglia (Bologna: Bononia University Press, 2009).

2.   Robert Hollander suggests that the fifty chapters of the *Comedia delle ninfe fiorentine* and the fifty *canti* of the *Amorosa visione* reflect Boccaccio's sense of inferiority vis-à-vis Dante: "To attempt half a *Commedia* seemed daring enough." See Hollander, *Boccaccio's Two Venuses* (New York: Columbia University Press, 1977), 205 n. 67. Cf. Victoria Kirkham, "Amorous Vision, Scholastic Vistas," in *The Sign of Reason in Boccaccio's Fiction* (Florence: Olschki, 1993), 67.

3.   Vittore Branca is one who notes the likely connection in his introduction to the Mondadori edition of the *Amorosa visione*, p. 11.

4.   Boccaccio's signature occupies the final verse of the first sonnet. The sonnets contain respectively seventeen verses, sixteen verses, and twenty-five verses, for a total of fifty-eight verses, the same as the regular number of

verse totals per canto in *Caccia di Diana*. Commenting on this connection, Francesco Bruni, *Boccaccio: L'invenzione della letteratura mezzana* (Bologna: Il Mulino, 1990), 213, aptly speaks of the *Visione*'s "gothic geometry." The third sonnet, longer, is technically both *rinterzato* and *caudato*, extended internally and "tailed." The poem teases us with its number symbolism, for which see Kirkham, "Amorous Vision, Scholastic Vistas," esp. 59, 102–10. Four of the eight manuscripts that transmit the text, which has a total of 4,406 verses (excluding the sonnets), contain three works in *terza rima* by Boccaccio (the *ternario* "Contento quasi ne' pensier d'amore," *Amorosa visione*, and *Caccia di Diana*), an anthology that Branca hypothesizes Boccaccio himself compiled; see Branca, "Per l'attribuzione della *Caccia di Diana* a Giovanni Boccaccio," in *Tradizione delle opere di Giovanni Boccaccio*, vol. 1, *Un primo elenco dei codici e tre studi* (Rome: Edizioni di Storia e Letteratura, 1958), 121–43. Victoria Kirkham has suggested that this trilogy was originally intended to carry the author's embedded signature just once, in the *Visione* set at the center and flanked by the two shorter works; see Kirkham, "Iohannes de Certaldo: La firma dell'autore," in *Gli zibaldoni di Boccaccio: Memoria, scrittura, riscrittura; Atti del Seminario internazionale di Firenze-Certaldo (26–28 aprile 1996)*, ed. Michelangelo Picone and Claude Cazalé Bérard (Florence: Franco Cesati, 1998), 455–68.

5. Sylvia Huot, "Poetic Ambiguity and Reader Response in Boccaccio's *Amorosa visione*," *Modern Philology* 83.2 (Nov. 1985): 109–22, demonstrates the "close relationship between lyric and narrative components" in what she calls the "composite text" of the *Amorosa visione*. The content in the sonnets connects meaningfully to their "unpacking" in the cantos of *terza rima*. Cf. Victoria Kirkham, "A New Flame," in *Fabulous Vernacular: Boccaccio's "Filocolo" and the Art of Medieval Fiction* (Ann Arbor: University of Michigan Press, 2001), 21–23: the letters GIOVANNI BOCCACCIO in the words of the prefatory sonnets correspond to the *terzine* in canto 15, where a fresco represents the poet's lady seated beside the enthroned god of love. They have "a tryst on the page" and "embrace acrostically."

6. Janet Smarr, "Boccaccio and the Choice of Hercules," *MLN* 92.1 (1977): 146–52.

7. There is a good account of Boccaccio's familiarity with, and indebtedness to, painters and sculptors in Creighton Gilbert, "La devozione di Giovanni Boccaccio per gli artisti e per l'arte," in *Boccaccio visualizzato: Narrare per immagini fra Medioevo e Rinascimento*, ed. Vittore Branca (Turin: Einaudi, 1999), 1:145–53. Another study, by Lucia Battaglia Ricci, *Ragionare nel giardino: Boccaccio e i cicli pittorici del "Trionfo della morte"* (Rome: Salerno, 2000), is particularly useful for the influence of fresco painting on Boccaccio.

8   For more on these *Decameron* tales involving fresco art, see Victoria Kirkham, "Painters at Play on the Judgment Day (*Dec.* VIII, 9)" *Studi sul Boccaccio* 14 (1983–84): 256–77, reprinted in *The Sign of Reason*; and Kirkham, "A Pedigree for Courtesy, or, How Boccaccio's Purser Cured a Miser," *Studi sul Boccaccio* 25 (1997): 213–38; reprinted as "The Tale of Guglielmo Borsiere (*Dec.* I, 8)," in *The "Decameron" First Day in Perspective*, ed. Elissa Weaver (Toronto: University of Toronto Press, 2004), 179–206.

9.   Alain of Lille, *Anticlaudianus sive De officiis viri boni et perfecti*, Biblioteca Augustana, http://www.hs-augsburg.de/~harsch/augustana.html. For the text in English, see *Anticlaudianus or the Good and Perfect Man*, trans. James J. Sheridan (Toronto: Institute of Pontifical Studies, 1973). Parallels are discussed by Kirkham, "Amorous Vision, Scholastic Vistas," 92–93.

10. Petrarch, *Africa*, Biblioteca Italiana, http://www.bibliotecaitaliana.it/xtf/view?docId=bibit000921/bibit000921.xml; *Petrarca's Africa*, trans. Thomas G. Bergin and Alice S. Wilson (New Haven, CT: Yale University Press, 1977).

11. Hayden B. J. Maginnis, "Boccaccio: A Poet Making Pictures," *Source: Notes in the History of Art* 15.2 (Winter 1996): 1–7, describes the varied internal arrangement of each mural and the unclear spatial—and thus programmatic—relationship among them.

12. Jonathan Usher, "An Autobiographical Phaethon: Boccaccio's *Allegoria Mitologica*," in *Petrarca e Boccaccio: Modelli letterari fra Medioevo e Umanesimo*, ed. Annalisa Cipollone and Carlo Caruso (Alexandria: Edizioni dell'Orso, 2005), 49–89.

13. Unless otherwise indicated, all translations are mine.

14. Many proposals have been advanced concerning the symbolic identity of the guide and the poet's lady, with divergent opinions on how to understand the seemingly ambiguous allegory of the *Visione* more generally. See, for an overview, Branca's introduction to the Mondadori edition, p. 16. He settles for seeing her as "the aspiration toward virtue deep in every good soul." Franca Petrucci Nardelli's notion of the *Amorosa visione* as burlesque verse in a sodomitic key, "*L'Amorosa visione* rivisitata," *Quaderni Medievali* 24 (Dec. 1987): 57–75, has not met with critical acceptance. Janet Smarr, *Boccaccio and Fiammetta: The Narrator as Lover* (Urbana: University of Illinois Press, 1986), chap. 5, takes the guide as Reason and Fiammetta as Wisdom, a reading in which Kirkham, "Amorous Vision, Scholastic Vistas," concurs. Smarr's view of a Neoplatonic ascent in the *Visione* counters Hollander, *Boccaccio's Two Venuses*, 77–91, who had emphasized the poem's erotic humor. Bruni, *Boccaccio*, 215–16, views the *Visione* as a "precarious" moral corrective to an overly permissive vernacular tradition (e.g., the *Romance of the Rose*, which culminates

with the Lover's sexual conquest of his "rose"). He calls the guide "Pietà" and Fiammetta Love-Charity.

15. Although the female guide reverses Dante's Virgil, she is a return to Virgil's own *Aeneid*, where Aeneas makes his journey to the underworld guided by the Sibyl.

16. Recall the Cacciaguida cantos, particularly *Par.* 17.128: "tutta tua visïon fa manifesta" (make manifest all your vision).

17. Branca sketches the father-son association as Bardi bankers at the court of King Robert in *Giovanni Boccaccio: Profilo biografico* (Florence: Sansoni, 1977), 16–26. His *Profilo biografico* had first appeared in Boccaccio, *Tutte le opere*, vol. 1 (Milan: Mondadori, 1968), 1–203.

18. Vittore Branca laid a useful foundation for beginning to sort out the reciprocal influences in Boccaccio and Petrarch's "game of mirrors" in "Implicazioni espressive, temi e stilemi fra Petrarca e Boccaccio," in *Boccaccio medievale e nuovi saggi sul "Decameron,"* 6th ed. (Florence: Sansoni, 1986), 300–332.

19. The debate continues on the question of whether or not Dante was the author of the *Fiore*, an Italian version in *ottava rima* of the *Romance of the Rose*. See, e.g., Zygmunt G. Barański and Patrick Boyde, eds., *The Fiore in Context*, The William and Katherine Devers Series in Dante Studies 2 (Notre Dame, IN: University of Notre Dame Press, 1997).

Chapter Eleven

1. Boccaccio, *Comedia delle ninfe fiorentine*, ed. Antonio Enzo Quaglio, in Boccaccio, *Tutte le opere*, ed. Vittore Branca, vol. 2 (Milan: Mondadori, 1964), 37.3: "sì come luogo abondevole di giovinette cavriuole e lascive, di damme giovani preste e più correnti, e di cerve mature, a ogni rete, cane o istrale avvisate." All citations are from this edition. Based on exhaustive study, Quaglio's edition of the *Comedia delle ninfe* is the first to number the separate prose and poetry sections as chapters (fifty all told). Citations here follow his numbering. Translations are my own unless otherwise indicated. See also Boccaccio, *L'Ameto*, trans. Judith Serafini-Sauli (New York: Garland, 1985), with brief but helpful notes; and Bernadette Marie McCoy, "An Annotated Translation of Boccaccio's *Ameto*" (PhD diss., New York University, 1971). The latter is marred by an overemphasis on the work's allusions to Christian conversion.

2. For an excellent introduction to and translation of the *Caccia*, see *Diana's Hunt / Caccia di Diana: Boccaccio's First Fiction*, ed. and trans. Anthony K. Cassell and Victoria Kirkham (Philadelphia: University of Pennsylvania Press, 1991), which notes parallels with the *Ameto* on pp. 30–33, concluding with the statement that it is, like the *Caccia*, "an allegory of virtue triumphant" (33).

3. *Comedia delle ninfe* 49.94–95: "Io mi tornai, dolendo de' miei mali, / al luogo usato."

4. *Comedia delle ninfe* 46.5: "d'animale bruto, uomo divenuto essere li pare." John Addington Symonds, in the nineteenth century, put it bluntly: the *Comedia* is an example of "the power of love to refine a rustic nature." See Symonds, *Italian Literature*, vol. 1, *Renaissance in Italy* (New York: Henry Holt, 1881), 126. Boccaccio will notably return to the theme in the story of *Decameron* 5.1, in which the rustic Cimone, far from being "humanized" by love, is notably dehumanized by it; see Millicent Marcus's article, "The Sweet New Style Reconsidered: A Gloss on the Tale of Cimone (*Decameron* V:1)," *Italian Quarterly* 81 (1980): 5–16.

5. See the introduction to Francesco Sansovino's sixteenth-century edition of the *Ameto*, in which he suggests that the prominence of tale-telling makes the work "quasi . . . un piccolo Decamerone"; *"Comedia delle ninfe fiorentine," di M. Giovanni Boccaccio da Certaldo*, ed. Francesco Sansovino (Venice: Giolito, 1558), fol. ii verso.

6. A number of works since the 1970s remark explicitly on close connections with Dante, among them Robert Hollander, *Boccaccio's Two Venuses* (New York: Columbia University Press, 1977). See, however, Hollander's remarks in *Boccaccio's Dante and the Shaping Force of Satire* (Ann Arbor: University of Michigan Press, 1997), 11: "The *Comedia delle ninfe fiorentine*, a work which may be less 'serious' than we have all assumed, has, because of its apparently orthodox religious sentiments, frequently been discussed as Dantean allegory"; and Robin Kirkpatrick, "The Wake of the *Commedia*," in *Chaucer and the Italian Trecento*, ed. Pietro Boitani (Cambridge: Cambridge University Press, 1983), 201–30: in the *Ameto*, Boccaccio, "like Dante, depicts a process of spiritual education and chooses a form that can only be described as a free variation upon the form of the *Commedia*" (205). More specifically, Giuseppe Velli, "L'*Ameto* e la pastorale: Il significato della forma," in *Boccaccio: Secoli di Vita; Atti del Congresso Internazionale: Boccaccio 1975, Università di California, Los Angeles, 17–19 ottobre 1975*, ed. Marga Cottino-Jones and Edward Tuttle (Ravenna: Longo, 1977), 67–80; and Janet Smarr, "Boccaccio pastorale tra Dante e Petrarca," in *Autori e lettori di Boccaccio*, ed. Michelangelo Picone (Florence: Cesati, 2002), 237–54, argue for the impact of *Purgatorio* on the *Ameto*, especially the cantos focusing on Matelda, Eden, and Beatrice. As the titles of these last two essays suggest, pastoral has been a formative generic model for discussing the *Ameto*, and the following remarks owe much to their insights.

7. *Comedia delle ninfe* 1.5: "ad Amore solo con debita contemplazione seguitare,

in una ho raccolte le sparte cure, i cui effetti se con discreta mente saranno pensati, non troverrò chi biasimi quel ch'io lodo."

8. The phrase "di quanto efficacia sia la bellezza" is Sansovino's, as a marginal note in the chapter where Ameto responds to Lia's first song. See Boccaccio, *Decameron*, ed. Sansovino, 7v.

9. For Nicolas Perella, *Midday in Italian Literature* (Princeton, NJ: Princeton University Press, 1979), 54, Ameto is the "secular descendant of Actaeon, whose initial enchantment and terror dissolve as *real* maidens instead of divinities welcome him."

10. As both their own songs and the final song of Ameto in chap. 47 partially identify them, the seven women can be said to be figures of the following virtues: Mopsa, Prudence; Emilia, Justice; Adiona, Temperance; Acrimonia, Fortitude; Agapes, Charity; Fiammetta, Hope; Lia, Faith. As with the *Caccia di Diana*, each woman belongs to a historical family, but not all the ladies have been fully identified.

11. This question is treated with varying degrees of explicitness in the *Caccia di Diana* and *Filocolo* as well, both of which deal with baptism and conversion, as Victoria Kirkham observes in the introduction to the translation of the *Caccia*, Cassell and Kirkham, *Diana's Hunt*, 24. That Boccaccio's contemporaries saw his work as linked to "baptism" is suggested by the presence of what Paul Watson and Victoria Kirkham convincingly argue is a baptismal font in an early fifteenth-century salver that shows several scenes from the *Comedia*. See their "Amore e virtù: Two Salvers Depicting Boccaccio's *Comedia delle ninfe fiorentine* in the Metropolitan Museum," *Metropolitan Museum Journal* 10 (1975): 35–50.

12. Examples of "redemptive metamorphoses" in the text can be found throughout, suggesting how Boccaccio conceived of his work as a corrective of Ovid.

13. *Comedia delle ninfe* 37.4: "estimando che gli audaci sieno aiutati dalla Fortuna." Cf. Virgil, *Aeneid* 10.284 and *Filocolo* 4.101.8, parallels noted by Quaglio in his commentary.

14. *Comedia delle ninfe* 49.37–44: "Così ne' miei pensieri e nel disio / conoscea que' d'Ameto . . . /. . . . / E di lui invidioso, palesare, / tal volta fu mi volli."

15. For further elaboration of the two Venuses in Boccaccio, see Hollander, *Boccaccio's Two Venuses*.

16. See more generally the comments of Nicolas J. Perella, "The World of Boccaccio's *Filocolo*," *PMLA* 76 (1961): 330–39, on the role of beauty in the *Filocolo* and elsewhere in Boccaccio's work, particularly as contrasted with the *stil novo* poets: "The beauty that strikes them is a reflection of an inner or spiritual beauty, and it is ultimately the lady's goodness that moves to virtue. For Boc-

caccio, on the other hand, it is beauty primarily as a physical quality that is made to have a refining or elevating effect" (335).

17. *Comedia delle ninfe* 42.1: "non quella Venere che gli stolti alle loro disordinate concupiscenzie chiamano dea." For Ficino, Venus is "that intellect . . . located in the Angelic Mind . . . entranced by an innate love for understanding the beauty of god," and the other "the power of procreation attributed to the World Soul"; cited in Patricia Rubin, "The Seductions of Antiquity," in *Manifestations of Venus: Art and Sexuality*, ed. Caroline Arscott and Katie Scott (Manchester: Manchester University Press, 2002), 24–38 (30).

18. *Comedia delle ninfe* 31.1: "Ameto rientrò ne' primi pensieri, ma con più temperato disio. Egli caccia da sé le imaginazioni vane, alle quali gli effetti conosce impossibili, e alle vere cose entra con dolce pensiero."

19. *Comedia delle ninfe* 46.3: "Similemente vede che sieno le ninfe, le quali più all'occhio che allo 'ntelletto erano piaciute, e ora allo 'ntelletto piacciono più che all'occhio."

20. It is "per salvatichezza o per disdegno" that Affren fails to respond to Mopsa (18.15).

21. *Comedia delle ninfe* 47.46–48: "Il qual s'avien che io voglia lasciare / a chi dietro verrà, sì che si possa, / sì come io, d'esse innamorare."

22. *Comedia delle ninfe* 43.7–12: "Svelin le luci oscure e nebulose / d'Ameto . . . / acciò che e', quanto all'umana gente/ è licito vederne, sappia dire / tra' suoi compagni poi, di me ardente."

23. The Italian, difficult to unravel, asks that his pages circulate widely, well bound and wrapped in silk, and that they not be used to wrap packages of woven wool or to line berets (47.51–60).

24. *Comedia delle ninfe* 31.8: "Oh quanto io ancora ho più di grazia che 'l misero Atteon, al quale non fu licito di potere ridire le vedute bellezze della vendicatrice Diana; e a me non fia tolto di potere in ciascun tempo narrare co' cari compagni il sentito bene."

25. The quotation is Tityrus's line in Virgil's first eclogue: "It is a god who gave us this peace"; *Virgil: Eclogues, Georgics, Aeneid I-VI*, trans. H. Rushton Fairclough, rev. G. P. Goold (Cambridge, MA: Harvard University Press, 2004), 1:6.

26. See the comment of Tobias Foster Gittes, *Boccaccio's Naked Muse: Eros, Culture, and the Mythopoeic Image* (Toronto: University of Toronto Press, 2008), 102–5, regarding the importance of Cadmus for the story of Florence's founding: he was both a "culture-hero" and inventor of writing.

27. These are poems that in any case owe a great deal to Polyphemus's song to Galatea in Ovid's *Metamorphoses* 13 and Virgil's *Eclogue* 2. Hence they share a common pastoral tradition.

28. Giovanni Claricio, the editor of the 1520 *Ameto*, in fact rewrote large sections of the *Comedìa* to place it more squarely within the tradition of Sannazaro—an act of editorial chutzpah that had scholars arguing for the next four centuries about the authentic *Comedìa*, at least until Quaglio's scholarly edition put the matter to rest. See Boccaccio, *Comedìa delle ninfe fiorentine*, ed. Antonio Enzo Quaglio (Florence: Sansoni, 1963), appendix, "Girolamo Claricio editore dell'*Ameto*," cclxxx-cccv. Sansovino (above, note 5) and subsequent editors and critics have been strongly influenced by the connections with Sannazaro; when Ameto leaves the gathering at the end of the text, Sansovino simply writes as a marginal annotation "Così il Sannazaro" (98).

29. *Comedie delle ninfe* 17.6: "Adunque, narranti, e chi noi siamo insieme ci facciamo conte, e, dicendo, faremo che noi oziose, come le misere fanno, non passeremo il chiaro giorno."

30. Again, see Sansovino, fol. vi verso, where he mentions the young Giovanni enamoured of a "Lucia."

31. *Comedìa delle ninfe* 39.73–78: "E se nella presente vita attiva / d'Aristotile avesser gli alti ingegni / inteso con tal fede operativa, / chi dubita che egli i lieti regni / ora terrebbe con gli altri seguaci."

32. *Purgatorio* 27.108: "lei lo vedere, e me l'ovrare appaga"; in the translation of Allen Mandelbaum (New York: Bantam, 1984).

33. *Purgatorio* 27.94–96.: "de l'oriente / prima raggiò nel monte Citerea, / che di foco d'amor par sempre ardente."

34. See Velli, "L'*Ameto* e la pastorale," 77–79, for a discussion of the virtues here and in connection with *Ameto* 45.1–9, in which we have another elaboration of the "stelle."

35. *Purgatorio* 1.19: "Lo bel pianeto che d'amar conforta."

36. *Paradiso* 2.16–18: "Que' gloriosi che passaro al Colco / non s'ammiraron come voi farete / quando Iason vider fatto bifolco."

37. Peter Hawkins, *Dante's Testaments: Essays in Scriptural Imagination* (Stanford, CA: Stanford University Press, 1999), 279: "Reaching far beyond the georgic poet's cultivation of well-known fields, Dante is instead an epic plowman whose men make one 'versus' after another. In so doing, he breaks open *terra incognita*, canto by canto. He is the unabashed master of the new."

38. *Comedìa delle ninfe* 44.5: "reggete la debole mente a tanta cosa . . . se possibile è che umana lingua narri le divine bellezze, la mia possa ancora ridire."

39. His ascent is capped here, suggesting the soundness of Guido di Pino's observation that Boccaccio's allegory "does not have the force and direction of an ascent: rather, it represents the confrontation on a human scale between virtue and sensuality." See Di Pino, *La polemica del Boccaccio* (Florence: Vallecchi, 1953), 69.

40. After listing the roles of the women in the *Comedia*, Sansovino, fol. iii, concludes: "One could say that the seven women represent the seven fields of learning, which like heavenly beings reveal themselves in lowly places to whoever devotes himself to them and confer greatness upon him. Such was perhaps the fate desired by Boccaccio, who took such great delight in poetry."

41. It is also known that Niccolò took part in an unsuccessful revolt some twenty years later against the Florentine current regime, for which he paid with his life. For comments, see the edition of Carlo Salinari and Natalino Sapegno, in *Decameron-Filocolo-Ameto-Fiammetta* (Milan: Ricciardi, 1966).

42. *Comedia delle ninfe* 50.2: "sacratissima chiesa di Roma."

43. *Comedia delle ninfe* 49. 4–6: "ad ascoltare i lieti e vaghi amori, / *nascosamente*, delle ninfe belle, / que' recitanti, e de' loro amadori."

44. Like Aeneas, Dido is mentioned frequently throughout the text, perhaps most memorably by the suicidal Caleone, who claims to Fiammetta that when his first beloved left him, "io estimo che 'l dolore della impaziente Didone fosse minore che 'l mio, quand'ella vide Enea dipartirsi" (35.83). If Caleone remains a double for Boccaccio in the *Comedia*, then this remark becomes especially pertinent when considering the narrator's poem in chap. 49 and his reflection on "the new flame that reawakens the old one, just as I experienced it [when hearing the nymphs]" (49.22–24).

45. *Comedia delle ninfe* 50.3: "prendi questa rosa, tra le spine della mia avversità nata, la quale a forza fuori de' rigidi pruni tirò la fiorentina bellezza, me nell'infimo stante delle tristizie."

46. In the foundational story told by Lia, Mars is called on to name the new town. He is about to give it some warlike name in keeping with his own identity, but when he sees Venus's dismay, he takes the flowers she is holding and announces, "Along with these flowers, the flowering season [of spring] moves me to name this city thusly, and so I give to her for all eternity the name Florenzia," thus restoring Venus's happiness and giving the citizens reason to hope in their future (*Comedia delle ninfe* 38.89).

47. *Comedia delle ninfe* 2.1–9: "Quella virtù che già l'ardito Orfeo / mosse a cercar le case di Plutone / . . . / per forza tira il mio debole ingegno / a cantar le tue lode, o Citerea, / insieme con le forze del tuo regno."

Chapter Twelve

1. The *Comedia delle ninfe* presents the foundation of Certaldo as a story of miscegenation. For a parallel between the two accounts, see Tobias Foster Gittes, *Boccaccio's Naked Muse: Eros, Culture, and the Mythopoeic Imagination* (Toronto: University of Toronto Press, 2008), 94–121.

2. These works are *Comedia delle ninfe fiorentine* (1341–42), *Amorosa visione*

(1342–43), *Elegia di madonna Fiammetta* (1343–44), and *Ninfale fiesolano* (1344–46).

3. Pier Giorgio Ricci dated the *Ninfale* much earlier, to Boccaccio's Neapolitan years; see Ricci, "Dubbi gravi intorno al 'Ninfale fiesolano,'" *Studi sul Boccaccio* 6 (1971): 109–24; reprinted in *Studi sulla vita e le opere del Boccaccio* (Milan: Ricciardi, 1985), 13–28. Vittore Branca cautiously follows the traditional attribution to the Florentine period and suggests a date between 1344 and 1346. This hypothesis prevails among scholars. See Branca, *Giovanni Boccaccio: Profilo biografico* (Florence: Sansoni, 1977), 69 n. 19. For a critical examination of Ricci's arguments, see Armando Balduino, "Sul *Ninfale fiesolano*," in *Boccaccio, Petrarca e altri poeti del Trecento* (Florence: Olschki, 1984), 249–66. This essay is a revised version of Balduino's introduction to *Ninfale fiesolano*, in Boccaccio, *Tutte le opere*, ed. Vittore Branca, vol. 3 (Milan: Mondadori, 1974), 275–82. See also Luigi Surdich, *Boccaccio* (Rome: Laterza, 2001), 88–95; and Bruno Porcelli, "Sull'unità compositiva del *Ninfale Fiesolano*," in *Dante maggiore e Boccaccio minore* (Pisa: Giardini, 1987), 160–73.

4. This crisis had affected Boccaccio's father, Boccaccino di Chellino, as agent of the Bardi house. According to Branca, Boccaccio was in Ravenna not before 1345 and possibly in 1346, before Ostasio's death in the same year. See Branca, *Giovanni Boccaccio*, 72–76. For the events in Florence during this period, see Giovanni Villani, *Cronica*, ed. Giovanni Porta, Fondazione Pietro Bembo (Parma: Guanda, 1991), 12.55.

5. On Boccaccio's activity during the period of composition of the *Ninfale* and the historical context, see Branca, *Giovanni Boccaccio*, 69–77.

6. In his literal commentary to *Inferno* 15.61–63, Boccaccio reports the story of the foundation of Florence according to the vulgate mythography of his times with a certain degree of skepticism about its historical truth. According to Stefano Baldassarri, Boccaccio's myth of the Florentine origins anticipates the need to re-elaborate the image of the city that prevailed in the Quattrocento. This essay argues that such a position is already present in the *Ninfale*. See Baldassarri, "A Tale of Two Cities: Accounts of the Origins of Fiesole and Florence from the Anonymous *Chronica* to Leonardo Bruni," *Studi Rinascimentali* 5 (2007): 29–56, 46–47.

7. Pier Massimo Forni sees in the illegitimacy of Pruneo's birth a possible projection of Boccaccio's own autobiographical theme; see Forni's edition of the *Ninfale fiesolano* (Milan: Mursia, 1991), 11.

8. Velli's remarks about the pastoral genre in the *Comedia delle ninfe* may be extended to the *Ninfale*: "La pastorale è anche . . . verifica delle complesse ragioni della vita associata mediante distacco e rifugio nella natura e dunque riporto a misura di esse contro valori originari ed elementari." Velli, "*L'Ameto* e

la pastorale," in *Petrarca e Boccaccio: Tradizione—memoria—scrittura* (Padua: Antenore, 1995), 196. See also Velli, "Tityrus redivivus: The Rebirth of Vergilian Pastoral from Dante to Sannazzaro (and Tasso)," in *The Western Pennsylvania Symposium on World Literatures, Selected Proceedings, 1974–1991: A Retrospective*, ed. Carla E. Lucente (Greensburg, PA: Eadmer, 1992), 107–18. See also Simona Lorenzini, "Rassegna di studi sul Boccaccio bucolico," *Studi sul Boccaccio* 38 (2010): 153–65.

9. The pastoral fable became a popular genre in Tuscany and in other Italian courts. Among the works influenced by Boccaccio are the *Driadeo d'amore* by Luca Pulci and Lorenzo the Magnificent's *Ambra* (as well as his parodic *Nencia da Barberino*). For the development of the genre in the Quattrocento, see Marzia Pieri, "La pastorale," in *Manuale di letteratura italiana: Storia per generi e problemi*, ed. Franco Brioschi and Costanzo Di Girolamo (Turin: Bollati Boringhieri, 1993), 1:273–92.

10. Joseph Tusiani, who translated the *Ninfale* into English octaves of blank verse with a final rhyming couplet, also emphasizes the *Ninfale*'s stylistic proximity to the *Decameron*. See *Nymphs of Fiesole*, trans. Tusiani (Rutherford, NJ: Fairleigh Dickinson University Press, 1971), 8, 17–18. See further Francesco Bruni, *Boccaccio: L'invenzione della letteratura mezzana* (Bologna: Il Mulino, 1990), 227–34; and Surdich, *Boccaccio*, 89. For a linguistic analysis of the *Ninfale*, see Balduino, "Sul *Ninfale*," 255–57. For Boccaccio's vital contribution to the evolution of the octave, see Guglielmo Gorni, "Un'ipotesi sull'origine dell'ottava rima," in *Metrica e analisi letteraria* (Bologna: Il Mulino, 1993), 153–70. See also Lorenzo Bartoli, "Considerazioni attorno ad una questione metricologica: Il Boccaccio e le origini dell'ottava rima," *Quaderns d'Italià* 4–5 (2000): 91–99.

11. On the specific traits of Boccaccio's pastoral with respect to Dante and Petrarch's, see Janet L. Smarr, "Boccaccio pastorale tra Dante e Petrarca," in *Autori e lettori di Boccaccio: Atti del Convegno internazionale di Certaldo (20–22 settembre 2001)*, ed. Michelangelo Picone (Florence: Franco Cesati Editore, 2002), 237–54.

12. According to Francesco Bruni the geographical names symbolize and guarantee the continuity between the archaic past and the present. See Bruni, *Boccaccio*, 227–34, 279–88. Bruno Porcelli observes that the Fiesolan space is at the center of the *Ninfale*; see Porcelli, "Sull'unità compositiva del *Ninfale fiesolano*," 171.

13. The second rubric introducing the beginning of the fable of Africo and Mensola is lost. See Balduino, *Ninfale fiesolano*, 275–89.

14. Boccaccio, *Ninfale* 2.8. Quotations from the *Ninfale* in Italian are from *Ninfale fiesolano*, ed. Balduino, in *Tutte le opere*, vol. 3. English translations are from

The Nymph of Fiesole, trans. Daniel J. Donno (New York: Columbia University Press, 1960). The theme of the *donna altera* associated with hunting—although in a different context but with the same tragic outcome—returns in the tale of Nastagio degli Onesti (*Decameron* 5.8).

15. The story presents the traditional opposition between Venus and Diana. On this theme see Robert Hollander, *Boccaccio's Two Venuses* (New York: Columbia University Press, 1977).

16. As Boccaccio explained in his commentary on *Inferno* 15.61–63, Atlas was a legendary king, descendant of Japheth, son of Noah. For Boccaccio's skepticism about the historical reality of Atlas as founder of Fiesole, see also *Genealogia deorum gentilium* 4.31.2.

17. Boccaccio based his account of the foundation and destruction of Fiesole and Florence on Giovanni Villani's *Cronica*. For the history of the two towns in medieval chroniclers, see Baldassarri, "Tale of Two Cities."

18. When Atlas founds Fiesole, he forces the nymphs to marry and disperses those who refuse to abandon Diana's cult. See *Ninfale* 437.

19. The same problematic relationship between myth and history is present in the *Genealogia deorum gentilium*, in which Boccaccio's vision of history emerges in a more structured form. As Giuseppe Mazzotta notes, "Boccaccio's *Genealogy of the Gentile Gods* is a humanistic theory of history whereby history, like the myths the text retrieves and glosses, is a work of imaginative reconstruction of the past, a reflection on origins so that a new beginning may be envisioned. The way to bring ancient myth and history to life is through the animating powers of poetry." Mazzotta, "Boccaccio: The Mythographer of the City," in *Interpretation and Allegory: Antiquity to the Modern Period*, ed. Jon Whitman (Leiden: Brill, 2000), 364.

20. Anna Cerbo, *Metamorfosi del mito classico da Boccaccio a Marino* (Pisa: ETS, 2001), 19: "il corpo mitologico deve essere uno, non due: uno barbarico e l'altro greco e latino, . . . al contrario della politica, la cultura non può e non deve dividere."

21. For the idea of miscegenation and its constant presence in Boccaccio's myths of origin, see Gittes, *Boccaccio's Naked Muse*, 89–121.

22. Boccaccio probably did not know Lucretian fragments directly; however, his vision of history is consonant with that of the Latin Epicurean. For a study on the possible influences of Epicurean philosophy on Boccaccio, see Marco Veglia, *"La vita lieta": Una lettura del "Decameron"* (Ravenna: Longo, 2000).

23. As Girafone explains to Africo, the Fiesolan hills pullulate with young lovers whom Diana has transformed into birds, springs, and trees (*Ninfale* 95).

24. See Armando Balduino, "Tradizione canterina e tonalità popolareggianti nel *Ninfale fiesolano*," *Studi sul Boccaccio* 2 (1964): 25–80. The *cantari* were narrative

poems in a popular register and in the same *ottava rima* as the *Ninfale*, "sung" or performed orally in the piazzas.

25. "Where is the pledged faith?" Pier Massimo Forni argues that the motive of the "ubi pacta fides?" is fundamental in the *Ninfale* and testifies to the Ovidian influence on the *poemetto* (from Hypsipyle's letter to Jason, *Heroïdes* 6.41–42; and cf. *Fasti* 3.485). See Forni, *Ninfale fiesolano*, 11.

26. Mensola and Africo are transgressive figures similar to many we find in the *Decameron*. They represent the possible disruption of social order that desire may trigger. It is possible to extend to the *Ninfale* Giuseppe Mazzotta's observation on the *Decameron*: "Sexual attraction, which is both fortuitous and 'natural,' is, from a social point of view, an indeterminate value because it can variously be both creative and disruptive of the balance of the world. . . . The effort must lie in finding the manner by which it can be accommodated to the conditions of social life." In the *Ninfale*, King Atlas, who imposes marriage on the nymphs, establishes these conditions. See Mazzotta, *The World at Play in Boccaccio's "Decameron"* (Princeton, NJ: Princeton University Press, 1986), 86.

27. Scholarship has cited also the myths of Jupiter and Calisto (quoted at *Ninfale* 334), Apollo and Daphne, Galatea, Actaeon (although in the *Ninfale* without the inversion we find in the *Comedia delle ninfe*), and Arethusa and Alpheus. Also significant are suggestions from Ovid's *Heroïdes* (the story of Canace and Macareus), and Statius's *Achilleides* for Africo's disguise as nymph. Still controversial is the possible influence of William of Blois's *Alda*. For Ovidian myths in the *Ninfale*, see the commentaries by Armando Balduino and Pier Massimo Forni. See also Linda Armao, "The *Ninfale fiesolano*: Ovidian Bravura Veiling Truth," in *Italiana 1988: Selected Papers from the Proceedings of the Fifth Annual Conference of the American Association of Teachers of Italian, Nov. 18–20, 1988*, ed. Albert N. Mancini, Paolo Giordano, and Anthony J. Tamburri (River Forest, IL: Rosary College, 1990), 35–49.

28. The "diaspora" of Africo's descendants and their transformation from Fiesolans into Florentines begins after the Romans' destruction of Fiesole and foundation of Florence. It ends only with Charlemagne's reconstruction of Florence centuries after Totila had destroyed it. See *Ninfale* 454–64.

29. See Forni's note as editor to *Ninfale* 413.

30. Ovid, *Metamorphoses* (Turin: Einaudi, 1994), 5.638.

31. For the unitary structure of the *Ninfale*, see Porcelli, "Sull'unità compositiva del *Ninfale fiesolano*."

32. On the idea of myth as "function," see Hans Blumenberg, *Work on Myth* (Cambridge, MA: MIT Press, 1985), 3–33. Enlightening are Mazzotta's observations on the use of myth in Boccaccio: "Boccaccio's mythography . . . radically departs from the views held by his predecessors of the Italian

Trecento. Myths are necessary for him because they express poetically the hazy, uncertain beginnings of culture." Mazzotta, "Boccaccio," 351.

Chapter Thirteen

1. The most recent edition of Boccaccio's eclogues, which is used here, is Boccaccio, *Buccolicum carmen*, ed. and trans. Giorgio Bernardi Perini, in Boccaccio, *Tutte le opere*, ed. Vittore Branca, vol. 5, pt. 2 (Milan: Mondadori, 1994), 689–1085. The standard English translation, also used here, is Boccaccio, *Eclogues*, trans. Janet L. Smarr (New York: Garland, 1987). A more recent, less scholarly translation is Boccaccio, *The Latin Eclogues*, trans. David R. Slavitt (Baltimore: Johns Hopkins University Press, 2010). The bibliography on the *Buccolicum carmen* and the pastoral is vast. Still useful are the early studies of Boccaccio and his works: Attilio Hortis, *Studi sulle opere latine del Boccaccio* (Trieste: Julius Dase, 1879), 1–68; Bonaventura Zumbini, "Le egloghe del Boccaccio," *Giornale Storico della Letteratura Italiana* 7 (1886): 94–152; Henri Hauvette, "Sulla cronologia delle egloghe latine del Boccaccio," *Giornale Storico della Letteratura Italiana* 28 (1896): 154–75; Oskar Hecker, *Boccaccio-funde* (Braunschweig: Georg Westermann, 1902), 43–92; Giacomo Lidonnici, "Il significato storico e psicologico del 'Buccolicum carmen' e la sua cronologia," in Boccaccio, *Il Buccolicum carmen*, ed. G. Lidonnici, (Città di Castello: S. Lapi, 1914), 159–312; and Enrico Carrara, *La poesia pastorale* (Milan: Vallardi, 1925), 111–31. For more recent readings of the entire work, which address among other things the complex issues of dating, historical identification, and literary sources, see Giorgio Bernardini Perini, introduction to Boccaccio, *Buccolicum carmen*, vol. 5, pt. 2, 691–704; Janet L. Smarr, introduction to Boccaccio, *Eclogues*, viii-lxxvi; Pier Giorgio Ricci, "Per la cronologia del *Buccolicum carmen*," in *Studi sulla vita e le opere del Boccaccio* (Milan: R. Ricciardi, 1985), 50–66; Gianvito Resta, "Codice bucolico boccacciano," in *I classici nel medioevo e nell'umanesimo* (Genoa: Istituto di Filologia Classica e Medievale, 1975), 59–90; Silvia Labagnara, *Il poema bucolico del Boccaccio* (Rome: L. Ambrosini, 1967); and Smarr, "Boccaccio pastorale tra Dante e Petrarca," in *Autori e lettori del Boccaccio: Atti del convegno internazionale di Certaldo (20–22 settembre 2001)*, ed. Michelangelo Picone (Florence: Cesati, 2002), 237–54. For studies of the pastoral in general that include a section on Boccaccio, see W. Leonard Grant, *Neo-Latin Literature and the Pastoral* (Chapel Hill: University of North Carolina Press, 1965), 80–86 and 97–110; Ellen Z. Lambert, *Placing Sorrow: A Study of the Pastoral Elegy Convention from Theocritus to Milton* (Chapel Hill: University of North Carolina Press, 1976), 61–68; Helen Cooper, *Pastoral: Medieval into Renaissance*, (Totowa, NJ: Rowman and Littlefield, 1977), 36–43; E. Kegel-Brinkgreve, *The Echoing Woods: Bucolic and*

Pastoral from Theocritus to Wordsworth (Amsterdam: Gieben, 1990), 273–83; Giuseppe Velli, "'Tityrus redivivus': The Rebirth of Virgilian Pastoral from Dante to Sannazaro (and Tasso)," in *Forma e parola: Studi in memoria di Fredi Chiappelli*, ed. Dennis J. Dutschke et al. (Rome: Bulzoni, 1992), 67–79; and Thomas K. Hubbard, *The Pipes of Pan: Intertextuality and Literary Filiation in the Pastoral Tradition from Theocritus to Milton* (Ann Arbor: University of Michigan Press, 1998), 235–46. For studies of individual eclogues, see Jonathan Usher, "Ischiro donatore di forti archi (*Buccolicum carmen* XIV, 129)," *Studi sul Boccaccio* 36 (2008): 111–15; Tobias Leuker, "Due maestri del Boccaccio: Il pappagallo e la fenice nel ritratto allegorico della Napoli di Roberto d'Angiò (*Buccolicum carmen* V.28–68)," *Studi sul Boccaccio* 35 (2007): 147–55; Mario Martelli, "'Nemo tibi secundus': Nota a *Buccolicum carmen* I, 93–4," *Studi sul Boccaccio* 19 (1990): 93–101; Giuseppe Chiecchi, "Per l'interpretazione dell'egloga *Olympia* di Giovanni Boccaccio," *Studi sul Boccaccio* 23 (1995): 219–44; and Arnaldo Foresti, "L'egloga ottava di Giovanni Boccaccio," *Giornale Storico della Letteratura Italiana* 78 (1921): 325–43. For more on the bibliography on Boccaccio's bucolic production, see Simona Lorenzini, "Rassegna di studi sul Boccaccio bucolico," *Studi sul Boccaccio* 38 (2010): 153–65.

2. *Genealogia deorum gentilium*, ed. Vittorio Zaccaria, in Boccaccio, *Tutte le opere*, ed. Vittore Branca, vols. 7–8 (Milan: Mondadori, 1998), 14.10.

3. For these commentaries on Petrarch's eclogues, see the classic edition by Antonio Avena, *Il "Bucolicum carmen" e i suoi commenti inediti* (1906; repr., Bologna: Forni, 1969).

4. The chronology of the composition and compilation of the eclogues that make up the *Buccolicum carmen* is still contested and largely unascertainable. The poems address historical events that go back to 1341 (Boccaccio's move from Naples to Florence, referred to in the first eclogue) and that cannot go beyond 1367 (the death of Donato Albanzani's son in 1368, who is referred to as living in the last eclogue). See Perini's notes on the chronology of each eclogue in Boccaccio, *Buccolicum carmen*, vol. 5, pt. 2, pp. 916–1085. Ricci, in "Per la cronologia," dates the first two eclogues to 1346–47, which corresponds to the traditional dating of the vernacular pastoral novel, the *Ninfale fiesolano*, as Smarr points out. Ricci breaks up the composition into three distinct parts: 1346–48 (eclogues 1–6), 1355 (eclogues 7–9), and 1367 (eclogues 10–16). See Smarr's discussion of the issues of dating and influence in "Boccaccio pastorale," 243–52.

5. Cf. Ricci, "Per la cronologia," 65–66.

6. For the letter to Martino da Signa, see *Epistola* 23 in Boccaccio, *Epistole*, ed. Ginetta Auzzas, with Augusto Campana, in Boccaccio, *Tutte le opere*, ed. Vittore Branca, vol. 5, pt. 1 (Milan: Mondadori, 1992), 712–23. For the dating,

see the discussion by Auzzas in *Epistole*, vol. 5, pt. 1, 841 n. 22. The history of the genre and Boccaccio's reading of the *Bucolica* as *humilis* is based on the proem to Servius's commentary on Virgil's *Bucolica*, in Servius Grammaticus, *In Virgilii "Bucolica" et "Georgica" commentarii*, ed. George Thilo (Leipzig: Teubner, 1887), 1–4.

7. *Epistola* 23.1.

8. The ancient and medieval poets are referred to as "other lowly poets about whom we must not bother" (alii, sed ignobiles, de quibus nil curandum est, *Epistola* 23.1). Those whom Boccaccio knew include Nemesianus, Calpurnius Siculus, Giovanni del Virgilio, and Dante. On Boccaccio's knowledge of Calpurnius and Nemesianus, see Hubbard, *Pipes of Pan*, 236; and Cooper, *Pastoral*, 238–40. On the difficult issue of determining Boccaccio's sources for the *Buccolicum carmen*, see also Giuseppe Velli, "A proposito di una recente edizione del 'Buccolicum carmen' del Boccaccio," *MLN* 105 (1990): 33–49. On Boccaccio's role in reviving the bucolic genre in the footsteps of Dante, Giovanni del Virgilio, and Petrarch, see Smarr, "Boccaccio pastorale"; Guido Martellotti, "La riscoperta dello stile bucolico (da Dante al Boccaccio)," in *Dante e Boccaccio e altri scrittori dall'umanesimo al romanticismo* (Florence: Olschki, 1983), 91–106; Giorgio Padoan, "Giovanni Boccaccio e la rinascita dello stile bucolico," *Il Boccaccio, le Muse, il Parnaso e l'Arno* (Florence: Olschki, 1978), 151–98; Velli, "'Tityrus redivivus'"; and Martellotti, "Dalla tenzone al carme bucolico: Giovanni del Virgilio, Dante, Boccaccio," *Italia Medioevale e Umanistica* 7 (1964): 325–36.

9. *Epistola* 23.1.

10. *Epistola* 23.2.

11. Cf. Smarr, intro. to *Eclogues*, xxvi.

12. Cf. Resta, "Codice bucolico," 64–65. In her introduction, Smarr rightly notes that Petrarch's high style was meant to reflect the height of his allegorical and didactic intentions (*Eclogues*, xxvi-vii). Boccaccio's championing of a mixed discourse (i.e., both humble and allegorical) here and in the *Buccolicum carmen* is a declaration of poetics that can be applied to works throughout his career. He was not a novice in the *modus humilis* of the pastoral nor in allegory. As many have noticed, the *Ninfale fiesolano, Commedia delle ninfe fiorentine, Filocolo*, and *Caccia di Diana*, among other of his vernacular works, each engage with the genre and its didactic possibilities. See Giuseppe Velli, "L'Ameto e la pastorale," in *Petrarca e Boccaccio: Tradizione — memoria — scrittura*, 2nd ed. (Padua: Antenore, 1995), 195–208; and Smarr, "Boccaccio pastorale," 237–44. For the frame of the *Decameron* as a "pastoral heterocosm," see Giuseppe Mazzotta, *The World at Play in Boccaccio's "Decameron"* (Princeton, NJ: Princeton Univer-

sity Press, 1986), 53. On the garden (including the *locus amoenus* and *hortus conclusus*) as an ethical and aesthetic symbol in the *Decameron*, see Robert P. Harrison, *Gardens: An Essay on the Human Condition* (Chicago: University of Chicago Press, 2008), 83–96.

13. This is a Virgilian location, but not a Virgilian doctrine, as Hubbard has noticed (*Pipes of Pan*, 236). If the doctrine behind the phrase "leviat mentes recitasse dolores" (the mind is lightened when its woes are told, *Buccolicum carmen* 1.27) had a classical predecessor, it must have been Ovid. There are various echoes of the conclusion of Virgil's *Bucolica*, in which Pan warns that Love cares not for the pain of men and will feed insatiably on men's tears (10.29–30) and in which Gallus responds that since love conquers all things, he must cede to love (10.69). Other Virgilian themes enter into play as well, such as the oppositions of cave and pasture and of exile and comfort, yet the classicism of the poem is counterbalanced by its medieval story of unrequited love. A pastoral episode from Ovid's *Metamorphoses* is alluded to when Damon compares Galla to Galatea (*Buccolicum carmen* 1.34).

14. See especially *Buccolicum carmen* 2.60–65 and 101 for the allusions to Virgil's second eclogue.

15. It is generally accepted that Boccaccio follows Petrarch's model of interpreting the purpose of the pastoral. See Velli, "'Tityrus,'" 347, where the author stresses that the *Ameto*, not the *Buccolicum carmen*, represents Boccaccio's greatest pastoral achievement; Martellotti, "Dalla tenzone," 336; and Smarr, "Boccaccio pastorale," 244–54, where the author argues that Dante was just as influential as Petrarch in the initial choice to write Latin eclogues. Resta points out that the version in the *Buccolicum carmen* follows Virgil's model much more closely than that of Petrarch ("Codice bucolico," 66–78). I tend to agree with Hubbard's assessment of the Petrarch-Boccaccio nexus: "Boccaccio was every bit as familiar with classical Latin poetry as Petrarch, but . . . he was able to mitigate his awe before the classic by conspicuously arraying Virgil as one of a series of poets culminating in a near contemporary (. . . for Boccaccio it was Petrarch). In so doing, Boccaccio creates a pastoral present that rivals and even transcends the weight of the past" (*Pipes of Pan*, 236–37).

16. For a detailed description of the differences between the two redactions and the extent of Petrarchan influence, see Giuseppe Velli, introduction to Boccaccio, *Carmina*, ed. Velli, in Boccaccio, *Tutte le opere*, ed. Vittore Branca, vol. 5, pt. 1 (Milan: Mondadori, 1992), 379–86; Martellotti, "Dalla tenzone," 334–36; Resta, "Codice bucolico," 66–69; and Konrad Krautter, *Die Renaissance der Bukolik in der lateinischen Literatur de XIV. Jahrhunderts: Von Dante bis Petrarca* (Munich: Wilhelm Fink, 1983), 69–80. See also the recent critical

edition of Boccaccio's pastoral exchanges with Checco: Simona Lorenzini, ed., *La corrispondenza bucolica di Giovanni Boccaccio e Checco di Meletto Rossi e l'egloga di Giovanni del Virgilio ad Albertino Mussato* (Florence: Olschki, 2009). For a comparative study of Boccaccio's language in these poems, see the "Glossario bucolico" at the end of Lorenzini's doctoral thesis, "Le corrispondenze bucoliche latine nel primo Umanesimo: Giovanni del Virgilio–Albertino Mussato e Giovanni Boccaccio–Checco di Meletto Rossi; Edizione critica, commento e introduzione, con un glossario della lingua bucolica di Dante, Petrarca e Boccaccio" (Tesi di Dottorato in "Civiltà dell'Umanesimo e del Rinascimento," Istituto Nazionale di Studi sul Rinascimento — Università di Pisa, 2008), 165–332.

17. *Buccolicum carmen* 4.1. Virgil, *Eclogues* 1.1 (trans. Fairclough, p. 83): "Quo te, Moeri, pedes?" (Whither afoot, Moeris?). Cf. Hubbard, *Pipes of Pan*, 238.

18. See Vittore Branca, *Giovanni Boccaccio: Profilo biografico* (Florence: Sansoni, 1977), 76.

19. As Hubbard has argued, however, Boccaccio inverts the tone of the Virgilian original, replacing Tityrus's optimism with Meliboeus's pessimism (*Pipes of Pan*, 237–38).

20. Boccaccio's sentiments toward the Grand Seneschal of Naples had changed drastically in the period between 1348 and 1355, when Acciaiuoli came to Florence in search of the military help of Charles IV and the Florentine government. During this visit he invited Boccaccio to come to Naples in order to replace Zanobi da Strada but did not follow up on his promise to help the aging humanist. The names of famous friends Damon and Pythias (Phytias), whom Boccaccio knew from Valerius Maximus, clearly make an appearance here to emphasize the contrast in the perjurious character of Acciaiuoli. Perini, following Foresti, notes that they denote possibly Boccaccio himself and Barbato da Sulmona (*Buccolicum carmen* vol. 5, pt. 2, p. 980).

21. Like Virgil before him, the author places himself within the frame of the poem by recounting indirectly the exchange between Mirtilis and Glaucus. Boccaccio alludes to and reworks classical material within the context of Christian universal history throughout. Cf. Smarr's note to the poem in Boccaccio, *Eclogues*, p. 237.

22. As Smarr notes, this typically Boccaccian conclusion marks a striking difference from Petrarch, who stages a similar competition (between himself and an inferior poet) in his fourth eclogue, *Daedalus*. For a comparative discussion of these two poems, see Smarr, intro. to *Eclogues*, xliv-v.

23. The forest is ruled by Theoschyros, which Hortis interpreted as *theos* and *kouros*, or "son of God," meaning Christ (*Studi*, 60). Perini has suggested that it comes from *theos* and *kyrios*, or the "Lord God." After Usher's study on the origin of the

name Ischyros ("strong" in Greek) in Olympia's description of heaven in the fourteenth eclogue, in which he argues that it is the same as that used in the Trisagion, I think it is more probable that the name Theoschyros (*theos* and *ischyros*) may mean simply "God the strong." See Usher, "Ischiro donatore."

24. Cf. Stefano Carrai, "Pastoral as Personal Mythology in History," in *Petrarch: A Critical Guide to the Complete Works*, ed. Victoria Kirkham and Armando Maggi (Chicago: University of Chicago Press, 2009), 167.

25. *Buccolicum carmen* 16.11: "Ter quinque capellas." On Ovid's engagement with the bucolic genre, see Alessandro Barchiesi, "Music for Monsters: Ovid's *Metamorphoses*, Bucolic Evolution, and Bucolic Criticism," in *Brill's Companion to Greek and Latin Pastoral*, ed. Marco Fantuzzi and Theodore Papanghelis (Leiden: Brill, 2006), 403–26. On landscape in Ovid's *Metamorphoses*, see Stephen Hinds, "Landscape with Figures: Aesthetics of Place in the *Metamorphoses* and Its Tradition," in *The Cambridge Companion to Ovid*, ed. Philip Hardie (Cambridge: Cambridge University Press, 2002), 122–49. On the particular importance of the number fifteen as a "marriage number," see Victoria Kirkham, "'*Chiuso parlare*' in Boccaccio's *Teseida*," in *The Sign of Reason in Boccaccio's Fiction* (Florence: Olschki, 1993), 17–55 (44–46). For Kirkham, the number fifteen is associated with Venus (3) and Mars (5). It is quite possible that there is some echo of the Teseida's "union between Venus and Mars" in the 15+1 poem structure of the *Buccolicum carmen* (45). Perhaps from such a union, the ewe in the envoy is pregnant. For the number fifteen in the *Amorosa visione*, see Kirkham, "Amorous Vision, Scholastic Vistas," in *Sign of Reason*, 105.

26. Ovid, *Metamorphoses* 15.169–72 (trans. Miller, p. 377): "utque novis facilis signatur cera figuris, / nec manet ut fuerat nec formas servat easdem, / sed tamen ipsa eadem est, animam sic semper eandem / esse sed in varias doceo migrare figuras."

27. The biographical references would be to the Neapolitan sojourn of the young Boccaccio, his move to Tuscany, and his subsequent nostalgia for the life of intellectual leisure that he had enjoyed in Naples. The possibility of a historical reference to the allegory of this poem and the other poems does not preclude other, "more sublime" allegorical meanings for Boccaccio, as is clear from his explanation of allegory in *Genealogia* 1.3.5–9.

28. Ernst Robert Curtius defines the *locus amoenus* in his classic *European Literature and the Latin Middle Ages*, trans. William Trask (1963; repr., Princeton: Princeton University Press, 1990), 195: "a beautiful, shaded natural site. Its minimum ingredients comprise a tree (or several trees), a meadow, and a spring or brook. Birdsong and flowers may be added. The most elaborate examples also add a breeze."

29. It is a commonplace that friendship and hospitality are classical Arcadian values. See, e.g., Robert Coleman's introduction to his edition of Virgil's *Eclogues* (Cambridge: Cambridge University Press, 1977), 32. In the case of Boccaccio's first eclogue, Tindarus offers Damon the cool quiet of his cave (1.22) in place of the pastures burnt by the midday sun (1.16), so that he may recount his misfortunes.

30. It is worth mentioning that there is a strong metaliterary dimension to Boccaccio's language here and in the previous quotation. The turn of phrase *sub cortice* is often used in the *Genealogia* when Boccaccio speaks of allegorical meaning. See, e.g., the chapter heading for the above-cited *Genealogia*, 14.10: "It's a Fool's Notion That Poets Convey No Meaning beneath the Surface of Their Fictions" (Stultum credere poetas nil sensisse sub cortice fabularum); trans. Charles G. Osgood, *Boccaccio on Poetry* (1930; New York: Liberal Arts Press, 1956), 52; and his letter to Fra Martino da Signa: "After him Virgil wrote in Latin, but he hid some meanings beneath the outer layer [lit. bark]" (Post hunc latine scripsit Virgilius, sed sub cortice nonnullos abscondit sensus, *Epistola* 23.2).

31. Although Boccaccio designates the first two eclogues as superficial allegories of his youthful indiscretions (*Epistola* 23.4: "et fere iuveniles lascivias meas in cortice pandunt") and urges Fra Martino da Signa to ignore them (ibid.: "de primis duabus eglogis . . . nolo cures"), he did care enough about them to include them in the late collection.

32. Caliopus even invokes the inhabitants of hell as a possible cause of the misfortune of Naples (5.91–92): "quis Orco / eduxit pestes in te?" (Who introduced to you such plagues from hell?).

33. The imagery at the opening of *Alcestus* (6.1–5) is reminiscent of the melting that takes place after Dante's ascent from Hell to the Mountain of Purgatory: "Pastores transisse nives et frigora leti / sub divo veteres stipula modulantur amores, / esculeas hedera nectunt de more corollas, / crateras Bromio statuunt et vina salutant / cantibus et multo protendunt carmine sacrum" (Happy that the snow and ice have passed / the shepherds pipe old lovesongs on their reeds / under the open sky; as is their custom, / oak garlands they entwine with ivy vines, / set bowls for Bacchus, honor the wines with songs, / and with much singing lengthen out the rite).

34. Besides the second of Petrarch's eclogues, *Argus*, which is often cited as the model that instigated the political and allegorical turn in Boccaccio's work, see, for example, his fifth and sixth eclogues, entitled respectively *Pietas pastoralis*, "The Shepherd's Filial Piety," and *Pastorum pathos*, "The Shepherd's Suffering."

35. This is evidenced by Boccaccio's own vagueness in explaining the allegory to Fra Martino, and in the varying historical interpretations offered for the interlocutors (cf. Perini, *Buccolicum carmen*, vol. 5, pt. 2, p. 997). For a list of interpretations that explain this sentiment, see Ricci, "Per la cronologia," 57, where he also argues that the poem should be read similarly to the *Corbaccio*.

36. Hubbard, *Pipes of Pan*, 238.

37. Cf. *Genealogia* 1.4, where Boccaccio writes that Pan originally signified the created world, or *natura naturata*, as it was formed by the combination of formless material (*Chaos*) and limitless time (*Eternitas*). He also mentions there that in time Pan became confused with the Demogorgon as creator of all things. See David Lummus, "Boccaccio's Poetic Anthropology: Allegories of History in the *Genealogie Deorum Gentilium Libri*," *Speculum* 87.3 (July 2012): 724–65 (741–52).

38. It has been duly noted that these geographical points refer to Boccaccio's historical voyage to Naples in 1355. The reference, however, is also internal. Cf. *Buccolicum carmen* 1.1–2.

39. In naming the acts of mercy, Boccaccio does not follow the scholastic list of seven corporal and seven spiritual works. Rather, he refers to the list of six acts enumerated in the "Judgment of Nations," in Matthew 25:31–46, five of which are corporal, and one of which is spiritual. Cf. Perini's note in Boccaccio, *Buccolicum carmen*, vol. 5, pt. 2, p. 1064.

40. In fact, in the letter to Fra Martino, when Boccaccio explains the meaning of Phylostropos, he writes (23.30): "By Phylostropos I mean my glorious teacher Francesco Petrarca, by whose admonitions I have very often been persuaded to abandon delight in temporal things and direct my mind to eternal ones, and thus he turned my loves, even if not completely, yet considerably toward the better." (Pro Phylostropo ego intelligo gloriosum preceptorem meum Franciscum Petrarcam, cuius monitis sepissime michi persuasum est ut omissa rerum temporalium oblectatione mentem ad eterna dirigerem, et sic amores meos, etsi non plene, satis tamen vertit in melius.) The adverb *sepissime* (very often) indicates frequent conversations between the two men in which Boccaccio was not always successful in implementing the other's advice. That the "conversion" was not complete, Boccaccio admits openly even to the Augustinian friar.

41. See Virgil, *Aeneid* 2.801 (trans. Fairclough, p. 371): "Iamque iugis summae surgebat Lucifer Idae / ducebatque diem" (And now above Ida's topmost ridges the day star was rising, ushering in the morn); and *Eclogues* 10.77 (trans. Fairclough, p. 95): "Ite domum saturae, venit Hesperus, ite capellae" (Get home, my full-fed goats, get home—the Evening Star draws on).

Chapter Fourteen

1. Boccaccio, *Elegia di madonna Fiammetta*, ed. Carlo Delcorno, in Boccaccio, *Tutte le opere*, vol. 5, pt. 2 (Milan: Mondadori, 1994), intro., 1. Delcorno, from whom I cite throughout, provides the standard edition and extensive commentary. An Italian school paperback version also exists: Boccaccio, *Elegia di madonna Fiammetta*, ed. Maria Pia Mussini Sacchi (Milan: Mursia, 1987). Boccaccio. *The Elegy of Lady Fiammetta*, ed. and trans. Mariangela Causa-Steindler and Thomas Mauch (Chicago: University of Chicago Press, 1990) is the translation I have used when citing in English throughout this essay. It replaces the older *Amorous Fiammetta*, rev. with intro. Edward Hutton (1926; repr., New York: Rarity Press, 1931), based on the first English translation, 1587.

2   See Francesco Bruni, *Boccaccio: L'invenzione della letteratura mezzana* (Bologna: Il Mulino, 1990), 218.

3. See Dario Rastelli, "La modernità della Fiammetta," *Convivium*, n.s., 1 (1947): 703–15. A majority of critics have considered it a "romance," since strictly speaking, the novel arises in later centuries.

4. Dario Rastelli, "Le fonti autobiografiche nell'*Elegia di madonna Fiammetta*," *Humanitas* 3 (1948): 790–802; Giuseppe Gigli, "Per l'interpretazione della Fiammetta," *Giornale Storico della Valdelsa* 21 (1913): 68–71.

5. Vittore Branca, *Boccaccio: The Man and His Works* (New York: New York University Press, 1976), 67–68.

6. Clorinda Donato, "Nota su l'*Elegia di Madonna Fiammetta* e la possibilità di una triplice analisi psicoanalitica: Autore, personaggio, pubblico," *Carte Italiane: A Journal of Italian Studies* 3 (1980): 29–38.

7. Mariangela Causa-Steindler, *The Elegy of Lady Fiammetta*, intro., xxi.

8. Victoria Kirkham, "Two New Translations: The Early Boccaccio in English Dress," review article in *Italica* 70 (1993): 79–88; see also Janet Levarie Smarr, *Boccaccio and Fiammetta: The Narrator as Lover* (Urbana: University of Illinois Press, 1986), 129–48.

9. Michael Calabrese, "Feminism and the Packaging of Boccaccio's Fiammetta," *Italica* 74 (1997): 20–42.

10. Salvatore Battaglia, "La tradizione di Ovidio nel Medioevo" and "Il significato della Fiammetta," in *La coscienza letteraria del Medioevo* (Naples: Liguori, 1965), 23–56 and 659–68; Vincenzo Crescini, *Contributo agli studi sul Boccaccio* (Turin: Loescher, 1887); Albert S. Cook, "Boccaccio: *Fiammetta*, chap. 1, and Seneca: *Hippolytus*, act 1," *American Journal of Philology* 28 (1907): 200–204; Giorgio Padoan, "Il Boccaccio fedele di Dante," in *Il Boccaccio, le Muse, il Parnaso e l'Arno* (Florence: Olschki, 1978), 229–46; Carlo Delcorno, "Note sui dantismi dell'*Elegia di madonna Fiammetta*," *Studi sul Boccaccio* 11 (1979): 251–94.

11. Dante Alighieri, *De vulgari eloquentia*, ed. and trans. Aristide Marigo (Florence: Le Monnier, 1957), 2.4.5–7: "Deinde in hiis que dicenda occurrunt debemus discretione potiri, utrum tragice, sive comice, sive elegiace sint canenda. Per tragediam superiorem stilum inducimus, per comediam inferiorem, per elegiam stilum intelligimus miserorum. Si tragice canenda videntur, tunc assumendum est vulgare illustre, et per consequens cantionem [oportet] ligare. Se vero comice, tunc quandoque mediocre, quandoque humile vulgare sumatur; et huius discretionem in quarto huius reservamus ostendere. Si autem elegiace, solum humile oportet nos sumere." I cite from *De vulgari eloquentia*, ed. and trans. Steven Botterill (Cambridge: Cambridge University Press, 1996), 56–59. The source is noted by Luigi Surdich, *La cornice di amore* (Pisa: ETS, 1987), 190–91; and Cesare Segre, "Strutture e registri nella *Fiammetta*," *Strumenti Critici* 6 (1972): 133–62 (135).

12. Surdich, *La cornice di amore*, 216, my trans.

13. *Elegia di madonna Fiammetta* 1.1: "Suole a' miseri crescere di dolersi vaghezza, quando di sé discernono o sentono compassione in alcuno. Adunque, acciò che in me, volonterosa più che altra a dolermi, di ciò per lunga usanza non menomi la cagione, ma s'avanzi, mi piace, o nobili donne, ne' cuori delle quali amore più che nel mio forse felicemente dimora, narrando i casi miei, di farvi, s'io posso, pietose"; trans. Causa-Steindler and Mauch, p. 1.

14. Suzanne C. Hagedorn, *Abandoned Women: Rewriting the Classics in Dante, Boccaccio, and Chaucer* (Ann Arbor: University of Michigan Press, 2004), 127.

15. Mary F. Wack, *Lovesickness in the Middle Ages: The Viaticum and Its Commentators* (Philadelphia: University of Pennsylvania Press, 1990), 149. One of the remedies prescribed in the *Viaticum* by Constantine was therapeutic intercourse, that is, the possibility of men having sex with prostitutes to balance the humor. Such a practice was, however, not available to women; Wack, 41.

16. See Jacques Ferrand, *A Treatise on Lovesickness*, ed. and trans. Donald A. Beecher and Massimo Ciavolella (Syracuse, NY: Syracuse University Press, 1990), 8. Interestingly in this manual the thirty-fourth chapter is dedicated to remedies to cure love melancholy in married persons, and the best treatment seems to be, in the author's opinion, procreation, which Fiammetta does not mention even once in her lamentations.

17. See Wack, *Lovesickness*, 41.

18. *Elegia di madonna Fiammetta* 5.17.1–5: "Quanto contraria medicina operava il mio marito alle mie doglie! . . . Quivi la maggior parte del tempo ozioso trapassa . . . quivi non s'usano vivande se non dilicate, e vini per antichità nobilissimi, possenti non che ad eccitare la dormente Venere, ma a risuscitare la morta in ciascun uomo. E quanto ancora in ciò la virtù de' bagni diversi adoperi, quelli il può saper che l'ha provato. Quivi i marini liti e i graziosi

giardini . . . amorose canzoni. . . . Tengasi adunque chi può quivi, tra tante
cose, contra Cupido, il quale quivi, per quello ch'io creda, sì come in luogo
principalissimo de' suoi regni, aiutato da tante cose, con poca fatica usa le
forze sue"; trans. Causa-Steindler and Mauch, pp. 72–73.

19. Dante Alighieri, *Vita nuova* (Milan: Garzanti, 1982), "Donne ch'avete intelletto d'amore," vv. 6–10; *Dante's Vita Nuova*, rev. ed., trans. with an essay by
Mark Musa (Bloomington: Indiana University Press, 1973), "Ladies who
have intelligence of love," p. 32: "Love lets me feel the sweetness of his presence, / and if at that point I could still feel bold, / my words could make all
mankind fall in love."

20. Boccaccio, *Decameron*, ed. Vittore Branca (Turin: Einaudi, 1992), Intro., 65:
"Io giudicherei ottimamente fatto che noi . . . a' nostri luoghi in contado . . .
ce ne andassimo a stare, e quivi quella festa, quella allegrezza, quello piacere
che noi potessimo, senza trapassare in alcun atto il segno della ragione,
prendessimo."

21. Victoria Kirkham, *The Sign of Reason in Boccaccio's Fiction* (Florence: Olschki,
1993), 7.

22. *Elegia di madonna Fiammetta* 1.22.2: "E però tra gli altri miei più sommi
pensieri, quanto che egli mi fosse gravissimo a fare, disposi di non preporre
alla ragione il volere, nel recare a fine cotale disio. E certo, quanto che io
molte volte fossi per diversi accidenti fortissimamente costretta, pur tanta di
grazia mi fu conceduta, che sanza trapassare il segno, virilmente sostenendo
l'affanno passai."

23. Dante, *Vita nuova*, trans. Musa, p. 74. For Boccaccio's debt to the *Vita nuova*,
see Delcorno's introduction to his edition, pp. 6, 18. Delcorno, "Note sui
dantismi," 253.

24. Charles S. Singleton, *An Essay on the "Vita nuova"* (Baltimore: Johns Hopkins
University Press, 1949), 7.

25. Monica Bardi, *Le voci dell'assenza: Una lettura dell'"Elegia di madonna Fiammetta"*
(Turin: Tirrenia, 1990), 30.1.

26. *Elegia di madonna Fiammetta* 5.1.4: "E in verità io non vi conforto tanto a
questo affanno, perché voi più di me divegnate pietose, quanto perché più la
nequizia di colui, per cui ciò m'avviene, conoscendo, divegnate più caute in
non commettervi a ogni giovine."

27. *Decameron*, ed. Branca, Proem, 14–15: "Nelle quali novelle piacevoli e aspri
casi d'amore e altri fortunati avvenimenti si vederanno così ne' moderni tempi
avvenuti come negli antichi; delle quali le già dette donne, che queste leg-
geranno, parimente diletto delle sollazzevoli cose in quelle mostrate e utile
consiglio potranno pigliare, in quanto potranno cognoscere quello che sia da
fuggire e che sia similmente da seguitare."

28. Smarr, *Boccaccio and Fiammetta*, 144.

29. Andreas Capellanus, *The Art of Courtly Love*, trans. John Jay Parry (New York: Columbia University Press, 1960), bk. 1, chap. 6, the seventh dialogue (p. 100): "Everybody knows that love can have no place between husband and wife. They may be bound to each other by a great and immoderate affection, but their feeling cannot take the place of love, because it cannot fit under the true definition of love. For what is love but an inordinate desire to receive passionately a furtive and hidden embrace?"

30. Andreas Capellanus, *Art of Courtly Love*, trans. Parry, bk. 2, chap. 8, "The Rules of Love," p. 185.

31. *Elegia di madonna Fiammetta* 6.8.6: "Solamente le cose liberamente possedute sogliono essere reputate vili, quantunque elle siene molto care, e quelle che con malagevolezza s'hanno, ancora che vilissime sieno, sono carissime reputate"; trans. Causa-Steindler and Mauch, p. 108.

32. Bardi, *Le voci dell'assenza*, 50.

33. *Elegia di madonna Fiammetta* 1.8.1.

34. *Elegia di madonna Fiammetta* 1.3.9–10: "non meno degl'iddii dolendomi, i quali con tanta oscurità alle grosse menti dimostrano li loro segreti, che quasi non mostrati, se non avvenuti, si possono dire!"; trans. Causa-Steindler and Mauch, p. 6.

35. *Elegia di madonna Fiammetta* 1.4.2: "io tutta mi mirava non altramente che il paone le sue penne." See Boccaccio, *Genealogia deorum gentilium*, ed. Vittorio Zaccaria, in Boccaccio, *Tutte le opere*, vols. 7–8 (Milan: Mondadori, 1998), 9.1.16: "Est enim clamosa avis pavo, in quo clamores, elatas voces. . . . Picta insuper penna nitet undique, et laudibus delectatur et ad ostentationem sui adeo trahitur, ut erecta in girum oculata cauda, nuda atque turpia posteriora relinquat"; Victoria Kirkham, *Fabulous Vernacular: Boccaccio's "Filocolo" and the Art of Medieval Fiction* (Ann Arbor: University of Michigan Press, 2001), 225: "Predictably the peacock as an invidious term of comparison for female vanity makes appearances in Boccaccio's unflattering portraits of the widow in the *Corbaccio* and amorous Fiammetta in the *Elegia di madonna Fiammetta*."

36. *Elegia di madonna Fiammetta* 1.1.4: "Conobbi che la mia bellezza, miserabile dono a chi virtuosamente di vivere desidera, più miei coetanei giovinetti e altri nobili accese di fuoco amoroso"; trans. Causa-Steindler and Mauch, p. 3.

37. Robert Hollander, *Boccaccio's Two Venuses* (New York: Columbia University Press, 1977), 47: "her performance of extravagances worthy of burlesque . . . After a while her insistence on her own pain becomes comic, not least of all because that pain is not a necessary one."

38. *Elegia di madonna Fiammetta* 1.15.

39. *Decameron*, Proem, 10–13.

40. *Elegia di madonna Fiammetta* 1.15: "Ora non veggiamo noi Venere santissima abitare nelle piccole case, sovenente solamente e utile al necessario nostro procreamento?"; trans. Causa-Steindler and Mauch, p. 15.

41. This is one of the main points of the *Decameron*, in which the author's compassion goes indeed to women in love: because of their lack of freedom they cannot access the diversions permitted to men. See *Decameron*, Proem, 13.

42. *Elegia di madonna Fiammetta* 1.14.

43. *Elegia di madonna Fiammetta* 1.17.

44. Surdich, like Hollander (and Boccaccio), distinguishes between two Venuses, one celestial and one worldly.

45. Walter Pabst, *Venus als Heilige und Furie in Boccaccios Fiammetta-Dichtung* (Krefiel: Scjerpe Verlag, 1958).

46. See Kirkham, *Fabulous Vernacular*, 251.

47. *Elegia di madonna Fiammetta* 1.4.

48. Surdich, *La cornice di amore*, 208–9.

49. Virgil, *Aeneid*, trans. H. R. Fairclough, Loeb Classical Library (Cambridge, MA: Harvard University Press, 1994), 4.101: "Ardet amans Dido traxique per ossa furorem."

50. Surdich, *La cornice di amore*, 176.

51. Vincenzo Crescini, *Contributo agli studi sul Boccaccio con documenti inediti* (Turin: Loescher, 1887), 160–61; and Cook, "Boccaccio: *Fiammetta*," 200–204.

52. *Elegia di madonna Fiammetta* 3.11.1–2: "Alcuna volta, se altro a fare non mi occorreva, ragunate le mie fanti con meco nella mia camera, e raccontava e faceva raccontare storie diverse, le quali quanto più erano di lungi dal vero, come il più così fatte genti le dicono, cotanto parea ch'avessono maggiore forza a cacciare i sospiri e a recare festa a me ascoltante; la quale alcuna volta, con tutta la malinconia, di quelle lietissimamente risi"; trans. Causa-Steindler and Mauch, p. 49.

53. *Elegia di madonna Fiammetta* 3.11.2–3: "in libri diversi ricercando le altrui miserie, e quelle alle mie conformando, quasi accompagnata sentendomi, con meno noia il tempo passava"; trans. Causa-Steindler and Mauch, p. 49.

54. *Elegia di madonna Fiammetta* 8.7.1: "Ricordami alcuna volta avere letti li franceschi romanzi, alli quali se fede alcuna si puote attribuire, Tristano e Isotta oltre ogn'altro amante essersi amati"; trans. Causa-Steindler and Mauch, p. 145.

55. Smarr, *Boccaccio and Fiammetta*, 143.

56. Smarr, *Boccaccio and Fiammetta*, 129–30.

57. *Elegia di madonna Fiammetta* 1.14.

58. *Elegia di madonna Fiammetta* 1.14.15: "La nostra mente tutta possiede e signoreggia Amore con la sua deità, e tu sai che non è sicura cosa alle sue potenze resistere"; trans. Causa-Steindler and Mauch, p. 14.

59. Hollander, *Boccaccio's Two Venuses*, 42.

60. *Elegia di madonna Fiammetta* 1.17.20: "Che mattamente fuggi? Se tanti iddii, tanti uomini, tanti animali da questi sono vinti, tu d'essere vinta da lui ti vergognerai?"; trans. Causa-Steindler and Mauch, p. 20.

61. Augustine, *De libero arbitrio*, ed. Franco Capitani (Milan: Pubblicazioni della Università Cattolica del Sacro Cuore, 1987), 1.7.16–1.11.21.

62. *Elegia di madonna Fiammetta* 6.107.

63. *Elegia di madonna Fiammetta* 5.20.4: "se forse alcuna v'era conforme alli miei mali, con orecchie l'ascoltava intentissima, di saperla disiderando, acciò che poi fra me ridicendola, con più ordinato parlare e più coperto mi sapessi e potessi in publico alcuna volta dolere."

64. "Perché cantando, il duol si disacerba"; Petrarch, *Canzoniere*, ed. Marco Santagata (Milan: Mondadori, 1996), 23.4.

65. Segre, "Strutture e registri nella *Fiammetta*," 115: "Fiammetta pare aggirarsi in una fredda galleria di statue: i personaggi a cui, nell'intensità del dramma, aveva chiesto parole, atteggiamenti, esempi, son ritornati marmi polverosi e muti."

66. Francesco De Sanctis, *Storia della letteratura italiana* (Naples: Morano, 1870), 1:310. "E se vuol consolarsi, cercando compagni al suo dolore si fa un trattato di storia antica, narrando tutti i casi infelici di amore negli antichi iddii ed eroi."

Chapter Fifteen

1. My heartfelt thanks to the editors for their considerable fine-tuning of an earlier draft of this essay, which has been greatly improved by their comments. Fundamental studies in the rehabilitation of Boccaccio's antifeminist satire are the following: *Il Corbaccio*, ed. Tauno Nurmela, with introduction and notes, Annales Academiae Scientiarum Fennicae, Series B, 146 (Helsinki: Suomalainen Tiedeakatemia, 1968); the more recent critical edition, here cited, with updated introduction, notes, and bibliography: *Corbaccio*, ed. Giorgio Padoan, in Boccaccio, *Tutte le opere*, ed. Vittore Branca, vol. 5, pt. 2 (Milan: Mondadori, 1994); Robert Hollander's monograph, which surveys and evaluates the history of criticism: *Boccaccio's Last Fiction: "Il Corbaccio"* (Philadelphia: University of Pennsylvania Press, 1988); and the sensitive English translation with introduction and notes of Anthony K. Cassell: *The Corbaccio* (Urbana: University of Illinois Press, 1975), reprinted as *The Corbaccio or The Labyrinth of Love*, 2nd rev. ed. (Binghamton, NY: Medieval & Renaissance Texts & Studies, 1993); and now on the *Decameron Web* (http://www.brown.edu/ Departments/Italian_Studies/dweb/texts/CorIndex.php), produced by the Department of Italian at Brown University, *The Corbaccio*, with discussion

of interpretations and bibliography, prepared by Guyda Armstrong. Although I cite Cassell's translation, I have frequently modified it to keep as close as possible to the Italian.

2. See Hollander, *Boccaccio's Last Fiction*, 333–35; Eugenio Giusti, *Dall'amore cortese alla comprensione: Il viaggio ideologico di Giovanni Boccaccio dalla "Caccia di Diana" al "Decameron"* (Milan: LED, 1999), 78–84; and Victoria Kirkham, "John Badmouth: Fortunes of the Poet's Image," in "Boccaccio 1990: The Poet and His Renaissance Reception," ed. Kevin Brownlee and Victoria Kirkham, special issue, *Studi sul Boccaccio* 20 (1991–92): 355–76.

3. See again Hollander, *Boccaccio's Last Fiction*, 26–33; and Guyda Armstrong, *The Corbaccio*, on *Decameron Web*.

4. *Lo Zibaldone boccaccesco Mediceo-Laurenziano Plut. XXIX-8: Riprodotto in facsimile*, edited by the R. Biblioteca Medicea Laurenziana, with preface by Guido Biagi (Florence: Olschki, 1915). The excerpt from *Adversus Jovinianum* (Against Jovinian) is an invective against a Roman priest who declared that marriage was as spiritually meritorious as virginity. Jerome maintained the opposite, denouncing marriage, the horrors of sexual intercourse, and women. This tract was used in the Middle Ages and Renaissance to defend the superiority of celibacy, virginity, and the religious life over marriage and life in the world. Jerome twisted a long excerpt from the pagan philosopher Theophrastus, a disciple of Aristotle, to his own Christian cause. See J. N. D. Kelly, *Jerome: His Life, Writings, and Controversies* (London: Duckworth, 1975).

5. Boccaccio labels them "Jeronimus contra Jovinianum . . . de non ducenda uxore" and "Dissuasio Valerii ad Rufinum ne ducat uxorem." *Zibaldone*, Jerome, fol. 52v; and Theophrastus, fols. 53r-54v.

6. For a modern introduction to rhetorical traditions, see James J. Murphy, *Rhetoric in the Middle Ages: A History of Rhetorical Theory from St. Augustine to the Renaissance* (Berkeley: University of California Press, 1974), esp. 10–14 on "praise and censure" in Cicero's *De inventione*; also A. J. Minnis and A. B. Scott, eds., with the assistance of David Wallace, *Medieval Literary Theory and Criticism, c. 1100-c. 1375: The Commentary Tradition* (Oxford: Clarendon Press, 1988), esp. index entries "blame" and "praise."

7. This kind of polemical invective has a distinguished pedigree: classical writers like Cicero and Juvenal; and Christian writers, too, especially Saint Jerome (admired and imitated by Boccaccio), who reminded critics that "the conventions of rhetoric permitted greater license in a polemical than in an instructional work." Kelly, *Jerome*, 189.

8. Virginia Brown, in her introduction to Boccaccio, *Famous Women*, trans. and ed. Brown, I Tatti Renaissance Library (Cambridge, MA: Harvard University Press, 2001), xi; the work features 106 *Lives* in all.

9. For multiple perspectives on Petrarch's relationship with Boccaccio, see Victoria Kirkham and Armando Maggi, eds., *Petrarch: A Critical Guide to the Complete Works* (Chicago: University of Chicago Press, 2009). For an overview of Petrarch's life with translations of some of his letters to Boccaccio and excerpts from the *Secretum*, see Peter Hainsworth, *The Essential Petrarch* (Indianapolis: Hackett, 2010). For Petrarch's Stoicizing view of the moral life, see Letizia A. Panizza, "Stoic Psychotherapy in the Middle Ages and Renaissance: Petrarch's *De Remediis*," in *Atoms, Pneuma, and Tranquillity: Epicurean and Stoic Themes in European Thought*, ed. Margaret Osler (Cambridge: Cambridge University Press, 1991), 39–65; a revised and updated version of the same article appears in Catherine Léglu and Stephen Milner, eds., *The Erotics of Consolation: Desire and Distance in the Late Middle Ages* (New York: Palgrave Macmillan, 2008), 117–39.

10. As he prepares to leave the Lover, the Spirit refers to her as "la malvagia femina, che mia moglie fu" (*Corbaccio*, ed. Padoan, 397).

11. *Corbaccio*, trans. Cassell, 1; ed. Padoan, 3: "Intendo di dimostrare nello umile trattato seguente una speziale grazia, non per mio merito, ma per solo benignità di Colei che, impetrandola da Colui . . . nuovamente mi fu conceduta." Here and throughout references are to page numbers in Cassell, and to section numbers in Padoan.

It was considered a problematic lapse of decorum for a Christian author to talk about himself except as a sinner, recipient of God's mercy, and confessor of his glory. Augustine's *Confessions* is the archetype, but Boccaccio would be even more familiar with Dante's strictures in *Convivio* 1.2.

12. *Corbaccio*, trans. Cassell, 77; ed. Padoan, 412: "Ingegnera'ti d'essere utile a coloro, e massamente a' giovani, li quali con gli occhi chiusi, per li non sicuri luoghi, troppo di sé fidandosi, senza guida si mettono."

13. *Corbaccio*, trans. Cassell, 77; ed. Padoan, 412: "Sopra ogni cosa ti guarda di non venire alle mani delle malvagie femine." Boccaccio uses the *envoi* or *congedo* in other verse and prose works; for example, *Filostrato, Filocolo*, and the *Teseida*, with the hope that his work *will* come into the hands of his beloved woman.

14. *Corbaccio*, trans. Cassell, 2; ed. Padoan, 6: "Giudicai che, senza alcuna mia colpa, io fossi fieramente trattato male da colei la quale io mattamente per mia singulare donna eletta avea."

15. *Corbaccio*, trans. Cassell, 2–3, 4; ed. Padoan, 9, 18: "Deh, stolto, che è quello a che il poco conoscimento della ragione, anzi più tosto il discacciamento di quella, ti conduce? . . . Etti possible, volendo essere uomo, di cacciarli; il che degli eterni [guai] non ti avverrebbe."

16. See, e.g., the introduction and commentary in Kenelm Foster and Patrick

Boyde, eds., *Dante's Lyric Poetry*, 2 vols. (Oxford: Oxford University Press, 1967). Nothing is asked of the idealized woman; she is praised—and loved—for her nobility of character.

17. See Boccaccio, *Esposizioni sopra la "Comedia" di Dante*, ed. Giorgio Padoan, vol. 6, *Tutte le opere* (Milan: Mondadori, 1965), *Inferno* 5.1.160–87. Boccaccio, commenting on the sin of lust (*lussuria*), explains that this otherwise "natural" act is punished so severely in human beings alone, because they have a rational soul and consequently should suppress sexual passion and have intercourse only for the sake of procreation (5.2.24–26). He next launches into invective against young contemporary women for their vanity, use of cosmetics, provocative dress, and lewd behavior (5.2.31–34), just as he does in *Il Corbaccio*.

18. Boccaccio, *Trattatello in laude di Dante*, ed. Pier Giorgio Ricci, in *Tutte le opere*, vol. 3 (Milan: Mondadori, 1974), 1.59: "Lascino i filosofanti lo sposarsi a' ricchi stolti, a' signori e a' lavoratori, e essi [filosofi] con la filosofia si dilettino, molto migliore sposa che alcuna altra." Boccaccio commends Dante for never trying to see his wife after his exile from Florence, for his saintliness in putting up with marriage, and for resolutely placing his studies before his wife and family (2.72–76). Boccaccio would seem to have followed his own advice by never marrying and by devoting his life to the Muses.

19. *Trattatello*, ed. Ricci, 1.173: "Che cosa non posseno le femine in noi [uomini]!" For "proof," Boccaccio lists biblical exempla of famous holy men, like Adam, who could not resist Eve; David, who killed Bathsheba's husband in order to possess her; and Solomon, notorious for his many wives (1.174). He omits to mention his own fathering of five illegitimate children. Ricci, in the introduction to his edition, pp. 426–27, dates the *Trattatello* between 1351 and 1355.

20. In fact, much research has been done on borrowings from the *Divina commedia* in *Il Corbaccio*. Hollander, who discusses Dante's presence there in *Boccaccio's Last Fiction*, 39–42, has compiled a list of specific passages, 59–71. This has been expanded by Guyda Armstrong, "Dantean Framing Devices in Boccaccio's *Corbaccio*," *Reading Medieval Studies* 27 (2001): 139–61.

21. *Corbaccio*, trans. Cassell, 10; ed. Padoan, 57: "Alcuni il chiamano 'il laberinto d'Amore,' altri 'la valle incantata,' e assai 'il porcile di Venere,' e molti 'la valle dei sospiri e della miseria.'"

22. *Corbaccio*, trans. Cassell, 12; ed. Padoan, 67: "Dalla qual conoscenza una contrizione sì grande e pentimento mi venne delle non ben fatte cose che . . . il cuore, non altrimenti che faccia la neve al sole, in acqua si risolvesse."

23. *Corbaccio*, trans. Cassell, 23; ed. Padoan, 128: "[Vedere adunque dovevi] amore essere una passione *accecatrice* dello animo, *disviatrice* dello 'ngegno, *ingrossatrice*, anzi *privatrice* della memoria, *dissipatrice* delle terrene facultà,

guastatrice delle forze del corpo, nemica della giovanezza, e della vecchiezza morte, *genitrice* de' vizi e *abitatrice* de' vacui petti; cosa senza ragione e senza ordine e senza stabilità alcuna; vizio delle menti non sane e *sommergitrice* della umana libertà" (italics mine). The above passage with its concentration of parallelisms and antitheses, repetitions and rhyme, found favor with preachers and censors.

24. *Corbaccio*, trans. Cassell, 52; ed. Padoan, 276: "Dèi dunque sapere né ogni infermità né ogni infermo potere essere sempre dal discreto medico da odoriferi unguenti medicato; . . . richeggiono cose fetide." Boccaccio could have found support for similar ideas—the need for foul medicines, and the technique of vituperation of the woman as a cure for erotic obsession—in Ovid's *Remedia amoris* 225–30 and 297–310.

25. *Corbaccio*, trans. Cassell, 24; ed. Padoan, 133–34: "La femina è animale imperfetto, passionato da mille passioni spiacevoli e abbominevoli pure a ricordarsene, non che a ragionarne: il che se gli uomini riguardassono, come dovessono, non altrimenti andrebbono a loro, né con altro diletto o apetito, che all'altre naturali e inevitabili oportune cose vadano. . . . Niuno altro animale è meno netto di lei; non il porco, quale ora è più nel loto, agiugne alla bruttezza di lei. E, se forse alcuno questo negasse, . . . ricerchinsi i luoghi secreti dove esse, vergognandosene, nascondono gli orribili strumenti li quali a tor via i loro umori superflui adoperano." The word *femina* here is meant to be discourteous; she is just like the female of any form of animal. See Mario Bonfante, "'Femmina' and 'donna,'" in *Studia philologica et litteraria in honorem L. Spitzer*, ed. A. G. Hatcher and K. L. Selig (Bern: Francke, 1958), 77–109.

26. *Corbaccio*, trans. Cassell, 27; ed. Padoan, 149: "Il fante, il lavoratore, il mugnaio, e ancora il nero etiopo, ciascuno è buono sol che possa." In this part of his invective, against wives, and against the scholar and philosopher taking a wife, Boccaccio is elaborating on the passages from Theophrastus quoted by Jerome that he copied in his *Zibaldone*.

27. *Corbaccio*, trans. Cassell, 29; ed. Padoan, 158: "Sì come animale a ciò inchinevole, subitamente in sì fervente ira discorrono che le tigre, i leoni, i serpenti hanno più d'umanità, adirati, che non hanno le femine."

28. *Corbaccio*, trans. Cassell, 35; ed. Padoan, 189: "Tu se' uomo fatta alla imagine e alla similitudine di Dio, animale perfetto, nato a signoreggiare e non ad essere signoreggiato." We have here a good example of the rhetorical license Boccaccio gives himself in insinuating that Eve was *not* made in the image and likeness of God. His mentor was again Jerome, who twisted scripture for his own ends. See Letizia Panizza, "Erasmus's *Encomium Matrimonii* of 1518 and the Italian Connections," in *Erasmus and the Renaissance Republic of Letters*, ed. Stephen Ryle (Turnhout: Brepols, 2013), for the efforts of Italian humanists

and Erasmus to upgrade marriage and the status of women in explicit opposition to Jerome.

29. *Corbaccio*, trans. Cassell, 55; ed. Padoan, 288: "due bozacchioni; che già forse acerbi pomi furono . . . tanto oltre misura dal loro natural sito spiccate e dilungate sono, se cascare le lasciasse . . . infino al bellìco l'agiugnerebbono, non altrimenti vote o vize che sia una viscica sgonfiata."

30. *Corbaccio*, trans. Cassell, 55–56; ed. Padoan, 291–93: "Come che nel vero io non sappia assai bene da qual parte io mi debbia cominciare a ragionare del golfo di Settalia, nella valle d'Acheronte riposto, sotto gli oscuri boschi di quella, spesse volte rugginosi e d'una gromma spiacevoli e spumosi, e d'animali di nuova qualità ripieni. . . . La bocca, per la quale nel porto s'entra, è tanta e tale che . . . avesse, senza sconciarmi di nulla, a un compagno, che con non minore albero di me navigato fosse, fatto luogo. . . . Ed è mirabile cosa che mai legno non v'entrò che non vi perisse e che, vinto e stanco, fuori non fosse gitato. . . . Egli è per certo quel golfo una voragine infernale."

31. *Corbaccio*, trans. Cassell, 60; ed. Padoan, 316: "Le sue orazioni e paternostri sono i romanzi franceschi e le canzoni latine, e' quali ella legge di Lancelotto e di Ginevra e di Tristano e d'Isotta e le loro prodeze e i loro amori e le giostre e i torniamenti e le semblee. Ella tutta si stritola quando legge Lancelotto o Tristano o alcuno altro colle loro donne nelle camere, segretamente e soli, raunarsi, sì come colei alla quale pare vedere ciò che fanno e che volentieri, come di loro imagina, così farebbe. . . . Legge [la Canzone] di Florio e di Biancifiore e simili cose assai."

32. Boccaccio here refers to a popular Italian versified version of the story he recast in a high style of vernacular prose, rescuing it, as Fiammetta requests, from the "fabulosi parlari degli ignoranti" (*Filocolo* 1.1.26). Prince Florio (Filocolo), a pagan, loves Biancifiore, a Christian. Only after many trials do they come together; Florio is converted, and they marry, after which they become the rulers of Spain and spread Christianity through their land. The romance was dedicated to Boccaccio's *donna*, Fiammetta. (See the essay by Elissa Weaver in this volume.)

33. *Corbaccio*, trans. Cassell, 69; ed. Padoan, 368: "Da virtù venne prima gentileza nel mondo."

34. *Corbaccio*, trans. Cassell, 72; ed. Padoan, 382–83: "A volere de' falli commessi satisfare interamente si conviene, a quello che fatto hai, operare il contrario; ma questo si vuole intendere sanamente. Ciò che tu hai amato, ti conviene avere in odio; e ciò, che tu per lo altrui amore t'eri a volere fare disposto, a fare il contrario, sì che tu odio acquisti, ti conviene disporre. . . . Tu hai amata costei perché bella ti pareva, perché dilettevole nelle cose libidinose l'aspettavi. Voglio che tu abbi in odio la sua bellezza, in quanto di peccare ti fu

cagione, o essere ti potesse nel futuro; voglio che tu abbi in odio ogni cosa che in le' in così fatto atto dilettevole la stimassi; la salute dell'anima sua voglio che tu ami e desideri."

35. *Corbaccio*, trans. Cassell, 72–73; ed. Padoan, 385: "Come a glorificarla [questa ingannatrice] eri disposto, così ad avvilirla ed a parvificarla ti disponi. . . . E, in quanto puoi, fa' che a le' nel tuo parlare lei medesima mostri e similmente la mostri ad altrui."

36. *Corbaccio*, trans. Cassell, 73; ed. Padoan, 390: "Se tempo da troppo affrettata morte non m'è tolto, io la farò, . . . ricredente della sua bestialità mostrandole che tutti gli uomini non sono da dovere essere scherniti ad uno modo, che ella vorrebbe così bene essere digiuna d'avermi mai veduto."

37. For the print history of *Il Corbaccio*, see Alberto Bacchi della Lega, *Serie delle edizioni delle opere di Giovanni Boccacci* (Bologna: Forni, 1875; reprint, 1967), 115–16. The 1487 title reads: *Invectiva di messer G. B. contra una malvagia donna: Dicto "Laberinto damore" et altrimenti "Il Corbaccio,"* published in Florence.

38. Letter of Messer Castorio Laurario of Padua, in *Invettiva di Messer Giovanni Boccaccio contra una malvagia donna, detto "Laberinto d'Amore," et altrimenti "Il Corbaccio"* (Milan: A. de Vicomercato, 1520), fols. Ivo–IIIvo. For this editor, marriage is a worthy union, especially if the woman is loved for her refinement, behavior, and virtue. He holds up Castiglione's *Book of the Courtier* as a fine work on true love, and Petrarch's Laura as the model *donna*, praising her, as if she were a real person, for placing chastity before wealth.

39. See *Il Corbaccio, altrimenti Labirinto d'amore*, ed. Lodovico Dolce (Venice: Gabriel Giolito, 1551), dedicatory letter.

40. Baldassare Castiglione, *Il cortegiano del conte Baldassare Castiglione*, ed. Antonio Ciccarelli da Fuligni (Venice: Bernardo Basa, 1584), 206. See Letizia Panizza, "Platonic Love on the Rocks: Castiglione Counter-Currents in Renaissance Italy," in *Laus Platonici Philosophi: Marsilio Ficino and His Influence*, ed. Stephen Clucas, Peter J. Forshaw, and Valery Rees (Leiden: Brill, 2011), 199–226.

41. See Letizia Panizza, "Plutarch's Camma: A Greek Literary Heroine's Adventures in Renaissance Italy," in *Italy and the Classical Tradition: Language, Thought, and Poetry, 1300–1600*, ed. Carlo Caruso and Andrew Laird (London: Duckworth, 2009), 101–17.

42. First printed in 1600, her polemic added a feminist critique of four specific misogynist treatises, beginning with *Il Corbaccio*. See Letizia Panizza, introduction to Lucrezia Marinella, *The Nobility and Excellence of Woman and the Defects and Vices of Men*, trans. Anne Dunhill (Chicago: University of Chicago Press, 1999), 1–34; and for Marinella's chapter on Boccaccio, 141–45. She begins by paraphrasing the Spirit's characterization of woman as an imperfect animal.

43. Hollander, *Boccaccio's Last Fiction*, 42.

44. See Millicent Marcus, "Misogyny as Misreading: A Gloss on *Decameron* VIII, 7," *Stanford Italian Review* 2.1 (Spring 1984): 23–40. The tale is about a scholar like our Narrator who exacts a cruel revenge on a widow who rejected him.

Chapter Sixteen

1. Giovanni Boccaccio, *Famous Women*, trans. and ed. Virginia Brown, I Tatti Renaissance Library 1 (Cambridge, MA: Harvard University Press, 2001), 3. My thanks to the editors of this volume for precious counsel and learned insights that have improved the present essay, and to Laurel Peacock for timely research assistance. All citations herein refer to chapter and text divisions in Brown's dual-language edition, which correspond to those in the definitive Italian version, on which Brown's translation is based: Giovanni Boccaccio, *De mulieribus claris*, ed. Vittorio Zaccaria, in *Tutte le opere*, vol. 10 (Milan: Mondadori, 1967). Stephen Kolsky's essential study of the *De mulieribus* suggests that work on this text was likely begun as early as 1359, during Boccaccio's visit with Petrarch in Milan. See Stephen D. Kolsky, *The Genealogy of Women: Studies in Boccaccio's "De mulieribus claris"* (New York: Peter Lang, 2003), 47. The present essay has benefited considerably from Kolsky's insightful analyses in *Genealogy of Women* as well as from his subsequent study, *The Ghost of Boccaccio: Writings on Famous Women in Renaissance Italy* (Turnhout: Brepols, 2005). Also valuable is Margaret Franklin, *Boccaccio's Heroines: Power and Virtue in Renaissance Society* (Aldershot, UK: Ashgate, 2006). Franklin offers an extended reading of the *De mulieribus* and traces the fortunes of Boccaccio's text in Italian literature and art through the mid-sixteenth century. For Boccaccio's biography, see Lucia Battaglia Ricci, *Boccaccio* (Rome: Salerno, 2000); Judith Powers Serafini-Sauli, *Giovanni Boccaccio* (Boston: Twayne, 1982).

2. One classical precedent, Plutarch's first-century B.C. *Mulierum virtutes*, was apparently unknown to Boccaccio. See Kolsky, *Genealogy of Women*, 42. On Petrarch's letter, *Familiares* 21.8, as a source and model for the *De mulieribus*, see Elsa Filosa, *Tre studi sul "De mulieribus claris"* (Milan: Edizioni Universitarie di Lettere Economia Diritto, 2012), 51–63. Filosa develops her argument from that of Kolsky, "La costituzione di una nuova figura letteraria: Intorno al *De mulieribus claris* di Giovanni Boccaccio," *Testo* 25 (1993): 36–52. The first monograph to appear in Italian on the *De mulieribus*, *Tre studi* appeared as the present essay was going to print, and is thus not substantially engaged here. Drawing on crucial philological and biographical coordinates for the *De mulieribus* and relating it to Boccaccio's other works, Filosa underscores the progressive, philogynous dimensions of this text. See especially Filosa, 39–44.

3. For essential philological information, see Vittorio Zaccaria, "Le fasi redazi-

onali del *De mulieribus claris*," *Studi sul Boccaccio* 1 (1963): 252–332, as well as the compendium of Zaccaria's authoritative studies (with valuable bibliography): Zaccaria, *Boccaccio narratore, storico, moralista e mitografo* (Florence: Olschki, 2001). See also Vittore Branca, *Tradizione delle opere di Giovanni Boccaccio*, vol. 1, *Un primo elenco dei codici e tre studi* (Rome: Edizioni di Storia e Letteratura, 1958); Franklin, *Boccaccio's Heroines*, 9–13; and Gilbert Tournoy, ed., *Boccaccio in Europe* (Louvain: Louvain University Press, 1977).

4. Among the most influential relevant studies, see Joan Kelly, *Women, History, & Theory: The Essays of Joan Kelly* (Chicago: University of Chicago Press, 1984); Constance Jordan, "Boccaccio's In-Famous Women: Gender and Civic Virtue in the *De mulieribus claris*," in *Ambiguous Realities: Women in the Middle Ages and Renaissance*, ed. Carol Levin and Neanie Watson (Detroit: Wayne State University Press, 1987), 34–40; Constance Jordan, *Renaissance Feminism: Literary Texts and Political Models* (Ithaca, NY: Cornell University Press, 1990). Nearly all of this first wave of feminist scholarship on the Renaissance was based on canonical, often prescriptive literary writings by men; much of it has been superseded by the research that it crucially inspired, which has focused on archival investigation and the editorial recuperation of texts by women. For explicit revisions of Kelly's influential conclusion that women did not "have a Renaissance," see Virginia Cox, *Women's Writing in Italy, 1400–1650* (Baltimore: Johns Hopkins University Press, 2008); Cox, *The Prodigious Muse: Women's Writing in Counter-Reformation Italy* (Baltimore: Johns Hopkins University Press, 2011). See also volumes in the series The Other Voice in Early Modern Europe, published by the University of Chicago Press and the University of Toronto, Centre for Reformation and Renaissance Studies.

5. On this later body of works, see Kolsky, *Ghost of Boccaccio*; and Franklin, *Boccaccio's Heroines*. Ruth Kelso lists 547 titles in the bibliography appended to her fundamental study, *Doctrine for the Lady of the Renaissance* (Urbana: University of Illinois Press, 1956). See also Giuseppe Zonta, ed., *Trattati del Cinquecento sulla donna* (Bari: G. Laterza, 1913).

6. See Christine de Pizan, *Le livre de la cité des dames*, trans. Eric Hicks and Thérèse Moreau (Paris: Stock, 1986); Pizan, *The Book of the City of Ladies*, trans. Rosalind Brown-Grant (London: Penguin, 1999).

7. For early interventions in this discussion, see David Hult, ed., *Debate of the Romance of the Rose* (Chicago: University of Chicago Press, 2010).

8. Stephen Kolsky argues that the character and significance of the *De mulieribus* have been distorted since the late twentieth century by a schematic tendency to place Boccaccio and Christine in conflicting traditions. See the introduction to his *Genealogy of Women* (especially 7–13) for his discussion

of negative readings of the *De mulieribus* in feminist scholarship. He cites as a judicious exception to this pattern Pamela Joseph Benson, *The Invention of the Renaissance Woman: The Challenge of Female Independence in the Literature and Thought of Italy and England* (University Park: Pennsylvania State University Press, 1992).

9. Named for the late fourth-century B.C. Greek mythographer Euhemerus and embraced by early Christians, euhemerism is the interpretation of mythology as a figural or distorted reflection of historical events and persons. Boccaccio's serious interest in Greco-Roman myth as an allegorical signifying system containing deep truths may be seen in a number of his works. In both the *Genealogia deorum gentilium* (*Genealogy of the Gentile Gods*), which he had begun to write by 1350 and continued to revise throughout his life, and his *Trattatello in laude di Dante*, begun in 1355, he adheres to ideas found in the ancients and in many medieval authors about the profoundly edifying capacities of poetry and other arts. Boccaccio is consistent with earlier Christian apologists for poetry (most famously Dante, in his *Letter to Cangrande della Scala*) who argued that one set of meanings beneath the poetic "veil," even of pagan texts, was Christian. For a concise discussion of Boccaccio's views, see the introduction to Boccaccio, *Boccaccio on Poetry: Being the Preface and Fourteenth and Fifteenth Books of Boccaccio's "Genealogia Deorum Gentilium,"* trans. Charles Osgood (1930; Indianapolis: Bobbs-Merrill, 1956), xi–xlix. On this practice in the *Filocolo*, see Victoria Kirkham, *Fabulous Vernacular: Boccaccio's "Filocolo" and the Art of Medieval Fiction* (Ann Arbor: University of Michigan Press, 2001), 10–11.

10. In a chapter titled "Boccaccio the Humanist," Kolsky observes: "The *De mulieribus claris* can be read as a conscious effort by Boccaccio to confirm his credentials as a humanist writer who was part of that avant-garde movement presided over by Petrarch" (*Genealogy of Women*, 39). Kolsky details the *De mulieribus*'s debt to Petrarch as well as to Tacitus, Livy, Valerius Maximus, and Homer, noting that "the fact of alluding to and making use of his knowledge of Greek was a sign of his commitment to extending humanism to include the study of Greek. Further, Boccaccio's deployment of Tacitus . . . may be seen as a conscious enlargement of the parameters of early humanism" (40).

11. Serafini-Sauli, *Giovanni Boccaccio*, 96.

12. The reference is to *De viris illustribus*. See Petrarch, *De viris illustribus*, in *Edizione nazionale delle opere di Francesco Petrarca*, vol. 2, pt. 1 (Florence: Sansoni, 1964).

13. Boccaccio, *Decameron*, ed. Vittore Branca (Milan: Mondadori, 1985), 4, Intro., 329; Giovanni Boccaccio, *The Decameron*, trans. G. H. McWilliam (London: Penguin, 1995), 4, Intro., 284.

14. Margaret Franklin notes that the chapter (644) on another prostitute, Flora,

counterbalances this positive portrait of Leaena. Boccaccio criticizes Flora for seeking to secure her own posthumous fame, even though her method for doing so was to finance festivals for public enjoyment. "Thus while both women were prostitutes, and both acted in the interest of civic welfare, Boccaccio condemns one for desiring public recognition and praises the other for silencing herself." Franklin, *Boccaccio's Heroines*, 50.

15. For more extended readings of Boccaccio's selective reporting in order to highlight the dangers of female ambition, see Franklin, *Boccaccio's Heroines*, 31–44.

16. Boccaccio's discouragement of second marriages here appears to go against the grain even of contemporary Florentine society, which, according to Christiane Klapisch-Zuber, considered widows an economic and social threat and therefore encouraged remarriage, especially of young widows. See Christiane Klapisch-Zuber, "The 'Cruel Mother': Maternity, Widowhood, and Dowry in Florence in the Fourteenth and Fifteenth Centuries," in *Women, Family, and Ritual in Renaissance Italy*, trans. Lydia Cochrane (Chicago: University of Chicago Press, 1985), 117–31. Behind these attitudes was a view of widows as prone to lust due to their sexual experience, and hence susceptible to lovers who might seize family assets. Boccaccio focuses on widows also in the *Filocolo*'s *quistioni d'amore* (question 9) and in the *Corbaccio*, where the woman under discussion is a widow. See Giovanni Boccaccio, *Il Filocolo*, trans. Donald Cheney (New York: Garland, 1985); Giovanni Boccaccio, *Corbaccio*, trans. Anthony K. Cassell (Urbana: University of Illinois Press, 1975). See also Franklin, *Boccaccio's Heroines*, 57–58.

Chapter Seventeen

1. All quotations are taken from Boccaccio, *Vita di Petrarca*, ed. Gianni Villani (Rome: Salerno Editrice, 2004), which also includes excellent annotations. The references in the body of the text are given by the paragraph numeration in the Latin text. Most scholarly studies on the *Vita* focus on the problem of the dating of the text. Foremost among them in authority and judgment is Renata Fabbri, ed., *Vite di Petrarca, Pier Damiani e Livio*, in *Tutte le opere*, ed. Vittore Branca, vol. 5, pt. 1 (Milan: Mondadori, 1992), 879–962. See also Vittore Branca, *Tradizione delle opere di Giovanni Boccaccio* (Rome: Edizioni di Storia e Letteratura, 1958), 116–17. Ernest Hatch Wilkins, "Boccaccio's Early Tributes to Petrarch," *Speculum* 38 (1963): 79–87, proposes an earlier date and also deals with the structure of the text. More significant in establishing the links between Boccaccio's biographical account of Petrarch and Petrarch's own self-dramatization is Giuseppe Velli, "Il *De Vita et Moribus Domini Francisci Petracchi de Florentia* e la biografia del Petrarca," *MLN* 102 (1987): 32–38.

2. The traditional traits of the biographical genre have been examined by Johann Bartuschat, *"De Vita et Moribus Domini Francisci Petracchi* de Boccace," *Chroniques Italiennes* 63–64 (2000): 81–93. On the tradition of the individual portrait, see Karl Enenkel, "Modelling the Humanist: Petrarch's 'Letter to Posterity' and Boccaccio's Biography of the Poet Laureate," in *Modelling the Individual: Biography and Portrait in the Renaissance, with a Critical Edition of Petrarch's "Letter to Posterity,"* ed. Karl Enenkel, Betsy De Jong-Crane, and Peter Liebregts (Amsterdam: Rodopi, 1998), 11–49.

3. Boccaccio, *De vita Petracchi* 72: "Franciscus Petracchi poeta, vir illustris ac vita moribusque et scientia clarus, sedente Benedicto XII pontifice maximo gloriosissima fama per orbem floruit universum."

4. For the role played by Dionigi da Borgo Sansepolcro in the intellectual interaction between Petrarch and Boccaccio, see the important work in Franco Suitner, ed., *Dionigi da Borgo Sansepolcro fra Petrarca e Boccaccio: Atti del Convegno di Studi, Sansepolcro, February 11–12, 2000* (Città di Castello: Petruzzi, 2001).

5. "Habita igitur laureatione, predictus cum Azone de Corrigio Parmam ivit; ibique secum integra amicitia iunctus, per aliquale tempus commoratus est, et moratur usque in hodiernum," *Vita Petracchi,* par. 17. This friendship with Azzo is recorded in Petrarch's "Letter to Posterity": "Inde ergo digressus parmam veni et cum illis de Corrigia . . ."; *Franciscu Petrarca Posteritati,* ed. Gianni Villani, in *Vita di Petrarca,* 123. Azzo was a powerful prince who cultivated the love of humane letters. Petrarch dedicated his *De remediis utriusque fortune* to him. See Fortunato Rizzi, *Francesco Petrarca e il decennio parmense (1341–1351)* (Turin: Paravia, 1934); and Ugo Dotti, *Vita del Petrarca* (Bari: Laterza, 1987), 130–35.

6. On this more shadowy side of Petrarch, including discussion of his relationship with Azzo da Correggio, see Victoria Kirkham, "Petrarch the Courtier: Five Public Speeches," in *Petrarch: A Critical Guide to the Complete Works,* ed. Victoria Kirkham and Armando Maggi (Chicago: University of Chicago Press, 2009), 141–50.

Chapter Eighteen

1. See the volume by Johannes Bartuschat, *Les "Vies" de Dante, Pétrarque et Boccace en Italie (XIV-XV, siècles) : Contribution à l'histoire du genre biographique* (Ravenna: Longo Editore, 2010).

2. For the dating of the three redactions, see Pier Giorgio Ricci, "Le tre redazioni del *Trattatello in laude di Dante,*" *Studi sul Boccaccio* 8 (1974): 197–214; and Carlo Paolazzi, "Petrarca, Boccaccio e il *Trattatello in laude di Dante,*" *Studi Danteschi* 55 (1983): 165–249. The first version is an autograph, Toledo, Biblioteca Capitolar de Toledo, MS 104.6; the second is also an autograph,

Vatican City, Biblioteca Apostolica Vaticana, Chigi MS 50.5.176; for the third, no autograph survives, but there are a number of Florentine copies (see Ricci's "Nota al testo," in *Tutte le opere*, 3:848–56). For the text in all its versions, see Boccaccio, *Trattatello in laude di Dante*, ed. Pier Giorgio Ricci, in *Tutte le opere*, vol. 3. For an English translation of the first redaction, see *Giovanni Boccaccio's The Life of Dante (Trattatello in laude di Dante)*, trans. Vincenzo Zin Bollettino (New York: Garland, 1990), from which I quote. Unless otherwise indicated, all references are to section numbers in the text, not page numbers. There are no English translations of the second and third versions of the *Trattatello*; translations for these versions are my own.

3. Boccaccio called Dante the "first guide and light of [his] studies" (*primus studiorum dux et prima fax*), as we learn from Petrarch, *Familiares* 21.15 (1359). For this and other citations, see Petrarch, *Letters on Familiar Matters*, trans. Aldo S. Bernardo (New York: Italica Press, 2005); the text in Latin follows Petrarch, *Le familiari*, ed. Vittorio Rossi and Umberto Bosco, in *Edizione Nazionale delle opere di Francesco Petrarca*, vols. 10–13 (Florence: Sansoni, 1933–42).

4. Boccaccio describes the meeting in a letter of 1353. See his *Epistole*, ed. Ginetta Auzzas, *Tutte le opere*, vol. 5, pt. 1 (Milan: Mondadori, 1992), 10.4–6. For Boccaccio's life see Vittore Branca, *Boccaccio: The Man and His Works* (New York: New York University Press, 1976); and for Petrarch's life see Ernst Hatch Wilkins, *Life of Petrarch* (Chicago: Chicago University Press, 1961).

5. The absence of the *Commedia* in Petrarch's library did not prevent words by Dante from entering Petrarch's works. Moreover, Dante "è stato uno dei maestri, per non dire *il* maestro, del Petrarca volgare" (has been one of the masters, not to say *the* master, of the vernacular Petrarch; my trans.). Petrarch, *Il Canzoniere*, ed. Marco Santagata (Milan: Mondadori, 2001), lxiv. On Dante's influence on Petrarch, see also Santagata, "Dante in Petrarca," in *Per moderne carte: La biblioteca volgare di Petrarca* (Bologna: il Mulino, 1990), 79–91; Giuseppe Velli, "Il Dante di Francesco Petrarca," in *Petrarca e Boccaccio: Tradizione — memoria — scrittura* (Padua: Antenore, 1993), 60–73; and Zygmunt G. Barański and Theodore J. Cachey, eds., *Petrarch and Dante: Anti-Dantism, Metaphysics, Tradition* (Notre Dame, IN: University of Notre Dame Press, 2009).

6. Vatican City, Biblioteca Apostolica Vaticana, MS Vat. Lat. 3199. For the occasion and the dating of *Ytalie iam certus honos*, see Aldo Francesco Massèra, "Di tre epistole metriche boccaccesche," *Giornale Dantesco* 30 (1927): 31–44; Gioacchino Paparelli, "Due modi opposti di leggere Dante: Petrarca e Boccaccio," in *Giovanni Boccaccio editore e interprete di Dante* (Florence: Olschki, 1979), 73–90; and the indispensable introduction to Boccaccio's Latin poems, the *Carmina*, by Giuseppe Velli, in *Tutte le opere*, vol. 5, pt. 1, pp. 386–91.

7. Boccaccio, *Carmina* 5.29–32 (my trans.): "Erit alter ab illo / quem laudas meritoque colis, per secula, Dantes, / quem genuit grandis vatum Florentia mater / atque veretur ovans."

8. Velli, introduction to Boccaccio, *Carmina*, p. 390 (my trans.).

9. "Because I have already written a brief treatise in praise of him, however, I shall refrain here from elaborating." Boccaccio, *Boccaccio's "Expositions on Dante's 'Comedy,'"* trans. Michael Papio (Toronto: University of Toronto Press, 2009), 44. In the *Accessus* of the *Expositions*, Boccaccio includes a brief life of Dante, recalling the *Trattatello* with this passage.

10. For more details on the medieval form of *accessi ad auctorem*, "introductions to the author," see Alastair J. Minnis, *Medieval Theory of Authorship*, 2nd ed. (Philadelphia: University of Pennsylvania Press, 1988).

11. Toledo, Biblioteca Capitolar, Toledo, Spain, MS 104.6, autograph.

12. *Trattatello* 1.8: "Come che io a tanta cosa non sia sufficiente, nondimeno secondo la mia picciola facoltà, quello che essa [città] dovea verso lui magnificamente fare, non avendolo fatto, m'ingegnerò di far io; non con istatua o con egregia sepoltura, delle quali è oggi appo noi spenta l'usanza, né basterebbono a ciò le mie forze, ma con lettere povere a tanta impresa. Di questo ho, e di questo darò, acciò che igualmente, e in tutto e in parte, non si possa dire, fra le nazioni strane, verso contanto poeta la sua patria essere stata ingrata."

13. See Jason M. Houston, *Building a Monument to Dante: Boccaccio as Dantista* (Toronto: University of Toronto Press, 2010).

14. *Trattatello* 1.1: "[Solone] affermava essere il destro [piede] il non lasciare alcuno difetto commesso impunito, e il sinistro ogni ben fatto remunerare; aggiugnendo che, qualunque delle due cose già dette per vizio o per negligenza si sottraeva, o meno che bene si servava, senza niuno dubbio quella repubblica, che 'l faceva, convenire andare sciancata: e se per isciagura si peccasse in ambedue, quasi certissimo avea, quella non potere stare in alcun modo."

15. The nature and origins of poetry have been one of the most discussed topics in studies of the *Trattatello*. Among the important contributions to the field, see Ernest Robert Curtius, "Theologische Poetik im italienischen Trecento," *Zeitschrift für Romanische Philologie* 60 (1940): 1–15; Claudio Mésoniat, *Poetica theologia: La "Lucula Noctis" di Giovanni Dominici e le dispute letterarie tra '300 e '400* (Rome: Edizioni di Storia e Letteratura, 1984); Giorgio Ronconi, *Le origini delle dispute umanistiche sulla poesia (Mussato e Petrarca)* (Rome: Bulzoni, 1976); Vittorio Zaccaria, "La difesa della poesia nelle 'Genealogie' del Boccaccio," *Lettere Italiane* 38.3 (1986): 281–311; and the recent work by Michael Papio, "Introduction: Boccaccio as *lector Dantis*," in *Boccaccio's "Expositions,"* 3–37.

16. Antimarriage invectives such as the *Adversus Jovinianum* by Saint Jerome and the *Dissuasio Valerii ad Rufinum* by Walter Map, copied into the *Zibaldone*

Laurenziano, undertake to establish the incompatibility between marriage and intellectual life, a topic further developed in the *Corbaccio*.

17. For biographies of Dante to date, see Giuseppe Mazzotta, "Life of Dante," in *The Cambridge Companion to Dante*, ed. Rachel Jacoff, 2nd ed. (Cambridge: Cambridge University Press, 2007), 1–13, with bibliography.

18. The list of authors starts with Virgil: "Vergilio mantovano infra costoro / conobb'i' quivi più ch'altro esaltato, / sì come degno, per lo suo lavoro" (Among them Virgil the Mantuan / I recognized, there exalted more than any other / and worthily so, by dint of his work); and ends with Dante: "Dentro dal coro delle donne adorno, / in mezzo di quel loco ove facieno / li savi antichi contento soggiorno, / riguardando, vid'io di gioia pieno / onorar festeggiando un gran poeta, / tanto che 'l dire alla vista vien meno. / Aveali la gran donna mansueta / d'alloro una corona in su la testa / posta, e di ciò ciascun'altra era lieta. / E vedend'io così mirabil festa, / per lui raffigurar mi fé vicino, / fra me dicendo: 'Gran cosa fia questa.' / Trattomi così innanzi un pocolino, / non conoscendol, la donna mi disse: / —Costui è Dante Alighieri fiorentino, / il qual con eccellente stil vi scrisse / il sommo ben, le pene e la gran morte: / gloria fu delle Muse mentre visse, / né qui rifiutan d'esser sue consorte." (Within the graceful group of ladies, / in the midst of that place where / the ancient wise men were happily dwelling, / as I gazed again, in full gladness, I saw / such joyous honors bestowed upon a great poet / that telling must fall short of sight. / That great, serene lady had placed / on his head a crown of laurel, / for which act all the other ladies seemed to rejoice. / And seeing so wonderful a celebration, / I drew near to make him out, / saying to myself: "What a great thing this must be." / Having thus drawn myself a bit forward / without recognizing him, I heard the lady say: / "This is Dante Alighieri the Florentine, / he who, with excellent style, for your sake / described the highest good, the torments, the damnations: / he was the glory of the Muses while he lived, / nor here do they decline to be his consorts.") Boccaccio, *Amorosa visione*, ed. Vittore Branca, in Boccaccio, *Tutte le opere*, ed. Vittore Branca, vol. 3 (Milan: Mondadori, 1974), A 5.7–9; 5.70–88; *Amorosa visione*, trans. Robert Hollander, Timothy Hampton, and Margherita Frankel (Hanover, NH: University Press of New England, 1986).

19. See at least Giuseppe Billanovich, "La leggenda dantesca del Boccaccio: Dalla lettera di Ilaro al *Trattatello in laude di Dante*," *Studi Danteschi* 28 (1949): 45–144; John Larner, "Tradition of Literary Biography in Boccaccio's *Life of Dante*," *Bulletin of the John Rylands Library* 72 (1990): 107–17; Victoria Kirkham, "The Parallel Lives of Dante and Virgil," *Dante Studies* 110 (1992): 241–53.

20. Billanovich, "La leggenda dantesca del Boccaccio," 78–80.

21. Ibid., 109 n. 1.

22. Ibid., 114–15.

23. For an analysis of the premonitory dream of Dante's mother, see Luigi Sasso, "La carne del pavone," in *Reinardus: Yearbook of the International Reynard Society* 4 (1991): 85–91; and for the dream's significance in the larger context of medieval peacock symbolism, Victoria Kirkham, "The Poisoned Peacock," in *Fabulous Vernacular: Boccaccio's "Filocolo" and the Medieval Art of Fiction* (Ann Arbor: University of Michigan Press, 2001), 200–250, esp. 221–40.

24. On the influence of hagiographic literature on the *Trattatello*, see Billanovich, "La leggenda dantesca del Boccaccio"; Larner, "Tradition of Literary Biography"; and more recently, Karen Elizabeth Gross, "Scholar Saints and Boccaccio's *Trattatello in laude di Dante*," *MLN* 124 (2009): 66–85.

25. *Trattatello* 1.180: "Come noi dovemo certissimamente credere a quello che Iddio dispone niuna cosa contraria la Fortuna potere operare."

26. *Trattatello* 1.180: "Questi fu quel Dante, del quale è il presente sermone; questi fu quel Dante, che a' nostri seculi fu conceduto di speziale grazia da Dio; questi fu quel Dante, il qual primo doveva al ritorno delle muse, bandite d'Italia, aprir la via. Per costui la chiarezza del fiorentino idioma è dimostrata; per costui ogni bellezza di volgar parlare sotto debiti numeri è regolata; per costui la morta poesì meritamente si può dir suscitata: le quali cose, debitamente guardate, lui niuno altro nome che Dante potere degnamente avere avuto dimostreranno." This passage, especially elevated in its rhetoric, has a double parallel *tricolon*: two sentences that consist of three syntactical units, all beginning with anaphora: *Questi fu quel Dante* (This was that Dante) and *Per costui* (Because of him) respectively, and in which the units of the second sentence parallel those of the first in an association of cause and effect.

27. *Trattatello* 1.24: "non curando né caldi né freddi, né vigilie né digiuni, né alcun altro corporale disagio."

28. *Trattatello* 1.28–29: "Gli studii generalmente sogliono solitudine e rimozione di sollecitudine e tranquillità d'animo desiderare . . . quasi dallo inizio della sua vita infino all'ultimo della morte, Dante ebbe fierissima e importabile passione d'amore, moglie, cura familiare e publica, esilio e povertà."

29. Petrarch considered them responsible for the death of his friend Mainardo Accorsi.

30. For the reference to "apology," see *Familiares* 21.15.4. Boccaccio's letter is no longer extant.

31. Paolazzi, "Petrarca, Boccaccio e il *Trattatello*," 183 (my trans.): "Il testo dell'epistola petrarchesca si riferisce a un 'corpus' di lodi ben definito, ugualmente presente ai due interlocutori epistolari . . . , che l'autore Boccaccio, timoroso di aver troppo innalzato Dante a scapito indiretto di Petrarca,

sottopone all'esame di quest'ultimo pregandolo di esaminarlo attentamente e di darne un giudizio, mentre Petrarca ricusa i sospetti di invidia e approva l'elogio dantesco, incoraggiando Boccaccio a rifinirlo e divulgarlo." Paolazzi shows how, conversely, the *Trattatello* influences some passages of *Familiares* 21.15. Scholars from Foscolo on have spilled rivers of ink on *Familiares* 21.15. Foscolo defined it as "extended by contradictions, ambiguities, and indirect apologies," in "A Parallel between Dante and Petrarca," in *Saggi e discorsi critici*, ed. Cesare Foligno (Florence: Le Monnier, 1953), 111; Gianfranco Contini talks about its "psychological ambiguity," in *Letteratura italiana delle origini* (Florence: Sansoni, 1970), 663; Paparelli exclaims, "Frankly, to me it looks like a masterpiece of hypocrisy!" (my trans.; "a me francamente pare un capolavoro d'ipocrisia!"), in "Due modi opposti di leggere Dante," 77. On *Familiares* 21.15 see the indispensable article "Francesco Petrarca," by Michele Feo, in *Enciclopedia Dantesca* (Rome: Istituto della Enciclopedia Italiana, 1943), 4:450–58; and for a more exhaustive bibliography, Paola Vecchi Galli, "Dante e Petrarca: Scrivere il padre," *Studi di Problemi e Critica Testuale* 79 (2009): 57–82.

32. Vatican City, Biblioteca Apostolica Vaticana, MS Chigi 50.5.176.

33. Boccaccio might have abbreviated the invective against Florence because of political events of 1360. An attempted coup d'état involved friends of his: "On December 30 [1360] Domenico Bandini and Nicolò di Bartolo del Buono (the dedicatee of the *Commedia delle Ninfe Fiorentine*) were hanged; the others took flight and were banished. Among these were Pino de' Rossi, Luca Ugolini, Andrea dell'Ischia—also friends of Boccaccio." Vittore Branca, *Boccaccio: The Man and His Works* (New York: New York University Press, 1976), 121. Diminishing the harsh tones of the invective against Florence was a good precaution, as was his move to Certaldo in 1361.

34. A detailed analysis of the individual differences between the two editing phases can be found in Giuseppe Billanovich, *Petrarca letterato* (Rome: Edizioni di Storia e Letteratura); and Paolazzi, "Petrarca, Boccaccio e il *Trattatello*."

35. Ricci, introduction to *Trattatello*, p. 431 (my trans.): "veramente gli era uscito dal cuore."

36. *Trattatello* 1.84: "la quale [la lingua volgare], secondo il mio giudicio, egli primo non altrimenti fra noi Italici esaltò e recò in pregio, che la sua Omero tra' Greci e Virgilio tra' Latini."

37. Petrarch, *Familiares* 21.15.22: "Cui tandem invideat qui Virgilio non invidet, nisi forte sibi fullonem et cauponum et lanistarum ceterorumve, qui quos volunt laudari vituperant, plausum et raucum murmur invideam, quibus cum ipso Virgilio cumque Homero carere me gratulor?"

38. For a detailed explanation of this gloss, see the analytic tables provided by Billanovich, *Petrarca letterato*, 270–71; and Paolazzi, "Petrarca, Boccaccio e il *Trattatello*," 202–6.

39. *Trattatello* 2.61 (my trans.): "Che diranno qui coloro, a gli studi de' quali non bastando della loro casa, cercano le solitudini delle selve? Che coloro, a' quali è riposo continuo, e a' quali l'ampie facoltà senza alcun pensiero ogni cosa oportuna ministrano? Che coloro che, soluti da moglie e da figliuoli posson vacare a lor piacere? De' quali assai sono che, se ad agio non sedessero, o udissero un mormorio, non potrebbon, non che meditare, ma leggere, né scrivere, se non stesse il gomito riposato."

40. Paolazzi, "Petrarca, Boccaccio e il *Trattatello*," 204 (my trans.): "una ironica facciata contro gli igegni troppo delicati."

41. Giuseppe Velli, "Petrarca e Boccaccio: L'incontro milanese," in *Petrarca e la Lombardia: Atti del Convegno di Studi, Milano, 22–23 maggio 2003*, ed. Giuseppe Frasso, Giuseppe Velli, and Maurizio Vitale (Padua: Antenore, 2005), 149 (my trans.): "Senza tener conto delle *solitudini delle selve*, del *continuo riposo*, non era Petrarca ad avere *ampie facultà*, ad essere *soluto da moglie e da figliuoli*? Non è questione di malizia di noi posteri. L'ambiguità è nel testo. Il meno che si possa dire è che esso sfugge al totale controllo dell'autore."

42. The Vatican Chigi manuscripts 50.5.176 and 50.6.213, whose unity has been demonstrated by Domenico De Robertis, transmit a singular autographic miscellany that collects the *Vita nuova*, the canon of fifteen *canzoni* by Dante, the *Divine Comedy*, the *Canzoniere* (Chigi form), the *canzone* "Donna me prega" with a commentary by Dino del Garbo, the *Trattatello*, and *Ytalie iam certus honos*. See Domenico De Robertis, *Il codice Chigiano L. V. 176 autografo di Giovanni Boccaccio* (Florence: Alinari, 1974); and De Robertis, "La tradizione boccaccesca delle Canzoni di Dante," in *Giovanni Boccaccio editore ed interprete di Dante* (Florence: Olschki, 1979), 5–13.

43. Simon Gilson, *Dante and the Renaissance* (Cambridge: Cambridge University Press, 2005), 27.

44. Theodore J. Cachey, "Between Petrarch and Dante: Prolegomenon to a Critical Discourse," in Barański and Cachey, *Petrarch and Dante*, 18.

45. On Boccaccio's influence on the composition of the *Canzoniere*, see Santagata, *Per moderne carte*; and Cachey, "Between Petrarch and Dante," 16–35.

46. Giorgio Padoan, "Il Boccaccio 'fedele' di Dante," in *Il Boccaccio, le Muse, il Parnaso, l'Arno* (Florence: Olschki, 1978), 229–46.

47. Billanovich, "Il più grande discepolo di Petrarca," in *Petrarca letterato*, 57–294.

48. Velli, "Petrarca e Boccaccio," 152.

49. It seems important to add that in the same period, 1371, Boccaccio also wrote a letter addressed to Iacopo Pizzinga, in which he again exalts Dante as the

one who awakened the sleeping Muses, and only "after him" (*post hunc, Epist.* 19.26–27) talks about Petrarch; indeed, this *post hunc* might be read not just in a chronological sense, but also in terms of merit.

Chapter Nineteen

1. Robert Hollander, "Boccaccio's Dante: Imitative Distance (*Decameron* I.1 and VI.10)," *Studi sul Boccaccio* 13 (1981–82): 169–98; Attilio Bettinzoli, "Per una definizione delle presenze dantesche nel *Decameron* I: I registri 'ideologici,' lirici, drammatici," *Studi sul Boccaccio* 13 (1981–82): 267–326; Kristina Marie Olson, "Resurrecting Dante's Florence: Figural Realism in the *Decameron* and the *Esposizioni*," *MLN* 124 (2009): 45–65.

2. See Elsa Filosa's essay on the *Trattatello* in this volume.

3. See Todd Boli's essay on the *Epistole* in this volume.

4. Carlo Paolazzi, "Petrarca, Boccaccio e il *Trattatello in laude di Dante*," *Studi Danteschi* 55 (1983): 165–249; Giuseppe Velli, "Il *De Vita et moribus domini Francisci Petracchi de Florentia* del Boccaccio e la biografia del Petrarca," *MLN* 102 (1987): 32–38; Todd Boli, "Boccaccio's *Trattatello in laude di Dante*, or *Dante Resartus*," *Renaissance Quarterly* 41 (1988): 389–412; Victoria Kirkham, "The Parallel Lives of Dante and Virgil," *Dante Studies* 110 (1992): 233–53; Karen Elizabeth Gross, "Scholar Saints and Boccaccio's *Trattatello in laude di Dante*," *MLN* 124 (2009): 66–85.

5. Benvenuto da Imola, *Comentum super Dantis Aldigherij Comoediam* (1887; Dartmouth Dante Project), http://dante.dartmouth.edu/, *Par.* 15.97–99: "Modo in interiori circulo est Abbatia monachorum sancti Benedicti, cuius ecclesia dicitur Sanctus Stephanus, ubi certius et ordinatius pulsabantur horae quam in aliqua alia ecclesia civitatis; quae tamen hodie est satis inordinata et neglecta, ut vidi, dum audirem venerabilem praeceptorem meum Boccacium de Certaldo legentem istum nobilem poetam in dicta ecclesia." While Benvenuto mentions Boccaccio and his works some two dozen times in his commentary, this is his only reference to the *Esposizioni*.

6. See Boccaccio, *Esposizioni sopra la "Comedia" di Dante*, ed. Giorgio Padoan, in Boccaccio, *Tutte le opere*, ed. Vittore Branca, vol. 3 (Milan: Mondadori, 1965), the edition cited throughout. Translations are mine. Cf. *Boccaccio's Expositions on Dante's "Comedy,"* trans. with introduction and notes by Michael Papio (Toronto: University of Toronto Press, 2009).

7. For an article that questions the general wisdom that Boccaccio ceased work on the *Esposizioni* because of the onslaught of his terminal illness, see Todd Boli, "Treatment of Orthodoxy and Insistence on the *Comedy*'s Allegory in Boccaccio's *Esposizioni*," *Italian Culture* 9 (1991): 63–74, arguing that fatigue with his own labor, in particular with the need to allegorize so many stub-

bornly resistant details, was responsible for the incomplete condition of the manuscript, a view shared, if with a quite different understanding of the reasons for the expositor's disgust, by Papio, *Boccaccio's Expositions*, 26–35.

8. Guyda Armstrong and Vika Zafrin, "Towards the Electronic *Esposizioni*: The Challenges of the Online Commentary," *Digital Medievalist* 1.1 (Spring 2005), http://www.digitalmedievalist.org/journal/1.1/armstrong/.

9. These "L" indications are present in only two of the four surviving early manuscripts, classified by Padoan as the Beta group. Both codices, with omissions and disagreements between them, are of the fifteenth century: Florence, Biblioteca Nazionale, MS 2.4.58 (F^1); and Florence, Biblioteca Riccardiana, MS 1053 (FR). See Padoan's textual notes, *Esposizioni*, pp. 713–28, esp. 728.

10. See the second sentence of *Inf.* 1, *esp. litt.* 1: "The present volume is divided into three principal parts, which are the three books [*cantiche*] in which the author himself has divided it."

11. Teodolinda Barolini establishes a critical framework for the term in quotes in *The Undivine Comedy: Detheologizing Dante* (Princeton, NJ: Princeton University Press, 1993), chap. 1.

12. The references to the *Epistle to Cangrande* in the *Esposizioni*, which appear in *Accessus* 7–13 (noted by Padoan, pp. 767–69, 771), are to paragraphs 17–19, 23–27, 28, 29–31, 39, and 41 in the letter. See Luis Jennaro-MacLennan, "Boccaccio and the Epistle to Cangrande," in *The Trecento Commentaries on the "Divina Commedia" and the Epistle to Cangrande* (Oxford: Clarendon, 1974), 105–23; and for a more recent treatment, Robert Hollander, *Dante's Epistle to Cangrande* (Ann Arbor: University of Michigan Press, 1993). Recently Carlo Ginzburg has proposed that the text of the *Epistle* that follows the introductory section that both Augusto Mancini and Bruno Nardi allowed to remain within the "authentic" canon of Dante's works was composed by none other than Boccaccio. See Ginzburg, "Dante's Epistle to Cangrande and Its Two Authors," *Proceedings of the British Academy* 139 (2006): 195–216. For a counterargument, see Hollander, "Due recenti contributi al dibattito sull'autenticità dell'*Epistola a Cangrande*," *Letteratura Italiana Antica* 10 (2009): 541–52, esp. 543–48, pointing out that Ginzburg has not dealt adequately with the force of Luca Azzetta's demonstration that the epistle, if it were not written by Dante, had to have been composed at least by 1343. Azzetta, "Le chiose alla *Commedia* di Andrea Lancia e altre questioni dantesche," *L'Alighieri* 21 (2003): 5–76. The result is that Boccaccio would have had to have composed his *epistola falsa* before he was thirty and in a Neapolitan cultural atmosphere that does not accord easily with such theoretical Dantean interests. The best single hypothesis remains that Dante himself wrote the epistle.

13. For consideration of these terms see Robert Hollander, "Dante *Theologus-Poeta*," *Dante Studies* 94 (1976): 91–136.

14. See, *inter alia*, *Inferno* 1.7 and 29.55–57; *Purgatorio* 24.52–54; *Paradiso* 1.13–21 and 25.1–2.

15. Jonathan Usher notes that this passage clearly reflects the *Epistle to Cangrande*, even if Boccaccio did not recognize that document as Dantean. See Usher, "Boccaccio on Readers and Reading," *Heliotropia* 1.1 http://scholar works.umass.edu/cgi/viewcontent.cgi?article=1004&context=heliotropia (2003); but see similar observations present in Padoan, 788 nn. 18–21.

16. Jennaro-MacLennan, "Boccaccio and the Epistle to Cangrande." For a later bibliographical note, giving some twenty references to work published between 1913 and 1979, see Robert Hollander, *Boccaccio's Dante and the Shaping Force of Satire* (Ann Arbor: University of Michigan Press, 1997), 22 n. 3.

17. Jennaro-MacLennan, "Boccaccio and the Epistle to Cangrande," 120–23.

18. Filippo Villani's spectacularly "theological" views were not yet circulating. Before Boccaccio's time, with the exception of a single commentator, Guido da Pisa, the tendency had been to avoid the more "theological" expression urged by the poem and the *Epistle*.

19. Boli, "Treatment of Orthodoxy."

20. Those interested will find the subjects of the various "allegories" examined by Boccaccio in one of the opening notes to each canto of the *Esposizioni* as they appear in the Dartmouth Dante Project.

21. Was Boccaccio responding to the historical referentiality of the scenes involving Farinata and Cavalcante?

22. For a recent and compelling reassessment of Petrarch's hostility to Dante, see a number of the essays gathered in Zygmunt G. Barański and Theodore J. Cachey, eds., *Petrarch and Dante: Anti-Dantism, Metaphysics, Tradition* (Notre Dame, IN: University of Notre Dame Press, 2009).

Chapter Twenty

1. For a general survey of the Renaissance history of the *Genealogia* as well as a list of texts and translations, see my introduction to Boccaccio, *Genealogy of the Pagan Gods*, vol. 1, ed. and trans. Jon Solomon, I Tatti Renaissance Library, vol. 46 (Cambridge, MA: Harvard University Press, 2011), viii–xiii. In the preparation of my edition, cited here unless otherwise indicated, I consulted Boccaccio, *Genealogia deorum gentilium*, ed. Vittorio Zaccaria, in Boccaccio, *Tutte le opere*, ed. Vittore Branca, vols. 7–8 (Milan: Mondadori, 1998). I also sometimes referred to the edition superseded by Zaccaria's: Boccaccio, *Genealogie deorum gentilium libri*, ed. Vincenzo Romano, 2 vols. (Bari: Laterza,

1951). Still useful for English students of medieval literary theory is *Boccaccio on Poetry: Being the Preface and the Fourteenth and Fifteenth Books of Boccaccio's "Genealogia Deorum Gentilium,"* trans. with intro. Charles G. Osgood (1930; repr., Indianapolis: Bobbs–Merrill, 1956). Editors have cited the title of the text as both *Genealogia* and *Genealogie*. I have chosen the singular form since all the gods descend from a single progenitor, "Demogorgon." See the discussion in my edition, xxiii-xxvi.

2. *Genealogia* 1, Preface 1.20–21: "et tu meis humeris, non dicam celum, quod illi tulere, quin imo et terram super addere cupis et maria, ac etiam celicolas ipsos, et cum eis sustentatores egregios. Nil aliud hoc est nisi velle ut pondere premar et peream."

3. The index Coluccio Salutati commissioned from Domenico Bandini lists 1,966 items. An electronic Latin word count tallies over 210,000.

4. For an English translation of Boccaccio's own recollection in *Genealogia* 15.6.8, see Marianne Pade, "The Fragments of Theodontius in Boccaccio's *Genealogie deorum gentilium libri*," in *Avignon & Naples: Italy in France, France in Italy in the Fourteenth Century*, ed. Marianne Pade, Hannemarie Ragn Jensen, and Lene Waage Petersen (Rome: "L'Erma" di Bretschneider, 1997), 151. For Paolo's own *Genealogie deorum* as well as his *Collectiones*, see Teresa Hankey, "Un nuovo codice delle 'Genealogie deorum' di Paolo da Perugia," *Studi sul Boccaccio* 18 (1989): 65–161. For a thorough investigation, see Pade, "Fragments of Theodontius," 149–82.

5. E.g., Virgil, *Aeneid* 6.273–89.

6. Boccaccio cites every book of the *Iliad* except 17 and 22, and every book of the *Odyssey* except 2, 4, 17, 18, and 20–24.

7. Boccaccio did not master the language. The transcriptions of Homeric Greek in the *Genealogia* contain many diacritical errors, and Leontius's Latin translations are imprecise. Federica Ciccolella, *Donati Graeci: Learning Greek in the Renaissance* (Leiden: Brill, 2008), 98–99, suggests that Leontius "aroused remarkable interest in Greek mythology, stimulating Boccaccio . . . to write his *Genealogia deorum gentilium*." This overlooks Boccaccio's autobiographical account, but Ciccolella's discussion puts Leontius's unsatisfactory pedagogical method into historical context. For Petrarch's dislike of Leontius, see Petrarch's *Seniles* 3.6 and 6.1. Cf. the still useful monograph by Ernest H. Wilkins, *The University of Chicago Manuscript of the "Genealogia Deorum Gentilium" of Boccaccio* (Chicago: University of Chicago Press, 1927), esp. chap. 2, "The Greek Quotations in the *Genealogia*."

8. Oskar Hecker, *Boccaccio-funde* (Braunschweig: George Westermann, 1902), vii, first identified this autograph.

9. For color illustrations and some commentary, see Maria Grazia Ciardi Dupré

Dal Poggetto, "L'iconografia nei codici miniati boccacciani dell'Italia centrale e meridionale," in *Boccaccio visualizzato: Narrare per parole e per immagini fra Medioevo e Rinascimento*, ed. Vittore Branca (Turin: Einaudi, 1999), 2:3–52, 57–62 (fig. 5), and 78–88 (figs. 12–18).

10. For Boccaccio's April 1372 letter to Pietro, see Boccaccio, *Epistole*, ed. Ginetta Auzzas, in *Tutte le opere*, ed. Vittore Branca, vol. 5 (Milan: Mondadori, 1992), 680 (20.23).

11. Vittorio Zaccaria, "Per il testo delle 'Genealogie deorum gentilium,'" *Studi sul Boccaccio* 16 (1987): 179–240; and Zaccaria, "Ancora per il testo delle 'Genealogie deorum gentilium,'" *Studi sul Boccaccio* 21 (1993): 243–73.

12. Giuseppe Billanovich, "Pietro Piccolo da Monteforte tra il Petrarca e il Boccaccio," in *Medioevo e Rinascimento: Studi in onore di Bruno Nardi* (Florence: Sansoni, 1955), 65–72.

13. *Genealogie*, ed. Zaccaria, 1596.

14. *Genealogia* 14.22.1 and 15.8.4.

15. Giovanni Gullace, "Medieval and Humanistic Perspectives in Boccaccio's Concept and Defense of Poetry," *Mediaevalia* 12 (1989 [for 1986]): 226.

16. Pade, "Fragments of Theodontius," 155, specifies some of the authors known in southern Italy, where the study of Greek continued, and to Theodontius: [Apollodorus], Hesiod, Pausanias, Scholia D on the *Iliad*, and scholia on Apollonius of Rhodes and Pindar.

17. See M. L. West, "Stesichorus Redivivus," *Zeitschrift für Papyrologie und Epigraphik* 4 (1969): 135–49.

18. Unfortunately Boccaccio errs in reporting Eusebius's account; see *Genealogie*, ed. Zaccaria, 1686 n. 70.

19. Homer, *Iliad* 2.104; Aeschylus, *Agamemnon* 60; Sophocles, *Electra* 10; Euripides, *Orestes* 4–32.

20. [Apollodorus], *Bibliotheca*, Epitome 2.10, and earlier sources include still another, Pittheus.

21. [Apollodorus,] Epitome 3.13, also offers the Atreus lineage. The Pl[e]isthenes tradition is found in Hesiod (frag. 194), Stesichorus (frag. 42), Bacchylides (15.48), and Euripides' lost *Cretan Women* — see also Euripides, *Orestes*, ed. and trans. M. L. West (Warminster: Aris & Philips, 1987), 182; and Hellanicus (4 F 157); cf. Aeschylus, *Agamemnon* 1569 and 1602. For the adoption motif, see Scholion D on *Iliad* 2.249 and the scholion on Euripides, *Orestes* 4. Boccaccio employs the same genealogy in *De casibus* 1.15.3.

22. Walter Burkert, *Homo Necans* (Berkeley: University of California Press, 1983), 108–9, does not cite this genealogical parallel.

23. Cf. Benjamin Garstad, "Belus in the 'Sacred History' of Euhemerus," *Classical Philology* 99 (2004): 246–57, esp. 250–51.

24. *Genealogia* 2.44.2: "Ex quibus comprehendi potest a similitudine nominis et forsan temporis exortum errorem, ut qui Beli Syriaci filius fuerit, creditus Beli Egyptiaci. Sed ex quocumque Belo natus sit, mens michi est hic Theodontii et Pauli opinionem sequi, cum de superiori non satis certus appareat autor. Hunc igitur dicunt ex Egypto in litus Syrium abiisse et Phenicibus imperasse et amplissima atque generosa prole claruisse."

25. Because we cannot verify the genealogical lineages sourced from either Theodontius or Paolo, and because we know that one of Paolo's own compositions was his *Genealogie deorum*, there is reason to suspect the validity of some of these generations, which serve primarily to connect a genealogical gap.

26. For the Semitic origins of many Theban myths, see Michael C. Astour, *Hellenosemitica: An Ethnic and Cultural Study in West Semitic Impact on Mycenaean Greece* (Leiden: E. J. Brill, 1967), 113–224.

27. Boccaccio (*Genealogia* 2.44) discusses several variants of Agenor; [Apollodorus] and Hyginus mention ten. Sophocles inserts Polydorus into the lineage, but Boccaccio (2.46), citing Lactantius [Placidus] and Theodontius, writes that he knows of no offspring.

28. By "fractal" I mean an arrangement that is the same in large and small degree, in this case Boccaccio's pattern of proceeding from divine to human.

29. Cf. the "uncertain Judean god" described by Lucan (*Pharsalia* 2.592–93) and the aniconic Cypriot meteorite described by Tacitus (*Histories* 2.2–3), for which see Boccaccio's discussion of Cypriot Venus (*Genealogia* 3.23.8–9).

30. For a survey of the tradition, see Christiane Klapisch-Zuber, "The Genesis of the Family Tree," *I Tatti Studies: Essays in the Renaissance* 4 (1991): 105–29.

31. He makes a similar progression in *De mulieribus claris*, beginning with Eve and approximately two dozen mythological goddesses and queens, and then cataloging as many as five dozen historical characters ranging from Sappho to his contemporary, Joan, queen of Jerusalem and Sicily. Other than beginning with Adam and Eve, Boccaccio does not use a similar progression in *De casibus*.

Chapter Twenty-One
"*So spoke Pyrrhus, and by 'Hera' he meant Fortune, the power we better and more rightly call 'divine providence.'*"

1. Boccaccio, *De casibus virorum illustrium*, ed. Pier Giorgio Ricci and Vittorio Zaccaria, in *Tutte le Opere*, ed. Vittore Branca, vol. 9 (Milan: Mondadori, 1983), 1, Proem, 7: "quid Deus omnipotens, seu—ut eorum loquar more—Fortuna, in elatos posit et fecerit . . . a mundi primordio in nostrum usque evum." For the manuscript count and description, in addition to this edition (ninety-two in Latin alone, not counting translations into the European ver-

naculars), see Vittore Branca, *Tradizione delle opere di Giovanni Boccaccio* (Rome: Edizioni di Storia e Letteratura, 1958), 84–90. No complete English translation is available, although "about half of the original tales and links have been selected" for translation in Boccaccio, *The Fates of Illustrious Men*, trans. Louis Brewer Hall (New York: Frederick Unger, 1965). A useful search tool is made available by the Università degli Studi di Roma 'La Sapienza', http://www.bibliotecaitaliana.it/exist/bibit/.

2. For the philological details, see Pier Giorgio Ricci, "Le due redazioni del *De Casibus*," *Rinascimento* 13 (1962): 3–29; and Vittorio Zaccaria, "Le due redazioni del *De casibus*," *Studi sul Boccaccio* 10 (1977–78): 1–26.

3. Book 7 ends with the Jewish *diaspora* after Titus destroyed the Temple of Jerusalem (A.D. 70), presented possibly as the last act of the Roman Empire in God's providential plan for mankind. Book 8 starts with a crowd of destitute emperors from the new age of Salvation that Christ's sacrifice opened for humanity. It is not easy to establish a criterion for historical periodization in Boccaccio's work, and the label "postclassical" is used here in an attempt to capture the potentially significant theological difference between pre- and post-Redemption ages. The same general sense of a divided history is at work in Dante's review of the Roman imperial mission in both *Paradiso* 6 and *Monarchia* 2. In these works, the destruction of the Temple in Jerusalem seems to be part of the historical sequence of events in which the Roman Empire was assigned a preparatory (rather than sustaining) role for the Christian Church.

4. For the iconographic suggestion, see Lucia Battaglia Ricci, "Immaginario trionfale: Petrarca e la tradizione figurativa," in *I "Triumphi" di Francesco Petrarca*, ed. Claudia Berra (Milan: Cisalpino, 1999), 255–98.

5. On the vast array of sources mobilized in the work, in addition to the rich introductory notes by Zaccaria (xx–xxv), see Vittore Branca, *Boccaccio medievale* (Florence: Sansoni, 1964), 158–63; Annalisa Carraro, "Tradizioni culturali e storiche nel *De casibus*," *Studi sul Boccaccio* 12 (1980): 197–262; Lowell Edmunds, "A Note on Boccaccio's Sources for the Story of Oedipus in *De casibus illustrium virorum* and in the *Genealogie*," *Aevum* 56 (1982): 248–52; Jonathan Usher, "*Magna pars abest*: A Borrowed *sententia* in Boccaccio's *De casibus*," *Studi sul Boccaccio* 21 (1993): 235–42; and Usher, "A Quotation from the *Culex* in Boccaccio's *De casibus*," *Modern Language Review* 97 (2002): 312–23.

6. Boccaccio, *De casibus* 1, Proem, 9: "ne continua hystoriarum series legenti possit fastidium aliquod inferre."

7. Boccaccio, *De casibus* 5.20.14, "De Iugurta Numidarum rege": "Sic qui fraude fratres occiderat, qui fraude bellum traxerat, qui luserat Romanos fraude, fraude irretitus est. Qui in thesauris et regni splendore ac in potentia magis quam in persuasa sibi virtute voluptatem ac spem omnem posuerat, pauper

obscurus impotens et, quod peius est, captivus ab aliena virtute factus est. Qui per fratrum sanguinem regni culmen ascenderat, per abrupta montis flumen ad imum descendit; et sic qui nimio concupiverat estu, alvei gurgitis frigiditate tepefactus est."

8. For a further extended meditation in this vein, a *contrapasso*-like analysis of history's mercilessly balanced ledger, see also *In Iudeos pauca* (7.9.1–8).

9. Boccaccio, *De casibus* 5.4.1, "In cives hominesque nequam": "Quid mirer imperium Occeano terminasse Romanos, dum tales intueor illi rei publice fuisse cives? Equidem adversus eos nulle fuere Fortune vires et argumento sit, videre volentibus, ubi virtus sit ibi nullas partes esse Fortune."

10. Zaccaria, introduction to *De casibus*, xxxiii–xxxiv.

11. On the complex question of Machiavelli's triad Fortune-virtue-occasion, in its relation to vernacular antecedents, see Vincenzo Cioffari, "The Function of Fortune in Dante, Boccaccio, and Machiavelli," *Italica* 24 (1947): 1–13.

12. For Cicero's treatment of virtues, see Andrew R. Dyck, *A Commentary to Cicero's "De officiis"* (Ann Arbor: University of Michigan Press, 1997), 100–102, 191–94, and 338–40. See Zaccaria's comment in his introduction (xxxvi) and his listing of the work among the "sources" for the Regulus episode in the gloss to 5.3 (p. 971).

13 The text is cited from *Carmina Burana*, ed. Edoardo Bianchini (Milan: Rizzoli, 2010), which contains a useful historical-cultural commentary. In that edition, the one-line poem in question closes the sequence of texts pertinent to the theme of Fortune. The formulaic quality of the life parabola, as Boccaccio describes it, is at times reflected on the level of style. See, for instance, the almost perfectly parallel statements closing the accounts of Arsinois's life, "se non debitas, sed quas exegit Fortuna . . . penas ostendens" (4.16.1), and the life of Alexander Balas, "etsi non debitas, quas tamen exegit Fortuna, penas dedit" (5.15.10). In the first instance, Boccaccio's diction may reflect and respond to Dante's in *Convivio* 1.3.4: "mostrando contra mia voglia la piaga de la fortuna, che suole ingiustamente molte volte al piagato essere imputata" (unwillingly displaying the wound of fortune, which is often unjustly blamed on the wounded).

14. For the potential relevance of Boccaccio's juridical and rhetorical training for the framing mechanisms of his narratives, see Giancarlo Mazzacurati, *All'ombra di Dioneo: Tipologie e percorsi della novella da Boccaccio a Bandello* (Florence: La Nuova Italia, 1996); and Lucia Battaglia Ricci, "*Decameron*: Interferenze di modelli," in *Autori e lettori di Boccaccio: Atti del Convegno internazionale di Certaldo (20–22 settembre 2001)*, ed. Michelangelo Picone (Florence: Franco Cesati, 2002), 179–94. The treatment of *casus* as a narrative form, in André Jolles, *Forme semplici* (1930), now in *I travestimenti della letteratura: Saggi critici e teorici (1897–1932)*, ed. S. Contarini (Milan: Mondadori, 2003), still proves useful.

15. For a detailed list, see Zaccaria's introduction, lii. At least two works, however, deserve explicit mention: Laurent de Premierfait's reworking of Boccaccio's text in his *Des cas des nobles hommes et femmes* and John Lygdate's *Fall of Princes*.

16. This line of inquiry is currently being pursued in several quarters. See the seminal work by Vittorio Zaccaria, *Boccaccio narratore, storico, moralista e mitografo* (Florence: Olschki, 2001). Particularly intriguing sections for this study may perhaps be found in 7.3 (the long and lively squabble among Messalina, Tiberius, and Caligula), 9.1 (the debate between Brunhilde, queen of the Franks, and the author), and 9.21 (the narrative on the deaths of the Knights Templar).

17. An interesting case of partial redistribution and shift is Boccaccio's Boniface VIII, who gnaws his hand like Dante's Ugolino. See, for visual examples of this act, Moshe Barasch, *Gestures of Despair in Medieval and Early Renaissance Art* (New York: New York University Press, 1976), figs. 1–3. In the *De casibus* Boniface appears only in a short cameo in 9.20.4, where he is portrayed as biting his hands in rage, an image recognizable from *Inferno* 33.58–60, only three paragraphs after Dante's Count Ugolino has appeared "inediam qua cum filiis perierat deflentem" (lamenting the starvation that killed him with his children). Dante's blast at Boniface, coming from the mouth of Guido da Montefeltro in *Inferno* 27.92–93, "né sommo officio né ordini sacri / guardò in sé" (paying no heed to his lofty office or sacred orders), is then redeployed in *De casibus* 9.7.12. "On Pope John XXII": "non obstante flammei pilei reverentia nec sacrorum que exercebat officiorum" (notwithstanding the reverence due both to the flame-red cap and the sacred duties he was performing). An intratextual gloss within the gloss may point to the further Dantean echo contained in Boccaccio's choice of *reverentia* to translate *guardò*, in the above passage. It evokes the balancing act achieved in Dante's antipapal (but not anti-institutional) tirade against Nicholas III in *Inferno* 19.100–103: "E se non fosse ch'ancor lo mi vieta / la reverenza de le somme chiavi / che tu tenesti ne la vita lieta / io userei parole ancor più gravi" (And were it not for the reverence of the supreme and holy keys you held in life above, I would use even harsher words).

18. A similar signal, entrusted to the endnotes, may also be found at 9.6.13, "Dolentes quidam et in superbos": "Quem si mente integra velimus inspicere"; the editor rightly flags this as an echo of Dante's phrase "se ben si guarda / con la mente sana" in *Purgatorio* 6.36.

19. Boccaccio, *De casibus* 1.11.4: "quis verba faciens, quod ob meritum, quis in quem facta, quo in loco, quo in tempore, iratus an quietus animo, hostis an amicus, infamis aut honestus homo sit."

20. The digressive quality of the move is suggested by the verb *svaria* that Zaccaria uses on p. 922 to characterize the way the chapter moves between two themes.

21. For this line of reasoning, see Regina Psaki, "The Play of Genre and Voicing in Boccaccio's *Corbaccio*," *Italiana* 5 (1993): 41–54; and Robert Hollander, *Boccaccio's Last Fiction: "Il Corbaccio"* (Philadelphia: University of Pennsylvania Press, 1988).

Chapter Twenty-Two

1. For Sicco Polenton's statement "Decades . . . tres T. Livii patrium in sermonem vertit" (he converted three decades of T. Livy into the speech of his country) and Bembo's 1533 letters referring to a "Deca di Livio tradotta in volgare dal Boccaccio" (Decade of Livy translated into the vernacular by Boccaccio), see Attilio Hortis, *Cenni di G. Boccacci intorno a Tito Livio* (Trieste: Lloyd Austro-Ungarico, 1887), 71–73.

2. Bembo writes in a letter from 1527: "e per quello che io stimar ne posso, per niente egli non è traduzione del Boccaccio" (and as far as I can tell, it is not at all a translation of Boccaccio's). For the text of the letter, see Francesco Maggini, "Le prime traduzioni di Tito Livio," in *I primi volgarizzamenti dai classici latini* (Florence: Le Monnier, 1952), 75.

3. A colophon tells us that it was translated in 1323 "di francesco in latino" by a certain Filippo di S. Croce in Puglia. See Charles Samaran, "Pierre Bersuire: La traduction française de Tite-Live," *Histoire Littéraire de la France* 39 (1962): 358–414, 364; and Luca Azzetta, "Tradizione latina e volgarizzamento della prima Deca di Tito Livio," *Italia Medioevale e Umanistica* 36 (1993): 175–97.

4. Giuseppe Billanovich, "Il Boccaccio, il Petrarca e le più antiche traduzioni in italiano delle decadi di Tito Livio," *Giornale Storico della Letteratura Italiana* 130 (1953): 311–37; Billanovich, *La tradizione del testo di Livio e le origini dell'umanesimo*, vol. 1, *Tradizione e fortuna di Livio tra Medioevo e Umanesimo*, pt. 1 (Padua: Antenore, 1981). Petrarch's Livy survives in London, British Library, MS Harley 2493.

5. Maria Teresa Casella, *Tra Boccaccio e Petrarca: I volgarizzamenti di Tito Livio e di Valerio Massimo* (Padua: Antenore, 1982).

6. Battaglia notes the resemblance of details and whole expressions in his notes to the *Filocolo*: Giovanni Boccaccio, *Filocolo*, ed. Salvatore Battaglia (Bari: Laterza, 1938), 572–73.

7. Antonio Enzo Quaglio, "Valerio Massimo e il *Filocolo* di Giovanni Boccaccio," *Cultura Neolatina* 20 (1960): 45–77; and Quaglio, "Tra fonti e testi del Filocolo," *Giornale Storico della Letteratura Italiana* 139 (1962): 321–69, 513–40; 140 (1963): 321–63, 489–551. See also Ernesto Parodi, "La cultura e lo stile del

Boccaccio," in *Lingua e letteratura: Studi di teoria linguistica e di storia dell'italiano antico*, vol. 2 (Venice: Pozza, 1957); and Vincenzo Pernicone, "Il *Filostrato* di Giovanni Boccaccio," *Studi di Filologia Italiana* 2 (1929): 77–128.

8. Casella, *Tra Boccaccio e Petrarca*, 10–12.

9. Giorgio Padoan, "Sulla genesi del *Decameron*," in *Boccaccio: Secoli di vita; Atti del Congresso Internazionale: Boccaccio 1975, Università di California, Los Angeles 17–19 Ottobre, 1975*, ed. Marga Cottino-Jones and Edward F. Tuttle (Ravenna: Longo, 1977), 143–76.

10. Vatican City, Biblioteca Apostolica Vaticana, MS Ferraioli 559. See Vanna Lippi Bigazzi, ed., *Un volgarizzamento inedito di Valerio Massimo* (Florence: Accademia della Crusca, 1996), xiv-vi: "oggi, nel 1326, la tiene il principe Filippo che fu sconfitto dal magnanimo Uguiccione da Faggiuola" (today, in 1326, it belongs to Prince Filippo, who was defeated by the magnanimous Uguiccione da Faggiuola). Maria Teresa Casella, "Sul volgarizzamento boccacciano di Valerio Massimo: Un codice rintracciato; Una chiosa imbarazzante?," *Studi sul Boccaccio* 19 (1990): 191–208.

11. Giuliano Tanturli, "Volgarizzamenti e ricostruzione dell'antico: I casi della terza e quarta Deca di Livio e di Valerio Massimo, la parte del Boccaccio (a proposito di un'attribuzione)," *Studi Medievali* 27 (1986): 811–88.

12. For characteristics of *volgarizzamento*, see Alison Cornish, *Vernacular Translation in Dante's Italy: Illiterate Literature* (Cambridge: Cambridge University Press, 2011).

13. Livy, *Le deche di T. Livio*, ed. Francesco Pizzorno, vol. 5 (Savona: Sambolino, 1842–45), 10: "Considerato, che, secondo che Aristotele vuole nel primo della rettorica sua, il sapere le antiche storie è utilissimo nelle cose civili; ho proposto di riducere di latino in volgare X libri di Tito Livio Patavino . . . acciò che da quello . . . possano li non letterati prendere e delle storie diletto, e delle magnifiche opere e virtuose grazioso frutto" (Having considered that, according to what Aristotle means in the first of his Rhetoric, knowing ancient stories is very useful in civil things, I proposed to bring over from Latin into vernacular ten books of the Paduan Titus Livy . . . so that from that . . . the unlettered can take delight from the stories and gracious profit from the magnificent and virtuous works).

14. Livy, *Le deche di T. Livio*, ed. Pizzorno, 5:10–11: "Nè è mio intendimento nella sposizione della predetta Deca seguire strettamente per tutto la lettera dell'Autore: perocché, ciò facendo, non veggio che io al fine intento potessi venire acconciamente, il quale è di voler far chiaro a' non intendenti la intenzione di T. Livio. Perciocchè non in luogo uno, ma in molti esso sì precisamente scrive, che se sole le sue parole, senza più, si ponessono, si rimarebbe tronco il volgare a coloro, dico, i quali non sono di troppo sottile avvedimento,

che così poco ne intenderebbero volgarizzato, come per lettera. Adunque acciocchè interissimamente ogni sua intenzione eziandio da' più materiali si comprenda, non partendomi dalla sua propria intenzione, estimo che utile sia in alcun luogo con più parole alquanto le sue adampiare."

15. Simone Marchesi, "Fra filologia e retorica: Petrarca e Boccaccio di fronte al nuovo Livio," *Annali d'Italianistica* 22 (2004): 361–74.

16. Carlo Dionisotti, *Geografia e storia della letteratura italiana* (Turin: Einaudi, 1967), 141: "La provenienza del testo di Livio, che il Boccaccio volgarizzò, non si identifica certo con una scuola che, non dirò suggerisse, ma tollerasse quel volgarizzamento. Di fatto nessuna più convincente prova può addursi della distanza che ancora a quella data, prima del 1346, separava i due grandi successori di Dante" (The provenance of the text of Livy that Boccaccio translated is certainly not identifiable with a school that would even tolerate, let alone suggest, that vernacularization. In fact, there can be no more convincing proof of the distance that still at that date, before 1346, separated Dante's two great successors).

17. In novella 66 in Franco Sacchetti, *Trecentonovelle*, ed. Valerio Marucci (Rome: Salerno, 1996), 191–93, Coppo di Borghese Domenichi reads the episode about the Roman matrons' protest against the Oppian law from the fourth decade. The narrator Fiammetta admires this same Coppo in *Decameron* 5.9 as "uomo di grande e di reverenda auttorità ne' dì nostri, e per costumi e per vertù molto più che per nobiltà di sangue chiarissimo e degno d'eterna fama" (man of great and venerable authority in our days, very renowned and worthy of eternal fame much more for both his customs and virtue than for nobility of blood). See Alison Cornish, "When Illiterates Read: The Anxiety of Volgarizzamento," *Mediaevalia* 26 (2005): 59–98; and Cornish, *Vernacular Translation*, 16–43.

18. Lorenzo Valla, *Discourse on the Forgery of the Alleged Donation of Constantine*, trans. Christopher B. Coleman (New Haven, CT: Yale University Press, 1922), 110–11.

19. Florence, Biblioteca Nazionale Centrale, MS Panciatichiano 58, fol. 5r, also found in Florence, Biblioteca Nazionale Centrale, MS Palatino 762. Text transcribed in Lippi Bigazzi, *Un volgarizzamento inedito*, xxi: "Maximo Valerio . . . il quale altra volta recai di gramatica in questa volgare lingua, ma però che certi savi religiosi, considerata l'afectione che ' layci [*sic*] portano a questo libro per le narrazioni de' fatti e detti degni di memoria che in esso sono, e considerata la brevitate d'esse storie, che tocca l'autore, la quale ingenera agli uditori sete di più steso stilo, fecion sopra esso, a modo di chiose, certi scritti, onde, pregato di mettere quelle chiose sopra questo testo e spezialmente perché in più parti per la povertà de la mia facultade non sentia

quello che li chiosatori sentono, mi conviene di novello ritrarlo a la detta lingua insieme con le chiose necessarie e utili; però non si meravigli chi vedrae diverso questo secondo volgare dal primo."

20. The "vulgate" version is available in Valerio Massimo, *De' fatti e detti degni di memoria della città di Roma e delle stranie genti*, ed. Roberto De Visiani (Bologna: Romagnoli, 1867–68).

21. Adriana Zampieri, "Una primitiva redazione del volgarizzamento di Valerio Massimo," *Studi sul Boccaccio* 10 (1977–78): 21–41. This redaction is preserved in two witnesses: Florence, Biblioteca Mediceo-Laurenziana, MS Ashburn 526 and Florence, Biblioteca Nazionale Centrale, MS Palatino 459. See also Concetto Marchesi, "Di alcuni volgarizzamenti toscani in codici fiorentini," *Studj Romanzi* 5 (1907): 123–236; repr. in Marchesi, *Scritti minori di filologia e di letteratura* (Florence, Olschki, 1978), 1:343–432, 391–92.

22. Florence, Biblioteca Nazionale Centrale, MS Panciatichiano 58 and MS Palatino 762. In briefer form they are also discernible in Florence, Biblioteca Mediceo-Laurenziana, MS Acquisti e Doni 418 and Vatican, Biblioteca Apostolica Vaticana, MS Ferrajoli 559.

23. Tanturli, "Volgarizzamenti e ricostruzione dell'antico," 875.

24. Tanturli, "Volgarizzamenti e ricostruzione dell'antico," 881, points out a passage in the *Filocolo* (1.10.4–11) imitating an episode in *Aeneid* 2.298–369 that has the same omissions as Andrea Lancia's translation. For Lancia's text, see Cesare Segre, *Volgarizzamenti del Due e Trecento* (Turin: UTET, 1964), 619–20.

25. Florence, Biblioteca Mediceo-Laurenziana, MS Gaddiano 71. Maurizio Perugi, "Chiose gallo-romanze alle 'Eroidi': Un manuale per la formazione letteraria del Boccaccio," *Studi di Filologia Italiana* 47 (1989): 101–48. Maria Gozzi, "Sulle fonti del *Filostrato*," *Studi sul Boccaccio* 5 (1968): 123–209, esp. 204–5. See also Gozzi's introduction to her edition of Binduccio dello Scelto, *La storia di Troia* (Milan: Luni, 2000), 40–43.

Chapter Twenty-Three

1. Pliny the Elder, *Natural History* 37.32.

2. On the early contacts between Europeans and Canary Islanders, see Charles Verlinden, "Lanzarotto Malocello et la découverte portugaise des Canaries," *Revue Belge de Philologie et d'Histoire* 36 (1958): 1173–1209; David Abulafia, "Neolithic Meets Medieval: First Encounters in the Canary Islands," in *Medieval Frontiers: Concepts and Practices*, ed. David Abulafia and Nora Berend (Burlington, VT: Ashgate, 2002), 255–78.

3. The text is preserved as autograph in one of his working notebooks, the *Zibaldone Magliabechiano* (Florence, Biblioteca Nazionale Centrale, MS Banco Rari 50, fols. 123v-124r). For its most recent modern edition, see Boccaccio,

De Canaria et insulis reliquis ultra Ispaniam in Occeano noviter repertis, ed. Manlio Pastore Stocchi, in Boccaccio, *Tutte le opere*, ed. Vittore Branca, vol. 5, pt. 1 (Milan: Mondadori, 1992), 963–86. The English translations from the *De Canaria* in this essay are my own. There is an unreliable English version of most of Boccaccio's text in Richard Henry Major's introduction to Pierre Bontier and Jean Le Verrier, *The Canarian; or, Book of the Conquest and Conversion of the Canarians in the Year 1402*, ed. and trans. with notes and intro. by Richard Henry Major (London: The Hakluyt Society, 1872), xiii–xix.

4. Versions of this important study have been published in English and, more recently, in Italian: Theodore J. Cachey Jr., "Petrarch, Boccaccio, and the New World Encounter," *Stanford Italian Review* 10 (1991): 45–59; Cachey, "Petrarca, Boccaccio e le Isole Fortunate: *Lo sguardo antropologico*," in *Boccaccio geografo: Un viaggio nel Mediterraneo tra le città, i giardini e . . . il "mondo" di Giovanni Boccaccio*, ed. Roberta Morosini with Andrea Cantile (Florence: Mauro Pagliai, 2010), 205–28. See also Cachey, *Le Isole Fortunate: Appunti di storia letteraria italiana* (Rome: "L'Erma" di Bretschneider, 1995), a monograph on the topos of the Fortunate Isles in Italian literature.

5. Manlio Pastore Stocchi, "Il 'De Canaria' boccaccesco e un *locus deperditus* nel 'De Insulis' di Domenico Silvestri," *Rinascimento* 10 (1959): 143–56 (152): "The *De Canaria* seems influenced by myths of an exclusively erudite sort, such as that of the noble savage." See also Pastore Stocchi, "La cultura geografica dell'umanesimo," in *Optima hereditas: Sapienza giuridica romana e conoscenza dell'ecumene* (Milan: Garzanti-Scheiwiller, 1993), 563–86. Pastore Stocchi's work on the *De Canaria* has been crucial, not least for the publication of the definitive text. Important contributions have also been made by Giorgio Padoan: his "Petrarca, Boccaccio e la scoperta delle Canarie," in *Il Boccaccio, le Muse, il Parnaso e l'Arno* (Florence: Olschki, 1978), 277–91, is an updated version of an article first published in 1964; on the *De Canaria*, see also Padoan, "Navigatori italiani nell'oceano fra XIII e XV secolo," in *Optima hereditas*, 527–60; J. K. Hyde, *Literacy and Its Uses: Studies in Late Medieval Italy*, ed. Daniel Waley (New York: Manchester University Press, 1993), 198–207; David Wallace, *Premodern Places: Calais to Surinam, Chaucer to Aphra Behn* (Malden, MA: Blackwell Publishing, 2004), 208–11, 224–25.

6. The most recent major study of Boccaccio's use of the Golden Age myth is Tobias Foster Gittes, *Boccaccio's Naked Muse: Eros, Culture, and the Mythopoeic Imagination* (Toronto: University of Toronto Press, 2008), 24–76. See also Gustavo Costa, *La leggenda dei secoli d'oro nella letteratura italiana* (Bari: Laterza, 1972), 20–25. On Renaissance reception of the Golden Age myth, see A. Bartlett Giamatti, *The Earthly Paradise and the Renaissance Epic* (Princeton, NJ: Princeton University Press, 1966); Harry Levin, *The Myth of the Golden*

Age in the Renaissance (Bloomington: Indiana University Press, 1969). Relevant material is also to be found in Frank E. Manuel and Fritzie P. Manuel, *Utopian Thought in the Western World* (Cambridge, MA: Harvard University Press, 1979).

7. Ovid, *Metamorphoses* 1.89–166; Virgil, *Aeneid* 6.792–97, 8.314–27; *Georgics* 1.125–55, 2.458–end; *Eclogues* 4; Horace, *Satires* 1.3.99–114; Seneca, *Epistles* 90; *Phaedra* 483–558; Juvenal, *Satires* 6.1–24, 13.28–59; Boethius, *Consolation of Philosophy* 2.5.

8. The *"Etymologies" of Isidore of Seville*, trans. S. Barney, J. Beach, and O. Berghof (Cambridge: Cambridge University Press, 2006), 294; W. M. Lindsay, ed., *Isidori Hispalensis Episcopi Etymologiarum sive Originum libri XX* (Oxford: Clarendon Press, 1911), 14.6: "unde gentilium error et saecularium carmina poetarum propter soli fecunditatem easdem esse Paradisum putaverunt."

9. See Arthur O. Lovejoy and George Boas, *Primitivism and Related Ideas in Antiquity* (1935; repr., Baltimore: Johns Hopkins University Press, 1997), chap. 11, "The Noble Savage in Antiquity." A more recent contribution is Stelio Cro, "Classical Antiquity, America, and the Myth of the Noble Savage," in *The Classical Tradition and the Americas*, vol. 1, *European Images of the Americas and the Classical Tradition*, ed. Wolfgang Haase and Meyer Reinhold, pt. 1 (Berlin: W. de Gruyter, 2004), 379–418.

10. Cicero, *Tusculan Disputations* 5.32, 90; Horace, *Odes* 3.24.1–32; Virgil, *Georgics* 3.349–83; Seneca, *De providentia* 4.14–15; Solinus, *Collectanea*, App. 22, 12–15.

11. Pliny, *Natural History* 4.89–91.

12. *De Canaria* 14: "Fidei et legalitatis videntur permaxime: nil enim esibile datur uni quin antequam gustet equis portionibus diviserit ceterisque portionem suam dederit."

13. *De Canaria* 12: "Honorabant se invicem: verum alterum eorum magis quam reliquos, et hic femoralia palme habet, reliqui vero iuncorum, picta croceo et rufo."

14. *De Canaria* 12: "Cantant dulciter et fere more gallico tripudiant. Ridentes sunt et alacres et satis domestici, ultra quam sint multi ex Ispanis."

15. *De Canaria* 13: "Ostensa sunt eis aurea et argentea numismata, omnino eis incognita. . . . Monilia aurea, vasa celata, enses, gladii ostensi eis non apparet ut viderint umquam vel se penes habeant."

16. *De Canaria* 15: "Mulieres eorum nubunt, et que homines noverunt more virorum femoralia gerunt; virgines autem omnino nude incedunt, nullam verecundiam ducentes sic incedere."

17. In Pomona's account of the Golden Age in Boccaccio's *Comedia delle ninfe fiorentine*, acorns are the food of choice. See *Comedia delle ninfe fiorentine*, ed. Antonio Enzo Quaglio, in Boccaccio, *Tutte le opere*, vol. 2 (Milan: Mondadori,

1964), 26.47: "E la terra, più copiosa di beni che di gente, per sé a' rozzi popoli fedele donava nutrimenti, però che le ramose querce abondanti di molte ghiande sodisfaceano a tutti i digiuni"; and for an English version, Boccaccio, *L'Ameto*, trans. Judith Serafini Sauli (New York: Garland, 1985), p. 67.

18. *De Canaria* 5: "ficus siccas in sportulis palmeis, bonas uti cesenates cernimus, et frumentum longe pulcrius nostro, habebat quippe grana longiora et grossiora nostro, album valde. . . . Frumentum autem et segetes aut more avium comedunt aut farinam conficiunt quam etiam absque panis confectione aliqua manducant aquam potantes."

19. For example, Ovid, *Metamorphoses* 1.89–96; Virgil, *Eclogues* 4.37–39.

20. *Seneca's Tragedies*, trans. Frank Justus Miller (Cambridge, MA: Harvard University Press, 1979), act 2, lines 329–78: "Candida nostri saecula patres / videre, procul fraude remota. / sua quisque piger litora tangens / patrioque senex factus in arvo, / parvo dives. . . . Nunc . . . / quaelibet altum cumba pererrat. / terminus omnis motus . . . : / Indus gelidum potat Araxen, / Albin Persae Rhenumque bibunt. / venient annis saecula seris, quibus Oceanus vincula rerum / laxet et ingens pateat tellus / Tethysque novos detegat orbes."

21. Translation mine; Boccaccio, *Genealogie deorum gentilium*, ed. Vittorio Zaccaria (Milan: Mondadori, 1998), bk. 10, Pr. 2–3: "Quid enim spectare, divino prestante lumine, rates, humano excogitatas ingenio et artificio fabrefactas? . . . quod minimum humani generis reipublice bonum est, his agentibus navigationibus maris huius, factum est ut Cymber et Celta altero orbis angulo non nunquam sentiant qui sint Arabes . . . sic et Hyspanus Maurusque visitatus visitet Persas et Yndos et Caucasum; et Tyles ultima calcet Taprobanis litora, et dum sua invicem permutant bona, non mores solum legesque et habitus mirentur fit, quin imo qui se, dum alterum intuetur ex altero quoniam sit mundo, nec uno eodemque se cum illo amiri oceano, arbitratur, ritus misceat, fidem mercimoniis comunicet, amicitias iungat."

22. See Cachey, "Petrarca, Boccaccio," 227–28; and Aldo Scaglione, "A Note on Montaigne's *Des Cannibales* and the Humanist Tradition," in *First Images of America: The Impact of the New World on the Old*, ed. Fredi Chiappelli with Michael J. B. Allen and Robert L. Benson (Berkeley: University of California Press, 1976), 1:63–70.

Chapter Twenty-Four

1. Boccaccio, *De montibus, silvis, fontibus, lacubus, fluminibus, stagnis seu paludibus et de diversis nominibus maris*, ed. Manlio Pastore Stocchi, in *Tutte le opere*, ed. Vittore Branca, vol. 8 (Milan: Mondadori, 1998), 1815–2122. All citations are from this edition.

2. Manlio Pastore Stocchi, introduction to Boccaccio, *De montibus*, in Branca, *Tutte le opere*, 8:1820. See also Pastore Stocchi, *Tradizione medievale e gusto umanistico nel "De Montibus" del Boccaccio* (Padua: CEDAM, 1963); and Pastore Stocchi, "La cultura geografica dell'umanesimo," in *Optima hereditas: Sapienza giuridica romana e conoscenza dell'ecumene* (Milan: Scheiwiller, 1992), 563–85.

3. Claudio Greppi, "Il dizionario geografico di Boccaccio: Luoghi e paesaggi nel *De Montibus*," in *Boccaccio geografico: Un viaggio nel Mediterraneo tra le città, i giardini e . . . il "mondo" di Giovanni Boccaccio*, ed. Roberta Morosini with Andrea Cantile (Florence: Mauro Pagliai, 2010), 89–102 (95).

4. Boccaccio, *De montibus*, "De fontibus," 3.1, p. 1881.

5. *De fluminibus, fontibus, lacubus, nemoribus, paludibus, montibus, gentibus per litteras libellus* is thought to have provided the classical model for Boccaccio's much more ambitious enterprise. See *Vibius Sequester*, ed. Remo Gelsomino (Leipzig: Teubner, 1962). For Petrarch's role and that of his "disciple" Boccaccio in the reception of Pliny, Pomponius Mela, and Vibius Sequester, see Giuseppe Billanovich, "Dall'antica Ravenna alle bibliotheche umanistiche," *Aevum* 30 (1956): 319–53.

6. Boccaccio, *De montibus*, "De stagnis et paludibus," 6.1–2, p. 1986.

7. Boccaccio, *De montibus*, "De diversis nominibus maris," 3.1–116, pp. 1996–2025.

8. Boccaccio, *De montibus* 1.1, p. 1827: "ocio vires restaurare cupiens."

9. Pastore Stocchi, introduction to Boccaccio, *De montibus*, 1817.

10. The concluding pages of the *De montibus* include the discussion of the hazards to which the geographical tradition is particularly subject because of both the textual fragility of the toponomastic record and the susceptibility of the sites themselves to modification over time. For Pastore Stocchi these pages testify to "una sua acutezza peculiare nel cogliere i lineamenti fondamentali di problematiche che solo più tardi l'umanesimo farà proprie e tenterà di risolvere" (introduction to Boccaccio, *De montibus*, 1819).

11. "celebres inter auctores quoscunque et potissime gentiles."

12. Boccaccio, *De montibus* 1.3, p. 1827.

13. Pastore Stocchi, introduction to Boccaccio, *De montibus*, 1822.

14. The *De montibus* appears at times to be implicitly engaged in a dialogue with contemporary cartography. See Greppi, "Il dizionario geografico," 95. See also Michelina Di Cesare, "Il sapere geografico di Boccaccio tra tradizione e innovazione: *L'imago mundi* di Paolino Veneto e Pietro Vesconte," in Morosini, *Boccaccio geografo*, 67–88.

15. Among the entries taken directly (rather than via some encyclopedic intermediary) from classical Greek and Latin authors, of particular interest

are those derived directly from the newly available Homer. For example, among the mountains: Ypoplacus (1.288, p. 1853) from *Iliad* 6.396–97, and Mimanta (1.354, p. 1857) from *Iliad* 2.868; and among the rivers: Symois (5.796, p. 1973) from *Odyssey* 3.172. For Boccaccio and Petrarch's knowledge of Homer, which was mediated by the translations of Leonzio Pilato, see Agostino Pertusi, *Leonzio Pilato fra Petrarca e Boccaccio* (Venice: Istituto per la Collaborazione Culturale, 1964). Boccaccio did learn enough Greek from Leonzio to cite Homer directly forty-five times in his *Genealogia deorum gentilium*. See the essay in this volume by Jon Solomon.

16. Boccaccio, *De montibus*, "Sinay," 1.502, p. 1868 and note.

17. See Greppi, "Il dizionario geografico," 95.

18. Boccaccio, *De montibus*, "Sorgia," 3.114, p. 1892; "Baiarum," 3.20, p. 1883. For a discussion of Boccaccio's Neapolitan haunts, see Roberta Morosini, "Napoli: Spazi rappresentativi della memoria," in Morosini, *Boccaccio geografo*, 179–204. See Petrarch's description of Baia in *Familares* 5.4.

19. Boccaccio displays a patriotic Florentine bias in several entries that reveal an anti-Venetian bias; for example, see "Tuscum mare" (p. 2022) and "Venetum mare" (p. 2023).

20. Boccaccio, *De montibus* 5.2, p. 1907: "De his potissime dico quos ad notitiam antiquorum deduxit solertia seu ipsi sumpsimus oculis regiones varias peragrantes."

21. Boccaccio, *De montibus*, p. 2101 n. 873. Boccaccio evidently anticipates here the discovery that Pastore Stocchi elsewhere attributes to later humanists such as Flavio Biondo, that is, "that historical geography is not only a recovery of ancient knowledge in the service of ancient writers, but it is also the reconnaissance and study of the physical transformations endured over the course of time by geographical entities" ("La cultura geografica," 583).

22. See Theodore J. Cachey Jr., "Petrarca, Boccaccio e le isole Fortunate: Lo sguardo antropologico," in Morosini, *Boccaccio geografo*, 205–28; and the essay by James Coleman in this volume.

23. See Theodore J. Cachey Jr., "Petrarch's Cartographical Writing," in *Humanisms in the Intellectual World: 12th-16th Century*, ed. Bert Roest and Stephen Gersh (Leiden: Brill, 2003), 73–91.

24. Boccaccio's independence of mind and greater modernity with respect to Petrarch in geographical matters is consistent with and not unrelated to his attitude toward the vernacular and toward Dante. See Theodore J. Cachey Jr., "Between Dante and Petrarch," in *Petrarch and Dante: Antidantism, Metaphysics, Tradition*, ed. Zygmunt G. Barański and Theodore J. Cachey Jr. (Notre Dame, IN: University of Notre Dame Press, 2009), 3–50.

25. Boccaccio, *De montibus* 7.117–26, pp. 2025–28.

26. Ambrogio Camozzi, "Il Veglio di Creta alla luce di Matelda: Una lettura comparativa di *Inferno* XIV e *Purgatorio* XXVIII," *The Italianist* 29 (2009): 3–49.

27. For "Appenninus," see Boccaccio, *De montibus* 1.52, pp. 1832–33; and Pastore Stocchi's n. 72 on p. 2041; for "Arnus," 5.3, pp. 1908–9. Franco Farinelli, "L'immagine dell'Italia," in *Geografia politica delle regioni italiane*, ed. Pasquale Coppola (Turin: Einaudi, 1997), 33–59. For the cartographic writing of the *Inferno*, see Theodore J. Cachey Jr., "Cartographic Dante," *Italica* 87.3 (2010): 325–54.

28. Boccaccio, *De montibus* 5.2, p. 1908: "quia patrie flumen sit et michi ante alios omnes ab ipsa infantia cognitus." For the Latin poem, see the essay by Velli in this volume.

29. Dante Alighieri, *The Divine Comedy*, trans. and comm. Robert Hollander and Jean Hollander (New York: Random House, 2002).

30. Boccaccio, *De montibus* 5.3; and Pastore Stocchi's n. 2 on pp. 2075–76.

31. Boccaccio, *De montibus* 5.3, p. 1908: "Anchisam, oppidum Florentinorum, preterfluat, maiorum eximii iubaris Francisci Petrarche poete conspicui vetustissimam sedem."

32. From a geobiographical point of view, the entry on another Tuscan river, the Elsa (*De montibus* 5.368, pp. 1932–33), taken together with the entry on the Arno, can be seen to reflect Boccaccio's more "mobile" origins when compared to Dante's.

33. The *Geographia* was the subject of intense interest and discussion among the humanists gathered at the Council of Constance (1414–18), including Guillaume Fillastre, who played an important role in utilizing Ptolemy's cartography to assess the changing image of the world in the wake of events such as the recent Béthencourt and La Salle expedition (1402) and the conquest of Ceuta (1415). The presence of Ptolemy at the council, according to Patrick Gautier Dalché, "L'oeuvre géographique du Cardinal Fillastre (d. 1428)," in *Humanisme et culture géographique à l'époque du Concile de Constance: Autour de Guillaume Fillastre* (Turnhout: Brepols, 2002), marks a turning point in the attitude of humanists throughout Europe: they began to reconsider the function of the world map in the light of its relationship to contemporary exploration and discovery.

Chapter Twenty-Five
This essay was translated by Michael Sherberg with the editorial collaboration of Victoria Kirkham and Janet Smarr.

1. Cf. Boccaccio, *Le rime*, ed. Antonio Lanza (Rome: Aracne Editrice, 2010), xi; for the criteria of Lanza's edition, see pp. lxi-ci. Lanza proposes a different order for the lyrics from that in prior editions, in particular the editions of

Vittore Branca (Bari: Laterza, 1939; Padua: Liviana, 1958; and most recently, Milan: Mondadori, 1992). Branca followed an edition by Aldo Francesco Massèra (Bologna: Romagnoli-Dall'Acqua, 1914), which undertook to put the lyrics in a chronological order, though without a philological basis. In the pages that follow I use Lanza's text and thus his numbering for the lyrics, but they are cross-referenced for convenience with Branca's 1992 edition.

2. See Vittore Branca, "L'atteggiamento del Boccaccio di fronte alle sue "Rime" e la formazione delle più antiche sillogi," in *Tradizione delle opere di Giovanni Boccaccio*, vol. 1, *Un primo elenco dei codici e tre studi* (Rome: Edizioni di Storia e Letteratura, 1958), 289–91; cf. *Le rime*, ed. Lanza, xii n. 1.

3. On this whole question see Lanza's *Nota al testo*, in *Le rime*, lxi-lxv.

4. In *Le rime*, lxiv-lxix, Lanza provides a table showing the correspondence between numbers in his and Branca's editions.

5. Lucia Battaglia Ricci, *Boccaccio* (Rome: Salerno Editrice, 2000), 72. Battaglia Ricci refers as well to Branca's writings, specifically the introduction and commentary to his 1992 edition of the *Rime*, pp. 3–31 and 208–46. The presence of Petrarch in Boccaccio before 1350 is significant; see Paolo Trovato, *Dante in Petrarca: Per un inventario dei dantismi nei "Rerum vulgarium fragmenta"* (Florence: Olschki, 1979), 23–25; Franco Suitner, "Sullo stile delle 'Rime' e sulle polemiche letterarie riflesse in alcuni sonetti," *Studi sul Boccaccio* 12 (1980): 95–128; Giuseppe Billanovich, "Tito Livio, Petrarca, Boccaccio," *Archivio Storico Ticinese* 25 (1984): 3–10; Marco Santagata, *Per moderne carte: La biblioteca volgare di Petrarca* (Bologna: Il Mulino, 1990), 246–51.

6. The *plazer* (cf. Italian *piacere*) and its opposite, the *enueg* (cf. Italian *noia*), describe two opposite types of Provençal poetry, the former being a wish list of delightful things, the latter a litany of the poet's complaints.

7. This "wish poem" derives as a genre from the *plazer*. See Dante Alighieri, *Dante's Lyric Poetry*, ed. and trans. Kenelm Foster and Patrick Boyde, 2 vols. (Oxford: Clarendon Press, 1967), no. 15 (1:30 for text, and for commentary, 2:52–54).

8. *Le rime*, ed. Lanza, no. 57; ed. Branca, no. 1. Traditionally, as in Branca, it was placed as no. 1.

9. See Roberto Fedi, *I poeti preferiscono le bionde: Chiome d'oro e letteratura* (Florence: Le Càriti, 2007).

10. Regarding the insistence on diminutives, Lanza rightly refers to the example of Boccaccio's *Comedia delle ninfe fiorentine* 49.1–14. And cf. Ilaria Tufano, *"Quel dolce canto": Letture tematiche delle "Rime" del Boccaccio* (Florence: Franco Cesati, 2006), 49–52.

11. This is also Battaglia Ricci's opinion; Battaglia Ricci, *Boccaccio*, 73.

12. *Le rime*, ed. Lanza, no. 21; ed. Branca, no. 74.

13. Lanza, no. 94; Branca, no. 83.

14. Petrarch, *Triumphi*, ed. Vinicio Pacca, 2nd ed. (Milan: Mondadori, 2000), *Triumphus Pudicitiae* 133–35: "Queste [Lucretia and Penelope] gli strali / avean spezato, e la pharetra a lato / a quel protervo, e spennacchiato l'ali."

15. Branca, no. 73.

16. I.e., the soul.

17. See Cavalcanti 5: "Li mie' foll'occhi, che prima guardaro"; and 12: "Perché non fuoro a me li occhi dispenti"; Cino 51: "Infin che gli occhi miei non chiude Morte," in *Poeti del dolce stil novo*, ed. Mario Marti (Florence: Le Monnier, 1969).

18. Foster and Boyde, *Dante's Lyric Poetry*, no. 79, vv. 31–36. For a few annotations on this text and others, see Roberto Fedi, "Il grande freddo," in *Il mito e la rappresentazione del nord nella tradizione letteraria, Atti del Convegno di Padova, 23–25 ottobre 2006* (Rome: Salerno Editrice, 2008), 219–56. See further Robert M. Durling and Ronald L. Martinez, *Time and the Crystal: Studies in Dante's Rime Petrose* (Berkeley: University of California Press, 1990), whose English translation of Dante's "Amor, tu vedi ben" (p. 284) is here cited.

19. Referring to the title of Petrarch's lyric collection, formally *Rerum vulgarium fragmenta*, also called *Canzoniere*.

20. For "di bel soggiorno" see *Purgatorio* 7.45. Cf. *Rime*, ed. Branca, no. 101. Cf. further Branca, no. 46: "Quante fiate indrieto mi rimiro / e veggio l'ore e i giorni e i mesi e gli anni / ch'io ho perduto seguendo gl'inganni / della folle speranza e del desiro, / veggio il pericol corso e il martiro / sofferto invan in gli amorosi affanni, / né trovar credo chi di ciò mi sganni, / tanto ne piango e contro a me m'adiro. // E maledico il dì che prima vidi / gli occhi spietati, che Amor guidaro / pe' miei nel cor, che lasso e vinto giace. / O crudel morte, perché non m'uccidi? / Tu sola puoi il mio dolor amaro / finire e pormi forse in lieta pace."

21. This is Durling's translation, as well as his edition of the original. See *Petrarch's Lyric Poems: The "Rime sparse" and Other Lyrics*, trans. and ed. Robert M. Durling (Cambridge, MA: Harvard University Press, 1976), no. 281, 460–61.

22. The twin peaks of Parnassus are Cyrrha and Nisa, the former sacred to Apollo, the latter to the Muses. Dante speaks of them as well (*Paradiso* 1.16–18). The Italian *collo* for "colle" is also attested in Dante (*Inferno* 23.43 and *Paradiso* 4.132). The Castalian font, on Parnassus, was sacred to the Muses. Verse 9 makes an obvious Dantean reference (*Inferno* 1.5), as well as an easy but significant one to Petrarch (*Rerum vulgarium fragmenta* 265.1 and 35.12).

23. Sennuccio died in 1349. Petrarch pays tribute to him in *Rerum vulgarium fragmenta* 287.

24. Lanza, no. 127; Branca, no. 126.

Chapter Twenty-Six

1. Boccaccio's twenty-four surviving prose epistles comprise twenty-one Latin
    epistles (one of which, except for its conclusion, survives only in a vernacular
    translation), a whimsical letter in Italian (beginning in Tuscan and ending in
    Neapolitan), a brief but gossipy business letter in Italian, and a longer Italian
    composition, apparently meant to circulate beyond its addressee, the so-called
    Epistola consolatoria a Pino de' Rossi (*Consolatory Epistle to Pino de' Rossi*). The
    Latin epistles are found in Giovanni Boccaccio, *Epistole*, ed. and trans. Ginetta
    Auzzas, with an appendix ed. Augusto Campana, in Giovanni Boccaccio, *Tutte
    le opere*, ed. Vittore Branca, vol. 5, pt. 1 (Milan: Mondadori, 1992), 493–856.
    The two shorter letters in Italian are found in Giovanni Boccaccio, *Lettere*, ed.
    and trans. Ginetta Auzzas, in *Tutte le opere*, ed. Branca, vol. 5, pt. 1, 857–78.
    The letter to Pino de' Rossi is found in Giovanni Boccaccio, *Consolatoria a
    Pino de' Rossi*, ed. Giuseppe Chiecchi, in Giovanni Boccaccio, *Tutte le opere*, ed.
    Vittore Branca, vol. 5, pt. 2 (Milan: Mondadori, 1994), 615–87. These editions
    furnish the texts cited here. In these editions, all of the Latin epistles, except
    the unnumbered epistle in Campana's appendix, are accompanied by Italian
    translations, and the Neapolitan section of the whimsical letter is accompanied
    by a translation in standard Italian. As of this writing, no English transla-
    tion of any of the letters appears to have been published, and the translations
    used here are accordingly the author's own. Boccaccio's metrical epistles and
    his four allegorical epistles (those numbered 1–4 in Boccaccio, *Epistole*, ed.
    Auzzas) are treated elsewhere in this volume. Nineteen of Boccaccio's let-
    ters, fifteen of which are known to have existed and four of which may have
    existed, are now lost and identified in Ginetta Auzzas, "Studi sulle 'Epistole':
    Testimonianze di testi irreperibili," *Studi sul Boccaccio* 6 (1971): 131–44.
2. Boccaccio, *Lettere*, 864: "abbate Ja' Boccaccio" (13). In this and all following
    citations, the number in parentheses refers to the numbered section of the let-
    ter cited.
3. Boccaccio, *Lettere*, 864: "nín juorno, ní notte perzì, fa schitto ca scribere" (13).
4. Boccaccio, *Lettere*, 864 (18).
5. See Vittore Branca, "Registri strutturali e stilistici," in *Boccaccio medievale e
    nuovi studi sul "Decameron*," 5th ed. (Florence: Sansoni, 1981), 93 and 133,
    where Branca uses the word *bifrontalità* in discussing Boccaccio's reduction of
    the three traditional medieval styles, low, middling, and high, to two divergent
    and opposing styles, the one comic and humble, the other grave and sublime.
6. Francesco Sabatini, *Napoli angioina: Cultura e società* (Naples: Edizioni Scienti-
    fiche Italiane, 1975), 107: "piccolo, precoce capolavoro."
7. The *cursus* is the practice prescribed by the *ars dictaminis* of ennobling the
    style of a prose composition by ending each sentence with one of three

conventional rhythmic cadences. For a description of the *cursus* and the *ars dictaminis* generally, see James J. Murphy, *Rhetoric in the Middle Ages: A History of Rhetorical Theory from Saint Augustine to the Renaissance* (Berkeley: University of California Press, 1974), esp. 220–24 (for division of epistolary contents) and 248–53 (for prose rhythms).

8. Boccaccio, *Epistole*, 546: "ipse mei predicti domini iussu, non armiger, sed—ut ita loquar—rerum occurrentium arbiter, sum iturus" (9).

9. Boccaccio, *Epistole*, 554: "cum nuper civitatem nostram veluti dextero pede claudicantem liberis carere studiis videremus" (12).

10. Boccaccio, *Epistole*, 550: "ad civitatis nostre leges et mores" (3); 554: "quod vix unquam hoc pacto alteri contigisse meminimus" (20).

11. See Ginetta Auzzas, "Studi sulle 'Epistole': L'invito della Signoria fiorentina al Petrarca," *Studi sul Boccaccio* 4 (1967): 203–44, esp. 226.

12. Boccaccio, *Epistole*, 580: "iusta indignatione motus" (25).

13. Boccaccio, *Consolatoria a Pino de' Rossi*, 651: "quelli conforti che a voi dono" (176).

14. Boccaccio, *Consolatoria*, 629–30: "lasciare la propia patria . . . la quale amavate" (9); "questo strale, ch'è 'l primo che l'esilio saetta" (10).

15. Dante Alighieri, *La "Commedia" secondo l'antica vulgata*, ed. Giorgio Petrocchi (Turin: Einaudi, 1975); Dante, *The Divine Comedy*, trans. Charles S. Singleton, 6 vols. (Princeton, NJ: Princeton University Press, 1970–75).

16. Boccaccio, *Epistole*, 592: "extrema mandata" (16).

17. Boccaccio, *Epistole*, 594: "sic enim egit impetus" (20).

18. Boccaccio, *Epistole*, 598: "larghe promesse" (7).

19. Giovanni Boccaccio, *Decameron*, ed. Vittore Branca (Turin: Einaudi, 1980), "Conclusione dell'autore" 24: "il lamento di Germia, la passione del Salvatore e il ramarichio della Magdalena."

20. See Boccaccio, *Epistole*, 599 (12): "la quale io spessissime volte teco, quasi d'uno grande navilio la più bassa parte, d'ogni bruttura recettacolo, 'sentina' chiamai" (the which [room], very often speaking with you, as though it were lowest part of a great ship, I called "the bilge").

21. Boccaccio, *Epistole*, 604: "una fetida cameruzza" (46).

22. Boccaccio, *Epistole*, 606: "quasi un vile schiavo" (59).

23. Boccaccio, *Epistole*, 606: "'di vetro'" (59).

24. Boccaccio, *Epistole*, 609: "E tu me figliuolo delle Muse chiami 'di vetro' . . . ?" (86).

25. Boccaccio, *Epistole*, 620: "ed il nimico delle Muse, dirollo io amico?" (175).

26. Boccaccio, *Epistole*, 636: "quadam modesta ac filiali affectione" (7).

27. Boccaccio, *Epistole*, 638: "manibus illis giganteis suis in brachiolum meum iniectis" (13).

28. Boccaccio, *Epistole*, 640: "quas nunquam habui" (19).

29. Ginetta Auzzas reports Petrarch's full heading in her commentary on Epistle 15 in Boccaccio, *Epistole*, 816: "Iohannis Boccaccii de Certaldo ad Franciscum Petrarcham laureatum familiaris epistola una ex mille" (Giovanni Boccaccio of Certaldo to Francesco Petrarca, laureate, a private letter, one of a thousand).

30. Boccaccio, *Epistole*, 656: "quodam occulto nexu astringi videbatur quam omnino solutam cupio libertas" (13).

31. Boccaccio, *Epistole*, 656: "non iam patiatur etas libertati assueta colla iugo subicere" (15).

32. Boccaccio, *Epistole*, 656: "Ea tamen qua in sede locatus sum, si quid spendori [*sic*] tuo accomodum queam, iniunge parato" (17).

33. Boccaccio, *Epistole*, 674: "veris atque sanctissimis rationibus" (5).

34. Boccaccio, *Epistole*, 680: "divulgatus est, ut auferatur a me spes omnis non perfectum opus in melius redigendi" (23).

35. Boccaccio, *Epistole*, 682: "insultus" (33).

36. Boccaccio, *Epistole*, 686: "profuse et inconsiderate" (42); "Multa mea vitia occultat et contegit fame mee tenuitas, ubi etiam nevum minimum illius splendida gloria accusaret" (43).

37. Boccaccio, *Epistole*, 688: "ni superveniat quod nondum viderim, circa finem mensis huius vel sequentis principium ad eum usque Patavum ire" (52).

38. Mainardo Cavalcanti is the Florentine friend whose hospitality rescued Boccaccio from the squalid quarters provided by Niccola Acciaiuoli as related in Epistle 13.42 and following.

39. Boccaccio, *Epistole*, 690: "et rerum omnium displicentia" (6).

40. Boccaccio, *Epistole*, 692: "breviter, in tristitiam tendunt omnia mea" (7).

41. Boccaccio, *Epistole*, 692: "adeo ossibus impressa pellis, ut Erysithon videar potius quam Iohannes" (10).

42. Boccaccio, *Epistole*, 692: "malorum finis omnium antequam gravior amicis efficiar" (13).

43. Boccaccio, *Epistole*, 694: "in finem meum me omnino iturum rebar" (18).

44. Boccaccio, *Epistole*, 706: "secondo . . . generosi animi tui testimonium, donum scilicet equum primo" (30).

45. Boccaccio, *Epistole*, 704: "libellos meos non legisse" (17).

46. Boccaccio, *Epistole*, 704: "Quod autem te hieme futura facturum scribis, laudo ni melior adsit cura" (18).

47. Boccaccio, *Epistole*, 704: "Sane, quod inclitas mulieres tuas domesticas nugas meas legere permiseris non laudo, quin imo queso per fidem tuam ne feceris" (19).

48. The unnamed "stories" (*libellos*) and "trifles" (*nugas*) to which this letter refers

have traditionally been indentified with the tales collected in Boccaccio's *Decameron*. That Petrarch's nearly contemporaneous *Epistole Seniles* 17.3 refers to the *Decameron* explicitly and characterizes it in terms very much like those used here by Boccaccio to characterize his "trifles" encourages this identification. See, however, Rhiannon Daniels, "Rethinking the Critical History of the *Decameron*: Boccaccio's Epistle XXII to Mainardo Cavalcanti," *Modern Language Review* 106.2 (2011): 423–47, for a reading that interprets *libellos* to mean not "collected stories" but rather "individual books" and understands those books to include not only the *Decameron* but also Boccaccio's vernacular romances and even the first two eclogues of his *Buccolicum carmen*.

49. For Salutati as Boccaccio's source for the news of Petrarch's death, see Vittore Branca, *Giovanni Boccaccio: Profilo biografico* (Florence: Sansoni, 1977), 180 n. 1.

50. Boccaccio, *Epistole*, 724: "postquam in patria publice legentem *Comediam* Dantis" (3).

51. Boccaccio, *Epistole*, 724: "Heu michi misero! longe alter tibi viderer quam is quem vidisti Venetiis" (4).

52. Boccaccio, *Epistole*, 726: "sed michi amicisque suis in hoc estuoso solo relictis" (6).

53. Boccaccio, *Epistole*, 728: "Heu! infelix patria, cui nati tam illustris servare cineres minime datum est . . . ! Equidem tanti fulgoris indigna es. Neglexisti, dum viveret, illum trahere et pro meritis in sinu collocare tuo" (16).

54. Boccaccio, *Epistole*, 732: "non, hercle! quod meruerim, verum quoniam illi sic mos fuit, ut quem semel in suum assumpserat, semper diligenter servarit: et ego quadraginta annis vel amplius suus fui" (28).

55. Branca, *Giovanni Boccaccio*, 165: "quinquaginta florenos auri de Florentia pro una veste hiemali ad studium lucubrationesque nocturnas."

56. Boccaccio, *Epistole*, 732: "sepissime severus nimium rerum suarum iudex minatus est vivens" (32).

57. Boccaccio, *Epistole*, 734: "sic et copiam ultime fabularum mearum quam suo dictatu decoraverat" (41).

58. Boccaccio, *Epistole*, 736: "tres fere dies totos . . . in scribendo hanc brevem epistolam consumpsi"; "Tuus *Iohannes Boccaccius*, si quid est" (44).

59. Boccaccio, *Epistole*, 724: "Flebilem epistolam tuam . . . , amantissime frater, suscepi, . . . et quam cito nomen tuum legi, sensi quid in eadem lecturus eram: felicem scilicet transitum incliti patris et preceptoris nostri" (1).

60. Giovanni Boccaccio, *De casibus virorum illustrium*, ed. Pier Giorgio Ricci and Vittorio Zaccaria, in Giovanni Boccaccio, *Tutte le opere*, ed. Vittore Branca, vol. 9 (Milan: Mondadori, 1983), 836: "pater optime" (9.23.7); "fili mi" (9.23.8).

61. See Pietro Bembo, *Prose della volgar lingua*, in Pietro Bembo, *Prose e rime*, ed. Carlo Dionisotti, 2nd ed. (Turin: UTET, 1966), 110, where Giuliano de' Medici asserts the excellence of the Florentine vernacular: "I miei due Toschi vi porrei dinanzi, il Boccaccio e il Petrarca senza più" (I would set before you my two Tuscans, Boccaccio and Petrarch—no one else).

62. Petrarch's *Seniles* close with his *Epistle to Posterity* (18.1). The final words of Petrarch's *Epistole Seniles* 17.4 are reported in Ernest H. Wilkins, *Petrarch's Later Years* (Cambridge: The Medieval Academy of America, 1959), 314: "Ualete amici ualete epistole." See also David Wallace, "Love between Men, Griselda, and Farewell to Letters *(Rerum senilium libri),*" in *Petrarch: A Critical Guide to the Complete Works*, ed. Victoria Kirkham and Armando Maggi (Chicago: University of Chicago Press, 2009), 321–30.

63. For more on Boccaccio's and Petrarch's differing views of rank and fame, see Petrarch, *Senile V 2*, ed. Monica Berté (Florence: Le lettere, 1998), a volume-length edition and study of Petrarch's letter to Boccaccio on the current literary scene and his and Boccaccio's place in it. Victoria Kirkham's essay "A Life's Work," which serves as the introduction to this book's companion volume, *Petrarch*, ed. Kirkham and Maggi, 1–30, underscores the near obsessiveness with which Petrarch compared his achievement with that of others and strove, in an early identification of Florence's "three crowns," to secure, though with varying shades of difference, pride of place for himself, Boccaccio, and Dante. As seen above in Boccaccio's Epistle 20 to Pietro Piccolo da Monteforte, Boccaccio, like Petrarch, is contemptuous of those who judge poetry without reading it. Nevertheless, as Epistle 20 also suggests, Boccaccio could not be more different from Petrarch in his asserted disregard for his own literary rank: while Boccaccio may lament the premature release of his *Genealogia deorum gentilium* and the subsequent impossibility of submitting the work to a final edit, he accepts it with the resignation of one who is ready, if not content, to accept a rank far inferior to that of his mentor, Petrarch. Similarly, while the aristocratic Petrarch of *Epistole seniles* 5.2 uses distinctions between vernacular and learned writers to categorize and rank them, the democratic Boccaccio of Epistle 24 sees the poetic calling as overriding such distinctions and uniting great writers in a single embrace.

Chapter Twenty-Seven

1. These three autograph manuscripts are the *Zibaldone Laurenziano* (Florence, Biblioteca Medicea-Laurenziana, Pl. 29.8; the *Miscellanea Laurenziana* (Florence, Biblioteca Medicea-Laurenziana, Pl. 33.31; and the *Zibaldone Magliabechiano* (Florence, Biblioteca Nazionale Centrale, Banco Rari, 50). See in this volume the essays by Giuseppe Velli on the *Elegia di Costanza*, Steven

Grossvogel on the *Allegoria mitologica*, Jason Houston on the *Epistole allegoriche*, and James Coleman on *De Canaria*. Originally planned as volumes 11 and 12 of Boccaccio, *Tutte le opere*, ed. Vittore Branca (which extended only through volume 10), they still await a comprehensive modern edition. A practical point of entry into the extensive scholarship on the *Zibaldoni* is the anthology that anchors this essay, *Gli zibaldoni di Boccaccio: Memoria, scrittura, riscrittura; Atti del Seminario internazionale di Firenze-Certaldo (26–28 aprile 1996)*, ed. Michelangelo Picone and Claude Cazalé Bérard (Florence: Franco Cesati, 1998), hereafter *Gli zibaldoni* (all translations from this volume are mine). *Lo zibaldone boccaccesco Mediceo-Laurenziano Plut. XXIX.8, Riprodotto in facsimile*, ed. R. Biblioteca Medicea Laurenziana [Enrico Rostagno], preface by Guido Biagi (Florence: Olschki, 1915), reproduces the second part of the manuscript.

2.   Henri Hauvette, "Notes sur des manuscrits autographes de Boccace à la Bibliothèque Laurentienne," *Mélanges d'Archéologie* 14 (1894): 87–145; repr. in *Études sur Boccace (1894–1916)*, intro. Carlo Pellegrini (Turin: Bottega di Erasmo, 1968), 87–146; Oscar Hecker, *Boccaccio-funde* (Braunschweig: George Westermann, 1902); Guido Traversari, *Le lettere autografe di Giovanni Boccaccio del codice laurenziano XXIX, 8* (Castelfiorentino: Società Storica della Valdelsa, 1905); Giuseppe Vandelli, "Lo Zibaldone Magliabechiano è veramente autografo del Boccaccio," *Studi di Filologia Italiana* 1 (1927): 69–86.

3   Filippo Di Benedetto, "Considerazioni sullo Zibaldone Laurenziano del Boccaccio e restauro testuale della prima redazione del 'Faunus,'" *Italia Medioevale e Umanistica* 14 (1971): 91–129; Bianca Maria Da Rif, "La miscellanea lauren-ziana XXXIII 31," *Studi sul Boccaccio* 7 (1973): 59–124; Aldo Maria Costan-tini, "Studi sullo Zibaldone Magliabechiano I: Descrizione e analisi," *Studi sul Boccaccio* 7 (1973): 21–58; Costantini, "Studi sullo Zibaldone Magliabechiano II: Il florilegio senechiano," *Studi sul Boccaccio* 8 (1974): 79–126; Costantini, "Studi sullo Zibaldone Magliabechiano III: La polemica con fra Paolino da Venezia," *Studi sul Boccaccio* 10 (1975–76): 255–76.

4.   Antonia Mazza, "L'inventario della 'parva libraria' di Santo Spirito e la biblioteca di Boccaccio," *Italia Medioevale e Umanistica* 9 (1966): 1–74; *Mostra di manoscritti, documenti e edizioni: VI Centenario della morte di Giovanni Boccaccio, Firenze-Biblioteca Medicea Laurenziana, 22 maggio–31 agosto 1975*, 2 vols. (Certaldo: Comitato Promotore, 1975); Vittore Branca, *Tradizione delle opere di Giovanni Boccaccio*, vols. 1 and 2 (Rome: Edizioni di Storia e Letteratura, 1958 and 1991).

5.   See Picone and Cazalé Bérard, *Gli zibaldoni di Boccaccio*; and Marco Palma, *Bibliografia degli zibaldoni di Boccaccio (1976–1995)* (Rome: Viella, 1996). See also the online bibliography at the website of the Biblioteca Laurenziana di Firenze, http://opac.bml.firenze.sbn.it.

6. Armando Petrucci, *Breve storia della scrittura latina* (Rome: Bugatto Libri, 1992), 162; Petrucci, "Il libro d'autore," in *Letteratura italiana*, vol. 2, *Produzione e consumo*, ed. Alberto Asor Rosa (Turin: Einaudi, 1983), 499–524; Petrucci, "Minuta, autografo, libro d'autore," in *Il libro e il testo: Atti del Convegno Internazionale d'Urbino (20–23 settembre 1982)*, ed. Cesare Questa and Renato Raffaelli (Urbino: Università degli Studi di Urbino, 1984), 397–414.

7. On the *zibaldone* as a genre and on its definitions, see Raul Mordenti, "Problemi e prospettive di un'edizione ipertestuale dello *Zibaldone Laurenziano*," in Picone and Cazalé Bérard, *Gli zibaldoni di Boccaccio*, 361–77 (362–63).

8. Stefano Zamponi, Martina Pantarotto, and Antonella Tomiello, "Stratigrafia dello Zibaldone e della Miscellanea Laurenziani," in Picone and Cazalé Bérard, *Gli zibaldoni di Boccaccio*, 181–243; Virginia Brown, "Boccaccio in Naples: The Beneventan Liturgical Palimpsest of the Laurentian Autographs (MS 29.8 and 33.31)," *Italia Medioevale e Umanistica* 34 (1991): 41–126; condensed in "Between the Convent and the Court: Boccaccio and the Beneventan Gradual from Naples," in *Gli zibaldoni*, 307–13.

9. Zamponi, Pantarotto, and Tomiello, "Stratigrafia dello Zibaldone," 183.

10. Eighty *Priapea* (to use the Latin title) are transmitted by the *Miscellanea Laurenziana*, fols. 39r-45v. See Remigio Sabbadini, *Le scoperte dei codici latini e greci ne' secoli XIV e XV* (Florence: Sansoni, 1905), 1:31 and 41. These Priapic poems are among the ancient texts rediscovered by Boccaccio.

11. Zamponi, Pantarotto, and Tomiello, "Stratigrafia dello Zibaldone," 190–91.

12. Ibid., 196.

13. Ibid., 241.

14. Filippo Di Benedetto, "Presenza di testi minori negli Zibaldoni," in Picone and Cazalé Bérard, *Gli zibaldoni di Boccaccio*, 13–28.

15. Doris Ruhe, "Boccace astronomien?" in Picone and Cazalé Bérard, *Gli zibaldoni di Boccaccio*, 65–79.

16. Claire Cabaillot, "La *Mavortis miles*: Petrarca in Boccaccio," in Picone and Cazalé Bérard, *Gli zibaldoni di Boccaccio*, 129–39.

17. Dennis Dutschke, "Il libro miscellaneo: Problemi di metodo tra Boccaccio e Petrarca," in Picone and Cazalé Bérard, *Gli zibaldoni di Boccaccio*, 95–112 (106).

18. Dutschke, "Il libro miscellaneo," 97.

19. Ibid., 101.

20. Da Rif, "La miscellanea laurenziana XXXIII 31," 59–60.

21. Robert Black, "Boccaccio, Reader of the *Appendix Vergiliana*: The *Miscellanea Laurenziana* and Fourteenth-Century Schoolbooks," in Picone and Cazalé Bérard, *Gli zibaldoni di Boccaccio*, 113–28 (115).

22. Black, "Boccaccio, Reader," 115.

23. The dating to 1351–56 is first proposed by Francesco Macrì-Leone, "Il

Zibaldone boccaccesco della Magliabechiana," *Giornale Storico della Lettera-tura Italiana* 10 (1877): 1–41; and confimed by Vittore Branca, "Boccaccio e i Veneziani bergoli," *Lingua Nostra* 3 (1941): 49–52. Antonio Enzo Quaglio prefers 1351–52: "Tra fonti e testo del *Filocolo*," *Giornale Storico della Lettera-tura Italiana* 140 (1963): 489–551; while Giorgio Padoan sets it back to 1345: "Petrarca, Boccaccio e la scoperta delle Canarie," *Italia Medioevale e Umanistica* 7 (1964): 263–77.

24. Giuseppe Vandelli, "Lo Zibaldone Magliabechiano è veramente autografo," *Studi di Filologia Italiana* 1 (1927): 69–86.

25. Giancarlo Savino, "Un pioniere dell'autografia boccaccesca," in Picone and Cazalé Bérard, *Gli zibaldoni di Boccaccio*, 333–48; Gabriella Pomaro, "Memoria della scrittura e scrittura della memoria: A proposito dello Zibaldone Maglia-bechiano," in Picone and Cazalé Bérard, *Gli zibaldoni di Boccaccio*, 259–82.

26. Aldo Maria Costantini, "Tra chiose e postille dello Zibaldone Magliabe-chiano: Un catalogo e una chiave di lettura," in Picone and Cazalé Bérard, *Gli zibaldoni di Boccaccio*, 29–35 (29).

27. Pier Giorgio Ricci, "Nota critica—*De casibus virorum illustrium*," in Giovanni Boccaccio, *Opere in versi, Corbaccio, In laude di Dante, Prose latine, Epistole*, ed. Ricci (Milan: Ricciardi, 1965), 1278–80.

28. Costantini, "Tra chiose e postille," 31.

29. Ibid., 31–32.

30. Isabelle Heullant-Donat, "Boccaccio lecteur de Paolino da Venezia: Lectures discursives et critiques," in Picone and Cazalé Bérard, *Gli zibaldoni di Boccaccio*, 37–52.

31. A. Teresa Hankey, "La *Genealogia deorum* di Paolo da Perugia," in Picone and Cazalé Bérard, *Gli zibaldoni di Boccaccio*, 81–94.

32. Vittore Branca and Pier Giorgio Ricci, *Un autografo del "Decameron" (Codice hamiltoniano 90)* (Florence: Olschki, 1962); Di Benedetto, "Considerazioni sullo Zibaldone"; *Mostra di manoscritti, documenti e edizioni*.

33. Giovanni Morello, "Disegni marginali nei manoscritti di Giovanni Boccac-cio," in Picone and Cazalé Bérard, *Gli zibaldoni di Boccaccio*, 161–71 (168–69). See also the essay by Victoria Kirkham in part 9 of this volume.

34. Morello, "Disegni marginali," 163. See also Costantini, "Tra chiose e postille," 29.

35. Victoria Kirkham, "Johannes de Certaldo: La firma dell'autore," in Picone and Cazalé Bérard, *Gli zibaldoni di Boccaccio*, 455–68 (456).

36. Di Benedetto, "Presenza di testi minori," 91–129.

37. Francesco Mazzoni, "Moderni errori di trascrizione nelle epistole dantesche conservate nello Zibaldone Laurenziano," in Picone and Cazalé Bérard, *Gli zibaldoni di Boccaccio*, 315–25.

38. Savino, "Un pioniere," 333–48; Giuseppe Billanovich, *Prime ricerche dantesche* (Rome: Edizioni di Storia e Letteratura, 1947), 335.

39. Savino, "Un pioniere," 348, referring to Sebastiano Ciampi, *Monumenti d'un manoscritto autografo di Gio. Boccacci da Certaldo* (Florence: Giuseppe Galletti, 1827).

40. Patrizia Rafti, "Riflessioni sull'*usus distinguendi* del Boccaccio negli Zibaldoni," in Picone and Cazalé Bérard, *Gli zibaldoni di Boccaccio*, 283–306 (283).

41. Michelangelo Picone, "La *Comedia Lidie* dallo Zibaldone al *Decameron*," in Picone and Cazalé Bérard, *Gli zibaldoni di Boccaccio*, 401–23 (401).

42. Di Benedetto, "Presenza di testi minori," 13–14.

43. Picone, "La *Comedia Lidie*," 403.

44. Robert Hollander, "Boccaccio, Ovid's *Ibis*, and the Satirical Tradition," in Picone and Cazalé Bérard, *Gli zibaldoni di Boccaccio*, 385–99. Cf. Boccaccio, *Elegia di madonna Fiammetta*, ed. Carlo Delcorno, in Boccaccio, *Tutte le opere*, ed. Vittore Branca, vol. 5, pt. 2 (Milan: Mondadori, 1994). Hollander cites Delcorno's identifications of parallels with *Ibis* at *Elegia* 6.12.9. 6.12.11, and 6.12.12.

45. Pier Massimo Forni, "La realizzazione narrativa in Boccaccio," in Picone and Cazalé Bérard, *Gli zibaldoni di Boccaccio*, 415–23.

46. Claude Cazalé Bérard, "L'*Allegoria mitologica* de Boccace: Un mythe entre Orient et Occident," in *Actes du Colloque Mythes et sociétés en Méditerranée orientale: Entre le sacré et le profane* (Lille: Université de Lille 3, 2005), 143–62.

47. Boccaccio, *Tutte le opere*, ed. Vittore Branca, vol. 5, pts. 1 and 2 (Milan: Mondadori, 1992 and 1994).

48. Tito Orlandi, "Teoria e prassi della codifica dei manoscritti," in Picone and Cazalé Bérard, *Gli zibaldoni di Boccaccio*, 349–59 (359).

49. Mordenti, "Problemi e prospettive," 361–77.

50. "Lest it vary"; Mordenti, "Problemi e prospettive," 367.

51. http://rmcisadu.let.uniroma1.it/boccaccio.

Chapter Twenty-Eight

1. Giuseppe Vandelli early advocated attention for Boccaccio as artist in his classic essay, "Un autografo del *Teseida*," *Studi di Filologia Italiana* 2 (1929): 5–76. The codex is MS Acquisti e Doni 325, Biblioteca Laurenziana, Florence. Bernhard Degenhart and Annegrit Schmitt, in their monumental and authoritative *Corpus der italienischen Zeichnungen 1300–1450* (Berlin: Mann, 1968–), cataloged the drawings in Boccaccio's *Zibaldone Laurenziano, Miscellanea Laurenziana*, and *Zibaldone Magliabechiano*. They further proposed Boccaccio as the artist of the catchwords in his autograph *Decameron* (MS Hamilton 90, Staatsbibliothek der Stiftung Preussischer Kulturbesitz, Berlin), and, on

the basis of resemblances with those catchwords, they believed that he could be assigned the incomplete cycle of illustrations in one of his autograph copies of the *Divine Comedy* (MS 1035, Biblioteca Riccardiana, Florence). Brieger and Meiss, however, called the little-studied illustrations of the Riccardiana Dante Venetian, second quarter of the fifteenth century, while noting alternative identifications—Florentine, Paduan, late Trecento; see Peter Brieger, Millard Meiss, and Charles S. Singleton, *Illuminated Manuscripts of the "Divine Comedy"* (Princeton, NJ: Princeton University Press, 1969), 1:249–50. Armando Petrucci, too, recognized the "deliziosi disegnini" in Hamilton 90 as Boccaccio's, since they are in the same colored inks as the text: Petrucci, "A proposito del Ms. Berlinese Hamiltoniano 90 (Nota descrittiva)," *MLN* 85 (1970): 1–12. Vittore Branca embraced the German team and Petrucci's attributions of the Hamilton 90 catchwords: Branca, "Prime interpretazioni visuali del *Decameron*," in *Boccaccio medievale*, 6th ed. (Florence: Sansoni, 1986), 395–432; Branca, "Interpretazioni visuali del *Decameron*," in Vittore Branca, Paul F. Watson, and Victoria Kirkham, "Boccaccio visualizzato," *Studi sul Boccaccio* 15 (1985–86): 87–119; and Branca, "Introduzione: Il narrar boccacciano per immagini dal tardo gotico al primo Rinascimento," in *Boccaccio visualizzato: Narrare per parole e per immagini fra Medioevo e Rinascimento*, ed. Branca (Turin: Einaudi, 1999), 1:3–20. For an overview of Branca's sweeping contributions over a fifty-year period to "Boccaccio visualized," see Victoria Kirkham, "Il poeta visualizzato," *Studi sul Boccaccio* 37 (2009): 39–77.

2.   No one seems to have made Boccaccio's decorative initials a target of careful study. For his late pen-flourished capitals (1370–72), see Boccaccio, *Decameron: Facsimile dell'autografo conservato nel codice Hamilton 90 della Staatsbibliothek Preussischer Kulturbesitz di Berlino*, ed. Vittore Branca (Florence: Alinari, 1975). Such embellishments, characterized by intricate, lacy ornamentation inside and around the letters and long-reaching racemes along the margins, appear throughout his autograph corpus. See, e.g., folios from MS Zelada 104.6, Archivo y Biblioteca Capitulares, Toledo, Spain (*Trattatello in laude di Dante, Vita nuova, Commedia, Argomenti in terza rima, Quindici canzoni dantesche*), ca. 1350–55, reproduced in Maurizio Fiorilla and Patrizia Rafti, "Marginalia figurati e postille di incerta attribuzione in due autografi del Boccaccio (Firenze, Biblioteca Medicea Laurenziana, Plut. 54.32; Toledo, Biblioteca Capitular, ms. 104.6)," *Studi sul Boccaccio* 29 (2001): 199–213, figs. 2b and 4c. Examples of the *sgraffito* initial appear in Boccaccio's early *Zibaldone Laurenziano*, MS Plut. 29.8, Biblioteca Laurenziana, Florence. Seminal insights on that manuscript, including its autograph drawings, came from Filippo Di Benedetto, "Considerazioni sullo Zibaldone laurenziano del Boccaccio e restauro testuale della prima redazione del 'Faunus,'" *Italia Medioevale e Umanistica* 14 (1971):

91–129; see further Giovanni Morello, "Disegni marginali nei manoscritti di Giovanni Boccaccio," in *Gli zibaldoni di Boccaccio: Memoria, scrittura, riscrittura; Atti del Seminario internazionale di Firenze-Certaldo (26–28 aprile 1996)*, ed. Michelangelo Picone and Claude Cazalé Bérard (Florence: Franco Cesati, 1998), 161–77.

3. For good discussions of such dots and dashes in Boccaccio's manuscripts, see A. C. De la Mare, *The Handwriting of Italian Humanists* (Oxford: Oxford University Press, 1973), 1:20; and Morello, "Disegni marginali."

4. William H. Sherman has a delightfully informative monograph on this ancestor of the computer cursor, *Used Books: Marking Readers in Renaissance England* (Philadelphia: University of Pennsylvania Press, 2009). Boccaccio's maniculeas are distinctive in their elegant grace and detail.

5. Marcello Ciccuto mentions these crowns in Boccaccio's genealogy of the Angevin dynasty in his *Zibaldone Magliabechiano*; Ciccuto, "Immagini per i testi di Boccaccio: Percorsi e affinità dagli Zibaldoni al *Decameron*," in Picone and Cazalé Bérard, *Gli zibaldoni di Boccaccio*, 153; as does Morello, "Disegni marginali." Attilio Hortis, *Studj sulle opere latine del Boccaccio* (Trieste: Dase, 1879), 334–35 n. 3, diagrammed the genealogy, indicating placement of the crowns; Giuseppe Billanovich, *Restauri boccacceschi* (Rome: Edizioni di Storia e Letteratura, 1945), 84–85 and note, connects them with "traditional custom."

6. Maria Grazia Ciardi Dupré Dal Poggetto expanded the number of attributions, claiming for Boccaccio the Capponi *Decameron* (MS 482, Bibliothèque Nationale, Paris). She was the first to define a "corpus" of Boccaccio's art, dividing it into two parts, one "minor" (the small, marginal drawings), one "major" (the narrative cycles in Dante's *Inferno* [MS Riccardiano 1035] and the Capponi *Decameron*), proposals enthusiastically endorsed by Branca in their joint publication: Ciardi Dupré and Branca, "Boccaccio visualizzato da Boccaccio I: 'Corpus' dei disegni e cod. Parigino It. 482," *Studi sul Boccaccio* 22 (1994): 197–225. Previously, Branca had contrasted the "amateurish" catchwords of Hamilton 90 with the lively drawings in the Capponi MS, which, following Degenhart and Schmitt, he characterized as the work of an unknown artist, professional, late Gothic, and Florentine: Vittore Branca, "Giovanni Boccaccio," in *Enciclopedia dell'arte medievale* (Rome: Istituto della Enciclopedia Italiana, 1992), 3:549–57. Experts today concur. See, e.g., Marco Cursi, *Il "Decameron": Scritture, scriventi, lettori; Storia di un testo* (Rome: Viella, 2007), 31–33; Lucia Battaglia Ricci, "Edizioni d'autore, copie di lavoro, interventi di autoesegesi: Testimonianze trecentesche," in *"Di mano propria": Gli autografi dei letterati italiani.* ed. G. Baldassari et al. (Rome: Salerno, 2010), 123–57; Martina Mazzetti, "Giovanni Boccaccio novelliere

disegnatore artista: Fare arte nella letteratura del Trecento" (Tesi di Laurea, Università di Pisa, 2009). For sharing this compendious preview of published studies, I thank Mazzetti, who makes a felicitous distinction regarding Paris MS 482: Boccaccio is the "intellectual author" of the drawings, but a different "material author" was responsible for their actual execution. See Mazzetti, "Boccaccio disegnatore: Per un'idea di 'arte mobile,'" *Letteratura e Arte* 10 (2012): 9–37, http://www.academia.edu/1897952/Boccaccio_disegnatore._Per_unidea_di_arte_mobile.

Meanwhile, Maurizio Fiorilla's *Marginalia figurati nei codici di Petrarca* (Florence: Olschki, 2005), with an extensive appendix on Boccaccio and plentiful color plates, brings thoughtful commentary to issues of attribution. Marco Petoletti, "Il Marziale autografo di Giovanni Boccaccio," *Italia Medioevale e Umanistica* 46 (2005): 35–55, adds five new drawings to the canon. Sandro Bertelli and Marco Cursi, "Novità sull'autografo Toledano di Giovanni Boccaccio: Una data e un disegno sconosciuti," *Critica del Testo* 15.1 (2012): 287–95, have announced the most recent addition to Boccaccio's drawing corpus, a full-folio profile bust of Homer, visible only with ultraviolet light, on the parchment back cover of Boccaccio's Toledo Dante anthology (MS Zelada 104.6). At the same time, others now are starting to shrink the corpus. As Alessandro Volpe sensibly argues, just because a manuscript is autograph does not mean that the drawings in it are (Fiorilla and Rafti, "Marginalia figurati," provide a good example). In his view, neither the Paris *Decameron* MS 482 nor the Riccardiana *Inferno* MS 1035 is by Boccaccio; neither are they by the same artist. See Volpe, "Boccaccio illustratore e illustrato," *Intersezioni* 31.2 (2011): 287–300. Finally, Francesca Rosa Pasut has announced (personal communication, December 2, 2012) that she is reevaluating Bertelli and Cursi's *Omero*, the Capponi *Decameron* miniatures, and the Riccardiana *Inferno*, all images "per le quali è sempre più debole la possibilità di un'autografia boccacciana." See Pasut, "Boccaccio disegnatore," in *Catalogo della mostra: Biblioteca Medicea Laurenziana*, ed. Teresa De Robertis, Carla Maria Monti, Marco Petoletti, Giuliano Tanturli, and Stefano Zamponi (Florence: Mandragora, forthcoming).

7.   Antonio Enzo Quaglio, ed., *Filocolo*, in Boccaccio, *Tutte le opere*, vol. 1, identifies "Calmeta pastore solenissimo" (5.8.16) as Andalò. Cf. Quaglio's *Scienza e mito nel Filocolo* (Padua: Liviana, 1967), which traces Boccaccio's transformation of his astrological knowledge into the stuff of fiction. Janet Levarie Smarr connects Boccaccio's epic to the zodiac in "Boccaccio and the Stars: Astrology in the *Teseida*," *Traditio* 35 (1979): 303–32.

8.   MS Plut. 29.8, fol. 5r, Biblioteca Laurenziana, Florence. Morello, "Disegni marginali," figs. 1, 12, 13, and 14, reproduces astrological diagrams, charts, and the bull from Andalò's *Tractatus spere materialis* and *Tractatus teorice*

planetarum in Boccaccio's notebook. For the text, see Filippo Di Benedetto, "Considerazioni sullo Zibaldone laurenziano del Boccaccio e restauro testuale della prima redazione del 'Faunus,'" *Italia Medioevale e Umanistica* 14 (1971): 105 n. 2: "Colurus autem dicitur a colon quod est membrum et uros quod est bos silvester, eo quod apparet nobis ad modum caude bovis erecte quod est membrum eius. Facit autem in sua erectione semicirculum." The bull, in the same ink as the text, resembles a catchword, which appears in the lower margin (*bas-de-page*) of a manuscript folio to announce the first word in the next quire so the gatherings can be bound in proper order. This drawing could be called a quasi catchword, since the script does not correspond exactly to the text. The folio ends "in sua erectione semicir-" with the rest of the hyphenated word presumably at the top of 6r: "culum."

9.   Charlton T. Lewis and Charles Short, *A Latin Dictionary* (1879; Oxford: Clarendon Press, 1969), s.v. "cauda."

10. Di Benedetto, "Considerazioni sullo Zibaldone laurenziano," 105.

11. On the *Priapeia* (fols. 39r-45v of the Laurentian miscellany), see Bianca Maria Da Rif, "La *Miscellanea Laurenziana* XXXIII 31," *Studi sul Boccaccio* 7 (1973): 59–124, esp. 84–86. The Martial (MS C 67 sup., Biblioteca Ambrosiana, Milan) turned up in 2006. Among books Boccaccio bequeathed to Santo Spirito, it is rich with glosses and drawings. Its discoverer, Petoletti, "Il Marziale autografo," quotes Boccaccio's mixed marginal comments, including a formulaic curse on Martial for his foul mouth: "Maledicatur poeta talis." He could have copied it from the library at Montecassino during a visit to Naples in 1362–63.

12. I take suggestions from G. H. McWilliam's translation of the *Decameron* (Harmondsworth, UK: Penguin, 1972) throughout. Cf. Alatiel's "St. Stiffen" (*San Cresci in Valcava*). Boccaccio is punning on the name of a real locale in the Mugello once called San Cresci in Valcava. Its medieval *pieve* still stands in Borgo San Lorenzo.

13. Morello, "Disegni marginali," traces with reproductions the development of Boccaccio's catchword drawings, from minimal dots and squiggles at each end to an enclosing rectangle or leaf, and eventually, the human half figures in his last *Decameron*.

14. MS Acquisti e Doni 325, fol. 64r. Biblioteca Laurenziana, Florence. The only illustrated catchword in the codex, it encloses "gli avesse," first words of the ninth gathering. See *Teseida delle nozze d'Emilia*, ed. Alberto Limentani, in Boccaccio, *Tutte le opere*, vol. 2 (Milan: Mondadori, 1964), 6.25.1–4: "seguieno il nobile Castore / e 'l suo fratel Polluce, tutti armati, / e ben mostravan che di gran valore / *gli avesse* 'l cigno [Jove] lor padre dotati." Each space for an illustration corresponds to fourteen lines of text. Keyed to specific episodes,

they are variously positioned, not just at folio top or bottom, but also within the columns of text.

15. Maria Grazia Ciardi Dupré Dal Poggetto, "L'iconografia dei codici miniati boccacciani dell'Italia centrale e meridionale," in Branca, *Boccaccio visualizzato*, 2:10–11, attributed this dedication scene and the two illuminated initials to Boccaccio. Cf. Maria Cristina Castelli's catalog description with color reproduction of fol. 1r, in Branca, *Boccaccio visualizzato*, 2:56–57, cat. no. 4; for Pasut, "Boccaccio disegnatore," the plan for the illustrations was Boccaccio's; the hand was professional.

16. MS 90, sup. 98[1], fol. 24v, Biblioteca Laurenziana, Florence, reproduced by Ciccuto, "Immagini per i testi," fig. 5, p. 160. For the modern text in Latin and English, see Boccaccio, *Famous Women*, trans. and ed. Virginia Brown, I Tatti Renaissance Library 1 (Cambridge, MA: Harvard University Press, 2001), 37.6, pp. 144–45: "Fecit [Zeuxis] ergo quod potuit; et quod *pinxerat*, tanquam celeste simulacri decus, posteritati reliquit." For a similar fourteenth-century catchword drollery, cf. the psalter, Harley MS 2888, London, British Library, fol. 32v, accessible online by searching "Harley 2888."

17. Thirteen of the original sixteen quires survive. For history of the attribution of the drawings, see above, note 1.

18. Illustrated catchwords, favored in the Trecento, were sometimes by the copyist, sometimes by the miniaturist. Degenhart and Schmitt, *Corpus* (1968), cat. no. 59 and plates, followed by Ciardi Dupré, "'Corpus' dei disegni," and "Il rapporto testo e immagini all'origine della formazione artistica e letteraria di Giovanni Boccaccio," in *Medioevo: Immagine e racconto; Atti del Convegno internazionale di studi Parma, 27–30 settembre 2000*, ed. Arturo Carlo Quintavalle (Milan: Electa, 2003), 456–73, mention a missal by the Master of the Dominican Effigies made for the Benedictine nuns at San Pier Maggiore in Florence as comparable to Hamilton 90 for the quality of its catchwords.

19. For Petrarch's Virgil (MS A.79 inf., Biblioteca Ambrosiana, Milan) and Simone's frontispiece, fol.1v, many reproductions are available online; for the *Divine Comedy*, see, e.g., Vatican MS lat. 4776, reproductions in Brieger, Meiss, and Singleton, *Illuminated Manuscripts*.

20. I am grateful to my colleague Paul F. Watson for many insights on Boccaccio as artist and for passing on to me before his death notes in a prospectus for an unrealized book, "Pictorial Narrating: Italian Renaissance Artists and Giovanni Boccaccio." He refers to the Hamilton 90 catchwords as "drawings of unexpected skill and great charm" that show Boccaccio's "flair for puns, verbal and visual." The catalog entry for Hamilton 90 in Branca, *Boccaccio visualizzato*, 2:62–66, has complete full-color illustrations but contains errors in the texts of the catchwords. Those that have faded can be reconstructed with

472   Notes to Pages 324–327

aid from Boccaccio, *Decameron: Edizione diplomatico-interpretativa dell'autografo Hamilton 90*, ed. Charles S. Singleton (Baltimore: Johns Hopkins University Press, 1974), also with full-color illustrations. They should read as follows: 8v: the abbot, 1.4 ("mente"); 16v: Landolfo Rufolo, 2.4 ("al suo [cammino]"); 23v: Alatiel, 2.7 ("vivere"); 31v: Bartolomea (or Neifile), 2.10 ("licentia"); fol. 39v: Tedaldo, 3.7 ("Tedaldo"); 47v: Filippo Balducci, 4, Intro. ("et Filippo"); 55v: soldier of the Signoria, 4.6 ("sia ardito"); 63v: armed infantryman, 5.3 ("et essendosi"); 71v: Pietro di Vinciolo, 5.10 ("che poco"); 79v: Gianni Lotteringhi, 7.1 ("pare"); 87v: the scholar Rinieri, 8.7 ("al suono"); 95v: Madonna Iancofiore, 8.10 ("che voi"); 103v: Donno Gianni, 9.10 ("tu dì").

21. A reproduction of the "Alatiel" catchword is available at the University of Zurich Romance Languages seminar site, http://www.rose.uzh.ch/static/decameron/seminario/II_07/testi/alatiel.htm.

22. The word is divided between the end of one quire and the beginning of the next: "piana-mente" (*Decameron* 1.4.7). Branca, ed. *Decameron*, 1021 n. 9, identifies the religious order and house, famous as the place where Dante reputedly met Frate Ilaro. Cf. Branca, *Boccaccio medievale*, 402.

23. The "Tedaldo" catchword appears as a logo of the American Boccaccio Association and its newsletter. See http://www.brown.edu/Departments/Italian_Studies/heliotropia/aba/about.shtml. Another good color reproduction appears with an informal review of Branca's *Boccaccio visualizzato* on the blog "Miglior acque," http://miglior-acque.blogspot.com/2010/03/boccaccio-visualizzato-ed-vittore.html. Paul Watson called the *pentimento* to my attention (personal communication). The tale is resonant of *Inferno* 23, prison to the hypocrites, and *Inferno* 26, where Ulysses speaks from a forked tongue of fire. See Victoria Kirkham, "The Word, the Flesh, and the *Decameron*," in *The Sign of Reason in Boccaccio's Fiction* (Florence: Olschki, 1993), 173–97, esp. 192–95.

24. MS ital. 482, Bibliothèque Nationale, Paris. See Florence Callu and François Avril, eds., *Boccace en France: De l'humanisme è l'érotisme* (Paris: Bibliothèque Nationale, 1975), cat. no. 63; Degenhart and Schmitt, *Corpus* (1968), cat. no. 65 and plates. Giovanni di Agnolo Capponi (d. 1392), who signed the table of contents, held high offices in the city government as consul of the wool guild and prior of the major guilds. Branca speculates that he transcribed the tales before 1364, when he entered the Arte della Lana. The manuscript history is complex, and authorship of its illustrations continues to be debated. Ciardi Dupré, "Boccaccio visualizzato da Boccaccio I: 'Corpus' dei disegni," attributed them to Boccaccio and found numerous parallels between them and his drawings in other manuscripts in "Il rapporto testo e immagini." Marco Cursi, "Authorial Strategies and Manuscript Tradition: Boccaccio and the *Decameron*'s Early Diffusion" (talk, presented at the conference "Boccaccio

at 700: Medieval Contexts and Global Intertexts," Binghamton, New York, April 26–27, 2013), has suggested that Boccaccio did not actually draw the images in MS 482 but supervised closely their production, which may have been based on a model book that he himself sketched. Mazzetti, "Boccaccio disegnatore," usefully distinguishes between "intellectual" and "material" paternity: Boccaccio may have sketched them, developing his ideas over a period of years; then he or Capponi assigned the actual execution to a professional artist.

25. *Decameron* 6, Concl., 19–28. The Valley, inside "six little mountains" from which water streams into a round clear lake at the center, resembles a fountain fashioned by Nature on a grand scale. It has symbolic features of the chaste Venus, sometimes symbolized by the number six, considered "perfect." See Martianus Capella, *The Marriage of Philology and Mercury*, trans. William Harris Stahl and Richard Johnson, with E. L. Burge, in *Martianus Capella and the Seven Liberal Arts* (New York: Columbia University Press, 1977), 280 ("Arithmetic," section 736): "Who would doubt that the number six is perfect and proportional, since it is the sum of its parts? . . . The number six is assigned to Venus, for it is formed of a union of the sexes: that is, of the triad, which is male because it is an odd number, and the dyad, which is female because it is even; and twice three makes six." For the associations of the Valle delle Donne with the "good," procreative Venus (not lust), see Edith Kern, "The Gardens in the *Decameron cornice*," *PMLA* 66 (1951): 505–23. Ciardi Dupré, "'Corpus' dei disegni," 212, mistakenly calls the fountain octagonal.

26. How society contains natural sexual urges is the subject of Thomas M. Greene's classic essay, "Forms of Accommodation in the *Decameron*," *Italica* 45 (1968): 297–313. For the *brigata*'s rationally ordered retreat, see Kirkham, "An Allegorically Tempered *Decameron*," in *Sign of Reason*, 131–71.

27. The first to identify this scene was Daniela Delcorno Branca, "'Cognominato prencipe Galeotto': Il sottotitolo del *Decameron*," *Studi sul Boccaccio* 23 (1995): 79–88. Horses (here; for 10.1, set at the court of King Alfonso of Spain; and in the epilogue) are signs of nobility, in contrast to Balducci's donkey (fol. 79v) and the ass skull impaled in Gianni Lotteringhi's vineyard (fol. 133v). See Ciardi Dupré, "'Corpus' dei disegni."

28. MS Plut. 34.49, fol. 1v, Biblioteca Laurenziana, Florence. This portrait belongs to Ciardi Dupré's "corpus," but its uncertain dating seems to be after Boccaccio's death. For her attribution, see Ciardi Dupré, "L'iconografia nei codici miniati," in Branca, *Boccaccio visualizzato*, 2:16–17. For descriptions, see Victoria Kirkham, "L'immagine del Boccaccio nella memoria tardo-gotica e rinascimentale," in Branca, *Boccaccio visualizzato*, 1:103; cat. no. 13, 1:120–21; and Castelli, in Branca, *Boccaccio visualizzato*, 2:73–74, cat. no. 8. Ciardi

Dupré, "L'iconografia nei codici," following Degenhart and Schmitt, *Corpus* (1980), cat. no. 707 and pl. 170, identifies one of its models in a Neapolitan manuscript of the mid-Trecento Pasut, "Boccaccio disegnatore," squelches any possibility of Boccaccio's hand in this.

29. Exceptions to the rule are the plague; the half tale of Filippo Balducci; the servants' quarrel, paired with Cisti the baker (not 6.1 but 6.2); 9.9 (only one column wide, with Solomon's advice to beat a recalcitrant wife); and the *brigata*'s cavalcade back to Florence.

30. MS Pal. lat. 1989, Biblioteca Apostolica Vaticana, Vatican City, made in Paris, ca. 1414–19, is the most beautiful and first fully illustrated *Decameron* (one hundred illuminations, one for each *novella*). See the catalog entry, no. 83, by Eberhard König, in Branca, *Boccaccio visualizzato*, 3:205–14, and p. 207, fig. 289. Horizontally flowing images in the Capponi *Decameron* may be indicative of Neapolitan influence, as documented by Ciardi Dupré, "Il rapporto testo e immagini," 469–71.

31. The attribution to Boccaccio is now challenged by Volpe and Pasut (see above, note 6). For Volpe, "Boccaccio illustratore," this imposing cycle is "incompatible" with Boccaccio's tiny, scattered marginalia.

32. MS 1035, Biblioteca Riccardiana, Florence. Degenhart and Schmitt, *Corpus* (1968), cat. no. 66, assigned it to Boccaccio on the basis of similarities with Hamilton 90 catchwords, but Brieger and Meiss, with good black-and-white reproductions of all seven drawings in *Illuminated Manuscripts*, 2:44, 62, 88, 123, 134, 162, and 203, thought it fifteenth-century Venetian (see above, note 1). Ciardi Dupré, "Il rapporto testo e immagini," vigorously defended Boccaccio's authorship. For the *bas-de-page* illustrations, compare Boccaccio's *Inferno*, for example, with MS 8530, Bibliothèque de l'Arsenal, Paris (Italian, mid-fourteenth century); MS 597.34, Musée Condé, Chantilly (Pisan, ca. 1345), reproduced in Brieger, Meiss, and Singleton, *Illuminated Manuscripts*, vol. 2.

33. Boccaccio, *Diana's Hunt / Caccia di Diana: Boccaccio's First Fiction*, ed. and trans. Anthony K. Cassell and Victoria Kirkham (Philadelphia: University of Pennsylvania Press, 1991).

34. It resembles in style the boats that carry Ifigenia's kidnappers in the Capponi *Decameron*, MS 482, Bibliothèque Nationale, Paris.

35. Other illuminators are not so precise—if they represent those coats of arms at all—and most do not depict the Centaur with horns, which make him more of a hybrid "marvel." See Brieger, Meiss, and Singleton, *Illuminated Manuscripts*, vol. 2, on cantos 12 and 27.

36. Josephus, *Antiquitates Judaicae*, MS Plut. 66.1, fol. 43r, Biblioteca Laurenziana, Florence. Boccaccio could have seen this early eleventh-century manuscript at Montecassino. For the iconography of Moses, see Ruth Mellinkoff,

The Horned Moses in Medieval Art and Thought (Berkeley: University of California Press, 1970).

37. Boccaccio took material for *Filocolo* 5.45ff. from the *Mirabilia Romae*, a popular compilation based on *De quatuor maioribus regnis* by the twelfth-century Dominican chronicler Martinus Polonus. See Quaglio's commentary on the *Filocolo*, 938 n. 5. Several times in his *Genealogy* and *Famous Women* Boccaccio cites Solinus, *De mirabilibus mundi* (The Wonders of the World). For "Dripetrua, queen of Laodicea," see Boccaccio, *Famous Women*, trans. Brown, p. 35, no. 315.

38. See his autograph copy of Ovid's collected works, MS 489, fol. 43r, Biblioteca Riccardiana, Florence; cf. in the same codex the head of a youth, fol. 53v, discussed by Ciccuto, "Immagini per i testi"; and Mazzetti, "Boccaccio disegnatore." For reproductions of both drawings, see Ciardi Dupré, "Boccaccio visualizzato," figs. 5 and 6.

39. Boccaccio's "Seneca" (MS C 67 sup., fol. 115v, Biblioteca Ambrosiana, Milan), a favorite ancient for his plays and *Letters to Lucilium*, results from a corrupt text, properly "Severo." Petoletti, "Il Marziale autografo" (see above, note 7), counts five drawings, noting that an unnamed laureate (fol. 10r) resembles Boccaccio's profile of Abraham in the Josephus manuscript (MS Plut. 61.1, fol. 11v, Biblioteca Laurenziana, Florence). Another tiny marginal drawing, a youth in profile, decorates Boccaccio's autograph Terence for the play *Adelphoe*: MS Plut. 38.17, fol. 53v, Biblioteca Laurenziana, Florence, reproduced in Ciardi Dupré, "Boccaccio visualizzato," fig. 4, also Degenhart and Schmitt, *Corpus* (1980), cat. no. 702, who identify this personage as the character Ctesipho (but Ciccuto, "Immagini per i testi," 152, identifies the figure as Demea, and his student Mazzetti, "Boccaccio disegnatore," 15, tentatively agrees). Beyond restoring lacunae in his *Thebaid* with commentary by Lactantius Placidus, (MS Plut. 38.6, Biblioteca Laurenziana, Florence, twelfth–thirteenth c.) Boccaccio drew his usual manicules and seems to have made small male heads on fols. 23r and 126r, the latter in a pointed Phrygian hat (Capaneus?). See Di Benedetto, "Considerazioni sullo Zibaldone laurenziano," pl. 9a.

40. MS Plut. 33.31, fol. 53r, Biblioteca Laurenziana, Florence, depicts conjoined male twins beside a gloss on Orosius, *History against the Pagans*, reporting that at the time of Theodosius they were born divided above the umbilical, lived two years, one toothless and sleeping, the other without eating or sleeping, and died within three days of each other; fol. 56v, an armless, sightless female with fish tail beside the chronicle of Martinus Polonus, putting her birth in 583; and fol. 59v, conjoined female twins, illustrating the same chronicle for around 940, born in Gascony with two chests and two heads, who lived a

long time and died together. See Ciccuto, "Immagini per i testi," 147–48 n. 26. Ciardi Dupré, "'Corpus' dei disegni" 200–201, connects Boccaccio's fascination with such phenomena to his library copy of Solinus.

41. Claudian, *Carmina*, MS lat. 8082, Bibliothèque Nationale, Paris. Above one of his elegant long-fingered manicules pointed directly at "Florentine," Boccaccio drew a tiny laureated profile to represent Florentinus, thought to be an emperor (fol. 4v), reproduced in color by Fiorilla, fig. 41. "Florentine" is actually a vocative, referring to Claudian's dedicatee.

42. Pliny, *Natural History*, MS lat. 6802, fol. 220v, Bibliothèque Nationale, Paris. Boccaccio drew Abraham's picture in the Josephus and diagrammed his genealogy opposite (MS Plut. 66.1, fols. 11v, 12r, Biblioteca Laurenziana, Florence), reproduced in Di Benedetto, "Considerazioni sullo Zibaldone laurenziano," pls. 5, 6 (see also below, note 46), and he makes "Abraam giudeo" a protagonist in *Decameron* 1.2. For the identification of the drawing in Petrarch's Pliny under "vultur" as Abraham, see Fiorilla, *Marginalia figurati*, 47–52. The incantation garbles Genesis 22:15, on the sacrifice of Isaac, at the moment the angel of the Lord called out to stay his father's hand: "vocavit autem *angelus Domini Abraham* secundo de caelo." Perhaps Boccaccio saw the Pliny when he visited Petrarch for a month in Milan in 1359.

43. Vincenzo Fera, "Le cipolle di Certaldo e il disegno di Valchiusa," in *Petrarca nel tempo: Tradizione lettori e immagini delle opere; Catalogo della mostra, Arezzo, Sottochiesa di San Francesco, 22 novembre 2003–27 gennaio, 2004*, ed. Michele Feo (Pontedera: Bandecchi and Vivaldi, 2003), 499–512, doubts as a Petrarchan that Boccaccio would have dared draw in manuscripts not his—but he did, even a three-hundred-year-old parchment of Josephus. Fiorilla, *Marginalia figurati*, 63, counters that when Boccaccio was going to sell all his manuscripts and abandon poetry, Petrarch wrote offering to share his books (*Seniles* 1.5), which are "non minus tuos" (no less yours), expressing the hope that after they died, their libraries would be united. MS lat. 5150, Bibliothèque Nationale, Paris, a historical miscellany, is another example of a book that belonged to Petrarch and preserves annotations by both him and Boccaccio. See Avril, *Mostra*, no. 108, in Callu and Avril, *Boccace en France*.

44. "Transalpina solitudo mea iocundissima." Those who assigned it to Petrarch are Pierre De Nolhac, "Pétrarque dessinateur," in *Pétrarque et l'humanisme* (Paris: Librairie Honoré Champion, 1907), 269–71; Lucia Chiovenda, "Die Zeichnungen Petrarcas," *Archivum Romanicum* 17 (1933): 1–61; Gianfranco Contini, "Petrarca e le arti figurative," in *Francesco Petrarca Citizen of the World: Proceedings of the World Petrarch Congress Washington, D.C., April 6–13 1974*, ed. Giuseppe Billanovich, Umberto Bosco, and Paolo Sambin (Padua: Antenore, 1980), 115–31; and Fera, "Le cipolle di Certaldo." François Avril first

suggested it was Boccaccio's, *Mostra di manoscritti*, p. 14, no. 20, in Callu and
Avril, *Boccace en France*. Ciardi Dupré corroborates him firmly on stylistic
grounds. Fiorilla, *Marginalia figurati*, 52–58, who recalls Petrarch's reference
to abundant fish in the Sorgue (*Familiares* 3.19.1), reviews the question, lean-
ing toward Boccaccio, as do I. So too Pasut, "Boccaccio disegnatore."

45. MS Plut. 52.9, Biblioteca Laurenziana, Florence. For color reproductions of
all thirteen images, which range in size down to about a half page, appearing
both above and below the text, see the description by Maria Cristina Castelli,
in Branca, *Boccaccio visualizzato*, 2:57–62, cat. no. 5. Blank spaces left for
initials indicate the codex was to be handsomely decorated throughout. See
further Ciardi Dupré, "Il rapporto testo e immagini"; Morello, "Disegni marginali," 170–71. I thank Jon Solomon for sharing with me electronic images
of several manuscript folios.

46. Lineage, beginning with the fictional one he claimed for himself as a grandson
of the king of France (*Filocolo* 5.8.2–14), had long intrigued Boccaccio. For
example, to the Beneventan copy of *Jewish Antiquities* he added a small profile
of Abraham (fol. 11v), and opposite (fol. 12r), he diagrammed that patriarch's descendants. The *Zibaldone Magliabechiano* contains the *Genealogie* by
Paolo da Perugia; another *Genealogie* by Franceschino degli Albizzi e Forese
Donati; little studied family genealogies for the Carolingians, the Normans,
and the Angevins (thirty-three names in three generations, with a crown
drawn beside each ruler); Countess Matilda; the Blessed Virgin; and Joseph.
See Aldo Maria Costantini, "Studi sullo Zibaldone Magliabechiano, I," *Studi
sul Boccaccio 7* (1973): 21–58; Ciardi Dupré, "'Corpus' dei disegni," 201, who
refers for cultural context of trees in Boccaccio's *Genealogia* to Christiane
Klapisch-Zuber, "The Genesis of the Family Tree," *I Tatti Studies: Essays in
the Renaissance 4* (1991): 105–29.

47. Boccaccio himself transcribed a high proportion of the manuscripts in his
library, not to mention others he gave as gifts. See De la Mare, *Handwriting of
Italian Humanists*, 1:20. For Boccaccio's sensitivity to *mise-en-page*, see especially Battaglia Ricci, "Edizioni d'autore."

48. Colored and decorated initials range in size from two lines to the length of
a full octave. Under rubricated chapter headings, alternating red and blue
parafs further subdivide the text in a Scholastic style of articulation. These
ancestors of the printer's pilcrow (a backward P) are for Boccaccio C-shaped
semicircles with the top horizontally extended, the back third of the C filled
in, and a vertical bar in front of the solid part that bisects the C from top to
bottom. Parafs and the yellow-washed initials signal his understanding of the
sonnet (8 + 3 + 3) and the octave (6 + 2) in their metrical divisions. Parafs
serve further to define voices in a dialogue, to mark new stages in narrative

advancement, or to emphasize Boccaccio's favorite passages—for example, a pithy *sententia*, or axiom, on love at 4.55. William E. Coleman, "The Knight's Tale," in *Sources and Analogues of the "Canterbury Tales,"* ed. Robert M. Correale and Mary Hamel (Cambridge: D.S. Brewer, 2005), 2:87–247, esp. 99–101, counts one hundred paraphs (but the total does not seem meaningful because the codex has lost some of its folios). Sublinear dots in the manuscript, he notes, indicate how spoken text is to be elided, making it both "a reading version and a performance version."

49. There is considerable scholarship on references to artists in their literature: e.g., Christie K. Fengler and William A. Stephany, "The Visual Arts: A Basis for Dante's Imagery in *Purgatory* and *Paradise*," *Michigan Academician* 10 (1977): 127–41; Christopher Kleinhenz, "A Nose for Art (*Purgatorio* VII): Notes on Dante's Iconographical Sense," *Italica* 52.3 (1975): 372–79; Kleinhenz, "Dante and the Tradition of Visual Arts in the Middle Ages," *Thought* 65 (1990): 17–26; Chiovenda, "Die Zeichnungen Petrarcas"; Contini, "Petrarca e le arti figurative"; Maurizio Bettini, *Francesco Petrarca sulle arti figurative: Tra Plinio e Agostino* (Città di Castello: Sillabe, 2002); Maria Monica Donato, "'Veteres' e 'novi,' 'externi' e 'nostri': Gli artisti di Petrarca; Per una rilettura," in *Medioevo: Immagine e racconto; Atti del convegno internazionale di studi, Parma, 27–30 settembre 2000*, ed. Arturo Carlo Quintavalle (Milan: Electa, 2003), 433–55; Creighton Gilbert, *Poets Seeing Artists' Work: Instances in the Italian Renaissance* (Florence: Olschki, 1991); Gilbert, "La devozione di Giovanni Boccaccio per gli artisti e l'arte," in Branca, *Boccaccio visualizzato*, 1:145–53; Mazzetti, "Giovanni Boccaccio novelliere disegnatore artista"; Paul F. Watson, "The Cement of Fiction: Giovanni Boccaccio and the Painters of Florence," *MLN* 99 (1984): 43–64.

50. In his will, he bequeathed the Giotto to his Carrara patron. See *Petrarch's Testament*, ed. and trans. Theodor E. Mommsen (Ithaca, NY: Cornell University Press, 1957).

Chapter Twenty-Nine

1. This early will, recorded in the Gabella dei Contratti (Libro E, Duomo 1364), was notarized on August 21, 1365, by Ser Filippo di Ser Piero Doni, the same notary who had drawn up the will of Nardo di Cione only months earlier. Nardo and his brother Andrea (called Orcagna) decorated the Strozzi Chapel of Santa Maria Novella, the church in which Boccaccio had set the opening of his *Decameron*. Vittore Branca, *Tradizione delle opere di Giovanni Boccaccio* 1 (Rome: Edizioni di Storia e Letteratura, 1958), 117–18, notes that the first will was probably contained in the Archivio dei Contratti, which was absorbed only partially into the Archivio di Stato.

2. *Annotationi et discorsi sopra alcuni luoghi del "Decameron"* (Florence: Giunti, 1573 [1574]). Domenico Maria Manni, *Istoria del "Decamerone"* (Florence: Antonio Ristori, 1742), 109–17, republished it (followed by a Latin version) and suggested that it was the lost will of 1365. In fact, it was only a vernacular draft of the 1374 will. [Gaetano Milanesi], *Il testamento di Giovanni Boccaccio secondo l'originale in pergamena dell'Archivio Bichi-Borghesi di Siena* (Siena: Alessandro e Landi, 1853), 4, noted that error, also corrected by Pietro Fanfani in *Annotazioni e discorsi sopra alcuni luoghi del "Decameron,"* 4th ed. (Florence, Le Monnier, 1857), 36–37. Milanesi's edition was twice reprinted: Siena: G. Landi, 1859; and Siena: Lazzeri, 1873. It was also reprinted (not without errors) by Francesco Corazzini, *Le lettere edite e inedite di messer Giovanni Boccaccio* (Florence: Sansoni, 1877), 419–33, who added a brief introduction and textual variants in notes. A photograph of Antonio Rossi's 1847 case in which the official document was housed, described in Milanesi, *Sulla storia dell'arte, scritti varij* (Siena: Lazzeri, 1873), 7–8 and 363–64, appears in Reale Archivio di Stato in Siena, 56.

3. Giovambattista Ubaldini, *Istoria della casa de gli Ubaldini* (Florence: Sermartelli, 1588), 43. Interestingly, Ubaldini later quotes (116) Boccaccio's description of his distant relative, Ottaviano degli Ubaldini, from *Esposizioni* 10.103–5.

4. For the inventory, see Antonia Mazza, "L'inventario della 'Parva libraria' di Santo Spirito e la biblioteca del Boccaccio," *Italia Medioevale e Umanistica* 9 (1966): 1–74.

5. I have worked from a digital version of Siena, Archivio di Stato, MS Diplomatico Bichi Borghesi, 28 agosto 1374. Alongside this document, I consulted the 1853 transcription in Milanesi, *Il testamento di Giovanni Boccaccio*, and took suggestions, on very few occasions, where I believed it was appropriate, from Manni, *Istoria del "Decamerone,"* 113–17, and from Florence, Biblioteca Nazionale, MS Magl. 9.123 (39r-43v), which is a later copy that Manni had first used. For descriptions of the testament and its extant copies, see *Mostra di manoscritti, documenti e edizioni: VI centenario della morte di Giovanni Boccaccio, Firenze-Biblioteca Medicea Laurenziana 22 maggio–31 agosto 1975* (Certaldo: Comitato Promotore, 1975), 1:166, no. 149; Branca, *Tradizione delle opere*, 1:117–18.

6. Jonathan Davies, *Culture and Power: Tuscany and Its Universities, 1537–1609* (Leiden: Brill, 2009), app. 5.

7. Milanesi, *Il testamento di Giovanni Boccaccio*, 4–6. For Borghesi, see above, note 2. Valuable observations regarding the history of Boccaccio's will were printed at the behest of Scipione Borghesi Bichi (1801–77), Italian senator and patron of the arts, in the very slim volume *Il testamento di Giovanni Boccaccio* (1853), prepared by Milanesi but published without his name.

8. Armando Maggi, "To Write as Another: The Testament," in *Petrarch: A Critical*

Guide to the Complete Works, ed. Victoria Kirkham and Armando Maggi (Chicago: University of Chicago Press, 2009), 333. See also Theodor E. Mommsen, *Petrarch's Testament* (Ithaca, NY: Cornell University Press, 1957).

9. Marcus Tullius Cicero, *Cicero Mannucciorum commentariis illustratus* (Venice: Aldus Manutius, 1581–83), 10:137–38. That the initial appearance of Boccaccio's will elicited surprise is clear from Michel de Montaigne's reaction to it, *Journal de voyage de Michel de Montaigne*, ed. François Rigolot (Paris: Presses Universitaires de France, 1992), 187: "On Friday, at the Giuntis' shop, I bought a bunch of copies of Dante's *Comedy*, eleven to be precise, and certain other little books. And there I saw Boccaccio's testament printed with certain discourses on the *Decameron*. The testament shows this great man's amazing poverty and degree of ill fortune. He leaves some sheets and a few bed parts to his relatives, and sisters. His books to a certain friar whom he orders to share them with whoever asks for them. He even takes into account containers and the vilest of furniture. He orders masses and a burial. It was printed just as it was found, written on parchment that was worn and ruined" (translation mine). The same sort of "religious refashioning" is clear in pages like those of Giovanni Battista Baldelli, *Vita di Giovanni Boccaccio* (Florence: Ciardetti, 1806), 211–12; Francesco Cateni, "Sopra la tomba di messer Gio. Boccaccio," *Nuovo Giornale de' Letterati* 11.23 (1825): 100–123, esp. 105–6; Ugo Foscolo, "Discorso storico sul testo del *Decamerone*," in Boccaccio, *Decameron* (Milan: Reina, 1849), vii–xxxvi, esp. xxxv; and Edward Hutton, *Giovanni Boccaccio: A Biographical Study* (New York: Lane, 1910), 289.

10. Manni, *Istoria del "Decamerone,"* 118–28.

11. Cf. Arnaldo Della Torre, *Storia dell'Accademia Platonica di Firenze* (Florence: Carnesecchi, 1902), 200–201; Manni, *Istoria del "Decamerone,"* 123–24.

12. Ibid., 119. The Giunti's Italian version begins at this paragraph.

13. Giuseppe Billanovich, *Restauri boccacceschi* (Rome: Edizioni di Storia e Letteratura, 1947), 167–70, in an appendix on "Boccaccio chierico," mentions the altarpieces Boccaccio commissioned for his parish church, on which see also Robert Williams, "Boccaccio's Altarpiece," *Studi sul Boccaccio* 19 (1990): 229–40. The state of Boccaccio's tomb received a great deal of attention, especially in the wake of Byron's *Childe Harold's Pilgrimage* 4.58. See Cateni, "Sopra la tomba"; Luigi De Angelis, "Il sepolcro del Boccaccio," *Nuovo Giornale de' Letterati* 11.24 (1825): 219–37; and Giuseppe De Poveda, *Del sepolcro di Mess. Giovanni Boccaccio e di varie sue memorie* (Colle: Pacini, 1827). More objective research was provided by Domenico Tordi, *Gl'inventari dell'eredità di Iacopo Boccaccio* (Orvieto: Rubeca e Scaletti, 1923), esp. 15–16. See also Ippolito Rosellini, "Della casa di Giovanni Boccaccio," *Antologia* 59.4 (1825): 86–92; and

Aldo Francesco Massèra, "Rassegna critica di studi boccacceschi," *Giornale Storico della Letteratura Italiana* 65 (1915): 370–421, esp. 414–20.

14. The unexpected word *tabolettas* (here translated as "shelves") earned a "*sic*" from Milanesi, *Il testamento di Giovanni Boccaccio*, and Corazzini, *Le lettere*. *Tabuletta* (Lat.) and *tavoletta* (Ital.) were words typically used to denote either a small writing surface (cf. Dante, *Vita nuova* 34.1) or another object with a flat surface, though not necessarily a table, as in modern Italian. By extension, it could be a panel (like the *tavoletta* of the Virgin that Boccaccio left to Sandra), shelf, bench, table, or slab. The description is unclear here. In fact, in the Italian version, as printed in the Giunti edition, these "two ordinary shelves three braccia [i.e., about six feet] in length" (duas tabolettas usitatas longitudinis trium brachiorum) are described as "two used tablecloths, each six braccia [i.e., about twelve feet] long" (ii tovaglie menate di lunghezza bra vi luna). Many quotations of this passage simply reproduce the Italian. If the Latin version preceded the vernacular, the switch from *tabolettas* to *tovaglie* would simply imply a similar lack of clarity in the mind of the transcriber/ translator. Otherwise, it is Tinello's Latin that is suspect. The translation here of the adjective follows Milanesi's text (*usitatas*, "ordinary"), but Corazzini (427), followed by Hutton, *Giovanni Boccaccio*, 351, has *usitatis longitudinis*, "of ordinary length." Both readings seem preferable to Manni's *usutaria*, in *Istoria del "Decamerone,"* 114.

15. Attilio Hortis, *Studij sulle opere latine del Boccaccio* (Trieste: Julius Dase, 1879), 295.

16. Boccaccio, *Opere in versi, Corbaccio, Trattatello in laude di Dante, Prose latine, Epistole*, ed. Pier Giorgio Ricci (Milan: Ricciardi, 1965), 674.

17. Boccaccio, *The Latin Eclogues*, trans. David R. Slavitt (Baltimore: Johns Hopkins University Press, 2010), 118.

18. See Hortis, *Studij*, 365–66; Berthold Louis Ullman, *The Public Library of Renaissance Florence: Niccolò Niccoli, Cosimo de' Medici, and the Library of San Marco* (Padua: Antenore, 1972), 8.

19. Adolfo Gaspary, "Il supposto incendio dei libri del Boccaccio a S. Spirito," *Giornale Storico della Letteratura Italiana* 9 (1887): 457. Cf. Vittorio Cian, "Il supposto incendio dei libri del Boccaccio a S. Spirito," *Giornale Storico della Letteratura Italiana* 10 (1887): 298–99; and Oskar Hecker, *Boccaccio-funde* (Braunschweig: G. Westermann, 1902), 6–9.

20. Mazza, "L'inventario della 'Parva libraria'"; and cf. A. Goldmann, "Drei italienische Handschriftenkataloge s. XIII–XV," *Zentralblatt für Bibliothekswesen* 4.2 (1887): 137–55; David Gutiérrez, "La biblioteca di Santo Spirito in Firenze nella metà del secolo XV," *Analecta Augustiniana* 23 (1962): 5–88. Cf. Hecker,

Boccaccio-funde, 9–11; Francesco Novati, review of Goldmann, *Giornale Storico della Letteratura Italiana* 10 (1887): 413–25; and Branca, *Tradizione delle opere*, 2:183.

21. Manni, *Istoria del "Decamerone*,*"* 102–7; Hortis, *Studij*, 298–99; and Giorgio Padoan, *L'ultima opera di Giovanni Boccaccio: Le "Esposizioni sopra il Dante"* (Padua: Cedam, 1959), 3–4. See also Domenico Guerri, *Il commento del Boccaccio a Dante: Limiti della sua autenticità e questioni critiche che n'emergono* (Bari: Laterza, 1926), 213–16; and Irene Hijmans-Tromp, ed., *Vita e opere di Agnolo Torini* (Leiden: Universitaire Pers, 1957), 16. Little more is known of Francesco di Lapo Bonamichi's life other than what has been stated here. Note that he is one of the guardians of Iacopo's children mentioned below and is the husband of Sandra, to whom Boccaccio left his image of the Virgin. On the judge of the case, see Giulio Giani, "Un antico pratese oggi dimenticato: Parente di Corrado da Prato," *Archivio Storico Pratese* 1 (1916–17): 149–56.

22. In the Italian version, Boccaccio stipulates that the recipients of these religious articles are to keep them for as long as they last and to pray to God for his soul.

23. Billanovich, *Restauri boccacceschi*, 167–80. See also Alfonso Bertoldi, "Del sentimento religioso di Giovanni Boccaccio e dei canti di lui alla Vergine," *Giornale Storico della Letteratura Italiana* 68 (1916): 82–107.

24. Domenico Moreni, *Notizie istoriche dei contorni di Firenze* (Florence: Cambiagi, 1791–95), 4:92–110; Giuseppe De Novaes, *Elementi della storia de' sommi pontefici da S. Pietro sino al felicemente regnante Pio Papa VII* (Siena: Rossi, 1802–15), 4:198–200; Emanuele Repetti, *Dizionario geografico fisico storico della Toscana* (Florence: Tofani, 1833–43), 1:336; Balbino Rano, "El monasterio de Santa María del Santo Sepulcro en Campora (Florencia) y la fundación de la Orden de San Jerónimo," *Yermo* 11 (1973): 41–68.

25. A curious footnote: on March 28, 1573, Vincenzo Borghini wrote to Giorgio Vasari asking him to search for one of these relics (preferably a piece of the cross) while in Rome. He apparently had reason to believe that Boccaccio's collection had been taken there by the friars and given away in trade. See Alessandro Del Vita, "Lettere di Don Vincenzo Borghini a Giorgio Vasari," *Il Vasari* 4.1–2 (1931): 79–88, esp. 88. Giuseppe Richa, *Notizie istoriche delle chiese Fiorentine divise ne' suoi quartieri* (Florence: Viviani, 1754–62), 1:102, believes they may have passed into the possession of the Florentine Badia. In the Giunti Italian version of the will, Boccaccio notes that they were to be given to the friars "so that, whenever they reverently behold the relics, they will pray to God for me."

26. What we do know is that she was the wife, as we read here, of Francesco di Lapo Buonamici, also known as Morello, and the daughter of Giovanni di

Lapo Sassetti of the San Pietro Buonconsigli parish. See Manni, *Istoria del "Decamerone,"* 125.

27. Much of the information in this paragraph comes from Manni, *Istoria del "Decamerone"*; Baldelli, *Vita di Giovanni Boccaccio*; and Tordi, *Gl'inventari*. It is largely taken for granted that Iacopo was a rather undependable brother and that their relationship was not infrequently strained.

28. Bianca was a member of the same Donati clan to which Dante's wife, Gemma, also belonged, a relationship that has caused some scholars to suggest she may have provided Boccaccio with material used in the *Trattatello* and *Esposizioni*, but she comes into Boccaccio's life too late for the former, and her influence on the latter is undemonstrable.

29. According to Tordi, *Gl'inventari*, 81–83, Iacopo's son Boccaccio was born in January 1367, and Antonio in October 1368.

30. This is the same Giovanni di Iacopo Boccaccio who copied MS Kynžvart 2D4, which contains a collection of Boccaccio's bucolic poems. See Giuseppe Billanovich and František Čáda, "Testi bucolici nella biblioteca del Boccaccio," *Italia Medioevale e Umanistica* 4 (1961): 201–22.

31. Vincenzo Crescini, *Contributo agli studi sul Boccaccio* (Turin: Loescher, 1887), 32–33.

32. Ibid., 260–61.

33. Tordi, *Gl'inventari*, 57, 65–67.

34. Ibid., 8–9, 73. The field in question does not appear in the Italian version of the will. This may in fact be the same property that was vandalized in 1352. See Ugo Dorini, "Contributi alla biografia del Boccaccio," *Miscellanea Storica della Valdelsa* 22 (1914): 73–91, esp. 76.

35. Barduccio di Cherichino, Francesco di Lapo Bonamichi, and Agnolo di Torino Bencivenni are all included in Iacopo's will as well. Crescini, *Contributo*, 261.

36. Marchionne di Coppo Stefani, *Cronaca fiorentina*, ed. Niccolò Rodolico (Città di Castello: Lapi, 1903), 158. See also Manni, *Istoria del "Decamerone,"* 127.

37. Guido Carocci, *Il comune di San Casciano in Val di Pesa* (Florence: Pia Casa di Patronato, 1892); Cateni, "Sopra la tomba," 68. Lapo Buonamici died in 1328 and was buried in Santa Croce.

38. Curiously, he also appears in legal documents accused of having wounded a man in a street brawl in 1344. See Emanuela Porta Casucci, "Le paci fra privati nelle parrocchie fiorentine di San Felice in Piazza e San Frediano: Un regesto per gli anni 1335–1365," *Annali di Storia di Firenze* 4 (2009): 195–241, esp. 213. The *podestà*, usually brought from another city for a term of six months to one year, administered justice as chief magistrate. The *vicario* was a representative sent by Florence to rule as vice-administrator over smaller

484 Notes to Pages 350–351

towns in the countryside (such as Certaldo and Pescia) that were its territorial dependencies.

39. The Canigiani family supposedly had its origins in ancient Fiesole and had come down to Florence very early on, settling by the fourteenth century on the Borgo Pidiglioso (now Via de' Bardi, 22–24) in the Oltrarno. The family had taken refuge in Lucca after the battle of Montaperti but returned once the Guelphs had regained power. Petrarch's mother, Eletta Canigiani, was a member of this family, which boasted twelve *gonfalonieri di giustizia* (heads of government) and fifty-five priors in Florence before going extinct in 1813.

40. Luigi Pecori, *Storia della terra di San Gimignano* (Florence: Tipografia Galileiana, 1853), 747. In 1375 he shared the Florentine ambassadorship in Pescia with Guido di Giovanni Machiavelli whose family home stood next door to Boccaccio's in Certaldo. Guido, a distant relative of Niccolò Machiavelli, died in 1390 after having held several important political offices in and around Florence. He is also mentioned in Franco Sacchetti's *Trecentonovelle* (*novella* 70).

41. Like many of the *grandi*, such as the Buondelmonti, the Altoviti, and the Soderini, the Canigiani family was on the horns of a dilemma at the time of the uprising. They were neither supporters of the wool carders nor backers of the party that wished to prolong conflict with the pope.

42. See Roberto Abbondanza, "Una lettera autografa del Boccaccio nell'archivio di stato di Perugia," *Studi sul Boccaccio* 1 (1963): 5–13. He was also one of Florence's priors the year after Boccaccio's death.

43. See Ghino Lazzeri, "Il testamento di Agnolo Torini," in *A Vittorio Cian: I suoi scolari dell'Università di Pisa (1900–1908)* (Pisa: Mariotti, 1909), 35–44. His chief occupation, however, was probably the sale of fine fabrics and cloths. See Hijmans-Tromp, *Vita e opere di Agnolo Torini*, 7–10.

44. Agnolo Torini, *Brieve meditazione sui beneficii di Dio*, ed. Francesco Zambrini (Bologna: Romagnoli, 1862); and Hijmans-Tromp, *Vita e opere di Agnolo Torini*, 20–38.

45. Hijmans-Tromp, *Vita e opere di Agnolo Torini*, 18–20.

46. Boccaccio, *Epistole*, ed. Ginetta Auzzas, in *Tutte le opere*, vol. 5, pt. 1 (Milan: Mondadori, 1992), 842.

47. Boccaccio, *Epistole* 24.8–9.

BIBLIOGRAPHY

PRIMARY LITERATURE

Aeschylus. *Oresteia*. With an English translation by Alan H. Sommerstein. Cambridge, MA: Harvard University Press, 2009.

Alain of Lille. *Anticlaudianus or the Good and Perfect Man*. Translated by James J. Sheridan. Toronto: Institute of Pontifical Studies, 1973.

———. *Anticlaudianus sive De officiis viri boni et perfecti*. Biblioteca Augustana. http://www.hs-augsburg.de/~harsch/augustana.html.

Andreas Cappellanus. *The Art of Courtly Love*. Translated by John Jay Parry. New York: Columbia University Press, 1960.

———. *De amore*. Munich: Eidos, 1964.

Anthologia latina. Edited by Franz Buecheler and Alexander Riese. Leipzig: Teubner, 1894–1926.

Apollodorus. *The Library*. With an English translation by James G. Frazer. 2 vols. Cambridge, MA: Harvard University Press, 1921.

Augustine. *De libero arbitrio*. Edited by Franco Capitani. Milan: Pubblicazioni della Università Cattolica del Sacro Cuore, 1987.

Bembo, Pietro. *Prose della volgar lingua*. In Pietro Bembo, *Prose e rime*, edited by Carlo Dionisotti, 73–309. Turin: UTET, 1966.

Binduccio dello Scelto. *La storia di Troia*. Edited by Maria Gozzi. Milan: Luni, 2000.

Boccaccio, Giovanni. *Allegoria mitologica*. Edited by Manlio Pastore Stocchi. In *Tutte le opere*, vol. 5, pt. 2. Milan: Mondadori, 1994.

———. *L'Ameto*. Translated by Judith Serafini-Sauli. New York: Garland, 1985.

———. *Amorosa visione*. Edited by Vittore Branca. In *Tutte le opere*, vol. 3. Milan: Mondadori, 1974.

———. *Amorosa visione*. Translated by Robert Hollander, Timothy Hampton, and Margherita Frankel. Hanover, NH: University Press of New England, 1986.

———. *Amorosa Visione e Caccia di Diana*. Italy, 1430. Wellesley College Library, Wellesley, MA. Plimpton MS 858, fols. 67–88.

———. *Amorous Fiammetta* [1587]. Revised by Edward Hutton. New York: Rarity Press, 1931.

———. "An Annotated Translation of Boccaccio's *Ameto*." Translated by Bernadette Marie McCoy. PhD diss., New York University, 1971.

———. *Boccaccio on Poetry: Being the Preface and Fourteenth and Fifteenth Books of Boc-*

caccio's "Genealogia Deorum Gentilium." Translated by Charles Osgood. 1930. Indianapolis: Bobbs-Merrill, 1956.

———. *Boccaccio's "Expositions on Dante's 'Comedy.'"* Translated by Michael Papio. Toronto: University of Toronto Press, 2009.

———. *The Book of Theseus: Teseida delle Nozze d'Emilia.* Trans. Bernadette Marie McCoy. New York: Medieval Text Association, 1974.

———. *Buccolicum carmen.* Edited and translated by Giorgio Bernardi Perini. In *Tutte le opere,* vol. 5, pt. 2. Milan: Mondadori, 1994.

———. *Il Buccolicum carmen.* Edited by Giacomo Lidonnici. Città di Castello: S. Lapi, 1914.

———. *Caccia di Diana.* Ed. Vittore Branca. In *Tutte le opere,* vol. 1. Milan: Mondadori, 1967.

———. *"La caccia di Diana," poemetto di Giovanni Boccaccio, ora per la prima volta pubblicata per cura di I. Moutier.* Florence: Stamperia Magheri, 1832.

———. *Carmina.* Edited by Giuseppe Velli. In *Tutte le opere,* vol. 5, pt. 1. Milan: Mondadori, 1992.

———. *Chaucer's Boccaccio: Sources of "Troilus" and the "Knight's" and "Franklin's Tales."* Edited and translated by N. R. Havely. Cambridge: D.S. Brewer, 1980.

———. *Comedia delle ninfe fiorentine.* Edited by Antonio Enzo Quaglio. In *Tutte le opere,* vol. 2. Milan: Mondadori, 1964.

———. *"Comedia delle ninfe fiorentine," di M. Giovanni Boccaccio da Certaldo.* Edited by Francesco Sansovino. Venice: Giolito, 1558.

———. *Consolatoria a Pino de' Rossi.* Edited by Giuseppe Chiecchi. In *Tutte le opere,* vol. 5, pt. 2, 615–87. Milan: Mondadori, 1994.

———. *Corbaccio.* Edited by Giorgio Padoan. In *Tutte le opere,* vol. 5, pt. 2. Milan: Mondadori, 1994.

———. *Il Corbaccio.* Edited by Tauno Nurmela. Annales Academiae Scientiarum Fennicae, Series B, 146. Helsinki: Suomalainen Tiedeakatemia, 1968.

———. *The Corbaccio.* Translated and edited by Anthony K. Cassell. Urbana: University of Illinois Press, 1975. Reprinted as *The Corbaccio or The Labyrinth of Love,* 2nd rev. ed. (Binghamton, NY: Medieval & Renaissance Texts & Studies, 1993).

———. *Il Corbaccio, altrimenti Labirinto d'amore.* Ed. Lodovico Dolce. Venice: Gabriel Giolito, 1551.

———. *La corrispondenza bucolica di Giovanni Boccaccio e Checco di Meletto Rossi e l'egloga di Giovanni del Virgilio ad Albertino Mussato.* Edited by Simona Lorenzini. Florence: Olschki, 2009.

———. *Decameron.* Edited by Vittore Branca. Turin: Einaudi, 1980.

_____ *Decameron.* Edited by Vittore Branca. Milan: Mondadori, 1985.

———. *Decameron.* Edited by Aldo Francesco Massèra. Bari: Laterza, 1927.

———. *Il Decameron*. Edited by Aldo Rossi. Bologna: Cappelli, 1977.

———. *The Decameron*. Translated by G. H. McWilliam. Harmondsworth, UK: Penguin, 1972.

———. *Decameron: Edizione critica secondo l'autografo Hamiltoniano*. Edited by Vittore Branca. Florence: Accademia della Crusca, 1976.

———. *Decameron: Edizione diplomatico-interpretativa dell'autografo Hamilton 90*. Edited by Charles S. Singleton. Baltimore: Johns Hopkins University Press, 1974.

———. *Decameron: Facsimile dell'autografo conservato nel codice Hamilton 90 della Staatsbibliothek Preussischer Kulturbesitz di Berlino*. Edited by Vittore Branca. Florence: Alinari, 1975.

———. *Decameron, Filocolo, Ameto, Fiammetta*. Edited by Carlo Salinari and Natalino Sapegno. Milan: Ricciardi, 1966.

———. *De Canaria et insulis reliquis ultra Ispaniam in Oceano noviter repertis*. Edited by Manlio Pastore Stocchi. In *Tutte le opere*, vol. 5, pt. 1. Milan: Mondadori, 1992.

———. *De casibus virorum illustrium*. Edited by Pier Giorgio Ricci and Vittorio Zaccaria. In *Tutte le opere*, vol. 9. Milan: Mondadori, 1983.

———. *De montibus, silvis, fontibus, lacubus, fluminibus, stagnis seu paludibus et de diversis nominibus maris*. Edited by Manlio Pastore Stocchi. In *Tutte le opere*, vol. 8. Milan: Mondadori, 1998.

———. *De mulieribus claris*. Edited by Vittorio Zaccaria. In *Tutte le opere*, vol. 10. Milan: Mondadori, 1967.

———. *Diana's Hunt / Caccia di Diana: Boccaccio's First Fiction*. Edited and translated by Anthony K. Cassell and Victoria Kirkham. Philadelphia: University of Pennsylvania Press, 1991.

———. *Eclogues*. Translated by Janet Levarie Smarr. New York: Garland, 1987.

———. *Elegia di madonna Fiammetta*. Edited by Carlo Delcorno. In *Tutte le opere*, vol. 5, pt. 2. Milan: Mondadori, 1994.

———. *Elegia di madonna Fiammetta*. Edited by Maria Pia Mussini Sacchi. Milan: Mursia, 1987.

———. *The Elegy of Lady Fiammetta*. Translated by Mariangela Causa-Steindler and Thomas Mauch. Chicago: University of Chicago Press, 1990.

———. *Epistole e lettere*. Edited and translated by Ginetta Auzzas with an appendix edited by Augusto Campana. In *Tutte le opere*, vol. 5, pt. 1. Milan: Mondadori, 1992.

———. *Esposizioni sopra la "Comedia" di Dante*. Edited by Giorgio Padoan. In *Tutte le opere*, vol. 6. Milan: Mondadori, 1965.

———. *Famous Women*. Translated and edited by Virginia Brown. I Tatti Renaissance Library 1. Cambridge, MA: Harvard University Press, 2001.

———. *The Fates of Illustrious Men*. Translated by Louis Brewer Hall. New York: Frederick Unger, 1965.

———. *Filocolo*. Edited by Salvatore Battaglia. Bari: Laterza, 1938.

———. *Filocolo*. Edited by Antonio Enzo Quaglio. In *Tutte le opere*, vol. 1. Milan: Mondadori, 1967.

———. *Il Filocolo*. Translated by Donald Cheney. Edited by Donald Cheney and Thomas G. Bergin. New York: Garland, 1985.

———. *Filostrato*. Edited by Vittore Branca. In *Tutte le opere*, vol. 2. Milan: Mondadori, 1964.

———. *Genealogia deorum gentilium*. Edited by Vittorio Zaccaria. In *Tutte le opere*, vols. 7–8. Milan: Mondadori, 1998.

———. *Genealogie deorum gentilium*. Edited by Vincenzo Romano. Bari: Laterza, 1951.

———. *Genealogy of the Pagan Gods*. Vol. 1. Edited and translated by Jon Solomon. I Tatti Renaissance Library 46. Cambridge, MA: Harvard University Press, 2011.

———. *Invettiva di Messer Giovanni Boccaccio contra una malvagia donna, detto "Laberinto d'Amore," et altrimenti "Il Corbaccio."* Edited by Messer Castorio Laurario of Padua. Milan: A. de Vicomercato, 1520.

———. *The Latin Eclogues*. Translated by David R. Slavitt. Baltimore: Johns Hopkins University Press, 2010.

———. *Lettere*. Edited and translated by Ginetta Auzzas. In *Tutte le opere*, vol. 5, pt. 1. Milan: Mondadori, 1992.

———. *The Life of Dante*. Translated by Vincenzo Zin Bollettino. New York: Garland, 1990.

———. *Ninfale fiesolano*. Edited by Armando Balduino. In *Tutte le opere*, vol. 3. Milan: Mondadori, 1974.

———. *Ninfale fiesolano*. Edited by Pier Massimo Forni. Milan: Mursia, 1991.

———. *The Nymph of Fiesole*. Edited and translated by Daniel J. Donno with illustrations by Angela Conner. New York: Columbia University Press, 1960.

———. *Nymphs of Fiesole*. Translated by Joseph Tusiani. Rutherford, NJ: Fairleigh Dickinson University Press, 1971.

———. *Opere in versi, Corbaccio, Trattatello in laude di Dante, Prose latine, Epistole*. Edited by Pier Giorgio Ricci. Milan: Ricciardi, 1965.

———. *Opere latine minori (Buccolicum carmen, Carminum et epistolarum quae supersunt, Scripta breviora)*. Edited by Aldo Francesco Massèra. Bari: Laterza, 1928.

———. *Opere minori in volgare*. Ed. Mario Marti. Milan: Rizzoli, 1958.

———. *Rime, Caccia di Diana*. Edited by Vittore Branca. Padua: Liviana, 1958.

———. *Rime*. Ed. Vittore Branca. In *Tutte le opere*, vol. 5, pt. 1. Milan: Mondadori, 1992.

———. *Le rime*. Edited by Antonio Lanza. Rome: Aracne, 2010.

———. *Le rime, L'amorosa visione, La caccia di Diana*. Edited by Vittore Branca. Bari: Laterza, 1939.

———. *Teseida delle nozze d'Emilia*. Edited by Alberto Limentani. In *Tutte le opere*, vol. 2. Milan: Mondadori, 1964.

———. *Il testamento di Giovanni Boccaccio secondo l'originale in pergamena dell'Archivio Bichi-Borghesi di Siena*. Siena: Alessandri e Landi, 1853. Later editions: Siena: G. Landi, 1859; Siena: Lazzeri, 1873. Reprinted in Corazzini, *Le lettere edite e inedite di messer Giovanni Boccaccio*, 419–33; and partially in Gaetano Milanesi, *Sulla storia dell'arte toscana: Scritti vari* (Siena: Lazzeri, 1873), 363–64.

———. *Trattatello in laude di Dante*. Edited by Pier Giorgio Ricci. In *Tutte le opere*, vol. 3. Milan: Mondadori, 1974.

———. *Tutte le opere di Giovanni Boccaccio*. Edited by Vittore Branca. 10 vols. Milan: Mondadori, 1964–98.

———. *Vita di Petrarca*. Edited by Gianni Villani. Rome: Salerno Editrice, 2004.

———. *Vite di Petrarca, Pier Damiani e Livio*. Edited by Renata Fabbri. In *Tutte le opere*, vol. 5, pt. 1. Milan: Mondadori, 1992.

———. *Lo zibaldone boccaccesco Mediceo-Laurenziano Plut. XXIX-8, Riprodotto in fac-simile*. Edited by the R. Biblioteca Medicea Laurenziana. Preface by Guido Biagi. Florence: Olschki, 1915.

———. *Zibaldoni: Edizione diplomatica interpretativa codificata*. http://rmcisadu.let .uniroma1.it/boccaccio.

Boethius. *Boethian Number Theory: A Translation of the "De institutione arithmetica."* Edited and translated by Michael Masi. Amsterdam: Rodopi, 1983.

———. *The Theological Tractates, The Consolation of Philosophy*. With English translations by H. F. Stewart, E. K. Rand, and S. J. Tester. Cambridge, MA: Harvard University Press, 1973.

Bonsignori da Città di Castello, Giovanni. *Ovidio Metamorphoseos Vulgare*. Edited by Erminia Ardissino. Bologna: Commissione per i Testi di Lingua, Casa Carducci, 2001.

Borghini, Vincenzo. *Annotationi et discorsi sopra alcuni luoghi del "Decameron."* Florence: Giunti, 1573.

Campanus of Novara. *Euclid's Elements*. Edited by H. L. L. Busard. 2 vols. Stuttgart: Steiner, 2005.

Il cantare di Fiorio e Biancifiore, edito e illustrato. Edited by Vincenzo Crescini. 2 vols. Bologna: Romagnoli-Dall'Acqua, 1889–99. Reprint, Bologna: Forni, 1967.

Cantari di Griselda. Edited by Raffaele Morabito. L'Aquila: L.U. Japadre, 1988.

Cantari fiabeschi arturiani. Edited by Daniela Delcorno Branca. Milan: Luni, 1999.

Carmina Burana. Edited by Edoardo Bianchini. Milan: Rizzoli, 2010.

Carmina latina epigrafica. Edited by Franz Buecheler. Leipzig: Teubner, 1897.

Cassiodorus. *De artibus ac disciplinis liberalium litterarum*, c. IV, *De arithmetica*. Paris: J.-P. Migne, 1865.

Castiglione, Baldassare. *Il cortegiano del conte Baldassare Castiglione*. Edited by Antonio Ciccarelli da Fuligni. Venice: Bernardo Basa, 1584.

Chaucer, Geoffrey. *The Riverside Chaucer*. Edited by Larry D. Benson. Boston: Houghton Mifflin, 1987.

———. *The Workes of Geffray Chaucer newly printed*. Edited by William Thynne. London, 1532.

Cicero. *Cicero Mannucciorum commentariis illustratus*. Venice: Aldus Manutius, 1581–83.

———. *Tusculan Disputations*. With an English translation by J. E. King. Cambridge, MA: Harvard University Press, 1927.

The Commentary on the First Six Books of the "Aeneid" Commonly Attributed to Bernardus Silvestris. Ed. Julian Ward Jones and Elizabeth Frances Jones. Lincoln: University of Nebraska Press, 1977.

Dante Alighieri. *La "Commedia" secondo l'antica vulgata*. Edited by Giorgio Petrocchi. Turin: Einaudi, 1975.

———. *Il Convivio*. Edited by Maria Simonelli. Bologna: Prof. Riccardo Pàtron, 1966.

———. *Dante's Lyric Poetry*. Edited by Kenelm Foster and Patrick Boyde. 2 vols. Oxford: Oxford University Press, 1967.

———. *De vulgari eloquentia*. Edited and translated by Steven Botterill. Cambridge: Cambridge University Press, 1996.

———. *De vulgari eloquentia*. Translated by Aristide Marigo. Florence: Le Monnier, 1957.

———. *The Divine Comedy*. Translated with commentary by Robert Hollander and Jean Hollander. 3 vols. New York: Random House, 2002–7.

———. *The Divine Comedy*. Edited and translated by Charles S. Singleton. 6 vols. Princeton, NJ: Princeton University Press, 1970–75.

———. *Rime*. Edited by Gianfranco Contini. Turin: Einaudi, 1965.

———. *Vita nuova*. Introduction by Eduardo Sanguineti. Milan: Garzanti, 1982.

———. *Vita nuova*. Edited by Domenico De Robertis. In *Opere minori*, vol. 1, pt. 1. Milan: Riccardo Ricciardi, 1995.

———. *Vita nuova*. Translated by Mark Musa. Bloomington: Indiana University Press, 1973.

Euclid. *Elements of Geometry*. The Greek Text of J. L. Heiberg. Edited and translated by Richard Fitzpatrick. 2008. http://farside.ph.utexas.edu/euclid.html.

———. *The First Latin Translation of Euclid's "Elements" Commonly Ascribed to Adelard of Bath*. Edited by H. L. L. Busard. Toronto: Pontifical Institute of Medieval Studies, 1983.

————. *The Medieval Latin Translation of the Euclid's "Elements" Made Directly from the Greek.* Translated by the Sicilian School of Translators of the Twelfth Century. Text based on Theon of Alexandria's version. Edited by H. L. L. Busard. Stuttgart: Steiner, 1987.

Euripides. *Orestes.* Edited and translated by M. L. West. Warminster: Aris & Philips, 1987.

Ferrand, Jacques. *A Treatise on Love Sickness.* Translated by Donald A. Beecher and Massimo Ciavolella. Syracuse, NY: Syracuse University Press, 1990.

Hesiod. *Theogony, Works and Days, Testimonia.* With an English translation by Glenn W. Most. Cambridge, MA: Harvard University Press, 2007.

Homer. *Iliad.* With an English translation by A. T. Murray. 2 vols. Cambridge, MA: Harvard University Press, 1924–25.

————. *Odyssey.* With an English translation by A. T. Murray. 2 vols. Cambridge, MA: Harvard University Press, 1919.

Horace. *Odes and Epodes.* With an English translation by Niall Rudd. Cambridge, MA: Harvard University Press, 2004.

————. *Selections: Satires, Epistles, and Ars Poetica.* With an English translation by H. Rushton Fairclough. Cambridge, MA: Harvard University Press, 1978.

Iamblichus. *The Theology of Arithmetic.* Edited and translated by Robin Waterfield. Grand Rapids, MI: Phanes Press, 1988.

Isidore of Seville. *The "Etymologies" of Isidore of Seville.* Translated by S. Barney, J. Beach, and O. Berghof. Cambridge: Cambridge University Press, 2006.

————. *Isidori Hispalensis Episcopi Etymologiarum sive Originum libri XX.* Edited by W. M. Lindsay. Oxford: Clarendon Press, 1911.

Juvenal. *Juvenal and Persius.* With an English translation by Susanna Morton Braund. Cambridge, MA: Harvard University Press, 2004.

Livy. *Le deche di T. Livio.* Edited by Francesco Pizzorno. 6 vols. Savona: Sambolino, 1842–49.

Lucan. *The Civil War (Pharsalia).* With an English translation by J. D. Duff. Cambridge, MA: Harvard University Press, 1928.

Marchiònne di Coppo Stefani. *Cronaca fiorentina.* Edited by Niccolò Rodolico. Città di Castello: Lapi, 1903.

Marinella, Lucrezia. *The Nobility and Excellence of Woman and the Defects and Vices of Men.* Translated by Anne Dunhill. Chicago: University of Chicago Press, 1999.

Martianus Capella. *Martianus Capella and the Seven Liberal Arts.* Edited and translated by William Harris Stahl, Richard Johnson, and E. L. Burge. 2 vols. New York: Columbia University Press, 1977.

Montaigne, Michel de. *Journal de voyage de Michel de Montaigne.* Edited by François Rigolot. Paris: Presses Universitaires de France, 1992.

Nicomachus of Gerasa. *Introduction to Arithmetic.* Translated by M. L. D'Ooge. Edited by F. E. Robbins and L. C. Karpinski. Ann Arbor: University of Michigan Press, 1938.

The *"Novellino," or, "One Hundred Ancient Tales": An Edition and Translation Based on the 1525 Gualteruzzi Editio Princeps.* Edited and translated by Joseph P. Consoli. New York: Garland, 1997.

Ovid. *Heroides and Amores.* Translated by Grant Showerman. Cambridge, MA: Harvard University Press, 1971.

———. *Metamorphoses.* Turin: Einaudi, 1994.

———. *Metamorphoses.* With an English translation by Frank Justus Miller. 2 vols. Cambridge, MA: Harvard University Press, 1977–84.

———. *Metamorphosis Ovidiana moraliter . . . explanata: Paris, 1509 / Pierre Bersuire, Libellus: Basel, 1543 / Albricus.* Edited by Stephen Orgel. New York: Garland, 1979.

———. *Ovide moralisé: Poème du commencement du quatorzième siècle.* Edited by Cornelis de Boer. Amsterdam: J. Müller, 1915–38.

———. *Ovidius moralizatus.* Edited by Joseph Engels. Utrecht: Instituut voor Laat Latijn der Rijksuniversiteit, 1962; 1966.

Petrarch. *Africa.* Biblioteca Italiana, http://www.bibliotecaitaliana.it/xtf/view? docId=bibit000921/bibit000921.xml.

———. *Il "Bucolicum carmen" e i suoi commenti inediti.* Edited by Antonio Avena. 1906. Reprint, Bologna: Forni, 1969.

———. *Canzoniere.* Edited by Marco Santagata. Milan: Mondadori, 1996.

———. *De viris illustribus.* Edited by Guido Martellotti. In *Edizione nazionale delle opere di Francesco Petrarca,* vol. 2, pt. 1. Florence: Sansoni, 1964.

———. *Le familiari.* Edited by Vittorio Rossi and Umberto Bosco. In *Edizione nazionale delle opere di Francesco Petrarca,* vols. 10–13. Florence: Sansoni, 1933–42.

———. *Letters on Familiar Matters.* Translated by Aldo S. Bernardo et al. 3 vols. 1975–85. Reprint, New York: Italica Press, 2005.

———. *Opere latine di Francesco Petrarca.* Edited by Antonietta Bufano. 2 vols. Turin: UTET, 1975.

———. *Petrarca's Africa.* Translated by Thomas G. Bergin and Alice S. Wilson. New Haven, CT: Yale University Press, 1977.

———. *Petrarch's Lyric Poems: The "Rime sparse" and Other Lyrics.* Translated and edited by Robert M. Durling. Cambridge, MA: Harvard University Press, 1976.

———. *Petrarch's Testament.* Edited and translated by Theodor Ernest Mommsen. Ithaca, NY: Cornell University Press, 1957.

———. *Res seniles: Libri V–VIII.* Edited by Silvia Rizzo. Florence: Casa Editrice Le Lettere, 2009.

———. *Senile V 2.* Edited by Monica Berté. Florence: Le lettere, 1998.

————. *Trionfi, Rime Estravaganti, Codice degli Abbozzi*. Edited by Vinicio Pacca and Laura Paolino. Milan: Mondadori, 1996.

————. *Triumphi*. Edited by Marco Ariani. Milan: Mursia, 1988.

————. *Triumphi*. Edited by Vinicio Pacca. 2nd ed. Milan: Mondadori, 2000.

Pizan, Christine de. *The Book of the City of Ladies*. Translated by Rosalind Brown-Grant. London: Penguin, 1999.

————. *Le livre de la cité des dames*. Edited and translated by Eric Hicks and Thérèse Moreau. Paris: Stock, 1986.

Pliny. *Natural History*. With an English translation by H. Rackham et al. 10 vols. Cambridge, MA: Harvard University Press, 1938–63.

Poeti del dolce stil novo. Edited by Mario Marti. Florence: Le Monnier, 1969.

Poeti minori del Trecento. Edited by Natalino Sapegno. Milan: Riccardo Ricciardi, 1962.

Pucci, Antonio. *Cantari della Reina d'Oriente*. Edited by Attilio Motta and William Robins. Bologna: Commissione per i Testi di Lingua, 2007.

————. *Cantari di Apollonio di Tiro*. Edited by Renzo Rabboni. Bologna: Commissione per i Testi di Lingua, 1996.

Robert of Chester. *A Thirteenth-Century Adaptation of Robert of Chester's Version of Euclid's "Elements."* Edited by H. L. L. Busard. Munich: Institut für Geschichte der Naturwissenschaften, 1996.

Sacchetti, Franco. *Il libro delle rime*. Edited by Franca Brambilla Ageno. Florence: Olschki, 1990.

————. *Trecentonovelle*. Edited by Valerio Marucci. Rome: Salerno, 1996.

————. *Il trecentonovelle*. Edited by Antonio Lanza. Florence: Sansoni, 1993.

Seneca. *Moral Essays*. With an English translation by John W. Basore. 3 vols. Cambridge, MA: Harvard University Press, 1928–35.

————. *Tragedies*. With an English translation by Frank Justus Miller. 2 vols. Cambridge, MA: Harvard University Press, 1979.

Servius Grammaticus. *In Virgilii "Bucolica" et "Georgica" commentarii*. Edited by George Thilo. Leipzig: Teubner, 1887.

Solinus. *Collectanea rerum memorabilium*. Edited by T. Mommsen. Berlin: Weidmann, 1958.

Sophocles. *Ajax, Electra, Oedipus Tyrannus*. With an English translation by Hugh Lloyd-Jones. Cambridge, MA: Harvard University Press, 1994.

Statius. *Thebaid*. Translated by J. H. Mozley. 2 vols. Cambridge, MA: Harvard University Press, 1967.

————. *Thebaid: A Song of Thebes*. Translated by Jane Wilson Joyce. Ithaca, NY: Cornell University Press, 2008.

Tacitus. *Histories*. With an English translation by Clifford H. Moore and John Jackson. 2 vols. Cambridge, MA: Harvard University Press, 1925–31.

Theon of Smyrna. *Expositio rerum mathematicarum ad legendum Platonem utilium.* Edited by Eduardus Hiller. Leipzig: Teubner, 1878.

Trattati del Cinquecento sulla donna. Edited by Giuseppe Zonta. Bari: Laterza, 1913.

Ubaldini, Giovambatista. *Istoria della casa de gli Ubaldini.* Florence: Bartolomeo Sermatelli, 1588.

Valerio Massimo. *De' fatti e detti degni di memoria della città di Roma e delle stranie genti.* Edited by Roberto De Visiani. Bologna: Romagnoli, 1867–68.

Valla, Lorenzo. *Discourse on the Forgery of the Alleged Donation of Constantine.* Translated by Christopher B. Coleman. New Haven, CT: Yale University Press, 1922.

Vibius Sequester. Edited by Remus Gelsomino. Leipzig: Teubner, 1962.

Villani, Giovanni. *Cronica.* Edited by Giovanni Porta. Fondazione Pietro Bembo. Parma: Guanda, 1991.

Virgil. *Eclogues.* Edited by Robert Coleman. Cambridge: Cambridge University Press, 1977.

———. *Eclogues, Georgics, Aeneid.* With an English translation by H. Rushton Fairclough. 2 vols. Cambridge, MA: Harvard University Press, 1994.

———. *Eclogues, Georgics, Aeneid I-VI.* With an English translation by H. Rushton Fairclough. Revised by G. P. Goold. Cambridge, MA: Harvard University Press, 2004.

Volgarizzamenti del Due e Trecento. Edited by Cesare Segre. Turin: UTET, 1964.

SECONDARY LITERATURE

Abbondanza, Roberto. "Una lettera autografa del Boccaccio nell'archivio di stato di Perugia." *Studi sul Boccaccio* 1 (1963): 5–13.

Abulafia, David. "Neolithic Meets Medieval: First Encounters in the Canary Islands." In *Medieval Frontiers: Concepts and Practices,* edited by David Abulafia and Nora Berend, 255–78. Burlington, VT: Ashgate, 2002.

Agostinelli, Edvige. "A Catalogue of the Manuscripts of *Il Teseida.*" *Studi sul Boccaccio* 15 (1985): 1–83.

Allenspach, Joseph, and Giuseppe Frasso. "Vicende, cultura e scritti di Gerolamo Squarzafico, alessandrino." *Italia Medioevale e Umanistica* 23 (1980): 233–92.

Almansi, Guido. *The Writer as Liar: Narrative Technique in the "Decameron."* London: Routledge & Kegan Paul, 1975.

Anderson, David. *Before the "Knight's Tale": Imitation of Classical Epic in Boccaccio's "Teseida."* Philadelphia: University of Pennsylvania Press, 1988.

———. "An Early Reference to the *Teseida.*" *Studi sul Boccaccio* 16 (1987): 325–28.

Annotationi et discorsi sopra alcuni luoghi del "Decameron." Florence: Giunti, 1573.

———. Edited by Pietro Fanfani. 4th ed. Florence: Le Monnier, 1857.

Le annotazioni e i discorsi sul "Decameron" del 1573 dei Deputati fiorentini. Edited by Giuseppe Chiecchi. Padua: Antenore, 2001.

Armao, Linda. "The *Ninfale fiesolano*: Ovidian Bravura Veiling Truth." In *Italiana 1988: Selected Papers from the Proceedings of the Fifth Annual Conference of the American Association of Teachers of Italian, Nov. 18–20, 1988*, edited by Albert N. Mancini, Paolo Giordano, and Anthony J. Tamburri, 35–49. River Forest, IL: Rosary College, 1990.

Armstrong, Guyda. "Boccaccio and the Infernal Body: The Widow as Wilderness." In Stillinger and Psaki, *Boccaccio and Feminist Criticism*, 83–104.

———. "Dantean Framing Devices in Boccaccio's *Corbaccio.*" *Reading Medieval Studies* 27 (2001): 139–61.

Armstrong, Guyda, and Vika Zafrin. "Towards the Electronic *Esposizioni*: The Challenges of the Online Commentary." *Digital Medievalist* 1.1 (Spring 2005). http://www.digitalmedievalist.org/journal/1.1/armstrong/.

Arscott, Caroline, and Katie Scott, eds. *Manifestations of Venus: Art and Sexuality.* Manchester: Manchester University Press, 2002.

Ascoli, Albert R. "Auerbach fra gli Epicurei: Dal Canto X dell'*Inferno* alla VI giornata del *Decameron.*" *Moderna* 11 (2009): 135–52.

———. "Pyrrhus' Rules: Playing with Power from Boccaccio to Machiavelli." *Modern Language Notes* 114 (1999): 14–57.

Asor Rosa, Alberto. "*Decameron* di Giovanni Boccaccio." In Asor Rosa, *Letteratura italiana*, 1:579–83. Milan: Einaudi, 1992.

———, ed. *Letteratura italiana: Le opere.* Vol. 1, *Dalle origini al Cinquecento.* Milan: Einaudi, 1992.

Astour, Michael C. *Hellenosemitica: An Ethnic and Cultural Study in West Semitic Impact on Mycenaean Greece.* Leiden: E. J. Brill, 1967.

Auerbach, Erich. *Mimesis: The Representation of Reality in Western Literature.* Translated by Willard R. Trask. New York: Doubleday, 1957.

Auzzas, Ginetta. "I codici autografi: Elenco e bibliografia." *Studi sul Boccaccio* 7 (1973): 1–20.

———. "Studi sulle 'Epistole': L'invito della Signoria fiorentina al Petrarca." *Studi sul Boccaccio* 4 (1967): 203–44.

———. "Studi sulle 'Epistole': Testimonianze di testi irreperibili." *Studi sul Boccaccio* 6 (1971): 131–44.

Azzetta, Luca. "Le chiose alla *Commedia* di Andrea Lancia e altre questioni dantesche." *L'Alighieri* 21 (2003): 5–76.

———. "Tradizione latina e volgarizzamento della prima Deca di Tito Livio." *Italia Medioevale e Umanistica* 36 (1993): 175–97.

———. "Vicende d'amanti e chiose di poema: Alle radici di Boccaccio interprete di Francesca." *Studi sul Boccaccio* 37 (2009): 155–70.

Bacchi della Lega, Alberto. *Serie delle edizioni delle opere di Giovanni Boccacci latine, volgari, tradotte e trasformate.* Bologna: Romagnoli, 1875. Reprint, Bologna: Forni, 1967.

Baldassarri, Stefano. "A Tale of Two Cities: Accounts of the Origins of Fiesole and Florence from the Anonymous *Chronica* to Leonardo Bruni." *Studi Rinascimentali* 5 (2007): 29–56.

Baldelli, Giovanni Battista. *Vita di Giovanni Boccaccio.* Florence: Ciardetti, 1806.

Balduino, Armando. *Boccaccio, Petrarca e altri poeti del Trecento.* Florence: Olschki, 1984.

———. "Tradizione canterina e tonalità popolareggianti nel *Ninfale fiesolano.*" *Studi sul Boccaccio* 2 (1964): 25–80.

Barański, Zygmunt G., and Patrick Boyde, eds. *The "Fiore" in Context.* The William and Katherine Devers Series in Dante Studies 2. Notre Dame, IN: University of Notre Dame Press, 1997.

Barański, Zygmunt G., and Theodore J. Cachey, eds. *Petrarch and Dante: Anti-Dantism, Metaphysics, Tradition.* Notre Dame, IN: University of Notre Dame Press, 2009.

Barasch, Moshe. *Gestures of Despair in Medieval and Early Renaissance Art.* New York: New York University Press, 1976.

Barbi, Michele. *La nuova filologia e l'edizione dei nostri scrittori da Dante al Manzoni.* Florence: Sansoni, 1973.

Barchiesi, Alessandro. "Music for Monsters: Ovid's *Metamorphoses,* Bucolic Evolution, and Bucolic Criticism." In *Brill's Companion to Greek and Latin Pastoral,* edited by Marco Fantuzzi and Theodore Papanghelis, 403–26. Leiden: Brill, 2006.

Bardi, Monica. *Le voci dell'assenza: Una lettura dell'"Elegia di madonna Fiammetta."* Turin: Tirrenia, 1990.

Barolini, Teodolinda. *Dante and the Origins of Italian Literary Culture.* New York: Fordham University Press, 2006.

———. *The Undivine Comedy: Detheologizing Dante.* Princeton, NJ: Princeton University Press, 1993.

Barsella, Susanna. "Boccaccio, Petrarch, and Peter Damian: Two Models of the Humanist Intellectual." *Modern Language Notes* 121.1 (2006): 16–48.

Bartoli, Lorenzo. "Considerazioni attorno ad una questione metricologica: Il Boccaccio e le origini dell'ottava rima." *Quaderns d'Italià* 4–5 (2000): 91–99.

Bartuschat, Johannes. "*De Vita et Moribus Domini Francisci Petracchi* de Boccace." *Chroniques Italiennes* 63–64 (2000): 81–93.

———. *Les "Vies" de Dante, Pétrarque et Boccace en Italie (XIV–XV siècles): Contribution à l'histoire du genre biographique.* Ravenna: Longo, 2010.

Battaglia, Salvatore. *La coscienza letteraria del Medioevo.* Naples: Liguori, 1965.

Battaglia Ricci, Lucia. *Boccaccio*. Rome: Salerno, 2000.

———. "*Decameron*: Interferenze di modelli." In Picone, *Autori e lettori di Boccaccio*, 179–94.

———. "Edizioni d'autore, copie di lavoro, interventi di autoesegesi: Testimonianze trecentesche." In *"Di mano propria": Gli autografi dei letterati italiani. Atti del Convegno internazionale di Forlì 24–27 novembre 2008*, edited by Guido Baldassari, Matteo Motolese, Paolo Procaccioli, Emilio Russo. 123–57. Rome: Salerno, 2010.

———. "Immaginario trionfale: Petrarca e la tradizione figurativa." In *I "Triumphi" di Francesco Petrarca*, edited by Claudia Berra, 255–98. Milan: Cisalpino, 1999.

———. *Ragionare nel giardino: Boccaccio e i cicli pittorici del "Trionfo della morte."* Rome: Salerno, 2000.

Bausi, Francesco. "Gli spiriti magni: Filigrane aristoteliche e tomistiche nella decima giornata del *Decameron*." *Studi sul Boccaccio* 27 (1999): 205–53.

Benson, Pamela Joseph. *The Invention of the Renaissance Woman: The Challenge of Female Independence in the Literature and Thought of Italy and England*. University Park: Pennsylvania State University Press, 1992.

Bergin, Thomas G. *Boccaccio*. New York: Viking Press, 1981.

Bernardi, Marco, and Carlo Pulsoni. "Primi appunti sulla rassettatura del Salviati." *Filologia Italiana* 8 (2011): 167–200.

Bernardo, Aldo. "Petrarch's Attitude toward Dante." *Publications of the Modern Language Association of America* 70 (1955): 488–517.

Berra, Claudia, ed. *Motivi e forme delle "Familiari" di Francesco Petrarca*. Milan: Cisalpino, 2003.

Bertelli, Sandro, and Marco Cursi. "Novità sull'autografo Toledano di Giovanni Boccaccio: Una data e un disegno sconosciuti." *Critica del Testo* 15.1 (2012): 287–95.

Bertoldi, Alfonso. "Del sentimento religioso di Giovanni Boccaccio e dei canti di lui alla Vergine." *Giornale Storico della Letteratura Italiana* 68 (1916): 82–107.

Bertoli, Gustavo. "Le prime due edizioni della seconda 'Rassettatura.'" *Studi sul Boccaccio* 23 (1995): 3–17.

Bettini, Maurizio. *Francesco Petrarca sulle arti figurative: Tra Plinio e Agostino*. Città di Castello: Sillabe, 2002.

Bettinzoli, Attilio. "Per una definizione delle presenze dantesche nel *Decameron* I: I registri 'ideologici,' lirici, drammatici." *Studi sul Boccaccio* 13 (1981–82): 267–326.

———. "Per una definizione delle presenze dantesche nel *Decameron* II: Ironizzazione e espressivismo antifrastico-deformatorio." *Studi sul Boccaccio* 14 (1983–84): 209–40.

Billanovich, Giuseppe. "Il Boccaccio, il Petrarca e le più antiche traduzioni in italiano delle decadi di Tito Livio." *Giornale Storico della Letteratura Italiana* 130 (1953): 311–37.

———. "Dall'antica Ravenna alle biblioteche umanistiche." *Aevum* 30 (1956): 319–53.

———. "La leggenda dantesca del Boccaccio dalla lettera di Ilaro al *Trattatello in laude di Dante.*" *Studi Danteschi* 28 (1949): 45–144.

———. *Petrarca letterato: Lo scrittoio del Petrarca.* Rome: Edizioni di Storia e Letteratura, 1947.

———. "Pietro Piccolo da Monteforte tra il Petrarca e il Boccaccio." In *Medioevo e Rinascimento: Studi in onore di Bruno Nardi*, 65–72. Florence: Sansoni, 1955.

———. *Prime ricerche dantesche.* Rome: Edizioni di Storia e Letteratura, 1947.

———. *Restauri boccacceschi.* Rome: Edizioni di Storia e Letteratura, 1947.

———. "Tito Livio, Petrarca, Boccaccio." *Archivio Storico Ticinese* 25 (1984): 3–10.

———. *La tradizione del testo di Livio e le origini dell'umanesimo.* Vol. 1, *Tradizione e fortuna di Livio tra medioevo e umanesimo.* Padua: Antenore, 1981.

Billanovich, Giuseppe, and František Čáda. "Testi bucolici nella biblioteca del Boccaccio." *Italia Medioevale e Umanistica* 4 (1961): 201–22.

Black, Robert. "Boccaccio, Reader of the *Appendix vergiliana*: The *Miscellanea Laurenziana* and Fourteenth-Century Schoolbooks." In Picone and Cazalé Bérard, *Gli zibaldoni di Boccaccio*, 113–28.

Bloom, Harold. *The Anxiety of Influence: A Theory of Poetry.* Oxford: Oxford University Press, 1997.

Blumenberg, Hans. *Work on Myth.* Cambridge, MA: MIT Press, 1985.

Boitani, Piero, ed. *Chaucer and the Italian Trecento.* Cambridge: Cambridge University Press, 1983.

———, ed. *The European Tragedy of Troilus.* Oxford: Clarendon Press, 1989.

———. "Style, Iconography, and Narrative: The Lesson of the *Teseida.*" In *Chaucer and the Italian Trecento*, edited by Piero Boitani, 185–99. Cambridge: Cambridge University Press, 1983.

Boli, Todd. "Boccaccio's *Trattatello in laude di Dante*, or '*Dante Resaurtus.*'" *Renaissance Quarterly* 41 (1988): 389–412.

———. "Treatment of Orthodoxy and Insistence on the *Comedy's* Allegory in Boccaccio's *Esposizioni.*" *Italian Culture* 9 (1991): 63–74.

Bonfante, Mario. "'Femmina' and 'donna.'" In *Studia philologica et litteraria in honorem L. Spitzer*, edited by A. G. Hatcher and K. L. Selig. 77–109. Bern: Francke, 1958.

Bontier, Pierre, and Jean Le Verrier. *The Canarian; or, Book of the Conquest and Conversion of the Canarians in the Year 1402.* Edited and translated with notes and introduction by Richard Henry Major. London: The Hakluyt Society, 1872.

Bragantini, Renzo, and Pier Massimo Forni, eds. *Lessico critico decameroniano*. Milan: Bollati Boringhieri, 1995.

Branca, Vittore. *"L'Amorosa Visione* (tradizione, significati, fortuna)." *Annali della Reale Scuola Normale Superiore di Pisa (Lettere, Storia e Filosofia)*, ser. 2, 11 (1942): 263–90.

———. "L'Atteone del Boccaccio fra allegoria cristiana, evemerismo trasfigurante, narrativa esemplare, visualizzazione rinascimentale." *Studi sul Boccaccio* 24 (1996): 193–208.

———. *Boccaccio: The Man and His Works*. Translated by Richard Monges. New York: New York University Press, 1976.

———. "Boccaccio e i Veneziani bergoli." *Lingua Nostra* 3 (1941): 49–52.

———. *Boccaccio medievale*. Florence: Sansoni, 1964.

———. *Boccaccio medievale e nuovi studi sul "Decameron"* (1956). Florence: Sansoni, 1990.

———, ed. *Boccaccio visualizzato: Narrare per parole e per immagini fra Medioevo e Rinascimento*. 3 vols. Turin: Einaudi, 1999.

———. "L'editio princeps dell'*Amorosa visione* del Boccaccio." *Bibliofilia* 40 (1938): 460–68.

———. "Giovanni Boccaccio." In *Enciclopedia dell'arte medievale*, 3:549–57. Rome: Istituto della Enciclopedia Italiana, 1992.

———. *Giovanni Boccaccio: Profilo biografico*. Florence: Sansoni, 1977.

———. "Introduzione: Il narrar boccacciano per immagini dal tardo gotico al primo Rinscimento." In Branca, *Boccaccio visualizzato*, 1:3–37.

———. "Per l'attribuzione della *Caccia di Diana* a Giovanni Boccaccio." *Annali della R. Scuola Normale Superiore di Pisa* 2.7 (1938): 287–302. Reprinted in Branca, *Tradizione delle opere di Giovanni Boccaccio*, 1:121–43.

———. *Tradizione delle opere di Giovanni Boccaccio*. Vol. 1, *Un primo elenco dei codici e tre studi*. Rome: Edizioni di Storia e Letteratura, 1958. Vol. 2, *Un secondo elenco di manoscritti e studi sul testo del "Decameron" con due appendici*. Rome: Edizioni di Storia e Letteratura, 1991.

———. "Tradizione letteraria e cultura medievale nella autobiografia romanzesca del Boccaccio." In *Formen der Selbstdarstellung: Analekten zu einer Geschichte des literarischen Selbstportraits; Festgabe für Fritz Neubert*, edited by Günter Reichenkron and Erich Haase, 16–34. Berlin: Duncker & Humblot, 1956.

Branca, Vittore, and Pier Giorgio Ricci. *Un autografo del "Decameron": Codice hamiltoniano 90*. Florence: Olschki, 1962.

Branca, Vittore, Paul F. Watson, and Victoria Kirkham. "Boccaccio visualizzato." *Studi sul Boccaccio* 15 (1985–86): 87–119.

Branch, Eren Hostetter. "Rhetorical Structures and Strategies in Boccaccio's *Teseida*." In *The Craft of Fiction: Essays in Medieval Poetics*, edited by Leigh A. Arrathoon, 143–60. Rochester, MI: Solaris Press, 1984.

Brieger, Peter, Millard Meiss, and Charles S. Singleton. *Illuminated Manuscripts of the "Divine Comedy."* 2 vols. Princeton, NJ: Princeton University Press, 1969.

Brioschi, Franco, and Costanzo Di Girolamo, eds. *Manuale di letteratura italiana: Storia per generi e problemi.* 4 vols. Turin: Bollati Boringhieri, 1993.

Brown, Virginia. "Boccaccio in Naples: The Beneventan Liturgical Palimpsest of the Laurentian Autographs (Ms 29.8 and 33.31)." *Italia Medioevale e Umanistica* 34 (1991): 41–126. Reprinted as "Between the Convent and the Court: Boccaccio and the Benevental Gradual from Naples," in Picone and Cazalé Bérard, *Gli zibaldoni di Boccaccio*, 307–13.

Bruni, Francesco. *Boccaccio: L'invenzione della letteratura mezzana.* Bologna: Il Mulino, 1990.

Bujanda, J. M de. *Index de Rome, 1557, 1559, 1564: Les premiers index romains et l'index du Concile de Trente.* Sherbrooke, QC: Centre d'études de la Renaissance, 1990.

Burkert, Walter. *Homo Necans.* Berkeley: University of California Press, 1983.

Cabaillot, Claire. "La Mavortis miles: Petrarca in Boccaccio." In Picone and Cazalé Bérard, *Gli zibaldoni di Boccaccio*, 129–39.

Cachey, Theodore J., Jr. "Between Petrarch and Dante: Prolegomenon to a Critical Discourse." In Barański and Cachey, *Petrarch and Dante*, 3–49.

———. "Cartographic Dante." *Italica* 87 (2010): 325–54.

———. *Le Isole Fortunate: Appunti di storia lettteraria italiana.* Rome: "L'Erma" di Bretschneider, 1995.

———. "Petrarca, Boccaccio e le Isole Fortunate: Lo sguardo antropologico." In Morosini, *Boccaccio geografo*, 205–28.

———. "Petrarch, Boccaccio, and the New World Encounter." *Stanford Italian Review* 10 (1991): 45–59.

———. "Petrarch's Cartographical Writing." In *Humanism in the Intellectual World: 12th–16th Century*, edited by Bert Roest and Stephen Gersh, 73–91. Leiden: Brill, 2003.

Calabrese, Michael. "Feminism and the Packaging of Boccaccio's Fiammetta." *Italica* 74 (1997): 20–42.

Callu, Florence, and François Avril, eds. *Boccace en France: De l'humanisme à l'érotisme.* Paris: Bibliothèque Nationale, 1975.

The Cambridge History of French Literature. Edited by William Burgwinkle, Nicholas Hammond, and Emma Wilson. Cambridge: Cambridge University Press, 2011.

The Cambridge History of Italian Literature. Edited by Peter Brand and Lino Pertile. Cambridge: Cambridge University Press, 1999.

The Cambridge History of Literary Criticism: The Middle Ages. Edited by Alastair Minnis and Ian Johnson. Cambridge: Cambridge University Press, 2005.

Camozzi, Ambrogio. "Il Veglio di Creta alla luce di Matelda: Una lettura comparativa di *Inferno* XIV e *Purgatorio* XXVIII." *The Italianist* 29 (2009): 3–49.

Candido, Igor. "Amore e Psiche dalle chiose del Laur. 29.2 alle due redazioni delle *Genealogie* e ancora in *Decameron* X.10." *Studi sul Boccaccio* 38 (2009): 171–96.

Carocci, Guido. *Il comune di San Casciano in Val di Pesa*. Florence: Pia Casa di Patronato, 1892.

Carrai, Stefano. "Pastoral as Personal Mythology in History." In Kirkham and Maggi, *Petrarch*, 165–77.

Carrara, Enrico. *La poesia pastorale*. Milan: Vallardi, 1925.

Carraro, Annalisa. "Tradizioni culturali e storiche nel *De casibus*." *Studi sul Boccaccio* 12 (1980): 197–262.

Casella, Maria Teresa. "Sul volgarizzamento boccacciano di Valerio Massimo: Un codice rintracciato; Una chiosa imbarazzante?" *Studi sul Boccaccio* 19 (1990): 191–208.

———. *Tra Boccaccio e Petrarca: I volgarizzamenti di Tito Livio e di Valerio Massimo*. Padua: Antenore, 1982.

Cassell, Anthony K. "Boccaccio's *Caccia di Diana*: Horizon of Expectation." *Italian Culture* 9 (1991): 85–102.

Castelli, Maria Cristina. "*Buccolicum carmen*." In Branca, *Boccaccio visualizzato*, 2:73–74.

———. "*Genealogie deorum*." In Branca, *Boccaccio visualizzato*, 2:57–62.

———. "*Teseida*." In Branca, *Boccaccio visualizzato*, 2:56–57.

Cateni, Francesco. "Sopra la tomba di messer Gio. Boccaccio." *Nuovo Giornale de' Letterati* 11.23 (1825): 100–123.

Cazalé Bérard, Claude. "*L'Allegoria mitologica* de Boccace: Un mythe entre Orient et Occident." In *Actes du Colloque Mythes et sociétés en Méditerranée orientale: Entre le sacré et le profane*, 143–62. Lille: UL3, 2005.

———. "Boccaccio e la *Poetica* ovvero l'apologia della finzione." *Testo e Senso* 1 (1998): 27–53; 2 (1999): 15–43. http://testoesenso.it.

———. "Filoginia/misoginia." In Bragantini and Forni, *Lessico critico decameroniano*, 116–41.

———. "Riscrittura della poetica e poetica della riscrittura." In Picone and Cazalé Bérard, *Gli zibaldoni di Boccaccio*, 425–53.

Cerbo, Anna. *Metamorfosi del mito classico da Boccaccio a Marino*. Pisa: ETS, 2001.

Charity, A. C. *Events and Their Afterlife: The Dialectics of Christian Typology in the Bible and Dante*. Cambridge: Cambridge University Press, 1966.

Cherchi, Paolo. *Andrea Cappellano, i trovatori e altri temi romanzi*. Rome: Bulzoni, 1979.

Chiecchi, Giuseppe. "Per l'interpretazione dell'egloga *Olympia* di Giovanni Boccaccio." *Studi sul Boccaccio* 23 (1995): 219–44.

Chiecchi, Giuseppe, and Luciano Troisio. *Il "Decameron" sequestrato: Le tre edizioni censurate nel Cinquecento*. Milan: Unicopli, 1984.

Chiovenda, Lucia. "Die Zeichnungen Petrarcas." *Archivum Romanicum* 17 (1933): 1–61.

Ciampi, Sebastiano. *Monumenti d'un manoscritto autografo di Gio: Boccacci da Certaldo.* Florence: Giuseppe Galletti, 1827.

Cian, Vittorio. "Il supposto incendio dei libri del Boccaccio a S. Spirito." *Giornale Storico della Letteratura Italiana* 10 (1887): 298–99.

Ciardi Dupré Dal Poggetto, Maria Grazia. "L'iconografia nei codici miniati boccacciani dell'Italia centrale e meridionale." In Branca, *Boccaccio visualizzato,* 2:3–52.

———. "Il rapporto testo e immagini all'origine della formazione artistica e letteraria di Giovanni Boccaccio." In *Medioevo: Immagine e racconto; Atti del Convegno internazionale di studi Parma, 27–30 settembre 2000,* edited by Arturo Carlo Quintavalle, 456–73. Milan: Electa, 2003.

Ciardi Dupré Dal Poggetto, Maria Grazia, and Vittore Branca. "Boccaccio visualizzato da Boccaccio I: 'Corpus' dei disegni e cod. Parigino It. 482." *Studi sul Boccaccio* 22 (1994): 197–225.

Ciavolella, Massimo. "Mediaeval Medicine and Arcite's Love Sickness." *Florilegium* 1 (1979): 222–41.

———. "La tradizione della 'aegritudo amoris' nel *Decameron.*" *Giornale Storico della Letteratura Italiana* 147 (1970): 496–517.

Ciccolella, Federica. *Donati Graeci: Learning Greek in the Renaissance.* Leiden: Brill, 2008.

Ciccuto, Marcello. "Immagini per i testi di Boccaccio: Percorsi e affinità dagli Zibaldoni al *Decameron.*" In Picone and Cazalé Bérard, *Gli zibaldoni di Boccaccio,* 141–60.

Cioffari, Vincenzo. "The Function of Fortune in Dante, Boccaccio, and Machiavelli." *Italica* 24 (1947): 1–13.

Cipollone, Annalisa, and Carlo Caruso, eds. *Petrarca e Boccaccio: Modelli letterari fra Medioevo e Umanesimo.* Alexandria: Edizioni dell'Orso, 2005.

Clagett, Marshall. "The Medieval Latin Translation from the Arabic of the *Elements* of Euclid, with Special Emphasis on the Versions of Adelard of Bath." *Isis* 44 (1953): 16–42.

Clubb, Louise George. "Boccaccio and the Boundaries of Love." *Italica* 37 (1960): 188–96.

Cocco, Ernesta. *Il "Filocolo" del Boccaccio e le sue fonti.* Naples: An. Chiurazzi & Figlio, 1935.

Coleman, William E. "The Knight's Tale." In *Sources and Analogues of the "Canterbury Tales,"* edited by Robert M. Correale and Mary Hamel, 2:87–247. Cambridge: D.S. Brewer, 2005.

Contini, Gianfranco. *Letteratura italiana delle origini.* Florence: Sansoni, 1970.

———. "Petrarca e le arti figurative." In *Francesco Petrarca Citizen of the World: Proceedings of the World Petrarch Congress, Washington, D.C., April 6–13, 1974*, edited by Giuseppe Billanovich, Umberto Bosco, and Paolo Sambin, 115–31. Padua: Antenore, 1980.

Cook, A. S. "Boccaccio, *Fiammetta*, Chap. 1, and Seneca, *Hyppolitus*, Act 1." *American Journal of Philology* 28 (1907): 200–204.

Cooper, Helen. *Pastoral: Medieval into Renaissance*. Totowa, NJ: Rowman and Littlefield, 1977.

Corazzini, Francesco. *Le lettere edite e inedite di messer Giovanni Boccaccio*. Florence: Sansoni, 1877.

Cornish, Alison. *Vernacular Translation in Dante's Italy: Illiterate Literature*. Cambridge: Cambridge University Press, 2011.

———. "When Illiterates Read: The Anxiety of Volgarizzamento." *Mediaevalia* 26 (2005): 59–98.

Costa, Gustavo. *La leggenda dei secoli d'oro nella letteratura italiana*. Bari: Laterza, 1972.

Costantini, Aldo Maria. "Studi sullo *Zibaldone Magliabechiano* I: Descrizione e analisi." *Studi sul Boccaccio* 7 (1973): 21–58.

———. "Studi sullo *Zibaldone Magliabechiano* II: Il florilegio senechiano." *Studi sul Boccaccio* 8 (1974): 79–126.

———. "Studi sullo *Zibaldone Magliabechiano* III: La polemica con fra Paolino da Venezia." *Studi sul Boccaccio* 10 (1975–76): 255–76.

———. "Tra chiose e postille dello *Zibaldone Magliabechiano*: Un catalogo e una chiave di lettura." In Picone and Cazalé Bérard, *Gli zibaldoni di Boccaccio*, 29–35.

Cottino-Jones, Marga, and Edward F. Tuttle, eds. *Boccaccio: Secoli di vita; Atti del Congresso Internazionale: Boccaccio 1975, Università di California, Los Angeles, 17–19 ottobre 1975*. Ravenna: Longo, 1977.

Coulter, Cornelia. "The Library of the Angevin Kings at Naples." *American Philological Association* 65 (1944): 141–55.

Cox, Virginia. *The Prodigious Muse: Women's Writing in Counter-Reformation Italy*. Baltimore: Johns Hopkins University Press, 2011.

———. *Women's Writing in Italy, 1400–1650*. Baltimore: Johns Hopkins University Press, 2008.

Crescini, Vincenzo. *Contributo agli studi sul Boccaccio con documenti inediti*. Turin: Loescher, 1887.

Cro, Stelio. "Classical Antiquity, America, and the Myth of the Noble Savage." In *The Classical Tradition and the Americas*, vol. 1, *European Images of the Americas and the Classical Tradition*, edited by Wolfgang Haase and Meyer Reinhold, pt. 1, 379–418. Berlin: W. de Gruyter, 2004.

Croce, Benedetto. *Poesia popolare and poesia d'arte*. Bari: Laterza, 1930.

Cursi, Marco. "Authorial Strategies and Manuscript Tradition: Boccaccio and the

Decameron's Early Diffusion." Talk presented at the conference "Boccaccio at 700: Medieval Contexts and Global Intertexts," Binghamton, New York, April 26–27, 2013.

———. *Il Decameron: Scritture, scriventi, lettori; Storia di un testo*. Rome: Viella, 2007.

———. Essay forthcoming in *Dentro l'officina del Boccaccio: Autografi dalla "Commedia" al "Decameron,"* edited by Sandro Bertelli and Davide Cappi. Vatican City: Biblioteca Apostolica Vaticana, 2013.

———. *La scrittura e i libri di Giovanni Boccaccio*. Rome: Viella, 2013.

Curtius, Ernst Robert. *European Literature and the Latin Middle Ages*. Translated by Willard R. Trask. New York: Harper, 1963.

———. "Theologische Poetik im italienischen Trecento." *Zeitschrift für Romanische Philologie* 60 (1940): 1–15.

Daniélou, Jean. *From Shadows to Reality: Studies in the Biblical Typology of the Fathers*. Translated by Wulstan Hibberd. Westminster, MD: Newman Press, 1960.

Daniels, Rhiannon. *Boccaccio and the Book: Production and Reading in Italy, 1340–1520*. London: Modern Humanities Research Association and Maney Publishing, 2009.

———. "Rethinking the Critical History of the *Decameron*: Boccaccio's Epistle XXII to Mainardo Cavalcanti." *Modern Language Review* 106 (2011): 423–47.

Da Rif, Bianca Maria. "La miscellanea laurenziana XXXIII 31." *Studi sul Boccaccio* 7 (1973): 59–124.

Davies, Jonathan. *Culture and Power: Tuscany and Its Universities, 1537–1609*. Leiden: Brill, 2009.

De Angelis, Luigi. "Il sepolcro del Boccaccio." *Nuovo Giornale de' Letterati* 11.24 (1825): 219–37.

"Il *Decameron* nella tradizione manoscritta: Boccaccio ed i suoi primi lettori, mercanti, monaci e lo stesso Petrarca; Una intervista a Marco Cursi." Il Centro culturale Gli Scritti, 9/13/2007. http://www. gliscritti.it/approf/2007/ conferenze/cursi290907.htm.

Degenhart, Bernhard, and Annegrit Schmitt. *Corpus der italienischen Zeichnungen 1300–1450*. Berlin: Mann, 1968–.

De la Mare, Albinia Catherine. *The Handwriting of Italian Humanists*. Oxford: Oxford University Press, 1973.

Delcorno, Carlo. "Note sui dantismi dell'*Elegia di madonna Fiammetta*." *Studi sul Boccaccio* 11 (1979): 251–94.

Delcorno Branca, Daniela. "'Cognominato prencipe Galeotto': Il sottotitolo del *Decameron*." *Studi sul Boccaccio* 23 (1995): 79–88.

———. "Il sottotitolo illustrato nel parigino it. 482." *Studi sul Boccaccio* 23 (1995): 79–88.

Della Torre, Arnaldo. *Storia dell'Accademia Platonica di Firenze.* Florence: Carnesecchi, 1902.

Del Vita, Alessandro. "Lettere di Don Vincenzo Borghini a Giorgio Vasari." *Il Vasari* 4.1–2 (1931): 79–88.

De Nolhac, Pierre. *Pétrarque et l'humanisme.* Paris: Librairie Honoré Champion, 1907.

De Novaes, Giuseppe. *Elementi della storia de' sommi pontefici da S. Pietro sino al felicemente regnante Pio Papa VII.* 16 vols. Siena: Rossi, 1802–15.

De Poveda, Giuseppe. *Del sepolcro di Mess. Giovanni Boccaccio e di varie sue memorie.* Colle: Pacini, 1827.

De Robertis, Domenico. "Nascita, tradizione e venture del cantare in ottava rima." In Picone and Predelli, *I cantari*, 9–24.

———. "Un nuovo carme del Boccaccio: L'epitaffio per Pino e Ciampi della Tosa." *Studi sul Boccaccio* 9 (1975–76): 43–101.

———. "Problemi di metodo nell'edizione dei cantari." In *Studi e problemi di critica testuale*, 119–38. Bologna: Commissione per i Testi di Lingua, 1961.

———. "La tradizione boccaccesca delle Canzoni di Dante." In *Giovanni Boccaccio editore ed interprete di Dante*, 5–13. Florence: Olschki, 1979.

De Sanctis, Francesco. *Storia della letteratura italiana.* Naples: Morano, 1870.

Desmond, Marilynn. "History and Fiction: The Narrativity and Historiography of the Matter of Troy." In *The Cambridge History of French Literature*, 139–44.

Di Benedetto, Filippo. "Considerazioni sullo *Zibaldone laurenziano* del Boccaccio e restauro testuale della prima redazione del 'Faunus.'" *Italia Medioevale e Umanistica* 14 (1971): 91–129.

———. "Presenza di testi minori negli Zibaldoni." In Picone and Cazalé Bérard, *Gli zibaldoni di Boccaccio*, 13–28.

Di Cesare, Michelina. "Il sapere geografico di Boccaccio tra tradizione e innovazione: *L'imago mundi* di Paolino Veneto e Pietro Vesconte." In Morosini, *Boccaccio geografo*, 67–88.

Di Girolamo, Costanzo, and Charmaine Lee. "Fonti." In Bragantini and Forni, *Lessico critico decameroniano*, 142–62.

Dionisotti, Carlo. *Geografia e storia della letteratura italiana.* Turin: Einaudi, 1967.

Di Pino, Guido. "Lettura del 'Teseida.'" *Italianistica* 8 (1979): 26–37.

———. *La polemica del Boccaccio.* Florence: Vallecchi, 1953.

Donato, Clorinda. "Nota su l'*Elegia di Madonna Fiammetta* e la possibilità di una triplice analisi psicoanalitica: Autore, personaggio, pubblico." *Carte Italiane*: A *Journal of Italian Studies* 3 (1980): 29–38.

Donato, Maria Monica. "'Veteres' e 'novi,' 'externi' e 'nostri': Gli artisti di Petrarca; Per una rilettura." In *Medioevo: Immagine e racconto; Atti del convegno internazionale di studi, Parma, 27–30 settembre 2000*, edited by Arturo Carlo Quintavalle, 433–55. Milan: Electa, 2003.

Dorini, Ugo. "Contributi alla biografia del Boccaccio." *Miscellanea Storica della Valdelsa* 22 (1914): 73–91.

Dotti, Ugo. *Vita del Petrarca*. Bari: Laterza, 1987.

Durling, Robert M. "Boccaccio on Interpretation: Guido's Escape (*Decameron* VI.9)." In *Dante, Petrarch, Boccaccio: Studies in the Italian Trecento in Honor of C. S. Singleton*, edited by Aldo S. Bernardo and Anthony L. Pellegrini, 273–304. Binghamton, NY: MRTS, 1983.

———. "A Long Day in the Sun: *Decameron* 8.7." In *Shakespeare's "Rough Magic": Renaissance Essays in Honor of C. L. Barber*, edited by Peter Erickson and Coppélia Kahn, 269–75. London: Associated University Presses, 1985.

Durling, Robert M., and Ronald L. Martinez. *Time and the Crystal: Studies in Dante's "Rime Petrose."* Berkeley: University of California Press, 1990.

Dutschke, Dennis. "Il libro miscellaneo: Problemi di metodo tra Boccaccio e Petrarca." In Picone and Cazalé Bérard, *Gli zibaldoni di Boccaccio*, 95–112.

Dyck, Andrew R. *A Commentary to Cicero's "De officiis."* Ann Arbor: University of Michigan Press, 1997.

Edmunds, Lowell. "A Note on Boccaccio's Sources for the Story of Oedipus in *De casibus illustrium virorum* and in the *Genealogie*." *Aevum* 56 (1982): 248–52.

Edwards, Robert R. "Medieval Literary Careers: The Theban Track." In *European Literary Careers: The Author from Antiquity to the Renaissance*, edited by Patrick Cheney and Frederick A. de Armas, 104–28. Toronto: University of Toronto Press, 2002.

Eisner, Martin. Review of Boccaccio, *Theseid of the Nuptials of Emilia (Teseida delle Nozze di Emilia)*, translated by Vincenzo Traversa. *Heliotropia* 5.1–2 (2008). http://www.brown.edu/Departments/Italian_Studies/heliotropia/05/eisner.pdf.

Encyclopedia of Italian Literary Studies. Edited by Gaetana Marrone. 2 vols. New York: Routledge, 2007.

Enenkel, Karl. "Modelling the Humanist: Petrarch's 'Letter to Posterity' and Boccaccio's Biography of the Poet Laureate." In *Modelling the Individual: Biography and Portrait in the Renaissance, with a Critical Edition of Petrarch's "Letter to Posterity,"* edited by Karl Enenkel, Betsy De Jong-Crane, and Peter Liebregts, 11–49. Amsterdam: Rodopi, 1998.

Faloci Pulignani, M. "L'arte tipografica in Foligno nel secolo XV." *La Bibliofilia* 2 (1900–1901): 23–35.

Farinelli, Franco. "L'immagine dell'Italia." In *Geografia politica delle regioni italiane*, edited by Pasquale Coppola, 33–59. Turin: Einaudi, 1997.

Fedi, Roberto. "Il grande freddo." In *Il mito e la rappresentazione del nord nella tradizione letteraria, Atti del Convegno di Padova, 23–25 ottobre 2006*, 219–56. Rome: Salerno, 2008.

———. *I poeti preferiscono le bionde: Chiome d'oro e letteratura*. Florence: Le Càriti, 2007.

————. "Il regno di Filostrato: Natura e struttura della giornata IV del *Decameron*." *Modern Language Notes* 102 (1987): 39–54.

Fengler, Christie K., and William A. Stephany. "The Visual Arts: A Basis for Dante's Imagery in *Purgatory* and *Paradise*." *Michigan Academician* 10 (1977): 127–41.

Feo, Michele. "Francesco Petrarca." In *Enciclopedia Dantesca*, 4:450–58. Rome: Istituto della Enciclopedia Italiana, 1943.

Fera, Vincenzo. *Antichi editori e lettori dell' "Africa."* Messina: Centro degli Studi Umanistici, 1984.

————. "Le cipolle di Certaldo e il disegno di Valchiusa." In *Petrarca nel tempo: Tradizione lettori e immagini delle opere; Catalogo della mostra, Arezzo, Sottochiesa di San Francesco, 22 novembre 2003–27 gennaio 2004*, edited by Michele Feo, 499–512. Pontedera: Bandecchi and Vivaldi, 2003.

————. *La revisione petrarchesca dell' "Africa."* Messina: Centro degli Studi Umanistici, 1984.

Fido, Franco. "Architettura." In Bragantini and Forni, *Lessico critico decameroniano*, 13–33.

————. *Il regime delle simmetrie imperfette: Studi sul "Decameron."* Milan: Franco Angeli, 1988.

Filosa, Elsa. "Intertestualità tra *Decameron* e *De mulieribus claris*: La tragica storia di Tisbe e Piramo." *Heliotropia* 3.1–2 (2005–6). www.heliotropia.org. Reprinted in *Tre studi sul "De mulieribus claris*,*"* 89–98.

————. *Tre studi sul "De mulieribus claris."* Milan: Edizioni Universitarie di Lettere Economia Diritto, 2012.

Fiorilla, Maurizio. *Marginalia figurati nei codici di Petrarca*. Florence: Olschki, 2005.

Fiorilla, Maurizio, and Patrizia Rafti. "Marginalia figurati e postille di incerta attribuzione in due autografi del Boccaccio (Firenze, Biblioteca Medicea Laurenziana, Plut. 54.32; Toledo, Biblioteca Capitular, ms. 104.6)." *Studi sul Boccaccio* 29 (2001): 199–213.

Folkerts, Menso. *The Development of Mathematics in Medieval Europe*. Aldershot, UK: Ashgate, 2006.

————. "The Importance of the Pseudo-Boethian *Geometria* during the Middle Ages." In *Boethius and the Liberal Arts*, edited by Michael Masi, 187–209. Bern: Peter Lang, 1981.

Foresti, Arnaldo. "L'egloga ottava di Giovanni Boccaccio." *Giornale Storico della Letteratura Italiana* 78 (1921): 325–43.

Forni, Pier Massimo. "La realizzazione narrativa in Boccaccio." In Picone and Cazalé Bérard, *Gli zibaldoni di Boccaccio*, 415–23.

Foscolo, Ugo. "Discorso storico sul testo del *Decamerone*." In Giovanni Boccaccio, *Decameron*, edited by Girolamo Tiraboschi, vii-xxxvi. Milan: Reina, 1849.

———. *Saggi e discorsi critici*. Edited by Cesare Foligno. Florence: Le Monnier, 1953.

Foster, Kenelm. *Petrarch: Poet and Humanist*. Edinburgh: Edinburgh University Press, 1984.

Franci, Raffaella. "L'insegnamento dell'aritmetica nel medioevo." In *Scienze matematiche e insegnamento in epoca medioevale: Atti del Convegno Internazionale di Studio, Chieti, 2–4 maggio, 1996*, edited by P. Freguglia, L. Pellegrini, and R. Paciocco, 112–51. Naples: Edizioni Scientifiche Italiane, 2000.

Franklin, Margaret. *Boccaccio's Heroines: Power and Virtue in Renaissance Society*. Aldershot, UK: Ashgate, 2006.

Frasso, Giuseppe, Giuseppe Velli, and Maurizio Vitale, eds. *Petrarca e la Lombardia: Atti del Convegno di Studi, Milano, 22–23 maggio 2003*. Padua: Antenore, 2005.

Freccero, Carla. "From Amazon to Court Lady: Generic Hybridization in Boccaccio's *Teseida*." *Comparative Literature Studies* 32 (1995): 226–43.

Freccero, John. *Dante: The Poetics of Conversion*. Edited by Rachel Jacoff. Cambridge, MA: Harvard University Press, 1986.

Freedman, Alan. "Il cavallo del Boccaccio: Fonte, struttura e funzione della metanovella di Madonna Oretta." *Studi sul Boccaccio* 9 (1975): 225–41.

Freedman, Luba. "A Note on Dante's Portrait in Boccaccio's *Vita*." *Studi sul Boccaccio* 15 (1985–86): 253–63.

Fukushima, Osamu. *An Etymological Dictionary for Reading Boccaccio's "Teseida."* Florence: Franco Cesati, 2011.

Gambera, Disa. "Women and Walls: Boccaccio's *Teseida* and the Edifice of Dante's Poetry." In Stillinger and Psaki, *Boccaccio and Feminist Criticism*, 39–68.

Gambin, Enrica. *Trivia nelle tre corone: I volti di Diana nelle opere di Dante, Petrarca, Boccaccio*. Padua: Il Poligrafo, 2009.

Garstad, Benjamin. "Belus in the 'Sacred History' of Euhemerus." *Classical Philology* 99 (2004): 246–57.

Gaspary, A. "Il supposto incendio dei libri del Boccaccio a S. Spirito." *Giornale Storico della Letteratura Italiana* 9 (1887): 457.

Gautier Dalché, Patrick. "L'oeuvre géographique du Cardinal Fillastre (d. 1428): Représentation du monde et perception de la carte à l'aube des découvertes." In *Humanisme et culture géographique à l'époque du Concile de Constance: Autour de Guillaume Fillastre; Actes du Colloque de l'Université de Reims, 18–19 novembre 1999*, edited by D. Marcotte, 293–355. Turnhout: Brepols, 2002.

Giamatti, A. Bartlett. *The Earthly Paradise and the Renaissance Epic*. Princeton, NJ: Princeton University Press, 1966.

Giani, Giulio. "Un antico pratese oggi dimenticato: Parente di Corrado da Prato." *Archivio Storico Pratese* 1 (1916–17): 149–56.

Giannetto, Nella. "Madonna Filippa tra *casus* e *controversiae.*" *Studi sul Boccaccio* 32 (2004): 81–100.

Gigli, Giuseppe. "Per l'interpretazione della *Fiammetta.*" *Giornale Storico della Valdelsa* 21 (1913): 68–71.

Gilbert, Creighton. "La devozione di Giovanni Boccaccio per gli artisti e l'arte." In Branca, *Boccaccio visualizzato*, 1:145–53.

———. *Poets Seeing Artists' Work: Instances in the Italian Renaissance.* Florence: Olschki, 1991.

Gilson, Simon. *Dante and the Renaissance.* Cambridge: Cambridge University Press, 2005.

———. "Notes on the Presence of Boccaccio in Cristoforo Landino's *Comento sopra la Comedia di Danthe Alighieri.*" *Italian Culture* 23 (2005): 1–30.

Ginsberg, Warren. *Chaucer's Italian Tradition.* Ann Arbor: University of Michigan Press, 2002.

Ginzburg, Carlo. "Dante's Epistle to Cangrande and Its Two Authors." *Proceedings of the British Academy* 139 (2006): 195–216.

Gittes, Tobias Foster. *Boccaccio's Naked Muse.* Toronto: University of Toronto Press, 2008.

Giusti, Eugenio. *Dall'amore cortese alla comprensione: Il viaggio ideologico di Giovanni Boccaccio dalla "Caccia di Diana" al "Decameron."* Milan: LED, 1999.

Goldmann, A. "Drei italienische Handschriftenkataloge s. XIII–XV." *Zentralblatt für Bibliothekwesen* 4 (1887): 137–55.

Gorni, Guglielmo. *Metrica e analisi letteraria.* Bologna: Il Mulino, 1993.

Gozzi, Maria. "Sulle fonti del *Filostrato.*" *Studi sul Boccaccio* 5 (1968): 123–209.

Grant, W. Leonard. *Neo-Latin Literature and the Pastoral.* Chapel Hill: University of North Carolina Press, 1965.

Greene, Thomas M. "Forms of Accommodation in the *Decameron.*" *Italica* 45 (1968): 297–313.

Greppi, Claudio. "Il dizionario geografico di Boccaccio: Luoghi e paesaggi nel *De Montibus.*" In Morosini, *Boccaccio geografico*, 89–102.

Grieve, Patricia E. *Floire and Blancheflor and the European Romance.* Cambridge: Cambridge University Press, 1997.

Gross, Karen Elizabeth. "Scholar Saints and Boccaccio's *Trattatelo in laude di Dante.*" *Modern Language Notes* 124 (2009): 66–85.

Grossvogel, Steven. *Ambiguity and Allusion in Boccaccio's "Filocolo."* Florence: Olschki, 1992.

Guerri, Domenico. *Il commento del Boccaccio a Dante: Limiti della sua autenticità e questioni critiche che n'emergono.* Bari: Laterza, 1926.

Gullace, Giovanni. "Medieval and Humanistic Perspectives in Boccaccio's Concept and Defense of Poetry." *Mediaevalia* 12 (1989 [for 1986]): 226–48.

Gutiérrez, David. "La biblioteca di Santo Spirito in Firenze nella metà del secolo XV." *Analecta Augustiniana* 23 (1962): 5–88.

Hagedorn, Suzanne C. *Abandoned Women: Rewriting the Classics in Dante, Boccaccio, & Chaucer*. Ann Arbor: University of Michigan Press, 2004.

Hainsworth, Peter. *The Essential Petrarch*. Indianapolis: Hackett, 2010.

Hankey, A. Teresa. "La *Genealogia deorum* di Paolo da Perugia." In Picone and Cazalé Bérard, *Gli zibaldoni di Boccaccio*, 81–94.

———. "Un nuovo codice delle 'Genealogie deorum' di Paolo da Perugia." *Studi sul Boccaccio* 18 (1989): 65–161.

Harrison, Robert P. *Gardens: An Essay on the Human Condition*. Chicago: University of Chicago Press, 2008.

Hart, Walter Morris. "The Lady in the Garden." *Modern Language Notes* 22 (1907): 241–42.

Hauvette, Henri. "Notes sur des manuscrits autographes de Boccace à la Bibliothèque Laurentienne." *Mélanges d'Archéologie* 14 (1894): 87–145. Reprinted in *Études sur Boccace (1894–1916)*, introduced by Carlo Pellegrini (Turin: Bottega di Erasmo, 1968), 87–146.

———. "Sulla cronologia delle egloghe latine del Boccaccio." *Giornale Storico della Letteratura Italiana* 28 (1896): 154–75.

Hawkins, Peter. *Dante's Testaments: Essays in Scriptural Imagination*. Stanford, CA: Stanford University Press, 1999.

Hecker, Oskar. *Boccaccio-funde: Stücke aus der bislang verschollenen Bibliothek des Dichters darunter von selner Hand geschriebenes Fremdes und Eigenes*. Braunschweig: George Westermann, 1902.

Henke, Robert. *Performance and Literature in the Commedia dell'Arte*. Cambridge: Cambridge University Press, 2002.

Heullant-Donat, Isabelle. "Boccaccio lecteur de Paolino da Venezia: Lectures discursives et critiques." In Picone and Cazalé Bérard, *Gli zibaldoni di Boccaccio*, 37–52.

Hijmans-Tromp, Irene, ed. *Vita e opere di Agnolo Torini*. Leiden: Universitaire Pers, 1957.

Hinds, Stephen "Landscape with Figures: Aesthetics of Place in the *Metamorphoses* and Its Tradition." In *The Cambridge Companion to Ovid*, edited by Philip Hardie, 122–49. Cambridge: Cambridge University Press, 2002.

Hollander, Robert. "Boccaccio, Ovid's *Ibis*, and the Satirical Tradition." In Picone and Cazalé Bérard, *Gli zibaldoni di Boccaccio*, 385–99.

———. "Boccaccio's Dante: Imitative Distance (*Decameron* I.1 and VI.10)." *Studi sul Boccaccio* 13 (1981–82): 169–98.

———. *Boccaccio's Dante and the Shaping Force of Satire*. Ann Arbor: University of Michigan Press, 1997.

———. *Boccaccio's Last Fiction: "Il Corbaccio."* Philadelphia: University of Pennsylvania Press, 1988.

———. *Boccaccio's Two Venuses.* New York: Columbia University Press, 1977.

———. *Dante's Epistle to Cangrande.* Ann Arbor: University of Michigan Press, 1993.

———. "Dante *Theologus-Poeta*." *Dante Studies* 94 (1976): 91–136.

———. "Due recenti contributi al dibattito sull'autenticità dell'*Epistola a Cangrande*." *Letteratura Italiana Antica* 10 (2009): 541–52.

———. "The Validity of Boccaccio's Self-Exegesis in His *Teseida*." *Medievalia et Humanistica* n.s., 8 (1977): 163–83.

Hortis, Attilio. *Cenni di Giovanni Boccacci intorno a Tito Livio.* Trieste: Lloyd Austro-Ungarico, 1887.

———. *Studij sulle opere latine del Boccaccio con particolar riguardo alla storia della erudizione nel medio evo e alle letterature straniere aggiuntavi la bibliografia delle edizioni.* Trieste: Libreria Julius Dase, 1879.

Houston, Jason M. *Building a Monument to Dante: Boccaccio as Dantista.* Toronto: University of Toronto Press, 2010.

Hubbard, Thomas K. *The Pipes of Pan: Intertextuality and Literary Filiation in the Pastoral Tradition from Theocritus to Milton.* Ann Arbor: University of Michigan Press, 1998.

Hughes, Ted. *Birthday Letters.* London: Faber, 1998.

Hult, David, ed. *Debate of the "Romance of the Rose."* Chicago: University of Chicago Press, 2010.

Huot, Sylvia. "Poetic Ambiguity and Reader Response in Boccaccio's *Amorosa visione*." *Modern Philology* 83 (1985): 109–22.

Hutton, Edward. *Giovanni Boccaccio: A Biographical Study.* New York: Lane, 1910.

Hyde, J. K. *Literacy and Its Uses: Studies on Late Medieval Italy.* Edited by Daniel Waley. New York: Manchester University Press, 1993.

Illiano, Antonio. "Per una rilettura della *Caccia di Diana*." *Italica* 61 (1984): 312–34.

Jennaro-MacLennan, Luis. "Boccaccio and the Epistle to Cangrande." In *The Trecento Commentaries on the "Divina Commedia" and the Epistle to Cangrande*, 105–23. Oxford: Clarendon Press, 1974.

Jolles, André. *I travestimenti della letteratura: Saggi critici e teorici (1897–1932).* Edited by Silvia Contarini. Milan: Mondadori, 2003.

Jordan, Constance. "Boccaccio's In-famous Women: Gender and Civic Virtue in the *De mulieribus claris*." In *Ambiguous Realities: Women in the Middle Ages and Renaissance*, edited by Carol Levin and Neanie Watson, 25–47. Detroit: Wayne State University Press, 1987.

———. *Renaissance Feminism: Literary Texts and Political Models.* Ithaca, NY: Cornell University Press, 1990.

Kahane, Henry, and Renée Kahane. "Akritas and Arcita: A Byzantine Source of Boccaccio's *Teseida*." *Speculum* 20 (1945): 415–25.

Kaske, Robert Earl. *Medieval Christian Literary Imagery: A Guide to Interpretation.* Toronto: University of Toronto Press, 1988.

Kegel-Brinkgreve, E. *The Echoing Woods: Bucolic and Pastoral from Theocritus to Wordsworth.* Amsterdam: Gieben, 1990.

Kelly, J. N. D. *Jerome: His Life, Writings, and Controversies.* London: Duckworth, 1975.

Kelly, Joan. *Women, History, & Theory: The Essays of Joan Kelly.* Chicago: University of Chicago Press, 1984.

Kelso, Ruth. *Doctrine for the Lady of the Renaissance.* Urbana: University of Illinois Press, 1956.

Kern, Edith. "The Gardens in the *Decameron cornice.*" *Publications of the Modern Language Association of America* 66 (1951): 505–23.

Kirkham, Victoria. *Fabulous Vernacular: Boccaccio's "Filocolo" and the Art of Medieval Fiction.* Ann Arbor: University of Michigan Press, 2001.

———. "L'immagine del Boccaccio nella memoria tardo-gotica e rinascimentale." In Branca, *Boccaccio visualizzato*, 1:85–143.

———. "Iohannes de Certaldo: La firma dell'autore." In Picone and Cazalé Bérard, *Gli zibaldoni di Boccaccio*, 455–68.

———. "John Badmouth: Fortunes of the Poet's Image." In "Boccaccio 1990: The Poet and His Renaissance Reception," edited by Kevin Brownlee and Victoria Kirkham, 355–76. Special issue, *Studi sul Boccaccio* 20 (1991–92).

———. "A Life's Work." In Kirkham and Maggi, *Petrarch*, 1–30.

———. "Maria a.k.a. Fiammetta: The Men behind the Woman." In Stillinger and Psaki, *Boccaccio and Feminist Criticism*, 13–27.

———. "Numerology and Allegory in Boccaccio's *Caccia di Diana.*" *Traditio* 34 (1978): 303–29.

———. "The Parallel Lives of Dante and Virgil." *Dante Studies* 110 (1992): 241–53.

———. "A Pedigree for Courtesy, or, How Boccaccio's Purser Cured a Miser." *Studi sul Boccaccio* 25 (1997): 213–38. Reprinted as "The Tale of Guglielmo Borsiere (*Dec.* I, 8)," in Weaver, *"Decameron" First Day in Perspective*, 179–206.

———. "Il poeta visualizzato." *Studi sul Boccaccio* 37 (2009): 39–77.

———. "Reckoning with Boccaccio's *Questioni d'Amore.*" *Modern Language Notes* 89 (1974): 47–59.

———. *The Sign of Reason in Boccaccio's Fiction.* Florence: Olschki, 1993.

———. "Le tre corone e l'iconografia del Boccaccio." In proceedings of "Convegno Internazionale: Boccaccio letterato," Firenze-Certaldo, 10–12 ottobre 2013. Forthcoming.

————. "Two New Translations: The Early Boccaccio in English Dress." *Italica* 70 (1993): 79–88.

Kirkham, Victoria, and Armando Maggi, eds. *Petrarch: A Critical Guide to the Complete Works*. Chicago: University of Chicago Press, 2009.

Kirkpatrick, Robin. "The Wake of the *Commedia*." 201–30. In Boitani ed., *Chaucer and the Italian Trecento*.

Klapisch-Zuber, Christiane. "The 'Cruel Mother': Maternity, Widowhood, and Dowry in Florence in the Fourteenth and Fifteenth Centuries." In *Women, Family, and Ritual in Renaissance Italy*, translated by Lydia Cochrane, 117–31. Chicago: University of Chicago Press, 1985.

————. "The Genesis of the Family Tree." *I Tatti Studies: Essays in the Renaissance* 4 (1991): 105–29.

Kleinhenz, Christopher. "Dante and the Tradition of Visual Arts in the Middle Ages." *Thought* 65 (1990): 17–26.

————. "A Nose for Art (*Purgatorio* VII): Notes on Dante's Iconographical Sense." *Italica* 52 (1975): 372–79.

Kolsky, Stephen D. "La costituzione di una nuova figura letteraria: Intorno al *De mulieribus claris* di Giovanni Boccaccio." *Testo* 25 (1993): 36–52.

————. *The Genealogy of Women: Studies in Boccaccio's "De mulieribus claris."* New York: Peter Lang, 2003.

————. *The Ghost of Boccaccio: Writings on Famous Women in Renaissance Italy*. Turnhout: Brepols, 2005.

König, Eberhard. "*Decameron*." In Branca, *Boccaccio visualizzato*, 3:205–14.

Krautter, Konrad. *Die Renaissance der Bukolik in der lateinischen Literatur de XIV. Jahrhunderts: Von Dante bis Petrarca*. Munich: Wilhelm Fink, 1983.

Labagnara, Silvia. *Il poema bucolico del Boccaccio*. Rome: L. Ambrosini, 1967.

Lambert, Ellen Z. *Placing Sorrow: A Study of the Pastoral Elegy Convention from Theocritus to Milton*. Chapel Hill: University of North Carolina Press, 1976.

Larner, John. "Tradition of Literary Biography in Boccaccio's *Life of Dante*." *Bulletin of John Rylands Library* 72 (1990): 107–17.

Lazzeri, Ghino. "Il testamento di Agnolo Torini." In *A Vittorio Cian: I suoi scolari dell'Università di Pisa (1900–1908)*, 35–44. Pisa: Mariotti, 1909.

Leuker, Tobias. "Due maestri del Boccaccio: Il pappagallo e la fenice nel ritratto allegorico della Napoli di Roberto d'Angiò (*Buccolicum carmen* V.28–68)." *Studi sul Boccaccio* 35 (2007): 147–55.

Levin, Harry. *The Myth of the Golden Age in the Renaissance*. Bloomington: Indiana University Press, 1969.

Lewis, Charlton T., and Charles Short. *A Latin Dictionary*. Oxford: Clarendon Press, 1969.

Librandi, Rita. "Corte e cavalleria della Napoli angioina nel *Teseida* del Boccaccio." *Medioevo Romanzo* 4 (1977): 53–72.

Limentani, Alberto. "Tendenze della prosa del Boccaccio ai margini del 'Teseida.'" *Giornale Storico della Letteratura Italiana* 135 (1958): 524–51.

Lippi Bigazzi, Vanna, ed. *Un volgarizzamento inedito di Valerio Massimo*. Florence: Accademia della Crusca, 1996.

Lorenzini, Simona. "Le corrispondenze bucoliche latine nel primo Umanesimo: Giovanni del Virgilio–Albertino Mussato e Giovanni Boccaccio–Checco di Meletto Rossi; Edizione critica, commento e introduzione, con un glossario della lingua bucolica di Dante, Petrarca e Boccaccio." Tesi di Dottorato in "Civiltà dell'Umanesimo e del Rinascimento," Istituto Nazionale di Studi sul Rinascimento — Università di Pisa, 2008.

———. *La corrispondenza bucolica di Giovanni Boccaccio e Checco di Meletto Rossi e l'egloga di Giovanni del Virgilio ad Albertino Mussato*. Florence: Olschki, 2009.

———. "Rassegna di studi sul Boccaccio bucolico." *Studi sul Boccaccio* 38 (2010): 153–65.

Lovejoy, Arthur O., and George Boas. *Primitivism and Related Ideas in Antiquity*. 1935. Reprint, Baltimore: Johns Hopkins University Press, 1997.

Lummus, David. "Boccaccio's Poetic Anthropology: Allegories of History in the *Genealogie deorum gentilium libri*." *Speculum* 87.3 (July 2012): 724–65.

Macri-Leone, Francesco. "Il Zibaldone boccaccesco della Magliabechiana." *Giornale Storico della Letteratura Italiana* 10 (1877): 1–41.

Maggi, Armando. "To Write as Another: The Testament." In Kirkham and Maggi, *Petrarch*, 333–46.

Maggini, Francesco. *I primi volgarizzamenti dai classici latini*. Florence: Le Monnier, 1952.

Maginnis, Hayden B. J. "Boccaccio: A Poet Making Pictures." *Source: Notes in the History of Art* 15.2 (Winter 1996): 1–7.

Manni, Domenico Maria. *Istoria del "Decamerone."* Florence: Antonio Ristori, 1742.

Manuel, Frank E., and Fritzie P. Manuel. *Utopian Thought in the Western World*. Cambridge, MA: Harvard University Press, 1979.

Marchesi, Concetto. "Di alcuni volgarizzamenti toscani in codici fiorentini." *Studj Romanzi* 5 (1907): 123–236.

———. *Scritti minori di filologia e di letteratura*. 2 vols. Florence: Olschki, 1978.

Marchesi, Simone. "Fra filologia e retorica: Petrarca e Boccaccio di fronte al nuovo Livio." *Annali d'Italianistica* 22 (2004): 361–74.

———. *Stratigrafie decameroniane*. Florence: Olschki, 2004.

Marcus, Millicent Joy. *An Allegory of Form: Literary Self-Consciousness in the "Decameron."* Saratoga, CA: ANMA Libri, 1979.

———. "Cross-Fertilizations: Folklore and Literature in *Decameron* 4.5." *Italica* 66 (1985): 383–98.

———. "Misogyny as Misreading: A Gloss on *Decameron* VIII, 7." *Stanford Italian Review* 2.1 (Spring 1984): 23–40.

———. "The Sweet New Style Reconsidered: A Gloss on the Tale of Cimone." *Italian Quarterly* 81 (1980): 5–16.

Martelli, Mario. "'Nemo tibi secundus': Nota a *Buccolicum carmen* I, 93–4." *Studi sul Boccaccio* 19 (1990): 93–101.

Martellotti, Guido. "Dalla tenzone al carme bucolico: Giovanni del Virgilio, Dante, Boccaccio." *Italia Medioevale e Umanistica* 7 (1964): 325–36.

———. *Dante e Boccaccio e altri scrittori dall'umanesimo al romanticismo.* Florence: Olschki, 1983.

———. "La riscoperta dello stile bucolico." In *Dante e la cultura veneta*, edited by Vittore Branca and Giorgio Padoan, 335–46. Florence: Olschki, 1966.

Marti, Mario. *Giovanni Boccaccio, Opere minori in volgare.* 4 vols. Milan: Rizzoli, 1958.

Martinez, Ronald L. "Apuleian Example and Misogynist Allegory in the Tale of Peronella (*Decameron* VII.2)." In Stillinger and Psaki, *Boccaccio and Feminist Criticism*, 201–16.

———. "Before the *Teseida*: Statius and Dante in Boccaccio's Epic." *Studi sul Boccaccio* 20 (1991): 205–19.

———. "The Tale of the Monk and His Abbot (I.4)." In Weaver, *"Decameron" First Day in Perspective*, 113–34.

Masséra, Aldo Francesco. "Di tre epistole metriche boccaccesche." *Giornale Dantesco* 30 (1927): 31–44.

———. "Rassegna critica di studi boccacceschi." *Giornale Storico della Letteratura Italiana* 65 (1915): 370–421.

———. "Il serventese Boccaccesco delle belle donne." *Miscellanea Storica della Valdelsa* 21 (1913): 55–67.

Mazza, Antonia. "L'inventario della 'parva libraria' di Santo Spirito e la biblioteca di Boccaccio." *Italia Medioevale e Umanistica* 9 (1966): 1–74.

Mazzacurati, Giancarlo. *All'ombra di Dioneo: Tipologie e percorsi della novella da Boccaccio a Bandello* Florence: La Nuova Italia, 1996.

Mazzetti, Martina. "Boccaccio disegnatore: Per un'idea di 'arte mobile.'" *Letteratura e arte* 10 (2012): 9–37. http://www.academia.edu/1897952/Boccaccio_disegnatore._Per_unidea_di_arte_mobile.

———. "Boccaccio e l'invenzione del libro illustrabile: Dal *Teseida* al *Decameron*." *Per Leggere* 21 (2011): 135–61.

———. "Giovanni Boccaccio novelliere disegnatore artista: Fare arte nella letteratura del Trecento." Tesi di Laurea, Università di Pisa, 2009.

Mazzoni, Francesco. "Moderni errori di trascrizione nelle epistole dantesche conservate nello *Zibaldone Laurenziano.*" In Picone and Cazalé Bérard, *Gli zibaldoni di Boccaccio*, 315–25.

Mazzotta, Giuseppe. "Boccaccio: The Mythographer of the City." In *Interpretation and Allegory: Antiquity to the Modern Period*, edited by Jon Whitman, 349–64. Leiden: Brill, 2000.

————. "Life of Dante." In *The Cambridge Companion to Dante*, edited by Rachel Jacoff, 1–13. 2nd ed. Cambridge: Cambridge University Press, 2007.

————. *The World at Play in Boccaccio's "Decameron."* Princeton, NJ: Princeton University Press, 1986.

McGregor, James. "Boccaccio's Athenian Theater: Form and Function of an Ancient Monument in *Teseida.*" *Modern Language Notes* 99 (1984): 1–42.

————. *The Image of Antiquity in Boccaccio's "Filocolo," "Filostrato," and "Teseida."* New York: Peter Lang, 1991.

————. *Shades of Aeneas: The Imitation of Vergil and the History of Paganism in Boccaccio's "Filostrato," "Filocolo," and "Teseida."* Athens: University of Georgia Press, 1991.

Mellinkoff, Ruth. *The Horned Moses in Medieval Art and Thought.* Berkeley: University of California Press, 1970.

Meneghetti, Maria Luisa. "Epico, romanzo, poema cavalleresca." 1: 697–761. In *Manuale di letteratura italiana: Storia per generi e problemi.* Edited by Franco Brioschi and Costanzo Di Girolamo. Turin: Bollati Boringhieri, 1993.

Mésoniat, Claudio. *Poetica theologia: La "Lucula Noctis" di Giovanni Dominici e le dispute letterarie tra '300 e '400.* Rome: Edizioni di Storia e Letteratura, 1984.

Migiel, Marilyn. "Beyond Seduction: A Reading of the Tale of Alibech and Rustico (*Decameron* III.10)." *Italica* 75 (1998): 161–77.

————. *A Rhetoric of the "Decameron."* Toronto: University of Toronto Press, 2003.

Minnis, A. J., and A. B. Scott, eds. *Medieval Literary Theory and Criticism c. 1100-c. 1375: The Commentary Tradition.* With the assistance of David Wallace. Oxford: Clarendon Press, 1988.

Minnis, Alastair J. *Medieval Theory of Authorship.* Philadelphia: University of Pennsylvania Press, 1988.

Mordenti, Raul. "Problemi e prospettive di un'edizione ipertestuale dello *Zibaldone Laurenziano.*" In Picone and Cazalé Bérard, *Gli zibaldoni di Boccaccio*, 361–77.

Morello, Giovanni. "Disegni marginali nei manoscritti di Giovanni Boccaccio." In Picone and Cazalé Bérard, *Gli zibaldoni di Boccaccio*, 161–77.

Moreni, Domenico. *Notizie istoriche dei contorni di Firenze.* 6 vols. Florence: Cambiagi, 1791–95.

Morosini, Roberta, ed. *Boccaccio geografo: Un viaggio nel Mediterraneo tra le citta, i giar-*

dini e . . . il "mondo" di Giovanni Boccaccio. With Andrea Cantile. Florence: Mauro Pagliai, 2010.

———. "Napoli: Spazi rappresentativi della memoria." In Morosini, *Boccaccio geografo*, 179–204.

———. *"Per difetto rintegrare": Una lettura del "Filocolo" di Giovanni Boccaccio*. Ravenna: Longo, 2004.

Mostra di manoscritti, documenti e edizioni: VI Centenario della morte di Giovanni Boccaccio, Firenze-Biblioteca Medicea Laurenziana, 22 maggio–31 agosto 1975. 2 vols. Certaldo: Comitato Promotore, 1975.

Murdoch, J. E. "The Medieval Euclid: Salient Aspects of the Translations of the *Elements* by Adelard of Bath and Campanus of Novara." *XIIe Congrès Internationale d'Histoire des Sciences, Colloques* 49–50 (1968): 67–94.

Murphy, James J. *Rhetoric in the Middle Ages: A History of Rhetorical Theory from Saint Augustine to the Renaissance*. Berkeley: University of California Press, 1974.

Muscetta, Carlo. *Giovanni Boccaccio*. Bari: Laterza, 1972.

Nardelli, Franca Petrucci. *"L'Amorosa visione* rivisitata." *Quaderni Medievali* 24 (1987): 57–75.

Neri, Ferdinando. *Storia e poesia*. Turin: Chiantore, 1944.

Noakes, Susan. *Timely Reading: Between Exegesis and Interpretation*. Ithaca, NY: Cornell University Press, 1988.

Novati, Francesco. Review of Goldmann, "Drei italienische Handschriftenkataloge s. XIII–XV." *Giornale Storico della Letteratura Italiana* 10 (1887): 413–25.

Olson, Glending. *Literature as Recreation in the Later Middle Ages*. Ithaca, NY: Cornell University Press, 1982.

Olson, Kristina Marie. "Resurrecting Dante's Florence: Figural Realism in the *Decameron* and the *Esposizioni*." *Modern Language Notes* 124 (2009): 45–65.

Optima hereditas: Sapienza giuridica romana e conoscenza dell'ecumene. Milan: Garzanti-Scheiwiller, 1993.

Orlandi, Tito. "Teoria e prassi della codifica dei manoscritti." In Picone and Cazalé Bérard, *Gli zibaldoni di Boccaccio*, 349–59.

Pabst, Walter. *Venus als Heilige und Furie in Boccaccios Fiammetta-Dichtung*. Krefeld: Scjerpe, 1958.

Pade, Marianne. "The Fragments of Theodontius in Boccaccio's *Genealogie deorum gentilium libri*." In *Avignon & Naples: Italy in France, France in Italy in the Fourteenth Century*, edited by Marianne Pade, Hannemarie Ragn Jensen, and Lene Waage Petersen, 149–82. Rome: "L'Erma" di Bretschneider, 1997.

Padoan, Giorgio. *Il Boccaccio, le Muse, il Parnaso e l'Arno*. Florence: Olschki, 1978.

———. "Giovanni Boccaccio." In *Enciclopedia Dantesca*, 1:645–60. Rome: Istituto della Enciclopedia Italiana, 1943.

————. "Navigatori italiani nell'oceano fra XIII e XV secolo." In *Optima hereditas*, 527–60.

————. "Petrarca, Boccaccio e la scoperta delle Canarie." *Italia Medioevale e Umanistica* 7 (1964): 263–77.

————. "Sulla genesi del *Decameron*." In Cottino-Jones and Tuttle, *Boccaccio*, 143–77. Reprinted in *Il Boccaccio le Muse il Parnaso e l'Arno*, 93–121.

————. *L'ultima opera di Giovanni Boccaccio: Le "Esposizioni sopra il Dante."* Padua: Cedam, 1959.

————. *Ultimi studi di filologia dantesca e boccacciana*. Edited by Aldo Maria Costantini. Ravenna: Longo, 2002.

Palma, Marco. *Bibliografia degli zibaldoni di Boccaccio (1976–1995)*. Rome: Viella, 1996.

Panizza, Letizia A. "Erasmus's *Encomium Matrimonii* of 1518 and the Italian Connections." In *Erasmus and the Renaissance Republic of Letters*, edited by Stephen Ryle. Turnhout: Brepols, 2013.

————. "Platonic Love on the Rocks: Castiglione Counter-Currents in Renaissance Italy." In *Laus Platonici Philosophi: Marsilio Ficino and His Influence*, edited by Stephen Clucas, Peter J. Forshaw, and Valery Rees, 199–226. Leiden: Brill, 2011.

————. "Plutarch's Camma: A Greek Literary Heroine's Adventures in Renaissance Italy." In *Italy and the Classical Tradition: Language, Thought, and Poetry, 1300–1600*, edited by Carlo Caruso and Andrew Laird, 101–17. London: Duckworth, 2009.

————. "Stoic Psychotherapy in the Middle Ages and Renaissance: Petrarch's *De Remediis*." In *Atoms, Pneuma, and Tranquility: Epicurean and Stoic Themes in European Thought*, edited by Margaret Osler, 39–65. Cambridge: Cambridge University Press, 1991. Reprinted in *The Erotics of Consolation: Desire and Distance in the Late Middle Ages*, edited by Catherine Léglu and Stephen Milner (New York: Palgrave Macmillan, 2008), 117–39.

Paolazzi, Carlo. "Petrarca, Boccaccio e il *Trattatello in laude di Dante*." *Studi Danteschi* 55 (1983): 165–249.

Paparelli, Gioacchino. "Due modi opposti di leggere Dante: Petrarca e Boccaccio." In Società Dantesca Italiana, *Giovanni Boccaccio*, 73–90.

Parodi, Ernesto. *Lingua e letteratura: Studi di teoria linguistica e di storia dell'italiano antico*. 2 vols. Venice: Pozza, 1957.

Pastore Stocchi, Manlio. "La cultura geografica dell'umanesimo." In *Optima hereditas*, 563–85.

————. "Il 'De Canaria' boccaccesco e un *locus deperditus* nel 'De Insulis' di Domenico Silvestri." *Rinascimento* 10 (1959): 143–56.

————. "Introduzione." In Boccaccio, *De montibus*, 1817–24.

————. *Tradizione medievale e gusto umanistico nel "De Montibus" del Boccaccio.* Padua: CEDAM, 1963.

Pasut, Francesca Rosa. "Boccaccio disegnatore." In *Catalogo della mostra: Biblioteca Medicea Laurenziana,* edited by Teresa De Robertis, Carla Maria Monti, Marco Petoletti, Giuliano Tanturli, and Stefano Zamponi. Florence: Mandragora, 2013.

————. Essay forthcoming in *Dentro l'officina del Boccaccio: Autografi dalla "Commedia" al "Decameron,"* edited by Sandro Bertelli and Davide Cappi, 000. Vatican City: Biblioteca Apostolica Vaticana, 2013.

Pecori, Luigi. *Storia della terra di San Gimignano.* Florence: Tipografia Galileiana, 1853.

Perella, Nicolas J. *Midday in Italian Literature.* Princeton, NJ: Princeton University Press, 1979.

————. "The World of Boccaccio's *Filocolo.*" *Publications of the Modern Language Association of America* 76 (1961): 330–39.

Pernicone, Vincenzo. "Il *Filostrato* di Giovanni Boccaccio." *Studi di Filologia Italiana* 2 (1929): 77–128.

————. "Girolamo Claricio collaboratore del Boccaccio." *Belfagor* 1 (1946): 474–86.

Pertusi, Agostino. *Leonzio Pilato fra Petrarca e Boccaccio: Le sue versioni omeriche negli autografi di Venezia e la cultura greca del primo umanesimo.* Venice: Istituto per la Collaborazione Culturale, 1964.

Perugi, Maurizio. "Chiose gallo-romanze alle *Eroidi*: Un manuale per la formazione letteraria del Boccaccio." *Studi di Filologia Italiana* 47 (1989): 101–48.

Petoletti, Marco. "Il Marziale autografo di Giovanni Boccaccio." *Italia Medioevale e Umanistica* 46 (2005): 35–55.

Petrucci, Armando. "Il ms. Berlinese Hamiltoniano 90: Note codicologiche e paleografiche." In Giovanni Boccaccio, *Decameron: Edizione diplomatico-interpretativa dell'autografo Hamilton 90.* Ed. Charles S. Singleton. 647–61. Baltimore: Johns Hopkins University Press, 1974.

————. *Breve storia della scrittura latina.* Rome: Bugatto Libri, 1992.

————. "Il libro d'autore." In *Letteratura italiana,* vol. 2, *Produzione e consumo,* edited by Alberto Asor Rosa, 499–524. Turin: Einaudi, 1983.

————. "Minuta, autografo, libro d'autore." In *Il libro e il testo: Atti del Convegno Internazionale d'Urbino (20–23 settembre 1982),* edited by C. Questa e R. Raffaelli, 397–414. Urbino: Università degli Studi di Urbino, 1984.

Piacentini, Angelo. "La vipera dei Visconti e il leone di Firenze: Per un esametro attribuito al Boccaccio." *Studi sul Boccaccio* 38 (2010): 145–52.

Picone, Michelangelo, ed. *Autori e lettori di Boccaccio: Atti del Convegno internazionale di Certaldo (20–22 settembre 2001).* Florence: Franco Cesati Editore, 2002.

————. *Boccaccio e la codificazione della novella: Letture del "Decameron."* Ravenna: Longo, 2008.

————. "La *Comedia Lidie* dallo Zibaldone al *Decameron.*" In Picone and Cazalé Bérard, *Gli zibaldoni di Boccaccio,* 401–23.

————. "Il *Decamerone* come macrotesto: Il problema della cornice." In Picone and Mesirca, *Introduzione al "Decameron,"* 9–34.

————. "The Tale of Bergamino (I.7)." In Weaver, *"Decameron" First Day in Perspective,* 160–78.

————. "Tipologie culturali: Da Dante a Boccaccio." *Strumenti Critici* 10 (1976): 263–74.

Picone, Michelangelo, and Maria Bendinelli Predelli, eds. *I cantari: Struttura e tradizione.* Florence: Olschki, 1984.

Picone, Michelangelo, and Claude Cazalé Bérard, eds. *Gli zibaldoni di Boccaccio: Memoria, scrittura, riscrittura.* Florence: Franco Cesati, 1998.

Picone, Michelangelo, and Margherita Mesirca, eds. *Introduzione al "Decameron."* Florence: Franco Cesati, 2004.

Pieri, Marzia. "La pastorale." In Brioschi and Di Girolamo, *Manuale di letteratura italiana,* 1:273–92.

Pomaro, Gabriella. "Memoria della scrittura e scrittura della memoria: A proposito dello Zibaldone Magliabechiano." In Picone and Cazalé Bérard, *Gli zibaldoni di Boccaccio,* 259–82.

Poole, Gordon. "Boccaccio's *Caccia di Diana.*" *Canadian Journal of Italian Studies* 5 (1982): 149–56.

Porcelli, Bruno. "Strutture e forme narrative nel *Filocolo.*" *Studi sul Boccaccio* 21 (1993): 207–33.

————. "Sull'unità compositiva del *Ninfale Fiesolano.*" In *Dante maggiore e Boccaccio minore,* 160–73. Pisa: Giardini, 1987.

Porta Casucci, Emanuela. "Le paci fra privati nelle parrocchie fiorentine di San Felice in Piazza e San Frediano: Un regesto per gli anni 1335–1365." *Annali di Storia di Firenze* 4 (2009): 195–241.

Potter, Joy Hambuechen. *Five Frames for the "Decameron": Communicative and Social Systems in the Cornice.* Princeton, NJ: Princeton University Press, 1982.

Psaki, Regina. "The Play of Genre and Voicing in Boccaccio's *Corbaccio.*" *Italiana* 5 (1993): 41–54.

Quaglio, Antonio Enzo. "Boccaccio e Lucano: Una concordanza e una fonte dal *Filocolo* all'*Amorosa visione.*" *Cultura Neolatina* 23 (1963): 153–71.

————. *Scienza e mito nel Boccaccio.* Padua: Liviana, 1967.

————. "Tra fonti e testo del *Filocolo.*" *Giornale Storico della Letteratura Italiana* 139 (1962): 321–69, 513–40; 140 (1963): 321–63, 489–551.

————. "Valerio Massimo e il *Filocolo* di Giovanni Boccaccio." *Cultura Neolatina* 20 (1960): 45–77.

Rada, Paola. *Cantari tratti dal "Decameron."* Pisa: Maria Pacini Fazzi, 2009.

Rafti, Patrizia. "Riflessioni sull'*usus distinguendi* del Boccaccio negli Zibaldoni." In Picone and Cazalé Bérard, *Gli zibaldoni di Boccaccio*, 283–306.

Raimondi, Ezio. "Il Claricio: Metodo di un filologo umanista." *Convivium* 17 (1948): 108–34, 258–311, 436–59.

————. *Il Claricio: Metodo di un filologo umanista.* Edited by Marco Veglia. Bologna: Bononia University Press, 2009.

Rajna, Pio. "Il cantare dei cantari e il servenstese del maestro di tutti l'arti." *Zeitschrift für romanische Philologie* 2 (1878): 220–54, 419–37.

————. "Le questioni d'amore nel *Filocolo*." *Archivum Romanicum* 31 (1902): 28–81.

Rano, Balbino. "El monasterio de Santa María del Santo Sepulcro en Campora (Florencia) y la fundación de la Orden de San Jerónimo." *Yermo* 11 (1973): 41–68.

Rastelli, Dario. "Le fonti autobiografiche nell'*Elegia di madonna Fiammetta*." *Humanitas* 3 (1948): 790–802.

————. "La modernità della *Fiammetta*." *Convivium* n.s., 1 (1947): 703–15.

Reale Archivio di Stato in Siena. *La sala della mostra e il Museo delle Tavolette Dipinte della Biccherina e della Gabella.* Siena: Lazzeri, 1911.

Repetti, Emanuele. *Dizionario geografico fisico storico della Toscana.* 5 vols. Florence: Tofani, 1833–43.

Resta, Gianvito. *I classici nel medioevo e nell'umanesimo.* Genoa: Istituto di Filologia Classica e Medievale, 1975.

Ricci, Pier Giorgio. "Dubbi gravi intorno al *Ninfale fiesolano*." *Studi sul Boccaccio* 6 (1971): 109–24. Reprinted in Ricci, *Studi sulla vita e le opere del Boccaccio*, 13–28.

————. "Le due redazioni del *De Casibus*." *Rinascimento* 13 (1962): 3–29.

————. "Per la dedica e la datazione del *Filostrato*." *Studi sul Boccaccio* 1 (1963): 333–47.

————. *Studi sulla vita e le opere del Boccaccio.* Milan: Ricciardi, 1985.

————. "Le tre redazioni del *Trattatello in laude di Dante*." *Studi sul Boccaccio* 8 (1974): 197–214.

Richa, Giuseppe. *Notizie istoriche delle chiese Fiorentine divise ne' suoi quartieri.* 10 vols. Florence: Viviani, 1754–62.

Richardson, Brian. *Print Culture in Renaissance Italy: The Editor and the Vernacular Text, 1470–1600.* Cambridge: Cambridge University Press, 1994.

Riva, Massimo. "*Hereos/Eleos*: L'ambivalente terapia del male d'amore nel libro chiamato *Decameron* cognominato *Prencipe Galeotto*." *Italian Quarterly* 38 (2000): 69–106.

Rizzi, Fortunato. *Francesco Petrarca e il decennio parmense (1341–1351)*. Turin: Paravia, 1934.

Ronconi, Giorgio. *Le origini delle dispute umanistiche sulla poesia (Mussato e Petrarca)*. Rome: Bulzoni, 1976.

Rosellini, Ippolito. "Della casa di Giovanni Boccaccio." *Antologia* 59 (1825): 86–92.

Rossi, Aldo. *Il "Decameron": Pratiche testuali e interpretative*. Bologna: Cappelli, 1982.

Rubin, Patricia. "The Seductions of Antiquity." In *Manifestations of Venus: Art and Sexuality*, edited by Caroline Arscott and Katie Scott, 24–38. Manchester: Manchester University Press, 2002.

Ruhe, Doris. "Boccace astronomien?" In Picone and Cazalé Bérard, *Gli zibaldoni di Boccaccio*, 65–79.

Sabatini, Francesco. *Napoli angioina: Cultura e società*. Naples: Edizioni Scientifiche Italiane, 1975.

Sabbadini, Remigio. *Le scoperte dei codici latini e greci ne' secoli XIV e XV*. 2 vols. Florence: Sansoni, 1905.

Samaran, Charles. "Pierre Bersuire: La traduction française de Tite-Live." *Histoire Littéraire de la France* 39 (1962): 358–414.

Sandal, Ennio, ed. *Dante e Boccaccio: Lectura Dantis Scaligera, 2004–2005, in memoria di Vittore Branca*. Padua: Antenore, 2006.

Santagata, Marco. *Per moderne carte: La biblioteca volgare di Petrarca*. Bologna: Il Mulino, 1990.

Sasso, Luigi. "La carne del pavone." *Reinardus: Yearbook of the International Reynard Society* 4 (1991): 185–91.

Savino, Giancarlo. "Un pioniere dell'autografia boccaccesca." In Picone and Cazalé Bérard, *Gli zibaldoni di Boccaccio*, 333–48.

Scaglione, Aldo D. *Nature and Love in the Late Middle Ages: An Essay on the Cultural Context of the "Decameron."* Berkeley: University of California Press, 1963.

———. "A Note on Montaigne's *Des Cannibales* and the Humanist Tradition." In *First Images of America: The Impact of the New World on the Old*, edited by Fredi Chiappelli with Michael J. B. Allen and Robert L. Benson, 1:63–70. Berkeley: University of California Press, 1976.

Segre, Cesare. *Semiotica filologica: Testi e modelli culturali*. Turin: Einaudi, 1979.

———. *Le strutture e il tempo*. Turin: Einaudi, 1974.

———. "Strutture e registri nella *Fiammetta*." *Strumenti Critici* 6 (1972): 133–62. Reprinted in Segre, *Le strutture e il tempo*, 87–115.

———. *Volgarizzamenti del Due e Trecento*. Turin: UTET, 1964.

Serafini-Sauli, Judith Powers. *Giovanni Boccaccio*. Boston: Twayne, 1982.

Sherberg, Michael. *The Governance of Friendship: Law and Gender in the "Decameron."* Columbus: Ohio State University Press, 2011.

Sherman, William H. *Used Books: Marking Readers in Renaissance England*. Philadelphia: University of Pennsylvania Press, 2009.

Silvestris, Bernardus. *The Commentary on the First Six Books of the "Aeneid" Commonly Attributed to Bernardus Silvestris*. Edited by Julian Ward Jones and Elizabeth Frances Jones. Lincoln: University of Nebraska Press, 1977.

Singleton, Charles. *An Essay on the "Vita nuova."* Baltimore: Johns Hopkins University Press, 1949.

Sinicropi, Giovanni. "Il segno linguistico del *Decameron.*" *Studi sul Boccaccio* 9 (1975–76): 169–224.

Smarr, Janet Levarie. "Boccaccio and the Choice of Hercules." *Modern Language Notes* 92 (1977): 146–52.

———. *Boccaccio and Fiammetta: The Narrator as Lover*. Urbana: University of Illinois Press, 1986.

———. "Boccaccio and Renaissance Women Writers." *Studi sul Boccaccio* 20 (1991–92): 279–97.

———. "Boccaccio and the Stars: Astrology in the 'Teseida.'" *Traditio* 35 (1979): 303–32.

———. "Boccaccio pastorale tra Dante e Petrarca." In Picone, *Autori e lettori di Boccaccio*, 237–54.

———. "Boccaccio's *Filocolo*: Romance, Epic, Allegory." *Forum Italicum* 12.1 (1978): 26–43.

———. "Symmetry and Balance in the *Decameron.*" *Mediaevalia* 2 (1976): 160–87.

Società Dantesca Italiana. *Giovanni Boccaccio editore e interprete di Dante*. Florence: Olschki, 1979.

Stewart, Pamela. "La novella di madonna Oretta e le due parti del *Decameron.*" In *Retorica e mimica nel "Decameron" e nella commedia del Cinquecento*, 19–38. Florence: Olschki, 1986.

Stillinger, Thomas C. *The Song of Troilus: Lyric Authority in the Medieval Book*. Philadelphia: University of Pennsylvania Press, 1992.

Stillinger, Thomas C., and F. Regina Psaki, eds. *Boccaccio and Feminist Criticism*. Chapel Hill, NC: Annali d'Italianistica, 2006.

Suitner, Franco, ed. *Dionigi da Borgo Sansepolcro fra Petrarca e Boccaccio: Atti del Convegno di Studi, Sansepolcro, February 11–12, 2000*. Città di Castello: Petruzzi, 2001.

———. "Sullo stile delle 'Rime' e sulle polemiche letterarie riflesse in alcuni sonetti." *Studi sul Boccaccio* 12 (1980): 95–128.

Surdich, Luigi. *Boccaccio*. Bari: Laterza, 2001.

———. *La cornice d'amore: Studi sul Boccaccio*. Pisa: ETS, 1987.

———. "La memoria di Dante nel *Decameron*: Qualche riscontro." *Letteratura Italiana Antica* 7 (2006): 325–40.

Symonds, John Addington. *Italian Literature.* Vol 1, *Renaissance in Italy.* New York: Henry Holt, 1881.

Tanturli, Giuliano. "Volgarizzamenti e ricostruzione dell'antico: I casi della terza e quarta Deca di Livio e di Valerio Massimo, la parte del Boccaccio (a proposito di un'attribuzione)." *Studi Medievali* 27 (1986): 811–88.

Tordi, Domenico. *Gl'inventari dell'eredità di Iacopo Boccaccio.* Orvieto: Rubeca e Scaletti, 1923.

Torini, Agnolo. *Brieve meditazione sui beneficii di Dio.* Edited by Francesco Zambrini. Bologna: Romagnoli, 1862.

Torraca, Francesco. "Giovanni Boccaccio a Napoli (1326–1339)." *Rassegna Critica della Letteratura Italiana* 21 (1916): 1–80.

———. *Giovanni Boccaccio a Napoli, 1326–1339.* Naples: L. Pierro e Figlio, 1915.

Tournoy, Gilbert, ed. *Boccaccio in Europe.* Louvain: Louvain University Press, 1977.

Traversari, Guido. *Le lettere autografe di Giovanni Boccaccio del codice laurenziano XXIX, 8.* Castelfiorentino: Società Storica della Valdelsa, 1905.

Trovato, Paolo. *Con ogni diligenza corretto: La stampa e le revisioni editoriali dei testi letterari italiani (1470–1570).* Bologna: Il Mulino, 1991.

———. *Dante in Petrarca: Per un inventario dei dantismi nei "Rerum vulgarium fragmenta."* Florence: Olschki, 1979.

Tufano, Ilaria. *"Quel dolce canto": Letture tematiche delle "Rime" del Boccaccio.* Florence: Cesati, 2006.

Ulivi, Elisabetta. "Le scuole d'abaco e l'insegnamento della matematica a Firenze nei secoli XIII–XVI." In *Scienze matematiche e insegnamento in epoca medioevale: Atti del Convegno Internazionale di Studio, Chieti, 2–4 maggio, 1996,* edited by P. Freguglia, L. Pellegrini, and R. Paciocco, 87–110. Naples: Edizioni Scientifiche Italiane, 2000.

Ullman, Berthold Louis. "Geometry in the Medieval Quadrivium." In *Studi di Bibliografia e di Storia in Onore di Tammaro De Marinis,* edited Romeo de Maio, 4:263–85. Amsterdam: Van Housden, 1964.

———. *The Public Library of Renaissance Florence: Niccolò Niccoli, Cosimo de' Medici, and the Library of San Marco.* Padua: Antenore, 1972.

Usher, Jonathan. "An Autobiographical Phaethon: Boccaccio's *Allegoria Mitologica.*" In *Petrarca e Boccaccio: Modelli letterari fra Medioevo e Umanesimo,* edited by Annalisa Cipollone and Carlo Caruso, 49–89. Alexandria: Edizioni dell'Orso, 2005.

———. "Boccaccio on Readers and Reading." *Heliotropia* 1.1 (2003). www.heliotropia.org.

———. "Desultorietà nella novella portante di Madonna Oretta (*Decameron* VI.1) e altri citazioni apuleiane nel Boccaccio." *Studi sul Boccaccio* 29 (2001): 67–103.

———. "Industria e acquisto erotico: La terza giornata." In Picone and Mesirca, *Introduzione al "Decameron,"* 99–113.

———. "Ischiro donatore di forti archi (*Buccolicum carmen* XIV, 129)." *Studi sul Boccaccio* 36 (2008): 111–15.

———. "*Magna pars abest*: A Borrowed *sententia* in Boccaccio's *De casibus*." *Studi sul Boccaccio* 21 (1993): 235–42.

———. "A Quotation from the *Culex* in Boccaccio's *De casibus*." *Modern Language Review* 97 (2002): 312–23.

———. "Le rubriche del *Decameron*." *Medioevo Romanzo* 10 (1985): 392–418.

———. "A 'ser' Cepparello, Constructed from Dante Fragments (*Decameron* I.1)." *The Italianist* 23 (2003): 181–93.

———. "'Sesto tra cotanto senno' and *appetentia primi loci*: Boccaccio, Petrarch, and Dante's Poetic Hierarchy." *Studi sul Boccaccio* 35 (2007): 157–98.

Vandelli, Giuseppe. "Un autografo della 'Teseide' (*Laurenziana, Doni e Acquisti, 305*)." *Studi di Filologia Italiana* 2 (1929): 5–76.

———. "Lo Zibaldone Magliabechiano è veramente autografo del Boccaccio." *Studi di Filologia Italiana* 1 (1927): 69–86.

Van Egmond, Warren. "The Commercial Revolution and the Beginnings of Western Mathematics in Renaissance Florence, 1300–1500." PhD diss., Indiana University, 1976.

———. "New Light on Paolo dell'Abbaco." *Annali dell'Istituto e Museo di Storia della Scienza di Firenze* (1977): 3–21.

———. *Practical Mathematics in the Italian Renaissance: A Catalog of Italian Abbacus Manuscripts and Printing Books to 1600*. Supplement to Annali dell'Istituto e Museo di Storia della Scienza (1980), fasc. 1, monograph 4. Florence: Istituto e Museo di Storia della Scienza, 1980.

Vecchi Galli, Paola. "Dante e Petrarca: Scrivere il padre." *Studi e Problemi di Critica Testuale* 79 (2009): 57–82.

Veglia, Marco. "La filologia di Zadig." *Ecdotica* 4 (2007): 134–57. Revised for the introduction to Raimondi, *Il Claricio*.

———. *"La vita lieta": Una lettura del "Decameron."* Ravenna: Longo, 2000.

Velli, Giuseppe. "*L'Ameto* e la pastorale: Il significato della forma." In Cottino-Jones and Tuttle, *Boccaccio*, 67–80. Reprinted in *Petrarca e Boccaccio*, 195–208.

———. "A proposito di una recente edizione del 'Buccolicum carmen' del Boccaccio." *Modern Language Notes* 105 (1990): 33–49.

———. "Il *De Vita et moribus domini Francisci Petracchi de Florentia* del Boccaccio e la biografia del Petrarca." *Modern Language Notes* 102 (1987): 32–38.

———. "Petrarca e Boccaccio: L'incontro milanese." In *Petrarca e la Lombardia*, edited by Giuseppe Frasso, Giuseppe Velli, and Maurizio Vitale, 145–64. Padua: Antenore, 2005

————. *Petrarca e Boccaccio: Tradizione—memoria—scrittura.* Padua: Antenore, 1995.

————. "Sull' 'Elegia di Costanza.'" *Studi sul Boccaccio* 4 (1967): 241–54. Reprinted in *Petrarca e Boccaccio*, 118–32.

————. "'Tityrus redivivus': The Rebirth of Vergilian Pastoral from Dante to Sannazzaro (and Tasso)." In *The Western Pennsylvania Symposium on World Literatures, Selected Proceedings, 1974–1991: A Retrospective*, edited by Carla E. Lucente, 107–18. Greensburg, PA: Eadmer, 1992. Also in *Forma e parola: Studi in memoria di Fredi Chiappelli*, edited by Dennis J. Dutschke et al. (Rome: Bulzoni, 1992), 67–79.

Verlinden, Charles. "Lanzarotto Malocello et la découverte portugaise des Canaries." *Revue Belge de Philologie et d'Histoire* 36 (1958): 1173–1209.

Vio, Giovanni. "Chiose e riscritture apuleiane." *Studi sul Boccaccio* 20 (1991–92): 139–65.

Vitale, Maurizio, and Vittore Branca. *Il capolavoro del Boccaccio e due diverse redazioni.* 2 vols. Venice: Istituto Veneto di Scienze, Lettere ed Arti, 2002.

Vittorini, Domenico. Review of Benedetto Croce, *Poesia popolare e poesia d'arte. Italica* 12 (1935): 139–41.

Volpe, Alessandro. "Boccaccio illustratore e illustrato." *Intersezioni* 31.2 (2011): 287–300.

Wack, Mary F. *Love Sickness in the Middle Ages: The Viaticum and Its Commentators.* Philadelphia: University of Pennsylvania Press, 1990.

Wallace, David. *Boccaccio's "Decameron."* Cambridge: Cambridge University Press, 1991.

————. *Chaucer and the Early Writings of Boccaccio.* Woodbridge, UK: D.S. Brewer, 1985.

————. *Chaucerian Polity: Absolutist Lineages and Associational Forms in England and Italy.* Stanford, CA: Stanford University Press, 1997.

————. "Love between Men, Griselda, and Farewell to Letters (*Rerum Senilium Libri*)." In Kirkham and Maggi ed., *Petrarch.* 321–30.

————. *Premodern Places: Calais to Surinam, Chaucer to Aphra Behn.* Malden, MA: Blackwell Publishing, 2004.

Watson, Paul F. "The Cement of Fiction: Giovanni Boccaccio and the Painters of Florence." *Modern Language Notes* 99 (1984): 43–64.

————. "Gathering of Artists: The Illustrations of a *Decameron* of 1427." *TEXT: Transactions of the Society for Textual Scholarship* 1 (1981): 147–55.

Watson, Paul F., and Victoria Kirkham. "Amore e virtù: Two Salvers Depicting Boccaccio's *Comedia delle ninfe fiorentine* in the Metropolitan Museum." *Metropolitan Museum Journal* 10 (1975): 35–50.

Weaver, Elissa B., ed. *The "Decameron" First Day in Perspective.* Toronto: University of Toronto Press, 2004.

West, M. L. "Stesichorus Redivivus." *Zeitschrift für Papyrologie und Epigraphik* 4 (1969): 135–49.

Wetherbee, Winthrop. "History and Romance in Boccaccio's *Teseida*." *Studi sul Boccaccio* 20 (1991): 173–84.

Whitfield, J. H. "Boccaccio and Fiammetta in the *Teseide*." *Modern Language Review* 33 (1938): 22–30.

Wilkins, Ernest Hatch. "Boccaccio's Early Tributes to Petrarch." *Speculum* 38 (1963): 79–87.

———. *Life of Petrarch*. Chicago: University of Chicago Press, 1961.

———. *Petrarch's Later Years*. Cambridge: The Medieval Academy of America, 1959.

———. *The University of Chicago Manuscript of the "Genealogia Deorum Gentilium" of Boccaccio*. Chicago: University of Chicago Press, 1927.

Williams, Robert. "Boccaccio's Altarpiece." *Studi sul Boccaccio* 19 (1990): 229–40.

Witt, Ronald G. "The Arts of Letter-Writing." In Minnis and Johnson, *The Cambridge History of Literary Criticism: The Middle Ages*, 68–83.

Zaccaria, Vittorio. "Ancora per il testo delle 'Genealogie deorum gentilium.'" *Studi sul Boccaccio* 21 (1993): 243–73.

———. *Boccaccio narratore, storico, moralista e mitografo*. Florence: Olschki, 2001.

———. "La difesa della poesia nelle *Genealogie* del Boccaccio." *Lettere Italiane* 38 (1986): 281–311.

———. "Le due redazioni del *De casibus*." *Studi sul Boccaccio* 10 (1977–78): 1–26.

———. "Le fasi redazionali del *De mulieribus claris*." *Studi sul Boccaccio* 1 (1963): 252–332.

———. "Per il testo delle 'Genealogie deorum gentilium.'" *Studi sul Boccaccio* 16 (1987): 179–240.

Zago, Esther. "Women, Medicine, and the Law in Boccaccio's *Decameron*." In *Women Healers and Physicians: Climbing the Long Hill*. Edited by Lilian Furst. 64–78. Lexington: University Press of Kentucky, 1997.

Zampieri, Adriana. "Una primitiva redazione del volgarizzamento di Valerio Massimo." *Studi sul Boccaccio* 10 (1977–78): 21–41.

Zamponi, Stefano, Martina Pantarotto, and Antonella Tomiello. "Stratigrafia dello *Zibaldone* e della *Miscellanea Laurenziana*." In Picone and Cazalé Bérard, *Gli zibaldoni di Boccaccio*, 181–258.

Zumbini, Bonaventura. "Le egloghe del Boccaccio." *Giornale Storico della Letteratura Italiana* 7 (1886): 94–152.

CONTRIBUTORS

Susanna Barsella is associate professor of Italian in the Department of Modern Languages and Literatures and the Center for Medieval Studies at Fordham University. With Italian medieval literature and early humanism in the light of continuities from antiquity to the Middle Ages as her main area of research, she has published on Dante, Petrarch, Boccaccio, and Michelangelo. Her work on the modern period includes articles on Pirandello, Gadda, and twentieth-century poetry. She serves as treasurer of the American Boccaccio Association. She is the author of *In the Light of the Angels: Angelology and Cosmology in Dante's "Divina Commedia"* (2010) and coeditor of *The Humanist Workshop: Essays in Honor of Salvatore Camporeale* (2012).

Todd Boli, an independent scholar living in Framingham, Massachusetts, has taught Italian at Columbia University, the University of Florida, Tufts University, and Regis College. A graduate of Harvard College, he holds a doctorate in Italian from Columbia University. He has been a Fulbright Scholar and Austin Oldrini Traveling Fellow and has served as secretary-treasurer and vice president of the Dante Society of America. His publications include works on Boccaccio and Dante, as well as articles for *The Dante Encyclopedia* (2000). He has contributed occasional public readings to Boston College's *Lectura Dantis* series.

Annelise M. Brody is a lecturer in Italian at Washington University in St. Louis. She received her PhD in Italian from Johns Hopkins University. Her main area of research is Italian medieval literature, in particular the influence of the church fathers on the writings of Petrarch and Boccaccio. She has published on Petrarch and is currently working on a rereading of the Griselda story in the *Decameron* in the context of its literary tradition.

Theodore J. Cachey Jr. is professor of Italian and chair of the Department of Romance Languages and Literatures at the University of Notre Dame. He specializes in Italian medieval and Renaissance literature, in particular Dante and Petrarch, the history of the Italian language, and the literature and history of travel. He is the author or editor of several books, including most recently *Petrarch's Guide to the Holy Land* (2002), *Le culture di Dante* (2004), and *Dante and Petrarch: Anti-Dantism, Metaphysics, Tradition* (2009), as well as essays and book chapters in *Annali d'Italianistica, Belfagor, Intersezioni, The History of Cartography, Modern Language Notes,* and *Schede Umanistiche,* among others. He is founder and coeditor (with Zygmunt G. Barański and Christian Moevs) of the William and Katherine Devers Series in Dante and Medieval Italian Literature and serves on the editorial boards of *Dante Studies, Letteratura Italiana Antica, Italian Studies: The Journal of the American Association for Italian Studies* (AAIS), and *Italica: The Journal of the American Association of Teachers of Italian* (AATI).

Claude Cazalé Bérard is professor emerita of Italian literature at the Université Paris Ouest-Nanterre-La Défense. A member of the Accademia Ambrosiana in Milan, her specialties are Italian medieval literature, nineteenth- and twentieth-century Italian literature, cultural and gender studies, comparative literature, and critical theory. She is the author of *Stratégie du jeu narratif: Le "Décaméron," une poétique du récit* (1985), *Les métamorphoses du récit, conteurs, prédicateurs, chroniqueurs des XIIIe et XIVe* (1987), and *Donne tra memoria e scrittura: Fuller, Weil, Sachs, Morante* (2009), and the coeditor of *Gli zibaldoni di Boccaccio: Memoria, scrittura, riscrittura* (1998). Among her articles are "Filoginia/Misoginia," in *Lessico critico decameroniano*, ed. Renzo Bragantini and Pier Massimo Forni (1995); "Boccace et Pétrarque: La culture encyclopédique comme horizon et enjeu pour la littérature italienne médiévale," in *L'entreprise encyclopédique*, ed. Jean Bouffartigues and Françoise Mélonio (1997); and "Il giardino di Fiammetta: Una *quête* amorosa sulle sponde del Mediterraneo," in *Boccaccio geografo*, ed. Roberta Morosini (2010).

James K. Coleman is currently visiting assistant professor of Italian at Johns Hopkins University. His main fields of research are medieval and Renaissance Italian literature and the humanist reception of ancient texts. He is the author of articles on literature and philosophy in Quattrocento Florence, on Ariosto's *Orlando furioso*, and on the thought of Giambattista Vico. He is currently working on a book project entitled *Orphic Poetry in Lorenzo de' Medici's Florence*.

Alison Cornish is professor of Italian in the Department of Romance Languages at the University of Michigan. She is the author of two books, one a study of the literary significance of Dante's use of astronomy (*Reading Dante's Stars*, 2000), and, most recently, a volume on the phenomenon and the mentality of vernacularization in late medieval Italy (*Vernacular Translation in Dante's Italy: Illiterate Literature*, 2011). She was a Fellow at the Harvard University Center for Italian Renaissance Studies at Villa I Tatti in 2005–6 and is currently occupied with reading manuscript miscellanies, especially of translated texts, and teaching Italian through opera.

Roberto Fedi is professor of Italian literature at the Università per Stranieri in Perugia, where he was formerly dean of the Faculty of Italian Language and Culture. He has published studies on Petrarch and the sixteenth-century lyrical tradition: *La memoria della poesia: Canzonieri, lirici e libri di rime nel Rinascimento* (1990), Giovanni Della Casa, *Le rime* (1978, 1993), and *Francesco Petrarca* (2002); on relations between literature and the figurative arts in the Renaissance: Iacopo da Pontormo, *Diario* (1996), and *I poeti preferiscono le bionde* (2007); and on the novel and short stories from Boccaccio to Verga: *Cultura letteraria e società civile nell'Italia unita* (1984) and *Scritture ottocentesche* (2011). He has also studied Boccaccio and the modern cultural tradition and coedited *Ariosto Today* (2003).

Elsa Filosa is assistant professor of Italian at Vanderbilt University. Her current research is on medieval Italian literature. She is the author of *Tre studi sul De mulieribus claris: I modelli letterari—I rapporti con il "Decameron"—La donna umanistica* (2012) and coeditor of *Boccaccio in America: Proceedings of the 2010 International Boccaccio Conference at the University of Massachusetts, Amherst* (2012). She has also published several articles and book chapters on Boccaccio, Petrarch, and Dante. She is now serving for the second time as executive secretary of the American Boccaccio Association, editing its biannual newsletter, and co-compiling the annual North American Boccaccio Bibliography.

Steven M. Grossvogel is associate professor of Italian at the University of Georgia. With research interests in medieval Italian literature, especially the works of Boccaccio and Dante, he is the author of *Ambiguity and Allusion in Boccaccio's "Filocolo"* (1992) and articles in the journals *Studi sul Boccaccio*, *Italiana*, *Il Veltro*, and *Modern Language Notes*, among others. He has also contributed to the Modern Language Association series volume *Approaches to Teaching Boccaccio's "Decameron"* (2000) and *Medieval Italy: An Encyclopedia* (2003).

Robert Hollander was professor in European literature at Princeton University from 1961 until his retirement in 2003. Founding director of the Dartmouth Dante Project (1982) and the Princeton Dante Project (1999), he has devoted his scholarship primarily to the study of Dante. His books include *Allegory in Dante's "Commedia"* (1969), *Studies in Dante* (1980), *Il Virgilio dantesco* (1983), and *Dante's Epistle to Cangrande* (1993), and more than a hundred articles, as well as an introductory study on Dante (*Dante Alighieri*, 2000; English edition, 2001). With his wife, the poet Jean Hollander, he has translated the *Commedia*, a text accompanied by his annotations (2000–2008; Italian edition of the commentary, 2011). On Boccaccio, he has authored *Boccaccio's Two Venuses* (1977), *Boccaccio's Last Fiction: "Il Corbaccio"* (1988), and *Boccaccio's Dante and the Shaping Force of Satire* (1997); translated the *Amorosa visione* (1986); and, most recently, published "The Struggle for Control among the *novellatori* of the *Decameron* and the Reason for Their Return to Florence," *Studi sul Boccaccio* 39 (2011): 1–72.

Jason Houston is associate professor of Italian at the University of Oklahoma at Norman and the director of the curriculum at University of Oklahoma in Arezzo. A medievalist with interests in Dante, Petrarch, and Boccaccio, as well as the relationships among the Three Crowns of Florence, he is the author of *Building a Monument to Dante: Boccaccio as Dantista* (2010) and articles on Dante, Boccaccio, and Petrarch. He has also cotranslated and edited *Giovanni Boccaccio: Minor Latin Works*, forthcoming in the I Tatti Renaissance Library series.

Victoria Kirkham is professor emerita of Romance languages at the University of Pennsylvania. She is the author of *The Sign of Reason in Boccaccio's Fiction* (1993) and *Fabulous Vernacular: Boccaccio's "Filocolo" and the Art of Medieval Fiction* (2001); and the coeditor and cotranslator of *Diana's Hunt / Caccia di Diana: Boccaccio's First Fiction* (1991). She has published articles on the *Divine Comedy*, Boccaccio, Renaissance culture, the Victorians' love of Italy, and Italian cinema. She is the coeditor of *Petrarch: A Critical Guide to the Complete Works* (2009) and the editor and translator of *Laura Battiferra degli Ammannati and Her Literary Circle: An Anthology* (2006). She has served twice on the Council of the Dante Society and is a past president of the American Boccaccio Association.

David Lummus is assistant professor of Italian at Stanford University, where he teaches medieval and early modern literature and culture. His research focuses on late medieval Italian literature and early Renaissance humanist thought, especially on interrelations between politics and poetry and on the mythographic tradition between the twelfth and sixteenth centuries. He has written on Boccaccio's *Genealogia deorum gentilium*, on Boccaccio's poetics, and on the question of Greek culture in Petrarch and Boccaccio, among other things. He is currently at work on a book about the political resonances of fourteenth- and fifteenth-century defenses of poetry.

Simone Marchesi is associate professor of French and Italian at Princeton University. His main research area is the dialogue of Italian medieval writers, especially Dante, Petrarch, and Boccaccio, with classical and late antique texts. His published work on medieval authors includes two monographs, *Stratigrafie decameroniane* (2004) and *Dante and Augustine: Linguistics, Poetics, Hermeneutics* (2011), and several articles and chapters in edited collections. Most recently, he edited and translated into Italian Robert Hollander's full commentary on Dante's *Commedia* (2011).

Ronald L. Martinez is professor of Italian studies at Brown University. In addition to more than forty articles on topics in Italian literature, from Guido Cavalcanti's lyrics to Ariosto's *Orlando furioso*, he has collaborated with Robert M. Durling on a monograph on Dante's lyric poetry, *Time and the Crystal: Studies in Dante's Rime Petrose* (1990), and on an edition, with translation and commentary, of Dante's *Divine Comedy* (1996, 2003, 2011). When residing in Minneapolis, he translated plays by Carlo Goldoni and Carlo Gozzi for professional productions. Martinez is currently writing a study on Dante's appropriation of medieval liturgy in the *Commedia* and in other works.

Giuseppe Mazzotta is the Sterling Professor in the Humanities for Italian at Yale University and a member of the American Academy of Arts and Sciences. His scholarly interests focus mainly on medieval, Renaissance, and Baroque literature and thought. He has written several books: *Dante, Poet of the Desert: History and Allegory in the "Divine Comedy"* (1979); *The World at Play in Boccaccio's "Decameron"* (1986); *The Worlds of Petrarch* (1993; repr., 2000); *Dante's Vision and the Circle of Knowledge* (1993); *The New Map of the World: The Poetic Philosophy of Giambattista Vico* (1999); and *Cosmopoiesis: A Renaissance Experiment* (2005). He has also edited several multiauthor volumes.

Letizia Panizza is a research fellow in Italian literature and culture at Royal Holloway, London. She has published studies on humanists, including Petrarch, Valla, and Erasmus; on rhetoric versus dialectic in the Renaissance; and on satirical political and religious literature of the sixteenth and seventeenth centuries. She is a contributor to *The Cambridge History of Italian Literature* (1996), editor of *Women in Renaissance Culture and Society* (2000), and coeditor of *The Cambridge History of Women's Writing in Italy* (2000), *Petrarch in Britain* (2007), and *Lucian of Samosata: Vivus and Redivivus* (2007). She wrote the introduction to Lucrezia Marinella's *The Nobility and Excellence of Women* (1999), edited Arcangela Tarabotti's *Women Are No Less Rational Than Men* (1994), and translated Tarabotti's *Paternal Tyranny* (2004) and *Convent Life as Hell* (forthcoming).

Michael Papio is professor of Italian studies at the University of Massachusetts, Amherst, where he is associate chair of the Department of Languages, Literatures, and Cultures. Author of *Keen and Violent Remedies: Social Satire and the Grotesque in Masuccio Salernitano's "Novellino"* (2000), he also translated and annotated *Boccaccio's Expositions on Dante's "Comedy"* (2009), translated and coedited *Pico della Mirandola's "Oration on the Dignity of Man": A New Translation and Commentary* (2012), and coedited *Boccaccio in America: Proceedings of the 2010 International Boccaccio Conference at the University of Massachusetts, Amherst* (2012). With a special interest in computing for the humanities, he is coeditor of the award-winning *Decameron Web*, the founding editor of *Heliotropia*, an online peer-reviewed journal in Boccaccio studies, and current president of the American Boccaccio Association.

Brian Richardson is emeritus professor of Italian language at the University of Leeds. His publications include *Print Culture in Renaissance Italy: The Editor and the Vernacular Text, 1470–1600* (1994), *Printing, Writers, and Readers in Renaissance*

Italy (1999), *Manuscript Culture in Renaissance Italy* (2009), and an edition of Giovanni Francesco Fortunio's *Regole grammaticali della volgar lingua* (2001). From 2003 to 2013, he was general editor of the *Modern Language Review*.

Arielle Saiber is associate professor of Italian at Bowdoin College. She publishes primarily on topics in medieval and Renaissance literature, science, and early print history, but she also works on electronic music and science fiction. She is the author of *Giordano Bruno and the Geometry of Language* (2005) and is completing a manuscript on the conversation between mathematics and literature in early modern Italy. She coedited and cotranslated an anthology of primary sources, *Images of Quattrocento Florence: Writings on Literature, History, and Art* (2000) and has coedited special issues such as "Mathematics and the Imagination" for *Configurations* (2009) and "Longfellow and Dante" for *Dante Studies* (2010). She is currently coediting an issue on "Italian sound" for *California Italian Studies* and compiling the first anthology in English of Italian science fiction.

Deanna Shemek is professor of literature at the University of California, Santa Cruz. Her main area of research is the Italian Renaissance. She is the author of *Ladies Errant: Wayward Women and Social Order in Early Modern Italy* (1998) and the coeditor of *Phaethon's Children: The Este Court and Its Culture in Early Modern Italy* (2005) and *Writing Relations: American Scholars in Italian Archives* (2008). She is also the cotranslator and editor of Adriana Cavarero's *Stately Bodies: Literature, Philosophy, and the Question of Gender* (2002). She is a founding member of the editorial board of the peer-reviewed online journal *California Italian Studies* and serves on the editorial board of *Italian Studies* (UK). She is preparing a volume of the selected letters of Isabella d'Este in English translation, and a monograph on Isabella d'Este as epistolary correspondent.

Michael Sherberg is professor of Italian at Washington University in St. Louis and chair of the Department of Romance Languages and Literatures. He is the author of *Rinaldo: Character and Intertext in Ariosto and Tasso* (1993) and, more recently, *The Governance of Friendship: Law and Gender in the "Decameron"* (2011). He has written extensively on Italian authors ranging from Dante to Carlo Collodi and is currently working on a translation of Iacopo Passavanti's *Specchio della vera penitenza*.

Janet Levarie Smarr is currently professor of theater history and Italian studies at the University of California, San Diego, and formerly a professor of comparative literature and Italian at the University of Illinois at Urbana-Champaign. She has published numerous essays on Boccaccio as well as the monograph *Boccaccio and Fiammetta: The Narrator as Lover* (1986) and an annotated translation of *Boccaccio's Eclogues* (1987), and has served as president of the American Boccaccio Association. Her *Joining the Conversation: Dialogues* *by Renaissance Women* (2005), and her most recent book, *Louise-Geneviève Gillot de Sainctonge: Dramatizing Dido, Circe, and Griselda* (2010), deal in part with Boccaccio's influence on Italian and French women writers of the sixteenth and seventeenth centuries.

Jon Solomon, Robert D. Novak Professor of Western Civilization and Culture and professor of classics at the University of Illinois at Urbana-Champaign, works on the classical tradition in opera and cinema, ancient Greek mythology and music, as well as ancient Roman cuisine and The Three Stooges. He recently published volume 1 of the I Tatti translation and edition of Boccaccio's *Genealogy of the Pagan Gods* (2011). His publications include Ptolemy's *Harmonics* (1999) and *The Ancient World in the Cinema* (1977, 2001). He is the coauthor of *Up the University* (1993) and is currently working on a book on Ben-Hur.

Jane Tylus is professor of Italian studies and comparative literature at New York University, where she also directs the Humanities Initiative. Her recent books include *Reclaiming Catherine of Siena: Literacy, Literature, and the Signs of Others* (2009) and a translation (with Troy Tower) of an edition of the complete poetry of Gaspara Stampa (2010). She is the coeditor (with Gerry Mulligan) of *The Poetics of Masculinity in Early Modern Italy and Spain* (2010) and is currently writing a book on Siena and pilgrimage in the Renaissance. She is the editor of the journal *I Tatti Studies in the Italian Renaissance*.

Jonathan Usher is emeritus professor of Italian at Edinburgh University. His work in the medieval field has concentrated largely on Boccaccio's knowledge and reinterpretation of the classical tradition. He is cotranslator of *The Decameron* in the Oxford World Classics series (1998), and his essays and reviews have appeared widely in print and electronic journals, including *Modern Language Review*, *Electronic Bulletin of the Dante Society of America*, *Studi sul Boccaccio*, *Heliotropia*, *Modern Language Notes*, *Modern Language Review*, and *Italian Studies*.

Giuseppe Velli, professor emeritus of modern philology at the University of Milan, has also taught at the University of California, Los Angeles, Smith College, and the University of Macerata. He has held the chairs of medieval and Renaissance philology at the University of Venice and of Italian literature at the University of Milan. A past honorary president of the American Association of Italian Studies, he has served as coeditor of the journal *Studi petrarcheschi* and codirector for the Petrarch editions sponsored by the Ente Nazionale Francesco Petrarca, of whose governing board he is a member. He is the author of *Petrarca e Boccaccio: Tradizione—memoria—scrittura* and *Tra lettura e creazione: Sannazaro—Alfieri—Foscolo,* and the editor of Boccaccio's Latin poetry (*Carmina*) for the Mondadori *Tutte le opere* series (1992).

David Wallace is Judith Rodin Professor of English at the University of Pennsylvania, with a subsidiary appointment in the German Department. He is the author of *Chaucer and the Early Writings of Boccaccio* (1985), *Giovanni Boccaccio: Decameron*, in the Cambridge Landmarks of World Literature Series (1991), and *Premodern Places* (2004); the coeditor of *The Cambridge Companion to Medieval Women's Writing* (2003); and the editor of *The Cambridge History of Medieval English Literature* (1999, 2002). His most recent book is *Strong Women* (2011), and he is currently editing a literary history of Europe (1348–1418).

Elissa Weaver, professor emerita in the Department of Romance Languages and Literatures at the University of Chicago, is a scholar of early modern Italian literature. She is the author of many articles on the Italian epic-chivalric tradition (Boiardo, Berni, and Ariosto), Boccaccio's *Decameron*, and the writing of women, especially convent women. She has published a monograph on a women's literary tradition, *Convent Theatre in Early Modern Italy: Spiritual Fun and Learning for Women* (2002), and a study of the life and work of Antonia Tanini Pulci, along with the Italian edition of Pulci's plays, *Saints' Lives and Bible Stories for the Stage* (2010). She has prepared other scholarly editions and edited several collections of essays, including *The "Decameron" First Day in Perspective* (2004) and *Arcangela Tarabotti, a Literary Nun in Baroque Venice* (2006).

INDEX

Abbondanza, Roberto, 484n42
Abulafia, David, 449n2
Acciaiuoli, Andrea, countess of Altavilla, 203
Acciaiuoli, Lapa, 41
Acciaiuoli, Niccola, 7, 16, 41, 65, 74, 158, 296, 299–300, 303, 305, 350, 355n35, 369n23, 410n20, 460n38
Accorsi, Mainardo, 434n29
Adam and Eve, 15, 34, 269
Aeschylus, 441n19
Agostinelli, Edvige, 383n5, 383n7
Alain of Lille, 55; *Anticlaudianus*, 121, 395n9
Albanzani, Donato degli, 155, 158, 407n4
Albizzi, Franceschino degli, 477n46
allegory, 4, 9–11, 58, 91–93, 115, 123, 158, 165, 224, 227, 229, 277, 378n3, 390n11, 395n14, 396n2, 397n6, 400n39, 408n12, 411n27, 413n35. *See also* Boccaccio, Giovanni: and allegory; Bocaccio, Giovanni: works: *Allegoria mitologica*
Allegretti, Ghinozzo di Tommaso, 43
Allenspach, Joseph, 365n7
Almansi, Guido, 356n1
Ambrose, 209
Andalò del Negro. *See* Negro, Andalò del
Anderson, David, 382n1
Andrea dell'Ischia, 435n31
Andrea di Cione (Orcagna), 478n1
Andreas Capellanus, 71, 175, 177,

181, 376n12, 380n16, 390n17, 417nn29–30
Andrew (prince of Hungary, husband of Joan). *See* Anjou, house of
Angevins. *See* Anjou, house of; Naples
Angiolieri, Cecco, 284, 287
Anjou, house of, 66, 78–79, 374n14; Andrew, husband of Joan, 57, 58, 355n30; Joan of Naples, granddaughter of Robert, 203, 355n30; Robert of Anjou, 10–11, 14, 57–58, 64, 65, 67, 79, 88, 89, 109, 112, 126–27, 157–58, 211, 367n3, 369n17, 371n7, 374n14, 379n7, 380n12, 396n17, 406n1. *See also* Naples
Apuleius, 71, 119, 238, 356n2; *Metamorphoses of Lucius*, 23, 31, 360n33
Aquinas. *See* Thomas Aquinas, Saint
Aquino, Maria d', 7, 78, 112. *See also* Fiammetta
Ardissino, Erminia, 372n8
Ariosto, Lodovico, 8, 97, 193
Aristotle, 3, 37, 121, 139, 187, 230, 244; *Ethics*, 354n17, 363n54, 381n20, 420n4, 447n13
Armao, Linda, 405n27
Armstrong, Guyda, 223, 363n57, 419n1, 422n20, 438n8
Arno, 146, 160, 161, 278, 366n2, 455n32
Arrathoon, Leigh A., 384n14
Arrigo da Settimello, 55
Arscott, Caroline, 399n17